THE NEW ENCYCLOPEDIA OF HOSTAS

DIANA GRENFELL
MICHAEL SHADRACK

Foreword by His Royal Highness
The Prince of Wales

TIMBER PRESS
Portland · London

For Roger and Kathy,
our spouses,
and all the other wonderful friends
we have made through the "friendship plant."

Diana Grenfell & Michael Shadrack

PAGE 1: *Hosta* 'Reptilian'

PAGE 2: *Hosta* 'Magic Fire'

PAGE 3: The garden of Fred and Audra Wilson, Ackworth, Iowa

PAGE 5: *Hosta* 'Cat's Eye'

This revised, expanded work incorporates portions of *The Color Encyclopedia of Hostas* (2004) and *Timber Press Pocket Guide to Hostas* (2007). Mention of trademark, proprietary product, or vendor does not constitute a guarantee or warranty of the product by the publisher or authors and does not imply its approval to the exclusion of other products or vendors.

Published in 2009 by Timber Press, Inc.

The Haseltine Building
133 S.W. Second Avenue, Suite 450
Portland, Oregon 97204-3527
www.timberpress.com

2 The Quadrant
135 Salusbury Road
London NW6 6RJ
www.timberpress.co.uk

Printed in China
Designed by Susan Applegate

Library of Congress Cataloging-in-Publication Data

Grenfell, Diana.
The new encyclopedia of hostas/Diana Grenfell, Michael Shadrack; foreword by His Royal Highness the Prince of Wales.
p. cm.
"This revised, expanded work incorporates portions of the Color encyclopedia of hostas (2004) and Timber Press pocket guide to hostas (2007)."
Includes bibliographical references and index.
ISBN 978-0-88192-960-7
1. Hosta. I. Shadrack, Michael. II. Title.
SB413.H73G7425 2009
635.9′3432—dc22 2009016603

A catalog record for this book is also available from the British Library.

CONTENTS

Hostas in the woodland garden at Highgrove House.
Copyright © A. G. Carrick Ltd. Used by permission.

FOREWORD

His Royal Highness
The Prince of Wales

CLARENCE HOUSE

Hostas have been one of my favourite plants for a long time and even more so when, at Highgrove, I discovered they did well and were not too badly plagued by slugs. The time came when I thought that growing them as collections in several carefully chosen sites would make more impact than having individual hostas or small plantings of hostas scattered all over the garden. I was also mindful of my role as Patron of the National Council for the Conservation of Plants and Gardens...

As the Stumpery was taking shape in the mind's eye, I could immediately envisage the potential of planting substantial groupings of a variety of different, huge-leafed hostas to contrast with the tough, spiny-leafed butcher's broom, and to act as a foil for the delicate tracery of the groups of ferns which would form the remainder of the planting plan. The Stumpery, a revival of the eighteenth century Picaresque movement, was planned as an enclosed glade and designed by Julian and Isabel Bannerman.

As these plantings matured, I began to see the possibilities and benefits of extending the Stumpery into the adjacent Woodland Garden which was about to undergo a long overdue revitalization programme.

It was suggested to me during the planning stage of this new Woodland Garden that I might apply for National Plant Collection status for my ever-increasing collection of very large-leafed hostas. This exciting prospect focused my mind still further on the genus which, although now among the most popular perennials both in the United Kingdom and the United States, has come a very long way from its humble far-eastern origins.

Different categories of National Plant Collections of Hosta already exist, but having the space at Highgrove and the support of a talented and enthusiastic gardening team, I felt that I, too, could play my part by helping to amass a comprehensive collection. In this way both the newest varieties can be assessed for their garden value and I can also help to conserve some almost forgotten varieties, raised and introduced by early pioneers of the genus, which must be saved from disappearing from our gardens. I need hardly say that I am indebted to Diana Grenfell for all the expert advice and help she has given with this particular garden project.

As Patron of the National Council for the Conservation of Plants and Gardens and the British Hosta and Hemerocallis Society, I warmly welcome the publication of such a comprehensive book written by a leading expert on the genus and illustrated with superb photographs, which cannot but tempt all gardeners who are attracted by exotic, luxuriant-leafed perennials to learn more about this supremely attractive foliage plant.

Charles

Hosta 'Regal Supreme'

PREFACE AND ACKNOWLEDGEMENTS

Hostas have moved on since my first book about them was published in 1990. During the research stage for that book, in addition to my own observations, I waded through all the learned publications available, sifted through the records of various societies, spent days in libraries and museums, wrote numerous letters, and made endless telephone calls. Now one only has to switch on the computer to find this information at the touch of a button, and communication is almost instantaneous.

Before the 1990s hosta enthusiasts were thirsting for knowledge and were less discerning, or less critical, about the available hostas, rarely discarding any which were considered less than perfect. Now, thanks to the expeditions being undertaken by more and more collectors, breeders, and nursery owners who study hostas in the wild in Japan, Korea, and China, we know more about the habitats and conditions in which the species live and so are better able to grow them more successfully in our gardens. We are also learning from scientific research which hostas should no longer be considered species, and that the input of taxonomists on hostas is still in its infancy—the ploidy of hostas being a topic of much interest and debate. There is even a recently approved National Plant Collection of tetraploid hostas. George Schmid is building on his work on the species by making generally available to all hosta growers his up-to-date research; this can be found on www.hostalibrary.org.

A number of *Hosta* hybridizers in the United States and Europe have made names for themselves by the introduction of their work to the trade. I am delighted to be able to include introductions such as *H.* 'Clovelly', *H.* 'Flemish Sky', and *H.* 'Hacksaw' and outstanding new sports such as *H.* 'Cat and Mouse' and *H.* 'Regal Supreme'. Many of these hybridizers first came to prominence by submitting their seedlings and sports to the American Hosta Society's Region 1 First Look, an annual competition held to showcase hostas before they become available commercially.

What is most exciting to the gardener is that hostas are now, and have been for several years, the number one perennial plant in the United States. There are, and always were, excellent reasons for this being so. First and foremost is the sheer sumptuousness of their leaves: they outshine the leaves of every other foliage plant in the garden. There is also the diversity of the size, shape, and color of the leaves, the ease of cultivation, and the quick response to a gardener's care and attention. Hostas have given shade gardening the recognition and cachet it deserves, especially in hot climates, where cool, shaded areas are prized over sunny borders. All these qualities have earned hostas their place as the supreme shade plant. Moreover, small and large nurseries as well as tissue-culture laboratories are springing up everywhere, making a huge and ever-increasing range of hostas available to the gardening public.

I have chosen to list the hostas described in this reference according to leaf color and type of variegation rather than alphabetically. An alphabetical listing would be an easier and more obvious way to tackle a book on colorful flowers, but I am suggesting that the leaves of hostas have such a special appeal that the descriptions deserve to be arranged in a directory by their leaf color and type of variegation. The penultimate chapter of the directory covers those hostas that experience tells us are mainly for connoisseurs, and I provide explanations in that chapter. Since publication of the first edition of this encyclopedia I have been aware that miniature hostas have become even more popular and sought after; therefore the final chapter is now devoted to miniature hostas and those with almost as small leaves which perform similarly in the garden. I hope this directory will enable readers to make more finely tuned hosta selections for their gardens as they consider how different-colored leaves perform in various garden situations and locations.

For a number of years I have been aware of a gap in the market for a hosta book that has an illustration accompanying each hosta featured. I am grateful to my constructive and patient editor, Anna Mumford, Timber Press's commissioning editor in the United Kingdom, for offering me the opportunity to write the comprehensively illustrated book I had always hoped to write one day. I am also grateful to my editor across the pond, Linda Willms, at Timber Press in Portland, Oregon, for her creative and helpful advice and input throughout this undertaking.

Hostas can look ravishing in pictures but only someone who knows them well and understands their garden value and cultural needs can fully capture their qualities. Over the years at hosta conventions and meetings on both sides of the Atlantic, I have been aware, while taking notes, of Mike Shadrack busy with his camera. The results of his work bore fruit when he won the Hostas and Their Companions section at the American Hosta Society's annual Hosta in Focus Photographic Weekend in 1997. His pictures feature regularly in the American Hosta Society's journals and, more recently, in the gardening press and hosta specialist nursery catalogues. Mike was undoubtedly the obvious person to collaborate with me on this project, and it has been a joy to work with such a professional and good-humored colleague.

Many people have helped me in the preparation of this book and I am grateful to them all, but I should like to single out Warren Pollock for his valuable contribution by vetting the text for American hosta growers.

The number of books on hostas now published has made researching them considerably easier. Nevertheless, a book of this complexity could not have been written without the help of hosta enthusiasts in many parts of the world, who have freely shared with me their knowledge and experience, much of it garnered over many years. I extend my thanks, in alphabetical order, to Barbara Alsop, Michelle and Tony Avent, John Baker and June Colley, Stephen Baker, Gwen Black, Ann and Roger Bowden, Sandra Bond, Leila Bradfield, Chris Brickell, Mary Chastain, Donald Church, Oscar and Peter Cross, Ian Crystal, Don Dean, Una Dunnett, Danny Van Eechaute, C. H. Falstad, Joyce and Marco Fransen, Roger Grounds, Joe Halinar, Brian Halliwell, Hans Hansen, Jack Hirsch and Gary Lindheimer, Jay Hislop, Jonathan Hogarth, David Howard, Bob Kuk, Jeroen Linneman, Ron Livingston, Ran Lydell, Bill Meyer, Alex Malloy, Lu and Dan Nelson, Hugo Philips, Peg and Ray Prag, Charles Purtymun, Ray Rodgers, Jean and Peter Ruh, Tim Saville, W. George Schmid, Jim Schwarz, Kathy Guest Shadrack, Barry Sligh, Nancy and Bob Solberg, Alex Summers, Derrick Targett, Jan van den Top, Susan and Alan Tower, The Virginia Tech Entomology Department, Shirley and Van Wade, Kevin Walek, Mary Walters, Jerry Webb, and James Wilkins.

Finally, and most importantly, we extend our most heartfelt and grateful thanks to His Royal Highness The Prince of Wales for graciously contributing the Foreword to this book.

Diana Grenfell

I would like to thank the countless hosta people in England, Belgium, Holland, France, Canada, and the United States who have allowed me to photograph their plants over the years. Special thanks are due to John Baker and June Colley, Doug Beilstein, Gwen Black, Sandra Bond, Ann and Roger Bowden, the late Margo and Udo Dargatz, the late Ed Elslager, C. H. Falstad and Walters Gardens, Marco and Joyce Fransen, Hans Hansen, Bob Kuk, Peter and Jean Ruh, W. George Schmid, Jan van den Top, Danny Van Eechaute, Van and Shirley Wade, Dick and Jane Ward, Jim and Sandy Wilkins, and Audra and Fred Wilson. They all allowed me unfettered access to their large hosta collections and gave so freely of their knowledge and advice.

Michael Shadrack

A beautiful blend of hostas.

Hosta hypoleuca

1

Hostas in the Wild

Hostas are natives of the Far East, with their center of distribution being Japan. Outlying species occur in China and Korea. Hostas are thought to have evolved from lilylike ancestors that migrated from east-central China by two different routes that recombined some time later to produce the hostas we know today. One group went by a northerly route through southeastern Russia and thence southward into Hokkaido and Honshu. The more primitive group, ancestors of the present-day *Hosta plantaginea*, migrated via a more southerly route through southern Manchuria into the Korean peninsula and from thence to southern Japan.

In the eons it took them to migrate, the two

populations became substantially differentiated, though not sufficiently so in their reproductive organs to prevent cross-pollination. The Japanese mainland, with its great diversity of physical and climatological habitats, encouraged further differentiation, although only those populations that were physically isolated have remained distinct. Plainly, most wild populations have been interbreeding for many centuries, whereas those that were geographically isolated have now been largely brought together by the intervention of man.

The wild species of *Hosta* are typically clump-forming perennial plants, most of which have broadly or narrowly heart-shaped leaves and clusters of lilylike flowers carried on upright stems just above the foliage mound. Typically, the wild species grow on forest margins or in open glades in woodlands, and it is from these that most garden varieties have been derived.

A number of lesser-known species have adapted to growing in quite different habitats. *Hosta hypoleuca*, for example, can grow in dense shade, enveloped in thick mist, but equally well clinging to near-vertical, sunbaked volcanic cliffs in which it produces just one large leaf, the back of which is covered in fine white powder that protects it from the sun's heat that is reflected off bare rocks. At the other extreme, the grassy-leaved *H. longissima* grows in damp, cloud-shrouded meadows at high altitudes where its thin leaves are shaded in summer by taller miscanthus grasses. A few diminutive species, such as *H. venusta*, with leaves no bigger than a thumbnail, grow as epiphytes on mossy tree trunks, while *H. alismifolia* forms extensive colonies in wet sphagnum bogs and *H. kiyosumiensis* perches on rocks or mossy tree roots at the edges of streams, trailing its roots in the water.

All the wild species of *Hosta* and the cultivated varieties too are reliably hardy. They require winter chilling to less than 40°F (4°C) for several weeks to achieve proper dormancy. The underground parts can remain unharmed even when the ground around them is frozen solid for long periods.

Most of the wild species grow in areas of dense shade with much higher rainfall than is typical in areas where they are most widely cultivated. On the main islands of Japan, the average annual precipitation is a little more than 62 in. (1575 mm), a figure that in America can only be matched or bettered by the Pacific Northwest, with 61 to 82 in. (1549 to 2083 mm), in Europe only by Scotland, with 51 to 61 in. (1295 to 1550 mm), and by the west coast of New Zealand, with 81 in. (2057 mm). By comparison, the U.S. Northeastern and Midwestern states receive only 20 to 40 in. (508 to 1016 mm) of rain, the same as most of Europe, including England, and southeastern Australia.

While a few *Hosta* species, typically those with thin leaves, naturally grow in marshy or boggy conditions, and a few in habitats where they are periodically or regularly submerged, the majority grow in moisture-retentive but free-draining soils or other media. The conditions favored by hostas are generally those with high relative humidity, especially in summer, when humidity can reach 75 to 80 percent. Inclement weather is not uncommon in the wild habitats of hostas. In addition to frosts and snowfalls, ice and hail storms also occur, as well as severe tropical storms. These events devastate the top growth of the hostas but seldom damage their roots so that in time the hostas recover.

Hosta sieboldii 'Kabitan'

2 Hostas in the West

LONG BEFORE HOSTAS REACHED THE West, they were selected for their ornamental value and cultivated in Japan and possibly in China and Korea for literally hundreds of years. The first Westerner ever to knowingly see a hosta, and certainly the first to draw and describe one, was Engelbert Kaempfer (1651–1715), a medical doctor with the Dutch East India Company stationed on Deshima, an artificial island in Nagasaki harbor. He was never allowed to visit the mainland, Japan still being fiercely hostile to foreigners, but he made reasonably accurate drawings of two hostas, one of which was later identified as *Hosta* 'Lancifolia'.

The first hosta to actually reach the West was *Hosta plantaginea*, seed of which was sent to the Jardin des Plantes in Paris by the French consul in Macao sometime between 1784 and 1789. With its large, pure white flowers and exotic fragrance, it was soon being grown by the thousands in public gardens throughout France, from whence it was distributed to the rest of Europe. A second Chinese species, *H. ventricosa*, followed soon after, and was first cultivated in a private botanic garden in London.

It was not until forty years later that hostas from Japan started reaching the West. The person responsible for their arrival was Philipp von Siebold

(1791–1866), another botanizing medical doctor with the Dutch East India Company. His first shipment arrived in Europe in 1829, and more shipments followed. The hostas, as well as other plants, were grown on in Siebold's nursery in Ghent and later dispersed to botanic and other gardens across Europe, some varieties eventually reaching the United States. Other notable plant hunters followed, such as Robert Fortune (1813–1880), and the collecting of hostas in their wild habitats goes on to this day, although it is now strictly controlled by international agreements.

In 1985 an expedition mounted by the U.S. National Arboretum in Washington, D.C., under the auspices of the Friends of the Arboretum and led by Barry Yinger, introduced two species not previously known in the West, and an expedition by members of the American Hosta Society (AHS) in 1995 introduced other, previously unknown varieties. In 1997 Tony Avent, Dan Hinkley, Darrell Probst, and Bleddyn and Sue Wynn-Jones undertook an expedition to South Korea, where several new forms of *Hosta* were collected. Both George Schmid and Mark Zilis, in preparation for the publication of their superb books, have also studied hosta species in their native habitats, which has greatly added to our knowledge. In Japan itself, new species and varieties are still being discovered, and there are probably more to be found in China and Korea.

The first major shipment of hostas to reach the United States directly from Japan was organized by Thomas Hogg Jr. The son of a London nurseryman of the same name who had migrated to America, Thomas was made a U.S. marshal by President Lincoln, who sent him to Japan in 1862. While there Hogg bought hostas, especially variegated ones, from street markets and it is likely that these hostas were included in the consignments of plants he sent back to the family nursery in Manhattan.

CLASSIFICATION

Hostas are monocotyledonous plants, meaning they produce one seed leaf, not two, and were for a long time placed in the family Liliaceae. This placement was not satisfactory since Liliaceae was a huge family embracing an extraordinarily varied selection of disparate plants. Under a new system of classifying the monocotyledons that was originally devised by R. M. T. Dahlgren, H. T. Clifford, and P. F. Yeo in 1985 and adopted by the Royal Botanic Gardens, Kew, in 1987, hostas are now placed in their own family, Hostaceae. This classification is generally accepted today.

The name *Hosta* was first applied to this genus in 1812. It honors the Austrian botanist Nicholas Thomas Host (1761–1834), who wrote a flora of Austria. The name was supplanted for some years, however, by the name *Funkia*, which honors Heinrich Christian Funk, a botanist of whom little is now known. The term *Funkia* will be found in books by Gertrude Jekyll, William Robinson, and their contemporaries, and it is still used as a vernacular name for hostas in many parts of Europe. Today the correct naming of plants is governed by two international

Hostas in the Rock Garden at the Royal Horticulture Society Garden, Wisley.

codes, the International Code of Nomenclature for Cultivated Plants and the International Code of Botanical Nomenclature. Under these codes, *Hosta* has been determined as the correct name for this genus.

When hostas first reached the West, botanists generally assumed that they were all species, even though many of them were variegated. It turns out that some of these hostas had been found by the early collectors not in the wild (where Westerners were seldom allowed to go) but in gardens, especially temple gardens, and that the plants were in fact garden varieties, having been selected and maintained in cultivation by gardeners. This has led to problems in their naming and in the way their names are expressed.

For example, *Hosta decorata* was so named when it was thought to be a species, even though it has white-margined leaves, and the species name was expressed in italics to denote its specific status. Now that it is known to be a garden variety, its second name is usually written in Roman type, inside single quotation marks, as in 'Decorata', to show that it is a cultivated variety. Taxonomists, however, seem unable to agree about this plant's status. The variegated form of *H.* 'Decorata' is sometimes known as *H. decorata* var. *decorata*, while the wild, green-leaved version is known as *H. decorata* f. *normalis*. Such terminological confusion may be unnecessary since the plants are plainly cultivated varieties.

BOTANY

Hostas are frost-hardy perennial herbs that arise from short, sometimes rhizomatous, white, fleshy roots. The leaves, which are stalked and varied in size from small to large, rise directly from the rootstock and form rounded or spreading mounds. The flowers are large by botanical standards, tubular, flared and funnel- or spider-shaped, usually with six spreading lobes called tepals. They vary in color from white to deep purple and are presented in a raceme at the top of a usually unbranched scape.

The reproductive organs at the heart of each flower consist of six stamens (the male organs) that rest on the tube of the flower and protrude from it, their tips upturned like an eyelash, and of a stigma, a style and an ovary (the female organs). If fertilized, the ovary will swell into an elongated, many-chambered capsule, and seed will mature in about six weeks. Plants start into growth as the ground warms in the spring, withering away at the onset of winter, perennating as roots with dormant buds.

The shape of a hosta is primarily determined by its root type. Hostas with compact root systems produce rounded mounds of foliage, whereas those with running rootstocks produce spreading colonies of foliage.

Leaves

Hosta leaves arise directly from the crown, the fibrous collar that connects the above-ground parts to the below-ground parts. The leaves are made up of two parts, the petiole (stalk) and the blade. The two parts are usually clearly differentiated, but in a few species and cultivars, such as *Hosta longissima*, the two are confluent. The size and shape of both can be diagnostic.

A plain-green hosta with unusual surface texture and an elegant margin accents a stone bird bath in the backyard of Jim and Sandy Wilkins, Jackson, Michigan.

The petioles are never quite flat but are, in varying degrees, U- or V-shaped. The color of the petiole is normally the color of the blade, possibly in a paler tone, and any variegation is carried down into the petiole. Some species, in particular *Hosta longipes* and *H. pycnophylla*, have distinctly red- or purple-dotted petioles. This trait was originally passed on automatically to many hybrids and considered of no particular significance. Among the first hybrids to be prized for this characteristic was *H.* 'Regal Rhubarb'. Now breeders are making crosses to create even brighter red petioles, such as *H.* 'Emeralds and Rubies' and *H.* 'Fire Island'. In the newer introductions, such as *H.* 'Katsuragawa Beni', the red dots are visible well into the base of the leaf blade.

Most hostas pass through both juvenile and adult phases producing both juvenile and adult leaves, and these usually differ in shape. For the purposes of this book, an adult (mature) hosta (one which produces adult leaves) is one that has completed its sixth growing season after root division. Many hostas also produce summer leaves that are different from their vernal leaves. In the directory section of this book, the leaves described are adult leaves unless otherwise stated.

Hosta leaves are classified by size, shape, leaf blade, venation, substance, finish, and color. They fall into one of five **general size categories**:

The intensely bright red-dotted petioles of *Hosta* 'Fire Island' retain their color throughout the season.

Class 1 (VERY LARGE)	144 sq. in. (900 sq cm) and larger
Class 2 (LARGE)	81–144 sq. in. (530–900 sq cm)
Class 3 (MEDIUM)	25–81 sq. in. (160–530 sq cm)
Class 4 (SMALL)	6–25 sq. in. (36–160 sq cm)
Class 5 (VERY SMALL)	about 4–10 sq. in. (26–65 sq cm)
Class 5 (MINIATURE)	about 4 sq. in. (26 sq cm)

Leaf shape is described in terms of leaf length-to-width ratios:

Round	1:1
Broadly oval	6:5
Oval	2:1 or 3:2
Elliptical	3:1
Lance-shaped	6:1

Definitions of the shapes of hosta leaves and the possible variations on tip and base shapes may seem very exact, but in practice the leaves in any one clump of hosta may vary considerably and fall between definitions. The **base of the leaf** or lobes may be

heart-shaped (cordate): having two equal, rounded lobes on each side of the petiole where the petiole joins the leaf blade. On round leaves, the lobes will be conspicuously overlapping or folded.
flat (truncate): where the leaf appears to have been cut straight across.
tapered or wedge-shaped (cuneate): with the leaf's sides straight but converging.
rounded (attenuate): with the sides of the leaf curved and converging.

The **tip of the leaf** may be

acuminate: coming to a long tapering point, as in *H.* 'Francheska'
mucronate: coming abruptly to a sharp point on a round leaf, as in *H.* 'Tokudama'.
cuspidate: terminating in a sharp point, as in *H. montana*.
acute: coming straight to a sharp point, as in *H.* 'Lancifolia'.

obtuse: rounded, as in *H*. 'Decorata'.

vestigial: a small trace of a point on a rounded leaf as in *H*. 'Cathedral Windows'.

The **margins** of hostas are usually entire; that is, they are rarely toothed, cut, or lobed. Occasionally there may be very slight serrations. Margins may also be flat, undulate, rippled, or evenly and deeply rippled, which in hosta parlance is known as "piecrusted."

The **midrib** is lighter in color than the blade, often colorless, and can appear to pierce the blade, particularly in glaucous, self-colored leaves.

The **leaf blade** may be level (flat), undulate (wavy), or twisted, and can be shallowly cupped, as in *H*. 'Sea Lotus Leaf' or deeply cupped, as in *H*. 'Abiqua Drinking Gourd'. The **surface** may also be smooth, as in *H*. 'Gay Blade', dimpled, as in *H*. 'Blue Wedgwood', seersuckered, as in *H*. 'Midas Touch', puckered, as in *H*. 'Millenium', or furrowed, as in *H. montana*. Although the veins may give a ridged effect, the **finish** of the blade's upper surface can be matt, as in *H*. 'Gold Standard', satiny (slightly shiny), as in

H. 'Fragrant Bouquet', very shiny, as in *H*. 'Bubba', or glaucous, as in *H. sieboldiana* 'Elegans'. The leaves are always smooth (glabrous), that is, without hairs or roughness.

The **veins** on hosta leaves are arranged in a form called campylodrome, which means the veins that

The smooth leaf of *Hosta ventricosa* has widely spaced veins and an evenly rippled to piecrusted margin.

Mature plants of *Hosta* 'Niagara Falls' have piecrusted leaf margins. Young plants do not.
'

enter the leaf at its base curve outward as the leaf widens and inward as the leaf narrows toward the tip. The veins can appear deeply impressed, or furrowed, when seen from above and prominently raised, or ribbed, when seen from below.

The area of the leaves between the veins may be thick or thin, and this is known as their **substance**. It is sometimes incorrectly called their texture. The greater the substance, the stiffer and more rigid are the leaves.

Leaf color of the wild species is normally green, though variegated sports do occasionally occur. The color arises from pigments carried in bodies called plastids, the dominant plastids throughout the plant kingdom being green ones called chloroplasts. Different colors are the result of other pigments carried in other chloroplasts, but since all chloroplasts are very similar, it takes only a minute change or error in replication for chloroplasts to slip from one color to another. This slippage seems to happen more frequently with hostas than with other plants.

The growing tip or **meristem** of a plant is always essentially the same, but different parts of the plant develop from different parts of the growing tip. Hosta leaves are made up of three layers known as L1, L2, and L3. The outer layer, L1, is also called the epidermis and is particularly important in the formation of leaf margins. If colored plastids occur in this layer,

the leaf will have a colored margin. If colored plastids arise in L2, the middle layer of the leaf, they will produce a colored center to the leaf. Perhaps surprisingly, plastids can move from one layer of a leaf to another. Colored plastids originating in L2 can move to L1, and this is what happens when a streaked hosta turns into a hosta with a variegated margin.

Plastids can lose their coloring as easily as they become colored, which is what happens when a variegated hosta leaf sports to a single color. All variegation is thus more or less unstable, though variegation in the margin is usually more stable than variegation in the center of the leaf. The currently popular "grass clippings" or flecked variegation occurs when the leaf starts reverting to all green.

Flowers

Hosta flowers are borne in racemes at the tops of **scapes** (stems) which arise directly from the rootstock or crown at the base of the leaf mound. The scapes themselves are usually round and solid, rarely hollow, as in *Hosta minor*, occasionally ridged, as in *H. minor* and *H. venusta*, and usually simple and rarely branched, as in *H. tibae*. They may be upright or leaning, and can be straight or curved. In the following descriptions, the measurement given for scapes refers to the length, not the height.

The individual flowers are held away from the scape

The heavily puckered leaf of *Hosta* 'Clearfork River Valley' has widely spaced veins and a flat margin.

The leaves of *Hosta* 'Fire and Brimstone', a collector's plant, are streaked in three shades of green and cream.

by short stems known as **pedicels**. These may hold the flower away from the scape at a right angle or may allow the flower to droop. The pedicels emerge from bracts on the scape, which are known as flower bracts. In some species and cultivars, these **flower bracts** are so small they can scarcely be seen with the naked eye, while in others they are so large that they may be taken for true leaves, as in *Hosta kikutii*. Most flower bracts fall between these extremes. They typically wither once flowering is over.

Some hostas have a second type of bract on the flower scape, and these are known as foliaceous or **leafy bracts**. They are also called inflorescence leaves. Leafy bracts can always be distinguished from flower bracts because they occur only on the lower part of the scape beneath the flowers. The largest leafy bracts normally occur toward the base of the scape, and the bracts are usually outward-facing, rarely small and stem-clasping. In several species and varieties, these bracts can be showy, and if the true leaves are variegated, the bracts will be similarly variegated, as in *Hosta* 'Undulata'.

The **raceme** or flower cluster may be dense, as in *Hosta* 'Blue Moon', or sparse, as in *H. tsushimensis*. The flowers are usually disposed to one side of the scape, called secund, an exception being *H.* 'Koryu', in which the flowers are disposed all around the scape, called whorled. Each hosta flower lasts only a day.

Hosta flowers are bisexual, the female organs consisting of an ovary (with three cavities) at the base of the flower from which arises a long, tubular style at the tip of which is a three-lobed stigma that receives pollen in season. These are surrounded by the male organs consisting of six stamens, at the tips of which are the anthers, which produce pollen. The style is usually longer than the stamens, but both usually protrude from the mouth of the flower.

All the male and female organs are surrounded by and contained within the flower (perianth), which consists of a narrow tube followed by a flaring section composed of six lobes. Three of them are exterior lobes (also known as the calyx), and three are interior lobes (the corolla), but they are scarcely differentiated and are called tepals or, more commonly, lobes or petals.

In outline, the flowers of hostas may be tubular or funnel-shaped (infundibuliform), bell-shaped

The funnel-shaped flowers of *Hosta plantaginea*.

The bell-shaped flowers of *Hosta ventricosa*.

The spider-shaped flowers of *Hosta laevigata*.

(campanulate), or spider-shaped (arachnoid), though the latter are basically funnel-shaped but with narrow, widely separated lobes. Many flowers fall between these two extremes, and most cultivars have more or less flaring flowers. In *Hosta clausa* the flowers remain closed and then fall away from the pedicel, except for *H. clausa* f. *normalis* in which the flowers are open.

Pollination occurs when the pollen of one plant reaches the stigma of another (mechanisms exist to prevent self-pollination). This activity is chiefly carried out by insects. After a grain of pollen lands on a stigma, it grows a pollen tube down through the hollow style to the ovary, carrying the male gametes with it. Once the tube reaches the ovary, it discharges the gametes and fertilization takes place.

Hosta flowers vary in color within a limited spectrum. Typically, most are described in terms of lavender, but they can vary from white through to deep purple, often with stripes of a deeper tone. The amount of red in the coloration will determine whether the flower color is perceived as leaning more toward blue or mauve.

Seed

If fertilized, the ovaries of hostas swell into oval, many-chambered pods that are usually the same color as the leaves (and often variegated if the leaves are variegated). The pods ripen about six weeks after fertilization. On opening they reveal three chambers, and in each chamber are two rows of flat, oval seeds that are shiny and black if fertile or pale beige or white if infertile. A few varieties produce pods that do not contain seeds or they produce no pods at all, in which case the scapes wither after flowering. Both are usually denoted as sterile varieties. Fertile seed usually germinates quickly and easily.

3 The Cultivation and Propagation of Hostas

THE ART OF GROWING GOOD HOSTAS lies in understanding their needs and in providing them. In broad terms, hostas need a fertile soil that is moist but well drained, a measure of protection against the heat of the sun, and shelter from strong winds. However, they vary greatly in their individual requirements, and fine-tuning is needed to get the best from a wide range of hostas.

GENERAL CONSIDERATIONS OF CLIMATE

Hostas are hardy perennial plants well adapted to cultivation throughout the temperate world and, to a lesser degree, in some subtropical regions. They are reliably frost tolerant to about 28°F (−2°C). They can tolerate summer temperatures as high as 100°F (38°C), and somewhat higher for short times. Heat dormancy occurs above temperatures of 95°F (35°C). All hostas require a measure of winter chilling to below 40°F (4°C) for several weeks as part of their annual cycle of growth and rest.

Since hostas in the wild receive far higher rainfall than they are likely to receive in cultivation in the West, that amount needs to be supplemented to raise it to about 1 in. (25 mm) per week while the hostas are in active growth. Hostas are also surprisingly drought tolerant, but when they are under stress from drought, their leaves will wither and burn. They are also tolerant of temporary flooding but will not stand long periods of inundation when dormant.

SOIL

Hostas are tolerant of a wide range of soil types but grow best in a rich, friable loam with a pH of about 6. They are less tolerant of shallow soils over chalk: green-leaved varieties tend to exhibit the typical symptoms of chlorosis (the areas between the veins turn yellow or yellowish while the veins remain green), and blue-leaved varieties assume a muddy tinge.

Large hostas, such as *Hosta sieboldiana*, grow well on heavy clay soils that are rich in plant nutrients, but they take time to become established. They will establish more quickly and grow better if the ground is thoroughly prepared before planting. Given that hosta roots spread out below ground to the edge of the leaf mound or beyond and that a mature specimen of *H. sieboldiana* or *H. montana* can be 6 to 8 ft. (1.8 to 2.4 m) across, a planting hole 6 to 8 ft. across should be prepared. Preparing the soil means incorporating lavish quantities of coarse grit and organic materials to a depth of at least one spit (the depth of a spade's blade) and in equal amounts by volume. Since clay soils tend to revert to clay over time, it is important to maintain the gains made by the incorporation of these materials by continuing to use them as a mulch in succeeding years.

The problems posed by sandy soils are quite different, though the remedy is much the same. Sandy soils are poor largely because they are free draining, meaning that nutrients quickly get washed through them. Hostas in such soils rapidly develop large root systems that go in search of water and nutrients, though the plant's top growth is often sparse. To grow good hostas on sandy soils, it is essential to add large amounts of organic matter and to mulch with similar materials in succeeding years. The hostas may also need regular feeding with packaged organic materials, such as pelleted chicken manure or animal manure, proprietary fertilizers, or a foliar feed.

Very small and miniature hostas have quite different

soil requirements from the larger ones and their needs will be fully discussed in chapter 13.

SUN AND SHADE

Hostas are widely thought of as shade-tolerant or even shade-loving plants but this is only part of the story. While shade seems essential for the protection of the large expanses of hosta leaves, more sun is required to produce good flowers. Many hostas will grow in a great deal more sunlight than the conditions in which they are normally planted, provided they receive sufficient moisture at the roots.

Shade is created whenever something intervenes between the sun and some third object. But shade is more than merely the absence of direct sunlight. The presence of shade modifies the climate in the shaded area, making it generally cooler and more humid, while at the same time moderating the extremes of diurnal and seasonal temperature fluctuations,

At the base of an ancient stone wall at the Old Kennels, Nunwick, near Hadrian's Wall in Northumberland, England, the brassy yellow leaves of *Hosta* 'Sun Power' are complemented by yellow-variegated *H.* 'Fortunei Aureomarginata' and white-edged *H.* 'Fringe Benefit'.

Hosta 'Lakeside Black Satin' needs a site in full shade to produce its exceptionally dark green leaves.

Hosta 'Hadspen Blue' holds its color well given good light to dappled shade, as seen here in the garden of Jim and Sandy Wilkins, Jackson, Michigan.

enabling the soil to retain a more constant level of moisture.

Most hostas in cultivation need to be grown in more or less shaded conditions, but this is partly because they seldom receive the amount of moisture at their roots that they really need. There are notable exceptions, however. *Hosta plantaginea* and its hybrids can be grown in full sun in most regions; indeed, in the United Kingdom this species will not flower unless grown in the sun. For most hostas, a balance has to be struck between the amount of moisture available and the amount of sun reaching the leaves. The more moisture at the roots, the more sun the leaves will tolerate. In an experiment conducted by the author, *H.* 'Francee' was grown for several years in a pot standing up to its crown in a pond in sunlight all day long without so much as a scorched margin. In normal soils, the same hosta has to be grown in dappled shade to prevent leaf burn.

Shade can vary considerably in its quality or intensity. The sort of shade cast by thin, high clouds is quite different from that cast by the canopy of dense, evergreen trees, a brick wall, or a solid fence. In general, hostas need good light such as the kind they would receive at the foot of a north wall (in the Northern Hemisphere) where they are shaded from direct sunlight yet receive good light from the open skies above. Light, dappled shade cast by a high tree canopy is also ideal. Hostas will not flourish in dense shade and should never be planted in parts of the garden that are too shaded for anything else to grow.

As a generalization, hostas with blue-green leaves succeed best in shaded places, as do hostas with white variegation, whether central or marginal. Hostas with green, chartreuse, or yellow leaves will take more sun provided that there is adequate moisture at the roots. Most hostas multiply best in sun because this gives them the maximum opportunity to photosynthesize, which is why hosta nurseries often grow their plants in rows in fields. The leaves may be scorched and deformed with such exposure, but they soon recover once in cultivation.

Creating and Reducing Shade

Shade is most naturally created by planting trees, although trees tend to go on growing beyond their desired size and have roots that may compete directly with the hosta roots. Using a felt bag coated with a copper solution will help to ameliorate competition from tree roots.

The choice of tree is important. Beeches (*Fagus*), birches (*Betula*), cherries (*Prunus*), large maples (*Acer*), and willows (*Salix*) have roots that run just below the soil's surface and are best avoided. Cherries, poplars (*Populus*), and wingnuts (*Pterocarya*) produce undesirable quantities of suckers. Some cherries and willows have roots that make an impenetrable mat, and it is hopeless to try to grow hostas near them. Gum trees (*Eucalyptus*) and shagbark hickory (*Carya ovata*) shed their bark in unsightly strips that can damage hostas as they fall. Lime trees (*Tilia*) attract aphids that drip honeydew on all beneath them. Oak trees (*Quercus*), by contrast, put their roots down deeply, well below

A high canopy of trees provides moderate shade for the spectacular leaves of *Hosta* 'Liberty'.

those of the hostas, as do many genera of small, ornamental trees.

Some suitable ornamental trees include service trees (*Amelanchier*), Japanese maple (*Acer palmatum* and its forms), pagoda tree or honey locust (*Cercidiphyllum japonicum*), silver bells tree (*Halesia monticola* var. *vestita*), apples and crabs (*Malus*), black tupelo (*Nyssa sylvatica*), *Gleditsia*, *Halesia*, *Liquidambar*, *Sorbus*, *Stuartia*, and *Styrax*. Several magnolias are also good companions: *Magnolia* ×*loebneri* and its fragrant white-flowered hybrid 'Merrill' or the pink-flowered 'Leonard Messel', *M.* ×*proctoriana*, *M. salicifolia*, as well as *M. sprengeri* and its hybrids 'Spectrum' and 'Star Wars'.

Many large shrubs that ultimately form small, multistemmed trees can cast enough shade for a small collection of hostas, or indeed a collection of small hostas. Among the best of these are the various witch hazels (*Hamamelis*), the taller, winter-flowering viburnums, hazel (*Corylus*) in its color-leaved forms, and photinias such as *Photinia* 'Birmingham' and *P.* 'Red Robin' with their new, red leaves.

If shade is too dense for hostas to flourish, whole trees may have to be removed, but all that is generally needed is to remove the lower branches, so raising the canopy and allowing light and air in.

Artificial Shade

One way to beat the problems created by trees with their ever-increasing shade cast and constantly invading roots is to use an artificial structure such as a pergola or a shade house (also known as a lath house). Shade houses look roughly like greenhouses but are usually constructed of stout uprights linked by less bulky tie-bars to which are attached roofing laths. In the Northern Hemisphere, lath houses should be oriented so that the ridge runs east to west, and the laths themselves run north to south. This alignment of the laths ensures that as the sun appears to move across the sky, the shadows cast by the laths move across the hostas at a steady rate. If the laths were aligned east to west, the movement of the shadows would be much less and the amount of sun reaching the hostas might be enough to damage the leaves. If 2-in. (5-cm) wide laths are used, then the spacing between them should be 2½ to 2¾ in. (6 to 7 cm). This spacing can be varied along the length of the house, thus allowing for hostas that like deeper shade to be grown at one end, and those that prefer more sun at the other.

Pergolas may seem in many ways an ideal compromise between living trees and artificial structures since, once covered in climbing plants, they can take on a fairly natural appearance. The problem, as is the case with trees, is that many climbers have greedy roots. Silver lace vine (*Fallopia baldschuanica*), for example, has roots that spread far and wide, while many honeysuckles (*Lonicera*) make dense mats of roots in which little else will grow. Moreover, many climbers soon cast too dense a shade, but if they are cut back, they will cast insufficient shade. It can be difficult to get the balance right.

WHAT TO LOOK FOR WHEN BUYING HOSTAS

The two factors which contribute most to the success of hostas are the buying of a good plant in the first place and the proper preparation of the ground.

The most important things to look for when buying a hosta are healthy leaves and healthy roots. The leaves, if they are present, should be turgid, of good color and not discolored; they should also not show signs of any physical damage. The roots should be plump and white, and plentiful enough to bind the soil without filling the pot or encircling its bottom. If the soil falls away from the roots, the plant has not been in the pot long enough to establish itself, and if the roots fill too much of the pot, the plant has probably been in the pot too long.

Reject any hosta that has poor, mainly brown roots or that shows any sign of damage to the roots. Particular care should be taken when buying tissue-cultured plants, as these are not always properly weaned.

PLANTING

As a general rule, hostas can be planted at any time when the soil is open and workable. Clearly this varies with local climatic conditions.

When to Plant
In a mild, maritime climate, planting can be undertaken at almost any time of year from mild spells in the depths of winter to damp periods in high summer, but in harsher continental climates, the planting season may be more limited. For example, in North Carolina the planting season is usually early May (late spring) and late August (late summer). Planting at these times enables the hostas to establish themselves before both the heat and droughts of summer and the frosts of winter.

The best time to plant hostas is when they are actively making new roots. This is not when they are creating the first flush of new leaves but a little later, when the first leaves have hardened off but before the second flush of leaves has started. Some hostas also make a second burst of root growth in late summer once the hottest weather is past.

The important thing is to plant hostas at least six weeks before the date of the first killing frost. This gives them time to settle in while the ground is still warm, and it gives the ground time to firm up before the frosts. If planting is left any later, the likely air gaps in the soil will allow the frost to penetrate directly to the roots of the hostas.

Preparing the Ground
The most important single factor in the success of any plant is the thorough prior preparation of the ground. No amount of watering and feeding after planting will make up for poor soil preparation. The ideal soil for hostas is one that is easily worked, is rich in plant foods, and retains moisture while draining well.

Most garden soils can be improved by adding organic matter such as peat or coir, finely chopped bark, farmyard manure, or good garden compost. Coarse grit should also be added to clays and other heavy soils. The goal of adding all this organic matter to the soil is to produce humus, which is a colloidal black or brown substance that can hold water and bind with the particles of clay soil, making it more open. The organic materials themselves are not humus, and their very coarseness helps create spaces in the soil through which roots can penetrate. However, the bacteria that convert organic matter to humus exhaust much of the available nitrogen in the process, thereby depriving the hostas of vital nitrogen. This means that whenever organic matter is added to the soil, some nitrogen fertilizer should also be applied.

If only a single hosta is to be planted, then a single hole should be dug that is proportional in size to the expected size of the hosta. For large hostas, the hole should be a minimum of 3 ft. (90 cm) in diameter, possibly as much as 5 ft. (1.5 m), but since hostas are not deep rooting, the hole need be no more than 18 in. (45 cm) deep. It is important to loosen the soil at the bottom of the hole before back-filling the holes with alternating 2¾-in. (7-cm) layers of soil and organic matter. Each layer that is added should be thoroughly mixed with the previous layers and then well firmed with the feet.

Where a larger number of hostas is to be planted, it is simpler to prepare the whole area, either by double-digging or with a mechanical tiller (rotovator). The tiller should be set to its maximum depth and the ground turned over. Any roots or large rocks thrown up in the process should be removed. The area should then be covered with 2 to 4 in. (5 to 10 cm) of organic matter and a scattering of balanced,

general purpose fertilizer, then tilled again. On all except sandy or gravelly soils, about 1 in. (2.5 cm) of coarse grit or pea-shingle should then be spread over the area, and this too should be tilled into the ground. The planting area or the individual holes should be left to settle for several weeks before planting begins.

If the area to be planted consists of light to moderate woodland the top soil can be removed and a 1- to 2-in. (2.5- to 5-cm) layer of sharp gravel put down with a layer of newspaper or landscape fabric placed over the top and the top soil, augmented by good quality potting compost, replaced. Landscape fabric deters tree roots from returning.

How to Plant

At planting time, dig a hole large enough to take all the hosta roots, well spread out, not bent nor folded. Then make a small mound in the middle of the hole so that the crown of the plant can rest on it with the roots running downhill. The roots of the hosta should

Avid plant collectors John Baker and June Colley maintain more than 800 hosta cultivars in their Hampshire garden, making it one of the largest collections in England.

be teased out and spread over the sides of the mound. It is particularly important to tease the roots of pot-grown hostas which may be very congested. Then return the soil to the hole, firming it with hands or feet. Finally, water the hosta thoroughly. The soil around the hosta should be mulched to keep the roots cool and to prevent water loss through its surface.

WATERING

Hostas being natives of areas of high rainfall demand plenty of water at the roots, a trait they have brought with them into cultivation and passed on to the modern hybrids grown in gardens. Leaves that are deprived of sufficient precipitation will wilt and turn yellow, and if the situation persists, the plants may die back to their overwintering buds. Although they may start into growth again once there is sufficient moisture in the soil, the leaves will be much smaller than before. Thus, for hostas to thrive, it is essential to ensure a sufficient and regular supply of water during the growing season.

While it may seem self-evident that the best way to water plants is by whatever means most nearly resembles rainfall, this is certainly not the case with hostas. Overhead artificial watering can lead to water lying on the leaves, which can in turn cause them to rot, become the focus of fungal infections, and attract slugs and snails. Overhead watering of blue-leaved hostas can severely damage the glaucous bloom, since the individual water droplets hitting the leaves actually erode the waxy coating. Even fine mist sprays, which do not cause actual physical damage, can leave unsightly chalky or other discolorations.

Lightly sprinkling hostas using overhead irrigation is also harmful because it only dampens the surface of the soil, resulting in roots that turn upward toward the surface to get what little water is available instead of in deep, life-sustaining roots. The hostas thus become extraordinarily vulnerable in times of drought.

Another view of the Baker-Colley garden.

Hosta 'Halcyon' combines beautifully with ground-hugging common dog violet (*Viola riviniana*), red-flowered giant wake robin (*Trillium chloropetalum*), and variegated-leaved golden dead nettle (*Laminum galeobdolon*) in Beth Chatto's garden, Essex, England.

A mulch of white stones sets off the rich blue-green leaves of the diminutive *Hosta* 'Blue Mouse Ears'. Note the striking raceme with buds swelling up like mini-balloons before partially opening.

Water is best applied directly to the roots of hostas, beneath the leaves, using a watering can without a rose, a watering wand attached to a hose, or a hose that is left trickling slowly for several hours. Seep hoses are an excellent means of applying water in the right place and can be looped around clumps of hostas, though the girth of the loop must be increased every year. Watering is best done in the early morning (especially in warmer climates) to give hostas maximum benefit. Watering in the evening and at night tends to encourage slugs and snails.

The same watering principles apply to hostas in containers. Potted hostas will need to be watered at least every two to three days from the time the leaves emerge in spring until they die down in the autumn. Very large hostas, especially those growing in sun or

A luxuriant planting of hostas, grasses, and unusual perennials by Wol and Sue Staines at Glen Chantry Garden near Colchester in Essex, England.

in a windy site, will need as much as 3 gallons (12 liters) of water every day, while hostas of average size will need at least 1 gallon (4.5 liters) a day.

FEEDING AND MULCHING

Hostas only achieve their sumptuous potential if, in addition to adequate supplies of water, they also receive plenty of nourishment from the soil. They are generally considered gross feeders and will respond well to liberal though not excessive applications of manures and fertilizers.

In this age of green awareness, organic feeds such farmyard manure, garden compost, or leaf-mold are much advocated. Excellent though they are as mulches and as contributors to soil humus levels, their nutritional value varies from batch to batch and is always unbalanced and often negligible. Generally, it is more useful to use artificial fertilizers whose nutritional values are known. These fertilizers may come in the form of granules, pellets, or powder; some are liquid feeds that are applied either to the roots or the foliage.

Ideally, hostas should be lightly mulched in spring and autumn and fed in spring and early summer. This guideline applies both to hostas in the ground and hostas in containers. Any heavy fertilization after midsummer will promote soft, sappy growth that will be enjoyed by slugs and snails.

The purposes of mulching are first to keep the roots cool, second to reduce water evaporation through the surface of the soil, and third to continue to add humus to the soil. The materials used for mulching tend to vary from area to area, largely depending on local availability and cost. Generally, farmyard manure, peat, coir, cocoa shells, garden compost, shredded bark, crushed corncobs, pine needles, seaweed, salt hay, and similar organic materials are suitable. These eventually decompose and contribute to the humus level in the soil, but inorganic mulches such as stones or gravel are sometimes used, as are plastic or woven materials that suppress weeds. A mulch of small gray slate offcuts can accentuate the brilliance of yellow hostas leaves, conversely a more somber mood can be created using gray gravel with blue leaves. Many different combinations can also be effective when

growing hostas mulched with gravel in contrasting colors.

Where hostas have been planted singly, the mulch should be applied in a ring around the plant. Care should be taken not to bury the crown itself as this might cause it to rot in the winter. The mulch should be spread up to or beyond the circumference of the leaf mound. While most hostas are frost hardy throughout the temperate world, it is sometimes expedient to cover the crowns lightly with straw, dry fern fronds, or salt hay to prevent heaving in alternating spells of cold and warmth. The mulch should not be too thick; a depth of no more than 1 in. (2.5 cm) for large hostas and ³⁄₁₆ to ³⁄₈ in. (5 to 10 mm) for small hostas is usually sufficient. The spread of the mulch should be slightly greater than the anticipated spread of the leaf mound.

Where hostas are planted together in large groups, the mulch should be spread over the whole area, again without covering the crowns. The petioles should not be covered as this can be a cause of fungal diseases, especially southern stem blight. Mulches that are laid too thickly will create an ideal nesting site for voles and other rodents. Undecayed organic matter, such as fresh lawn mowings and fresh vegetable waste from the house, should be composted before being used in the garden.

GROWING IN CONTAINERS

The first essential when growing hostas in containers is to make sure that the containers are large enough to take the roots with room to spare for two or three years of development. The containers should have large enough holes in the bottom to ensure good drainage, but the holes themselves should be covered with crocks (pieces of broken terracotta pots or roof tiles), wire screening, or porous matting so that the growing mix does not slip through them.

In general, medium to large and very large hostas are best grown in a soil-based growing mix, though medium and small hostas do better in soil-less potting mixes with coarse grit added. If large and very large hostas are grown in soil-less mixes, special care must be taken not to let the mix dry out as it is difficult to then rewet, a particular problem for large-leaved hostas that metabolize huge quantities of water daily.

As a result of so much watering, any nutrients in the soil are soon leached out and will need to be replaced. With very large hostas, it is a good idea to put a layer of organic manure such as farmyard manure over the crocks before adding the potting mix and then to mix some organic manure in with the growing mix. Some growing mixes contain fertilizer, but it is usually designed to last for only a few weeks. Several-month controlled-release fertilizer granules or pellets should then be scattered on the growing mix under the plant's leaves, but this should not be done more than once or twice in the growing season, and never after midsummer. An alternative is a weekly, dilute foliar feed, but again this should not be used after midsummer.

Any healthy hosta will outgrow its pot sooner or later. It will then need to be moved on to a larger

Container-grown hostas arranged at varying heights add interest to the otherwise level garden of Pat and George Raeder, Akron, Ohio.

container or split and put back in the same pot but in fresh growing mix. If this is not done, the leaves of the hostas will diminish in size and may become misshapen.

While most hostas are suitable for cultivation in containers, hostas of the Elegans Group, the Golden Medallion Group, and the Tokudama Group are usually less successful in containers because they develop a fibrous core at the crown, which impedes their development if they are kept in containers for more than two or three years. Hostas of the Fortunei Group, however, with their finer root system, remain in good condition in containers for longer than average.

Many hosta gardeners bring their containerized hostas into a garage or garden room for winter protection since ice will form at the bottom of an unprotected pot and rainwater will freeze over the soil at the top. Containers can be tightly packed together on shelves with a mulch spread around and over the top to give even more protection in the coldest regions.

PROPAGATION

Hostas can be readily increased by seed or division, but the only way to be certain that the newly propagated hosta will be an exact replica of its parent is to divide it.

Division

The easiest way to increase a large hosta from a well-established clump is to take a slice out of it rather as one would take a slice from a circular cake, using a sharp spade. The slice, once removed, can then be broken down or cut into smaller pieces. For smaller hostas a knife is usually all that is required. Whatever instrument is used should be dipped in a fungicidal solution before and after use, and the cut surfaces of the hostas should also be dusted with a fungicidal powder. The newly separated pieces can then be potted up or planted out to grow on. The hole left by the removal of the original slice should be filled with good garden soil, and after a season or so, the clump will look as though it has never been disturbed.

Alternatively, the whole clump can be dug out of the ground and split by using two forks back-to-back as levers to tease the clump into two or more parts. Once the clumps are out of the ground they can be split down to individual buds or fans of leaves using a sharp knife or saw. Some hostas with a tough, dense and almost woody crown, such as *Hosta sieboldiana*, must be split with a sharp knife or saw, but other hostas with looser, more diffuse root systems, such as *H. sieboldii*, can simply be shaken or pulled apart. The roots of most hostas lie somewhere between these extremes.

The number of new plants that can be obtained from an established clump is limited to the number of buds or fans in that clump. The main buds of hostas are normally cone-shaped and mauve or violet (sometimes they are dark brown or almost black, as in *Hosta nigrescens*), but careful examination of the white rootstock just below the bud will usually reveal a number of much smaller, latent buds. If the main bud is damaged or destroyed, some of these latent buds may start into growth and make new fans of leaves after several weeks. The simplest way of provoking these latent side buds into growth is to trample on the emerging crowns and destroy the shoots as soon as they poke up through the earth in the spring. Alternatively, hostas can be "mown," which involves cutting the leaves off ³⁄₁₆ to ³⁄₈ in. (5 to 10 mm) above the ground. Mowing, which is a more certain method of provoking growth than trampling, can be done twice in any one growing season.

A further technique, which can be useful with rare or particularly slow-growing hostas, is known as the "Ross method" after its American inventor, Henry Ross. The earth is scraped away from around the hosta revealing its rootstock. A knife is inserted into a fan of leaves at the point where the leaves emerge from the rootstock and then pushed down through the roots into the soil. The knife is removed and inserted into the same fan of leaves but at right angles to the original insertion, then again pushed down through the roots into the earth. This method of dividing each fan into four without taking the hosta out of the earth can be repeated for every fan of leaves. The soil should be returned around the roots and the plant left to grow on. Some leaves will turn yellow and blotchy over the following weeks, but the plant will soon return to its usual, healthy self. Many

nursery people employ a further technique of growing hostas for division in full sunlight since they grow faster that way.

Hostas are usually divided in spring just as the shoots are coming through the surface of the soil, but this is more a counsel of convenience than of perfection: it is easy to see what one is trying to separate when no leaves are in the way. Some people prefer to divide in high summer (July or August in the Northern Hemisphere) when the plants are in full leaf because it gives the cut surfaces time to heal and the young plantlets time to make new roots while the soil or growing medium is still warm and before the winter chill sets in. If hostas are divided in high summer their leaves should be cut off to within ³⁄₁₆ to ³⁄₈ in. (5 to 10 mm) the crown. They will then produce new leaves.

The typical reason for wanting to divide a hosta is simply to increase it, but one might also want to

The emerging shoots of *Hosta* 'El Capitan'.

The expanding shoots of *Hosta* 'El Capitan'.

33

divide a hosta because it has produced a sport. A sport is a part of a plant that is different in character from the original plant, as for example when a stem with double flowers or variegated leaves appears on an otherwise nonvariegated plant. It is usually wise to wait until the sport has appeared in more than one season, and then, rather than removing the piece that has sported, remove the parts of the plant that have not sported. Ultimately, the piece that has sported can be lifted and divided, then potted up or grown on.

Tissue Culture

Tissue culture propagation, also known as micropropagation, is merely a form of division. Cells are usually taken from meristematic tissue, for hostas most often a shoot tip, and grown on in a sterile jelly in a test tube under sterile conditions in a laboratory. Temperature, lighting, and feeding are manipulated to persuade these cells to grow on into tiny plantlets which, once weaned and further grown on, will exactly resemble the parent plant. Once the cells are established in test tubes, they can be divided again and again, making it possible to produce huge numbers of the same plant far more quickly than by conventional means.

A small proportion of the plants produced in this way sometimes fail to conform to the character of the parent plant, and these are usually rogued out and destroyed. Sometimes a plantlet departs from the required true-to-type uniformity in a way that actually makes it more attractive than the original plant. Such sports are then themselves grown on and in due course may be named and tissue cultured. *Hosta* 'June' arose in this way, as have a great many of the new varieties of hosta now coming on the market.

Seed

Most hostas produce abundant seed, and if the seed heads are left standing through the fall for their decorative winter effect, seedlings will likely appear. Hostas are promiscuous, and it is most unlikely that any seedling will have more than a passing resemblance to the seed or pod parent, or any particular merit of its own. Few will be worthy of space in the garden unless they are the results of crosses deliberately made in pursuit of clear breeding objectives. So high have hosta breeders raised expectations that only the very best seedlings are now good enough. The only hosta that will come true from seed is *Hosta ventricosa*, which is apomictic.

Not all hostas produce fertile seed, however, and not all seed in any one pod is necessarily fertile. Pods should be picked as soon as they start to open and placed in clearly labeled paper (not plastic) bags. If the pods are picked too soon, the immature seeds are likely to rot, but if picked too late, they may already have been shed. Seed should be allowed to fall in the bag and then carefully winnowed. This involves tipping the seeds from the paper bag onto a sheet of white paper so that they can be clearly seen. The husks, any infertile seeds, and other debris should be removed because any non-seed matter that remains with the seeds is likely to rot or become infected once sown, which could cause the loss of an entire batch of seed.

Seed can be either sown to overwinter and germinate in the spring or stored for spring sowing. Stored seed should be placed in a suitable envelope and clearly labeled, not only with the name of the hosta or the cross, but also with the year. The envelope should be placed in an airtight tin that is stored in a refrigerator until it is needed. Seed normally remains fully viable for six months, though viability varies from variety to variety. The seed of large-flowered, fragrant hostas seems to be much less viable than that of other varieties and should be sown within a month of ripening. The viability of the seed of all other hostas will start to decline after six months, even if it has been stored properly.

Since hosta seeds are fully frost hardy they can be sown out of doors at any time of the year. Other problems, however, may prevent their successful germination. If periods of frost alternate with periods of milder weather, heaving of the soil or growing mix could expose the seeds to the elements, and they may then be eaten by vermin or become desiccated. Sowing seeds in frames or under glass allows for greater control over such hazards.

Once the seed has germinated, the seedlings should be kept shaded and watered until they are large enough to prick out into individual pots. Eventually they should be lined out in beds or planted where they are to grow in the garden. Many professional growers grow their hostas on under artificial lights since this enhances their photosynthetic rate.

HYBRIDIZING

The purpose of hybridizing hostas is to try to raise new hostas that seem, if only in the eyes of the breeder, to be an improvement on other hostas. Breeders should be clear in their own minds about what improvement or improvements they are seeking so that they can select the most suitable parents and also have a yardstick by which to judge whether the objective has been achieved.

Crossing plants is a simple matter of transferring the pollen from the anthers of the pollen parent to the stigma of the pod parent. The real skill, however, lies first in preventing the pod parent from being pollinated beforehand by unwanted insects, and second in getting the timing right. The usual practice is to slit open the bud of the pod parent with a razor blade before the bud opens naturally and then to cut away the petals, sepals, and male reproductive organs to prevent self-pollination. Since hostas can only be pollinated by visiting insects and the insects have no platform on which to land, pollination by insects cannot now take place.

The transfer of pollen to the pod parent is most simply done by brushing the anther (using the filament as a handle) across the tip of the stigma. Some breeders prefer to transfer the pollen using a small, camel-hair paintbrush, but if the brush is used more than once there is always the danger that pollen from a previous cross may remain on the brush, even when the brush is sterilized in methylated spirits and air dried. Whatever means is used, timing is critical. Ripe pollen has a dry, dustlike texture: if it is sticky it has lost its potency. The tip of the stigma becomes sticky and slightly swollen when it is receptive, but once moisture (like a drop of dew) appears at the tip, the moment has been missed. The most successful matings generally take place in the middle of the morning, particularly if the same flower is pollinated two or three times during the morning.

While most hostas may be crossed with relative ease, *Hosta plantaginea* and most of its fragrant derivatives are notoriously difficult to cross. This may be

partly because *H. plantaginea* is a nocturnally opening species and is not therefore sexually receptive at the same time as other hostas. Some breeders have found that crosses made at 4 p.m. the day before the flower opens are more successful than those made the following morning. Some growers find that putting pollen of *H. plantaginea* around the rim of the stigma and the pollen of the desired pollen parent on the tip of the stigma is more successful than just the pollen parent's own. Each cross should be clearly labeled, the label carrying the name of both parents and stating clearly which is the pod parent. The label should also state the date on which the cross was made.

Buds of *Hosta* 'Deep Blue Sea' are beginning to open.

Hosta 'Cinnamon Sticks', with its red-spotted petioles, is useful as either a pod or pollen parent for introducing red features into leaves, petioles, and scapes.

Seed usually takes six to eight weeks to ripen. Once sown it generally germinates quickly, within two to six weeks. Seed that is not sown out of doors as soon as it is gathered can be stored in an air-tight tin in a refrigerator through the winter and then sown indoors or out as spring begins. Raising seedlings indoors allows the grower greater control over pests and diseases.

Seedlings should be grown on for two or even three years before even the most elementary evaluation is made, and at that stage all worthless seedlings should be discarded. Worthless seedlings will not improve with time and should be ruthlessly trashed. Even highly successful breeders find that, in general, less than 5 percent of seedlings are worth keeping at this stage. A higher proportion of seedlings should be kept

if the hostas are being bred for their flowers since the first flowers are seldom typical. When breeding for foliage, breeders should retain the best seedlings until they produce mature leaves, which may take as long as seven years.

If after all this effort you succeed in producing a seemingly worthwhile hosta, you may want to name it, but it is worth remembering that there are currently approximately 7500 named cultivars, of which around 4000 are registered. To be worth naming, a hosta needs to be really special. If it is to be registered with the International Cultivar Registration Authority for *Hosta*, that authority will require it to be distinct from all other hostas, to be uniform and stable in its characteristics, and to maintain those characteristics when propagated.

The former garden of Gwen Black in Cumbria, England.

4 Gardening with Hostas

HOSTAS ARE, IN THE MAIN, easy, adaptable garden plants, and the range available is now so diverse that hostas can be grown in most gardens and in a wide variety of garden habitats. But any plant as bold or as brightly colored as the hosta—or at least most of them—draws the eye very strongly. It is therefore often helpful to look at their placing in the garden through the eyes of a garden designer who can see the overall picture rather than through the eyes of a hostaphile who is forever comparing the merits or defects of different varieties. Even the eyes of an ecologist are not helpful because ecologists will try to fit the hosta to its habitat rather than consider the esthetics of its placement.

CONSIDERATIONS OF DESIGN

Gardens replete with little else but hostas are for collectors and breeders, and there is nothing wrong with that. But for most gardeners, hostas gain by being set in the context of other plants and in a strong garden framework. Essentially, design is about manipulating space, keeping a balance between voids and solids, voids being open spaces like lawns, grass, or water, solids being big, bulky objects like trees, shrubs (including hedges), or buildings. Gardens are most enjoyable to be in when the voids predominate.

The first principle of planting is not to mix like with like but to contrast like with unlike. Most hostas have solid leaves with entire margins, so plants with many-fingered leaves, such as Lenten rose (*Helleborus orientalis*), dicentras with their finely divided leaves, and ferns with their lacy fronds, afford a contrast, as do many sedges (*Carex*) with their linear leaves. In his book on botanical Latin, William Stearn (1996) listed no less than 138 different leaf shapes; in addition, he mentioned 27 variations on the leaf tip, 12 on the base of the leaf, with a further 9 on the form of the margin and 10 on the ways the leaf may be cut or divided. The diversity is there for those who have the desire to seek it out.

The size of the leaf also matters. Large leaves look larger when grown next to small leaves, which makes the small leaves look smaller too. Next to giant rhubarb (*Gunnera manicata*), the leaves of even the largest hostas look quite small, though the leaves of baby's tears (*Soleirolia soleirolia*, syn. *Helxine soleirolii*) are minute when compared with the leaves of even tiny hostas such as *Hosta venusta*.

Texture matters too. Further interesting associations are created by contrasting plants with shiny leaves with those that have matt or furry leaves. Hosta leaves offer a number of interesting leaf surfaces, from the lustrously oily *Hosta* 'Bubba' to the almost rough-to-the-touch *H*. 'Rhino Hide'. Some have raised, fused areas, such as *H*. 'Koryu' or *H*. 'Praying Hands', while others such as *H*. 'Azure Snow' and *H*. 'Winfield Blue' have leaves that look like frosted icing.

The same principle of contrasting size and texture applies to hostas that are grown in both the sun or shade, though many of the most suitable companions for sun-loving hostas are monocotyledons such as agapanthus, crocosmias, and grasses, which tends to limit the range of foliage to strap-shaped or linear leaves. The most suitable companions for shade-loving hostas are dicotyledons, and these generally have a far wider range of leaf forms. While the leaves of shade-loving plants are often large or finely divided (the better to catch what little sunlight reaches them), the internal economy of sun-loving plants is quite different. Their leaves are often small, often pungent, and sometimes covered in a layer of fine, silvery hairs. While most hostas will flower better in the sun than in shade, one species, *Hosta plantaginea*, is better adapted to growing in the sun than other hostas and in cooler climates its leaves can become etiolated if it is grown in shade all day.

HOSTAS IN WOODLAND

Hostas have always been considered shade-loving plants, though shade-tolerant is a more accurate term since they are plants of woodland and forest margins, rather than of the dark, deep heart of the forest. Most hostas, particularly the larger sorts, grow best in light, open woodland with high, filtered shade and shelter from desiccating winds. Their natural companions are native oaks (*Quercus*) and pines (*Pinus*), together with exotics such as larch (*Larix*) and spruce (*Picea*), and an understory of lace-cap hydrangeas, rhododendrons, azaleas, and butcher's broom (*Ruscus aculeatus*). Beneath the feet of the ground-level story of larger ferns, such as *Woodwardia fimbriata*, *Dryopteris goldiana*, and *D. ludoviciana*, would be a scattering of Solomon's seal (*Polygonatum*), feathery false lily of the valley (*Maianthemum racemosum*, syn. *Smilacina racemosa*), and Japanese fairy bells (*Disporum sessile*), as well as ground-covering ivies and early spring bulbs.

Generally, large groups of hostas with muted, solid colors, mid-green or gray-blue leaves blend better into a landscape of natural woodland, public parks,

and the wilder areas of large country estates than hostas of brighter hues. *Hosta* 'Blue Angel' for example, may eventually achieve a spread of at least 9 ft. (2.7 m) across and will look majestic under a stand of oaks, with smaller hostas (such as drifts of *H. sieboldii* or *H.* 'Decorata') weaving around groups of low-growing ferns on the woodland floor. More formal public parks and open spaces tend to use hostas as ribbon planting or as edging in the foreground and use varieties like *H*. 'Bold Edger' or *H*. 'Resonance' as ground cover, which can also help prevent soil erosion on steep banks or slopes.

Woodland glades in suburban or small country gardens, where the trees are often ornamental rather than native, are much better suited to the more sophisticated and colorful hostas. Plant associations here are likely to be more thoughtful, with color contrasts or echoes involving foliage, bark, and stem. Such associations can be just as effective as flower power, though on a more subtle level.

THE MIXED BORDER

The mixed border has largely taken over from the traditional herbaceous border, mainly because it needs less maintenance. If thoughtfully planted it gives at least three seasons of enjoyment, starting with early spring bulbs and ending with the dying embers of late autumn foliage. It also ensures that in regions where it is impossible to garden (where it is too cold, for example) for several months of winter, there is an outline of shrubs and trees, albeit a fairly stark one, to look at from the house.

Provided there is shade for part of the day, preferably after midday, hostas will associate well with a wide variety of small ornamental trees, shrubs, roses, traditional cottage garden flowers, and bulbs in a harmonious arrangement. The hostas in such a setting can be used for either their foliage or their flowers; some can be used for both.

Preeminent among hostas grown for their flowers are *Hosta* 'Royal Standard', whose leaves look good for the whole season and whose fragrant white flowers provide a long, mid- to late summer display; *H*. 'Tall Boy' with its towering spires of mauve-blue flowers; and the much smaller *H. clausa* f. *normalis* with its

The garden of Judy Springer, Staunton, Virginia.

Don Dean's garden in Ramsey, Minnesota.

dense heads of vivid purple flowers. Hostas with colored or variegated foliage can be used to draw the eye to a flowering group or to reinforce the coloring of a flower group.

HOSTAS IN CONTAINERS

The increasing popularity of growing hostas in pots is partly because the leaf mound of most hostas is the perfect complement to a typical pot and partly because it is easier to prevent leaf damage by slugs and snails when the hosta is being grown in a container.

Generally, it is the largest hostas that look best in pots but, as always, where several pots are grouped together, it is important to vary the size of the hostas as well as their leaf shape and coloring or variegation, especially if all the pots contain hostas. This is slightly less important if the hostas are already being grown in a setting of quite different plants, which might be the case near a house with a foundation planting largely of shrubs. Similarly, varied associations might be less

important if hostas are growing among other sorts of potted plants such as yuccas, agaves, dasylirions, phormiums and even opuntias in sun, or ferns, carices, aspidistras, and rhododendrons in shade.

Hostas in containers can also be used more informally in cottage gardens by sprinkling seed of trailing lobelia into the soil as it begins to warm up in late spring. The contrast of dark blue lobelia with all shades of hosta leaves will be very pleasing.

While the first choice of hostas to grow in pots and other containers may be the large and medium-sized varieties, small and miniature hostas grown in containers of the correct scale can be equally effective.

HOSTAS AT THE WATERSIDE

While it is true that certain hostas do grow in the wild in water meadows and in other very wet conditions, they are mostly smaller species and scarcely what one would choose to grow in the rampant vegetation that normally surrounds a lake or pond or, to a lesser degree, a stream. Whether by nature or nurture,

Flowering hostas in the garden of Cindy and Clarence Nance in Morton, Illinois.

A trough planting of tiny hostas at the former Hosta Choice Nursery and Gardens in Ontario, Canada.

The charming leaves of *Hosta* 'Albomarginata' are simply beautiful in their watery reflection at Longstock Water Garden near Stockbridge in Hampshire, England.

most of us tend to expect the vegetation around water to grow larger and be more vigorous than vegetation in drier ground. Medium-sized, large, and even giant hostas are very much in keeping with this expectation and may indeed have even more sumptuous leaves than many genuinely riverine plants. They are certainly bold enough to compete with waterside irises, ferns, ligularias, rodgersias, and the other familiar denizens of damp garden habitats.

A problem is that relatively few gardens have natural ponds or streams. The water in most gardens is held in place by concrete, butyl, or some other artificial material so that there is no natural transitional zone of dampness between the water and the dry land. But this does not mean that waterside hostas cannot be grown; it simply means that a little more trouble has to be taken to meet their cultural needs.

The simplest way to overcome the problem of dry soil outside the pond is to enrich the soil with copious quantities of organic matter and to water it with a seep (or leaky) hose hidden under mulch. Alternatively, the ground can be dug out and a liner placed in the depression as though for a pond but with a few holes in the liner that is then backfilled with earth, the objective being to impede drainage, not prevent it altogether. Either method creates conditions in which hostas and moisture-loving plants will thrive. Artificial ponds are usually sited in full sun, so it may also be necessary to plant a tree or two to cast light, filtered shade over the hostas. Avoid willows whose roots form impenetrable mats.

There is little in the literature about growing hostas directly in water, but the author's own early experiments show that *Hosta* 'Francee', *H. longissima*, and *H.* 'Undulata' and its several forms will succeed. Presumably, *H. kiyosumiensis* and its forms would also succeed if their pots were stood in water with the crown above water level throughout the summer.

Hostas among other waterside plants at Cambridge Botanic Garden, England.

5 Pests, Diseases, and Other Threats to Hostas

THE THREE BEST DEFENSES against the pests and diseases that can trouble hostas are to grow healthy, vigorous plants, to study the needs of each particular hosta so as to grow it in optimum conditions, and to be vigilant in checking for the presence of pests and diseases so that they can be dealt with using a minimum of chemicals.

SLUGS AND SNAILS

Slugs and snails are notorious for being the most troublesome pests of hostas. Both are classified in phylum Mollusca, class Gastropoda, and are known collectively as mollusks, but several different genera are involved.

Slugs remain active throughout the whole year and can feed whenever the temperature rises above 41°F (5°C). Snails, by contrast, become inactive at the onset of cold weather and take shelter for the winter, typically in flowerpots and logs or against walls. They seal their shells onto a hard surface with mucilage that dries to become hard, in effect gluing the shell to a chosen surface.

There are some 25 species of slugs in the United Kingdom and more in the United States, but only 5 species eat leaf foliage, the rest being carnivores that eat other slugs or worms. The real enemies of hostas are the little black and brown slugs that eat both shoots and roots.

Although slugs and snails are hermaphrodite, they still need to pair up to breed. Breeding usually occurs in spring or autumn when the weather is mild and moist. Small white or creamy spherical eggs up to 1/50 in. (2 mm) long are laid in batches of up to 50 in cavities in the soil. These eggs hatch into tiny versions of their parents and take about three years to reach maturity. When young, they are susceptible to death through desiccation if the soil dries out and also to being eaten by song thrushes, hedgehogs, snakes, frogs and toads, shrews, and slowworms. Some beetles, such as ground (carabid) beetles and rove (staphylinid) beetles feed on them, as do some insects including glowworms and sciomyzid fly larvae.

Human Intervention

The most effective way of reducing slug and snail populations in most gardens is to go out at night with a light and collect these pests in a container that is suitable for destruction. They are particularly easy to find when the garden is wet after rain or when there is a heavy dew. Unless you have done this nighttime collecting, you may well be unaware of the sheer size of the mollusk population in your garden.

The most widely used poisons for controlling slugs and snails are metaldehyde and methiocarb slug pellets. (A Certified Applicator's Permit is required for purchase of methiocarb in the United States.) Introduced into the United States some years ago are small pellets containing one percent iron phosphate; these are less toxic to wild life and their use is becoming widespread. A German company manufacturers the pellets and ships them around the world where they are packed under other companies' labels. In Europe it is Ferramol; in the United States it is Sluggo and Escar-Go!. Slug baits are most effective when applied around the garden on mild evenings, particularly in warm weather in early spring. Slugs are inactive in very hot and very dry weather, so there is little point in using the pellets then.

Baits with iron phosphate reportedly can be used around domestic animals and wildlife, but metaldehyde and methiocarb pellets can be fatal to cats, dogs, and prowling wildlife. It is unlikely, however, that cats or dogs will find pellets that are concealed under a roofing slate or tile propped up on a stone, placed in the angle between the earth and a wall or a fence or laid across the gutter between lawn and border. Moreover, using slates or tiles in this way creates the cool, damp conditions that slugs and snails find most attractive, thereby ensuring they find the pellets. Some slug pellets are blue, which is a difficult color for birds to see, thus making it unlikely that they will eat the pellets. Also, some baits have a very bitter chemical added, making it highly unlikely they will be ingested by children, domestic animals, and wildlife.

Another chemical, one that is far less toxic to pets than metaldehyde and methiocarb, is aluminum sulfate. It comes in the form of crystals that can be scattered on the surface of the soil around hostas. It acts as a contact poison and is particularly effective among germinating hosta seeds.

Hanging hostas in the garden of John Baker and June Colley, Hampshire, England. Such an arrangement allows for more plants to be cultivated in a limited space.

A number of other substances are also poisonous to slugs and snails. Among these are salt, borax, ammonia, a home-made garlic wash, and caffeine. These act as contact poisons and are most effective when applied directly onto the slug, snail, or their eggs instead of when scattered on the soil. Applying a 10-percent solution of household ammonia to the crown and nearby area when shoots first emerge in the spring can be an effective preventive. There are some reports of used coffee grounds being effective when applied to the soil around hostas. A home-made garlic wash, used regularly, can be very successful and less damaging to wild life.

An alternative to using poisons in deterring slugs and snails is the use of barriers since mollusks avoid surfaces that are sharp, hairy, or very absorbent. Several substances are used, most of which are commonly occurring. Among those that deter because of their sharpness are sand, coarse grit, sharp cinders, wood ashes, diatomaceous earth, broken eggshells, and crushed oyster and scallop shells. Many proprietary products such as porous volcanic rock (which is marketed in England, Europe, and Australia as Mollbar) are also suitable. Other types of barriers, such as continuous strips or tapes of copper or aluminum placed around the hostas, cause a chemical reaction which makes the mollusks overproduce mucilage resulting in their desiccation. Although they are effective as deterrents, they are expensive and suffer the same shortcomings as other types of barriers. The hosta leaves arch over the barrier and then touch the ground, thereby affording slugs and snails a bridge over the barrier.

Where hostas are growing in containers, slugs and snails can be deterred to some extent if the containers are raised off the ground on small feet and if a band of petroleum jelly or fruit-tree grease is placed around the outside of the container, since slugs and snails will not be able to motor across it. Penetrating oils (one proprietary product is WD-40) act as deterrents if

About 500 named cultivars are on display at Hosta Hillside, a world-class collection created and maintained by the Michigan Hosta Society at Hidden Lake Gardens in Tipton, Michigan.

they are sprayed on the outsides of containers. Copper tape tied round the outside of pots will also deter slugs and snails.

A third way of dealing with slugs and snails is through biological controls. Biological control through a pathogenic nematode, *Phasmarhabditis hermaphrodita*, has been available for some years but is not equally successful in all gardens. The nematodes are most effective when applied in spring and are more effective on light sandy soils than on heavy clay soils.

An additional measure of control over slugs and snails can be achieved by understanding their needs and then denying them. This means removing dead and dying leaves and not allowing a litter of decaying vegetation to build up in the garden. Hosta leaves should be removed as soon as they start to turn yellow or show signs of decay. Ideally, one should be just as vigilant with the leaves of other plants in the garden. The slug and snail problem is, unfortunately, exacerbated by the fact that hostas seem to grow best in soils rich in organic matter, which is usually supplied in the form of mulches (vegetable matter in one form or another) or as animal manure. Both types of organic matter provide ideal breeding grounds for slugs and snails.

Controlling these pests is also helped if other sorts of garden rubbish are kept to a minimum. Bricks or planks of wood, for example, that are left lying around the garden provide ideal breeding sites. The continual cultivation of the soil's surface can also keep slug and snail populations down by exposing their eggs to the air, thereby destroying them.

Another method of limiting the number of snails and slugs is by making use of plant associations. Hosta foliage is attractive to slugs and snails at all times, and the more hostas one grows, the more one seems to attract slugs and snails; however, not all plants are equally attractive since some have a texture or chemical content that slugs and snails dislike. Hairy-leaved plants are often left well alone. Where hostas are mixed among such plants, the levels of damage to the hostas may be considerably lessened. The following is a list of plants that, while not immune to damage from slugs and snails, tend to survive unscathed in most gardens.

Acanthus mollis
Achillea filipendulina
Agapanthus hybrids and cultivars
Alchemilla mollis
Anemone hupehensis
Anemone ×hybrida
Antirrhinum majus
Aquilegia species
Armeria species
Aster amellus
Aster ×frikartii
Aster novae-angliae
Astilbe ×arendsii
Astrantia major
Bergenia
Centaurea dealbata
Centaurea montana
Corydalis lutea
Cynara cardunculus
Dicentra spectabilis
Digitalis purpurea
Eryngium species
Euphorbia species
Ferns
Foeniculum vulgare
Fuchsia cultivars
Gaillardia aristata
Geranium species
Geum chiloense
Liatris spicata
Lysimachia punctata
Myosotis species
Nepeta ×fassenii
ornamental grasses
Papaver nudicaule
Papaver orientale
Pelargonium
Phlox paniculata
Physostegia virginiana
Polemonium foliosissimum
Polygonatum species
Potentilla hybrids and cultivars
Pulmonaria species
Rudbeckia fulgida
Salvia ×superba
Saxifraga ×urbium
Scabiosa caucasica
Sedum spectabile
Sempervivum species
Sisyrinchium species
Solidago species
Stachys macrantha
Tanacetum coccineum
Thalictrum aquilegiifolium
Tradescantia virginiana
Tropaeolum species
Verbascum species

VINE WEEVILS

Vine weevils (*Otiorhynchus sulcatus*), sometimes called black vine weevils to distinguish them from clay-colored weevils, are highly damaging to hostas both in the larval and adult stages, though the larvae do most damage. These are fat, creamy white, C-shaped, legless grubs about ⅜ in. (1 cm) long that have tiny heads of a malicious shade of burnt sienna. They feed on the roots of hostas and many other plants, especially when the plants are growing in pots. They sometimes destroy all the roots, thereby causing the leaves to turn yellow and the plant to wilt and usually die. The adult weevils are quite distinct in their waisted shape and are dull black, minutely speckled with tiny tufts of yellow hairs. They have roughened wing-cases beneath which are no wings. They feed at night, hiding by day in the basal leaves of low-growing plants and under stones and suchlike.

Vine weevils are often more of a problem in pots than in the open ground, especially if the pots are in tunnels or under glass and if the plants are growing in a soil-less growing mix and have not been repotted for over a year. They can also be a considerable problem in damp or ill-drained ground. Once vine weevils become established, they can be difficult to eradicate completely.

Human Intervention

Although hostas are sometimes decimated by vine weevil, there are other plants that vine weevils prefer both as hosts for their grubs and as food for the adults.

Among these are adiantums, begonias, bergenias, cyclamen, primulas, saxifrages, and sedums. Some nursery people place pots of one or other of these plants at the entrance to their tunnels in the hope that the vine weevils will go to them rather than to the hostas.

Adult vine weevils can also be trapped, especially under glass or in tunnels, by placing rolls of corrugated paper, old sacking, or canvas on or near the ground to provide daytime refuge for the weevils. These materials should be inspected daily and shaken out over a clean surface where the weevils can be spotted and destroyed. The adults can also be seen quite easily by torchlight after dark, picked off the plants, and destroyed.

Potted plants that are yellowing or wilting should be tipped out of their containers and the remaining roots, if any, washed off under running water and then repotted in fresh growing mix. The original soil

Hundreds of hosta varieties densely planted in the former suburban garden of Randy Goodwin, Indianapolis, Indiana.

should be burned or otherwise sterilized before being reused or put on the garden.

Vine weevils once were controlled by highly toxic organochlorine insecticides. These chemicals are very persistent in the soil, have found their way into the food chain, and have also killed beneficial insects. They are now banned and no effective alternatives have been found. Acephate, ranked among the best insecticide available to home gardeners, is only somewhat effective. Treatment with acephate requires application in springtime, and a second and third application later on to help control emerging adults.

The best mitigation for vine weevils is to kill the larvae, that is, their grubs. The chemical imidacloprid, which kills these and several other grubs on contact, is now available in nurseries and garden centers. In the United Kingdom it can be found as a packet specifically marketed for vine weevil control. In the United States and some other countries, home gardeners wanting to use imidacloprid for vine weevil control will need to purchase this chemical as an insecticide for the white grubs of Japanese beetles in lawns and gardens. It is available as both a granule and a liquid, and is easily spread or sprayed onto hosta beds as well as containers. It is best to apply imidacloprid to the soil in advance of when larvae will be feeding. Some nurseries use a potting compost containing imidacloprid or other grub-killing chemicals already mixed into it.

A parasitic nematode, *Heterorhabditis megidis*, provides the most effective control of vine weevil. It is usually bought by mail order and is applied in the same way as the nematode for the control of slugs.

FOLIAR NEMATODES

All hosta gardeners in the United States are likely to experience outbreaks of foliar nematodes (*Aphelenchoides fragariae* and *Ditylenchus dipsaci*), which can cause severe damage to hostas. These pests were virtually unknown in the United States until about 1991, apparently having been brought into the country on imported plants.

Foliar nematodes are microscopic segmented roundworms which feed on spongy live tissue inside the leaf. They are spread by splashing water. The roundworms overwinter in the crowns of hostas, migrating in the spring to the leaf blade, where they feed and multiply between the veins, causing the characteristic interveinal browning of the leaves appearing as brown stripes fading to just a slight discoloration. This browning is often not apparent until mid- or late summer.

Removing affected foliage may limit the infestation but will not be a complete remedy. Mildly infested plants can be ridded of the nematode and its eggs by soaking individual divisions in water held at a temperature of 120°F (49°C) for 15 to 20 minutes, after which they should be potted up and grown on in isolation from other hostas for at least six months.

According to a nematologist at Ohio State University, significant success was reported following applications of trichlorfon (as Dylox 80 powder) and ethoprop, and moderate success with applications of oxamyl (a restricted pesticide), diazinon (now banned from U.S. markets), trichlorfon (as Dylox 6.2 granular), a proprietary hydrogen dioxide (also called hydrogen peroxide) solution and insecticidal soap. Some growers claim that treating hostas the year after the affliction is noticed first when the shoots just emerge and then several times later in the season, with disulfoton (Di-Syston), a systemic organophosphate insecticide, decreases the foliar nematode population in the plants. No product available to the home gardener completely eradicates this problem.

LEAF SPOTTING AND PETIOLE ROT

Necrotic spots appear on the leaves of hostas for various reasons. Spots can appear in late spring if early spring was particularly cold and damp. These appear as minute brown spots with a tiny pinhole in the middle. Damage can usually be averted by ensuring good frost drainage. Once damaged, the leaves cannot be made whole again, though unsightly leaves can be cut off. With warmer weather, new leaves should come through normally.

Leaf spotting can also be caused by the fungi *Alternaria*, *Phyllostricta*, and *Colletotrichum omnivorum*. Further damage can be prevented by two or three sprays of thiophanate-methyl or thiram fungicide at two-week intervals; however, the careless use of garden chemicals can also cause leaf spotting.

A number of fungi and bacteria can cause petiole blight and crown rot in hostas. Southern stem blight or rot, also called petiole rot, caused by the fungi *Sclerotium rolfsii* and *S. rolfsii* var. *delphinii*, seems to be the most common of these infestations. It was first observed in the southern United States but appears to be traveling northwards as summers get longer and hotter and is more prevalent in times of high humidity. Seldom occurring before June, its identifying characteristics are spherical balls–hard, white then brown, and about the size of mustard seeds–where the petioles meet the crown, as well as white cottony mycelium masses in the area. The affected leaves usually have fallen over and easily detach if pulled gently. The plant should be dug up, all soil removed, and all affected parts scraped away with a sharp knife and burned. It should then be soaked in a 3-percent solution of hydrogen peroxide or 10-percent solution of household bleach for up to two hours. (Use the same treatment for hostas growing in pots.) The hostas should then be isolated at least until the end of the season, and no hostas should be planted where the infection occurred.

Fungicides that are both preventive and curative are azoxystrobin, kresoxim-methyl, and trifloxystrobin, which are strobilurins, and flutolanil, a benzamide. Flutolanil is listed specifically for control of *Sclerotium rolfsii*. Several applications will be required. Tebuconazole, a systemic triazole fungicide, is available to home gardeners for both curing and preventing Southern stem blight; it is highly effective and usually only one application is required each season. This chemical is listed as an all-purpose disease control for roses, flowers, and shrubs. A soil drench, such as bleach solution or pentachloronitrobenzene (PCNB), is sometimes helpful.

Anthracnose is a fungal disease appearing on the leaf as tiny to very large irregular rust-colored spots. Warm temperatures and wet conditions promote this disease. Usually anthracnose is most visible on yellow

The garden of hosta growers Van and Shirley Wade, Bellville, Ohio.

or light-colored (medio-variegated) hosta leaves. The best method of prevention is to avoid crowding plants together.

Crown rot is a term for the rotting disease that primarily affects the crowns of hostas, usually in early season. The hosta's crown is soft, mushy, or deteriorated. Affected tissue is usually light brown or reddish. Frequently an unpleasant rotting odor is noted. The roots in this area may also be affected. Crown rot is caused by bacterial and fungal (but not *Sclerotium rolfsii*) organisms believed to enter through some kind of plant damage. Corrective action is similar to that for stem blight: dig up the plant, trim away all rotted tissue, then soak the plant in bleach solution, and plant it in fresh soil. A preventative and curative fungicide is thiophanate-methyl; several applications may be required. A bleach solution or PCNB as a soil disinfectant is often applied.

Fungal infestations are sometimes caused by too many applications of high-nitrogen fertilizer and by overly dense mulches packed tightly around the hosta clump. Dense mulches prevent the movement of air or sufficient drainage of the soil and thus should be avoided.

In the southern United States, where humidity is very high, *Fusarium oxysporum* and *Verticillium alboatrum* are the causes of progressive yellowing of the outer to the inner leaves of a hosta clump. Fungicides can be used as prophylactics, but they need to be applied regularly and frequently.

VIRAL INFECTIONS

Viral infections are more likely to infect hostas that are in poor health or have been damaged by insects. It is much more difficult to contain the spread of a virus in large collections of a single genus, where it quickly spreads from plant to plant. Single plants found to be infected can be easily isolated and treated, or they can be burned if too badly infected to save. Prevention is better than cure, so it is always prudent when dividing hostas to dip the knife in alcohol or a bleach solution before making the cut, and again afterwards.

The most common viral infections affecting hostas are Hosta Virus X (HVX), tobacco rattle virus, and

Virus infecting the leaves of *Hosta* 'Gold Standard'.

tomato ring spot virus. HVX can be identified by a procedure developed at the University of Minnesota. The Arabic mosaic virus, which produces chlorotic leaves with some stunting, may also affect hostas. Sometimes what appears to be a viral infection in the form of stunted or deformed leaves is actually drought damage, and the mosaic patterning is often mistaken for a mottled sport.

CUTWORMS

Many species of cutworms exist. They are up to 1¼ in. (3 cm) long, are soft bodied and smooth, and curl up tightly when disturbed. They can be dull gray, brown, or black and may be striped or spotted. These night-feeders can cut off plants either at or below the soil surface. Some cutworms feed on the leaves or buds of hostas, while others feed on the roots. They are particularly destructive early in the season.

Cutworms can be prevented from causing damage without an insecticide being used. A stiff, 2¾-in. (7-cm) cardboard collar should be placed around the plant stem. The collar should extend about 1 in. (2.5 cm) into the soil and protrude 2 in. (5 cm) above the soil, clearing the stem by about ⅜ in. (1 cm). A newly patented, reusable cutworm shield can be purchased to protect the stems.

If damage is to the leaf surface, shine a torch on the leaves at night while these pests are feeding and squash them as they fall. *Bacillus thuringiensis* will kill cutworms and is safe to use. If cultural control fails, a proprietary insecticide should be applied.

The garden of Sue Mills, Chesterland, Ohio.

FUNGUS GNATS

Fungus gnats (families Fungivoridae and Sciaridae) are black with long, thin wings. They are very small, usually less than 1/50 in. (2 mm) in length, although some species may reach ¼ in. (6 mm). They are not a problem as adults, but in the larval stage they feed on the roots and can cripple and topple hosta seedlings.

Fungus gnats can be controlled indoors with pyrethrin as a surface drench, backed up by yellow sticky cards 2¾ × 4 in. (7 × 10 cm), cut in 1 in. (2.5 cm) strips and placed horizontally at soil level. These cards actually catch the emerging adult before it can fly and lay eggs.

Disulfoton systemic granules can be spread on the surface of the soil or, after the planting tray has been half filled with soil, it can be spread in a layer and then covered with the remaining soil. Seed would then be sown. Watering activates the granules, creating a vapor that could escape into the room if used on top of the soil.

DEER

Of all the four-legged creatures that have a taste for hostas, deer are by far the most voracious and can be a considerable problem in the country in certain regions of both Europe and the United States. Their depredations can start in the spring, when they often chew hostas right down to the ground and then continue through the growing season, eating almost any part of a hosta. They are most attracted to hostas with fragrant flowers, especially *Hosta plantaginea* and its hybrids.

A number of folk cures for deer exist, including hair (preferably human), urine (preferably human), lion and tiger dung (obtainable from some zoos), scarecrows, various shiny things such as CD discs suspended from strings so that they move in the wind, pepper sprays, and large dogs. When using commercial or home-made deer repellents, be sure to frequently change products so that the deer do not get used to them. The traditional wisdom is that barriers are only effective when they are over 8 ft. (2.4 m) tall. Where space permits, a sequence of lower barriers is effective, especially if they are too close together for the deer to gather themselves to spring over the next one.

RODENTS

Mice, rats, gray squirrels, rabbits, and voles can all wreak havoc in a bed of hostas. Most merely chew the foliage, making clumps unsightly, but voles actually devour the roots and can thus do a vast amount of damage. They often move into polytunnels and greenhouses for warmth during the winter. Since the plants are dormant and not under a gardener's constant observation (as they would be when in leaf), rodents can do plenty of harm before their presence is noticed. Vigilance, therefore, is essential.

Various traps and baits are available for the control of these creatures, and a measure of control can be attained with chlorophacinone formulated as paraffinized pellets. This chemical is on restricted sale, and in some states requires an applicator's license. Some growers bury a wire cage into the ground at planting depth and plant the hosta into this, combining the growing mix with sharp gravel as voles do not like this on their noses when burrowing. Raccoons will be deterred by an electric fence 18 in. (45 cm) high; they will also become disorientated and confused by fishing line wrapped between trees and posts, and the fishing line will be all but invisible to human eyes.

CLIMATIC AND OTHER DAMAGE

Sudden late frosts in some regions can cause unsightly damage to the newly emerged leaves of some hostas. *Hosta* 'Lancifolia', *H. montana* 'Aureomarginata', and *H. plantaginea* and its forms are particularly vulnerable.

Damage can often be averted by planting hostas in places where there is good frost drainage. Placing a plastic bucket over emerging hosta leaves in early evening and then removing it in the morning can also prevent damage to plants. If the damaged leaves are cut off, the new leaves will be unscathed unless further frosts occur. Repeated damage over the years will reduce the size and vigor of the hostas.

Spring burn is mainly a problem with forms of *Hosta sieboldiana* that have yellow in their leaves and is the result of a combination of conditions. It occurs in spring when the leaves are growing rapidly, when night temperatures drop down close to freezing, and when the leaves are then subsequently exposed to direct sunlight or strong winds. The yellow parts of the leaves are desiccated and they turn orange-brown and look as though they have developed rust. Oddly, the blue areas of the leaves do not seem to be affected, nor do the white-margined or white-centered forms of *H. sieboldiana*.

The problem of spring burn is largely solved by planting susceptible varieties out of the wind and where they will not be in direct sunlight in the early mornings. In Britain, where the climate is both cooler than in much of the United States, this kind of damage is seldom seen.

Melting out is a phenomenon usually seen only in hosta leaves with white centers. The middle of the white area turns brown and desiccates, eventually decaying and leaving one or several holes at the center of the brown area. In some varieties, the damage can reduce the leaf blade to brown, white, and green shreds. It used to be thought that the problem was caused by growing susceptible plants in too much sun, but the problem can occur with hostas growing in positions where direct sunlight never reaches them. The problem is less likely to occur in plants growing in moist soils and bright light.

Leaf scorch or sunburn is revealed when large sections of the leaves turn light yellow and then become crisp and brown. The problem is simply the result of hostas being grown in too much sun. It often occurs in gardens where shade for the hostas is created by trees, but either the hostas leaf-up early or the trees are late into leaf.

Center-clump dieback, also called centering out, though unsightly in the garden, is not a disease but merely a consequence of the natural development of a hosta clump. Like most perennial plants, hostas usually grow from the center outward in an ever-expanding ring. The center of the clump, being the oldest part, suffers senescence, exhausts the soil beneath it, and gets deprived of light by the more vigorous leaves of younger parts of the clump around it. In a sense there is no cure. The worry when this happens to hostas in the garden is that the moribund parts of the plant will develop a pernicious rot that might destroy the rest of the clump, though in fact this seldom happens. All that can be done is to dig up and divide the plant, replanting it in another part of the garden, but you will have a smaller plant in subsequent years. The soil where the plant was growing should be enriched with organic matter and fertilizer, and if no rot has occurred, another hosta can be planted there.

An island bed of hostas in the garden of Marcia Niswonger, Piqua, Ohio.

Hosta 'Hirao Splendor'

This directory has been compiled primarily to help gardeners choose which hostas to place where in the garden. Some hostas would fit easily into three different categories, but for ease of reference they are placed in the category deemed most important. Thus, for example, although the species and their sports are now listed in a special section at the beginning of the connoisseurs chapter, they are cross-referenced in other relevant chapters.

Mature hostas in Hans Hansen's garden in Waseca, Minnesota.

6

Hostas with Green Leaves

Hostas with plain green leaves must have very special qualities to capture the interest of modern hosta growers. In the 1950s and 1960s, very few variegated hostas were available, and there were virtually none with golden-yellow leaves and only a few with a central variegation. Any and all hosta introductions were eagerly welcomed and quickly disseminated. Today, however, our expectations are much higher, and if a green-leaved hosta is to rank on the popularity polls, it must be in the class of *Hosta* 'Clovelly', *H.* 'Devon Green', or *H.* 'Empress Wu'; that is, it must have an unusual surface texture, an interesting leaf shape or plant habit, or an exceptional characteristic such as heavy racemes of flower, an intensely white back, or outstanding red petioles and scapes, or it must carry genes that make it a good breeding plant.

Many older hostas have been omitted from this chapter as they have long been superseded by more attractive garden varieties. Such hostas will now usually only be found growing in National Plant Collections or as part of special species or early hybrid collections so that their unique genetic characteristics do not disappear forever.

Hosta 'Apple Green' (K. Anderson 1982)

SMALL

Origin: *H. nakaiana* hybrid.

Description: A compact, symmetrical mound 20 in. wide × 14 in. high (50 × 35 cm). Leaf blade 4 × 3 in.(10 × 8 cm), of average substance, light green to chartreuse, matt above and thinly glaucous below, dimpled, veins ribbed when mature, edge flat, leaf slightly cupped, widely oval with a cuspidate tip and heart-shaped overlapping lobes. Petiole narrow, pale green. Flower bell-shaped, pale lavender, on an upright, bare, light green, 18-in. (45-cm) scape in midsummer; fertile.

Cultivation Notes: Site in dappled shade. Exposure to strong sunlight turns the leaves more yellow. Increases rapidly.

Distinguishing Features: The flowers are widely spaced down the scape, almost reaching the leaf mound.

Hosta 'Bennie McRae' (N. Suggs 1989)

MEDIUM

Origin: *H. plantaginea* hybrid.

Description: An asymmetrical mound 30 in. wide × 24 in. high (75 × 60 cm). Leaf blade 11 × 4½ in. (28 × 11 cm), thin, glossy, light to mid-green, edge undulate, leaf arching, somewhat pinched toward the recurved tip, with narrowly oval, rounded to heart-shaped pinched lobes. Petiole mid-green. Flower funnel-shaped, fragrant, lavender, on an oblique, leafy,

*An asterisk before a name indicates that the plant is fully described elsewhere in this book.

Hosta 'Apple Green'

Hosta 'Bennie McRae'

green, 24-in. (60-cm) scape from late summer to early autumn; fertility unknown.

Cultivation Notes: Tolerates several hours of morning sun even in hot climates if provided with plenty of moisture at the roots. Exposure to sun turns the leaves a muted chartreuse.

Similar: *★H.* 'Honeybells' has wider leaves.

Hosta 'Betsy King' (F. Williams/AHS 1986)

MEDIUM

Origin: *★H.* 'Decorata' × *H. sieboldii* hybrid.

Description: An upright mound 24 in. wide × 16 in. high (60 × 40 cm). Leaf blade 5 × 2½ in. (13 × 6 cm), of average substance, glossy, dark green, some dimpling when mature, closely veined, edge shallowly undulate, leaf flat, oval with an obtuse tip and tapered open to pinched lobes. Petiole dark green. Flower widely flared, rich purple, in abundance, on an upright, leafy, dark green, 30-in. (75-cm) scape in late summer.

Cultivation Notes: Site in light to moderate shade.

Distinguishing Features: The rhizomatous root structure, small leafy bracts, and superb flowers.

Similar: *H.* 'Decorata Normalis' has slightly smaller leaves.

Hosta 'Black Hills' (R. Savory 1983)

LARGE

Origin: *H.* 'Green Gold' hybrid.

Description: An unruly mound 50 in. wide × 30 in. high (126 × 75 cm). Leaf blade 8 × 7 in. (20 × 18 cm), thick, very dark green with a blue-black cast, shiny above and thickly glaucous below, seersuckered and deeply puckered, edge almost flat, leaf shallowly cupped, widely oval to nearly round with a mucronate tip and heart-shaped overlapping lobes. Petiole glaucous lighter green, appearing to pierce the blade. Flower widely funnel-shaped, lilac, opening from a darker bud, on an upright, leafy, glaucous paler green, 40-in. (100-cm) scape in midsummer; fertile.

Cultivation Notes: Site in light to full shade. Pest resistant.

Distinguishing Features: Intense puckering or even distortion of the leaves appears only with maturity.

Similar: *H.* 'Big Top'; *H.* 'Birchwood Elegance'; *H.*

'Black Beauty'; *H.* 'Lakeside Prophecy' has a wavier leaf edge.

Hosta 'Bridegroom' (H. & D. Benedict/H. Gowen 1990)

SMALL–MEDIUM

Origin: Seedling from *H.* 'Holly's Honey' selfed.

Description: A low mound 34 in. wide × 16 in. high (85 × 40 cm), the leaves held in an upward stance. Leaf blade 5 × 4 in. (13 × 10 cm), thin, glossy, dark olive green, smooth, prominently veined, edge

Hosta 'Betsy King', attractive in leaf and flower.

Hosta 'Black Hills'

rippled, leaf triangular, the side sloping downward, the center and the twisted tip curving upward, the lobes heart-shaped and open. Petiole narrow, dark green, with purple dots toward the crown. Flower funnel-shaped, lavender, on an upright, bare, green, 18-in. (45-cm) scape in late summer; sterile.

Cultivation Notes: Site in light to moderate shade. Slow to moderate growth. Vulnerable to pests but worth the extra effort to preserve the leaves intact since this is one of the best of the newer green-leaved hostas.

Distinguishing Features: The leaves uniquely curve upward (hence the name).

Similar: *H.* 'Stirfry'.

Sports: *H.* 'Bestman' has wider leaves.

Hosta 'Bubba' (T. Avent 1998)

SMALL–MEDIUM

Origin: *H.* 'Sum and Substance' hybrid.

Description: A dense mound 24 in. wide × 12 in. high (60 × 30 cm). Leaf blade 6 × 4½ in. (15 × 11 cm), thick, olive green, glossy above and satiny below, dimpled, edge flat, leaf slightly folded, widely oval with a cuspidate to mucronate tip and rounded pinched lobes. Petiole short, lighter green, with red dots toward the crown. Flower bell-shaped, pale lavender, on an upright, green, 20-in. (50-cm) scape in late summer; sterile.

Cultivation Notes: Site in bright light to moderate shade. Grow with glaucous blue-leaved hostas to set

off the exceptionally lustrous leaf surface. Moderate growth rate.

Hosta 'Candy Dish' (A. Summers/A. Wrede 2003)

MEDIUM

Origin: *H.* 'Urajiro Hachijo' hybrid.

Description: A flattish, dense mound 24 in. wide × 12 in. high (60 × 30 cm). Leaf blade 5 × 4 in. (13 × 10 cm), of heavy substance, glossy, dark spinach green, smooth, prominent veins widely spaced, edge distinctively and evenly rippled, leaf flat, broadly ovate to nearly round with a mucronate tip and heart-shaped pinched lobes. Petiole purple-dotted dark green. Flower funnel-shaped, pale lavender, on an oblique, bare, green, 11- to 12-in. (28- to

Hosta 'Bubba'

Hosta 'Bridegroom'

Hosta 'Candy Dish'

30-cm) scape from late summer into autumn; fertility unknown.

Cultivation Notes: Site in moderate shade. Increases rapidly. May exceed its registered dimensions. A superb new introduction which will delight collectors of green-leaved hostas. Grow with *Saxifraga* 'Black Ruby' to echo the attractive leaf edges, against a lighter background such as white stone chippings.

Distinguishing Features: Precisely rippled edges on platterlike leaves.

Similar: *H.* 'Warwick Ballerina' has larger leaves and its margins are not so distinctly and evenly piecrusted.

Hosta 'Candy Hearts' (E. Fisher/P. Ruh 1998)

MEDIUM

Origin: *H. nakaiana* hybrid.

Description: A dense, spreading mound 30 in. wide × 15 in. high (75 × 38 cm). Leaf blade 4½ × 3½ in. (11 × 9 cm), of good substance, dark green with a gray cast, matt to satiny above and glaucous below, slightly dimpled when mature, edge slightly undulate, leaf widely oval with a mucronate tip and heart-shaped overlapping lobes. Petiole slightly arching, light green. Flower tubular, lavender, opening from a large ballooning bud, on an upright or oblique, bare, gray-green, 25-in. (63-cm) scape in midsummer; fertile.

Cultivation Notes: Site in dappled shade, where the leaves will retain their early, attractive blue-gray cast for longer into the summer. Good in pots and also

excellent for mass landscaping in light woodland since it increases rapidly.

Similar: *H.* 'Happy Hearts'; *H.* 'Heartleaf' is larger; *H.* 'Minnie Klopping' has slightly grayer leaves; ★*H.* 'Pearl Lake'.

Sports: ★*H.* 'Amber Maiden'; ★*H.* 'Fair Maiden'; *H.* 'Heartsong'.

Hosta 'Chodai Ginba' (Kajigawa/Gotemba Nursery/P. & J. Ruh 2003)

MEDIUM–LARGE

Origin: Unknown other than from Japan. Also known as 'Chodai Gihyo'.

Description: An overlapping mound 27 in. wide × 11 in. high (68 × 28 cm). Leaf blade 10 × 7 in. (25 × 18 cm), of good substance, blue-influenced gray-green, glossy above after the pruinosity has disappeared and thickly pruinose below, seersuckered, prominent veins widely spaced, edge slightly undulate, leaf broadly ovate with a mucronate tip and heart-shaped pinched to folded lobes. Petiole long, stout, gray-green turning green. Flower funnel-shaped, lavender-striped pale lavender to near-white, in a long, heavy raceme, on an oblique to upright, leafy, blue-green to green, 37-in. (94-cm) scape in high summer; seedpods blue-green, fertile.

Cultivation Notes: Tolerates some sun but remains a better leaf color for longer if grown in high, filtered light. Used for flower arrangement in Japan.

Distinguishing Features: Marked color change of

Hosta Candy Hearts

Hosta 'Chodai Ginba'

the leaves in summer from blue-influenced gray-green to darkish green.

Hosta 'Cinnamon Sticks' (R. Herold N/R)

SMALL–MEDIUM

Origin: *H. longipes* 'Hypoglauca' × *H.* 'Maruba Iwa'.

Description: A low, open mound 24 in. wide × 10 in. high (60 × 25 cm). Leaf blade 6 × 4½ in. (15 × 11 cm), thick, leathery, gray-green, matt above and thickly glaucous below, veins widely spaced, edge flat but kinked toward the overlapping lobes, leaf heart-shaped to nearly round with a cuspidate tip. Petiole wide, shallowly channeled, with cinnamon-red dots on back and front. Flower bell-shaped, lavender, in dense clusters, on a leaning, leafy, cinnamon-red-dotted, 14-in. (35-cm) scape from late summer to early autumn; fertile.

Cultivation Notes: Site in light to moderate shade with the petioles at eye level. Lovely with *Heuchera* 'Cathedral Windows', whose pewter and burgundy marbling affords a fine contrast with the hosta's cinnamon-red petioles. Lasts well into the fall. A useful breeding hosta for red-dotted petioles and scapes, both pod and pollen fertile for introducing red features into leaves, petioles, and scapes. Autumn temperatures in cooler climates may not be high enough for the seeds to set.

Distinguishing Features: Red dots continue from the petiole into the palm of the blade. Leafy scape bracts are also cinnamon red.

Hosta 'Cinnamon Sticks'

Similar: *H.* 'Chopsticks' has rounder leaves with a heavy white underside; *★H.* 'One Man's Treasure' has deeper colored flowers and scapes, and more intense purple dotting.

Hosta 'Clear Fork River Valley' (V. Wade 2007)

LARGE–VERY LARGE

Origin: *H.* 'Puckered Giant' × *H.* 'Woodland Blue'.

Description: An impressive mound 50 in. wide × 26 in. high (126 × 65 cm). Leaf blade 14 × 11 in. (35 × 28 cm), thick, heavy, blue-influenced dark green, glossy above and satiny below, heavily seersuckered and puckered, edge almost flat, leaf widely ovate to rounded with pinched heart-shaped lobes. Petiole stout, medium green. Flower funnel-shaped, near white, on an upright, light green, leafy, 32-in. (80-cm) scape in high summer; fertility unknown.

Cultivation Notes: Site in moderate shade where the superb intricate-textured leaf surface may be

Hosta 'Clear Fork River Valley', a juvenile plant.

appreciated. Slow to moderate growth but leave plenty of space for future increase. Pest resistant.

Distinguishing Features: One of the most heavily puckered hostas. The blueness in the leaf color disappears as summer progresses.

Similar: *H.* 'Cloudburst' is smaller; *H.* 'Jurassic Park' has blue-green leaves; *H.* 'Lothar The Giant'.

Hosta 'Clovelly' PPAF (K. Terpening 2005)

MEDIUM−LARGE

Origin: *H.* 'Split Decision' selfed.

Description: A diffuse mound of horizontal leaves 30½ in. wide × 18½ in. high (76 × 46 cm). Leaf blade 11 × 9 in. (28 × 23 cm), of good substance, matt, elm green, seersuckered, furrowed veins widely spaced, edge deeply and evenly piecrusted, leaf arching, lightly cupped, broadly ovate to nearly round with an extended cuspidate tip and pinched to folded heart-shaped lobes. Petiole long, arching, pale green. Flower funnel-shaped, pale lavender, on a stout, upright, bare, dark green, 18- to 24-in. (45- to 60-cm) scape in midsummer; seedpods green, fertile.

Cultivation Notes: Site in moderate shade. Grow as a specimen plant with plain-leaved foliage as a contrast. Also suitable for a large container such as a navy-blue ceramic cache-pot or a stone bowl placed on a 36-in. (90-cm) column so that the plant's many attributes can be enjoyed close-up. Winner of the Mildred Seaver Award at a *First Look* event.

Distinguishing Features: Piecrust leaf edge that stands out from the crowd.

Similar: *★H.* 'Cutting Edge' has bluer, narrower leaves; *★H.* 'Devon Discovery' has a less regular piecrust edge; *H.* 'Split Decision' is a seedling of *H.* 'Split Personality'.

Hosta 'Corkscrew' (R. Solberg 2003)

SMALL

Origin: *★H.* 'Tortifrons' × *★H.* 'One Man's Treasure'.

Description: A strikingly asymmetrical, upright to arching mound 22 in. wide × 9 in. high (55 × 23 cm). Leaf blade 7 × 2 in. (18 × 5 cm), thick, olive green, glossy above and very shiny below, smooth, veins closely ribbed, edge undulate, leaf arching, lanceolate, contorted with a recurved exaggeratedly acute tip, burgundy-purple dots toward the base. Petiole short, narrowly channeled, green, decurrent with the leaf blade. Flower funnel-shaped, lavender, on an upright, leafy, brownish-green, 18-in. (45-cm) scape in early autumn; fertile.

Cultivation Notes: Site in light to moderate shade. The contorted leaves give a restless countenance. Best in a container or in a border with ferns or plants of unusual leaf shape. Increases rapidly. Pest resistant. Winner of the Best Seedling Award at a *First Look* event. Also winner of the 2003 Alex J. Summers Distinguished Merit Award.

Distinguishing Features: Exceptionally contorted leaves with elongated tips.

Hosta 'Clovelly'

Hosta 'Corkscrew'

Similar: *H. 'Praying Hands' is larger, more upright, and less contorted; *H. 'Tortifrons' is smaller and has narrower leaves.

Hosta 'Crocodile Rock' (S. Wilkins/J. Wilkins 2000)

MEDIUM–LARGE

Origin: Unknown.

Description: An upright mound 30 in. wide × 18 in. high (75 × 45 cm). Leaf blade 7 × 4 in. (18 × 10 cm), thick, satiny, light green, evenly seersuckered, edge flat with occasional kinks, leaf flat to slightly undulate, spoon-shaped, with an acute tip and rounded to tapered open lobes. Petiole narrow, arching, very pale green. Flower funnel-shaped, rich deep purple, on an upright, bare, green, 30-in. (75-cm) scape in high summer; seedpods green, fertile.

Cultivation Notes: Site in light to medium shade. Moderate to rapid growth.

Distinguishing Features: Intensely seersuckered leaves with a pebbly texture resembling a crocodile's skin when mature.

Hosta 'Devon Discovery' (J. Goater/A. & R. Bowden/P. & J. Ruh 2005)

LARGE

Origin: Unknown.

Description: An arching mound 60 in. wide × 36 in. high (150 × 90 cm). Leaf blade 18 × 11 in. (45 × 28 cm), thick, matt, light to mid-green, veins deeply furrowed, edge rippled to kinked, leaf arching,

folded, oval with a twisted cuspidate tip and heart-shaped open to pinched lobes. Petiole stout, light green. Flower funnel-shaped, near white, on a thin, upright, leafy, pale green, 45-in. (113-cm) scape in midsummer; fertility unknown.

Cultivation Notes: Site in shade or light woodland. Makes a shapely background plant. Pest resistant.

Similar: H. 'Fluted Fountain' has broader leaves; H. 'Green Acres' has less-rippled, wider leaves.

Hosta 'Devon Green' (A. & R. Bowden/P. & J. Ruh 2005)

MEDIUM

Origin: Sport of *H. 'Halcyon'.

Description: A dense, overlapping mound 36 in. wide × 18 in. high (90 × 45 cm). Leaf blade 7 × 4 in. (18 × 10 cm), thick, glossy, dark olive green, smooth, closely veined, edge flat, leaf widely oval with an acute tip and heart-shaped pinched lobes. Petiole purple-dotted, lighter olive green, appearing to pierce the blade. Flower: see *H. 'Halcyon'.

Cultivation Notes: Site in light to moderate shade. A moderately rapid increaser. Lovely in a cream stone

Hosta 'Crocodile Rock'

Hosta 'Devon Discovery'

container. Still the best-selling green-leaved hosta in Europe.

Distinguishing Features: Purple-dotted, dark green scapes.

Similar: *H.* 'Canadian Shield'; *H.* 'Peridot'; *H.* 'Valerie's Vanity'.

Sports: *H.* 'Dax' has dark green leaves with a pale green center which bleeds into the outside edge; *H.* 'Silver Shadow' has a narrow, silver-white leaf margin.

Hosta 'Donahue Piecrust' (T. Donahue/P. Ruh 1999)

VERY LARGE

Origin: *H. montana* hybrid.

Description: A symmetrical mound 60 in. wide × 28 in. high (150 × 70 cm). Leaf blade 11½ × 7½ in. (29 × 19 cm), of good substance, mid-green to dark green, satiny above and glaucous below, prominently veined, edge distinctly rippled and turning upward, leaf slightly arching or convex, widely oval with an often-pinched cuspidate tip and heart-shaped pinched lobes. Petiole light green, appearing to pierce the blade. Flower bell-shaped, near white, opening from a lavender bud, on an upright to oblique, leafy, green, 27-in. (68-cm) scape in midsummer; fertile.

Cultivation Notes: Site in moderate shade. Slow to increase. The spectacular piecrust edge takes several years to develop fully. This parent of earlier introductions with piecrust edges has been superseded as a garden plant.

Similar: *H.* 'Green Piecrust'; *H.* 'Green Ripples'; *H.* 'Mesa Fringe'; *H.* 'Orinoco Flow'.

Hosta 'Dragon Wings' (W. Lefever 1996)

LARGE

Origin: ★*H. montana* × *H.* 'Fortunei'.

Description: A semi-upright, flowing mound 60 in. wide × 24 in. high (150 × 60 cm). Leaf blade 18 × 10½ in. (45 × 27 cm), of average substance, satiny,

Hosta 'Donahue Piecrust'

Hosta 'Devon Green'

Hosta 'Dragon Wings'

63

mid-green to dark green, prominently veined, edge evenly rippled, arching, broadly oval with a pinched cuspidate tip and heart-shaped open lobes. Petiole dark green. Flower funnel-shaped, palest lavender, on a leaning, leafy, green, 5-ft. (1.5-m) scape in late summer; fertile.

Cultivation Notes: Site in moderate shade. Slow to moderate growth rate. Grow as a specimen where the graceful leaves can be seen close up.

Distinguishing Features: Elegantly elongated, pinched tips that cause the leaves to droop.

Hosta 'Edge of Night' (R. Savory 1988)

LARGE

Origin: H. 'Green Gold' × ★H. 'Halcyon'.

Description: An unruly mound 49 in. wide × 24 in. high (122 × 60 cm). Leaf blade 9 × 8½ in. (23 × 21 cm), thick, dark olive to spinach green with a blue cast, matt above and glaucous below, dimpled and puckered, edge flat, leaf deeply cupped, nearly round with a mucronate tip and heart-shaped overlapping lobes. Petiole glaucous light olive green. Flower flared, lavender, on an upright, leafy, green, 23-in. (58-cm) scape in high summer; fertility unknown.

Cultivation Notes: Site in light to moderate shade. Increases slowly to moderately. Eventually makes superb plant and still a favorite. Pest resistant.

Similar: H. 'Biggie', ★H. 'Black Hills'; H. 'Deep Pockets'; H. 'Ming Jade'; H. 'Peter The Rock'; H. 'Pete's Dark Satellite'; H. 'Surf and Turf'.

Sports: H. 'Applause'; H. 'Awesome Illusion'; H. 'Ice Castle'; H. 'Night Shades'.

Hosta 'Elatior' (F. Maekawa/P. & J. Ruh 2002)

VERY LARGE

Origin: Now considered a probable hybrid of H. montana.

Description: An immense, semi-upright, wide-spreading mound 69½ in. wide × 31 in. high (174 × 78 cm). Leaf blade 14 × 9½ in. (35 × 24 cm), thick, light to mid-green, shiny above and glossy below, barely puckered, prominent veins widely spaced, edge shallowly undulate, broadly oval with a cuspidate tip and heart-shaped open lobes. Petiole oblique, stout, light green. Flower funnel-shaped, lavender, patterned near white, on an upright, leafy, light green, 69-in. (172-cm) scape in late summer; fertile.

Cultivation Notes: Site in light to moderate shade. A superb specimen for a woodland setting. Can suffer from stem blight.

Distinguishing Features: The tallest flower scape of any hosta. Small near-white bracts on the flower scape.

Similar: H. fluctuans; ★H. 'Green Sheen'; H. 'Green Wedge'.

Sports: H. 'Incognito' has a cream margin; H. 'Justice' has misted and streaked leaves; H. 'Victory' has widely cream-margined leaves and is somewhat similar to ★H. 'Sagae'.

Hosta 'Edge of Night'

Hosta 'Elatior'

Hosta **'Empress Wu'** (B. & V. Skaggs N/R)

VERY LARGE

Origin: *H.* 'Big John' hybrid.

Description: An impressive, upright, layered mound 50 in. wide × 30 in. high (126 × 75 cm). Leaf blade 18 × 15 in. (45 × 38 cm), thick, blue-influenced dark green, glaucous above and thinly glaucous below, dimpled, veins furrowed, edge flat to randomly and slightly kinked, leaf flat to slightly wavy, broadly ovate with a mucronate tip and pinched to folded heart-shaped lobes. Petiole upright, stout, pale green. Flower funnel-shaped, near white, on a semi-upright, leafy, light green, 36- to 40-in. (90- to 100-cm) scape from mid- to late summer; fertility unknown.

Cultivation Notes: Site in light to moderate shade in light woodland or at the back of a large border. Allow plenty of space for eventual increase. Slow to moderate increase.

Distinguishing Features: Puckered, folded leaves. One of the largest hostas.

Similar: *H.* 'Biggie' has leaves with a white underside; ★*H.* 'Big John' has grayer leaves; *H.* 'Stonewall'.

Hosta **'Essence of Summer'** (J. van den Top/M. Fransen/D. Van Eechaute 2004)

LARGE

Origin: Sport, possibly tetraploid, of *H.* 'Warwick Essence'.

Description: An irregular, open mound 51 in. wide × 24 in. high (127 × 60 cm). Leaf blade 11 × 9 in. (28 × 23 cm), very thick, matt, slightly blue-influenced medium green, seersuckered, prominently veined, edge flat to shallowly undulate, leaf broadly ovate with a mucronate tip and heart-shaped pinched lobes. Petiole green. Flower large, funnel-shaped, near-white, opening from a palest mauve bud, in a dense raceme, on an oblique, leafy, green, 30- to 36-in. (75- to 90-cm) scape in late summer; seedpods green; fertility unknown.

Hosta 'Empress Wu'

Cultivation Notes: Tolerates sun in cooler climates as long as adequate moisture is available.

Distinguishing Features: Leaves thicker and slightly darker green than those of its parent, indicating the likelihood of it being a tetraploid. Longish-tubed flowers reflect its *H. plantaginea ancestry.

Hosta 'Fall Bouquet' (P. Aden 1986)

SMALL

Origin: H. "Aden 322" × H. "Aden 324."

Description: A dome-shaped mound 18 in. wide × 12 in. high (45 × 30 cm). Leaf blade 5½ × 2¾ in.(14 × 7 cm), of average to good substance, satiny, mid-

Hosta 'Essence of Summer'

Hosta 'Fall Bouquet'

green to dark green, smooth, edge flat to shallowly rippled, leaf lanceolate to widely oval with a cuspidate tip and heart-shaped open lobes. Petiole narrow, purple-tinted green. Flower funnel-shaped, lavender, in a dense raceme, on an upright, bare, claret-colored, 16-in. (40-cm) scape in early autumn; sterile.

Cultivation Notes: Tolerates some sun everywhere except in the hottest climates. A thoroughly undervalued hosta considering its many attributes.

Distinguishing Features: Late season of flower combined with the claret petiole and scape.

Similar: *H. 'Cinnamon Sticks' has more noticeably red petioles and scapes.

Hosta 'Fried Green Tomatoes' (R. Solberg 1995)

MEDIUM

Origin: *H. 'Guacamole' sport.

Description: An open, semi-upright mound 18 in. wide × 10 in. high (45 × 25 cm). Leaf blade 8 × 6 in. (20 × 15 cm), of good substance, olive green, glossy, slightly dimpled when mature, prominent veins widely spaced, edge flat with an occasional kink, leaf slightly arching, widely oval with a mucronate tip and rounded open to pinched lobes. Petiole pale olive green. Flower: see *H. 'Fragrant Bouquet'.

Cultivation Notes: Tolerates some sun even in the hottest climates provided plenty of water is available. Large, fragrant, near-white flowers are a bonus.

Similar: H. 'Fried Bananas' has glossy, old-gold leaves.

Sports: H. 'Fragrant King' has green leaves with a white margin; H. 'Fragrant Queen' PP19,508 is a new tetraploid sport of H. 'Fragrant King' with wider margins.

Hosta 'Grand Slam' (H. Benedict & H. Gowen 1990)

SMALL–MEDIUM

Origin: Selfed clone of H. longipes 'Latifolia', from Japan.

Description: A dome-shaped, rippled mound 26½ in. wide × 10 in. high (66 × 25 cm). Leaf blade 7 × 6½ in. (18 × 16 cm), very leathery, dark olive green, shiny above and thickly glaucous below, slightly dimpled, edge distinctly and evenly rippled, leaf flat with a cuspidate tip and heart-shaped overlapping lobes. Petiole narrow, purple-tinted green. Flower funnel-

Hosta 'Fried Green Tomatoes'

Hosta 'Fragrant King'

shaped, rich violet, on an upright, leafy, purple, 20½-in. (51-cm) scape from early to mid-autumn; fertile.

Cultivation Notes: Site in light to moderate shade. Grow at eye level for best effect. Moderate growth rate. Pest resistant. Good pollen parent for leaf substance and shape.

Similar: ★*H.* 'One Man's Treasure'.

Sports: ★*H.* 'Mighty Mite' is smaller.

Hosta '**Green Fountain**' (P. Aden 1979)

MEDIUM—LARGE

Origin: *H.* 'Green Wedge' × ★*H. longipes*.

Description: A cascading mound 56 in. wide × 40 in. high (140 × 100 cm). Leaf blade 12 × 3½ in. (30 × 9 cm), moderately thick, olive green, shiny above and very glossy below, smooth, prominent veins widely spaced, edge heavily rippled, leaf oblong to elliptic, pinched just above the recurved tip, lobes tapered and pinched. Petiole green with red streaks. Flower funnel-shaped, lilac-colored, in large trusses, on a drooping, leafy, intensely red-streaked, green, 51-in. (127-cm) scape in late summer; fertile.

Cultivation Notes: Site in light to moderate shade all day. A very graceful hosta, best appreciated cascading down walls or from terracotta chimney pots, but also valuable for its showy late flowers.

Similar: *H. kikutii* var. *caput avis*.

Sports: *H.* 'Fountain of Youth' and *H.* 'Three Coins' both have white-margined leaves.

Hosta 'Grand Slam'

Hosta 'Green Fountain'

Hosta 'Green Sheen' (P. Aden 1978)

VERY LARGE

Origin: *H.* 'Green Wedge' × *H.* 'Chartreuse Wedge'.

Description: A dense mound 48 in. wide × 36 in. high (120 × 90 cm). Leaf blade 18 × 12 in. (45 × 30 cm), very thick, bright light green, a waxy sheen above and intensely glaucous below, veins furrowed, edge almost flat to slightly rippled, leaf folded, oval to nearly round with a mucronate tip and heart-shaped pinched to overlapping lobes. Petiole wide, pale green. Flower bell-shaped, near white, on an upright, bare, green, 5-ft. (1.5-m) scape from late summer to early autumn; fertile.

Cultivation Notes: Tolerates sun in cooler climates, but leaf color darkens when grown in shade. Pest resistant.

Similar: *H.* 'Green Wedge'

Hosta 'Green Velveteen' (R. Klehm 1999)

LARGE

Origin: Sport of ★*H.* 'Embroidery'.

Description: A low, graceful mound 32 in. wide × 16 in. high (80 × 40 cm). Leaf blade 13 × 8½ in. (33 × 21 cm), of average substance, elm green, glossy above and matt below, smooth, prominently veined, edge evenly rippled with small indentations, leaf arching to drooping, elongate to ovate with a recurved cuspidate tip and tapered to heart-shaped open to pinched lobes. Petiole arching, light green. Flower: see *H.* 'Embroidery'.

Cultivation Notes: Site in high, filtered light to moderate shade in semi-woodland or at the back of a border leaving plenty of space for the leaves to spread. Moderate growth rate. A very shapely hosta with much to recommend it.

Similar: ★*H.* 'Elatior' is taller and larger.

Hosta 'Hacksaw' (R. Livingston N/R)

SMALL

Origin: *H.* 'Atom Smasher' × ★*H.* 'Stiletto'.

Description: A semi-upright, stoloniferous mound 17 in. wide × 9 in. high (43 × 23 cm). Leaf blade 5½ × 1 in. (14 × 2.5 cm), of good substance, elm green turning chartreuse to almost yellow, veins ribbed, edge intensely rippled and serrated, leaf lanceolate

Hosta 'Green Velveteen'

Hosta 'Green Sheen'

Hosta 'Hacksaw'

with an acuminate tip. Petiole decurrent with the leaf blade. Flower lavender, opening from a violet bud, on a semi-erect, leafy, light green, 27-in. (68-cm) scape from late summer to early autumn; fertile both ways.

Cultivation Notes: Tolerates some morning sun although the leaves will fade. Increases rapidly. Winner of the William and Eleanor Lachman Award at a *First Look* event.

Distinguishing Features: Leaf blade edged with sawlike teeth and extremely narrow.

Similar: *H.* 'Atomic Needle' also has a serrated leaf edge; *H.* 'Drunken Boy'; *H.* 'Jaws' has much wider leaves with a serrated edge; *H.* 'Lizard's Lick' has a nonserrated leaf edge.

Hosta 'Harry van der Laar' (C. Visser N/R)

MEDIUM

Origin: *H. longipes* 'Hypoglauca' × *H.* 'Maruba Iwa'.

Description: An upright, open mound 24 in. wide × 12 in. high (60 × 30 cm). Leaf blade 7½ × 5 in. (19 × 13 cm), of good substance, mid-green, matt above and thickly glaucous below, smooth, veins widely spaced, edge undulate to rippled, leaf ovate with an elegant cuspidate tip and rounded open to pinched lobes. Petiole intensely dotted in claret-pink. Flower funnel-shaped, lavender, opening from a violet bud, on an upright, leafy, claret-pink dotted, green, 16-in. (40-cm) scape in late summer; fertility unknown.

Cultivation Notes: Site in light to moderate shade at eye level to enjoy the intensely white leaf undersides and the strikingly colored petioles.

Distinguishing Features: Claret-pink dots along the midrib at the base of the leaf.

Similar: *★H.* 'Marilyn Monroe'.

Hosta 'Heideturm' (U. Fischer N/R)

MEDIUM–LARGE

Origin: Unknown. The German name means "heath tower."

Description: A dense mound 24 in. wide × 18 in. high (60 × 45 cm). Leaf blade 9 × 6½ in. (23 × 16 cm), of good substance, bright apple-green, matt above and satiny below, dimpled to seersuckered, veins closely ribbed, edge slightly rippled, leaf undulate, widely oval, pinched toward the slightly cuspidate tip, lobes open to pinched. Petiole light green.

Hosta 'Harry van der Laar'

Hosta 'Heideturm'

Flower funnel-shaped, near white, on an upright, leafy, sometimes branched, 73-in. (183-cm) scape from mid- to high summer; fertility unknown.

Cultivation Notes: Tolerates full sun in cooler climates, especially if grown with moisture at its roots.

Distinguishing Features: The scapes, which occasionally branch, tower above the foliage mound.

Similar: *H.* 'Twiggie', raised by the same breeder, also has scapes that tower above the foliage and are sometimes branched.

Hosta 'Hirao Majesty' (S. Hirao/M. Zilis/P. Ruh 1997)

VERY LARGE

Origin: Seed sent from S. Hirao in Japan to a nursery in the United States.

Description: A swirling mound 66 in. wide × 26 in. high (165 × 65 cm). Leaf blade 15 × 9 in. (38 × 23 cm), thick, mid-green, shiny above and glossy below, smooth, veins widely spaced, edge widely rippled, leaf undulate, arching or drooping, recurved at the cuspidate tip, widely oval with heart-shaped open lobes. Petiole widely channeled. Flower open funnel-shaped, pale lavender, in dense clusters, in a habit like those of *H. kikutii, on a leaning, leafy, two-tone light green, 40-in. (100-cm) scape in high summer; occasionally fertile.

Cultivation Notes: Site in light to medium shade in cooler climates, in full shade in warmer climates.

Distinguishing Features: The floppy, pinched leaf

blade cascades downward as does the dense raceme of flowers on a long scape.

Similar: *H.* 'Colossal'; *H.* 'Hirao Supreme' is also thought to be a tetraploid.

Hosta 'Hirao Splendor' (S. Hirao/M. Zilis/P. Ruh 1997)

SMALL

Origin: Seed sent from S. Hirao in Japan to a U.S. nursery.

Description: A dense mound 18 in. wide × 12 in. high (45 × 30 cm). Leaf blade 5½ × 2 in. (14 × 5 cm), of average substance, light green, shiny above and satiny below, prominent veins, edge flat to sometimes shallowly rippled, leaf lanceolate with an acute tip and tapered open lobes. Petiole green, with red dots at the base. Flower funnel-shaped, purple-striped lavender, on an upright, leafy, red-tinted dark green, 21½-in. (54-cm) scape in autumn; sterile.

Cultivation Notes: Site in light to full shade. Increases slowly.

Hosta 'Holly's Honey' (G. Holly/AHS 1986)

LARGE

Origin: *H. ventricosa* hybrid.

Description: A dense mound 41 in. wide × 23 in. high (102 × 58 cm). Leaf blade 9 × 6½ in. (23 × 16 cm), thin, satiny, dark green, veins widely spaced, edge evenly but shallowly rippled to piecrusted, leaf widely oval, pinched at the drooping cuspidate tip,

Hosta 'Hirao Majesty'

Hosta 'Hirao Splendor'

convex, with heart-shaped pinched lobes. Petiole dark green. Flower bell-shaped, purple, in high summer; fertile.

Cultivation Notes: Site in moderately dense shade. Moderate to rapid growth rate. Vulnerable to pests because of the thin-leaved ★*H. ventricosa* in its ancestry.

Distinguishing Features: Dome-shaped, puckered leaves.

Hosta 'Holly's Honey'

Sports: *H.* 'Holly's Dazzler', from *H.* 'Holly's Honey' selfed.

Hosta 'Honeybells' (A. Cummings & AHS 1986) ♀
MEDIUM–LARGE

Origin: ★*H. plantaginea* × ★*H. sieboldii*.

Description: A lax mound 51 in. wide × 26½ in. high (127 × 66 cm). Leaf blade 10 × 6½ in. (25 × 16 cm), thinnish, olive green, satiny to glossy above and shiny below, veins widely spaced, edge shallowly undulate, leaf arching to drooping from the base, oval with an obtuse tip and rounded open to pinched lobes. Petiole narrow, light olive green. Flower open funnel-shaped, slightly fragrant, palest lavender, on an upright, leafy, green, 45-in. (113-cm) scape from late summer to early autumn; fertile.

Cultivation Notes: Tolerates full sun, which brings out the elusive fragrance of the flowers. Flowers open as the temperature rises, but the leaves turn a sickly green unless they receive plenty of water. Now superseded as a garden specimen and mainly used for landscaping. Leaves are said to be attractive to deer.

Hosta 'Honeybells'

Similar: ★*H*. 'Bennie McRae'; *H*. 'Buckwheat Honey'; ★*H*. 'Royal Standard'; *H*. 'Savannah Emerald'; *H*. 'Sweet Marjorie'; *H*. 'Sweet Susan'.

Sports: *H*. 'Sugar and Cream'; *H*. 'Sweet Standard'.

Hosta 'Invincible' (P. Aden 1986)

MEDIUM–LARGE

Origin: Unknown.

Description: A dense mound 49 in. wide × 20 in. high (122 × 50 cm). Leaf blade 8½ × 6½ in. (21 × 16 cm), leathery, olive green, glossy, veins widely spaced, edge distinctly rippled, leaf folded, wedge-shaped with a cuspidate tip and heart-shaped open to folded lobes. Petiole narrow, lightly red-dotted green.

Flower funnel-shaped, lightly fragrant, palest lavender, on a leaning, very leafy, pale green, 25-in. (63-cm) scape in late summer; fertile.

Cultivation Notes: Emerges early. Best in morning sun but tolerates sun all day in cooler climates if given plenty of water. Not as pest resistant as its name might suggest in spite of the excellent substance of the leaves, but nonetheless a superb hosta.

Distinguishing Features: Has been known to have multibranched scapes in wet summers. Scapes are stained red where the leafy bracts are attached and immediately above the bracts. Occasionally produces hose-in-hose double flowers.

Similar: *H*. 'Fragrant Star' has bluer leaves; *H*. 'Polished Jade'; *H*. 'Rippled Honey' has a more rippled leaf edge; ★*H*. 'Sweet Bo Peep'.

Sports: ★*H*. 'Devon Cloud'; *H*. 'Grasshopper'; *H*. 'Morning Angel'; *H*. 'Red Stepper' has darker mahogany-red petioles and scapes; *H*. 'Sugar and Spice' has dark green leaves margined cream turning white.

Hosta 'Invincible'

Hosta 'Fragrant Star'

Hosta 'Jade Cascade'

Hosta **'Jade Cascade'** (D. Heims N/R)

VERY LARGE

Origin: *H. montana* f. *macrophylla* seedling.

Description: A dramatically arching, open mound 60 in. wide × 40 in. high (150 × 100 cm). Leaf blade 21 × 8½ in. (53 × 21 cm), of good substance, glossy, bright olive green, slightly dimpled, veins conspicuous, edge widely rippled, leaf elongated lanceolate to oval with an acute tip and heart-shaped pinched lobes. Petiole deeply channeled, green, up to 15 in. (38 cm) long. Flower funnel-shaped, pale lavender, on a leaning, leafy, green, 42-in. (105-cm) scape from mid- to late summer; fertility unknown.

Cultivation Notes: Site in light to moderate shade. An ideal woodland hosta. Very slow to become established but well worth the wait.

Distinguishing Features: Deeply furrowed veining. Widely spaced individual flowers on scapes which are mahogany tinted below the distinct floral bracts.

Similar: ★*H.* 'Devon Discovery'.

Hosta **'Joseph'** (Kuk 1990)

MEDIUM

Origin: Sport of *H.* 'Josephine'.

Description: An arching mound 30 in. wide × 16 in. high (75 × 40 cm). Leaf blade 6½ × 5½ in. (16 × 14 cm), thick, glossy, very dark olive green, some seersuckering, veins ribbed, edge slightly rippled, leaf convex, widely oval to nearly round with a mucronate tip and heart-shaped open lobes. Petiole narrow, light olive green with maroon dots on the reverse. Flower flared,

lavender, on an upright, leafy, maroon-dotted, 16½-in. (42-cm) scape in late summer; fertility unknown.

Cultivation Notes: Site in light to moderate shade. Slower growing than *H.* 'Josephine'.

Similar: ★*H.* 'Black Hills'; *H.* 'Lakeside Accolade'; ★*H.* 'Lakeside Black Satin'; ★*H.* 'Second Wind'; *H.* 'Spinach Patch'; ★*H. ventricosa*.

Hosta **'Katsuragawa Beni'** (H. Masaoka N/R)

SMALL

Origin: Shikoku Island, Japan. Thought to be related to ★*H. kikutii*.

Description: An open, upright mound 20 in. wide × 12 in. high (50 × 30 cm). Leaf blade 7 × 3 in. (18 × 8 cm), of average to good substance, dark green with mahogany-crimson dots, smooth, with deeply impressed veins widely spaced, edge undulate, leaf arching, widely lanceolate with an acuminate tip and tapered open lobes. Petiole dotted mahogany-crimson on front and back. Flower funnel-shaped, pale lavender with deeper lavender tubes and a crimson pedicel, on an oblique to upright, leafy, deep mahogany-crimson, 16-in. (40-cm) scape from mid- to late summer; fertile.

Cultivation Notes: Site in moderate shade. An excellent breeding plant. Moderate growth rate.

Distinguishing Features: One of the best hostas in which the red dots extend up and onto each side of the midrib of the leaf blade.

Sports: *H.* 'Miss Ruby' has wedge-shaped green leaves with mahogany-red speckles extending from the petioles into the middle of the leaf on both surfaces.

Hosta 'Joseph' sporting to ★*H.* 'Queen Josephine'.

Hosta 'Katsuragawa Beni'

Hosta 'King Michael'

Hosta 'Komodo Dragon'

Hosta 'King Michael' (G. Krossa/A. Summers/P. Ruh 1992)

VERY LARGE

Origin: *H. montana* f. *macrophylla* hybrid.

Description: A huge, arching mound 47 in. wide × 33½ in. high (118 × 84 cm). Leaf blade 12½ × 9 in. (31 × 23 cm), thick, leathery, mid-green, satiny above and glossy and rough-textured below, veins deeply furrowed, edge rippled, leaf arching, widely oval with a cuspidate tip and heart-shaped open lobes. Petiole stout, light green. Flower flared, white, on an upright, bare, pale green, 75-in. (188-cm) scape in early summer; fertile.

Cultivation Notes: Site in light to medium shade. A superb background hosta for woodland gardens. It also makes the perfect single specimen in a paved courtyard.

Distinguishing Features: The noticeably cascading mound of foliage.

Similar: *H.* 'Bee's Colossus'; *H.* 'Big Boy'; *H.* 'Colossal'; *H.* 'Green Acres'; *H.* 'King James'; *H.* 'Mikado' is a sport of ★*H. montana* 'Aureomarginata'.

Hosta 'Komodo Dragon' (M. Seaver 2004)

VERY LARGE

Origin: Unknown.

Description: An open, almost vase-shaped mound 73 in. wide × 28 in. high (183 × 70 cm). Leaf blade 15 × 11 in. (38 × 28 cm), thick, blue-tinted dark green, matt above and glaucous below, dimpled, distinct veins widely spaced, edge conspicuously and evenly rippled, leaf widely oval with a cuspidate tip when mature, lobes heart-shaped and open. Petiole stout, blue-green. Flower funnel-shaped, palest lavender, on an upright, leafy, light green, 36-in. (90-cm) scape in midsummer; fertility unknown.

Cultivation Notes: Site in light to moderate shade. Increases rapidly. Pest resistant. An impressive specimen for the woodland garden.

Distinguishing Features: The attractive regular, shallow piecrust leaf edge.

Similar: *H.* 'Big Sam'; *H.* 'Brutus' has darker green leaves; *H.* 'Green Ripples'; *H.* 'Lakeside Ripples'; *H.* 'Sea Drift'.

Sports: *H.* 'Chinese Dragon' has streaked leaves.

Hosta 'Lakeside Black Satin' (M. Chastain 1993)
MEDIUM

Origin: *H. ventricosa* hybrid.

Description: An open mound 41 in. wide × 18 in. high (102 × 45 cm). Leaf blade 9 × 8½ in. (23 × 21 cm), thin, lustrous black-green, very glossy below, smooth, veins widely spaced, edge closely and evenly rippled, leaf widely oval with a mucronate tip and heart-shaped open lobes. Petiole dark green. Flower widely spaced, bell-shaped, white-striped, deep purple, on an upright, bare, dark green, 34¾-in. (87-cm) scape from mid- to late summer; fertility unknown.

Hosta 'Lakeside Black Satin'

Hosta 'Lakeside Lollipop'

Cultivation Notes: Site in full shade all day. First of the "black-leaved hostas."

Distinguishing Features: Exceptionally dark green leaves with very widely spaced veins.

Similar: ★*H.* 'Holly's Honey'; *H.* 'Lakeside Coal Miner' has blacker twisted leaves and smaller purple flowers; *H.* 'Lakeside Pillow Talk' has marginally greener leaves with more distinct leaf tips; ★*H. ventricosa.*

Sports: *H.* 'Stained Satin' has attractive medio-variegated leaves but is not as vigorous as its parent.

Hosta 'Lakeside Lollipop' (M. Chastain 1993)
SMALL

Origin: Unknown.

Description: A low, spreading mound 16 in. wide × 8½ in. high (40 × 21 cm). Leaf blade 3½ × 2¾ in. (9 × 7 cm), thick, shiny dark green, seersuckered, prominently veined, edge flat, leaf nearly round with a mucronate tip and rounded open lobes. Petiole lighter green, appearing to pierce the blade. Flower funnel-shaped, pure white, on an upright, leafy, dark green, 16-in. (40-cm) scape in midsummer; fertile.

Cultivation Notes: Site in light to moderate shade. Increases slowly. Grow in the foreground of a border. Ideal for a gravel garden.

Distinguishing Features: The almost perfectly round leaf blade and the petiole which together form the shape of a lollipop.

Hosta 'Lancifolia' (Engler 1887) ♆
SMALL–MEDIUM

Origin: In doubt, but often confused with *H. cathayana* and ★*H. sieboldii.*

Description: A dense, spreading mound 41 in. wide × 16 in. high (102 × 40 cm). Leaf blade 7 × 2½ in. (18 × 6 cm), thin, mid- to dark green, shiny above and glossy below, edge slightly undulate, leaf elliptic to narrowly oval with an acute tip and tapered open to pinched lobes. Petiole green, with purple dots toward the crown. Flower narrowly bell-shaped, lavender, in a dense raceme, on an upright, leafy, purple-dotted green, 20-in. (50-cm) scape in late summer; fertility limited.

Cultivation Notes: Emerges early, so the leaves may be damaged by spring frost. Vigorous and floriferous.

Has been used for mass planting in both public and private gardens since its introduction to the United States in the 1800s. An excellent beginner's hosta and also lovely in large wooden containers.

Similar: *H. cathayana* is more fertile but not as well known.

Sports: *H.* 'Change of Tradition' has green leaves with a fine white margin; *H.* 'Lancifolia Aurea' has chartreuse-yellow leaves.

Hosta 'Manhattan' (W. Brincka & O. Petryszyn 1994)

MEDIUM–LARGE

Origin: *H.* 'Sea Frolic' hybrid.

Description: A compact mound 36 in. wide × 14 in. high (90 × 35 cm). Leaf blade 11 × 8 in. (28 × 20 cm), thick, light gray-green turning darker green with bluish overtones, shiny above and matt below, intensely seersuckered and puckered, edge distinctly piecrusted, leaf arching toward the cuspidate tip, widely oval with heart-shaped pinched lobes. Petiole stout, light green, appearing to pierce the blade. Flower funnel-shaped, lavender, opening from an attractive bulging purple bud, on an upright, leafy, blue-green to purple, 36-in. (90-cm) scape in early summer; fertile.

Cultivation Notes: Site in light to medium shade. Very slow to increase. An interesting hosta with almost too many good features.

Distinguishing Features: The combination of the intensely rippled edge and the deeply seersuckered

Hosta 'Manhattan'

Hosta 'Lancifolia'

surface texture of the leaf. The ball-like purple buds enclosed by purple bracts.

Similar: *⋆H.* 'Niagara Falls' has similar piecrusted leaf edges but a smooth surface texture; *H.* 'Sea Current' has slightly rounder leaves.

Hosta 'Maraschino Cherry' (M. Zilis/R. Solberg 1999)

MEDIUM

Origin: Sport of *⋆H.* 'Cherry Berry'.

Description: An upright mound 36 in. wide × 16 in. high (90 × 40 cm). Leaf blade 7 × 2¾ in. (18 × 7 cm), thin, glossy, dark green, veins ribbed when mature, edge flat to occasionally kinked, blade elliptic with an acute tip and tapered pinched lobes. Petiole green with purple dots. Flower: see *H.* 'Cherry Berry'.

Cultivation Notes: Site in light to full shade. Increases rapidly. Vulnerable to pests although a sturdier plant than its parent.

Distinguishing Features: Remarkable dark red scapes towering above the leaf mound, followed by red seedpods, in contrast to the dark green leaves.

Similar: *⋆H.* 'Sparkling Burgundy' has slightly broader leaves.

Hosta 'Marilyn Monroe' (J. Hawes/P & J. Ruh 2005)

MEDIUM

Origin: Seed acquired from Japan of *H. rupifraga* 'Urajiro'.

Description: An upright mound 24 in. wide × 12 in. high (60 × 30 cm). Leaf blade 7 × 5 in. (18 × 13 cm), thick, pale grayish green, matt above and glaucous white below, smooth to occasionally puckered, widely veined, edge evenly piecrusted, leaf ovate to nearly round with a cuspidate tip and heart-shaped pinched to folded lobes. Petiole pale green, dotted red. Flower funnel-shaped, purple-striped pale lavender, on an upright, leafy, purple-dotted pale green, 18-in. (45-cm) scape in high summer; very fertile.

Cultivation Notes: Site in light to moderate shade at eye level to best appreciate the undersides of the leaves and the purple-dotted petioles and scapes. Vigorous. Produces exceptionally good seedlings.

Distinguishing Features: The ruffled leaf edge recurves, revealing the white underside of the leaf. The dark purple anthers contrast with the paler lavender petals.

Similar: *⋆H.* 'Candy Dish'; *⋆H.* 'Harry van der Laar' has narrower, grayer leaves.

Hosta 'Mighty Mite' (D. Dean 2004)

SMALL

Origin: *H.* 'Grand Slam' seedling.

Description: A low mound 18½ in. wide × 7 in. high (46 × 18 cm). Leaf blade 4 × 3 in. (10 × 8 cm), of good substance, elm green, glossy above and glaucous below, smooth, prominent veins widely spaced, edge attractively rippled, leaf undulate, folded toward the petiole, broadly ovate with a noticeably extended tip. Petiole dark purple-spotted pale green. Flower funnel-shaped, pale lavender, with a purple interior center stripe, the

Hosta 'Maraschino Cherry'

Hosta 'Marilyn Monroe'

reverse pattern on the exterior, the edges speckled purple, opening from a purple bud, on an oblique, leafy, densely deep purple-dotted green, 15½- to 17-in. (39- to 43-cm) scape from late summer to autumn; seedpods glossy, bright green; fertility unknown.

Cultivation Notes: Site in moderate to full shade, preferably at eye level to best observe the purple petioles and the thick indumentum on the leaf underside. Lovely as a single specimen in a square wooden container placed on a plinth to set off the very attractive leaves. One of the last to flower. Slow to moderate growth rate.

Distinguishing Features: Evenly rippled edges on highly glossy, leathery leaves.

Similar: *H.* 'Grand Slam' is larger.

Hosta 'Mighty Mite'

Hosta 'Moongate Little Dipper'

Hosta 'Moongate Little Dipper' (C. Issacs/R. Solberg 1996)

SMALL—MEDIUM

Origin: *H.* 'Serendipity' × ★*H.* 'Blue Blazes'.

Description: A low mound 18 in. wide × 12 in. high (45 × 30 cm). Leaf blade 4½ × 3½ in. (11 × 9 cm), thick, dark green with a slight blue cast, glossy above and matt below, dimpled to seersuckered, edge flat, leaf deeply cupped, nearly round with a mucronate tip and heart-shaped pinched to overlapping lobes. Petiole green. Flower: tubular, lavender, on a thin, upright to oblique, leafy, glaucous mauve, 15-in. (38-cm) scape in midsummer; fertile.

Cultivation Notes: Site in light to moderate shade. Slowish growth rate. Pest resistant. Place it where its distinctively cupped leaves contrast with linear-leaved hostas.

Distinguishing Features: Small, deeply cupped green leaves.

Similar: *H.* 'Serendipity'.

Hosta 'Neat and Tidy' (L. Simpers 1980)

LARGE—VERY LARGE

Origin: *H. sieboldiana* 'Golden Circles' hybrid.

Description: An unruly mound 32 in. wide × 30 in. high (80 × 75 cm). Leaf blade 9 × 8 in. (23 × 20 cm), thick, blue-tinted dark green, matt to shiny above and glaucous below, crumpled and puckered, veins conspicuous, edge slightly rippled, leaf convex with the midrib grooved, occasionally cupped, near round

Hosta 'Neat and Tidy'

with a mucronate tip and heart-shaped pinched lobes. Petiole glaucous light green. Flower bell-shaped, pale lavender, on an upright, leafy, 3-ft. (90-cm) scape in late summer; fertile.

Cultivation Notes: Site in light to moderate shade. At its best as a young plant. Can achieve larger dimensions in optimum growing conditions.

Distinguishing Features: Crumpled, rather distorted leaves.

Similar: *H.* 'Black Hills' has less-exaggerated leaf crumpling.

Hosta 'Niagara Falls' (W. Brincka & O. Petryszyn 1991)

LARGE

Origin: *H. montana* f. *macrophylla* × *H.* 'Sea Drift'.

Description: An open, spreading mound 30 in. wide × 20 in. high (75 × 50 cm). Leaf blade 15 × 8¾ in. (38 × 22 cm), thick, dark green, matt to glaucous above and shiny below, smooth, veins deeply impressed, edge with small, even ripples, leaf arching, widely oblong to oval with a cuspidate tip and heart-shaped pinched lobes. Petiole stout, pale green. Flower flared, pale violet, on a leaning, leafy, 4-ft. (1.2-m) scape; fertility unknown.

Cultivation Notes: Site in light to full shade all day. Dimensions are much larger in optimum growing conditions.

Distinguishing Features: Glaucous bloom on the leaf surface assumes a waxy sheen later in the season. Piecrust edges are not present on the leaves of young plants.

Similar: *H.* 'Lakeside Ripples'.

Sports: *H.* 'Hoosier Dome' has more pronounced, inverted cupping on rounder leaves; *H.* 'War Paint', one of the best introductions for the early season, has creamy yellow leaves in spring which fade gradually to green, enhanced by many chartreuse splashes and streaks.

Hosta 'One Man's Treasure' (H. Benedict/R. Solberg 1999)

MEDIUM

Origin: *H. longipes* 'Hypoglauca' hybrid.

Description: An open, arching mound 24 in. wide × 14 in. high (60 × 35 cm). Leaf blade 6½ × 5½ in.

Hosta 'Niagara Falls'

Hosta 'War Paint'

Hosta 'One Man's Treasure'

79

(16 × 14 cm), thick, leathery, mid- to dark green, matt above and glossy below, veins widely spaced, edges undulate, leaf widely oval with a twisted cuspidate tip and heart-shaped to flat open lobes. Petiole shallowly channeled, olive green, intensely dotted burgundy. Flower bell-shaped, violet, white-striped inside, on a stout, upright, leafy, deep burgundy-red, 20- to 24-in. (50- to 60-cm) scape in early autumn; seedpods purple; fertile.

Cultivation Notes: Site in light to moderate shade. Moderate growth rate. Grow with burgundy-veined *Mitella stylosa*, which also has burgundy leaf stems, as an echo. An outstanding hosta; among the best of all hostas in flower. Excellent hybridizing potential for passing on its red petioles and even darker scapes.

Distinguishing Features: Purple-black scapes, purple-stained flower bracts, deep violet pedicels and flower tubes, violet bell-shaped flowers, and mahogany-purple dotting on both sides of the petiole, the dotting reaching well into the palm of the blade.

Similar: *★H.* 'Cinnamon Sticks' has paler-colored flowers and scapes; *H.* 'Granddaddy Redlegs' is a sister seedling; *H.* 'Judy Rocco' has paler green leaves; *H.* 'Swizzle Sticks'.

Hosta 'Pearl Lake' (Piedmont Gardens 1982)
MEDIUM

Origin: Unknown, thought to be a hybrid of *H. nakaiana.*

Description: A dense, dome-shaped mound 36 in. wide × 15 in. high (90 × 38 cm). Leaf blade 5 × 4½ in. (13 × 11 cm), of average substance, mid- to dark green with a gray cast, matt to glaucous above and shiny below, slight dimpling, edge slightly undulate, leaf slightly folded, with a mucronate tip and heart-shaped pinched to overlapping lobes. Petiole narrow, green. Flower bell-shaped, purple-striped, pale lavender, in a dense raceme, on a narrow, upright, leafy, light green, 20-in. (50-cm) scape in early summer; fertile.

Hosta 'Pearl Lake'

Cultivation Notes: Grow in dappled shade. A vigorous, rapid increaser. Ideal as ground cover or for woodland margins. Has never become a favorite in spite of receiving the Alex J. Summers Distinguished Merit Hosta Award in 1982.

Similar: ★*H.* 'Candy Hearts'; *H.* 'Drummer Boy'; *H.* 'Happy Hearts'; ★*H. nakaiana*; *H.* 'Pasture's New'; *H.* 'Saint Fiacre'; *H.* 'Twiggie'.

Sports: ★*H.* 'Veronica Lake'.

Hosta 'Potomac Pride' (T. Avent 1995)

LARGE

Origin: ★*H. yingeri* × ★*H.* 'Blue Umbrellas'.

Description: A rounded, semi-upright mound 49 in. wide × 28 in. high (122 × 70 cm). Leaf blade 12 ×

Hosta 'Potomac Pride'

Hosta 'Quill'

8½ in. (30 × 21 cm), thick, leathery, very dark green with a blue cast, glossy above and a powdery bloom below, crumpled and puckered, veins ribbed, edge almost flat to slightly rippled, leaf mostly convex, widely oval with a mucronate tip and rounded open to pinched lobes. Petiole pale green, appearing to pierce the blade. Flower small, spider-shaped, lavender, on an upright, leafy, pale green, 34-in. (85-cm) scape from mid- to late summer; fertile.

Cultivation Notes: Tolerates full sun for half to three-fourths of the day. A vigorous, rapid increaser. Performs equally well in cooler regions although raised in a warmer climate. This superb hosta gets better with each succeeding season.

Similar: *H.* 'Flower Power' has flowers that extend down the scape and leaves that are greener, more oval, and more dimpled than seersuckered.

Sports: *H.* 'Capitol Hill' has a yellow margin; *H.* 'Potomac Glory' is medio-variegated; *H.* 'Potomac River' has pale green leaves and red-dotted petioles; *H.* 'Potomac Splash' is streaked.

Hosta 'Quill' (R. Herold 1996)

SMALL–MEDIUM

Origin: ★*H. pycnophylla* × ★*H. yingeri*.

Description: A dense mound 18 in. wide × 9 in. high (45 × 23 cm). Leaf blade 6½ × 2 in. (16 × 5 cm), thick, green with a blue cast, matt above and thickly glaucous below, veins closely ribbed, edge widely rippled, leaf arching, lanceolate with an acute tip and tapered open lobes. Petiole light green, appearing to pierce the blade. Flower small, spider-shaped, lavender, on an upright, leafy, light green, 15-in. (38-cm) scape from mid- to high summer; fertile.

Cultivation Notes: Tolerates at least half a day's sun in cooler climates.

Similar: *H.* 'Purple Passion' is darker colored in all its parts; *H.* 'Sahara Nights'; *H.* 'The Razor's Edge' has noticeably red petioles.

Hosta 'Quilting Bee' (R. O'Harra 1999)

SMALL

Origin: Unknown.

Description: A low, neat, dense mound 26½ in. wide × 8¾ in. high (66 × 22 cm). Leaf blade 4 × 2¾ in. (10 × 7 cm), thick, dark olive green, satiny above and matt below, dimpled to seersuckered, edge flat to slightly rippled, leaf cupped or convex, widely oval to nearly round with a mucronate tip and heart-shaped open lobes. Petiole flattish, light olive green. Flower near bell-shaped, striped lavender, on an upright, bare, green, 18-in. (45-cm) scape from mid- to late summer; fertility unknown.

Cultivation Notes: Site in shade all day. Moderate growth rate. Pest resistant.

Distinguishing Features: Scapes rising well above a pleasing mound of attractively shaped leaves with a quilted surface texture.

Similar: *H.* 'Lakeside Neat Petite' has less-quilted leaves; *H.* 'Peedee Elfin Bells'.

Hosta 'Quilting Bee'

Hosta 'Raspberry Sorbet'

Hosta 'Raspberry Sorbet' (D. Lohman/M. Zilis 1999)

SMALL—MEDIUM

Origin: *★H. rupifraga* × *★H.* 'Shining Tot'.

Description: A rippled mound 34 in. wide × 12 in. high (85 × 30 cm). Leaf blade 7 × 3½ in. (18 × 9 cm), thick, dark green, very glossy above and shiny gray-white below, edge rippled, leaf slightly arching, cupped at the base, widely lanceolate with a cuspidate tip and tapered open lobes. Petiole bright red toward the crown. Flower flared, purple-striped mauve, widely spaced, on an upright, leafy, 20-in. (50-cm) scape that is bright red toward the raceme, in late summer; fertile.

Cultivation Notes: Site in light to moderate shade. A moderate to rapid increaser.

Distinguishing Features: Red scapes contrasting with rich mauve flowers.

Similar: *H.* 'Red Neck Heaven' is *★H. kikutii* selfed; *H.* 'Red Salamander'.

Hosta 'Regal Rhubarb' (V. Sellers 1983)

LARGE

Origin: Thought to be of *★H. nigrescens* ancestry.

Description: An open, upright to vase-shaped mound 56 in. × 31 in. high (140 × 78 cm). Leaf blade 7 × 4 in. (18 × 10 cm), thick, mid- to dark green, matt to satiny above and thinly glaucous below, some dimpling, veins conspicuous, edge slightly undulate, leaf flat nearer the tip, arching, oval with a cuspidate

Hosta 'Regal Rhubarb'

tip and tapered pinched lobes. Petiole stout, dark green with scarlet dots. Flower funnel-shaped, purple, opening from a darker purple bud, on an upright, bare, 4-ft. (1.2-m) scape that is burgundy-purple toward the crown, in high summer; fertile.

Cultivation Notes: Site in light to full shade all day. One of the first hostas introduced for its burgundy-red petioles. Still worth growing though many others now have this trait in a more pronounced form. Grow with the petioles at eye level for the most impact. Underplant with *Heuchera* 'Mint Chocolate', whose strong vein markings echo the color of the hosta's petioles.

Distinguishing Features: There can be noticeable red dots piercing the blade from the petiole.

Similar: *H.* 'Flower Power'; *H.* 'Tall Boy'.

Sports: *H.* 'Rhubarb Pie' is a superb new introduction with red petioles, a distinctly piecrusted leaf edge, and white indumentum on the leaf underside.

Hosta 'Ringtail' (K. Terpening/J. Maier 2005)

MEDIUM

Origin: *H.* 'Green Fountain' seedling.

Description: An arching mound 28 in. wide × 16 in. high (70 × 40 cm). Leaf blade 10 × 4 in. (25 × 10 cm), of good substance, olive green, shiny above and highly glossy below, smooth, prominent veins widely spaced, edge heavily rippled, leaf lanceolate to elliptic with an acuminate tip extending in a thin curl and with tapered open lobes. Petiole pale green. Flower

widely funnel-shaped, palest lavender to near-white, opening from a long purple bud, on an upright, leafy, green, 28- to 30-in. (70- to 75-cm) scape from late summer to autumn; fertility unknown.

Cultivation Notes: Site in moderate to full shade, preferably in a container at eye level.

Distinguishing Features: The long, thin curl extending from the leaf tip. Exceptionally long and narrow flower buds and inflorescence leaves.

Similar: ★*H.* 'Green Fountain' does not have the curl at the leaf tip.

Hosta 'Rosedale Barnie' (J. Hadrava 1999)

MEDIUM

Origin: ★*H. ventricosa* × ★*H.* 'Invincible'.

Description: An open mound 36 in. wide × 15 in. high (90 × 38 cm). Leaf blade 6½ × 5 in. (16 × 13 cm), of average substance, dark green, matt above and slightly shiny below, slight dimpling, edge rippled, leaf nearly round with a cuspidate tip and tapered open lobes. Petiole dark green. Flower long, bell-shaped, violet-striped pale lavender, opening from a deep violet bud, in a dense raceme, on a stout, slightly leaning, leafy, green, 9½- to 16-in. (24- to 40-cm) scape from mid- to late summer; fertility unknown.

Cultivation Notes: Site in light to moderate shade. Can reach 40 in. (100 cm) wide in optimum growing conditions but is slow-growing. The excellent display of flowers shows the ★*H. ventricosa* ancestry.

Hosta 'Ringtail'

Hosta 'Rosedale Barnie'

Hosta 'Royal Standard' (J. Grulleman/Wayside/ AHS 1986) ♥

LARGE

Origin: *H. plantaginea × *H. sieboldii.

Description: A dense mound 51 in. wide × 36 in. high (127 × 90 cm). Leaf blade 9 × 5 in. (23 × 13 cm), of average substance, bright green, satiny above and shiny below, slightly dimpled when mature, edge slightly undulate, leaf slightly arching, oval with an acute tip and tapered open to pinched lobes. Petiole light green. Flower funnel-shaped, fragrant, white, opening from a lavender-tinted bud, on an upright to slightly oblique, leafy, pale green, 42-in. (105-cm) scape from late summer to autumn; fertile.

Hosta 'Royal Standard'

Cultivation Notes: Site in morning sun in the hottest climates and three-quarters of a day's sun in cooler regions; water and feed copiously throughout the growing season. Vigorous, fast growing. Leaves will turn chartreuse when exposed to full sunlight. Less likely to bloom well in cooler, wetter regions. First hosta to receive a plant patent.

Distinguishing Features: Very fragrant, waxy, white flowers that are far more abundant than those of its *H. plantaginea parent.

Similar: *H. 'Honeybells'; H. 'Sweet Susan' has fragrant, purple flowers; H. 'White Knight' has leaves with dull undersides.

Sports: *H. 'Hoosier Harmony'; H. 'Prairieland Memories' has yellow leaves; H. 'Royal Accolade' does not hold its central variegation for as long as H. 'Hoosier Harmony'.

Hosta 'Sea Monster' (M. Seaver 1978)

VERY LARGE

Origin: H. 'Brookwood Blue' hybrid.

Description: An unruly mound 51 in. wide × 28 in. high (127 × 70 cm). Leaf blade 16 × 12 in. (40 × 30 cm), very thick, bright green, matt to shiny above and glaucous below, seersuckered and puckered, edge flat to slightly rippled, leaf shallowly cupped or convex, flat, widely oval to rounded with a mucronate tip and heart-shaped overlapping lobes. Petiole deeply channeled, pale green, appearing to pierce the blade. Flower bell-shaped, white-striped pale lavender, on an upright to leaning, bare, pale green, 30½-in. (76-cm) scape in midsummer; fertile.

Cultivation Notes: Site in shade all day. Very slow to establish, taking up to seven years for the crumpled appearance of the leaves to reach their best. Pest resistant. Much used as a parent in the Seaver hybridizing programs.

Similar: H. 'Birchwood Green'; H. 'Wrinkles and Crinkles' is smaller.

Sports: H. 'Lochness Monster' has intensely seersuckered, yellow-margined leaves.

Hosta 'Sea Monster'

Hosta 'Second Wind' (J. Kulpa 1991)

MEDIUM

Origin: Sport of *H.* 'Whirlwind'.

Description: A dense mound 22 in. wide × 11 in. high (55 × 28 cm). Leaf blade 6½ × 4½ in. (16 × 11 cm), thick, leathery dark green, waxy to glossy above and thinly glaucous below, dimpled when mature, veins widely spaced, edge almost flat, leaf widely oval with a mucronate tip and heart-shaped pinched lobes. Petiole dark green. Flower: see *H.* 'Fortunei Hyacinthina' from which *H.* 'Whirlwind' mutated.

Cultivation Notes: Site in light to moderate shade. Among the best of the hostas with dark green leaves. Easily exceeds its registered dimensions.

Distinguishing Features: Leaves are a much darker green than those of its parent.

Similar: *H.* 'Black Beauty'; *H.* 'Rosedale Spoons'.

Hosta 'Sparkling Burgundy' (R. Savory 1982)

MEDIUM

Origin: *H.* 'Ginko Craig' hybrid.

Description: An upright mound 36 in. wide × 18 in. high (90 × 45 cm). Leaf blade 7½ × 4 in. (19 × 10 cm), thick, mid-green to dark olive green, glossy above and whitish satiny below, slightly dimpled, veins ribbed, edge widely kinked, leaf elliptic with an acute tip and flat to tapered lobes. Petiole olive green. Flower widely flared, pale lilac, opening from a violet bud, on an upright, leafy, dark red-purple, 23-in. (58-cm) scape in late summer; fertile.

Cultivation Notes: Site in light to full shade. Pest resistant.

Distinguishing Features: Long racemes of flowers poised almost at right angles to the scape well above the leaf mound.

Similar: *H.* 'Maraschino Cherry'.

Sports: *H.* 'Obsession' has mid-green leaves margined with a near black, jagged border pattern.

Hosta 'Sweet Bo Peep' (H. Benedict N/R)

MEDIUM

Origin: *H.* 'Invincible' hybrid.

Description: An open mound 41 in. wide × 16 in. high (102 × 40 cm). Leaf blade 6½ × 4½ in. (16 × 11 cm), thick, leathery, mid- to dark olive green, glossy

Hosta 'Second Wind'

Hosta 'Sparkling Burgundy'

Hosta 'Sweet Bo Peep'

above and shiny below, smooth, veins widely ribbed, edge slightly rippled, leaf slightly folded, oval with a mucronate tip and heart-shaped pinched lobes. Petiole olive green, red-stained toward the crown. Flower funnel-shaped, slightly fragrant, pale lavender, on an upright or oblique, leafy, olive green, 34-in. (85-cm) scape in late summer; fertility unknown.

Cultivation Notes: Site in morning sun in all but the hottest climates.

Distinguishing Features: Leaves are smaller and rounder than its parent.

Hosta 'Tardiflora' (Irving N/R)

SMALL–MEDIUM

Origin: Japanese gardens. Once considered a species.

Description: A dense mound 26 in. wide × 12 in. high (65 × 30 cm). Leaf blade 6 × 3 in. (15 × 8 cm),

thick, leathery, dark olive green, satiny above and glossy below, smooth, edge shallowly rippled, leaf oval with an acute tip and rounded open lobes. Petiole narrow, purple-streaked olive green. Flower narrowly funnel-shaped, lavender, in a dense raceme, disposed all around an upright, purple-streaked, 24-in. (60-cm) scape in autumn; fertile.

Cultivation Notes: Site in good light to dappled shade. Most memorable for being the pod parent of the Tardiana Group, the well-known hybrids between ★*H.* 'Tardiflora' and ★*H. sieboldiana* 'Elegans' raised in the 1960s and 1970s. Autumn flowers make *H.* 'Tardiflora' a very valuable hosta. Use it with low-growing asters and colchicums. Excellent for warmer climates as it has a long life cycle. Pest resistant.

Sports: *H.* 'National Velvet' has somewhat heart-shaped leaves with a velvety sheen; *H.* 'Tardiflora Honey Glaze' has leaves overlaid in honey-gold.

Hosta 'Tardiflora'

Hosta 'Teaspoon' (F. Nyikos 1998)

SMALL

Origin: *H.* 'Birchwood Parky's Gold' × *H.* 'Golden Tiara'.

Description: An upward-facing mound 21 in. wide × 7½ in. high (53 × 19 cm). Leaf blade 3½ × 3 in. (9 × 8 cm), of average substance, bright mid-green, matt above and satiny below, noticeably rugose when mature, edge irregularly serrated, leaf cupped, folded, heart-shaped to round with a mucronate tip and open lobes. Petiole long, narrow, pale green, appearing to pierce the blade. Flower tubular, pinkish, on an upright, bare, pale green, 20- to 22-in. (50- to 55-cm) scape in midsummer; fertile.

Cultivation Notes: Site in light to full shade. Moderate growth rate. A superb small hosta. Good in a rounded pot to echo the distinct leaf shape or in a square pot to contrast the leaf shape. Equally good in the front of a border.

Distinguishing Features: Leaves have a fancied resemblance to a coffee spoon rather than the teaspoon for which the plant is named.

Similar: *H.* 'Cody'; *H.* 'Quilting Bee'.

Hosta 'T Rex' (D. & J. Ward 1999)

VERY LARGE

Origin: *H. montana* f. *macrophylla* × *H.* 'Big John'.

Description: A huge, impressive mound 80 in. wide × 30 in. high (200 × 75 cm). Leaf blade 18 × 14 in. (45 × 35 cm), of heavy substance, matt, mid-green with a slight blue cast, seersuckered, prominently veined, edge slightly undulate, leaf ovate with a cuspidate tip and heart-shaped overlapping lobes. Petiole thick, pale green. Flower tubular, near-white, on an oblique, leafy, 34½-in. (86-cm) scape in early summer; fertile.

Cultivation Notes: Site in light shade with plenty of moisture to keep the massive leaves turgid as lack of sufficient water can cause wilting. Slow to start but eventually huge. Pest resistant. The immense, heavy leaves cascade downwards becoming creased and pleated. Lovely in a woodland among plants with variegated leaves.

Similar: *H.* 'Big John'.

Hosta 'Teaspoon'

Hosta 'T Rex'

Hosta 'Great Lakes Gold'

Hosta 'Daybreak'

7

Hostas with Chartreuse, Yellow, and Gold Leaves

THIS CATEGORY EMBRACES HOSTAS whose leaves range through shades of yellow from chartreuse to deep, rich gold. Yellowness in hostas is genetically determined, the relevant gene acting as a classical Mendelian inhibitor. The gene blocks or significantly slows down the production of chlorophyll or its precursors in the leaves, and this absence of chlorophyll makes the leaves appear yellow in varying degrees.

The phenomena of lutescence and viridescence are also caused by this or related genes that are sensitive to temperature. With viridescence, rising temperatures slow down the activity of the inhibitor gene, so that

89

increasingly more chlorophyll is produced as temperatures rise. With lutescence, the gene or genes become more and more inhibiting as temperatures rise so that less and less chlorophyll is produced.

The first yellow-leaved hostas came on the market in the late 1960s and were at once seized upon by hosta enthusiasts, but it was many years before such plants were generally available. They are now appearing on the market in ever-increasing numbers, not only because of their undoubted popularity but also because of the high yield of yellow seedlings.

Where possible I am noting which hostas are viridescent and which lutescent, and I hope this will be a useful guide as to where to place them in the garden. Lutescent hostas need more sunlight than viridescent hostas to bring out their coloring to its fullest. Lutescent hostas, especially the brightest lemon to golden yellows, will light up dark areas of the garden and will actually draw the eye to that spot. Experience tells that it is best not overdo the use of yellow, however, as too many individual, yellow-leaved hostas scattered over a border among darker shades can produce a spotty, inharmonious effect and can appear agitating in an otherwise restful garden.

Yellow hostas, if planted sensitively, will blend in well with hostas of other colors, especially blues, grays, and those with gold margins. Hostas with yellow leaves that are particularly sensitive to strong sunlight are at their most vulnerable early in the season when the leaves are expanding. Such hostas need temporary shade if they put on their leaves before the trees.

Hosta 'Abiqua Recluse' (Walden-West 1989)

MEDIUM–LARGE

Origin: *H.* 'White Vision' × **H.* 'Sum and Substance'.

Description: An unruly mound 36 in. wide × 18 in. high (90 × 45 cm). Leaf blade 12½ × 9 in. (32 × 23 cm), thick, metallic golden yellow, shiny above and thinly glaucous below, lightly seersuckered, veins ribbed, edge almost flat, leaf cupped or convex, oval with a mucronate tip and heart-shaped pinched to overlapping lobes. Petiole pale chartreuse yellow.

*An asterisk before a name indicates that the plant is fully described elsewhere in this book.

Flower widely funnel-shaped, palest lavender to near white, on an upright, leafy, chartreuse, 20-in. (50-cm) scape in late summer; fertile.

Cultivation Notes: Lutescent. Colors best in some sun, but site in afternoon shade in very hot climates. A slow to moderate increaser. Pest resistant.

Similar: *H.* 'Abiqua Gold Shield'; **H.* 'August Moon'; **H.* 'City Lights'; *H.* 'Faith', *H.* 'Radiance'; *H.* 'White Vision'.

Sports: *H.* 'Academy Blushing Recluse' and *H.* 'Wooden Nickel' have yellow-margined dark-green leaves; *H.* 'Appalachian Beauty' has yellow-margined blue-green leaves; **H.* 'Electrum Stater'; *H.* 'Glitter' has pale gray-green leaves.

Hosta 'Alice Gladden' (D. & J. Ward 1998)

MEDIUM–LARGE

Origin: *H.* 'White Vision' × *H. montana* f. *macrophylla*.

Description: Matures into an open, arching mound 60 in. wide × 24 in. high (150 × 60 cm). Leaf blade 14 × 11 in. (35 × 28 cm), thick, golden yellow, shiny above and dull below, dimpled, veins furrowed, edge and blade shallowly undulate, leaf oval with a cuspidate tip and heart-shaped open or pinched lobes. Petiole stout, wide, chartreuse-yellow. Flower funnel-shaped, near white, on an upright, leafy, pale yellow, 26-in. (65-cm) scape in midsummer; seedpods green, fertile.

Cultivation Notes: Lutescent. Color is better in light to moderate shade for half the day. Vigorous.

Hosta 'Abiqua Recluse'

Pest resistant. An arresting specimen or border plant needing space around it to set off its distinctive poise. Lovely when backed by shrubs with dark green leaves.

Similar: *H.* 'Blaze of Glory'; *H.* 'Midnight Sun' has leaves that unfurl bright yellow and remain yellow; ★*H.* 'Solar Flare'; *H.* 'Stardust'; *H.* 'Summer Warrior' has distinctively rippled margins; *H.* 'Templar Gold'.

Hosta 'Aspen Gold' (V. Grapes 1986)

MEDIUM–LARGE

Origin: Open-pollinated seedling of *H.* 'Golden Medallion'.

Description: A stiff, spreading mound 36 in. wide × 20 in. high (90 × 50 cm). Leaf blade 10 × 8½ in. (25 × 21 cm) thick, chartreuse to bright yellow, matt above and glaucous pale yellow below, intensely

Hosta 'Alice Gladden', before showing its yellow coloring.

Hosta 'Aspen Gold'

seersuckered, edge slightly undulate, leaf deeply cupped, nearly round with a mucronate tip and heart-shaped pinched to overlapping lobes. Petiole glaucous pale yellow. Flower funnel-shaped, palest lavender to near white, on an upright, leafy, glaucous pale yellow, 21-in. (53-cm) scape, barely overtopping the foliage, in midsummer; fertile.

Cultivation Notes: Lutescent. Color is best in some sun and takes several weeks for the yellow to brighten. In cooler, shady gardens the leaves will always have an underlying green tint. Slug resistant. Slow to increase. Grow as a specimen or accent among darker-leaved hostas or ferns, or with *Geranium pratense* Victor Reiter Junior Strain as a complete contrast. Has received the attention it deserves only since the late 1990s.

Distinguishing Features: In mature plants the leaves become so deeply cupped that the glaucous undersides offer a contrast with the golden-yellow upper surfaces.

Similar: *H.* 'Golden Delight' has leaves with less cupping; *H.* 'Lime Krinkles' has paler, more lime-tinted leaves; ★*H.* 'Midas Touch', *H.* 'Sun Glow', ★*H.* 'Super Bowl'; *H.* 'Thai Brass' has flatter, more pointed leaves.

Sports: *H.* 'Aspen Breeze' has heavily cupped, narrowly white-margined gold leaves; *H.* 'Dawn Treader' has cream leaves with irregular light green margins; *H.* 'Hoosier Homecoming' has a narrow white margin; ★*H.* 'Millie's Memoirs'; *H.* 'On The Edge' has a narrow green margin; *H.* 'Tranquility' has yellow-margined medium green leaves.

Hosta 'August Moon' (R. Langfelder/A. Summers/P. Ruh 1996)

MEDIUM–LARGE

Origin: Unknown.

Description: A dense, somewhat asymmetrical mound 42 in. wide × 20 in. high (105 × 50 cm). Leaf blade 9 × 8 in. (23 × 20 cm), thick, matt, chartreuse turning soft yellow then glowing golden yellow, seersuckered and puckered, veins strongly marked, edge slightly undulate, leaf usually slightly convex, widely oval to nearly round with a cuspidate tip and heart-shaped open to pinched lobes. Petiole chartreuse. Flower large, bell-shaped, soft lavender to near white, on an upright, leafy, glaucous grayish yellow, 32 in. (80 cm) scape in high summer; seedpods greenish, fertile.

Cultivation Notes: Lutescent. Except in the U.S. Deep South, where it grows exceptionally well, it colors best in four to five hours of morning sun. Vigorous, fast growing. Among the first yellow-leaved hostas introduced. Although considered a classic, it has never quite hit the headlines in spite of its many good qualities, such as its sun tolerance, but is better known for its many glamorous sports.

Distinguishing Features: Blooms three weeks later than many yellow-leaved ★*H. sieboldiana* types and increases faster. Has a great propensity for throwing sports, of which only a few of the best are mentioned here.

Sports: ★*H.* 'Abiqua Moonbeam'; ★*H.* 'Crystal Moon'; *H.* 'Devon Cloud', ★*H.* 'Gemini Moon'; *H.* 'Indiana Knight'; *H.* 'Indiana Moonshine'; *H.* 'Jupiter'; *H.* 'Lunar Magic'; *H.* 'Lunar Orbit'; *H.* 'Lunar Sea'; *H.* 'Mayan Moon'; *H.* 'Moon Over Lake Erie'; *H.* 'Polar Moon'; ★*H.* 'September Sun'; *H.* 'Watermark'; *H.* 'Xanadu Paisley' is a newly introduced streaked form.

Hosta 'Birchwood Parky's Gold' (F. Shaw & AHS 1986)

SMALL–MEDIUM

Origin: *H. nakaiana* hybrid.

Description: A dense, spreading mound 41 in. wide × 17 in. high (102 × 43 cm). Leaf blade 6 × 5 in. (15 × 13 cm), thin, chartreuse turning old gold, matt above and thinly glaucous below, smooth, edge nearly flat to slightly undulate, leaf widely oval to heart-shaped with a mucronate tip and heart-shaped open lobes. Petiole narrow, chartreuse. Flower funnel-shaped, lavender, on an upright, bare, chartreuse, 36-in. (90-cm) scape in midsummer; fertile.

Cultivation Notes: Site in some morning sun in cooler climates, otherwise light to medium shade. Vigorous, a rapid increaser. A classic hosta, still one of the best for lighting up woodland areas. Grow with ★*H.* 'Blue Cadet' or ★*H.* 'Pearl Lake'.

Similar: *H.* 'Gold Cadet'; ★*H.* 'Gold Edger'.

Sports: *H.* 'Parky's Prize', *H.* 'Patricia', and *H.*

Hosta 'August Moon'

'Zuzu's Petals' all have yellow-margined green leaves; *H. 'Sweet Home Chicago'.

Hosta 'Blackfoot' (M. Plater-Zyberk/R. Solberg 1994)

SMALL–MEDIUM

Origin: *H. sieboldii* 'Kabitan' hybrid.

Description: A moderately dense, rhizomatous mound 16 in. wide × 10 in. high (40 × 25 cm). Leaf blade 6 × 4 in. (15 × 10 cm), of average substance, chartreuse turning yellow, matt above and satiny below, slightly dimpled when mature, veins closely ribbed, edge flat, leaf slightly arching, slightly convex, narrowly oval with an acute tip and rounded open to pinched lobes. Petiole narrow, mahogany brown. Flower funnel-shaped, purple-veined lavender, on an upright, bare, burgundy, 16-in. (40-cm) scape from high to late summer.

Cultivation Notes: Viridescent. Site in good light rather than exposed to sunlight. Performs best in hotter, humid climates.

Distinguishing Features: A colorful hosta with brown petioles, red scapes, and purple flowers that make a great contrast with the intensely yellow leaves.

Hosta 'Blond Elf' (P. Aden N/R)

SMALL

Origin: Sport of *H*. 'Fresh'.

Description: A dense, dome-shaped mound 24 in. wide × 8½ in. high (60 × 21 cm). Leaf blade 4½ × 2 in. (11 × 5 cm), thin, chartreuse to muted yellow-gold, matt above and shiny below, veins closely spaced, edge widely rippled, leaf oval with an acute tip and tapered open lobes. Petiole narrow, chartreuse, appearing to pierce the blade. Flower funnel-shaped, lavender, on an upright, leafy, chartreuse, 14-in. (35-cm) scape from high to late summer; fertile.

Cultivation Notes: Lutescent. Tolerates morning sun in spite of its thin substance, except in warmer climates. Increases rapidly. Useful as an edging hosta or at the front of the border. Leaf color holds well into autumn.

Hosta 'Blackfoot'

Hosta 'Birchwood Parky's Gold'

Hosta 'Blond Elf'

Similar: *H.* 'Devon Gold'; ★*H.* 'Lemon Lime'.

Sports: *H.* 'Dumb Blonde' has streaked leaves.

Hosta 'Centerfold' (G. Kamp 1994)

LARGE

Origin: Unknown.

Description: A dense, unruly mound 46 in. wide × 24 in. high (116 × 60 cm). Leaf blade 10 × 9 in. (25 × 23 cm), thick, satiny, chartreuse turning golden yellow, intensely seersuckered, edge slightly rippled, leaf convex or slightly cupped, folded, widely oval with a cuspidate tip and heart-shaped overlapping lobes. Petiole light green. Flower flared, near white, on an upright, bare green, 18-in. (45-cm) scape from mid- to high summer; fertility unknown.

Cultivation Notes: Lutescent. Site in good light to dappled shade. A moderate growth rate.

Distinguishing Features: Leaf blades markedly folded down the center (and hence its name).

Similar: ★*H.* 'Aspen Gold'; ★*H.* 'Golden Waffles'; ★*H.* 'Midas Touch' has rounder leaves; *H.* 'Rosedale Golden Goose' has outstanding sun tolerance.

Hosta 'Christmas Gold' (M. Seaver N/R)

MEDIUM

Origin: Sport of ★*H.* 'Christmas Tree'.

Description: An unruly mound 41 in. wide × 18 in. high (102 × 45 cm). Leaf blade 9 × 8½ in. (23 × 21 cm), thick, emerging chartreuse turning first lemon yellow and finally golden yellow, holding its

color into autumn, satiny above and glaucous below, intensely seersuckered, crumpled, and puckered, edge almost flat, leaf cupped or convex, widely oval to nearly round with a mucronate tip and heart-shaped overlapping lobes. Petiole light green. Flower funnel-shaped, near white, on an upright, leafy, glaucous gray-green turning mahogany-purple, 22¾-in. (57-cm) scape from mid- to high summer; seedpods deep purple, fertile.

Cultivation Notes: Lutescent. Colors best in sun, which it will take all day except in the hottest climates. Adequate moisture is essential to prevent leaf scorch. Slow to increase. Pest resistant.

Distinguishing Features: Mature leaves can be crumpled to the point of distortion. The mahogany-purple scape and deep purple seedpods.

Sports: *H.* 'Jason and Katie' has yellow-margined green leaves; ★*H.* 'Lucy Vitols'.

Hosta 'City Lights' (P. Aden 1978)

LARGE

Origin: *H.* 'White Vision' × ★*H.* 'Golden Prayers'.

Description: An open mound 49 in. wide × 25 in. high (122 × 63 cm). Leaf blade 9 × 8½ in. (23 × 21 cm), thick, emerging glaucous chartreuse turning a pale metallic yellow gold, intensely seersuckered, strongly veined, edge almost flat, leaf shallowly cupped or convex, widely oval with a mucronate tip and heart-shaped open lobes. Petiole stout, very light green. Flower open funnel-shaped, near white, on

Hosta 'Centerfold'

Hosta 'Christmas Gold'

an upright, bare, pale green, 31-in. (78-cm) scape in midsummer; fertile.

Cultivation Notes: Lutescent. Site in light to medium shade all day. The glaucous bloom soon burns off the upper surface of the leaf leaving a satiny finish. Slow to increase. Pest resistant.

Similar: *★H.* 'Golden Waffles'; *H.* 'Harriette Ward'; *H.* 'Rosedale Lost Dutchman' has exceptionally puckered leaves; *H.* 'White Vision' is less popular now as a garden plant but important because it is the parent of many good yellow-leaved introductions; *★H.* 'Zounds' has slightly darker golden-yellow leaves.

Sports: *H.* 'Peedee Dew Catcher'.

Hosta 'Dalton's Pick' (K. Terpening 2005)

MEDIUM

Origin: Unknown.

Description: An upright mound 25 in. wide × 12 in. high (63 × 30 cm). Leaf blade 9 × 6 in. (23 × 15 cm), of good substance, matt, bright yellow, deeply and evenly seersuckered, veins widely spaced, edge flat, leaf folded, ovate with a cuspidate tip and pinched to folded heart-shaped lobes. Petiole chartreuse to

pale yellow. Flower pale lavender, on an upright, bare, chartreuse, 15- to 18-in. (38- to 45-cm) scape in early and midsummer; fertility unknown.

Cultivation Notes: Viridescent. Excellent sun tolerance. Site in sunlight and the color will hold for

Hosta 'Dalton's Pick'

Hosta 'City Lights'

the season, but provide plenty of moisture to prevent scorching; shade will turn the leaves chartreuse to green much sooner. Slow to moderate growth rate. The full effect of the intense seersuckering taking several seasons to develop. Voted Best in Section at *First Look 2*.

Distinguishing Features: The deep, uniform seersuckering which remains chartreuse in the hollows of the leaves.

Hosta 'Dancing Queen' (K. Terpening/A. Scheer 2005)

LARGE

Origin: *H.* 'Split Personality' seedling.

Description: An open mound 51 in. wide × 26 in. high (127 × 65 cm). Leaf blade 13 × 7 in. (33 × 18 cm), of good substance, brilliant golden yellow, satiny above and matt below, dimpled when mature, prominent veins widely spaced, edge evenly piecrusted, leaf folded when young, convex when mature, broadly ovate with a recurved cuspidate tip and pinched heart-shaped lobes. Petiole chartreuse yellow. Flower funnel-shaped, pale lavender, on an upright, leafy, chartreuse 44½-in. (112-cm) scape from mid- to late summer; fertility unknown.

Cultivation Notes: Slightly viridescent. The bright color of the leaves fades to pale yellow at the end of the summer. Site in light to moderate shade. A moderate increaser. Allow plenty of space so that the superb shape, color, and texture of the leaves are not hidden by other plants.

Distinguishing Features: Exceptionally attractive piecrust edges from its parent, a hosta whose leaves can be either blue or yellow.

Similar: *H.* 'Golden Gate' has slightly rounder leaves and is lutescent.

Hosta 'Dawn's Early Light' (O. Petryszyn 1998)

MEDIUM–LARGE

Origin: *H.* 'Sea Fire' hybrid.

Description: A pleasing, symmetrical mound 36 in. wide × 20 in. high (90 × 50 cm). Leaf blade 9 × 8 in. (23 × 20 cm), of average substance, matt lemon yellow above, glaucous pale green below, seersuckered when mature, prominently veined, edge distinctly piecrusted, leaf convex, nearly round with a slightly recurved vestigial tip and heart-shaped open to pinched lobes. Petiole narrowly channeled, chartreuse. Flower tubular, pale lavender, opening from a pink bud, on an upright, leafy, brownish chartreuse, 29-in. (73-cm) scape in midsummer; sterile.

Cultivation Notes: Viridescent. Leaves do not scorch but site in light to moderate shade where it will retain the exceptionally brilliant leaf color in spring. Moderate to rapid growth rate. Lovely with early flowering Japanese azaleas. Contrasts dramatically with *Heuchera* 'Obsidian'.

Distinguishing Features: The startling bright yellow leaf color.

Similar: *H.* 'Abiqua Gold Shield'; ★*H.* 'Sea Gulf Stream'.

Hosta 'Dancing Queen'

Hosta 'Dawn's Early Light'

Hosta **'Daybreak'** (P. Aden 1986)

LARGE

Origin: Unknown.

Description: A low, wide-spreading mound of horizontal leaves 60 in. wide × 12 in. high (150 × 30 cm). Leaf blade 14 × 10⅜ in. (35 × 26 cm), thick, chartreuse yellow turning deep golden yellow, shiny above and thinly glaucous below, veins closely spaced, some dimpling when mature, edge shallowly undulate, leaf slightly convex toward the tip, broadly ovate with a cuspidate tip and heart-shaped pinched lobes. Petiole light chartreuse yellow. Flower funnel-shaped, deep lavender-blue, on a drooping, leafy, dark green, 34-in. (85-cm) scape from mid- to late summer; fertile.

Cultivation Notes: Lutescent. Site in afternoon shade, particularly in hot climates. Among the best in this category. Pest and weather resistant. Will light up dark borders.

Distinguishing Features: Flowers are densely packed toward the tip of the scape. The leaf tip pinches and droops in maturity.

Similar: *★H.* 'Alice Gladden'; *★H.* 'Solar Flare' has oval leaves that are more distinctly undulate.

Sports: *H.* 'Day's End' has mid-green leaves with irregular golden-yellow margins that widen considerably as the plant matures; *H.* 'Mid Afternoon'; *H.* 'Midsummer Morning' has the reverse variegation.

Hosta **'Midsummer Morning'**

Hosta **'Daybreak'**

Hosta 'Dee's Golden Jewel' (K. Walek 1996)

MEDIUM—LARGE

Origin: ★*H.* 'Royal Standard' × ★*H.* 'Galaxy'.

Description: An upright, rhizomatous mound 18 in. wide × 24 in. high (45 × 60 cm). Leaf blade 6½ × 8 in. (16 × 20 cm), very thick, chartreuse to golden yellow, matt above and glaucous below, dimpled to seersuckered, veins ribbed, edge rippled, leaf folded or shallowly cupped, widely oval with a cuspidate tip and heart-shaped pinched lobes. Petiole chartreuse. Flower funnel-shaped, near white, in a dense raceme, on a slightly leaning, leafy, chartreuse, 30-in. (75-cm) scape in midsummer; barely fertile.

Cultivation Notes: Lutescent. Its sun tolerance, even in warmer climates, and its heavy leaf substance more than compensate for the less-than-spectacular leaf color. Very slow growth rate.

Similar: *H.* 'Fiesta'.

Sports: ★*H.* 'Jewel of the Nile'.

Hosta 'Drawn Butter' (Belle Gardens 1994)

MEDIUM

Origin: *H.* 'Whoopie' hybrid.

Description: An open, semi-upright mound 25 in. wide × 16½ in. high (63 × 42 cm). Leaf blade 5½ × 2¾ in. (14 × 7 cm), thick, greenish gold turning pale yellow then a rich deep gold, matt above and glaucous below, dimpled when mature, veins closely ribbed, edge rippled, leaf flat to slightly undulate, oval with a mucronate tip and rounded pinched lobes. Petiole

chartreuse, with purple dots toward the crown. Flower funnel-shaped, pale purple, on an arching, leafy, maroon-dotted, 20- to 24-in. (50- to 60-cm) scape in late summer; fertile.

Cultivation Notes: Lutescent. Best in dappled to medium shade, where it lights up darker-leaved shrubs. Slow to increase. Pest resistant.

Hosta 'Eola Salad Bowl' (S. Hottovy/Monrovia/L. Hottovy 2004)

SMALL

Origin: Unknown.

Description: A loose, unruly mound 24 in. wide × 8½ in. high (60 × 21 cm), the leaves held in an upward and outward stance. Leaf blade 4 × 2 in. (10

Hosta 'Drawn Butter'

Hosta 'Dee's Golden Jewel'

Hosta 'Eola Salad Bowl' in dense shade.

× 5 cm), thin, chartreuse to old gold, matt above and shiny below, veins widely spaced, edge nicely rippled, leaf slightly cupped or folded, elliptic to oval with a cuspidate tip and tapered or flat open lobes. Petiole narrowly channeled, chartreuse, appearing to pierce the blade. Flower funnel-shaped, purple, on an upright, leafy, light green, 14-in. (35-cm) scape in midsummer; fertility unknown.

Cultivation Notes: Lutescent. Needs good light in the morning to enhance the color, then light shade. Not suitable for containers but ideal for a raised bed with other small hostas, such as ★*H.* 'Little Wonder' or *H.* 'Island Charm'. Deserves to be better known.

Distinguishing Features: Distinctly rippled margins on a small leaf that is not lanceolate.

Similar: *H.* 'Osiris Petit Prince' has smaller, deeper yellow leaves.

Hosta 'Eye Catcher' (G. Goodwin 1996)

SMALL

Origin: Unknown, open-pollinated seedling.

Description: A rigid, low mound 24 in. wide × 12 in. high (60 × 30 cm). Leaf blade 4 × 3 in. (10 × 8 cm), thick, vivid golden yellow fading to chartreuse, matt above and glaucous below, intensely seersuckered and puckered, prominently veined, edge flat, leaf cupped, near round with a mucronate tip and heart-shaped open to pinched lobes. Petiole pale chartreuse, appearing to pierce the blade. Flower funnel-shaped, pale lavender, opening from a dark chartreuse bud,

on an upright, leafy, thick, chartreuse, 18-in. (45-cm) scape; seedpods light green, fertile.

Cultivation Notes: Viridescent. A brilliant golden yellow in spring, quite living up to its name, but equally attractive later on if grown in some morning sun followed by good light. Increases rapidly, often with a second flush of leaves. Pest resistant. Among the very best of the small-leaved golden yellows and deserves to be better known.

Distinguishing Features: Resembles a golden yellow-leaved ★*H.* 'Tokudama' but is much smaller, and the margins remain a slightly deeper gold but there are hints of green in the depths of the seersuckering. The first few flowers are tucked into the base of the scape leaves, the opening blooms creating the impression of a Christmas tree.

Similar: *H.* 'Banana Muffins' is a brighter shade of golden yellow; *H.* 'Dixieland Heat' has leaf shoots with red sheaths; *H.* 'Golden Friendship' has the same upright habit but larger, more-rugose leaves; *H.* 'Lemon Leaf' is a brighter color; ★*H.* 'Maui Buttercups' is slightly larger.

Hosta 'Feather Boa' (R. O'Harra 1991)

SMALL

Origin: ★*H. sieboldii* derivative.

Description: A dense mound 15 in. wide × 9 in. high (38 × 23 cm). Leaf blade 4 × 2 in. (10 × 5 cm), thin, bright pale yellow becoming chartreuse, matt above and shiny below, edge rippled to kinked, leaf

Hosta 'Eye Catcher'

Hosta 'Feather Boa'

arching, elliptic with a cuspidate tip and tapered open lobes. Petiole narrow, light yellow. Flower bell-shaped, purple-striped lavender, on a thin, upright, leafy, 16-in. (40-cm) scape in high summer; fertile.

Cultivation Notes: Viridescent. Site in good light all day or in morning sun to maintain the leaf color. Increases rapidly. Requires plenty of moisture.

Similar: *H.* 'Estrellita'; *H.* 'Gingee'; *H.* 'Lime Shag' has smaller leaves and is virtually identical to *H. sieboldii* 'Subcrocea'; *H.* 'Yellow Boa'.

Hosta 'Fire Island' (W. Brincka 1998)

MEDIUM

Origin: *H. longipes* 'Hypoglauca' × ★*H.* 'Crested Surf'.

Description: A dense mound 34 in. wide × 14 in. high (85 × 35 cm). Leaf blade 6½ × 4½ in. (16 × 11 cm), of moderate substance, bright, pale acid yellow turning chartreuse, shiny above and matt below, intensely seersuckered, edge distinctly rippled, leaf widely oval with a cuspidate tip and flat to tapered pinched lobes. Petiole intensely dotted and streaked

bright red, this color persisting throughout the season. Flower funnel-shaped, lavender, on an upright, leafy, chartreuse, 18- to 20-in. (45- to 50-cm) scape in late summer; seedpods green, fertile.

Cultivation Notes: Viridescent. Site in shade all day. Increases rapidly. Most effective when grown at eye level.

Distinguishing Features: One of the few yellow-leaved hostas with red dots on the leaf blade.

Similar: ★*H.* 'Ogon Iwa'.

Sports: ★*H.* 'Eye Declare', *H.* 'Paradise Island' has a stunningly beautiful combination of dark green-margined bright chartreuse leaves and dark red petioles.

Hosta 'Fortunei Albopicta Aurea' (N. Hylander & AHS 1987) ♀

MEDIUM

Origin: Natural sport of ★*H.* 'Fortunei Albopicta'.

Description: A dense mound 41 in. wide × 18 in. high (102 × 45 cm). Leaf blade 8½ × 5 in. (21 × 13 cm), of average substance, palest ivory-green to soft butter yellow, netted with thin green veins, gradually

Hosta 'Fire Island'

turning green, matt above and glaucous below, dimpled when mature, edge slightly rippled, leaf convex, widely oval with a cuspidate tip and heart-shaped overlapping lobes. Petiole light chartreuse. Flower: see *H.* 'Fortunei Albopicta'.

Cultivation Notes: Viridescent. A hosta for cooler climates, where the exquisite leaf color will be maintained for much longer. Site in light shade all day. Leaves are not suitable for flower arrangement as the petioles are too floppy. One of the first yellow-leaved hostas to be used for hybridizing but has now been superseded by the introduction of lutescent cultivars.

Similar: *H.* 'Gold Haze'; *H.* 'Gold Leaf'; *H.* 'Granary Gold' retains the yellow leaf color for a longer period; *H.* 'Zitronenfalter'.

Hosta 'Fragrant Gold' (P. Aden 1982)

LARGE

Origin: *H.* 'Sum and Substance' hybrid.

Description: A rounded mound 44½ in. wide × 22 in. high (112 × 55 cm). Leaf blade 10 × 8½ in. (25 × 21 cm), thick, chartreuse green slowly turning muted old gold, dimpled, prominently veined, edge almost flat, leaf convex, widely oval with a cuspidate tip and heart-shaped pinched lobes. Petiole stout, chartreuse. Flower widely flared, funnel-shaped, slightly fragrant, pale lavender, on an upright, bare, chartreuse, 34-in. (85-cm) scape in late summer; fertile.

Cultivation Notes: Lutescent. Site in morning sun followed by dappled shade or the leaves will not turn

Hosta 'Fragrant Gold'

Hosta 'Fortunei Albopicta Aurea'

golden yellow. Pest resistant. Floral fragrance is only apparent in hot, humid climates.

Distinguishing Features: Midrib and veins remain green when the leaves turn golden yellow.

Similar: *H.* 'Fried Bananas' has leaves of a clearer color.

Hosta 'Glory' (R. Savory 1985)

MEDIUM

Origin: *H.* 'August Moon' seedling.

Description: A rounded mound 24 in. wide × 11 in. high (60 × 28 cm). Leaf blade 5 × 5 in. (13 × 13 cm), thick, glaucous chartreuse turning bright yellow, intensely seersuckered and puckered, veins ribbed, edge rippled, leaf convex or cupped, almost round with a cuspidate tip and heart-shaped pinched or overlapping lobes. Petiole chartreuse. Flower bell-shaped, purple, in a cluster near the top on an upright, leafy, green, 19-in. (48-cm) scape in midsummer; fertile.

Cultivation Notes: Lutescent. Site in shade. Increases rapidly and will easily exceed its registered dimensions. Grow with *Geranium* 'Black Ice' for color contrast.

Distinguishing Features: Leaf edges are more rippled than its parent, and the midrib and veins remain green.

Sports: *H.* 'Old Glory' PP12,503 has a dark green margin.

Hosta 'Gold Edger' (P. Aden 1978)

SMALL

Origin: *H.* 'Blue Cadet' × *H.* 'Gold Cadet'.

Description: A dense, symmetrical mound 25 in. wide × 9–12 in. (63 × 23–30 cm). Leaf blade 3½ × 2½ in. (9 × 6 cm), thick, muted golden yellow fading to chartreuse, matt to glaucous above and glaucous below, dimpled, edge sometimes kinked, leaf cupped, widely oval with a mucronate tip and heart-shaped overlapping lobes. Petiole narrow, chartreuse. Flower bell-shaped, lavender, on an oblique to upright, bare, chartreuse, 12-in. (30-cm) scape in late summer; fertile.

Cultivation Notes: Viridescent. Tolerates full sun all day except in warmer climates. Leaf color is very dependent upon the quality of the light. Usually exceeds its registered dimensions. As its name implies, it is a popular edging hosta.

Similar: *H.* 'Birchwood Parky's Gold'; *H.* 'Gold

Hosta 'Gold Edger'

Hosta 'Glory'

Hosta 'Olympic Edger'

Drop' has a slightly less-pebbled leaf surface; *H.* 'Golden Spider'; *H.* 'Midwest Gold' has a slightly duller leaf color.

Sports: *H.* 'Gold Edger Supreme', with greenish gold leaves and a thin white margin, and *H.* 'Gold Edger Surprise', which has bluish green leaves narrowly margined white, are recommended for only the most avid collectors; *★H.* 'Hawkeye'; *H.* 'June Bug' has green-margined leaves; *H.* 'Olympic Edger' has narrow, cream-margined chartreuse to yellow leaves; *H.* 'Pacific Blue Edger' has blue leaves; *H.* 'Radiant Edger' has very wide yellow margins; *★H.* 'Royal Tiara'; *H.* 'Royal Wave'; *H.* 'Timothy' has green leaves with muted yellow margins; *★H.* 'X-Ray'.

Hosta **'Golden Empress'** (Kuk 1990)

SMALL–MEDIUM

Origin: *H.* 'Wayside Blue' seedling.

Description: A compact mound 18 in. wide × 10 in. high (45 × 25 cm). Leaf blade 4½ × 3½ in. (11 × 9 cm), thick, glaucous bright chartreuse to light yellow gold, seersuckered, edge slightly undulate, leaf slightly folded, widely oval with a cuspidate tip and heart-shaped pinched lobes. Petiole thin, chartreuse. Flower funnel-shaped, lavender, on a thin, purple-tinted green, leafy, 18-in. (45-cm) scape, towering above the leaf mound, in late summer; fertile.

Cultivation Notes: Lutescent. Site in sun in cooler climates, which is unusual in a plant of *★H.* 'Tokudama' ancestry. Site in dappled to full shade in hotter climates. Increases rapidly. Leaf color is muted because of the heavy glaucous bloom.

Hosta **'Golden Medallion'** (M. Eisel & AHS 1984)

MEDIUM

Origin: Group name embracing all yellow-leaved natural sports of *★H.* 'Tokudama'.

Description: A rounded mound 41 in. wide × 16 in. high (102 × 40 cm). Leaf blade 7 × 6½ in. (18 × 16 cm), thick, glaucous chartreuse turning bright golden yellow, intensely seersuckered with some puckering, edge almost flat, leaf shallowly cupped, nearly round with a mucronate tip and heart-shaped overlapping lobes. Petiole chartreuse. Flower: see *H.* 'Tokudama'.

Hosta 'Golden Empress'

Cultivation Notes: Lutescent. Site in light to medium shade all day, otherwise the edges can scorch. Among the first yellow-leaved hostas introduced. Needs plenty of moisture. Slow to increase. Pest resistant. Now largely superseded by gold-leaved hostas, which do not scorch.

Distinguishing Features: Leaf cupping is not as deep as in *H. 'Aspen Gold' or *H. 'Midas Touch'.

Similar: H. 'Golden Bullion' is another group name embracing all naturally occurring gold-leaved sports of *H. 'Tokudama Flavocircinalis' which have longer, narrower leaves; H. 'Lime Krinkles' has slightly larger leaves; H. 'Moon Lily'.

Hosta 'Golden Medallion'

Hosta 'Golden Oriole'

Hosta 'Golden Oriole' (E. Smith & BHHS 1988)

MEDIUM

Origin: *H. 'Lancifolia' × *H. sieboldii 'Kabitan'.

Description: An arching mound 41 in. wide × 18 in. high (102 × 45 cm). Leaf blade 9 × 4 in. (23 × 10 cm), of average substance, shiny, rich golden yellow fading to drab chartreuse, strongly veined, some dimpling when mature, edge slightly rippled, leaf arching, widely lanceolate with an acute tip and open heart-shaped lobes. Petiole chartreuse with burgundy dots. Flower funnel-shaped, purple, on an upright, leafy, olive-green, 25-in. (63-cm) scape in late summer; fertile.

Cultivation Notes: Viridescent. Site in good light or dappled shade. The brilliant golden leaves are at their best in early summer. Requires plenty of moisture.

Similar: H. 'Goldsmith' is one of Eric Smith's best-known introductions but in danger of being lost to cultivation.

Hosta 'Golden Prayers' (P. Aden 1976)

MEDIUM

Origin: Seedling of *H. 'Golden Waffles'. Registration details are at variance with what is now thought to be the "true" *H. 'Golden Prayers'.

Description: An upright mound 16–18 in. wide × 10–12 in. high (40–45 × 25–30 cm). Leaf blade 8 × 6½ in. (20 × 16 cm), thick, glaucous chartreuse turning golden yellow, intensely seersuckered with occasional puckering, edge almost flat, leaf deeply cupped or folded, widely oval with a mucronate tip and rounded pinched lobes. Petiole chartreuse to yellow. Flower funnel-shaped, near white, on an upright,

Hosta 'Golden Prayers' in deep shade.

bare, yellow, 20-in. (50-cm) scape in midsummer; fertility uncertain.

Cultivation Notes: Lutescent. Site in shade all day to prevent scorching of the leaf edge. Slow to moderate growth rate. Pest resistant.

Similar: *H.* 'Golden Bullion'; ★*H.* 'Golden Medallion'; ★*H.* 'Golden Waffles'; ★*H.* 'King Tut'; ★*H.* 'Little Aurora', with which it has been confused in the trade, is smaller; *H.* 'Thai Brass'.

Hosta 'Golden Scepter' (R. Savory 1983)

SMALL

Origin: Natural sport of ★*H.* 'Golden Tiara'.

Description: A spreading mound 18 in. wide × 12 in. high (45 × 30 cm). Leaf blade 4¾ × 4 in. (12 × 10 cm), thin, chartreuse turning deep golden yellow, matt above and shiny below, slightly dimpled when mature, edge almost flat, leaf widely oval to heart-shaped with a cuspidate tip and open to pinched lobes. Petiole long, thin, pale green. Flower: see *H.* 'Golden 'Tiara'.

Cultivation Notes: Lutescent. Site in dappled to full shade all day. Lovely when grown near dark-flowered rhododendrons and other shrubs with an open habit.

Distinguishing Features: Slower growing than its parent.

Similar: *H.* 'Sweet Tater Pie', a hybrid between *H.* 'Golden Scepter' and ★*H.* *yingeri*, has the burnished golden leaf color of the former and the plant habit of the latter.

Sports: ★*H.* 'Emerald Tiara'; ★*H.* 'Platinum Tiara'.

Hosta 'Golden Sculpture' (K. Anderson 1982)

LARGE

Origin: *H. sieboldiana* 'Elegans' hybrid.

Description: A vase-shaped mound 50 in. wide × 26 in. high (126 × 65 cm). Leaf blade 11 × 10 in. (28 × 25 cm), thick, sharp chartreuse yellow fading to lighter yellow, thinly glaucous evenly seersuckered, edge widely undulate, leaf convex when mature, widely oval with a slightly arching cuspidate tip and heart-shaped overlapping lobes. Petiole chartreuse. Flower funnel-shaped, near white, in a dense raceme, on an upright, leafy, green, 41-in. (102-cm) scape in midsummer; fertile.

Cultivation Notes: Lutescent. Site in some morning sun in cooler climates, otherwise in shade all day to prevent scorching of the leaf edge. Easily exceeds its registered dimensions although it is slow to increase; it is well worth the wait as it is a most impressive hosta. Pest resistant. Winner of the 1991 Alex J. Summers Distinguished Merit Hosta Award.

Distinguishing Features: Midrib and veins remain green.

Similar: *H.* 'Fort Knox'; ★*H.* 'High Noon'.

Sports: *H.* 'Garden Party' has narrow green margins and is slow to increase.

Hosta 'Golden Spades' (Kuk 1986)

SMALL

Origin: Open-pollinated *H. sieboldii* 'Kabitan' seedling.

Description: A dense mound 20 in. wide × 7 in. high (50 × 18 cm). Leaf blade 4 × 2¾ in. (10 × 7 cm),

Hosta 'Golden Scepter'   *Hosta* 'Golden Sculpture'

thin, deep golden yellow fading to chartreuse yellow, with green veins, matt above and shiny below, edge widely undulate, leaf slightly folded, wedge-shaped with a cuspidate tip and rounded open lobes. Petiole narrow, chartreuse. Flower funnel-shaped, violet-striped palest mauve, opening from a mauve bud, on a thin, upright, chartreuse, 16-in. (40-cm) scape from mid- to high summer; fertile.

Cultivation Notes: Viridescent. Achieves the best leaf color in high, filtered shade, the color being brightest early in the season. Lovely with glossy, dark green hostas or with contrasting burgundy foliage such as that of *Berberis thunbergii* 'Nana' and *Coleus* 'Pineapple'.

Distinguishing Features: Leaves have a fancied resemblance to the outline of a spade.

Hosta 'Golden Teacup' (J. & J. Wilkins 1989)

SMALL

Origin: ★*H.* 'Aspen Gold' × ★*H.* 'Gold Regal'.

Description: An upright mound 18 in. wide × 12 in. high (45 × 30 cm). Leaf blade 5 × 4½ in. (13 × 11 cm), thick, bright yellow turning chartreuse, matt above and glaucous below, intensely seersuckered, edge flat, leaf folded to deeply cupped, widely oval to round with a cuspidate tip and heart-shaped pinched to overlapping lobes. Petiole narrow, chartreuse. Flower flaring, white, on an upright, bare, 12-in. (30-cm) scape from mid- to late summer; fertile.

Cultivation Notes: Viridescent. Golden color remains longer if grown in some morning sun. Slow but worth the wait as the leaves have an attractive shape and surface texture. Pest resistant.

Similar: ★*H.* 'Eye Catcher'; ★*H.* 'Little Aurora' has more closely spaced seersuckering; ★*H.* 'Maui Buttercups' is less cupped and also has a distinctive white flower.

Sports: *H.* 'Gilded Teacup', a worthy new introduction, has dark green-margined bright gold leaves and is more vigorous than its parent.

Hosta 'Golden Teacup'

Hosta 'Golden Waffles'

Hosta 'Golden Spades'

Hosta **'Golden Waffles'** (P. Aden 1976)

MEDIUM

Origin: *H.* "Aden 381" × *H.* "Aden 388."

Description: A layered mound 24 in. wide × 16 in. high (60 × 40 cm). Leaf blade 9 × 8½ in. (23 × 21 cm), very thick, chartreuse to bright gold depending on light levels, satiny above and thinly glaucous below, intensely seersuckered, strongly veined, edge shallowly rippled, leaf convex to occasionally cupped, arching toward the tip, widely oval with a mucronate tip and heart-shaped overlapping lobes. Petiole chartreuse. Flower open funnel-shaped, purple-striped pale lavender, borne in profusion on an oblique, bare, olive-green, 30-in. (75-cm) scape in high summer; fertile.

Cultivation Notes: Lutescent. Easily exceeds its registered dimensions. One of the earliest registered yellow-leaved hybrids. Much used as a parent because of its heavy substance and deeply seersuckered leaf. A classic.

Hosta **'Gold Regal'** (P. Aden 1974)

LARGE—VERY LARGE

Origin: Unknown.

Description: A semi-upright, dense, overlapping mound 51 in. wide × 36 in. high (127 × 90 cm). Leaf blade 8½–11 × 7½–8½ in. (21–28 × 19–21 cm), thick, chartreuse to old gold, matt above and thickly glaucous below, dimpled, veins deeply impressed, edge flat, leaf slightly folded, widely oval with a cuspidate tip and tapered pinched lobes. Petiole stout, glaucous chartreuse, appearing to pierce the blade. Flower large, bell-shaped, grayish mauve on a stout, leafy, upright, glaucous green, 30- to 39-in. (75- to 98-cm) scape in midsummer; fertile.

Cultivation Notes: Lutescent. Tolerates long exposure to sun in most regions but morning sun only in the hottest climates. Leaves will remain chartreuse if grown in shade all day. Superb flowers are only one of this hosta's many attributes. An excellent breeding plant. Pest resistant.

Similar: *H.* 'Shade Master' also has superb flowers; ★*H.* 'Starboard Light' has more-wavy leaves.

Sports: ★*H.* 'Alex Summers'; *H.* 'David Reath' has yellow-margined dark green leaves; *H.* 'Golden Torch' is brighter and has a more vase-shaped habit; *H.* 'Independence Day' has pale green leaves with a muted yellow margin; *H.* 'Misty Regal' has green-margined, streaky chartreuse leaves; *H.* 'Rascal'; ★*H.* 'Ultraviolet Light' is similar in clump and leaf shape but the leaves are brighter gold and smaller.

Hosta **'Great Lakes Gold'** (D. & J. Ward 2000)

LARGE

Origin: *H.* 'White Vision' × *H. montana* f. *macrophylla*.

Description: An open, tiered mound 66 in. wide × 22 in. high (165 × 55 cm). Leaf blade 12 × 10 in. (30 × 25 cm), of good substance, matt, chartreuse turning

Hosta 'Gold Regal'

Hosta 'Great Lakes Gold'

golden yellow, some dimpling, veins furrowed, edge distinctly and attractively rippled, leaf arching toward the tip, oval with a cuspidate tip and deeply heart-shaped open to pinched lobes. Petiole stout, yellow. Flower funnel-shaped, pale lavender, on an upright, leafy, green, 27- to 29-in. (68- to 73-cm) scape in early summer; seedpods green, fertile.

Cultivation Notes: Lutescent. Needs morning sun (with plenty of moisture) everywhere except the hottest climates to maintain the leaf color. Pest resistant.

Distinguishing Features: One of very few large golden-yellow hostas having distinctly rippled edges.

Similar: ★*H*. 'Jimmy Crack Corn'.

Hosta 'Hadspen Samphire' (E. Smith/A. Eason/P. Ruh 1997)

SMALL—MEDIUM

Origin: ★*H. sieboldiana* 'Elegans' × ★*H. sieboldii* 'Kabitan'.

Description: A dense, rippled mound 41 in. wide × 18 in. high (102 × 45 cm). Leaf blade 9 × 4 in. (23 × 10 cm), thinnish, lustrous bright yellow with green

undertones toward the base, fading to green, smooth, edges deeply rippled, leaf narrowly oval when mature, with an acute tip and rounded to tapered lobes. Petiole chartreuse. Flower narrowly funnel-shaped, lavender, on a thin, arching, leafy, shiny green, 20-in. (50-cm) scape in late summer; seedpods green, fertile.

Cultivation Notes: Viridescent, but among the hostas with the brightest golden-yellow leaves early in summer. Keeps its color best in high, filtered shade. Slow to establish.

Similar: *H*. 'Chiquita'.

Hosta 'Heartache' (H. Benedict N/R)

MEDIUM—LARGE

Origin: *H. ventricosa* seedling × ★*H*. 'Gold Regal'.

Description: An unruly, rounded mound 42 in. wide × 20 in. high (105 × 50 cm). Leaf blade 9 × 8 in. (23 × 20 cm), of good substance, bright creamy yellow to golden yellow with chartreuse undertones appearing later in the summer, seersuckered and puckered, veins widely spaced, edge almost flat, leaf convex or cupped, nearly round with a mucronate

Hosta 'Hadspen Samphire'

tip and heart-shaped pinched to overlapping lobes. Petiole yellow. Flower superb, funnel-shaped, rich purple-striped violet, on an upright, stout, leafy, chartreuse, 40-in. (100-cm) scape in late summer; seedpods abundant; fertility unknown. Pest resistant.

Cultivation Notes: Viridescent. Site in good light or moderate shade. A deservedly very popular hosta having a great color contrast between its yellow leaf and deep purple flower.

Similar: *H.* 'Golden Friendship'.

Hosta 'High Noon' (M. Seaver 2004)

LARGE

Origin: Unknown. Initially known as *H.* 'Sea High Noon'.

Description: An upright, open mound 41–48 in.

Hosta 'Heartache'

Hosta 'High Noon'

wide × 26 in. high (102–120 × 65 cm). Leaf blade 14 × 9 in. (35 × 23 cm), moderately thick, chartreuse to golden yellow, matt above and slightly glaucous below, seersuckered, edge shallowly undulate, leaf cupped at the base then arching, widely oval with a cuspidate tip and heart-shaped folded lobes. Petiole chartreuse. Flower funnel-shaped, lavender, on an upright, 32-in. (80-cm) scape from mid- to late summer; seedpods very long, fertile.

Cultivation Notes: Lutescent. Site in some morning sun to brighten the color and remove the early season chartreuse hue. Pest resistant.

Distinguishing Features: Leaves are more elegantly pointed than most hostas with similar characteristics.

Similar: *H.* 'Fort Knox'; *H.* 'Rising Sun'.

Sports: *H.* 'Afternoon Delight' has green leaves with chartreuse to yellow margins.

Hosta 'Jimmy Crack Corn' (R. Sawyer N/R)

LARGE

Origin: *H.* 'Piedmont Gold' hybrid.

Description: An upright, open mound of horizontal leaves 44 in. wide × 24 in. high (110 × 60 cm). Leaf blade 8½ × 5 in. (21 × 13 cm), of good substance, chartreuse to bright golden yellow, satiny above and thinly glaucous below, dimpled when mature, veins conspicuously furrowed, edges heavily rippled, leaf slightly folded and arching, oval with a cuspidate tip and heart-shaped pinched lobes. Petiole chartreuse. Flower funnel-shaped, near white, in a dense cluster, on an upright, leafy, chartreuse, 24- to 30-in. (60- to 75-cm) scape in early summer; fertile.

Hosta 'Jimmy Crack Corn'

Cultivation Notes: Lutescent. Site in good light or dappled shade in the morning, then full shade. Pest resistant.

Distinguishing Features: The gracefully rippled edge is unusual on a hosta with golden-yellow leaves of this size.

Similar: *H.* 'Golden Gate' has deeper yellow flowers; *H.* 'Lime Piecrust' has slightly more-ovate leaves.

Hosta 'King Tut' (G. Harshbarger) 1981

MEDIUM

Origin: *H.* 'Tokudama Aureonebulosa' hybrid.

Description: A symmetrical mound 30 in. wide × 18¾ in. high (75 × 47 cm). Leaf blade 8 × 6½ in. (20 × 16 cm), thick, unfurling green to chartreuse slowly turning yellow, matt above and glaucous below, seersuckered, edge almost flat, leaf cupped, widely oval with a mucronate tip and heart-shaped open to pinched lobes. Petiole chartreuse. Flower narrowly funnel-shaped, lavender-striped near white, on an upright, leafy, chartreuse, 34¾-in. (87-cm) scape in midsummer; fertile.

Cultivation Notes: Lutescent. Slow to establish. Pest resistant. Considered among the best of the golden yellow-leaved Tokudama Group as it forms

Hosta 'Mister Watson'

Hosta 'King Tut'

a shapely mound. Also notable for throwing good offspring.

Distinguishing Features: The flower scapes are tall for a hosta of this ancestry.

Similar: *H.* 'Corn Muffins' has a rippled leaf margin; ★*H.* 'Golden Medallion'; *H.* 'Golden Nugget'; ★*H.* 'Golden Waffles'; *H.* 'Treasure'.

Sports: *H.* 'Mister Watson' has a barely discernible green margin; *H.* 'Tut Tut'.

Hosta **'Kiwi Gold Rush'** (B. Sligh 1999)

MEDIUM

Origin: Unknown.

Description: An open mound 24 in. wide × 15 in. high (60 × 38 cm). Leaf blade 6½ × 5 in. (16 × 13 cm), thick, matt, chartreuse turning golden yellow, seersuckered and puckered, veins prominently ribbed, edge undulate, leaf flat to arching, oval with a mucronate tip and rounded open to pinched lobes. Petiole chartreuse. Flower long funnel-shaped, pale lavender, on an upright, leafy, chartreuse, 25-in. (63-cm) scape in midsummer; fertile.

Cultivation Notes: Lutescent. Makes an enchanting group grown with *Dicentra spectabilis* 'Gold Bullion', *Filipendula* 'Aurea', and *Heuchera* 'Chocolate Ruffles' in filtered shade. Also tolerates sun in cooler climates. Vigorous, a rapid increaser.

Hosta **'Krugerrand'** (R. Balitewicz N/R)

VERY LARGE

Origin: ★*H.* 'High Noon' × ★*H.* 'Big John'.

Description: An impressive, upright mound 72 in. wide × 30 in. high (180 × 75 cm). Leaf blade 14 × 10 in. (35 × 25 cm), thick, matt, chartreuse becoming bright yellow, dimpled when mature, veins widely spaced, edge slightly undulate, leaf concave toward the base, widely oval with a recurved mucronate tip and heart-shaped pinched lobes. Petiole stout, semi-erect, olive green. Flower funnel-shaped, lavender, on an upright to leaning, leafy, olive-green, 40-in. (100-cm) scape in midsummer; fertile.

Cultivation Notes: Lutescent. Site in dappled to light shade. Moderately slow to increase. Pest resistant. Lovely backed with dark green ferns in a shaded courtyard where the leaves will hold their brilliant color.

Similar: ★*H.* 'Zounds' has rounder, deeper yellow leaves.

Hosta **'Lakeside San Kao'** (M. Chastain 1995)

LARGE

Origin: *H.* 'Piedmont Gold' hybrid.

Description: An open mound 46 in. wide × 18 in. high (116 × 45 cm). Leaf blade 11½ × 8½ in. (29 × 21 cm), very thick, satiny, emerging lime-white, becoming yellowish, then turning parchment, strongly veined, edge rippled, leaf slightly convex at the base and slightly arching toward the tip, widely oval with a cuspidate tip and heart-shaped pinched lobes. Petiole chartreuse. Flower long, tubular, lavender, on a bare, arching, burgundy, 15- to 19-in. (38- to 48-cm) scape in midsummer; fertile.

Hosta 'Kiwi Gold Rush'

Hosta 'Krugerrand', a young plant.

Cultivation Notes: Lutescent. Site in morning sun or light shade all day except in warmer climates. Pest resistant. Has many assets.

Distinguishing Features: Bright green veins embedded in the contrasting cream leaves. The contrasting burgundy scapes are an additional embellishment.

Similar: *H.* 'Lemon Chiffon'.

Hosta 'Lemon Meringue' (P. Ruh 1991)

MEDIUM–LARGE

Origin: *H. hypoleuca* hybrid.

Description: A somewhat unruly mound 27 in. wide × 19 in. high (68 × 48 cm). Leaf blade 11½ × 10 in. (29 × 25 cm), thick, chartreuse to light yellow, glaucous above and powdery white below, dimpled

Hosta 'Lakeside San Kao'

to seersuckered, edge rippled, leaf nearly round with a mucronate tip and heart-shaped open lobes. Petiole chartreuse. Flower funnel-shaped, palest lavender, on an oblique, bare, glaucous chartreuse, 22-in. (55-cm) scape from mid- to late summer; fertile.

Cultivation Notes: Site in morning sun in all but the hottest regions to boost plant vigor. Very slow to increase. Pest resistant. A beautiful hosta that is well worth persevering with.

Distinguishing Features: Areas of puckering either side of the midrib as well as hints of chartreuse in the seersuckering.

Similar: ★*H.* 'Glory'.

Hosta 'Little Aurora' (P. Aden 1978)

SMALL

Origin: Registered as *H.* 'Tokudama Aureonebulosa' × ★*H.* 'Golden Waffles', although there is now some disagreement about this.

Description: A compact mound 25 in. wide × 10 in. high (63 × 25 cm). Leaf blade 4½ × 3½ in. (11 × 9 cm), thick, chartreuse turning rich gold with a metallic sheen, thinly glaucous below, seersuckered when mature, some puckering, edge almost flat, leaf shallowly cupped, widely oval with a mucronate tip and heart-shaped overlapping lobes. Petiole narrow, chartreuse. Flower widely flared, pale lavender to near white, on an upright to leaning, olive-green, 10- to 18-in. (25- to 45-cm) scape in midsummer; fertile.

Cultivation Notes: Lutescent. Site in good light or

Hosta 'Lemon Meringue'

Hosta 'Little Aurora'

light shade for best color. Scape is often no higher than the top of the foliage mound and the flowers tend to nestle among the leaves. Although the dimensions given are an average size, plants can become somewhat larger. Moderate to good growth rate but is more successful in cooler gardens. Pest resistant.

Distinguishing Features: Much confused in the trade with *H*. 'Golden Prayers', which is larger and produces upright leaves in a praying position. The identity of many sports attributed to *H*. 'Little Aurora' is therefore in doubt.

Similar: *H*. 'Bright Glow' has a deeper leaf color.

Sports: *H*. 'Border Favourite' has thick, round, dark green leaves margined yellow; *H*. 'Delia'; *H*. 'Goldbrook Grace'; *H*. 'Just So'; *H*. 'Lakeside Leprechaun'; *H*. 'Little Sunspot'; *H*. 'Not So'; *H*. 'Subtlety'; *H*. 'Sultana'; *H*. 'Tattoo'; *H*. 'Vanilla Cream' is a paler yellow.

Hosta **'Little Black Scape'** (T. Avent 1995)

MEDIUM

Origin: Open-pollinated seedling of *H*. 'Sum and Substance'.

Description: A compact mound 24 in. wide × 10 in. high (60 × 25 cm). Leaf blade 5 × 4 in. (13 × 10 cm), of good substance, matt, chartreuse green turning golden yellow, dimpled, veins widely spaced, edge mainly flat but kinked toward the base, leaf oval with an acute tip and tapered open lobes. Petiole short, light green. Flower funnel-shaped, lavender, opening

from a violet bud, on an upright or oblique, occasionally leafy, glossy, darkest purple to black, 22 in. (55 cm) scape in midsummer; not fertile in the U.S. South, unknown elsewhere.

Cultivation Notes: Lutescent. Grow in morning sun to enhance the leaf and scape color. Moderate growth rate. Plant with *Hemerocallis* 'Sir Blackstem' and *Ophiopogon planiscapus* 'Nigrescens' to create an eye-catching effect.

Distinguishing Features: The unusual color combination of chartreuse-yellow leaves, dusky scapes, and violet flower buds.

Hosta **'Little Miss Magic'** (R. Solberg 2004)

SMALL

Origin: *H*. 'Estrellita' × *H*. 'Tardiflora'.

Description: A sturdy, tight, upright mound 16–18 in. wide × 8 in. high (40–45 × 20 cm). Leaf blade 7 × 2 in. (18 × 5 cm), of average substance, satiny, bright yellow turning chartreuse green, veins closely ribbed, edge less undulate in mature leaves, leaf lanceolate with an exaggeratedly acute tip and tapered open lobes. Flower funnel-shaped, purple striped pale lavender on an acute, bare, olive green, 14- to 18-in. (35- to 45-cm) scape in late summer; seedpods light green, fertile.

Cultivation Notes: Viridescent. Site in dappled to full shade.

Distinguishing Features: Sends out multiple sets of leaves throughout the summer, thus creating a multi-toned yellow, chartreuse, and green leaf mound.

Hosta 'Little Black Scape'

Hosta 'Little Miss Magic'

Hosta 'Marilyn' (M. Zilis 1990)

SMALL–MEDIUM

Origin: *H. 'Gold Drop' × H. 'Green Piecrust'.

Description: A dense mound 30 in. wide × 12 in. high (75 × 30 cm). Leaf blade 8½ × 3½ in. (21 × 9 cm), of average to good substance, chartreuse soon turning golden yellow finally becoming bright gold by high summer, slight dimpling, veins distinctly ribbed, edge widely undulate and rolled under, leaf heart-shaped with a cuspidate tip and tapered open to pinched lobes. Petiole chartreuse to yellow. Flower funnel-shaped, pale lavender, on an upright, bare, chartreuse, 24-in. (60 cm) scape in high summer; fertility unknown.

Hosta 'Marilyn'

Hosta 'Katie Q'

Cultivation Notes: Lutescent. Increases rapidly and easily exceeds its registered dimensions. In cooler climates, protect the early emerging leaves from late frosts; elsewhere morning sun enhances the leaf color. A hosta with nice movement to its leaves.

Sports: H. 'Katie Q' has dark green leaves with a wide yellow margin.

Hosta 'Marrakech' (K. Terpening N/R)

SMALL

Origin: Unknown.

Description: A rippled mound 18 in. wide × 10 in. high (45 × 25 cm). Leaf blade 5½ × 2 in. (14 × 5 cm), of good substance, soft pale yellow turning green toward midsummer, matt above and thickly glaucous below, edge very attractively rippled, leaf folded, lanceolate with an acuminate tip and tapered open lobes. Petiole narrowly channeled, soft yellow turning chartreuse. Flower funnel-shaped, pale lavender, on an oblique, leafy, pink, 15-in. (38-cm) scape in midsummer; fertility unknown.

Cultivation Notes: Viridescent. Vigorous. Won Best of Section at *First Look*.

Distinguishing Features: The thick, white wax on the back of the leaf which is unusual on yellow-leaved hostas. The red-dotted pink scapes and flower buds.

Similar: H. 'Cherry Tart' has lutescent yellow leaves on deep red petioles; H. 'Peppermint Sticks' has yellow leaves on vivid scarlet petioles.

Hosta 'Marrakech'

Hosta **'Maui Buttercups'** (W. Vaughn 1991)

SMALL

Origin: *★H. sieboldiana* 'Frances Williams' × *★H.* 'August Moon'.

Description: A diffuse, upward-facing mound 14 in. wide × 10 in. high (35 × 25 cm). Leaf blade 5 × 4 in. (13 × 10 cm), thick, chartreuse to bright yellow, shiny above and glaucous below, intensely seersuckered and puckered toward the tip, edge flat, leaf deeply cupped to folded, nearly round with a mucronate tip and heart-shaped pinched to overlapping lobes. Petiole wide, flattish, chartreuse to yellow. Flower flared to bell-shaped, green-tipped virtually white, on an upright, sturdy, leafy, glaucous chartreuse, 18-in. (45-cm) scape in late summer; seedpods large, greenish purple, fertile.

Cultivation Notes: Lutescent. Tolerates early morning sun followed by dappled shade in cooler climates, denser shade in warmer climates. Slow to establish but eventually has a moderate growth rate. A superb small yellow-leaved hosta having great presence in the garden.

Distinguishing Features: A noticeable hyaline line around the leaf edge. Very large leafy bracts along the scape and around the raceme.

Similar: *★H.* 'Eye Catcher'; *★H.* 'Golden Teacup'; *★H.* 'Little Aurora'.

Sports: *H.* 'Rainforest Sunrise' has dark green leaves with yellow margins and its much sought-after sport, *H.* 'Blue Maui', has blue-green leaves.

Hosta **'May'** (H. Hansen 1999)

SMALL

Origin: Tissue-cultured sport of *★H.* 'June'.

Description: An overlapping mound 16 in. wide × 7 in. high (40 × 18 cm). Leaf blade 5 × 3½ in. (13 × 9 cm), thick, bright golden yellow softening to chartreuse green by midsummer but remaining bright in good light, matt above and glaucous below, smooth, edge slightly rippled, leaf oval with a cuspidate tip and pinched heart-shaped lobes. Petiole gray. Flower: see *★H.* 'Halcyon'.

Cultivation Notes: Viridescent. Site in morning sun to keep the yellow color in the leaf for a longer time. Like its parent, it needs careful placing in the garden to get the best from the available light.

Similar: *H.* 'Cha Cha'; *H.* 'Early Times'; *H.* 'English Sunrise'; *H.* 'Valley's Lemon Ice' has citron-yellow leaves.

Hosta **'Maya Swingtime'** (A. Scheer N/R)

MEDIUM

Origin: Unknown.

Description: A dense mound 30 in. wide × 16–20 in. high (75 × 40–50 cm). Leaf blade 7 × 5 in. (18 × 13 cm), of average substance, chartreuse with a blue bloom gradually turning bright yellow, satiny above and thickly glaucous below, smooth, prominent deep blue veins widely spaced, edge attractively rippled, leaf somewhat twisted, lightly folded toward the crown, arching toward the tip, widely ovate to

Hosta 'Maui Buttercups'   *Hosta* 'May'

rounded with a very extended, recurved cuspidate tip and pinched heart-shaped lobes. Petiole blue-influenced chartreuse. Flower funnel-shaped, violet-striped near-white with lavender tubes, opening from a lavender bud, on a stout, upright, leafy, green,

Hosta 'Maya Swingtime'

26- to 30-in. (65- to 75-cm) scape in midsummer; fertile.

Cultivation Notes: Lutescent. Tolerates full sun in cooler climates but a plentiful supply of moisture is essential. Moderate growth rate.

Distinguishing Features: The veins in the unfurling leaves are blue giving a very soft effect. As the blue effect disappears, the leaves become bright yellow. The heavy white indumentum on the underside of the leaf is often apparent, giving this superb new introduction even more interest.

Hosta 'Midas Touch' (P. Aden 1978)

MEDIUM

Origin: *H.* 'Gold Cup' × ★*H.* 'Golden Waffles'.

Description: A dense mound 40 in. wide × 20 in. high (100 × 50 cm). Leaf blade 9 × 8 in. (23 × 20 cm), thick, emerging soft pale green to chartreuse slowly turning bright yellow, matt above and glaucous below, intensely seersuckered to deeply puckered, edge

Hosta 'Midas Touch', early in the season before it assumes its yellow leaf color.

shallowly undulate, leaf deeply cupped, nearly round with a mucronate tip and heart-shaped pinched lobes. Petiole chartreuse to old gold. Flower flared, pale lavender-striped near white, opening from a gray bud, in a dense raceme, on an upright, leafy, pale green, 24-in. (60-cm) scape in early summer; fertility unknown.

Cultivation Notes: Lutescent. Leaves will always have a green undertone, especially the midrib and veins, if grown in full shade, but will assume a brassy, metallic hue if exposed to strong sunlight for long periods. Slow to establish but has never been bettered. Pest resistant.

Distinguishing Features: The heavily pebbled surface texture of the leaf and the deep cupping that causes exposure of the leaf underside.

Similar: *H.* 'Aspen Gold'; *H.* 'King Tut'; *H.* 'Lime Krinkles' is paler and more lime-colored; *H.* 'Thai Brass' has flatter, more-pointed leaves.

Hosta 'Miki' (P. Ruh & W. Zumbar 1991)

LARGE

Origin: *H.* 'Hirao Majesty' × *H.* 'Hirao Supreme'.

Description: A dense, somewhat unruly mound 50 in. wide × 22 in. high (126 × 55 cm). Leaf blade 11 × 8½ in. (28 × 21 cm), thick, chartreuse turning bright yellow, matt above and shiny below, prominently veined, some dimpling when mature, edge slightly undulate, leaf convex, ovate with a cuspidate tip and heart-shaped open to pinched lobes. Petiole sturdy, chartreuse green. Flower funnel-shaped, lavender, on an oblique to upright, leafy, olive-green, 36-in. (90-cm) scape in high summer; fertile.

Cultivation Notes: Lutescent. Site in light shade to retain the brilliant golden-yellow leaf color. Slow to moderate growth rate. Good as a specimen. Grow in light woodland with *Heuchera* 'Caramel' to lighten up a dark area. Pest resistant.

Distinguishing Features: Some leaves exhibit pleating toward the tip when mature if there is enough moisture available.

Similar: *H.* 'Alice Gladden'; *H.* 'Solar' Flare'.

Hosta 'Moon Waves' (M. Plater-Zyberk/R. Solberg 1994)

MEDIUM

Origin: *H.* 'August Moon' hybrid.

Description: A dense mound 24 in. wide × 16 in. high (60 × 40 cm). Leaf blade 10 × 5 in. (25 × 13 cm), of good substance, chartreuse to golden yellow, waxy above and glaucous below, veins closely ribbed, edge intensely rippled, leaf widely lanceolate with a twisted cuspidate tip and rounded to tapered open lobes. Petiole chartreuse. Flower funnel-shaped, near white, on an upright, yellow, 30-in. (75-cm) scape in high summer; fertility unknown.

Cultivation Notes: Lutescent. Should tolerate morning sun . An eye-catching hosta which needs careful placing. Very effective with *Heuchera* 'Cappuccino' and *Carex testacea*.

Hosta 'Miki'

Hosta 'Moon Waves'

Distinguishing Features: Exaggerated rippling almost distorts the leaf shape.

Similar: *H.* 'Ophir' has purple-dotted petioles and mahogany streaking on the lower half of the scape.

Hosta 'Nancy' (A. Tower 2005)

SMALL–MEDIUM

Origin: Unknown.

Description: An open mound 27 in. wide × 11 in. high (68 × 28 cm). Leaf blade 6½ × 3½ in. (16 × 9 cm), very thick, glossy, golden yellow, smooth, veins widely spaced, edge heavily rippled, leaf lightly twisted with a cuspidate tip and tapered to heart-shaped open lobes. Petiole chartreuse yellow. Flower funnel-shaped, purple-striped lavender, on an upright, bare, green, 15- to 24-in. (38- to 60-cm) scape from high to late summer; sterile.

Cultivation Notes: Viridescent. Site in light shade to light up woodland areas in late spring to early summer when the leaf color is at its brightest. Lovely with blue-flowered corydalis as a contrast in color and leaf shape. Moderate growth rate.

Distinguishing Features: It is unusual for a medium to small yellow-leaved hosta to have such good substance.

Similar: *H.* 'Goldsmith' has a less-rippled leaf edge.

Hosta 'Ogon Iwa' (N/R)

MEDIUM

Origin: Thought to be a seedling of *H. longipes* emanating from the Watanabe Nursery in Japan.

Previously known in the trade as *H. longipes* 'Aurea', an invalid name.

Description: A rhizomatous mound 36 in. wide × 15 in. high (90 × 38 cm). Leaf blade 7½ × 3½ in. (19 × 9 cm), of average substance, golden yellow, matt above and shiny below, veins widely spaced, edge undulate to rippled, arching, broadly oval with a cuspidate tip and heart-shaped open lobes. Petiole golden yellow, intensely dotted red. Flower funnel-shaped, lavender, on a leaning, leafy 20- to 28-in. (50- to 70-cm) scape from late summer to early autumn; fertile.

Cultivation Notes: Viridescent. For the best effect, plant beside rocks in a naturalistic setting that are shaded from afternoon sun. A useful breeding plant, yielding a high percentage of yellow-leaved seedlings when it is selfed.

Similar: *H.* 'Ogon Amagi' has leaves that are not as bright golden yellow.

Hosta 'Piedmont Gold' (F. Payne 1982)

LARGE

Origin: Unknown.

Description: An overlapping mound 36 in. wide × 24 in. high (90 × 60 cm). Leaf blade 8 × 6 in. (20 × 15 cm), thick, chartreuse soon turning golden yellow, matt above and thinly glaucous below, prominently veined, dimpled when mature, edge slightly undulate, leaf arching, convex, oblong to broadly oval with a cuspidate tip and heart-shaped pinched lobes. Petiole deeply channeled, chartreuse. Flower funnel-shaped,

Hosta 'Nancy'

Hosta 'Ogon Iwa'

near white, on an upright or oblique, bare, gray-chartreuse, 30-in. (75-cm) scape in midsummer; fertile.

Cultivation Notes: Lutescent. Site in bright light but not direct sunlight to enhance the golden-yellow leaf color. The color assumes a paler yellow hue in autumn. Becomes much larger given optimum growing conditions. Pest resistant. A classic hosta, the parent of many sports, and used as both a pod and pollen parent in hybridizing.

Distinguishing Features: Leaves of juvenile plants are smooth, only becoming ribbed and seersuckered as the plant matures.

Similar: *★H.* 'Solar Flare'.

Sports: *H.* 'David Stone' has green-margined yellow leaves; *H.* 'Evening Magic' suffers from the drawstring effect; *H.* 'Everglades' has gold-margined green leaves; *★H.* 'Lakeside Symphony'; *H.* 'Moonshine' has green-margined yellow leaves; *★H.* 'Satisfaction'; *H.* 'Sentimental Journey' has yellow-margined chartreuse leaves; *H.* 'Summer Serenade'; *H.* 'Tyler's Treasure' has gold-margined green leaves.

Hosta 'Prairie Fire' (Kuk 1994)

SMALL–MEDIUM

Origin: *★H.* 'Gold Regal' × *H.* "Tokudama gold seedling."

Description: A dense, semi-upright mound 15–18 in. wide × 12–15 in. high (38–45 × 30–38 cm). Leaf blade 7 × 3½ in. (18 × 9 cm), thick, chartreuse turning rich, deep gold, matt above and glaucous below, seersuckered, prominently veined, edge distinctly rippled and twisted, leaf oval with a cuspidate tip and rounded pinched lobes. Petiole stout, deeply channeled, chartreuse. Flower long, funnel-shaped, near white, opening from a chartreuse bud, on an upright, leafy, chartreuse, 20-in. (50-cm) scape in late summer; fertile.

Cultivation Notes: Lutescent. Site in morning sun, except in the hottest climates, to enhance the fiery,

Hosta 'Piedmont Gold'

deep golden color of the leaves, which intensifies as the season progresses.

Similar: *H. 'Alice Gladden'; *H. 'Jimmy Crack Corn'.

Hosta 'Richland Gold' (V. Wade 1987)

MEDIUM

Origin: Sport of *H. 'Gold Standard'.

Description: A dense mound 36 in. wide × 18 in. high (90 × 45 cm). Leaf blade 7½ × 4½ in. (19 × 11 cm), of good substance, chartreuse turning rich yellow, matt above and glaucous below, slight dimpling, veins ribbed when mature, edge slightly undulate, leaf widely oval with a cuspidate tip and heart-shaped

pinched to overlapping lobes. Petiole chartreuse. Flower: see *H. 'Fortunei Hyacinthina'.

Cultivation Notes: Lutescent. Site in morning sun followed by dappled to light shade. Leaves are late to emerge. Plant size exceeds the given measurements if grown in optimum conditions. Vigorous, a rapid increaser. Ideal at the edge of light woodland. Suitable for container growing.

Sport: H. 'Zodiac'.

Hosta 'Sea Bunny' (M. Seaver 1986)

MEDIUM

Origin: Unknown.

Description: A dome-shaped mound 30 in. wide × 14 in. high (75 × 35 cm). Leaf blade 10 × 5½ in. (25 × 14 cm), thick, glossy, blue-tinted, iridescent golden yellow turning chartreuse green by midsummer, heavily seersuckered and puckered, edge slightly kinked, leaf folded, widely oval with an acute tip and tapered pinched lobes. Petiole chartreuse to olive green. Flower funnel-shaped, lavender-striped near white, on an upright, green, 28-in. (70-cm) scape in high summer; fertility unknown.

Cultivation Notes: Viridescent. Site in morning sun to achieve the best leaf color. Slow to moderate growth rate.

Distinguishing Features: This unusual multi-toned hosta has different leaf color combinations at different stages of the summer. Seersuckering is so intense that the leaf can become almost distorted.

Hosta 'Prairie Fire'

Hosta 'Richland Gold' sporting from *H.* 'Gold Standard'

Hosta 'Sea Bunny'

Hosta **'Sea Fire'** (M. Seaver 2004)

MEDIUM

Origin: Unknown.

Description: An arching mound 45½ in. wide × 18 in. high (114 × 45 cm). Leaf blade 10 × 8½ in. (25 × 21 cm), of average substance, emerging fiery golden yellow from red shoots, fading to light green by late summer, matt above and thinly glaucous below, dimpled, edge slightly rippled, leaf widely oval to nearly round with a mucronate tip and heart-shaped pinched to overlapping lobes. Petiole chartreuse, with red dots toward the crown. Flower funnel-shaped, pale lavender, opening from a purple bud, on an upright, chartreuse, 24- to 38-in. (60- to 95-cm) scape in midsummer; fertile.

Cultivation Notes: Viridescent, but one of the brightest gold-leaved hostas in spring. Increases rapidly. Easily exceeds registered dimensions in optimum growing conditions. Is an ideal ground cover in a lightly shaded woodland. Best known for its seedlings and sports.

Distinguishing Features: Dramatic color contrast among yellow leaves that turn green, purple flower buds, red shoots, and chartreuse petioles.

Similar: *H.* 'Golden Gate'.

Sports: ★*H.* 'Dawn's Early Light' has golden-yellow leaves; ★*H.* 'Eye Declare'; ★*H.* 'Saint Elmo's Fire'.

Hosta **'Sea Gulf Stream'** (M. Zilis/M. Seaver/A. Malloy 1999)

MEDIUM

Origin: Sport of *H.* 'Sea Gold Star'.

Description: A cascading mound 28 in. wide × 13 in. high (70 × 33 cm). Leaf blade 9 × 6½ in. (23 × 16 cm), thick, vivid chartreuse turning yellow, matt above and thickly glaucous below, dimpled to seersuckered, veins furrowed, edge saw-toothed, piecrusted, and twisted, leaf arching, folded, oval with a cuspidate tip and heart-shaped open to pinched lobes. Petiole deeply channeled, chartreuse. Flower funnel-shaped, pale lavender to near white, subtended by purple-gray bracts, on a narrow, arching, leafy, 22- to 24-in. (55- to 60-cm) scape in early summer; fertility unknown.

Cultivation Notes: Lutescent. Site in morning sun to enhance the yellowness of the leaves. Lovely with blue-leaved *H.* 'Rock and Roll' to echo the midrib and veins which are noticeably blue early in the season.

Hosta 'Sea Gulf Stream'

Hosta 'Sea Fire'

Hosta 'Spartacus'

Similar: *H.* 'Golden Gate'; *H.* 'Sea Gold Star' has a less-rippled leaf edge.

Sports: *H.* 'Spartacus' has yellow-margined green leaves.

Hosta 'Solar Flare' PP7,046 (Gardenview Horticultural Park 1981)

VERY LARGE

Origin: Unknown, although it has many of the characteristics of ★*H. montana*.

Description: An arching mound 53 in. wide × 28 in. high (132 × 70 cm). Leaf blade 14 × 10 in. (35 × 25 cm), thick, chartreuse turning golden yellow, thinly glaucous above early in the season and glaucous below, dimpled with some puckering at the midrib when mature, held horizontal to the petiole, veins closely ribbed, edge attractively rippled, leaf widely undulate and sometimes pinched along the midrib toward the tip, widely oval with a mucronate tip and heart-shaped open to pinched lobes. Petiole stout, chartreuse. Flower funnel-shaped, pale lavender, on an upright, leafy, chartreuse, 36-in. (90-cm) scape in early summer; fertile.

Cultivation Notes: Lutescent. Site in morning sun, except in the hottest climates, followed by light shade. Leaves become flatter with the edges more widely undulate when grown in full shade. Midrib and veins usually remain green. Can easily exceed its given dimensions. Best in cooler climates. Pest resistant.

Similar: ★*H.* 'Alice Gladden'; ★*H.* 'Jimmy Crack Corn'; ★*H.* 'Miki'; ★*H.* 'Piedmont Gold'; *H.* 'Stardust'; *H.* 'Templar Gold'.

Hosta 'Squash Casserole' (T. Avent 1995)

MEDIUM–LARGE

Origin: *H.* 'Hirao Elite' × ★*H.* 'August Moon'.

Description: A dense, flattish mound 46 in. wide × 20 in. high (116 × 50 cm). Leaf blade 11 × 6 in. (28 × 15 cm), of good substance, matt, chartreuse green turning old gold, seersuckered, prominently veined, edge rippled, leaf slightly undulate, widely oval with a cuspidate tip and rounded to heart-shaped open to pinched lobes. Petiole stout, chartreuse. Flower long, funnel-shaped, lavender, on an arching or oblique, leafy, olive-green, 22-in. (55-cm) scape in high summer; fertile.

Cultivation Notes: Although lutescent, the leaves of this cultivar remain a muted color even when exposed to sunlight. Ideal for warmer gardens, even in sun, if plenty of moisture is available.

Hosta 'Squash Casserole'

Hosta 'Solar Flare'

Hosta 'Jujen'

Sports: *H.* 'Jujen' is half the size of its parent; ★*H.* 'Key Lime Pie'; *H.* 'Yesterday's Memories' has a thin, dark green margin.

Hosta 'Starboard Light' (C. Seaver 1994)

LARGE

Origin: *H.* 'Komodo Dragon' hybrid.

Description: An open, upright mound 28 in. wide × 24 in. high (70 × 60 cm). Leaf blade 11 × 5 in. (28 × 13 cm), of good substance, matt, chartreuse turning rich, deep yellow, slightly dimpled, veins narrowly ribbed, edge rippled, leaf folded, widely oval with a cuspidate tip and heart-shaped open lobes. Petiole chartreuse. Flower funnel-shaped, near white, on an upright, leafy, chartreuse, 40-in. (100-cm) scape from mid- to late summer; fertile.

Cultivation Notes: Lutescent, the midrib and veins

Hosta 'Yesterday's Memories'

Hosta 'Starboard Light' in dappled shade.

usually remaining green. Site in morning sun, except in the hottest climates, where it is best suited to dappled shade. Pest resistant.

Distinguishing Features: The scape is bent near the tip.

Similar: ★*H.* 'Gold Regal'; *H.* 'Squire Rich'.

Hosta 'Sum and Substance' (P. Aden 1980)

VERY LARGE

Origin: Unknown but thought to have ★*H.* 'Elatior' and ★*H. hypoleuca* in its parentage.

Description: A spreading mound 60 in. wide × 36 in. high (150 × 90 cm). Leaf blade 18 × 15 in. (45 × 38 cm), thick, light green turning chartreuse to muted gold depending on light levels, shiny to waxy above and thinly glaucous below, barely dimpled, veins ribbed, edge slightly rippled, leaf cupped or convex, widely oval with a strongly cuspidate tip and heart-shaped overlapping lobes. Petiole stout, shallowly channeled, pale green. Flower funnel-shaped, pale lavender, on a drooping, chartreuse, leafy, 44-in. (110-cm) scape in late summer; fertile.

Cultivation Notes: Lutescent. Colors best in sun, which it tolerates for most of the day in cooler climates. In warmer climates, site it in morning sun and provide plenty of moisture. Can suffer from stem blight. Rapidly exceeds its registered dimensions and can become one of the largest hostas of all. Thought to be triploid. Selfs very easily. It is a fine parent and has produced many sports. A classic hosta. Named Hosta of the Year by the American Hosta Growers Association in 2004.

Distinguishing Features: Mahogany-brown shoots. Huge leaves which can make a man's hand look small.

Sports: *H.* 'Beauty Substance', *H.* 'Bottom Line', *H.* 'David A. Haskell', the smaller ★*H.* 'Eagle's Nest', ★*H.* 'Lady Isobel Barnett', *H.* 'Lodestar', *H.* 'Sum It Up', *H.* 'Sum of All', *H.* 'Sum Total', *H.* 'Titanic' PP12,402, and *H.* 'Zebson' all have green leaves with a yellow margin (with slight variations); *H.* 'Domaine de Courson' has satiny dark green leaves with a blue cast; *H.* 'Green Gables' has glossy, pale green leaves; *H.* 'Sum Cup-O-Joe' has green leaves with a thin white margin; *H.* 'Vim and Vigor' has darker green leaves; *H.* 'Small Sum' has waxy, bright yellow leaves; *H.* 'Caliban' has crumpled, muted yellow leaves with a pale green margin; *H.* 'Fran Godfrey' has yellow leaves with a dark blue-green margin; ★*H.* 'Parhelion' and ★*H.* 'Winter Snow' have chartreuse-yellow leaves with a white margin; *H.* 'Final Summation' PPAF, *H.* 'Something Good', and *H.* 'Variable Sum' have chartreuse-yellow leaves with a green margin; ★*H.* 'Gunther's Prize' has streaked leaves.

Hosta 'Sun Catcher' (R. Solberg 2004)

MEDIUM

Origin: ★*H.* 'Ogon Tsushima' × ★*H. yingeri.*

Description: A tight mound 29 in. wide × 12 in. high (73 × 30 cm). Leaf blade 6 × 3½ in. (15 × 9 cm), of good substance, leathery, glossy, bright yellow, slightly dimpled, veins widely spaced, edge lightly rippled, leaf lightly wavy, elliptic with an acute tip and tapered open lobes. Petiole short, dark olive green. Flower spider-shaped, purple-striped lavender,

Hosta 'Sun Catcher'

Hosta 'Sum and Substance'

124

on an upright, dark green, leafy, 22- to 24-in. (55- to 60-cm) scape from high to late summer; seedpods green, fertile.

Cultivation Notes: Viridescent. Site in morning sun in cooler climates to prolong the brilliant yellow leaf color, but shade elsewhere. Moderate growth rate.

Distinguishing Features: Persistent keel-shaped bracts on the inflorescence. The purple flowers are a very striking feature but do not appear until the leaves have turned green.

Hosta 'Sun Power' (P. Aden 1986)

LARGE

Origin: Unknown.

Description: A dense, upright mound 36 in. wide × 24 in. high (90 × 60 cm). Leaf blade 12 × 7 in. (30 × 18 cm), thick, chartreuse turning bright golden yellow, matt above and thinly glaucous below, slightly dimpled, prominently veined, edge widely undulate, leaf oval with a cuspidate tip and heart-shaped pinched lobes. Petiole chartreuse. Flower funnel-shaped, lavender, on an oblique, leafy, chartreuse, 36-in. (90-cm) scape from mid- to late summer; sterile.

Cultivation Notes: Lutescent. Achieves its best color early and holds it until frosts occur. Site in morning sun even in the hottest climates with high humidity, and provide an abundant supply of moisture at the roots in high summer. Becomes much larger given optimum growing conditions. Pest resistant. A classic hosta.

Distinguishing Features: In late summer the paler colored petiole seems to dramatically pierce the brassy golden leaf blade.

Sports: ★*H.* 'Abba Dabba Do'; *H.* 'Abba Dew' has yellow-margined light green leaves; *H.* 'Abba Windows'; *H.* 'Dab-a-Green' has a narrow, but distinct green margin; ★*H.* 'Paradise Power'.

Hosta 'Sun Power'

Hosta 'Super Bowl' (P. Aden N/R)

LARGE

Origin: *H.* 'Tokudama' hybrid.

Description: An upright mound 22 in. wide × 18 in. high (55 × 45 cm). Leaf blade 10½ × 10½ in. (27 × 27 cm), very thick, glaucous chartreuse turning golden yellow, intensely seersuckered and puckered, edge nearly flat to just rippled, leaf deeply cupped, nearly round with a mucronate tip and heart-shaped overlapping lobes. Petiole chartreuse to yellow. Flower bell-shaped, white, on an upright, bare, chartreuse, 26- in. (65-cm) scape from mid- to late summer; fertile.

Cultivation Notes: Lutescent. Site in morning sun except in the hottest climates. Slow to increase. Becomes much larger if given optimum growing conditions. Pest resistant.

Distinguishing Features: Leaves are even more deeply cupped than similar hostas, sometimes as much as 3½ in. (9 cm), causing the undersides to be visible.

Similar: ★*H.* 'Aspen Gold'; ★*H.* 'Midas Touch' has less cupping of the leaves; *H.* 'World Cup' has longer leaves.

Hosta 'Sweet Sunshine' (R. Solberg 1997)

SMALL–MEDIUM

Origin: *H.* 'Sweet Susan' × *H.* 'Tokudama Aureonebulosa'.

Description: An upright mound 24 in. wide × 14 in. high (60 × 35 cm). Leaf blade 5 × 4½ in. (13 × 11 cm), of average substance, thick, satiny, bright chartreuse barely turning yellow, seersuckered to puckered, prominently veined, edge flat, leaf cupped, nearly round with a mucronate tip and heart-shaped overlapping lobes. Petiole narrow, chartreuse. Flower funnel-shaped, fragrant, white, on an upright, leafy, chartreuse, 22-in. (55-cm) scape from mid- to late summer; fertile.

Cultivation Notes: Lutescent. Tolerates sun in cooler climates, but needs good light in warmer climates to encourage the production of the two to three flushes of leaves of which it is capable. A vigorous, moderate increaser given plenty of moisture. Pest resistant.

Similar: *H.* 'Sunny Delight', a sister seedling, has oval leaves and tolerates heat and sun even in the hottest climates.

Sport: *H.* 'Sun Kissed'.

Hosta 'Tangerine' (E. Elslager 1998)

SMALL–MEDIUM

Origin: *H.* 'Sea Sunrise' hybrid.

Description: An upright mound 21 in. wide × 12 in. high (53 × 30 cm). Leaf blade 8½ × 6½ in. (21 × 16 cm), thick, shiny, chartreuse to rich, deep golden yellow, dimpled and puckered near the midrib, prominently veined, edge slightly rippled, leaf nearly round with a mucronate tip and heart-shaped overlapping lobes. Petiole glaucous yellow. Flower funnel-shaped, purple-striped pale lavender, on an upright, 16-in.

Hosta 'Super Bowl'

Hosta 'Sweet Sunshine'

(40-cm) scape in midsummer; seedpods green; fertility uncertain.

Cultivation Notes: Lutescent. Holds it color well. Best grown in high, filtered shade. Slow to increase. Pest resistant.

Hosta 'Tequila Sunrise' (G. Johnson 2004)

MEDIUM

Origin: *★H.* 'Spritzer' × *★H. pycnophylla.*

Description: An upright, spreading mound 32 in. wide × 12 in. high (80 × 30 cm). Leaf blade 8 × 3½ in. (20 × 9 cm), of average substance, bright acid yellow, matt above and very glaucous below, smooth, veins widely spaced, edge most attractively piecrusted, leaf broadly lanceolate with a recurved acute tip and tapered open lobes. Petiole heavily dotted red. Flower funnel-shaped, dark smoky purple, on an upright, leafy, pale chartreuse yellow, 27- to 30-in. (68- to 75-cm) scape from late summer to early autumn; fertility unknown.

Cultivation Notes: Viridescent. Site in moderate shade. Grow with Japanese azaleas which flower when this hosta is producing its best leaf color.

Distinguishing Features: Although the brilliant yellow color fades, the leaves are very shapely and have a heavy indumentum on the under sides. The flower buds are encased in long, showy chartreuse-ivory bracts.

Similar: *★H.* 'Fire Island' has wider leaves; *★H.* 'Sun Catcher'.

Hosta 'Tijuana Brass' (K. Vaughn 1988)

LARGE

Origin: Seedling of *H.* 'Golden Waffles' × *H.* 'Polly Bishop'.

Description: A dense, unruly mound 25–28 in. wide × 20 in. high (63–70 × 50 cm). Leaf blade 10 × 8 in. (25 × 20 cm), thick, emerging chartreuse turning bright, brassy golden yellow with green undertones, shiny above and thinly glaucous below, intensely seersuckered and puckered, edge almost flat but sometimes with slight undulations, cupped or twisted, nearly round with a mucronate tip and heart-shaped overlapping lobes. Petiole olive green. Flower flared, pale

Hosta 'Tequila Sunrise'

Hosta 'Tangerine'

Hosta 'Tijuana Brass'

lavender, on an upright or slightly oblique, leafy, olive-green, 32-in. (80-cm) scape in high summer; fertile.

Cultivation Notes: Site in light shade. Easily exceeds its registered dimensions. Makes a statement in any garden.

Distinguishing Features: Probably has the most puckered and unruly leaves of any yellow-leaved hosta.

Similar: *H.* 'Aztec Treasure'.

Hosta 'Tortilla Chip' (R. Solberg 2002)

MEDIUM–LARGE

Origin: Sport of *H.* 'Stained Glass'.

Description: An overlapping mound 30 in. wide × 22 in. high (75 × 55 cm). Leaf blade 9 × 6½ in. (23 × 16 cm), of good substance, chartreuse turning muted golden yellow, glossy above and thinly glaucous below, prominently veined, edge almost flat, leaf slightly convex, broadly ovate with a recurved mucronate tip and heart-shaped pinched to overlapping lobes. Petiole chartreuse to muted golden yellow. Flower: see ★*H.* 'Fragrant Bouquet'.

Cultivation Notes: Lutescent. Tolerates sun in cooler climates, morning sun elsewhere. Increases rapidly. The flowers have some fragrance, particularly in hotter climates.

Similar: *H.* 'Fried Bananas' is a relative with larger, duller-colored leaves.

Hosta 'Tortilla Chip'

Hosta 'Ultraviolet Light' (J. & J. Wilkins 1989)

MEDIUM

Origin: *H.* 'Gold Regal' hybrid.

Description: A dense, tiered mound 42 in. wide × 18–24 in. high (105 × 45–60 cm). Leaf blade 8 × 5 in. (20 × 13 cm), of good substance, emerging rich golden yellow turning chartreuse yellow, satiny above and thinly glaucous below, prominently veined, some dimpling when mature, edge flat, leaf slightly undulate, widely oval with a cuspidate tip and heart-shaped open lobes. Petiole chartreuse, widening toward the blade. Flower funnel-shaped, rich purple, on an upright, leafy, chartreuse, 36-in. (90-cm) scape in late summer; seedpods numerous; fertile.

Cultivation Notes: Viridescent. Site in light to full shade all day, except in cooler regions where two hours of morning sun will retain the golden color for longer. A superb hosta.

Distinguishing Features: Considerably smaller than its parent and a much brighter color.

Similar: *H.* 'Fort Knox', another hybrid from ★*H.* 'Gold Regal', is more dimpled, has more and larger bracts encircling the raceme, and flowers a few weeks later.

Hosta 'Vanilla Cream' (P. Aden 1986)

SMALL

Origin: *H.* "Aden 456" × ★*H.* 'Little Aurora'.

Description: A somewhat rhizomatous mound 15 in. wide × 9 in. high (38 × 23 cm). Leaf blade 4½ × 4 in. (11 × 10 cm), of average substance, pale lemon-green becoming brighter yellow finally turning cream, matt above and thinly glaucous below, seersuckered, prominently veined, edge flat, leaf convex or slightly cupped, nearly round with a mucronate tip and flat to heart-shaped open to pinched lobes. Petiole pale green. Flower funnel-shaped, lavender, on an upright, bare, red-tinted, 12-in. (30-cm) scape in high summer; fertile.

Cultivation Notes: Lutescent. Site in morning sun followed by dappled shade to give the best leaf color. Lovely as a foreground to Japanese azaleas in early summer. A classic hosta and still very popular.

Distinguishing Features: Differs from most golden-yellow hostas in having pale creamy chartreuse leaves.

Similar: *★H.* 'Eye Catcher', *★H.* 'Golden Teacup', *★H.* 'Little Aurora', and *★H.* 'Maui Buttercups' all have brighter yellow leaves.

Sports: *H.* 'Heart and Soul' emerges pale green to chartreuse becoming creamy white with a dark green margin; *★H.* 'Ice Cream'; *H.* 'Ladybug' has brighter chartreuse coloring; *H.* 'Peppermint Cream'; *H.* 'Pistachio Cream' has dark green leaves; *★H.* 'Wylde Green Cream'.

Hosta 'Whiskey Sour' (R. Solberg 2002)

MEDIUM

Origin: *★H.* 'Ogon Tsushima' × *★H. yingeri.*

Description: A dense mound 24 in. wide × 15 in. high (60 × 38 cm). Leaf blade 6 × 3½ in. (15 × 9 cm), of good substance, satiny, chartreuse turning bright yellow, dimpled, veins widely spaced, edge slightly undulate, leaf convex, broadly ovate with a recurved mucronate tip and tapered to heart-shaped open to

Hosta 'Vanilla Cream'

Hosta 'Ultraviolet Light'

pinched lobes. Petiole pale yellow with red dots at the base. Flower tubular, violet-striped lavender, opening from a violet bud, on an upright, leafy, green, 32- to 36-in. (80- to 90-cm) scape from late summer to autumn; seedpods green, fertile.

Cultivation Notes: Viridescent. A good performer in all regions but needs shade in the hottest climates to prevent bleaching out or scorching.

Distinguishing Features: The bright yellow leaves are at their best in early summer. The flowers are widely spaced down the raceme.

Hosta 'Zounds' (P. Aden 1978)

LARGE

Origin: *H.* 'Golden Waffles' × *H.* 'Golden Prayers'.

Description: A dense mound 30 in. wide × 20 in. high (75 × 50 cm). Leaf blade 8½–10 × 8½–9 in. (21–25 × 21–23 cm), thick, chartreuse turning metallic golden yellow, satiny above and thinly glaucous pale yellow below, strongly veined on the underside, strongly seersuckered to puckered when mature, edge almost flat to shallowly rippled, leaf

Hosta 'Whiskey Sour'

shallowly cupped or convex, nearly round with a mucronate tip and heart-shaped pinched to overlapping lobes. Petiole stout, chartreuse. Flower funnel-shaped, pale lavender, on an upright, chartreuse, leafy, 30-in. (75-cm) scape from mid- to high summer; fertile.

Cultivation Notes: Lutescent. Site in good light or filtered to light shade, where it glows like a beacon when surrounded by dark green-leaved plants. Usually greatly exceeds the registered dimensions if given optimum growing conditions. Slow to moderate growth rate. Good pest resistance. A classic hosta.

Similar: *H.* 'Abiqua Zodiac'; *H.* 'Bumblebee'; *H.* 'City Lights'; *H.* 'Golden Rajah'; ★*H.* 'Golden Waffles'; *H.* 'Olive Oil' has glossier leaves; ★*H.* 'Tijuana Brass'; *H.* 'White Vision'.

Sports: ★*H.* 'American Eagle'; ★*H.* 'Dick Ward'; *H.* 'Gilded Cup' and *H.* 'Laura and Darrell' both have yellow-margined dark green leaves; *H.* 'Goldbrook Glory' has dark green margins and a bright cream center which turns white.

Hosta 'Zounds'

The garden of Michael and Susan Weber, Champaign, Illinois.

Hosta 'Deane's Dream'

8

Hostas with Glaucous Blue, Blue-Gray, Blue-Green, and Gray-Green Leaves

Hostas with blue leaves have long been prized by gardeners and collectors, but the blueness is only skin deep. It is produced by an epidermal wax coating which can easily be rubbed away between finger and thumb or by rough handling in the garden, revealing the greenness of the leaf underneath. It can also melt away if the leaves are exposed to too much sun.

The thicker the layer of wax, the bluer the leaf appears. The phenomenon is unusual in the plant world since hostas are shade tolerant, and most plants with a blue surface coating have it as protection against the heat of the sun. The underside of these leaves is also coated, but with a grayish white bloom that appears as a much lighter version of the upper surface. Some hostas have a thick, white, velvetlike surface on the underside of the leaf that protects the leaf from being scorched by heat radiating off the surface of the volcanic rocks on which they are growing.

Hostas with glaucous leaves perform best in temperate climates with high rainfall and a protracted spring season. Where springs are shorter, the year going straight from winter to summer, the blueness lasts for a shorter time. In the U.S. Midwest and South, hostas with blue-toned leaves, even those in full shade, will all start to turn green as early as the end of May. In the Pacific Northwest, particularly Washington and Oregon, the lack of frosts, the high rainfall, and the temperate climate provide hostas with ideal growing conditions. There is just enough winter cold to initiate dormancy and just enough heat, together with the rainfall, to grow the biggest hostas in the world, apart from those in New Zealand. The U.S. inland Northwest is almost as good a growing region because of the slightly hotter summers, but more watering and soil amendment are needed to produce huge hostas.

Growing hostas with blue leaves in full, hot sun melts the coating, and the leaves soon turn a streaky gray-green. Some emerge less blue, more green or gray, and many turn green after midsummer. I have placed the following hostas in this section of the directory in the color category which best represents them at midsummer. I have not included those with a slight bluish cast early in the season (for example, some *Hosta nakaiana* seedlings) because I think they belong in the green category. I have also not mentioned the underside of the leaf in this section; it is always somewhat glaucous, unless it has exceptionally thick or white powdering.

Most of the bluest hostas are dark blue (such as *Hosta* 'Blue Wedgwood'), but there are a few striking light blue varieties. *Hosta* 'Camelot' is one such example. Some are borderline blue to blue-green, such as *H.* 'Blue Arrow', which I have placed in the blue-green section.

Hosta 'Blue Danube'

BLUE LEAVES

HOSTAS IN THIS COLOR GROUP appear to have really blue leaves at midsummer, not blue-gray, blue-green, or gray-green leaves. They are usually derived from the very blue *Hosta* 'Tokudama' or *H. sieboldiana* 'Elegans', which is a hybrid of *H. sieboldiana* × *H.* 'Tokudama'. Most hostas in this group will assume a blue-green tinge earlier or later in the growing season, but some will remain almost blue until autumn. This phenomenon, which depends on genetic make-up, light levels, and degree of summer heat, will be discussed under the "Cultivation Notes" subheading.

*An asterisk before a name indicates that the plant is fully described elsewhere in this book.

Hosta 'Abiqua Blue Crinkles' (Walden-West 1999)

MEDIUM–LARGE

Origin: Unknown.

Description: A dense mound 36 in. wide × 24 in. high (90 × 60 cm), reaching 48 in. wide × 28 in. high (120 × 70 cm) in the Pacific Northwest. Leaf blade 9 × 6½ in. (23 × 16 cm), thick, intense pale blue, strongly seersuckered, edge flat, leaf distinctly cupped, widely oval with a cuspidate tip and rounded to tapered open lobes. Petiole wide, flattish, pale gray-blue, appearing to pierce the blade. Flower bell-shaped, near white, on an upright, leafy, glaucous gray-blue, 30- to 32-in. (75- to 80-cm) scape from mid- to late summer; fertility unknown.

Cultivation Notes: Site in good light and high, filtered shade to retain the blue color well into late summer. Fast growing, which is unusual for this type of hosta. Pest resistant.

Similar: *H.* 'Betcher's Blue' has shallower leaf cupping; *H.* 'Big Change' is a paler blue.

Hosta 'Abiqua Drinking Gourd' (Walden-West 1989)

MEDIUM–LARGE

Origin: ★*H.* 'Tokudama' × ★*H. sieboldiana* 'Elegans'.

Description: An open mound of deeply cupped leaves 36 in. wide × 20 in. high (90 × 50 cm). Leaf blade 8½ × 8½ in. (21 × 21 cm), thick, rich dark blue,

Hosta 'Abiqua Drinking Gourd'

Hosta 'Abiqua Blue Crinkles'

strongly seersuckered and puckered, edge flat, leaf deeply cupped, nearly round with a mucronate tip and tapered overlapping lobes. Petiole stout, gray-blue, appearing to pierce the blade. Flower tubular, near white, on an upright, leafy, gray-blue, 22-in. (55-cm) scape in midsummer; fertile.

Cultivation Notes: Site in good light. Protect from strong wind. Avoid planting directly under a tree canopy to prevent detritus falling into the leaves.

Distinguishing Features: Depth of the leaf cupping

Hosta 'Am I Blue'

Hosta 'Arctic Blast', fading to turquoise.

can be up to 4 in. (10 cm). The powdery gray underside of the leaves is often visible because of the cupping.

Similar: ★*H.* 'Blue Canoe'; *H.* 'Kayak' has longer leaves.

Hosta 'Am I Blue' (D. & J. Ward 1998)
VERY LARGE

Origin: *H.* 'Reginald Kaye' hybrid.

Description: A dense mound 44 in. wide × 30 in. high (110 × 75 cm). Leaf blade 13 × 12 in. (33 × 30 cm), thick, intense blue, seersuckered, prominently veined, edge flat, leaf slightly convex, nearly round with a mucronate tip and heart-shaped overlapping lobes. Petiole oblique, glaucous blue-gray. Flower small, bell-shaped, pale lavender, on an upright, bare, glaucous blue-green, 27- to 31-in. (68- to 78-cm) scape in midseason; fertility unknown.

Cultivation Notes: Site in light to full shade to maintain the wonderful leaf color. Slow to moderate growth. Pest resistant.

Similar: ★*H.* 'Big Daddy'; *H.* 'Bressingham Blue'.

Hosta 'Arctic Blast' (M. Carlson N/R)
MEDIUM–LARGE

Origin: ★*H.* 'Komodo Dragon' × ★*H.* 'Elvis Lives'.

Description: An upright, vase-shaped mound 43 in. wide × 20 in. high (108 × 50 cm). Leaf blade 7½ × 4 in. (19 × 10 cm), thick, frosty blue fading to turquoise green as summer progresses, glaucous above and heavily pruinose below, smooth, veins widely spaced, edge noticeably rippled, leaf slightly arching, narrowly ovate when mature, with a recurved acuminate tip and tapering pinched lobes. Petiole glaucous turquoise-blue. Flower funnel-shaped, lavender, on an upright, leafy, dark blue-green, 30-in. (75-cm) scape in midsummer; fertility unknown.

Cultivation Notes: Site in good light to moderate shade but not under a leaf canopy as falling detritus would soon mar the leaf surface. Grow in front of a larger dark green-leaved hosta as a contrast. A moderate increaser. A most desirable recent introduction which will be welcomed by all collectors of blue-leaved hostas.

Distinguishing Features: Leaves larger than those of the ★*H.* 'Elvis Lives' parent and with more-pronounced rippled edges.

Hosta **'Azure Snow'** (P. Ruh 1991)

MEDIUM–LARGE

Origin: The first blue-leaved *H. hypoleuca* hybrid.

Description: A low, open mound 30 in. wide × 15 in. high (75 × 38 cm). Leaf blade 12½ × 8 in. (31 × 20 cm), thick, powdery turquoise to pale blue above, powdery white below, dimpled, veins widely spaced, edge rippled, leaf shallowly undulate, arching, oval to triangular with a cuspidate tip and heart-shaped to rounded pinched lobes. Petiole narrow, pale green. Flower flared, lavender, on an arching, leafy, mauve, 16½-in. (42-cm) scape from mid- to late summer; fertile.

Cultivation Notes: Site in light to full shade all day. Moderate growth rate.

Distinguishing Features: Leaves have exceptionally thick, white undersides.

Similar: ★*H.* 'Blue Betty Lou' has the same distinctive leaf color; *H.* 'Maekawa' is a selection of ★*H. hypoleuca*.

Hosta **'Baby Blue Eyes'** (R. Solberg 2006)

SMALL

Origin: *H.* 'Cody' × ★*H.* 'Dorset Blue'.

Description: A tight, flattish mound 16 in. wide × 6 in. high (40 × 15 cm). Leaf blade 3½ × 2¾ in. (9 × 7 cm), thick, waxy, glaucous intense blue, dimpled, veins widely spaced, edge flat with an occasional kink on young plants, leaf folded, broadly ovate with a mucronate tip and open to pinched heart-shaped lobes. Petiole light turquoise-green, appearing to pierce the blade. Flower funnel-shaped, pale lavender, on an upright, bare, gray-green, 10- to 14-in. (25- to 35-cm) scape in high summer; fertility unknown.

Cultivation Notes: Site in good light to moderate shade. Slow to moderate growth rate. Pest resistant.

Distinguishing Features: Smaller, with leaves not as seersuckered as its ★*H.* 'Dorset Blue' parent but keeping their excellent blue color well through the summer.

Similar: ★*H.* 'Blue Ice' has grayer leaves; ★*H.* 'Kiwi Blue Baby' has a smoother surface texture.

Hosta **'Big Daddy'** (P. Aden 1978)

LARGE

Origin: Sport of a variegated *H.* "Robusta" seedling.

Description: A dense mound 41 in. wide × 26 in. high (102 × 65 cm). Leaf blade 12 × 11½ in. (30 × 29 cm), very thick, glaucous rich blue turning green toward late summer, strongly seersuckered and puckered, edge almost flat, leaf distinctly cupped, nearly round with a mucronate tip and heart-shaped folded to overlapping lobes. Petiole stout, paler blue-green, appearing to pierce the blade. Flower funnel-shaped, near white, on an upright, bare, paler blue-green, 28-in. (70-cm) scape in midsummer; fertile.

Hosta 'Azure Snow'

Hosta 'Baby Blue Eyes'

Cultivation Notes: Remains a chalky dark blue in a well-shaded site for most of the season, becoming less blue in brighter light. Very slow to increase, especially from a young tissue-cultured plant. Pest resistant.

Distinguishing Features: Among the most distinctly cupped, larger, blue-leaved hostas.

Similar: *H.* 'Aksarben'; *H.* 'Aqua Velva' has a darker color; *H.* 'Bressingham Blue' is larger; *H.* 'Lakeside Blue Jeans' has a less-cupped leaf; *H.* 'Skylight' is a paler blue.

Sports: ★*H.* 'Ice Age Trail' and *H.* 'Sugar Mama', a rarity, have streaked leaves; *H.* 'Papa' has blue-margined golden-yellow leaves that hold their color for most of the summer; *H.* 'Sugar Daddy' has white-margined blue leaves.

Hosta 'Blueberry Tart' (R. Solberg 2005)

SMALL

Origin: ★*H.* 'Blue Cadet' × ★*H.* 'Fall Bouquet'.

Description: A tight, dome-shaped mound 22 in. wide × 8 in. high (55 × 20 cm). Leaf blade 4½ × 3 in. (11 × 8 cm), of good substance, intense glaucous light blue, smooth, edge slightly rippled, leaf deeply folded, lightly wavy, broadly ovate with a cuspidate tip and tapered to rounded pinched lobes. Petiole long, pale blue-green. Flower small, funnel-shaped, orchid-lavender, on an upright, bare, blue-green, 11- to 12-in. (28- to 30-cm) scape in high summer; seedpods blue-green; fertile.

Cultivation Notes: Site in full shade to retain the deep blue leaf color throughout the summer. Increases rapidly. Plant in the front of a border with *Heuchera* 'Burgundy Frost' or as a single specimen in a container where the attractive leaf color and shape can be enjoyed. It has very long petioles for the small size of the leaf.

Hosta 'Blue Blush' (E. Smith & BHHS 1988)

SMALL

Origin: ★*H.* 'Tardiflora' × ★*H. sieboldiana* 'Elegans Alba'.

Description: An upright mound 15 in. wide × 11 in. high (38 × 28 cm). Leaf blade 6½ × 3 in. (16 × 8 cm), thick, dark blue, smooth, edge flat to slightly undulate, leaf slightly folded, twisted, widely lanceolate with an acute tip and tapered open lobes. Petiole narrow, gray-blue. Flower bell-shaped, rich lavender, on an upright, bare, gray-blue, 14-in. (35-cm) scape in high summer; fertile.

Hosta 'Blueberry Tart'

Hosta 'Big Daddy'

Hosta 'Blue Blush'

Cultivation Notes: Grow in high, filtered shade to medium shade. Good growth rate. Among the smaller members of the Tardiana Group, taking time to increase in size.

Similar: *H.* 'Hadspen Heron'; ★*H.* 'Sherborne Swift'.

Hosta **'Blue Danube'** (E. Smith & BHHS 1988)

MEDIUM

Origin: ★*H.* 'Tardiflora' × ★*H. sieboldiana* 'Elegans Alba'.

Description: A moderately dense mound 36 in. wide × 12 in. high (90 × 30 cm). Leaf blade 6½ × 5 in. (16 × 13 cm), thick, intense dark blue, seersuckered, edge almost flat, leaf shallowly cupped or convex, nearly round with a mucronate tip and heart-shaped open lobes. Petiole pale green. Flower funnel-shaped, pale lavender, on an upright, bare,

mauve-gray, 18-in. (45-cm) scape in high summer; fertile.

Cultivation Notes: Site in dappled to light shade to retain the blue leaf color for longer. Very slow to increase. Pest resistant.

Similar: ★*H.* 'Brother Ronald' has a more deeply cupped leaf; *H.* 'Dimple'; ★*H.* 'Hadspen Blue' is larger; *H. sieboldiana* 'Elegans', which it resembles, is larger.

Hosta **'Blue Hawaii'** (O. Petryszyn 1999)

LARGE–VERY LARGE

Origin: Unknown.

Description: An upright, outward-facing mound 42 in. wide × 30 in. high (105 × 75 cm). Leaf blade 10 × 8 in. (25 × 20 cm), thick, heavily glaucous rich powdery blue, seersuckered to puckered, prominently veined, edge flat, leaf ovate to heart-shaped with

Hosta 'Blue Danube'

a mucronate tip and open to pinched lobes. Petiole blue-green. Flower bell-shaped, lightly fragrant, white, in a prolific display, on an upright, leafy, pale blue-green, 44-in. (110-cm) scape from mid- to late summer; fertile.

Cultivation Notes: Site in light to full shade to retain good leaf color which can hold till summer's end. Vigorous. Pest resistant. A superb specimen or border plant. From the breeder's program designed

Hosta 'Blue Hawaii'

Hosta 'Blue Ice'

to raise hostas with leaves which hold their blue color throughout the summer.

Hosta 'Blue Ice' (H. Benedict 1987)
SMALL

Origin: *H. 'Dorset Blue' × *H. 'Blue Moon'.

Description: A low, flattish mound 8½–10 in. wide × 4–6 in. high (21–25 × 10–15 cm). Leaf blade 3½ × 3½ in. (9 × 9 cm), very thick, intense pale to mid-blue, dimpled to seersuckered, edge almost flat, leaf folded to cupped, heart-shaped to round with a cuspidate tip and open lobes. Petiole short, flattish, gray-blue. Flower bell-shaped, near white to very pale lavender, in a dense cluster, on an upright, bare, glaucous gray, 4- to 5-in. (10- to 13-cm) scape in late summer; fertile.

Cultivation Notes: Very slow to increase so worth exposing to morning sun as a young plant to boost its vigor even though it will temporarily lose its superb leaf color. Grow in a free-draining, moisture-retentive soil. Good in containers. Excellent pest resistance.

Similar: *H. 'Baby Blue Eyes'; *H. 'Blue Moon'.

Hosta 'Blue Jay' (H. Benedict 1987)
SMALL

Origin: *H. 'Dorset Blue' selfed.

Description: A compact mound 25 in. wide × 10 in. high (63 × 25 cm). Leaf blade 6 × 4 in. (15 × 10 cm), thick, intense dark blue turning dark green, dimpled, edge almost flat, leaf folded to cupped, widely oval to nearly round with a mucronate tip and heart-shaped pinched to overlapping lobes. Petiole narrow, blue-green. Flower bell-shaped, white, on an upright, bare, pale blue-green, 12-in. (30-cm) scape in high summer; fertile.

Cultivation Notes: Site in dappled to medium shade. Slow growth rate. Pest resistant. In essence a derivative of the Tardiana Group.

Similar: *H. 'Dorset Blue'.

Hosta 'Blue Moon' (E. Smith & P. Aden 1976)
SMALL

Origin: *H. 'Tardiflora' × *H. sieboldiana 'Elegans Alba'. Initially known as H. 'Halo' by Eric Smith.

Description: A neat, flattish mound 12 in. wide × 8½ in. high (30 × 21 cm). Leaf blade 4½ × 4½ in. (11 × 11 cm), very thick, rich dark blue, some dimpling when mature, edge slightly undulate, leaf cupped, widely oval to nearly round with a mucronate tip and heart-shaped open to folded lobes. Petiole short, near horizontal, blue-gray. Flower flared, near white to lavender-gray, in a dense raceme, on an upright, bare, blue-gray, 9-in. (23-cm) scape from mid- to high summer; fertile.

Cultivation Notes: Site in dappled to medium shade. Slow growth rate. Pest resistant.

Similar: ★*H.* 'Dorset Blue', with which is it often confused in the trade, is slightly larger; ★*H.* 'Kiwi Blue Baby'.

Sport: *H.* 'Full Moon' has larger, dark blue-green leaves.

Hosta 'Blue My Mind' (H. Gowen/H. Hansen 2003)

MEDIUM

Origin: *H.* 'Dorset Clown' hybrid.

Description: A dense, layered mound 34 in. wide × 22 in. high (85 × 55 cm). Leaf blade 8 × 6½ in. (20 × 16 cm), thick, glaucous chalky blue, dimpled, prominently veined, edge widely undulate, leaf broadly ovate to rounded with a cuspidate tip and open to pinched heart-shaped lobes. Petiole arching, gray-blue. Flower bell-shaped, pale lavender-striped near-white, on an upright, bare blue-green, 28-in. (70-cm) scape in midsummer; fertility unknown.

Cultivation Notes: Site in moderate to full shade to retain the exceptionally blue leaf color. Slow to moderate growth rate. Pest resistant. Grow in a border with green, purple, or variegated foliage plants such as *Polygonatum odoratum* 'Variegatum' or *Rodgersia pinnata* 'Chocolate Wing'.

Similar: Many of the Tardiana Group from which it is descended; ★*H.* 'Blue Wedgwood' has more-undulate margins and more cupping.

Hosta 'Blue Wedgwood' (E. Smith & BHHS 1988)

MEDIUM

Origin: ★*H.* 'Tardiflora' × ★*H. sieboldiana* 'Elegans Alba'.

Description: A dense mound 36 in. wide × 14 in. high (90 × 35 cm). Leaf blade 6½ × 5½ in. (16 × 14 cm), thick, bright to deep powdery blue, smooth, becoming strongly dimpled when mature, edge widely rippled, leaf oval to wedge-shaped with a mucronate tip and kinked to flattish overlapping

Hosta 'Blue Jay'

Hosta 'Blue Moon'

Hosta 'Blue My Mind'

lobes. Petiole blue-green with burgundy dots. Flower bell-shaped, soft lavender, on an upright, bare, 16-in. (40-cm) scape from mid- to high summer; fertile.

Cultivation Notes: Site in light to full shade all day, but even so the leaves will turn dark green early. Pest resistant.

Similar: *H.* 'Blue Dimples', with which it has been confused in the trade, has leaves that are similar but more dimpled and not wedge-shaped; *H.* 'Buffy'.

Hosta 'Brother Ronald' (E. Smith & BHHS 1988)
MEDIUM

Origin: *H.* 'Tardiflora' × *H. sieboldiana* 'Elegans Alba'.

Description: A dense mound 20 in. wide × 15 in. high (50 × 38 cm). Leaf blade 6 × 4 in. (15 × 10 cm), thick, intense mid- to dark blue, dimpled, veins slightly ribbed, edge slightly undulate, leaf cupped, widely oval with a mucronate tip and heart-shaped overlapping lobes. Petiole pale blue-green. Flower bell-shaped, white, in a dense cluster, on an upright, bare, glaucous gray-green, 18¾-in. (47-cm) scape in late summer; fertile.

Cultivation Notes: Among the bluest of the Tardiana Group. Rated one out of six on the Zilis blue scale, one being the bluest, but not the most shapely hosta in leaf or clump. Site in light to full shade. A moderate increaser.

Hosta 'Buckshaw Blue' (E. Smith & BHHS 1986)
MEDIUM

Origin: *H. sieboldiana* 'Elegans' × *H.* 'Tokudama'.

Description: An outward-facing mound 35 in. wide × 14 in. high (88 × 35 cm). Leaf blade 5 × 4½ in. (13 × 11 cm), thick, dark blue, heavily seersuckered, veins deeply impressed, edge almost flat, leaf markedly cupped toward the lobes, nearly round with a mucronate tip and heart-shaped folded or overlapping lobes. Petiole coarse, shallow, pale green, appearing to pierce the blade. Flower bell-shaped, near white, on an upright, bare, pale green, 18-in. (45-cm) scape in midsummer; fertile.

Cultivation Notes: The standard by which all blue-leaved hostas should be judged. Heavy, waxy coating on the leaves is retained until late summer in cooler climates, where it produces its best color if grown in full shade. Clear light gives the leaves a much lighter blue appearance. Avoid planting beneath a tree canopy because falling detritus can damage the attractive bloom on the leaves. Very slow to increase. Pest resistant. A classic hosta.

Similar: *H.* 'Blue Velvet'; *H.* 'Moscow Blue'; *H.* 'Tokudama'.

Hosta 'Blue Wedgwood'

Hosta 'Brother Ronald'

Hosta 'Camelot' (E. Smith & BHHS 1988)

MEDIUM

Origin: ⋆*H.* 'Tardiflora' × ⋆*H. sieboldiana* 'Elegans Alba'.

Description: An open layered mound 34 in. wide × 16 in. high (85 × 40 cm). Leaf blade 7 × 5 in. (18 × 13 cm), thick, intense light blue, seersuckered and puckered when mature, edge flat to slightly undulate, leaf shallowly cupped or convex, heart-shaped to nearly round with a cuspidate tip and heart-shaped overlapping lobes. Petiole long, light blue-green. Flower bell-shaped, palest lavender on an upright, bare, blue-green, 18-in. (45-cm) scape in late summer; fertile.

Cultivation Notes: Site in dappled to light shade. Slow to moderate increase. Pest resistant.

Distinguishing Features: The best of the lighter blue hostas in the Tardiana Group with a rounder, more pleasing leaf shape.

Similar: ⋆*H.* 'Brother Ronald'; ⋆*H.* 'Hadspen Blue'; *H.* 'Serena'; *H.* 'Sherborne Songbird'.

Hosta 'Deep Blue Sea' (C. Seaver 1994)

MEDIUM

Origin: *H.* 'Blue Moon' hybrid.

Description: A stiff, open mound 30 in. wide × 13 in. high (75 × 33 cm). Leaf blade 8 × 7 in. (20 × 189 cm), very thick, rich dark blue, intensely seersuckered and puckered, edge flat, leaf distinctly cupped, nearly round with a mucronate to cuspidate tip and heart-shaped open lobes. Petiole coarse, flattish, pale green, appearing to pierce the blade. Flower bell-shaped, rich lavender, in a dense raceme, on an upright, bare, lilac-gray, 15-in. (38-cm) scape in high summer; fertile.

Cultivation Notes: Site in good light to dappled shade. Leaves unfurl light green soon becoming a superb blue and keeping their color for most of the summer.

Distinguishing Features: Exaggeratedly rugose to seersuckered toward central midrib, almost distorting the symmetry of the leaf. Lobes are sometimes twisted behind the petioles.

Hosta 'Camelot'

Hosta 'Buckshaw Blue'

Hosta 'Deep Blue Sea'

143

Similar: *H.* 'Willy Nilly' has leaves that are slightly less blue and somewhat twisted.

Hosta 'Dorset Blue' (E. Smith & P. Aden 1977)

SMALL

Origin: ★*H.* 'Tardiflora' × ★*H. sieboldiana* 'Elegans Alba'.

Description: An open mound 24 in. wide × 10 in. high (60 × 25 cm). Leaf blade 5 × 4 in. (13 × 10 cm),

Hosta 'Dorset Blue'

thick, intense bright blue, seersuckered, edge slightly undulate, leaf cupped, heart-shaped to nearly round with a mucronate or cuspidate tip and heart-shaped pinched lobes. Petiole long, narrow, greenish blue. Flower bell-shaped, grayish white, in a dense raceme, on an upright, bare, 14-in. (35-cm) scape from high to late summer; very fertile.

Cultivation Notes: Site in dappled shade. Slow to increase. Pest resistant. Much used in breeding for small, blue-leaved hostas. The attractive silver overlay on the leaves makes this small member of the Tardiana Group a must-have for collectors of the bluest-leaved hostas.

Similar: *H.* 'Blue Eyes'; *H.* 'Blue Lollipop'; ★*H.* 'Blue Moon', with which it has been mistaken in the trade, is slightly smaller and not as blue; *H.* 'King of Spades'.

Sports: *H.* 'Blue Chip' is a selfed *H.* 'Dorset Blue'; ★*H.* 'Dorset Clown'.

Hosta 'Dorset Charm' E. Smith & P. Ruh 1990)

SMALL–MEDIUM

Origin: ★*H.* 'Tardiflora' × ★*H. sieboldiana* 'Elegans Alba'.

Hosta 'Dorset Charm'

Description: An open mound 30 in. wide × 10–12 in. high (75 × 25–30 cm). Leaf blade 5 × 3 in. (13 × 8 cm), very thick, dark blue, dimpled, closely veined, edge slightly rippled but widely undulate when mature, leaf arching, broadly ovate with a cuspidate tip and rounded open to pinched lobes. Petiole dark blue-green. Flower bell-shaped, pale lavender, on an upright, leafy, dark blue-green, 18-in. (45-cm) scape in late summer; fertile.

Cultivation Notes: Site in moderate shade. Leaves are truly dark blue in cooler climates; in hotter climates they are considered to be dark blue-green. Rated three out of six on the Zilis blue scale, one being the bluest. Although slow to establish, it can easily exceed its registered dimensions. A good breeding plant. Pest resistant.

Similar: *H.* 'Blue Baron' has longer and narrower steel-blue leaves.

Hosta 'Fragrant Blue' (P. Aden 1988)

MEDIUM

Origin: Unknown.

Description: A dome-shaped mound 36 in. wide × 15 in. high (90 × 38 cm). Leaf blade 8½ × 6½ in. (21 × 16 cm), thick, powdery light blue, dimpled, edge almost flat, leaf convex, widely oval with a cuspidate tip and heart-shaped open lobes. Petiole blue-green. Flower funnel-shaped, slightly fragrant, white, opening from a rich violet bud, on an upright 30-in. (75-cm) scape in high summer; very fertile.

Cultivation Notes: Site in good light to dappled shade to maintain the waxy bloom on the leaf. Vigorous. Pest resistant. Among the few blue-leaved hostas with fragrant flowers, although the fragrance is only perceptible in hot climates.

Similar: *H.* 'Indigo' is smaller.

Sports: ★*H.* 'Blue Flame'.

Hosta 'Hadspen Blue' (E. Smith & P. Ruh 1976)

MEDIUM

Origin: ★*H.* 'Tardiflora' × ★*H. sieboldiana* 'Elegans Alba'.

Description: An open mound 34 in. wide × 18 in. high (85 × 45 cm). Leaf blade 7 × 6½ in. (18 × 16 cm), thick, rich blue, smooth with some dimpling when mature, edge almost flat, leaf slightly

cupped or convex, heart-shaped to nearly round with a mucronate tip and overlapping lobes. Petiole stout, pale blue-gray. Flower bell-shaped, lavender-gray to near white, on an upright, bare, glaucous gray-blue, 18-in. (45-cm) scape from mid- to high summer; fertile.

Cultivation Notes: Leaves do not form a symmetrical mound but the wonderful leaf color makes this a very worthwhile garden plant. Less shapely than the leaves of the illustrious ★*H.* 'Halcyon' but of a thicker substance and more glaucous with a suggestion of rugosity on the leaf surface. One of the most intense blues of the Tardiana Group, keeping its color for longer than most. Early to emerge. Slow to increase. Pest resistant.

Hosta 'Fragrant Blue'

Hosta 'Hadspen Blue'

Similar: *H.* 'Dorset Flair' has a better leaf shape; *H.* 'Happiness'.

Sports: *H.* 'Aristocrat' PP11,286; *H.* 'Holy Grail'; *H.* 'Honeysong Blue and Gold'; ★*H.* 'Kiwi Blue Marble'; *H.* 'Nobility' is the reverse form of *H.* 'Aristocrat' and not easy to grow; *H.* 'Robyn's Choice'.

Hosta 'Halcyon' (E. Smith & BHHS 1988) ♀

MEDIUM

Origin: ★*H.* 'Tardiflora' × ★*H. sieboldiana* 'Elegans Alba'.

Description: A symmetrical mound 41 in. wide × 18 in. high (102 × 45 cm). Leaf blade 6½ × 4 in. (16 × 10 cm), thick, intense blue, smooth to barely rugose, edge almost flat, leaf widely oval with a cuspidate tip and heart-shaped pinched to overlapping lobes. Petiole flattish, blue-green, appearing to pierce the blade. Flower bell-shaped, near white, in a dense raceme, on a thick, upright, bare, mauve-gray, 22-in. (55-cm) scape in midsummer; seedpods pale green, fertile.

Cultivation Notes: Holds its color well into late summer given good light to dappled shade. A benchmark for all hostas in the Tardiana Group. The original *H.* 'Halcyon' is usually now only seen in older collections, since seed-raised strains and the advent of tissue have bastardized it. Juvenile leaves are conspicuously narrow, especially in micropropagated plants. A much used breeding plant. Superb in a container. Rated two out of six on the Zilis blue scale, one being the bluest. Winner of the 1987 Alex J. Summers Distinguished Merit Hosta Award.

Distinguishing Features: Attractive, small gray-green and mauve flower bracts.

Similar: *H.* 'Canadian Blue'.

Sports: *H.* 'Blue Ivory' PPAF has exceptionally wide ivory margins; *H.* 'Canadian Shield', *H.* 'Peridot', and *H.* 'Valerie's Vanity' have dark green leaves; ★*H.* 'Devon Green'; *H.* 'First Frost', its sport *H.* 'Valley's Glacier', and ★*H.* 'Great Escape' have white-margined leaves; ★*H.* 'El Niño' and *H.* 'Sleeping Beauty' have cream-margined leaves; *H.* 'Goldbrook Glimmer'; ★*H.* 'June'.

Hosta 'Halcyon'

Hosta **'Kiwi Blue Baby'** (G. Collier/B. Sligh 1999)

SMALL

Origin: ★*H.* 'Halcyon' selfed.

Description: A rounded, symmetrical mound 19 in. wide × 8 in. high (48 × 20 cm). Leaf blade 4 × 3 in. (10 × 8 cm), thick, frosty to dark blue, prominently veined, edge nearly flat, leaf flat to convex, widely oval with a cuspidate tip and heart-shaped pinched to overlapping lobes. Petiole blue-green. Flower bell-shaped, palest lavender, on an upright, bare, blue-green, 10-in. (25-cm) scape in midsummer; sterile.

Cultivation Notes: Site in good light or dappled to medium shade. Slow to increase. Pest resistant.

Hosta **'Love Pat'** (P. Aden 1978) ♀

MEDIUM–LARGE

Origin: *H.* 'Blue Velvet' × *H.* 'Blue Vision'.

Description: A dense mound 40 in. wide × 20 in. high (100 × 50 cm). Leaf blade 8½ × 8 in. (21 × 20 cm), thick, rich blue, intensely seersuckered, edge almost flat, leaf deeply cupped, nearly round with a mucronate tip and heart-shaped overlapping lobes. Petiole stout, blue-green. Flower near bell-shaped, palest lavender to nearly white, in a dense raceme, on a leafy, grayish mauve, 22-in. (55-cm) scape, barely rising above the leaf mound, in midsummer; fertile.

Cultivation Notes: Site in good light to light shade all day, but plant well away from a tree canopy. In the hottest climates the leaves turn dark green after midsummer. Slow to increase in its early years but much faster growing in maturity. Pest resistant.

Distinguishing Features: Leaves upwardly poised and very cupped, so the glaucous undersides are often visible.

Similar: *H.* 'Blue Rock'; *H.* 'Blue Splendor' is somewhat larger; *H.* 'Rock and Roll' has slightly grayer leaves; *H.* 'Silver Bowl' has blue-green leaves.

Sports: *H.* 'Breeder's Love' has yellow-streaked leaves; *H.* 'Love Affair'; *H.* 'Love Burst' has streaked leaves; *H.* 'Love Potion No. 9'.

Hosta **'Moscow Blue'** (A. Arett 1986)

MEDIUM–LARGE

Origin: ★*H.* 'Tokudama' hybrid.

Description: A dense mound 41 in. wide × 21 in. high (102 × 53 cm). Leaf blade 10 × 8 in. (25 × 20 cm), thick, intense blue, dimpled to seersuckered, puckered when mature, edge almost flat, leaf widely

Hosta 'Love Pat'

Hosta 'Kiwi Blue Baby'

Hosta 'Moscow Blue'

oval to nearly round with a mucronate tip and heart-shaped overlapping lobes. Petiole stout, light blue-green. Flower bell-shaped, white, on an upright, bare, 26-in. (65-cm) scape from mid- to late summer; fertile.

Cultivation Notes: Site in good light to light shade all day. Slow to increase. Pest resistant. Considered to be among the best of the many similar ★*H.* 'Toku-dama' hybrids.

Similar: ★*H.* 'Abiqua Blue Crinkles'; *H.* 'Betcher's Blue'; ★*H.* 'Buckshaw Blue'; *H.* 'Groo Blue'.

Hosta 'Powderpuff' (F. Nyikos 2002)

MEDIUM

Origin: ★*H.* 'Halcyon' × *H.* 'Blue Dimples'.

Description: An open mound 24 in. wide × 11 in. high (60 × 28 cm). Leaf blade 5 × 4 in. (13 × 10 cm), thick, intensely glaucous pale blue, prominently veined, edge widely kinked in juvenile plants but flat when mature, leaf moderately cupped and folded, broadly ovate to rounded with a mucronate tip and pinched heart-shaped lobes. Petiole thinly glaucous light blue-green. Flower funnel-shaped, pale lavender-striped creamy white, on an upright,

bare, glaucous pale blue-green, 13- to 15-in. (33- to 38-cm) scape from mid- to high summer; rarely sets seed, none viable yet.

Cultivation Notes: Site in moderate to full shade away from strong winds and away from trees to prevent falling detritus damaging the thick powdery indumentum covering the leaf surface. Best in a container in a sheltered position where the leaf color will hold well throughout the summer. Slow to moderate growth rate. Pest resistant.

Distinguishing Features: The intensely pale blue powdery leaves. The flowers are often deformed, the stamens and pistil being distorted.

Hosta 'Prairie Sky' PP17,309 (H. Hansen 2005)

SMALL–MEDIUM

Origin: *H.* 'Blue Jay' hybrid.

Description: A compact mound 36 in. wide × 14 in. high (90 × 35 cm). Leaf blade 7 × 6 in. (18 × 15 cm), thick, glaucous powdery pale blue, seersuckered, puckered when mature, edge flat, leaf slightly concave, broadly ovate with a vestigial tip and heart-shaped pinched lobes. Petiole light blue. Flower funnel-shaped, near-white to pale lavender, on an oblique to upright, bare, pale blue, 18- to 24-in. (45- to 60-cm) scape from mid- to late summer; fertility unknown.

Cultivation Notes: Best in shade where lower light levels help retain the bluest leaf color, but not under

Hosta 'Powderpuff' has an exceptionally powdered leaf surface.

Hosta 'Prairie Sky'

trees where raindrops and falling debris might spoil the appearance of the leaves. Moderately vigorous.

Similar: *★H.* 'Blue Danube' has darker blue leaves.

Hosta 'Samual Blue' (G. Krossa/P. Ruh 1981)

LARGE

Origin: Unknown.

Description: An upright mound 36 in. wide × 27 in. high (90 × 68 cm). Leaf blade 10½ × 8½ in. (27 × 21 cm), thick, rich sapphire-blue, intensely seersuckered, edge slightly undulate, leaf shallowly cupped, widely oval to nearly round with a mucronate tip and heart-shaped pinched lobes. Petiole stout, light green, appearing to pierce the blade. Flower funnel-shaped, rich lavender, on an upright, leafy, glaucous light green, 29-in. (73-cm) scape in midseason; fertile.

Cultivation Notes: Very heavy bloom makes the leaf color exceptionally blue, so shade is essential. Slow to establish. Pest resistant. A classic older introduction but never bettered.

Similar: *H.* 'Blue Velvet'; *H.* 'Skookumchuck'.

Hosta 'Sea Blue Leather' (M. Seaver 1994)

VERY LARGE

Origin: Unknown.

Description: An upright mound 51 in. wide × 34 in. high (127 × 85 cm). Leaf blade 14 × 12¾ in. (35 × 32 cm), very thick, leathery dark blue, seersuckered

Hosta 'Sea Blue Leather'

Hosta 'Samual Blue'

and puckered, edge almost flat, leaf shallowly cupped or convex, widely oval to nearly round with a mucronate tip and heart-shaped overlapping lobes. Petiole light blue-green. Flower bell-shaped, white, in a sparse raceme, on an upright or oblique, 36-in. (90-cm) scape in midsummer; fertile.

Cultivation Notes: Site in good light to light shade all day. Slow to increase. Pest resistant.

Distinguishing Features: Pruinose bloom soon fades from the upper leaf surface, leaving a pronounced leathery texture.

Similar: *H*. 'Lakeside Sapphire Pleats'.

Hosta sieboldiana 'Elegans' (G. Arends/N. Hylander/AHS 1987) ♛

LARGE–VERY LARGE

Origin: ★*H. sieboldiana* × ★*H*. 'Tokudama'.

Description: A dense mound 51 in. wide × 26 in. high (127 × 65 cm). Leaf blade 14½ × 10½ in. (36 × 27 cm), very thick, rich medium blue, intensely seersuckered and puckered when mature, edge almost flat to slightly undulate, leaf cupped or convex, widely oval to heart-shaped with a mucronate tip and heart-shaped overlapping lobes. Petiole light green-blue. Flower funnel-shaped, pale lavender-striped near white, in a dense raceme, on an upright, bare, light blue-green, 27-in. (68-cm) scape from mid- to high summer; very fertile.

Cultivation Notes: Site in good light to light shade all day. Most effective, like all hostas of this type, in cooler climates where the superb leaf color will be maintained for longer. Feed in early spring. Slow to establish. Pest resistant. Over the years this name has been applied to a variety of *H. sieboldiana* selections and it is likely that none of the plants in tissue culture under this name is the correct plant, which may now only be found in older collections and is likely to be superior in leaf color and shape. The white-flowered form of this selection is known as *H. sieboldiana* 'Elegans Alba' and is the pollen parent of the Tardiana Group.

Distinguishing Features: Flowers are bunched at the top of the scape, which rises only just above the foliage mound.

Similar: *H*. 'Edina Heritage'; ★*H*. 'Gray Cole'; *H*. 'Ryan's Big One' has slightly larger leaves; ★*H*. 'Samual Blue'.

Sports: *H*. 'Borwick Beauty'; *H*. 'Forncett Frances' has muted central variegation which gradually appears during summer; *H*. 'Helen Doriot' has slightly smaller leaves; ★*H. sieboldiana* 'Frances Williams'; ★*H. sieboldiana* 'George Smith'; *H. sieboldiana* 'Golden Meadows', the only sport with attractively piecrusted leaf margins that fold inwards, tolerates some sun; ★*H. sieboldiana* 'Great Expectations'; *H. sieboldiana* 'Northern Halo'; *H. sieboldiana* 'Northern Lights'; ★*H. sieboldiana* 'Northern Mist'; *H*. 'Temptation' has blue-green margined lutescent chartreuse to cream leaves.

Hosta sieboldiana 'Elegans'

Hosta 'Silver Bay'

Hosta **'Silver Bay'** (D. Dean 1999)

MEDIUM

Origin: *H.* 'Silver Frost' × ★*H.* 'Blue Moon'.

Description: A dense, flat-topped mound 34 in. wide × 13 in. high (85 × 33 cm). Leaf blade 7 × 6½ in. (18 × 16 cm), thick, intense silver-blue, seersuckered, edge slightly undulate, leaf folded to slightly cupped, widely oval to nearly round with a mucronate tip and heart-shaped pinched to overlapping lobes. Petiole light blue-green, appearing to pierce the blade. Flower bell-shaped, pale lavender, on an upright, bare, blue-green, 21- to 23-in. (53- to 58-cm) scape in high summer; seedpods light green, fertile.

Cultivation Notes: Site in good light to light shade where, like its parent *H.* 'Silver Frost, it is one of the few ★*H. sieboldiana* 'Elegans' cultivars that retains its blue color into the autumn. Moderate growth rate. Pest resistant. Lovely grown with variegated dead nettle or yellow-leaved hostas. Selected by the winner of the Alex J. Summers Distinguished Merit Award 2008 as his most outstanding introduction.

Distinguishing Features: Among the best of the more recently introduced blue-leaved hostas.

Hosta **'Tokudama'** (F. Maekawa N/R)

MEDIUM

Origin: Japanese gardens. Once considered a species.

Description: A loose mound 30 in. wide × 16 in. high (75 × 40 cm). Leaf blade 8½ × 6½ in. (21 × 16 cm), thick, rich dark blue, closely seersuckered, closely veined, edge slightly undulate, leaf shallowly cupped toward the edge, widely oval to nearly round with a mucronate tip and heart-shaped overlapping lobes. Petiole flattish, light green, appearing to pierce the blade. Flower narrowly funnel-shaped, near white, in mid- to high summer; fertile.

Cultivation Notes: Site out of direct sunlight but not under a tree canopy to avoid detritus falling into the leaves. Keeps its color for longer in shady sites. Very slow to increase. Pest resistant. Frequently produces sports. An excellent breeding plant.

Similar: ★*H.* 'Abiqua Blue Crinkles'; *H.* 'I'm So Blue'; ★*H.* 'Moscow Blue'.

Sports: *H.* 'Betcher's Blue'; ★*H.* 'Buckshaw Blue'; *H.* 'Tokudama Aureonebulosa' has cloudy blue-streaked yellow leaves (*H.* 'Robin Hood' is similar); ★*H.* 'Tokudama Flavocircinalis'; *H.* 'Warwick Cup'.

Hosta **'True Blue'** (P. Aden 1978)

LARGE—VERY LARGE

Origin: *H.* 'Chartreuse Wedge' × (★*H. nigrescens* × *H.* 'Blue Vision').

Description: An arching mound 51 in. wide × 30 in. high (127 × 75 cm). Leaf blade 12 × 10 in. (30 × 25 cm), thick, intense light blue above, glaucous gray-blue below, seersuckered, edge slightly undulate,

Hosta 'Tokudama'

Hosta 'True Blue'

leaf arching, mostly convex, widely oval to heart-shaped with a cuspidate tip and pinched lobes. Petiole oblique, wide, light green. Flower widely funnel-shaped, near white, in a dense raceme, on an oblique, bare, blue-green, 32-in. (80-cm) scape in midsummer; fertile.

Cultivation Notes: Site in good light to light shade. Not suitable for container growing. Moderate growth rate. Pest resistant.

Distinguishing Features: The inner leaves are rounder, the outer leaves noticeably longer. Leaves arch downward from oblique petioles.

Hosta 'Ultramarine'

Hosta 'Winfield Blue'

Hosta 'Winfield Mist'

Similar: *H.* 'Lakeside Maestro'; *H.* 'Perry's True Blue' may be identical to *H.* 'True Blue'; *H.* 'Singin' The Blues' has boat-shaped leaves with a distinctive "pinch."

Sports: *★H.* 'Blue River'.

Hosta 'Ultramarine' (M. Zilis 2003)

MEDIUM

Origin: *★H.* 'Sea Lotus Leaf' × *H. kikutii* f. *leuconota.*

Description: A low, dense mound 40 in. wide × 18 in. high (100 × 45 cm). Leaf blade 9 × 6 in. (23 × 15 cm), thick, rich powdery blue, intensely glaucous below, veins impressed, edge smooth, leaf flat, ovate with a cuspidate tip and open to pinched lobes. Petiole narrow, glaucous blue-gray. Flower funnel-shaped, pale lavender, on a semi-erect, leafy, 24-in. (60-cm) scape in late summer; fertility unknown.

Cultivation Notes: Site in moderate shade to retain the wonderful blue coloring of the leaf. Rapid growth rate. Pest resistant.

Distinguishing Features: The leaf edge is bordered by a distinct hyaline line. The veins are so deeply impressed that they resemble corduroy fabric. Both the raceme and the scape have long, white, leafy bracts.

Hosta 'Winfield Blue' (M. Zilis 1999)

SMALL–MEDIUM

Origin: An unnamed Tardiana Group seedling.

Description: An open mound 45½ in. wide × 18 in. high (114 × 45 cm). Leaf blade 7½ × 5 in. (19 × 13 cm), thick, powdery blue, slightly dimpled, edge distinctly rippled, leaf slightly arching, oval with a cuspidate tip and tapered open lobes. Petiole flattish, light blue. Flower tubular, palest lavender, on an upright, bare, light blue-green, 28-in. (70-cm) scape in high summer; fertile.

Cultivation Notes: Outstanding blue leaf color holds late into the summer provided the plant is grown in light to full shade. The best results occur in cooler climates.

Distinguishing Features: Among the bluest of the hostas with all-blue leaves and quite distinct.

Similar: *★H.* 'Elvis Lives' has leaves not quite as blue later in the season.

Sports: *H.* 'Winfield Mist'.

Hosta 'Gunsmoke'

BLUE-GRAY LEAVES

HOSTAS IN THIS CATEGORY are often as sophisticated as the purer blues and require careful placing in the garden. They are best used near the house, either as container specimens or planted to set off stonework or paving. These grayish blue leaves are due either to the basic leaf color or sometimes to the denseness of a glaucous gray indumentum on a blue leaf. The latter group of plants can quickly lose their bloom if exposed to hot sun, leaving a shiny or blotched surface on the leaves.

Hosta 'Babbling Brook' (K. Vaughn N/R)

MEDIUM–LARGE

Origin: (★*H.* 'Donahue Piecrust' × ★*H. pycnophylla*) × *H.* 'Regal Ruffles'.

Description: A low, spreading mound 30 in. wide × 16 in. high (75 × 40 cm). Leaf blade 14 × 11 in. (35 × 28 cm), of good substance, gray-blue later turning dark green, thickly glaucous below, veins widely spaced, edge distinctly rippled, leaf widely oval with a cuspidate tip and heart-shaped pinched lobes. Petiole pale green-gray. Flower narrowly funnel-shaped, lavender, on an upright then arching to horizontal, pale green-gray, 25-in. (63-cm) scape from mid- to high summer; fertile.

Cultivation Notes: Site in light to medium shade all day. Gray to silvery blue leaf color is retained for longer in cooler climates.

Distinguishing Features: When the raceme is heaviest, the scape arches down toward the ground in an unattractive manner.

Hosta 'Blue Angel' (P. Aden 1986) ♆

VERY LARGE

Origin: *H.* "Aden 365" × *H.* "Aden 361."

Description: A graceful, cascading mound 71 in. wide × 36 in. high (178 × 90 cm) and exhibiting characteristics from its ★*H. montana* heritage. Leaf blade 16 × 12 in. (40 × 30 cm), thick, dark blue-gray to dark blue-green, slightly dimpled when mature, prominent veins closely ribbed, edge rippled, leaf arching, convex, widely oval to wedge-shaped with a cuspidate tip and heart-shaped pinched lobes. Petiole gray-green. Flower open funnel-shaped, long-lasting, palest lavender to near white, in a dense raceme, on a stout, upright, leafy, gray-green, 4-ft. (1.2-m) scape in midsummer; fertile.

Cultivation Notes: Grow in a few hours of morning sun in cooler climates followed by light shade. Among the best large, blue-leaved hostas for gardens in warmer climates. Tolerates quite dry soil when fully established. If carefully sited, it almost attains the bluest category. A classic hosta.

Distinguishing Features: Among the largest blue-leaved hostas.

Similar: *H.* 'Bodacious Blue' increases more quickly and is more vigorous.

Hosta 'Blue Sliver'

Hosta 'Babbling Brook'

Hosta 'Blue Angel'

Sports: *H.* 'Angel Eyes'; *★H.* 'Beckoning' and *H.* 'Chesières Jasmin's Hope' have dark blue-gray margins with a viridescent white to light green center; *H.* 'Confused Angel' has streaked leaves; *H.* 'Dream Maker' has yellow-streaked and blotched blue leaves; *H.* 'Duke of Cornwall' and *★H.* 'Earth Angel' have cream-margined blue-gray leaves; *H.* 'Fallen Angel' emerges white with green speckling and turns green; *H.* 'Grey Ghost' has ghostly ivory leaves which turn bright yellow then fade to blue; *★H.* 'Guardian Angel'.

Hosta **'Blue Sliver'** (H. Benedict N/R)

SMALL

Origin: *H.* 'Dorset Blue' hybrid.

Description: An unruly mound 15 in. wide × 6 in. high (38 × 15 cm). Leaf blade 4½ × 2 in. (11 × 5 cm), of good substance, glaucous rich blue-gray, slightly dimpled, edge flat when mature, leaf lanceolate to cuneate with a strongly acute tip. Petiole narrow,

glaucous blue-gray, decurrent with the leaf blade. Flower bell-shaped, lavender to grayish white, on an upright, bare, glaucous blue-gray, 12-in. (30-cm) scape in late summer; fertility unknown.

Cultivation Notes: Site in light shade. Slow growing. Pest resistant. An ideal specimen for a small container or grown at the front of a border with ferns and foliage of a contrasting color.

Similar: *H.* 'Hadspen Heron' has greener leaves.

Hosta **'Chesapeake Bay'** (O. Petryszyn 2004)

LARGE

Origin: (*H.* 'Maui Rains' × *★H.* 'Blue Arrow') × *★H.* 'Blue Betty Lou'.

Description: An unruly mound 40 in. wide × 25 in. high (100 × 63 cm). Leaf blade 10 × 7 in. (25 × 18 cm), of good substance, glaucous gray-blue, dimpled, prominently veined, edge slightly undulate, leaf lightly wavy, moderately folded, broadly ovate with a

Hosta 'Chesapeake Bay'

mucronate tip and folded to overlapping heart-shaped lobes. Petiole glaucous blue-gray. Flower funnel-shaped, near white, on an upright, bare, blue-green, 31-in. (78-cm) scape from mid- to high summer; seed is set but viability unknown.

Cultivation Notes: Site in good light to moderate shade, leaving plenty of room for its rapid increase. Pest resistant.

Distinguishing Features: The emerging leaves are very bright blue and gradually turn a muted blue-gray. The leaf separation on the clump is distinctive.

Hosta 'Devon Blue' (A. & R. Bowden 1988)

MEDIUM–LARGE

Origin: A Tardiana Group seedling, not named by Eric Smith.

Description: An arching mound 40 in. wide × 20 in. high (101 × 50 cm). Leaf blade 10 × 6½ in. (25 × 16 cm), thick, blue-gray, veins closely ribbed, edge undulate, leaf arching toward the tip, lanceolate to oval with a cuspidate tip and rounded open lobes. Petiole pale blue-green, appearing to pierce the blade. Flower bell-shaped, palest lavender, on an upright, bare, 30-in. (75-cm) scape from mid- to high summer; fertile.

Hosta 'Devon Blue'

Hosta 'Devon Mist'

Cultivation Notes: Site in dappled to full shade. Quickly turns green if exposed to sunlight. Vigorous. Pest resistant.

Similar: ★*H.* 'Halcyon' is smaller and has a better-defined leaf shape.

Hosta 'Devon Mist' (A. & R. Bowden/P. & J. Ruh 2005)

MEDIUM

Origin: *H.* 'Buckshaw Blue' hybrid.

Description: A congested mound 28 in. wide × 15 in. high (70 × 38 cm). Leaf blade 6½ × 4 in. (16 × 10 cm), thick, leathery, dark blue-gray turning green later, veins closely ribbed, edge rippled, leaf widely oval to heart-shaped with a cuspidate tip and open lobes. Petiole narrow, blue-green. Flower bell-shaped, palest lavender, produced in profusion on an upright, bare, dark green, 20-in. (50-cm) scape from mid- to high summer; fertile.

Cultivation Notes: Site in good light to dappled shade. Slow to increase. Pest resistant.

Similar: ★*H.* 'Blue Wedgwood' has darker blue leaves; *H.* 'Ice Prancer' has narrower, even grayer leaves.

Hosta 'Flemish Sky' (D. Van Eechaute 2004)

MEDIUM

Origin: Unknown.

Description: An open mound 16 in. wide × 8 in. high (40 × 20 cm). Leaf blade 5 × 3 in. (13 × 8 cm), of good substance, glaucous intense gray-blue, smooth, veins widely spaced, edge widely rippled, leaf lightly cupped, broadly ovate with a recurved acuminate tip and pinched to overlapping heart-shaped lobes. Petiole glaucous, gray-green. Flower funnel-shaped, white-margined pale lavender, on an upright, glaucous blue-green, 12- to 20-in. (30- to 50-cm) scape from late summer to autumn; seedpods green, fertile.

Cultivation Notes: Site in good light to full shade to retain the ethereal gray-blue leaf coloring but not under a tree canopy as falling detritus could soon

Hosta 'Flemish Sky'

spoil the leaf surface. Best grown in a container set in front of a red brick wall for color contrast and where the exquisite beauty of the leaves can be seen close up. Moderate growth rate.

Distinguishing Features: The leaves appear almost pale gray due to the exceptionally thick pruinose coating, especially heavy on the reverse which, due to the leaf shape, is often visible. Leaf tip is very long.

Similar: *H. 'Sky Dancer' has more tightly ruffled leaves.

Hosta 'Goldbrook Grayling' (S. Bond N/R)

SMALL

Origin: *H.* 'Happiness' hybrid.

Description: A diffuse mound 18 in. wide × 8½ in. high (45 × 21 cm). Leaf blade 5½ × 1½ in.(14 × 4 cm),

Hosta 'Goldbrook Grayling'

thick, gray-blue, edge undulate to kinked, leaf folded, lanceolate with an acute tip and tapered open lobes. Petiole gray-green. Flower bell-shaped, lilac-pink, on an upright, bare, gray-green, 10-in. (25-cm) scape in late summer; fertility unknown.

Cultivation Notes: Site in some morning sun in cooler climates. Moderate growth rate. Pest resistant. Lovely in a container.

Distinguishing Features: Although it has many characteristics of Tardiana Group hostas, it is quite distinct in its gray leaves and pinkish flowers.

Hosta 'Great Plains' (W. Brincka & O. Petryszyn 1994)

LARGE–VERY LARGE

Origin: *H.* 'Sagae' × *H.* 'Tokudama Flavocircinalis'.

Description: A semi-upright mound 41 in. wide × 25 in. high (102 × 63 cm). Leaf blade 16 × 12 in. (40 × 30 cm), thick, gray-blue, upper surface with a waxy coating that soon vanishes, leaving a satiny, blue green upper surface that finally turns green, while the underside remains a light glaucous blue, veins furrowed, edge rippled to piecrusted, leaf undulate, widely oval with a cuspidate tip and heart-shaped open lobes. Petiole stout, light green. Flower long, tubular, pale lavender, in a dense raceme, on an upright or oblique, leafy, blue-green, 41-in. (102-cm) scape from mid- to high summer; fertile.

Cultivation Notes: Site in dappled to moderate shade.

Hosta 'Great Plains'

Hosta 'Gunsmoke', flowers

Similar: *H.* 'Grey Piecrust' does not have the outstanding qualities of *H.* 'Great Plains'.

Hosta 'Gunsmoke' (R. Herold 2000)

VERY LARGE

Origin: *★H.* 'Sagae' × *H.* 'Grey Piecrust'.

Description: An impressive, arching mound 65 in. wide × 30 in. high (163 × 75 cm). Leaf blade 14 × 10 in. (35 × 25 cm), leathery, emerging light blue-green, gradually turning rich deep blue-green with a grayish cast, satiny above and glaucous below, slightly dimpled, prominent veins widely spaced, edge rippled, leaf broadly ovate to rounded with a mucronate tip and heart-shaped open to pinched lobes. Petiole blue-green. Flower funnel-shaped, lavender, in a long truss, on an almost horizontal, leafy, 36-in. (90-cm) scape from late spring to midsummer; seedpods green, fertility unknown.

Cultivation Notes: Site in light to moderate shade to retain the best leaf color. Use as a background plant or single specimen. Vigorous. Pest resistant.

Distinguishing Features: Leaves are slow to assume their optimum width.

Similar: *H.* 'Moonlight Sonata' has a longer leaf.

Hosta 'Krossa Regal' (G. & A. Krossa 1980)

LARGE–VERY LARGE

Origin: *H. nigrescens* hybrid.

Description: An upright, arching mound, 71 in. wide × 32 in. high (178 × 80 cm), spreading with maturity. Leaf blade 11 × 7 in. (28 × 18 cm), of good substance, soft gray-blue, smooth, widely veined, edge slightly undulate, leaf slightly arching, oval with a cuspidate tip and rounded open lobes. Petiole upright, gray-green. Flower funnel-shaped, lavender, on an upright, bare, light gray-green, 5-ft. (1.5-m) scape from mid- to high summer; sterile.

Cultivation Notes: Site in dappled to light shade.

Hosta 'Gunsmoke', leaves

Hosta 'Krossa Regal'

Hosta 'Metallic Sheen'

Hosta 'Mississippi Delta', showing scape branching.

Slug resistant. Of great architectural merit as a specimen and good in a large container, which must be kept well-watered. Outstanding in leaf and flower. Winner of the 2001 Alex J. Summers Distinguished Merit Hosta Award.

Similar: ★*H.* 'Mikawa-no-Yuki' has white-backed green-gray leaves; ★*H.* 'Pewter Frost'; *H.* 'Phoenix' has a more refined leaf; ★*H.* 'Snowden'; *H.* 'Tenryu', collected from near the river Tenryu in Japan and, although closely related to ★*H. nigrescens*, looks more like *H.* 'Krossa Regal'.

Sports: *H.* 'Regal Chameleon' has a viridescent, pale green, central variegation; ★*H.* 'Regalia'; *H.* 'Regal Splendor'; ★*H.* 'Regal Supreme'; ★*H.* 'Tom Schmid'.

Hosta 'Metallic Sheen' (M. Zilis 1999)

LARGE–VERY LARGE

Origin: ★*H.* 'Sum and Substance' × ★*H. sieboldiana* 'Elegans'.

Description: An open mound 60 in. wide × 28 in. high (150 × 70 cm). Leaf blade 14 × 10 in. (35 × 25 cm), very thick, metallic gray-blue, turning dark green, seersuckered and puckered, edge almost flat, leaf shallowly cupped or convex, widely oval to nearly round with a mucronate tip and heart-shaped open to overlapping lobes. Petiole stout, light blue-gray to green, appearing to pierce the blade. Flower funnel-shaped, glaucous pale lavender, on an upright or leaning, leafy, 30- to 40-in. (75- to 100-cm) scape in late summer; fertile.

Cultivation Notes: Site in some morning sun in cooler climates, otherwise light shade all day. Slow to moderate growth rate. Pest resistant.

Distinguishing Features: The huge leaves of the *H.* 'Sum and Substance' parent and the thickness and surface texture of the ★*H. sieboldiana* 'Elegans' parent combine to make this an impressive hosta.

Similar: *H.* 'Carolina Blue' has smaller leaves.

Hosta 'Mississippi Delta' (O. Petryszyn 1998)

VERY LARGE

Origin: *H.* 'Sea Gold' × *H.* 'Golden Torch'.

Description: An open, upright, outward-facing mound 56 in. wide × 36 in. high (140 × 90 cm). Leaf blade 13 × 12 in. (33 × 30 cm), very thick, rubbery, blue-gray, dimpled and puckered, edge slightly undulate, flat to shallowly cupped, leaf nearly round with a mucronate tip and heart-shaped pinched to folded lobes. Petiole stout, blue-green. Flower long, tubular, near white, in a dense raceme, on an upright or oblique, light blue-green, 40-in. (100-cm) scape in high summer; seedpods green, fertile.

Cultivation Notes: Upper leaf surface soon loses its glaucous coating leaving a rubbery effect, but the best color is maintained if grown in light shade. Moderate growth rate. Pest resistant.

Distinguishing Features: Scape branching can occur on mature plants.

Hosta 'Osprey' (E. Smith & BHHS 1988)

MEDIUM

Origin: ★*H.* 'Tardiflora' × ★*H. sieboldiana* 'Elegans Alba'.

Description: A compact mound 36 in. wide × 17 in. high (90 × 43 cm). Leaf blade 7 × 5 in. (18 × 13 cm), thick, light gray-blue with a hint of green, moderately seersuckered, veins widely spaced, edge flat with occasional kinks, leaf folded to cupped, widely oval to nearly round with a mucronate tip and heart-shaped overlapping lobes. Petiole pale gray-green, appearing to pierce the blade. Flower bell-shaped, white, on a leafy, upright, pale gray-green, 24-in. (60-cm) scape from early to midsummer; fertile.

Cultivation Notes: Tolerates two hours of morning sun in cooler climates, elsewhere prefers good light to light shade. Slow to increase. Pest resistant.

Hosta 'Pewter Frost' (J. Dishon 1996)

MEDIUM

Origin: ★*H. pycnophylla* × ★*H. montana*.

Description: An upright mound 40 in. wide × 13 in. high (100 × 33 cm). Leaf blade 10 × 7 in. (25 × 18 cm), of moderate substance, intense blue-gray, prominently veined, edge slightly undulate, leaf slightly arching, oval with a cuspidate tip and heart-shaped pinched lobes. Petiole glaucous light green with scattered purple dotting. Flower long, funnel-shaped, near white, on an upright or oblique, leafy, glaucous light green, 33-in. (83-cm) scape from high to late summer; seedpods green, fertile.

Cultivation Notes: Site in light shade. The thick glaucous bloom soon disappears from the upper leaf surface, which is then very shiny, giving a gunmetal-like appearance. Moderate growth rate.

Distinguishing Features: The gracefully shaped leaves.

Hosta 'Pewterware' (D. Dean 1999)

SMALL

Origin: *H.* 'Urajiro Hachijo' × ★*H.* 'Blue Moon'.

Description: A dense mound 24 in. wide × 8 in. high (60 × 20 cm). Leaf blade 5½ × 4½ in. (14 × 11 cm), thick, gray-blue, edge widely undulate, leaf

Hosta 'Pewter Frost'

Hosta 'Osprey'

heart-shaped to almost round with a cuspidate tip and heart-shaped pinched lobes. Petiole light gray-green. Flower long, bell-shaped, lavender-striped near white, on an upright, bare, glaucous light green, 14- to 19-in. (35- to 48-cm) scape in early autumn; seedpods green, fertility unknown.

Hosta 'Pewterware'

Cultivation Notes: Site in dappled to full shade. Slow to increase. Pest resistant. A superb recent introduction.

Distinguishing Features: Leaves with a heavy glaucous bloom and of an exceptionally heavy substance.

Hosta 'Queen of the Seas' (M. Seaver 2001)

LARGE

Origin: Unknown.

Description: A layered mound of great architectural beauty 48 in. wide × 24 in. high (120 × 60 cm). Leaf blade 11½ in. × 9 in. (29 × 23 cm), thick, intensely glaucous rich blue-gray, some seersuckering when mature, veins furrowed, edge strongly piecrusted and slightly serrated, leaf twisted toward the tip, folded, broadly oval with a cuspidate tip and heart-shaped open to folded lobes. Petiole arching, glaucous pale green. Flower funnel-shaped, near-white, on an oblique, leafy, glaucous blue-gray, 27-in. (68-cm) scape in midsummer; fertile.

Hosta 'Queen of the Seas'

Cultivation Notes: Site in low light to shade with plenty of moisture to boost the plant's special characteristics. In hot climates, the blue cast disappears from the leaf surface. Grow with plain-leaved hostas to accentuate the attractively rippled edges. Pest resistant. Won Best in Show Award at the American Hosta Society's National Convention in 1997.

Distinguishing Features: The most dramatic blue-leaved hosta with rippled margins which will stand out in any collection.

Similar: *H.* 'Blue Piecrust', ★*H.* 'Donahue Piecrust', and *H.* 'Grey Piecrust', none of which compare in leaf shapeliness or color.

Hosta 'Sherborne Swift' (E. Smith & BHHS 1988)

SMALL–MEDIUM

Origin: ★*H.* 'Tardiflora' × ★*H. sieboldiana* 'Elegans Alba'.

Description: A diffuse mound 30 in. wide × 8½ in. high (75 × 21 cm). Leaf blade 5½ × 2½ in. (14 × 6 cm),

thick, blue-gray, edge almost flat with occasional kinks, leaf arching toward the tip, lanceolate with a cuspidate tip and tapered open to pinched lobes. Petiole narrow, gray-green. Flower bell-shaped, near white, in a dense raceme on an upright, leafy scape in midsummer.

Cultivation Notes: Site in light to full shade all day. Lovely with *Cimicifuga* 'Brunette'.

Distinguishing Features: Intensely gray-blue foliage.

Similar: *H.* 'Hadspen Hawk' has smaller, darker blue leaves.

Hosta sieboldiana 'Gray Cole' (Kuk 1985)

VERY LARGE

Origin: An early selected form of ★*H. sieboldiana* 'Elegans'.

Description: A billowing mound 84 in. wide × 36 in. high (210 × 90). Leaf blade 15 × 13 in. (38 × 33 cm), thick, gray-blue turning gray-green, seersuckered and puckered, edge slightly undulate, leaf shallowly cupped or slightly convex, widely oval to nearly

Hosta 'Sherborne Swift'

Hosta sieboldiana 'Gray Cole'

Hosta 'Silberpfeil'

Hosta 'Sky Dancer'

round with a mucronate tip and raised heart-shaped overlapping lobes. Petiole stout, gray-green, appearing to pierce the blade. Flower funnel-shaped, near white, on an upright, bare, glaucous green, 39-in. (98-cm) scape in midsummer; fertile.

Cultivation Notes: Tolerates morning sun but leaf color is better when grown in dappled to full shade. Of moderate increase once established. Pest resistant.

Distinguishing Features: Bloom scape can be branched. Petaloid stamen double flowers are sometimes produced. Slightly larger than its parent.

Hosta 'Silberpfeil' (H. Klose/P. & J. Ruh 2005)

SMALL—MEDIUM

Origin: ★*H.* 'Tardiflora' × ★*H. sieboldiana* 'Elegans'.

Description: An open mound 25 in. wide × 10 in. high (63 × 25 cm). Leaf blade 5 × 1⅜ in. (13 × 3.5 cm), thick, pale silver-blue, closely veined, edge almost flat to widely undulate, leaf slightly arching, lanceolate with an acute to cuspidate tip and tapered open lobes. Petiole narrow, pale silver-blue, appearing to pierce the blade. Flower bell-shaped, near white, on an upright, bare, blue-gray, 12-in. (30-cm) scape in midsummer; fertile.

Cultivation Notes: One of a collection of unnumbered and unnamed Tardiana Group seedlings acquired by the German nurseryman and hosta collector, the late Heinz Klose.

Similar: *H.* 'Hadspen Hawk' has darker leaves.

Hosta 'Sky Dancer' (D. Van Eechaute 2003)

MEDIUM

Origin: *H.* 'Paradise Red Delight' hybrid.

Description: An overlapping mound 18 in. wide × 14 in. high (45 × 35 cm). Leaf blade 7 × 6¾ in. (18 × 17 cm), of good substance, gray-blue, heavily pruinose above and glaucous below, smooth, veins widely spaced, edge markedly rippled, leaf flat, nearly round with a mucronate tip and open to pinched lobes. Petiole gray-blue, with burgundy-red dots. Flower funnel-shaped, lavender-striped pale lavender, on an upright, bare, grayish-green, 14- to 18-in. (35- to 45-cm) scape in late summer and autumn; seedpods grayish green, fertile.

Cultivation Notes: Site in full shade for best leaf color.

Distinguishing Features: The ethereal gray-blue leaf gradually loses the heavy indumentum on its upper surface, as the leaf turns gray-green.

Similar: *H. 'Flemish Sky' has a less-rippled leaf edge.

Sports: *H.* 'Exotic Dancer' has cream- and white-streaked leaves; *H.* 'Private Dancer' has leaves with very thick indumentum.

Hosta 'Something Blue' (L. Simpers & P. Ruh 1991)

MEDIUM–LARGE

Origin: *H.* 'Blue Beauty' × *H.* 'Blue Boy'.

Description: An open mound 51 in. wide × 22 in. high (127 × 55 cm). Leaf blade 9 × 8½ in. (23 × 21 cm), of good substance, blue-gray, deeply seersuckered and puckered, edge attractively rippled, leaf folded to cupped, widely oval with a cuspidate to mucronate tip and heart-shaped lobes. Petiole narrow, blue-green. Flower tubular, rich lavender, on an upright, bare, light blue-green, 26-in. (65-cm) scape in high summer; fertile.

Cultivation Notes: Site in good light to light shade all day. Increases more rapidly than many similar blue-leaved hostas.

Distinguishing Features: Attractive blue-gray leaf color.

Similar: *H.* 'Blue Betty Lou'.

Hosta 'Tomoko' (H. Klose/P. & J. Ruh 2003)

MEDIUM–LARGE

Origin: *H.* 'Tardiflora' × *H. sieboldiana* 'Elegans Alba'. Initially an unnumbered and unnamed Tardiana Group seedling, one of several given to the late Heinz Klose.

Description: A dense mound 32 in. wide × 20 in. high (80 × 50 cm). Leaf blade 10 × 8½ in. (25 × 21 cm), thick, rich dark blue-gray, dimpled, closely veined, edge almost flat, leaf convex, widely oval to

Hosta 'Something Blue'

nearly round with a mucronate tip and deeply heart-shaped pinched lobes. Petiole blue-gray. Flower bell-shaped, near white, on an upright, bare, gray-blue, 22-in. (55-cm) scape in midsummer; fertile.

Cultivation Notes: Site in dappled to light shade. Slow to establish. Pest resistant. Widely grown in European gardens.

Distinguishing Features: Closely resembles its *H. sieboldiana* 'Elegans Alba' parent but is somewhat smaller.

Hosta 'Turning Point' (R. Lydell 2001)

SMALL—MEDIUM

Origin: Streaked seedling of *H.* "Minuta," which is thought to be a large form of ★*H. venusta.*

Description: A dense mound 30 in. wide × 12 in. high (75 × 30 cm). Leaf blade 5 × 1⅜ in. (13 × 3.5 cm), thick, smooth, blue-gray, edge flat with an occasional kink, leaf slightly folded, lanceolate with an acute tip and tapered open lobes. Petiole narrow, blue-gray. Flower bell-shaped, lavender, on an upright, leafy, light purple, 24- to 30-in. (60- to 75-cm) scape from high summer to early autumn; fertile.

Cultivation Notes: Site in good light to dappled shade where the leaf color is long-lasting. Tolerates sun in cooler climates but the leaf surface will lose its pruinose coating. A moderate to good increaser.

Distinguishing Features: Leaves are upright then abruptly horizontal. Numerous flower scapes arise from the center of the mound and tower above the leaves.

Hosta 'Turning Point'

Hosta 'Tomoko'

Hosta 'Bigfoot'

BLUE-GREEN LEAVES

THIS CATEGORY EMBRACES all those hostas that are not quite blue enough to belong in the very blue section and yet are definitely too blue to belong in the green or gray-green sections. Many leaves unfurl green, turn blue for a few weeks, and finally take on greenish tints; others start blue but hold this color for a very short time, soon becoming greener.

Hosta 'Abiqua Trumpet' (Walden-West 1987)
SMALL

Origin: *H. 'Tokudama' selection.

Description: A flattish, dense mound 21 in. wide × 8½ in. high (53 × 21 cm). Leaf blade 4 × 3 in. (10 × 8 cm), thick, blue-green, dimpled to seersuckered, edge almost flat, folded to cupped, widely oval to nearly round with a mucronate tip at maturity and with

Hosta 'Abiqua Trumpet'

Hosta 'Andrew Jackson'

Hosta 'Barbara May'

Hosta 'Bette Davis Eyes'

rounded open to pinched lobes. Petiole narrow, light green, appearing to pierce the blade. Flower bell-shaped, pale lavender, on an upright, leafy, glaucous green, 14-in. (35-cm) scape in late summer; fertile.

Cultivation Notes: Site in some morning sun in cooler climates, otherwise in light to medium shade. Floriferous. A vigorous, moderately rapid increaser. Ideal in a container or as an edging plant. Pest resistant.

Distinguishing Features: Spoon-shaped leaves give the plant a pinwheel effect when seen from above. Leaves are bluer at the edges and greener toward the midrib.

Similar: *H.* 'Heart Throb' remains bluer-leaved for longer; *H.* 'Peter Pan' is slightly larger.

Hosta 'Andrew Jackson' (H. Sugita/M. Zilis/P. & J. Ruh 2001)

LARGE—VERY LARGE

Origin: Unknown. From Japanese seed.

Description: An upright mound 54 in. wide × 30 in. high (135 × 75 cm). Leaf blade 12¾ × 9 in. (32 × 23 cm), very thick, intense blue-green, seersuckered, edge distinctly rippled, leaf undulate and slightly twisted, deeply folded, oval with a cuspidate tip and rounded pinched lobes. Petiole glaucous pale blue, appearing to pierce the blade. Flower long, tubular, lavender-blushed near white, in a dense raceme, on an upright, leafy, glaucous blue-green, 31-in. (78-cm) scape from early to midsummer; fertility unknown.

Cultivation Notes: Site in light to full shade. Pest resistant.

Distinguishing Features: Prominent white lines overlay the veins.

Similar: *H.* 'Ulysses S. Grant' has slightly wavy leaves.

Hosta 'Barbara May' (R. Solberg 2004)

MEDIUM

Origin: (*H. pycnophylla* × *H.* 'Harvest Dandy') × (*H.* 'Blue Arrow' × *H.* 'Sea Fire').

Description: An open mound 30 in. wide × 14 in. high (75 × 35 cm). Leaf blade 8 × 5½ in. (20 × 14 cm), thick, smooth, emerging an intense glaucous blue soon turning rich blue-green, prominently veined, edge slightly rippled, leaf moderately wavy, triangular with a cuspidate tip and tapered to flat open lobes. Petiole glaucous blue-green. Flower funnel-shaped, pale lavender, on a semi-erect, leafy, blue-green, 24- to 26-in. (60- to 65-cm) scape from high to late summer; seedpods blue-green, fertile.

Cultivation Notes: Site in moderate to full shade. Moderate growth rate. One of a range of blue-leaved hybrids raised by its introducer to produce leaves which hold their color well through the summer.

Distinguishing Features: As it receives less light, the underside of the leaf retains its heavy white indumentum for longer than the upper surface.

Similar: ★*H*. 'Blue My Mind'.

Hosta 'Bette Davis Eyes' (K. Vaughn 1987)
MEDIUM

Origin: Sibling to *H*. 'Summer Fragrance' × ★*H*. 'Christmas Tree'.

Description: A dense mound 24 in. wide × 12 in. high (60 × 30 cm). Leaf blade 7½–9 × 4½ in. (19–23 × 11 cm), thick, dark blue-green, strongly veined, edge distinctly rippled, leaf arching, widely oval with a cuspidate tip and heart-shaped pinched to

overlapping lobes. Petiole blue-green. Flower funnel-shaped, fragrant, purple-tipped near white, on an oblique, leafy, dark green, 25-in. (63-cm) scape from mid- to late summer; fertile.

Cultivation Notes: Site in light to medium shade to retain the blue sheen on the leaves. Best in cooler climates and with plenty of moisture. A moderate increaser. Pest resistant.

Distinguishing Features: Long-blooming, fragrant flowers.

Hosta 'Bigfoot' (R. Duback 1998)
LARGE–VERY LARGE

Origin: Unknown.

Description: A tiered mound 68 in. wide × 30 in. high (172 × 75 cm). Leaf blade 19 × 12 in. (48 × 30 cm), thick, mid-blue-green, dimpled, moderately prominent veins widely spaced, edges slightly rippled, leaf nearly flat, widely oval with a cuspidate tip and heart-shaped overlapping lobes. Petiole gray-green. Flower large, tubular, near white, on an upright, bare, glaucous green, 31-in. (78-cm) scape in midsummer; fertile.

Hosta 'Bigfoot'

Cultivation Notes: Site in shade, Protect from harsh winds that can damage the slightly floppy leaves. Slow to start, then moderate growth. Pest resistant.

Distinguishing Features: The lack of cupping sets this cultivar apart from other similar hostas.

Hosta 'Big Mama' (P. Aden 1978)

LARGE—VERY LARGE

Origin: H. 'Blue Tiers' × ⋆H. 'Blue Angel'.

Description: An overlapping mound 60 in. wide × 26 in. high (150 × 65 cm). Leaf blade 18 × 14 in. (45 × 35 cm), thick, dark blue-green, seersuckered and puckered, veins deeply ribbed, edge rippled, leaf arching to convex, undulate near the cuspidate tip and widely oval with heart-shaped pinched lobes. Petiole stout, pale blue-green. Flower bell-shaped, palest lavender, on an upright, bare, gray-green, 42-in. (105-cm) scape in midsummer; fertile.

Cultivation Notes: Site in good light to full shade. Tolerates some morning sun in cooler climates but

with more sun the blue leaf color will disappear. Very floriferous. A useful background hosta. Slow to get started. Pest resistant.

Distinguishing Features: Leaves are thicker and more rigid than those of the ⋆H. 'Blue Angel' parent.

Hosta 'Blue Arrow' (K. Anderson 1982)

MEDIUM

Origin: Unknown.

Description: A semi-upright, arching mound 24 in. wide × 18 in. high (60 × 45 cm). Leaf blade 8½ × 3½ in. (21 × 9 cm), of good substance, blue-green above, pale glaucous green below, smooth, veins widely spaced, edge widely undulate and slightly upturned, leaf widely lanceolate with a cuspidate tip and heart-shaped open broad lobes. Petiole pale green, appearing to pierce the blade. Flower bell-shaped, near white, on an upright, bare, 20-in. (40-cm) scape in high summer; very fertile.

Cultivation Notes: Tolerates some morning sun in

Hosta 'Big Mama', the leaves are becoming green with exposure to sunlight.

cooler climates but the leaves remain bluer for longer in dappled to light shade. Pest resistant. Much used as a breeding plant.

Distinguishing Features: Although not one of the Tardiana Group, it has similar characteristics.

Similar: ★*H.* 'Blue Blush'; *H.* 'Gemstone' has turquoise-blue leaves; *H.* 'Hadspen Heron'; *H.* 'Happiness' has similar leaf shape but leaf is not as undulate, it turns green later, and has a generally coarser appearance; *H.* 'Kiwi Blue Heron'; *H.* 'Rhythm and Blues'; *H.* 'Salute'; ★*H.* 'Sherborne Swift'.

Sports: ★*H.* 'Deane's Dream'.

Hosta 'Blue Betty Lou' (C. Owens 1987)

LARGE

Origin: ★*H.* 'True Blue' × ★*H.* 'Gold Regal'.

Description: A semi-upright mound 32 in. wide × 24 in. high (80 × 60 cm). Leaf blade 10½ × 9 in. (27 × 23 cm), thick, light blue-green (almost turquoise), seersuckered, puckering from the midrib, edge

shallowly undulate, leaf deeply cupped, nearly round with a mucronate tip and kinked pinched lobes. Petiole sturdy, turquoise. Flower bell-shaped, lavender, on an upright, bare, 32-in. (80-cm) scape from mid- to late summer; fertile.

Hosta 'Blue Arrow'

Hosta 'Blue Betty Lou'

Cultivation Notes: Site in light to full shade all day. Performs well in warmer climates. Slow to establish. Pest resistant. Lovely with *Heuchera* 'Velvet Night'.

Distinguishing Features: Among the most turquoise-hued hostas.

Similar: *H.* 'Blue Bayou' is slightly greener.

Hosta 'Blue Blazes' (K. Vaughn 1988)

LARGE–VERY LARGE

Origin: ★*H.* 'Blue Boy' × *H.* 'Polly Bishop'.

Description: An unruly mound 35 in. wide × 30 in. high (88 × 75 cm). Leaf blade 13 × 12½ in. (33 × 31 cm), thick, rich, dark blue-green, intensely seersuckered and puckered, edge slightly undulate, leaf cupped or convex, widely oval to nearly round with a mucronate tip and deeply heart-shaped overlapping lobes. Petiole light blue-green, appearing to pierce the blade. Flower bell-shaped, pale lavender to near white, on a chunky, upright, bare, pale blue-green, 32-in. (80-cm) scape in midsummer; fertile.

Cultivation Notes: Site in light to full shade. Much faster growing than most blue-leaved hostas. Pest resistant.

Distinguishing Features: Flower buds are level with the top of the foliage. Large bracts cluster round the raceme. Leaf color remains an unusually rich, dark blue-green if grown in full shade all day.

Similar: ★*H.* 'Big Daddy' and *H.* 'Sea Grotto' are both bluer in color.

Sports: *H.* 'Blue Blazes Supreme' has streaked leaves.

Hosta 'Blue Boy' (D. Stone & AHS 1986)

MEDIUM

Origin: ★*H. nakaiana* × ★*H. sieboldiana* 'Elegans'.

Description: A dense mound 45 in. wide × 15 in. high (113 × 38 cm). Leaf blade 8½ × 5 in. (21 × 13 cm), of average substance, soft blue soon turning green, smooth, prominently veined, edge slightly rippled, leaf folded, widely oval with a cuspidate tip and heart-shaped pinched to overlapping lobes. Petiole thin, light blue-green. Flower funnel-shaped, pale lavender to near white, in profusion, on an upright, leafy, light green, 22-in. (55-cm) scape in midsummer; fertile.

Cultivation Notes: Site in dappled shade. A vigorous, rapid increaser. A useful ground cover and edging plant.

Similar: *H.* 'Fond Hope'; *H.* 'Goldbrook Genie'.

Hosta 'Blue Cadet' (P. Aden 1974)

MEDIUM

Origin: Although registered as a seedling of ★*H.* 'Tokudama', it has many of the characteristics of ★*H. nakaiana*.

Description: A neat, dense mound 30 in. wide × 15 in. high (75 × 38 cm). Leaf blade 5 × 4 in. (13 × 10 cm), of average substance, blue-green, matt above and glaucous below, slight dimpling when mature, edge flat, leaf folded, heart-shaped with a cuspidate tip and cupped lobes. Petiole narrow, light gray-green. Flower funnel-shaped, rich lavender, in a long, dense

Hosta 'Blue Blazes'

Hosta 'Blue Boy'

raceme, on an upright, bare, light green, 22-in. (55-cm) scape from mid- to late summer; fertile.

Cultivation Notes: Site in light shade all day. Leaves will turn dark green by late summer even if grown in good light to light shade. A vigorous, rapid increaser. A wonderful breeding plant and the parent of several miniature hostas introducing a blue cast to their leaves.

Distinguishing Features: Magnificent display of flowers atop the symmetrical mound. Good autumn color.

Similar: *H.* 'Abiqua Blue Edger'; *H.* 'Banyai's Dancing Girl'; ★*H.* 'Blue Boy'; *H.* 'Drummer Boy'; *H.* 'Goldbrook Genie'; *H.* 'My Blue Heaven'; *H.* 'Pacific Blue Edger'; *H.* 'Saint Fiacre'; *H.* 'Sherborne Profusion'.

Sports: *H.* 'Baby Doll' is an exciting new mini resembling a small *H.* 'June'; *H.* 'Medal of Honour' has a cream margin; *H.* 'Red Cadet' is a seedling of *H.* 'Blue Cadet' with gray-green leaves and red petioles and scapes; *H.* 'Serendipity'; ★*H.* 'Toy Soldier'.

Hosta 'Blue Clown' (H. & D. Benedict/J. & E. Stratton 1996)

SMALL

Origin: *H.* 'Dorset Blue' seedling selfed.

Description: An asymmetrical mound 15 in. wide × 10 in. high (38 × 25 cm). Leaf blade 2½ × 2 in. (6

Hosta 'Blue Clown'

Hosta 'Blue Cadet'

× 5 cm), thick, blue-green, moderately seersuckered, veins closely ribbed, edge slightly rippled, leaf slightly folded to cupped, widely oval with a mucronate tip and heart-shaped overlapping lobes. Petiole light green. Flower flared, white, on an upright, bare, light green, 8½-in. (21-cm) scape in midsummer; fertile.

Cultivation Notes: Site in good light to light shade. Very slow to increase. Pest resistant. Best grown in a pot until it has established a root system.

Similar: *H.* 'Blue Monday'; *H.* 'Blue Skies' is slightly larger and keeps its color better in cooler gardens.

Hosta 'Blue Diamond'

Hosta 'Blue Haired Lady'

Hosta 'Blue Diamond' (E. Smith & BHHS 1988)
MEDIUM

Origin: ★*H.* 'Tardiflora' × ★*H. sieboldiana* 'Elegans Alba'.

Description: A dense mound 17 in. wide × 12 in. high (43 × 30 cm). Leaf blade 7 × 5 in. (18 × 13 cm), thick, soft blue-green, dimpled when mature, edge slightly undulate, leaf slightly arching, lanceolate to oval with a cuspidate tip and rounded open to pinched lobes. Petiole light blue-green. Flower bell-shaped, pale lavender, on an upright, bare, lightly glaucous green, 18-in. (45-cm) scape in midsummer; fertile.

Cultivation Notes: Site in good light to light shade. Leaf color is much bluer in cooler climates. Moderate growth rate. Pest resistant.

Similar: *H.* 'Hadspen Heron' has a more rippled leaf edge.

Hosta 'Blue Haired Lady' (G. Johnson 2004)
MEDIUM

Origin: ★*H.* 'Sum and Substance' × ★*H. yingeri*.

Description: An open mound 34 in. wide × 14 in. high (85 × 35 cm). Leaf blade 9 × 5 in. (23 × 13 cm), of good substance, emerging soft blue turning mid-green to dark green, glossy above and shiny below, veins widely spaced, edge slightly rippled, leaf slightly arching, elongate to narrowly ovate with a cuspidate tip and tapered to heart-shaped open lobes. Petiole pale green. Flower moderately spider-shaped, pale lavender, striped near-white, opening from a lavender bud, on an upright, leafy, green, 30- to 34-in. (75- to 85-cm) scape from late summer into autumn; fertility unknown.

Cultivation Notes: Site in full shade to help retain the blue leaf color. Best in spring. Moderate growth rate. Pest resistant.

Distinguishing Features: Early leaves are matt above and glaucous below. The leaves change from blue to dark green during the summer. The flowers are widely spaced down the scape.

Hosta 'Blue Horizon' (L. Englerth 1985)
MEDIUM

Origin: *H.* 'Tokudama' hybrid.

Description: An open mound 32 in. wide × 17 in. high (80 × 43 cm). Leaf blade 8½ × 7½ in. (21 × 19 cm), very thick, rich blue-green, intensely seersuckered with some puckering, edge almost flat, leaf mainly convex, nearly round with a mucronate tip and heart-shaped pinched to overlapping lobes. Petiole light blue-green. Flower bell-shaped, white, on an upright, bare, lightly glaucous green, 18-in. (45-cm) scape in midsummer; fertile.

Cultivation Notes: Worth the trouble of placing carefully in light to moderate shade to retain the superb leaf color for as long as possible. Avoid positions under trees or in windy sites.

Similar: *H.* 'Blue Dome'; *H.* 'Blue Velvet'; *H.* 'Lady In Waiting' is larger.

Hosta **'Blue Seer'** (P. Aden N/R)

LARGE—VERY LARGE

Origin: *H. sieboldiana* 'Elegans' hybrid.

Description: An upright mound of horizontally poised leaves 51 in. wide × 30 in. high (127 × 75 cm). Leaf blade 14 × 13½ in. (35 × 34 cm), thick, light blue-green, intensely but shallowly seersuckered, puckered when mature, edge almost flat but sometimes with a kink at the lobes, leaf shallowly cupped, nearly round with a mucronate tip and heart-shaped pinched to overlapping lobes. Petiole stout, upright,

paler blue-green, appearing to pierce the blade. Flower funnel-shaped, white, abundantly produced, on an upright, bare, blue-green, 34-in. (85-cm) scape in midsummer; fertile.

Cultivation Notes: Site in light to full shade.

Distinguishing Features: Large flowers are compacted on the scape.

Similar: *H.* 'Evelyn McCafferty' has leaves more deeply and widely seersuckered and more puckered; *H.* 'Fantastic' has greener leaves; *H.* 'Will of Fortune'.

Hosta **'Blue Seer'**

Hosta **'Blue Horizon'**

Hosta 'Blue Umbrellas' (P. Aden 1978)

VERY LARGE

Origin: ★*H.* 'Tokudama' × ★*H. sieboldiana* 'Elegans'.

Description: An upright, stiff, open mound 54 in. wide × 36 in. high (135 × 90 cm). Leaf blade 14 × 10 in. (35 × 25 cm), very thick, blue-green turning dark green, seersuckered and puckered, veins widely spaced, edge flat, leaf usually convex but sometimes cupped, almost round with a mucronate tip and heart-shaped folded to overlapping lobes. Petiole pale blue-green, appearing to pierce the blade. Flower bell-shaped, almost white, on an upright, bare, pale green, 36-in. (90-cm) scape in midsummer; fertile.

Cultivation Notes: Tolerates some morning sun in cooler climates but the leaf color will remain bluer in light to moderate shade. Slow to increase. Pest resistant.

Distinguishing Features: Leaves, which soon turn shiny dark green, droop downward at the edges, giving an umbrella-like appearance.

Similar: ★*H.* 'Millenium'; *H.* 'Placemat'; ★*H.* 'Sea Lotus Leaf'.

Sports: ★*H.* 'Blue Lightning' is streaked; ★*H.* 'Dancing in the Rain'; *H.* 'Singing in the Rain' PP19,565 is the reverse sport.

Hosta 'Cutting Edge' (H. Gowen/R. Benedict 1999)

MEDIUM–LARGE

Origin: *H.* 'Salute' × ★*H. pycnophylla*.

Description: A dense, tiered mound 27 in. wide × 22 in. high (68 × 55 cm). Leaf blade 11½ × 6½ in. (29 × 16 cm), of good substance, mid-blue-green, satiny above and distinctly glaucous below, dimpled when mature, veins closely spaced, edge heavily rippled, leaf folded, slightly arching, oval with a cuspidate tip and rounded to tapered open to pinched lobes. Petiole glaucous pale gray-green, appearing to pierce the blade. Flower funnel-shaped, pale lavender, on an upright, bare, glaucous gray-green, 28-in. (70-cm) scape in high summer; fertility unknown.

Cultivation Notes: Site in light to moderate shade.

Hosta 'Singing In the Rain'

Hosta 'Cutting Edge'

Hosta 'Blue Umbrellas'

176

Slow to assume its mature characteristics but well worth the wait. Reasonably pest resistant.

Distinguishing Features: The leaf edge sometimes furls upward revealing the distinctly thickly powdered white underside.

Similar: *H.* 'Totally Twisted'.

Hosta 'Deane's Dream' (R. Solberg 2000)

MEDIUM

Origin: ★*H.* 'Blue Arrow' × ★*H.* 'Sea Fire'.

Description: An upright mound 28 in. wide × 16 in. high (70 × 40 cm). Leaf blade 9 × 4 in. (23 × 10 cm), thick, aquamarine to turquoise, edge slightly rippled, leaf folded, widely oval with a graceful cuspidate tip and tapered to heart-shaped open to pinched lobes. Petiole narrow, bright purple. Flower tubular, pale lavender, on an upright, glaucous blue, 22- to 26-in. (55- to 65-cm) scape in late summer; seedpods green, fertile.

Cultivation Notes: Performs well in warmer climates, but needs light to full shade all day. Moderate growth rate. Grow at eye level to feature the attractive mauve petioles, which are unusual in a hosta with this leaf color.

Distinguishing Features: The combination of attractive turquoise leaves with bright purple petioles that are more intensely purple-dotted than those of *H.* 'Venetian Blue'.

Similar: ★*H.* 'Blue Arrow'; *H.* 'Hadspen Heron'; ★*H.* 'Pineapple Poll'.

Hosta 'Devon Giant' (A. & R. Bowden N/R)

VERY LARGE

Origin: *H.* 'Hadspen Blue' hybrid.

Description: A dense mound 70 in. wide × 36 in. high (175 × 90 cm). Leaf blade 18¾ × 18 in. (47 × 45 cm), thick, dark blue-green, seersuckered and puckered toward the midrib, edge almost flat to slightly undulate, leaf almost round with a mucronate tip and deeply heart-shaped overlapping lobes. Petiole stout, green. Flower bell-shaped, near white to lavender, on an upright, leafy, green, 38-in. (95-cm) scape from mid- to high summer; fertile.

Cultivation Notes: Site in light to moderate shade. Slow to establish but eventually will become one of the largest hostas. Pest resistant. A superb background specimen or for a woodland garden.

Similar: *H.* 'Viking Ship' has slightly serrated leaves and a more rugose leaf surface.

Hosta 'Dusty Waters' (Naylor Creek Nursery N/R)

MEDIUM

Origin: Sport of *H.* 'Lakeside Cupcake'.

Description: An open mound 16 in. wide × 10 in. high (40 × 25 cm). Leaf blade 5½ × 5 in. (14 × 13 cm), thick, glaucous to matt, blue-green, dimpled to seersuckered, veins widely spaced, edge almost

Hosta 'Deane's Dream'

Hosta 'Devon Giant'

Hosta 'Dusty Waters', a juvenile plant in which the cupping and seersuckering have not yet developed

Hosta 'Elvis Lives'

Hosta 'Gentle Giant'

flat, leaf noticeably cupped, almost round with a mucronate tip and heart-shaped open lobes. Petiole flattish, blue-green. Flower funnel-shaped, near-white, on an upright, bare, blue-green, 12-in. (30-cm) scape in midsummer; fertility unknown.

Cultivation Notes. Site in moderate to full shade to preserve the blueness of the leaf. Best not grown under trees where detritus could fall into and spoil the deeply cupped leaves. Moderate growth rate. Pest resistant. Lovely planted next to its most attractively variegated parent.

Distinguishing Features: The deep cupping on the leaves.

Similar: ★*H.* 'Deep Blue Sea' is slightly larger with leaves even more deeply cupped.

Hosta 'Elvis Lives' (T. Avent 1995)

MEDIUM

Origin: *H.* 'Peter Pan' × ★*H.* 'Green Fountain'.

Description: A moderately dense mound 36 in. wide × 18 in. high (90 × 45 cm). Leaf blade 11 × 4½ in. (28 × 11 cm), of good substance, rich powdery blue, smooth, veins widely spaced, edges distinctly rippled and twisted, leaf arching toward the tip, lanceolate to oval with a cuspidate tip and rounded open lobes. Petiole blue-green. Flower long, tubular, lavender, on an upright, bare, light green, 22-in. (55-cm) scape from early to midsummer; fertile.

Cultivation Notes: Site in dappled to light shade. Blue suedelike upper surface of the leaf is apparent for longer in cooler climates. A moderate increaser.

Similar: *H.* 'Venetian Blue'; ★*H.* 'Winfield Blue' has bluer leaves for longer in the season.

Hosta 'Gentle Giant' (P. Black 2005)

VERY LARGE

Origin: *H. sieboldiana* 'Frances Williams' × unknown seedling.

Description: A huge, upright mound 68 in. wide × 45½ in. high (170 × 114 cm). Leaf blade 13 × 12 in. (33 × 30 cm), thick, intensely glaucous blue-green, seersuckered to puckered, prominent veins widely spaced, edge flat, leaf deeply cupped to folded, widely ovate to nearly round with overlapping lobes. Petiole very deeply channeled, pale frosted green. Flower tubular, lavender, on an oblique to upright, leafy, frosted green, 49- to 58-in. (122- to 147-cm) scape in midsummer; very fertile.

Cultivation Notes: Tolerates sun in cooler climates although strong sunlight melts the wax off the leaves angled directly at its rays turning them green; leaves in shade are not affected and hold their blue color through the summer. Best not planted under trees as falling debris will collect in the deeply cupped leaves. Easily exceeds its registered dimensions and one of the largest hostas with blue leaves. Increases rapidly. Pest resistant.

Distinguishing Features: The deep cupping of the leaves allows the thickly coated white undersides to be easily visible. The leafy bracts are small.

Similar: *H. nigrescens* is smaller and has grayer leaves.

Hosta 'H. D. Thoreau' (Walden-West 1999)
VERY LARGE

Origin: *H.* 'Sagae' × *H. hypoleuca*.

Description: A monumentally large, upright mound 84 in. wide × 38 in. high (210 × 95 cm). Leaf blade 18 × 15 in. (45 × 38 cm), very thick, leathery, intense blue-green with a silvery cast, dimpled, veins widely spaced, edge slightly rippled, leaf nearly convex, nearly round with a mucronate tip and heart-shaped overlapping lobes. Petiole sturdy, light green-blue. Flower long, bell-shaped, light lavender, on an upright, bare, glaucous green, 46½-in. (117-cm) scape from high to late summer; fertile.

Cultivation Notes: Site in light to medium shade.

Slow to increase. Pest resistant. Thought to be tetraploid. An outstanding hosta which should be better known.

Distinguishing Features: Leaves are almost rubbery. Very large, semi-double flowers have a glaucous bloom.

Hosta 'High Tide' (H. Hansen 2005)
SMALL–MEDIUM

Origin: *H. longipes* 'Latifolia' × *H.* 'Dorset Blue'.

Description: An open, overlapping mound 38 in. wide × 13 in. high (95 × 33 cm). Leaf blade 7 × 6 in. (18 × 15 cm), of good substance, glaucous blue-green, prominently veined, edge gently rippled, leaf broadly ovate with a cuspidate tip and heart-shaped open to pinched lobes. Petiole light blue-green, deeply grooved. Flower bell-shaped, lavender, on an upright, glaucous lavender, 16- to 21-in. (40- to 53-cm) scape from late summer to early autumn; fertility unknown.

Cultivation Notes: Site in good light to moderate shade. Slow to increase. Pest resistant. Grow at the front of a border or as an edging plant if there is plenty of space.

Distinguishing Features: Differs from its *H.* 'Dorset Blue' parent in having less cupped, smoother leaves with a very pronounced tip.

Hosta 'H. D. Thoreau'

Hosta 'High Tide'

Hosta 'Incredible Hunk' (E. Elslager 1998)

VERY LARGE

Origin: Unknown.

Description: An upright mound 58 in. wide × 35 in. high (147 × 88 cm). Leaf blade 16 × 14 in. (40 × 35 cm), very thick, rich blue-green, intensely seersuckered to puckered, edge distinctly rippled, leaf deeply cupped, almost round with a mucronate tip and heart-shaped overlapping lobes. Petiole thick, glaucous green. Flower tubular, near white with lavender stripes, on an upright, leafy, 38-in. (95-cm) scape in high summer; fertile.

Cultivation Notes: Site in light shade to full shade all day. Pest resistant.

Distinguishing Features: Leaf noticeably cupped. Underside of the leaf has a thick, white pruinose coating.

Hosta 'Kingfisher' (E. Smith & BHHS 1988)

MEDIUM

Origin: *H. 'Tardiflora' × *H. sieboldiana 'Elegans Alba'.

Description: An open mound 30 in. wide × 12¾ in. high (75 × 32 cm). Leaf blade 7 × 3½ in. (18 × 9 cm), thick, dark gray-blue becoming dark green, dimpled, edge widely undulate, leaf folded to slightly cupped, widely oval with a cuspidate tip and heart-shaped open lobes. Petiole dark purple-gray. Flower funnel-shaped, pale lavender, on an upright, bare, glaucous green, 14-in. (35-cm) scape in late summer to autumn; fertile.

Cultivation Notes: Keep out of direct sunlight to retain the unusual glaucous dark blue-green for as long as possible. Prized for its late-blooming flowers.

Distinguishing Feature: Distinct from other hostas in the Tardiana Group in that it dramatically changes color from dark blue-gray to very dark green early in the season.

Hosta 'Lakeport Blue' (C. Tompkins 1984)

LARGE

Origin: *H. sieboldiana* 'Elegans' hybrid.

Description: An upright mound 64 in. wide × 27 in. high (160 × 68 cm). Leaf blade 16 × 14 in. (40 × 35 cm), thick, intense blue-green, seersuckered, edge

Hosta 'Kingfisher'

Hosta 'Incredible Hunk'

Hosta 'Lakeport Blue'

almost flat, leaf deeply cupped, widely oval to nearly round with a mucronate tip and heart-shaped overlapping lobes. Petiole stout, light blue-green. Flower bell-shaped, white, in a dense raceme, on an upright, bare, glaucous mauve-gray, 36-in. (90-cm) scape in late summer; fertile.

Cultivation Notes: Site in light to full shade. Performs well in hot, humid climates, the good blue-colored leaves holding far into summer. Pest resistant. A classic hosta.

Similar: *H.* 'Blue Ox', a seedling of *H.* 'Lakeport Blue', has rounder, grayer leaves.

Hosta **'Lakeside Blue Cherub'** (M. Chastain 1991)

SMALL

Origin: Sport of *H.* 'Honey Moon'.

Description: A neat, compact mound 36 in. wide × 6½ in. high (90 × 16 cm). Leaf blade 3½ × 2½ in. (9 ×

6 cm), thick, leathery, pale blue-green, dimpled, veins closely ribbed, edge slightly undulate, leaf folded, widely oval to round with a mucronate tip and heart-shaped pinched lobes. Petiole light green. Flower funnel-shaped, lavender, on an upright, leafy, blue-green, 26-in. (65-cm) scape from mid- to high summer; fertile.

Cultivation Notes: Turquoise-hued leaves retain their attractive color in fairly low light. Vigorous. An excellent edging hosta.

Hosta **'Lederhosen'** (H. Benedict N/R)

MEDIUM

Origin: Unknown.

Description: A flattish, horizontally poised mound 24 in. wide × 12 in. high (60 × 30 cm). Leaf blade 7½ × 5 in. (19 × 13 cm), thick, rubbery, matt to shiny, rich blue-green, smooth, veins widely spaced, edge

Hosta 'Lakeside Blue Cherub'

deeply undulate, leaf ovate with a recurved and elongated cuspidate tip and open lobes. Petiole near horizontal, blue-green. Flower funnel-shaped, fragrant, white, opening from a very pale lavender bud, on an upright, leafy, green, 15-in. (38-cm) scape in late summer; fertility unknown.

Cultivation Notes: Site in shade in the hottest climates or in some morning sun in cooler gardens to promote maximum growth. The leaves turn midgreen in bright light. Vigorous.

Distinguishing Features: The tough, leathery leaves have a fancied resemblance to the German britches known as "lederhosen."

Similar: *H.* 'Bob Deane'.

Hosta 'Metallica' (W. & E. Lachman 1991)

MEDIUM

Origin: *H.* 'Beatrice' hybrid × ★*H.* 'Blue Moon'.

Description: A dense mound 21 in. wide × 16 in. high (53 × 40 cm). Leaf blade 7½ × 4 in. (19 × 10 cm), of average to good substance, dark blue-green turning shiny dark green by high summer, slightly dimpled, veins closely ribbed, edge rippled, leaf slightly twisted, folded, widely oval with a cuspidate tip and heart-shaped pinched to overlapping lobes. Petiole light blue-green. Flower widely funnel-shaped, rich lavender, on an upright, leafy, blue-green, 25- to 30-in. (63- to 75-cm) scape in high summer; fertility unknown.

Cultivation Notes: Easily exceeds its registered dimensions.

Similar: *H.* 'Lakeside Old Smoky' has thicker leaves; *H.* 'Neptune' has brighter blue-green leaves.

Hosta 'Millennium' (J. & J. Wilkins 1995)

VERY LARGE

Origin: *H.* 'Herb Benedict' × ★*H.* 'Sagae'.

Description: An upright, open mound 54 in. wide × 36 in. high (135 × 90 cm). Leaf blade 17 × 14 in. (43 × 35 cm), thick, intense blue-green turning green, seersuckered, puckered, and crimped, prominently veined, edge slightly undulate, leaf shallowly cupped or convex, widely oval to nearly round with a mucronate tip and heart-shaped pinched to overlapping lobes. Petiole stout, light green, appearing to

Hosta 'Lederhosen'

Hosta 'Metallica'

Hosta 'Millennium'

pierce the blade. Flower long, tubular, white, on a thick, upright, bare, 45- to 50-in. (113- to 126-cm) scape in high summer; fertile.

Cultivation Notes: Site in cool, moist shade all day. Slow to increase. Pest resistant.

Similar: *H. 'Metallic Sheen' is slightly smaller and its leaves are not as blue.

Hosta 'Moongate Flying Saucer' (C. Issacs/R. Solberg 1996)

SMALL–MEDIUM

Origin: *H.* 'Serendipity' × *H.* 'Blue Blazes'.

Description: An open mound 22 in. wide × 11 in. high (55 × 28 cm). Leaf blade 5 × 3 in. (13 × 8 cm), thick, blue-green turning dark green, seersuckered, edge almost flat, leaf folded to cupped, oval with a cuspidate tip and heart-shaped to round open lobes. Petiole light green, appearing to pierce the blade. Flower long, funnel-shaped, pale lavender, on an upright, bare, glaucous light green, 22-in. (55-cm) scape in early summer; fertile.

Cultivation Notes: Site in good light to light shade to retain the blue color for as long as possible. A moderate increaser.

Hosta 'Mr. Big' (Walden-West N/R)

VERY LARGE

Origin: *H. montana* × *H. sieboldiana* 'Elegans'.

Description: An open, layered, wide-spreading mound. 80 in. wide × 40 in. high (200 × 100 cm).

Leaf blade 22 × 20 in. (55 × 50 cm), up to 28 × 24 in. (70 × 60 cm), very thick, light blue-green, pale glaucous blue below, making the upper surface appear bluer, puckered, crumpled, and pleated when mature, veins widely spaced, edge nearly flat, convex, widely oval to nearly round with a mucronate tip and heart-shaped overlapping lobes. Petiole stout, glaucous dark green. Flower funnel-shaped, near white, on an upright, leafy, glaucous green, 45-in. (113-cm) scape in midsummer; fertility not known.

Cultivation Notes: The whole leaf becomes bluer with maturity. Very slow. Pest resistant.

Distinguishing Features: Uneven shirring along the veins is apparent in some leaves when mature. Among the largest hostas ever introduced, probably rivaling *H.* 'Sum and Substance'.

Hosta 'Party Favor' (R. Solberg 2000)

MEDIUM

Origin: *H.* 'Donahue Piecrust' × *H.* 'Akebono'.

Description: A flattish mound 28 in. wide × 14 in. high (70 × 35 cm). Leaf blade 6 × 3 in. (15 × 8 cm), of good substance, blue-green, conspicuous veins ribbed, edge serrated, evenly and closely rippled, leaf undulate, flat to slightly arching, oval with a cuspidate tip and heart-shaped pinched lobes. Petiole oblique, light green, appearing to pierce the blade. Flower funnel-shaped, lavender, on an upright, leafy, blackish, 26-in. (65-cm) scape in midsummer; seedpods green, fertile.

Cultivation Notes: Increases rapidly.

Hosta 'Moongate Flying Saucer'

Hosta 'Mr. Big'

Distinguishing Features: Has the piecrust ruffled edges of both parents and blackish scapes that gradually turn blue-green.

Similar: *H.* 'Neptune', ★*H.* 'Restless Sea'.

Hosta 'Powder Blue' (H. Sugita/P. Ruh 1998)

LARGE

Origin: Unknown.

Description: An overlapping mound 38 in. wide × 27 in. high (95 × 68 cm). Leaf blade 14 × 11 in. (35 × 28 cm), thick, emerging chartreuse becoming light powder blue, powdery above and heavily glaucous below, deeply and closely seersuckered, edge slightly undulate, leaf arching, broadly oval with a vestigial tip and heart-shaped pinched to folded lobes. Petiole stout, light blue turning light green. Flower bell-shaped, pale lavender, on an upright, leafy, 34-in. (85-cm) scape from early to midsummer; fertile.

Cultivation Notes: Tolerates hot, humid conditions and excessive rainfall but best in cooler gardens sited in moderate shade to maintain the almost unearthly leaf coloring and surface texture. Grow with lacy ferns and other contrasting dark green foliage or as a

Hosta 'Party Favor'

Hosta 'Powder Blue'

Hosta 'Reptilian'

specimen sited where the powdered leaves with their suedelike finish will be best appreciated.

Distinguishing Features: The very heavily powdered leaf surface which gradually diminishes after flowering. The attractive flower trusses are noticeable for their length.

Hosta 'Reptilian' (R. Sawyer N/R)

MEDIUM

Origin: Unknown.

Description: Mound 30 in. wide × 16 in. tall (75 × 40 cm). Leaves 8 × 4 in., thick, grayish blue-green, puckered and cupped, heart-shaped with a twisted and pointed tip, edge wavy and piecrusted. Petiole red. Flower pale lavender, on a reddish-purple-spotted scape in summer.

Cultivation Notes: Site in part to full shade. Pest resistant.

Hosta 'Rhapsody in Blue' (R. Benedict/J. & J. Wilkins 1995)

MEDIUM

Origin: *H. rupifraga* hybrid.

Description: An open mound 30 in. wide × 14 in. high (75 × 35 cm). Leaf blade 7½ × 7 in. (19 × 18 cm), thick, leathery, intense dark blue-green, smooth, widely spaced veins, edge undulate, nearly round with an exaggeratedly mucronate tip and heart-shaped open lobes. Petiole flattish, light green. Flower flared, white-striped rich mauve, surrounded by purple-tinted glossy, green bracts, on a thick, leafy, upright or oblique, purple-tinted, 22-in. (55-cm) scape from late summer to early autumn; fertile.

Cultivation Notes: Site in light shade to full shade to retain the exquisite blue-green leaf color for as long as possible, although during hot summers the leaves will soon turn shiny dark green.

Similar: *H.* 'Maruba Iwa'; *H.* 'Moonlight Sonata' is larger and has slightly fragrant, deep violet flowers; ★*H. rupifraga*.

Hosta 'Sea Lotus Leaf' (M. Seaver 1985)

MEDIUM–LARGE

Origin: *H.* 'Wagon Wheels' hybrid.

Description: A stiff, oblique to upright, horizontally poised mound 60 in. wide × 25 in. high (150 × 63 cm). Leaf blade 9 × 9 in. (23 × 23 cm), very thick, blue-tinted green turning green, evenly seersuckered, edge flat, leaf shallowly cupped, round with a vestigial tip and heart-shaped open to pinched lobes. Petiole stout, shallow, light green. Flower narrowly funnel-shaped, pale lavender, on a leaning, leafy, light green, 24-in. (60-cm) scape in late summer; very fertile.

Cultivation Notes: Site in dappled to full shade. Slow to increase at first, vigorous when established. Pest resistant. A useful parent for cupped leaf seedlings.

Similar: ★*H.* 'Blue Umbrellas'; *H.* 'Roundabout'.

Hosta 'Rhapsody in Blue', a juvenile plant.

Hosta 'Sea Lotus Leaf'

Hosta 'Silvery Slugproof'

Hosta 'Tutu'

Hosta 'Twilight Time'

Hosta 'Silvery Slugproof' (D. Grenfell 1996)

MEDIUM

Origin:★*H.* 'Tardiflora' × ★*H. sieboldiana* 'Elegans Alba'.

Description: A dense mound 40 in. wide × 16 in. high (100 × 40 cm). Leaf blade 7 × 5 in. (18 × 13 cm), thick, silvery blue-green, smooth, edge undulate, leaf flat to slightly folded, widely oval with an acute tip and heart-shaped pinched lobes. Petiole gray-green with red dots. Flower bell-shaped, pale lavender, on an upright, sometimes branched, leafy, gray-green, 22-in. (55-cm) scape in high summer; fertile.

Cultivation Notes: Tolerates some morning sun in cooler climates, otherwise light to moderate shade. Moderate growth rate. Very pest resistant.

Hosta 'Tutu' (K. Vaughn N/R)

LARGE

Origin: ★*H.* 'Donahue Piecrust' × ★*H. pycnophylla*.

Description: An open, tiered mound 46 in. wide × 16 in. high (116 × 40 cm). Leaf blade 9 × 7 in. (23 × 18 cm), thick, dark blue-green, dimpled and puckered, distinct veins widely spaced, edge ruffled, leaf flat, slightly folded to cupped, oval with a cuspidate tip and heart-shaped overlapping lobes. Petiole narrow, light green with purple dots, appearing to pierce the blade. Flower funnel-shaped, lavender, on an oblique, glaucous green, 43-in. (108-cm) scape in late summer; fertile.

Cultivation Notes: Site in light shade to retain the blue-toned leaf color. Use as a specimen or in a woodland setting with *Asplenium scolopendrium*, whose strap-shaped leaves have a contrasting shape but echo the ruffled edges of the hosta.

Distinguishing Features: Evenly piecrusted margins of the leaves are intensely glaucous on the undersides. Scapes are weighed down by the dense racemes.

Similar: *H.* 'Blue Piecrust'.

Hosta 'Twilight Time' (G. Johnson 2004)

MEDIUM

Origin: *H.* 'Spritzer' seedling.

Description: A flattish mound 38 in. wide × 12 in. high (95 × 30 cm). Leaf blade 8 × 4 in. (20 × 10 cm), of average substance, blue-green, matt above and glaucous below, smooth, veins deeply impressed, edge extravagantly rippled, leaf twisted, lanceolate with an extended acute tip and tapered open lobes. Petiole narrow, light blue-green. Flower funnel-shaped, pale lavender, on an almost upright, leafy, pale green, 18- to 26-in. (45- to 65-cm) scape from late summer to early autumn; seedpods green, fertile.

Cultivation Notes: Site in light to moderate shade. Increases rapidly. Lovely near rocks or in gravel. Grow with heart-shaped variegated hostas for a contrast.

Distinguishing Features: The leaves become bluer as the summer progresses.

Similar: *H.* 'Rhythm and Blues' is smaller.

Hosta 'War Party' (G. Goodwin 2000)

LARGE

Origin: Unknown.

Description: An upright, vase-shaped mound 36 in. wide × 30 in. high (90 × 75 cm). Leaf blade 14 × 7 in. (35 × 18 cm), of heavy substance, rich glaucous

blue-green, seersuckered, veins widely spaced, edge distinctively rippled, leaf cupped, elongate to cuneate with a cuspidate tip and flat to heart-shaped open to pinched lobes. Petiole blue-green. Flower funnel-shaped, pale lavender-striped near white, on an upright, bare, glaucous blue-green 30- to 41-in. (75- to 102-cm) scape in midsummer; seedpods blue-green, fertile.

Cultivation Notes: Site in good light to moderate shade for best effect. Holds its blue leaf color well.

Distinguishing Features: The intensely rippled leaves on a large blue-green hosta.

Hosta 'Yankee Blue' (R. Balitewicz 1999)

LARGE

Origin: *H.* 'Blue Arrow' × *H.* 'Elatior'.

Description: A dome-shaped mound 56 in. wide × 20 in. high (140 × 50 cm). Leaf blade 10 × 6 in. (25 × 15 cm), of good substance, rich blue-green, closely

Hosta 'War Party'

veined, edge flat with occasional kinks, leaf slightly arching, widely lanceolate to oval with an acute tip and tapered open lobes. Petiole light blue-green. Flower long, tubular, near white, on an upright, leafy, green, 20- to 24-in. (50- to 60-cm) scape from mid- to high summer; seedpods green, fertile.

Cultivation Notes: Site in light to moderate shade all day. A vigorous, rapid increaser for a blue-leaved hosta.

Similar: *H.* 'Biddy's Blue' also has long leaves but they are of a more turquoise blue and with rippled edges.

Hosta 'Yankee Blue'

Hosta 'Mikawa-no-Yuki'

GRAY-GREEN LEAVES

NLIKE THE BLUE-GRAY HOSTAS, which have a thick glaucous bloom on their leaves, hostas in this category have a thinner surface bloom and thus they appear to have greener leaves. In some hostas, the bloom disappears rapidly, even on plants growing in shade, and their distinctive grayness gives way to green. There are, however, some outstandingly good hostas with gray-green leaves, and they look their best when grown in naturalistic plantings or on the waterside.

Hosta 'Big John' (C. Owens 1986)

VERY LARGE

Origin: *H. sieboldiana* 'Mira' hybrid.

Description: A dense, overlapping mound 50 in. wide × 26 in. high (126 × 65 cm). Leaf blade 18 × 15 in. (45 × 38 cm), thick, dark bluish green soon becoming dark green, dimpled, edge flat to slightly

Hosta 'Big John'

kinked, leaf arching, widely oval with a mucronate tip and heart-shaped overlapping lobes. Petiole stout, glaucous light green. Flower bell-shaped, white-striped pale lavender, in a dense cluster, on an upright, bare, glaucous green, 32-in. (80-cm) scape, level with or just above the leaf mound, from mid- to late summer; fertile.

Cultivation Notes: Rapidly exceeds its registered dimensions to become one of the largest hostas both in clump and individual leaf size.

Distinguishing Features: Most of the glaucous bloom on the upper leaf surface is toward the midrib. The underside of the leaf is gray-green, and the general effect of the leaves is gray-green.

Hosta 'Dragon Fire' (W. Lefever/R. Solberg 2005)

LARGE

Origin: *H.* 'Riptide' seedling.

Description: An open mound 48 in. wide × 26 in. high (120 × 65 cm). Leaf blade 11½ × 10 in. (29 × 25 cm), of good substance, glaucous blue-influenced gray-green, smooth, prominent veins widely spaced, edge gently rippled, leaf lightly folded when young, convex when mature, broadly ovate with a twisted and recurved cuspidate tip and heart-shaped open to pinched lobes. Petiole purple with a white wax overlay. Flower funnel-shaped, recurved, pale lavender, on an upright, leafy, purple-gray, 38- to 42-in. (95- to 105-cm) scape from high to late summer; fertility unknown.

Cultivation Notes: Site in moderate to full shade to preserve the waxy leaf surface. Grow at eye level to expose the purple petioles which contrast well with the bluish leaves. Moderate growth rate.

Distinguishing Features: Leaves larger and slightly bluer than its parent.

Hosta 'Eric Smith' (E. Smith & J. Archibald 1987)

SMALL—MEDIUM

Origin: An Eric Smith seedling, probably not a *H.* 'Tardiana' hybrid, although given a number.

Description: A dense mound 36 in. wide × 16 in. high (90 × 40 cm). Leaf blade 5½ × 4½ in. (14 × 11 cm), of good substance, dark gray-green, slight dimpling, edge slightly undulate, leaf heart-shaped with a mucronate tip and pinched lobes. Petiole light green. Flower bell-shaped, rich lavender, in a dense raceme, on an upright, leafy, light green, 30-in. (75-cm) scape in high season; fertile.

Cultivation Notes: Site in good light or moderate shade. Vigorous.

Distinguishing Features: Probably the greenest leaved of the numbered Tardiana Group hostas, now thought to have ★*H. nakaiana* and not ★*H. sieboldiana* 'Elegans' as a parent.

Hosta 'Fortunei Hyacinthina' (N. Hylander & AHS 1987) ♀

MEDIUM—LARGE

Origin: Unknown but thought to have evolved in a European garden in the mid-nineteenth century.

Description: A dense mound 45 in. wide × 20 in. high (113 × 50 cm). Leaf blade 8½ × 6½ in. (21 × 16 cm), of good substance, dark gray-green turning green, thickly glaucous below, dimpled, edge slightly undulate with a distinct hyaline line, leaf slightly cupped, widely oval with a cuspidate tip and heart-shaped pinched to overlapping lobes. Petiole dark green. Flower funnel-shaped, pinkish lavender, opening from a rich violet bud, in a dense raceme, on an upright, leafy, glaucous green, 28-in. (70-cm) scape, purple-tinted toward the raceme, in high summer; fertility poor.

Cultivation Notes: Tolerates morning sun, which enhances the already excellent flowers but causes the

Hosta 'Dragon Fire'

Hosta 'Eric Smith'

Hosta 'Fortunei Hyacinthina'

slight blueness in the leaves to disappear. Adaptable. A vigorous, rapid increaser. Is currently grown less for its garden value than its propensity to throw sports, the classic being ★*H.* 'Gold Standard', the parent of a multitude of other sports. Only a few of the best sports are listed here.

Distinguishing Features: Flowers that resemble hyacinth and are among the best in the genus.

Similar: *H.* 'Fortunei Rugosa' has grayer, more deeply seersuckered leaves.

Sports: *H.* 'Arctic Rim' (creamy white margin); ★*H.* 'Gold Standard' (yellow center turning green); *H.* 'Heliarc' (khaki-gold margin); *H.* 'Julia' (creamy white margin); *H.* 'Mountain Green' (creamy yellow margin); *H.* 'Phyllis Campbell' (yellow center turning green); ★*H.* 'Sharmon' (yellow center turning green); *H.* 'Sheila West' (yellow center turning green); *H.* 'Thelma M. Pierson' (bright yellow leaves).

Hosta 'Goblin' (R. Lydell N/R)

MEDIUM

Origin: *H.* 'Halcyon' hybrid.

Description: A dense mound 36 in. wide × 14 in. high (90 × 35 cm). Leaf blade 7 × 4½ in. (18 × 11 cm), thick, gray-green, dimpled, edge slightly rippled, leaf folded, wedge-shaped to widely oval with a cuspidate tip and tapered open lobes. Petiole narrow, graygreen. Flower funnel-shaped, pale lavender, on a thin, upright, leafy, green, 20- to 22-in. (50- to 55-cm) scape from early to midsummer; fertile.

Cultivation Notes: Site in some morning sun in cooler climates. A vigorous, good performer.

Distinguishing Features: Scapes are leaning at the tips.

Hosta 'Mikawa-no-Yuki' (H. Sugita/P. Ruh 1997)

MEDIUM

Origin: ★*H. kikutii* (white-backed leaves) × ★*H. longipes* (white-backed leaves). Also known as *H.* 'Ozaki Special'.

Description: A graceful, cascading mound 30 in. wide × 14 in. high (75 × 35 cm). Leaf blade 8½ × 3 in. (21 × 8 cm), of good substance, rich gray-green, matt to satiny above and thickly glaucous below, prominent veins ribbed, edge slightly undulate, leaf arching, widely lanceolate to oblong with a slightly

recurved acuminate tip and rounded open to pinched lobes. Petiole glaucous gray-green, red speckled at the base. Flower bell-shaped, near-white, opening from a pale lavender bud, on an oblique, leafy, red-speckled gray-green 14- to 16-in. (35- to 40-cm) scape in late summer; fertile.

Cultivation Notes: Site in moderate shade. Increases rapidly. Grow in a container on a pedestal, preferably in a border, so that the undersides of the leaves can be fully appreciated.

Hosta 'Goblin'

Hosta 'Mikawa-no-Yuki'

Distinguishing Features: The back of the petiole is covered in white indumentum.

Similar: *H. kikutii* f. *leuconota* has a narrower leaf; *H.* 'Awakening Angel', a hybrid, has blue spear-shaped leaves.

Hosta 'Phantom' (R. Solberg/J. & J. Wilkins 1995)

MEDIUM

Origin: *H.* 'Riptide' hybrid.

Description: A moderately dense mound 33 in. wide × 18 in. high (83 × 45 cm). Leaf blade 10 × 7½ in. (25 × 19 cm), of good substance, dark gray-green above, glaucous light green below, slight dimpling when mature, veins ribbed, edge rippled to piecrusted, leaf arching, oval with a cuspidate tip and round to heart-shaped open to pinched lobes. Petiole wide, red-dotted and -backed. Flower superb, near bell-shaped, lavender, opening from a rich violet bud, on an oblique to upright, leafy, glaucous mauve-purple, 32-in. (80-cm) scape in late summer; sterile.

Cultivation Notes: Site in good light to dappled shade. Best grown at eye level to appreciate its virtues.

Distinguishing Features: Ghostly, gray-coated leaves, intensely red-dotted and -backed petioles, and thickly glaucous scapes make this an extremely garden-worthy hosta.

Similar: ★*H. pycnophylla* has less obviously red-dotted petioles and scapes.

Hosta 'Pineapple Poll' (E. Smith & BHHS 1988)

MEDIUM

Origin: ★*H. sieboldiana* 'Elegans' × ★*H.* 'Lancifolia'.

Description: An open mound 45 in. wide × 18 in. high (113 × 45 cm). Leaf blade 9 × 3½ in. (23 × 9 cm), thick, green with a gray cast, smooth, edge conspicuously rippled, leaf slightly twisted, upward- and outward-pointing, widely lanceolate with an acute tip and tapered open lobes. Petiole flattish, light green.

Hosta 'Phantom'

Flower funnel-shaped, purple-striped near white, on an upright, leafy, heavily glaucous green, 34-in. (85-cm) scape in late summer; fertile.

Cultivation Notes: Site in light shade to full shade. Increases rapidly.

Distinguishing Features: Mound of leaves resembles the tuft of leaves at the top of a pineapple.

Similar: ★*H.* 'Blue Arrow'; *H.* 'Hadspen Heron'.

Hosta 'Prince of Wales' (D. Grenfell 2003)

VERY LARGE

Origin: ★*H. sieboldiana* × ★*H. montana*.

Description: A stately, dense mound 71 in. wide × 36 in. high (178 × 90 cm). Leaf blade 20 × 14 in. (50 × 35 cm), thick, silvery gray-green with a slight blue cast in early season, seersuckered, strongly veined, edge slightly undulate, leaf slightly arching, elliptic to oval with a cuspidate tip and heart-shaped overlapping lobes. Petiole oblique, stout, grayish white.

Flower funnel-shaped, lavender-gray, in a heavy truss, on an upright to leaning, swan-necked, leafy, glaucous gray-green, 35-in. (88-cm) scape in midsummer; seedpods gray-brown, fertile.

Cultivation Notes: Site in some morning sun in cooler climates, otherwise light to moderate shade.

Hosta 'Pineapple Poll'

Hosta 'Prince of Wales'

Moderate growth rate. Grow with purple-leaved *Heuchera* 'Purple Petticoats' at its feet for an outstanding contrast of foliage color.

Distinguishing Features: Long leaf blade and impressive flower scape weighed down by the long, heavy raceme.

Hosta 'Quilted Hearts' (M. Soules 1989)

LARGE

Origin: *H. sieboldiana* hybrid.

Description: A dense mound 46 in. wide × 20 in. high (116 × 50 cm). Leaf blade 11 × 9½ in. (28 × 24 cm), very thick, matt dark gray-green above, with a slight blue cast early in the season, thickly glaucous pale green below, intensely seersuckered, edge almost flat, leaf slightly convex, nearly round with a mucronate tip and heart-shaped overlapping lobes. Petiole stout, light green, appearing to pierce the blade. Flower funnel-shaped, pink-tinted white, on an upright, leafy, glaucous light green, 20-in. (50-cm) scape in late summer; fertile.

Cultivation Notes: Site in light to moderate shade all day. Slow to establish but eventually makes an impressive clump. Pest resistant.

Distinguishing Features: Intensely seersuckered leaves are shirred along the veins, giving a pebbled effect.

Similar: *H.* 'Quilted Skies' has leaves that are longer, narrower, and blue-gray, and flowers that are bell-shaped.

Hosta 'Red October' (R. Herold N/R)

SMALL–MEDIUM

Origin: Unknown.

Description: An upright, open mound 28 in. wide × 10 in. high (70 × 25 cm). Leaf blade 8½ × 3½ in.

Hosta 'Quilted Hearts'

(21 × 9 cm), thick, dark gray-green, smooth, veins closely ribbed, edge rippled to kinked, leaf arching, widely lanceolate with an acute tip and tapered open lobes. Petiole gray-green, streaked and speckled with red, the speckling extending 1 in. (2.5 cm) into the leaf blade. Flower funnel-shaped, lavender, in a dense raceme, on an upright or slightly oblique, leafy, reddish, 24-in. (60-cm) scape in late autumn; fertility unknown.

Cultivation Notes: Among the best of the newer introductions with red petioles and scapes.

Distinguishing Features: Leaf underside covered in a thick, white coating.

Similar: *H.* 'Paradise Red Delight' has broader leaves; *H.* 'Red Dragon', a superb new introduction, has intense red petioles, purple scapes, and purple flowers.

Hosta 'Restless Sea' (H. Hansen 2006)

SMALL–MEDIUM

Origin: *H.* 'Salute' seedling.

Description: An upright mound 32 in. wide × 17 in. high (80 × 43 cm). Leaf blade 7½ × 4 in. (19 × 10 cm), of good substance, blue-gray to blue-green, matt above and glaucous below, prominently veined, edge serrated and undulate, leaf folded, cuneate with an elongated twisted tip and tapered folded lobes. Petiole gray-green with red dots. Flower bell-shaped, lavender, with a lavender-striped near-white interior, on an upright, leafy, gray-green 18- to 24-in. (45- to

60-cm) scape from late summer to early autumn; seedpods green, fertile.

Cultivation Notes: Site in good light to moderate shade, but even so the glaucous gray leaf surface will disappear over the summer. Moderate growth rate. Pest resistant. Grow with hostas and other plain-leaved plants to emphasize the "restlessness" of the leaves.

Hosta 'Red October', leaves

Hosta 'Red October', petioles

Hosta 'Restless Sea'

Distinguishing Features: The leaf edges are much more undulate than those of its parent.

Similar: ★*H.* 'Cutting Edge' has narrower leaves; ★*H.* 'Party Favor'.

Hosta 'Snowden'

Hosta 'Snowden' (E. Smith & BHHS 1988)

LARGE–VERY LARGE

Origin: ★*H.* 'Fortunei Albopicta Aurea' × ★*H. sieboldiana* 'Elegans'.

Description: An upright mound 53 in. wide × 32 in. high (132 × 80 cm). Leaf blade 14 × 10 in. (35 × 25 cm), thick, gray-green with a faint blue cast early in the season, dimpled, veins closely ribbed when mature, edge slightly undulate, leaf flat to convex, oval with a cuspidate tip and heart-shaped pinched lobes. Petiole gray-green. Flower widely funnel-shaped, white, on an upright, bare, 4-ft. (1.2-m) scape from mid- to high summer; occasionally sets seed.

Cultivation Notes: Site in good light or moderate shade. Slow to establish but eventually forms a magnificent specimen. Can be grown in a container if profusely watered.

Similar: ★*H.* 'Krossa Regal'; *H. sieboldiana* 'Mira'.

Hosta 'Theo's Blue'

Hosta 'Theo's Blue' (T. Leydens/B. Zonnenfeld N/R)

MEDIUM

Origin: *H. pycnophylla* × blue-leaved seedling.

Description: An open mound 25 in. wide × 14–18 in. high (63 × 35–45 cm). Leaf blade 6 × 5 in. (16 × 13 cm), of good substance, powdery blue–influenced gray-green, glaucous above and thickly glaucous below, dimpled, veins ribbed, edge gently undulate, leaf broadly ovate to rounded with a cuspidate tip and flattish to heart-shaped open to pinched lobes. Petiole long, thin, burgundy-purple. Flower funnel-shaped, purple-striped near-white, on an oblique, red-dotted, glaucous green, 25-in. (63-cm) scape in late summer and autumn; fertility unknown.

Cultivation Notes: Site in moderate to full shade to preserve the powdery coating on the leaf surfaces. Best grown at eye level to appreciate the plant's many qualities, but away from tree canopies to avoid falling detritus from marking the leaves. Moderate growth rate. Ideal for situations where leaves with only a hint of blue are wanted.

Distinguishing Features: Leaf underside is covered with a thick, white coating. Most of the leaf blade undulations occur along the base and the lower half of the leaf.

Hosta 'Great Escape'

Hosta 'Sagae'

9
Hosta Leaves with Variegated Margins

part from selected seedlings, most hostas with variegated margins are natural or tissue-cultured sports of plants already in existence. The hostas described in this category have, or are likely to become, classic or popular hostas in their own right, a prime example being *Hosta sieboldiana* 'Frances Williams'. Less popular or little-known sports are referred back to the hosta from which they sported or mutated. The hostas in this chapter include all those whose central leaf coloring is darker than the margin.

*An asterisk before a name indicates that the plant is fully described elsewhere in this book.

Hosta 'Abba Dabba Do' (T. Avent 1998)

LARGE

Origin: Sport of ★*H*. 'Sun Power'.

Description: An upright, rippled mound 70 in. wide × 24 in. high (175 × 60 cm). Leaf blade 12 × 6 in. (30 × 15 cm), thick, leathery, olive green, narrowly and irregularly margined yellow, matt above and thinly glaucous below, strongly veined, slightly dimpled, edge widely rippled, leaf elliptic with a cuspidate tip and rounded open lobes. Petiole light olive green. Flower: see *H*. 'Sun Power'.

Cultivation Notes: Performs well in sun even in hotter climates. A moderate to good increaser. Pest resistant.

Distinguishing Features: Leaves emerge green but quickly develop the attractive, bright yellow margin.

Sports: *H*. 'Abba Dew' has much wider yellow margins; ★*H*. 'Atlantis' is a tetraploid; *H*. 'Eclipse Power' has green leaves with a narrow white margin; *H*. 'Zippity Do Dah' has green leaves with a creamy margin.

Hosta 'Abby' (P. Ruh 1990)

SMALL

Origin: Sport of ★*H*. 'Gold Drop'.

Description: A ground-hugging, open mound 16½ in. wide × 6½ in. high (42 × 16 cm). Leaf blade 4 × 2½ in.(10 × 6 cm), of good substance, dark green, irregularly margined chartreuse to yellow, smooth,

Hosta 'Abby'

Hosta 'Abba Dabba Do' '

strongly veined, edge shallowly undulate, leaf folded at the lobes, widely oval with a cuspidate tip and heart-shaped open to pinched lobes. Petiole short, narrow, almost imperceptibly outlined in cream. Flower: see *H.* 'Gold Drop'.

Cultivation Notes: Site in light to full shade. Increases rapidly. A superb small hosta. One of the most popular sports of *H.* 'Gold Drop'.

Sports: *H.* 'Amy Elizabeth' has yellow leaves with a green margin.

Hosta 'Abiqua Moonbeam' (Walden-West 1987)

MEDIUM–LARGE

Origin: Sport of ★*H.* 'August Moon'.

Description: A dense mound 32 in. wide × 26 in. high (80 × 65 cm). Leaf blade 7 × 6½ in. (18 × 16 cm), thick, glaucous green, widely and irregularly margined chartreuse turning yellow, dimpled, edge almost flat, leaf widely oval with a cuspidate tip and heart-shaped overlapping lobes. Petiole glaucous light green. Flower: see *H.* 'August Moon'.

Cultivation Notes: Lutescent. Site in morning sun in cooler climates to promote the lutescent habit of the leaves, but the color looks richer when the plant is grown in shade. A moderate to fast increaser.

Distinguishing Features: Leaves emerge yellow, the center gradually turning green.

Similar: *H.* 'August Beauty'; *H.* 'Carolina Moon' is more intensely seersuckered and puckered; *H.* 'Mayan Moon' appears identical.

Sports: ★*H.* 'Gemini Moon'; *H.* 'Velvet Moon' has much thicker, very wide-margined green leaves.

Hosta 'Alex Summers' (V. Santa Lucia 1989)

LARGE–VERY LARGE

Origin: Sport of ★*H.* 'Gold Regal'.

Description: A striking, vase-shaped mound 60 in. wide × 32 in. high (150 × 80 cm). Leaf blade 9 × 7½ in. (23 × 19 cm), thick, mid-green, with very wide chartreuse margins turning creamy yellow and jetting toward the midrib, dimpled, closely veined when mature, edge slightly undulate, leaf slightly concave, oval with a cuspidate tip and heart-shaped open to pinched lobes. Petiole stout, oblique, glaucous green. Flower: see *H.* 'Gold Regal'.

Cultivation Notes: Site in morning sun in cooler climates to intensify the leaf color. In deep shade, the color remains muted. Slow to moderate growth rate.

Similar: *H.* 'David Reath'; *H.* 'Independence Day' has a narrower leaf margin and is more muted in color.

Sports: *H.* 'Summer Olympics' has yellow leaves.

Hosta 'Alligator Shoes' (H. Benedict/H. Hatfield N/R)

MEDIUM

Origin: ★*H.* 'Dorothy Benedict' × ★*H. montana*.

Description: A well-poised mound 24 in. wide × 18 in. high (60 × 45 cm). Leaf blade 7½ × 5 in. (19 × 13 cm), thick, blue-green to olive green, irregularly

Hosta 'Abiqua Moonbeam'

Hosta 'Alex Summers'

and narrowly margined cream to white, with random gray-green streaks jetting toward the midrib, matt above and glaucous below, seersuckered, veins closely spaced, edge unevenly rippled, leaf arching, convex, widely oval with a twisted cuspidate tip and heart-shaped open lobes. Petiole shallow, gray-green. Flower open, funnel-shaped, palest lavender, on a leaning, leafy, green, 36-in. (90-cm) scape from mid- to late summer; fertile.

Cultivation Notes: Site in morning sun for best growth. Increases moderately well. Takes several seasons for the unusual surface texture to appear. Pest resistant.

Distinguishing Features: The extremely pebbled leaf surface, reminiscent of alligator skin, is both unusual and attractive.

Sports: *H.* 'See Ya Later' has yellow leaves.

Hosta 'Alvatine Taylor' (Fairway Enterprises 1990)

LARGE–VERY LARGE

Origin: Sport of *H.* 'Lady In Waiting'.

Description: A colorful, dense mound 48 in. wide × 30 in. high (120 × 75 cm). Leaf blade 9–10 × 7–8 in. (23–25 × 18–20 cm), thick, glaucous blue-gray, widely and irregularly margined muted golden yellow, developing an attractive sheen by the end of summer, seersuckered and puckered when mature, prominently veined, edge slightly undulate, leaf widely oval with a cuspidate to mucronate tip and heart-shaped rounded to flat lobes. Petiole stout, light

green. Flower funnel-shaped, white, on an upright, leafy, glaucous green, 32-in. (80-cm) scape in high summer; fertile.

Cultivation Notes: Tolerates morning sun in cooler climates. Slow to moderate growth rate. Pest resistant. Winner of the 1998 Alex J. Summers Distinguished Merit Hosta Award.

Distinguishing Features: Differs from similar hostas in having a muted, golden-yellow leaf margin, longer leaves, and an ability to withstand sun damage.

Similar: *H.* 'Cinderella'; ★*H. sieboldiana* 'Frances Williams'.

Sports: *H.* 'Doubloons' has bright golden-yellow leaves.

Hosta 'A Many-splendored Thing' (E. Elslager 1999)

LARGE

Origin: ★*H.* 'Dorothy Benedict' × ★*H. hypoleuca*.

Description: An upright mound 43 in. wide × 24 in. high (108 × 60 cm). Leaf blade 11½ in. × 9½ in. (29 × 24 cm), thick, dark green, with wide yellow margins jetting toward the midrib, shiny above and glaucous below, rugose, veins noticeably ridged, edge almost flat to lightly rippled, leaf slightly convex or cupped, widely ovate to nearly round with a mucronate tip and heart-shaped folded lobes. Petiole deeply grooved, green, outlined in yellow. Flower funnel-shaped, near-white striped mauve-pink, in a dense cluster, on an upright, bare, pale green, 28- to

Hosta 'Alligator Shoes'

Hosta 'Alvatine Taylor'

32-in. (70- to 80-cm) scape in midsummer; seedpods green, fertile.

Cultivation Notes: Tolerates two hours of morning sun in cooler regions, otherwise dappled shade. Requires plenty of moisture. Slow to increase but eventually makes a superb specimen plant. Pest resistant.

Distinguishing Features: The glossy leaves of heavy substance emphasize the attractive marginal variegation which, in well-cultivated plants, exhibits some celadon and chartreuse streaks in the transitional areas.

Hosta 'American Dream' (V. Wade 1999)

MEDIUM–LARGE

Origin: Sport of ★*H*. 'High Fat Cream'.

Description: A dense, upright mound 40 in. wide × 24 in. high (100 × 60 cm). Leaf blade 10 × 7½ in. (25 × 19 cm), of good substance, chartreuse turning golden creamy yellow, widely and irregularly margined white, matt above and thinly glaucous below, seersuckered, edge slightly rippled, leaf cupped or convex, widely oval with a mucronate tip and heart-shaped folded lobes. Petiole chartreuse, outlined in cream. Flower: see *H*. 'High Fat Cream'.

Cultivation Notes: Site in morning sun in cooler climates to prevent the white margin from burning. Slow to increase but a strong grower. A superb recent introduction.

Distinguishing Features: The variegated margin can be up to 2¾ in. (7 cm) wide, which is wider than that of hostas with similar coloring.

Similar: *H*. 'Lakeside April Snow'; *H*. 'Moon Glow', a seedling of *H*. 'August Moon', was among the first hostas with yellow and white variegation, although it has now been superseded; ★*H*. 'Sea Dream'; *H*. 'Sunshine Glory'; *H*. 'Zodiac'.

Hosta 'American Eagle' (V. Wade 1999)

LARGE

Origin: Natural sport of ★*H*. 'Zounds'.

Description: An upright mound 30 in. wide × 20 in. high (75 × 50 cm). Leaf blade 9 × 8½ in. (23 × 21 cm), thick, very dark green, with wide, 2-in. (5-cm), irregular golden-yellow margins jetting toward the midrib, matt above and glaucous below, seersuckered, edge almost flat, leaf shallowly concave, nearly round

Hosta 'American Dream'

Hosta 'A Many-splendored Thing'

Hosta 'American Eagle'

Hosta 'American Icon'

Hosta 'Angel Feathers'

Hosta 'Antioch'

with a mucronate tip and heart-shaped pinched lobes. Petiole dark green, finely outlined in creamy yellow. Flower: see *H.* 'Zounds'.

Cultivation Notes: Site in some morning sun in cooler climates. Slow growth rate. Pest resistant. An outstanding newer introduction.

Distinguishing Features: The wide yellowish leaf margin is a striking contrast to the exceptionally dark green base color.

Similar: *H.* 'Laura and Darrell'.

Hosta 'American Icon' PP17,441 (H. Hansen 2004)

LARGE

Origin: Sport of *H.* 'Choo Choo Train'.

Description: A rounded mound 62 in. wide × 22 in. high (157 × 55 cm). Leaf blade 12 × 8 in. (30 × 20 cm), of average substance, mid- to dark green, exceptionally widely and irregularly margined bright golden yellow with some feathering toward the midrib, matt above and thinly glaucous below, veins conspicuous, edge evenly rippled, leaf arching, broadly ovate with a cuspidate tip and rounded overlapping lobes. Petiole green, outlined in yellow. Flower funnel-shaped, palest lavender to near white, on an upright, 30-in. (75-cm) scape from early to midsummer; seedpods green, fertile.

Cultivation Notes: Site in moderate shade to enhance the dramatic contrast between the strongly variegated leaf margin and the base color. Good growth rate. A superb specimen plant.

Distinguishing Features: The leaf emerges golden yellow, the green center appears gradually after a few weeks.

Similar: *H.* 'Afternoon Delight'; ★*H.* 'Climax' has wider leaves.

Hosta 'Angel Feathers' (K. Vaughn N/R)

MEDIUM

Origin: (★*H.* 'William Lachman' × sibling) × self.

Description: A dense, somewhat upright mound 34 in. wide × 16 in. high (85 × 402 cm). Leaf blade 7 × 4½ in. (18 × 11 cm), thick, medium green, widely and irregularly margined golden yellow to creamy white, with feathering toward the midrib, satiny above and glaucous below, dimpled, edge widely rippled, leaf triangular with a cuspidate tip and round to tapered pinched lobes. Petiole green, outlined in creamy yellow. Flower pale purple, on an upright, leafy, 24-in. (60-cm) scape in midseason; fertility unknown.

Cultivation Notes: Site in shade all day. Increases rapidly. A colorful hosta with attractively shaped leaves.

Distinguishing Features: The leaf edge becomes flatter with maturity.

Hosta 'Antioch' (C. Tompkins/P. Hofer/P. Ruh 1979)

MEDIUM–LARGE

Origin: *H.* 'Fortunei' hybrid.

Description: A dense mound 49 in. wide × 22 in. high (122 × 55 cm). Leaf blade 10 × 5½ in. (25 × 14 cm), of good substance, mid- to dark green, irregularly margined chartreuse turning creamy yellow and finally white, with celadon streaks jetting toward the midrib, satiny above and thinly glaucous below, strongly veined, edge undulate, leaf arching to the ground, convex, oval with a cuspidate tip and heart-shaped pinched lobes. Petiole dark green, outlined in creamy white. Flower narrowly funnel-shaped, lavender, in a dense raceme, on an upright, leafy, green, 29-in. (73-cm) scape in high summer; fertility low.

Cultivation Notes: Site in light to moderate shade for vigorous and rapid growth. Well-nourished soil and plenty of moisture increase the amount of variegation. Emerges late. Winner of the 1984 Alex J. Summers Distinguished Merit Hosta Award.

Distinguishing Features: Longer, more pointed leaves and wider variegation than *H.* 'Fortunei Albomarginata'.

Similar: *H.* 'Kiwi Treasure Trove'; *H.* 'Moerheim'; *H.* 'Rhapsody'; *H.* 'Shogun'; *H.* 'Silver Crown'; *H.* 'Spinners'.

Sports: *H.* 'Ice Follies' has a very wide creamy margin and requires full shade.

Hosta 'Arc de Triomphe' (E. Elslager 2000)

LARGE

Origin: *H.* 'Foxy Doxy' × *H. hypoleuca*.

Description: A graceful, arching mound 35 in. wide × 24 in. high (88 × 60 cm). Leaf blade 12 × 9 in. (30 × 23 cm), of heavy substance, dark grayish green, widely and irregularly margined cream to ivory, with streaks of celadon and cream jetting toward the midrib, satiny above and glaucous below, veins prominently ribbed, edge widely undulate, leaf slightly convex, ovate with a cuspidate tip and heart-shaped pinched to folded lobes. Petiole green, outlined in ivory. Flower purple-striped pale lavender, on an upright, leafy, 36-in. (90-cm) scape from mid- to late summer; fertile.

Cultivation Notes: Site in light shade as strong sunlight damages the marginal variegation. Slow to increase. Grow with blue-leaved hostas as a contrast.

Distinguishing Features: Some leaf edges are upturned showing the distinctly glaucous undersides inherited from the *H. hypoleuca* parent.

Similar: *H.* 'Celestial'.

Hosta 'Atlantis' PP17,093 (H. Hansen 2004)

VERY LARGE

Origin: Tetraploid sport of *H.* 'Abba Dabba Do'.

Description: A graceful, arching mound 70 in. wide × 30 in. high (175 × 75 cm). Leaf blade 13 × 8 in. (33 × 20 cm), of very good substance, bright mid-green, very widely margined and slightly streaked yellow to cream, matt above and glaucous below, veins deeply furrowed, edge widely undulate, leaf twisted, ovate with a recurved tip and overlapping heart-shaped lobes. Petiole coarse, flattish, green, outlined in cream. Flower: see *H.* 'Abba Dabba Do'.

Hosta 'Arc de Triomphe'

Cultivation Notes: Site in moderate shade to accentuate the depth of color of the variegation. Thrives in hotter climates.

Distinguishing Features: Leaves with heavier substance and wider margins than its parent. The eye-catching wide, even band of golden-yellow variegation with only slight feathering into the green base color.

Similar: *H.* 'American Icon' has a pale green base color.

Hosta 'Band of Gold' (E. Elslager 1999)

LARGE

Origin: *H.* 'Dorothy Benedict' × *H. hypoleuca.*

Description: An upright mound 26 in. wide × 22 in. high (65 × 55 cm), with vividly contrasting leaf colors. Leaf blade 10 × 8 in. (25 × 20 cm), thick, dark green,

Hosta 'Atlantis'

very widely margined chartreuse turning yellow and finally ivory white, with feathering along the transition and some celadon streaks, matt above turning glossy and glaucous below, seersuckered, prominently veined, edge slightly rippled, leaf lightly cupped, rounded with a mucronate tip and heart-shaped pinched lobes. Petiole dark green, outlined in yellow. Flower funnel- to bell-shaped, white with a translucent margin, opening from a palest lavender bud, on an upright, leafy, green, 24-in. (60-cm) scape from early to midsummer; seedpods green, fertility unknown.

Cultivation Notes: Site in moderate shade for most dramatic leaf color. Moderate growth rate. Reasonably pest resistant.

Distinguishing Features: The wide ivory-white margin is a striking contrast to the spinach green base color which the feathering enhances. The raceme is very attractive and enhanced by the pale anthers.

Similar: *H.* 'Formal Attire' and *H.* 'Robert Frost' both have narrower leaves.

Hosta 'Blazing Saddles' (T. Avent 2000)

MEDIUM–LARGE

Origin: *H.* 'Beatrice' seedling × *H.* 'Blue Umbrellas'.

Description: A symmetrical mound 44 in. wide × 18 in. high (110 × 45 cm). Leaf blade 9 × 8 in. (23 × 20 cm), of good substance, emerging light green turning dark green, widely and irregularly margined pale cream to white, with celadon streaking, glaucous above and matt below, seersuckered, veins widely

Hosta 'Band of Gold'

Hosta 'Blazing Saddles'

spaced, edge almost flat, leaf lightly cupped, oblong to ovate with a cuspidate tip and flat pinched lobes. Petiole narrowly channeled, dark green, outlined in white. Flower bell-shaped, lavender, on an upright, bare, green, 28-in. (70-cm) scape in midsummer; fertile.

Cultivation Notes: Site in dappled to full shade. Tolerates some morning sun in cooler gardens. A vigorous, slow to moderate grower. Pest resistant. Makes a superb border plant when accentuated by accompanying contrasting lacy foliage.

Distinguishing Features: The vivid color contrast between the margin and the base color of the leaf.

Similar: *H. 'Bobbie Sue' has wider leaves.

Hosta 'Blue Flame' (Naylor Creek Nursery 2004)

SMALL–MEDIUM

Origin: Sport of *H. 'Fragrant Blue'.

Description: A dome-shaped mound 22 in. wide × 16 in. high (55 × 40 cm). Leaf blade 6 × 4½ in. (15 × 11 cm), of good substance, powdery pale blue, irregularly margined cream turning yellow with celadon streaking and white flashes along the outer rim of the margin, dimpled, edge almost flat, leaf flat to convex, widely oval with a cuspidate tip and heart-shaped open to pinched lobes. Petiole blue, outlined in cream. Flower: see *H.* 'Fragrant Blue'.

Cultivation Notes: Site in good light to dappled shade to maintain the powdery bloom on the leaf surface. The floral fragrance is only perceptible in hot climates. Vigorous. Pest resistant.

Distinguishing Features: The marginal variegation

appears after the leaves have expanded and the attractive tricolored effect is only visible on mature plants.

Hosta 'Blue River' (D. Reath/R. Klehm 1998)

LARGE

Origin: Sport of *H. 'True Blue'.

Description: An arching mound 30 in. wide × 15 in. high (75 × 38 cm). Leaf blade 9 × 7½ in. (23 × 19 cm), thick, rich dark blue, widely and irregularly margined chartreuse turning yellow, with streaks jetting toward the midrib, shiny above and a thick glaucous blue-gray below, seersuckered, edge slightly undulate, leaf arching, convex, broadly ovate with a cuspidate to mucronate tip and heart-shaped pinched to folded lobes. Petiole stout, glaucous, blue-green. Flower: see *H.* 'True Blue'.

Cultivation Notes: Site in moderate shade to retain the subtle contrasts between the leaf margin, leaf center, and intermediate chartreuse streaking. Not suitable for containers. Slow to moderate growth rate. Pest resistant.

Distinguishing Features: Considerably smaller than its parent with a shiny upper leaf surface.

Similar: *H.* 'Bingo' and *H. 'Brave Amherst' have narrower leaf margins; *H.* 'Fleeta Brownell Woodroffe'; *H. 'Tokudama Flavocircinalis'.

Hosta 'Bobbie Sue' (C. Owens 1994)

MEDIUM–LARGE

Origin: Sport of *H.* 'Marbled White'.

Description: A spreading mound 46 in. wide × 16

Hosta 'Blue Flame'

Hosta 'Blue River'

in. high (116 × 40 cm). Leaf blade 9 × 4 in. (23 × 10 cm), thick, dark olive green, irregularly margined creamy white with chartreuse transitional splashing, satiny above and glossy below, slightly dimpled when mature, edge randomly rippled, leaf slightly undulate, oval with a cuspidate tip and rounded to tapered open lobes. Petiole flat, olive green, finely outlined in cream. Flower tubular, 2¾ in. (7 cm) long, purple-striped rich lavender, on an upright, leafy, green, 32-in. (80-cm) scape in midsummer; fertile.

Cultivation Notes: Site in shade in the hottest climates; elsewhere some morning sun is beneficial. Moderate to fast growth rate. A superb recent introduction.

Distinguishing Features: Leaves become flatter and wider with maturity.

Hosta 'Bobbie Sue', in deep shade

Hosta 'Bob Olson' (H. & D. Benedict 1995)

SMALL

Origin: *H.* 'Yellow Splash' selfed.

Description: An upright mound 12 in. wide × 5 in. high (30 × 13 cm). Leaf blade 3 × 2 in. (8 × 5 cm), of good substance, satiny, dark olive green, irregularly margined creamy white, veins moderately prominent, edge slightly rippled, leaf slightly undulate, somewhat folded, broadly elliptic with an acute tip and rounded open to pinched lobes. Petiole dark green, outlined in creamy white. Flower bell-shaped, on an upright, leafy, purple-flecked green, 16-in. (40-cm) scape in late summer; fertility unknown.

Cultivation Notes: Performs well in a sunny position for half a day except in the hottest regions. Fast growing.

Distinguishing Features: The conspicuously upright habit.

Hosta 'Bold Edger' (K. Vaughn 1983)

medium

Origin: *H.* 'Beatrice' × *H. sieboldiana* 'Frances Williams'.

Description. A fairly dense, irregular mound 20 in. wide × 20 in. high (50 × 50 cm). Leaf blade 6½ × 4 in. (16 × 10 cm); of good substance, mid- to dark olive-green widely and irregularly margined, yellow turning white, matt above and glaucous below, prominently veined; edge shallowly rippled, widely undulate, arching to convex, widely oval with a cuspidate tip, heart-shaped open lobes. Petiole dark green,

Hosta 'Bob Olson'

Hosta 'Bold Edger'

208

outlined in cream. Flower widely funnel-shaped, purple striped lavender on an upright, leafy, green, 30 in. (75 cm) scape in late summer; fertile.

Cultivation Notes: Site in moderate shade. Increases rapidly.

Distinguishing Features: Clump habit does not live up to the very attractive individual leaves.

Similar: *H.* 'Emily Dickinson'; *H.* 'Queen Josephine'; *H.* 'Tambourine'.

Hosta 'Border Bandit' (W. & E. Lachman 1992)

SMALL

Origin: *H.* 'Halcyon' hybrid.

Description: A compact mound 15 in. wide × 9 in. high (38 × 23 cm). Leaf blade 5½ × 3½ in. (14 × 9 cm), thick, blue-green, widely and irregularly margined creamy white with much celadon streaking, glossy above and matt below, edge slightly rippled but kinked toward the base, leaf convex, spear-shaped with a cuspidate tip and rounded open lobes. Petiole dark green, finely outlined in cream. Flower funnel-shaped, lavender, on an upright, leafy, dark green, 18-in. (45-cm) scape in late summer; fertile.

Cultivation Notes: Slow to increase at first but becomes a superb plant. A dramatic presence in the shaded border because of the slightly twisted leaves. An ideal pot plant.

Distinguishing Features: The slight twist to the leaves.

Hosta 'Brave Amherst' (W. & E. Lachman 1993)

MEDIUM

Origin: *H.* 'Christmas Tree' × *H.* 'Reversed'.

Description: A dense mound 25 in. wide × 18 in. high (63 × 45 cm). Leaf blade 9 × 6½ in. (23 × 16 cm), very thick, light blue-green, narrowly and irregularly margined and streaked yellow turning cream, matt above and glaucous below, seersuckered, veins moderately prominent, edge slightly rippled, leaf slightly cupped or convex, widely oval with a mucronate tip and heart-shaped overlapping lobes. Petiole stout, glaucous green, outlined in cream. Flower tubular, near white, on an upright, leafy, glaucous, green, 24-in. (60-cm) scape in early summer; fertile.

Cultivation Notes: Site in light to full shade. Very slow to establish. Pest resistant. A great improvement

on similar hostas since the margins do not scorch.

Distinguishing Features: Has longer, somewhat smaller leaves than *H. sieboldiana* 'Aurora Borealis' or *H. sieboldiana* 'Frances Williams' and is a better performer than the latter.

Hosta 'Brim Cup' (P. Aden 1986)

SMALL–MEDIUM

Origin: *H.* 'Wide Brim' hybrid.

Description: An open mound 15 in. wide × 12 in. high (38 × 30 cm). Leaf blade 6½ × 5 in. (16 × 13 cm), thick, dark green with a blue cast and with wide, irregular chartreuse margins that turn yellow and finally creamy white jetting toward the midrib, matt above and glaucous below, seersuckered, edge slightly rippled, leaf cupped, widely oval to nearly round with

Hosta 'Border Bandit'

Hosta 'Brave Amherst'

a mucronate tip and heart-shaped open to pinched lobes. Petiole shallow, dark green, outlined in cream. Flower funnel-shaped, opening light blue turning white, on an upright, bare, green, 18-in. (45-cm) scape in midsummer; fertile.

Cultivation Notes: Site in two hours of morning sun in cooler gardens. Slow to increase. Superb as a young plant but the edges can split or tear in maturity; nonetheless it remains popular, especially as a pot plant, because of the strikingly variegated leaves.

Distinguishing Features: Particularly wide and well-defined variegation for a hosta of this size.

Hosta 'Candy Cane' (E. Elslager 1995)

SMALL

Origin: Unknown but undoubtedly has *H. sieboldii* in its ancestry.

Description: A diffuse, cascading mound 14 in. wide × 7 in. high (35 × 18 cm). Leaf blade 6 × 2½ in. (15 × 6 cm), of average to good substance, satiny, dark green, irregularly and variably margined golden yellow fading to cream, some dimpling on mature outer leaves, edge rippled, leaf arching, lanceolate to oval with an acute tip and tapered open lobes. Petiole flattish, dark green, outlined in cream. Flower tubular, dark purple-striped lavender, on an upright, leafy, dark green, 13- to 16-in. (33- to 40-cm) scape in late summer; fertility unknown.

Cultivation Notes: Site in light to moderate shade since the margin will turn white if exposed to direct

sunlight. Vigorous, fast growing. Suitable for the edge of light woodland. Not suitable as a pot plant.

Similar: *H. 'Resonance'; H. 'White Dove'* has white-margined leaves.

Hosta 'Carnival' (W. & E. Lachman 1986)

MEDIUM–LARGE

Origin: *H. 'Beatrice'* × *H. sieboldiana* 'Frances Williams'.

Description: An open mound 41 in. wide × 16–18 in. high (102 × 40–45 cm). Leaf blade 9 × 7½ in. (23 × 19 cm), thick, mid- to dark green-blue to green-gray, widely and irregularly margined yellow to cream with celadon streaking and mottling jetting toward the midrib, matt above and glaucous below,

Hosta 'Candy Cane', in deep shade

Hosta 'Brim Cup'

Hosta 'Carnival', in deep shade

mature leaves intensely seersuckered, edge slightly rippled, leaf convex, oval to heart-shaped with a mucronate tip and heart-shaped open lobes. Petiole wide, green, strongly outlined in cream. Flower long-lasting, funnel-shaped, near-white to lavender, on a stout, upright, leafy, glaucous gray-green, 30-in. (75-cm) scape, poised well above the leaf mound, in mid-summer; fertile.

Cultivation Notes: Site in light to full shade as leaves lose their intense color if exposed to too much sun. Slow to establish but eventually becomes a strikingly colorful mound.

Distinguishing Features: Wide margins are distinctly feathered with two-tone mottling. Flower scapes have very attractive large variegated bracts surrounding the purple flower buds.

Similar: *H.* 'Carousel' is smaller and has less shapely leaves; *H.* 'Cavalcade' has leaves without mottling and streaking; *H.* 'Standing Ovation'.

Hosta 'Carolina Sunshine' (T. Avent 1999)

MEDIUM

Origin: *H. tibae* hybrid.

Description: A diffuse mound 41 in. wide × 14 in. high (102 × 35 cm). Leaf blade 9 × 5 in. (23 × 13 cm), of thin to average substance, glossy, mid- to dark green, widely and very irregularly margined and splashed butterscotch-yellow turning cream, veins widely spaced, edge conspicuously rippled, leaf arching, elliptic with an acute tip and tapered pinched

lobes. Petiole narrow, dark green, finely outlined in cream. Flower tubular, near-white striped lavender, on an upright, leafy, green, 20-in. (50-cm) scape in late summer; fertile.

Cultivation Notes: Very sun tolerant even in warmer climates. Increases rapidly. Easy to grow.

Distinguishing Features: The deeply rippled leaf edge.

Hosta 'Carrie Ann' (D. Stone & P. Ruh 1988)

SMALL

Origin: Unknown but has characteristics of ★*H. sieboldii*.

Description: An open mound 24 in. wide × 9 in. high (60 × 23 cm). Leaf blade 4½ × 2 in. (11 × 5 cm), of average substance, medium gray-green, narrowly and irregularly margined light yellow to white, smooth, strongly veined, edge widely rippled or kinked, leaf slightly undulate, lanceolate with an acute tip and tapered open lobes. Petiole green, outlined in white. Flower funnel-shaped, white, on an upright, leafy, green, 20-in. (50-cm) scape in late summer; fertility unknown.

Cultivation Notes: Site in some morning sun in cooler climates to boost the rather poor vigor. Slow to increase but worth the wait since there are so few white-margined hostas with white flowers.

Distinguishing Features: The blade is set obliquely on the petiole. The white flowers have green tips.

Similar: *H.* 'Emerald Isle' and *H.* 'Louisa' are

Hosta 'Carolina Sunshine'

Hosta 'Carrie Ann'

slightly smaller, have white flowers on upright, leafy, dark green, 34-in. (85-cm) scapes from mid- to high season, and are known to be fertile.

Hosta 'Celestial' (E. Elslager 2000)

VERY LARGE

Origin: *★H.* 'Dorothy Benedict' × *★H. hypoleuca*.

Description: An upright mound 43 in. wide × 31 in. high (108 × 78 cm). Leaf blade 15 × 14 in. (38 × 35 cm), thick, medium green, widely and irregularly margined chartreuse yellow with some streaking, satiny above and glaucous below, seersuckered, veins furrowed, edge slightly undulate, leaf arching, broadly ovate to rounded with a recurved mucronate tip and pinched to overlapping flat to heart-shaped lobes. Petiole green, outlined in cream. Flower funnel-shaped, pale lavender with a translucent margin, on an upright, bare, green, 33- to 36-in. (83- to 90-cm) scape from mid- to high summer; seedpods green, fertile.

Cultivation Notes: Site in light to moderate shade. Slow growth rate. Needs plenty of space as it eventually makes a huge clump.

Distinguishing Features: The huge arching leaves have attractive variegation and good surface texture.

Similar: *H.* 'Hippodrome' has bluer leaves with narrower, more undulate margins and is just as attractive.

Hosta 'Chantilly Lace' (W. & E. Lachman 1988)

SMALL

Origin: *H.* 'Calypso' × *★H.* 'Halcyon'.

Description: A dense, upright mound 41 in. wide × 16 in. high (102 × 40 cm). Leaf blade 6½ × 3 in. (16 × 8 cm), of average substance, smooth, dark gray-green, randomly margined and streaked white, matt above and glaucous below, edge rippled or kinked, leaf elliptic to oval with a cuspidate tip and rounded pinched lobes. Petiole narrow, olive green, finely outlined in white. Flower large, flared, almost white, on an upright, leafy, olive-green, 18-in. (45-cm) scape from mid- to late summer; fertility unknown.

Cultivation Notes: Site in light to moderate shade. Good growth rate but not easy in every garden.

Distinguishing Features: The leaf blade is held horizontally.

Similar: *H.* 'Everlasting Love'; *H.* 'Lacy Belle' has an upturned leaf edge.

Hosta 'Childhood Sweetheart' (H. Hansen 2005)

SMALL

Origin: (*★H.* 'Neat Splash' × *★H.* 'Tardiflora') × *★H.* 'Shining Tot'.

Description: A flattish mound 32 in. wide × 16 in. high (80 × 40 cm). Leaf blade 5 × 3 in. (13 × 8 cm), of average to good substance, dark green with a cream to ivory margin and many paler green streaks, matt above and shiny below, edge lightly undulate, leaf ovate with an acute tip and tapering pinched lobes.

Hosta 'Celestial'

Hosta 'Chantilly Lace'

Petiole dark green, outlined in ivory. Flower funnel-shaped, pale lavender, on an upright, bare, sometimes branched green, 21-in. (53-cm) scape from late summer to mid-autumn; seedpods green, fertile.

Cultivation Notes: Site in good light to moderate shade. Moderate growth rate. A robust border plant.

Similar: ★*H.* 'Beatrice' (the marginally variegated form).

Hosta 'Christmas Tree' (K. Vaughn & M. Seaver 1982)

MEDIUM–LARGE

Origin: ★*H. sieboldiana* 'Frances Williams' × ★*H.* 'Beatrice'.

Description: A somewhat unruly mound 36 in. wide × 20 in. high (90 × 50 cm). Leaf blade 8½ × 6½ in. (21 × 16 cm), very thick, olive green to dark green with a slight blue cast early in the season, narrowly and irregularly margined cream turning white, with some transitional celadon streaks jetting toward the midrib, matt above and glaucous below, intensely seersuckered when mature, edge slightly rippled, leaf widely oval to nearly round with a mucronate tip and heart-shaped pinched lobes. Petiole dark green, finely outlined in white. Flower funnel-shaped, pale lavender, on an upright, leafy, glaucous green, 18-in. (45-cm) scape from mid- to late summer; seedpods red, fertile.

Cultivation Notes: Tolerates two hours of morning sun in cooler climates. Pest resistant. Grow as a specimen plant in a large container.

Distinguishing Features: In full bloom, the plant outline is pyramidal, having a fancied resemblance to a Christmas tree.

Similar: *H.* 'Grand Master'; *H.* 'Sea Mist' is a seedling with a gentle, misty yellow leaf color and an almost imperceptible muted chartreuse margin; *H.* 'Van Wade'.

Sports: *H.* 'Chesières Green Christmas'; ★*H.* 'Christmas Gold'; *H.* 'Christmas Lights' and *H.* 'Christmas Pageant' have much wider margins and thicker substance indicating polyploidy.

Hosta 'Christmas Pageant'

Hosta 'Childhood Sweetheart'

Hosta 'Christmas Tree'

Hosta 'Climax' (G. Jones 2000)

LARGE

Origin: Sport of ★*H.* 'High Noon'.

Description: A striking, vase-shaped mound 40 in. wide × 26 in. high (100 × 65 cm). Leaf blade 14 × 9 in. (35 × 23 cm), of very good substance, rich mid- to dark green, widely and irregularly margined chartreuse turning golden yellow, with transitional chartreuse streaks jetting toward the midrib, matt above and slightly glaucous below, seersuckered, edge shallowly undulate, leaf cupped at the base then arching, nearly round with a cuspidate tip and folded heart-shaped lobes. Petiole mid-green, outlined in yellow. Flower: see *H.* 'High Noon'.

Hosta 'Climax'

Cultivation Notes: Site in dappled to light shade. Tolerates morning sun in cooler gardens. Pest resistant. Best planted in a border with other hostas or foliage plants of a plainer color.

Distinguishing Features: The striking, variegated leaf margin is 1 in. (2.5 cm) wide and later fades to ivory white.

Similar: *H.* 'Afternoon Delight'; *H.* 'Tyler's Treasure' has longer leaves.

Hosta 'Coquette' (H. Benedict 1987)

MEDIUM

Origin: ★*H.* 'Neat Splash' selfed.

Description: An open mound 41 in. wide × 16 in. high (102 × 40 cm). Leaf blade 6½ × 4½ in. (16 × 11 cm), of average substance, light, bright green, almost evenly and widely margined and streaked chartreuse to ivory white, matt above and glossy below, dimpled when mature, veins widely spaced, edge slightly and widely undulate, leaf oval with an obtuse tip and rounded open to pinched lobes. Petiole wide, green, outlined in white. Flower narrowly funnel-shaped, rich purple, opening from a purple bud, on an oblique, bare, green, 30-in. (75-cm) scape in late summer; fertile.

Cultivation Notes: Site in light to moderate shade. Moderate growth rate.

Distinguishing Features: Conspicuously margined, paddlelike leaves.

Similar: *H.* 'Avalanche' has a wider leaf margin; ★*H.*

Hosta 'Coquette'

Hosta 'Cordelia'

'Bold Edger'; *H.* 'City Slicker' has thicker leaves; ★*H.* 'Decorata'; *H.* 'Hertha'; ★*H.* 'Tea and Crumpets'.

Hosta 'Cordelia' (Kuk 1991)

MEDIUM

Origin: Open-pollinated seedling of *H.* 'Neat Splash'.

Description: A dense mound 36 in. wide × 14 in. high (90 × 35 cm). Leaf blade 6½ × 3 in. (16 × 8 cm), of average substance, smooth, glossy, dark green, fairly regularly margined creamy yellow turning ivory white and jetting toward the midrib, veins widely spaced, edge slightly undulate, leaf narrowly ovate with an acute tip and rounded open to pinched lobes. Petiole dark green, dotted in purple, outlined in cream. Flower funnel-shaped, vivid deep purple, on an upright, leafy, green, 26-in. (65-cm) scape in late summer; fertile.

Cultivation Notes: Site in light to moderate shade. A rapid grower with outstanding flowers. Ideal in light woodland or a border accompanied by ferns.

Similar: ★*H.* 'Don Stevens'; ★*H.* 'Queen Josephine'.

Hosta 'Crepe Suzette' (W. & E. Lachman 1986)

SMALL

Origin: *H.* 'Flamboyant' hybrid.

Description: An open mound 15 in. wide × 7 in. high (38 × 18 cm). Leaf blade 5 × 2 in. (13 × 5 cm), of moderate substance, dark green, widely margined crisp white, matt above and slightly shiny below, strongly veined, edge slightly undulate, leaf oval with an obtuse tip and tapered open lobes. Petiole flat, wide, dark green, outlined in white. Flower funnel-shaped, lavender, on a leaning, leafy, dark green, 10- to 12-in. (25- to 30-cm) scape in late summer; seedheads dark green, fertile.

Cultivation Notes: Site in light to moderate shade. Slow to increase.

Distinguishing Features: The margins on this distinctly oval-leaved hosta turn cream toward the end of the season and are exceptionally wide for a hosta of this size.

Similar: ★*H.* 'Crepe Soul'; ★*H.* 'Decorata'.

Sports: *H.* 'Cream Cheese' is slightly smaller; ★*H.* 'Moon River'.

Hosta 'Crested Surf' (H. & D. Benedict 1990)

SMALL

Origin: ★*H.* 'Neat Splash' selfed.

Description: A dense mound 30 in. wide × 10 in. high (75 × 25 cm). Leaf blade 5½ × 2½ in. (14 × 6 cm), thin, gold turning green, margined yellow to creamy white and transitionally splashed gray-green, satiny above and glaucous below, edge conspicuously rippled, leaf arching, twisting, kinked toward the tip, lanceolate to oval with an obtuse tip and tapered open to pinched lobes. Petiole kinked, green, outlined in white. Flower funnel-shaped, purple, on an upright, leafy, 16-in. (40-cm) scape in late summer; seedpods reddish purple, fertile.

Hosta 'Crepe Suzette'

Hosta 'Crested Surf'

Cultivation Notes: Site in light to moderate shade. A fast grower suitable for covering large areas. Needs dividing every four to five years in garden borders. Rippled leaf blades become less marked as the hosta matures.

Distinguishing Features: Attractive combinations of leaf color are at their best toward the end of the most active growth period when white-margined gold and green leaves are visible at the same time.

Similar: ★*H.* 'Resonance' has less-rippled leaves; *H.* 'Suzanne' has narrower leaves.

Hosta 'Crispula' (F. Maekawa/W. G. Schmid/AHS 2001) ♈

LARGE

Origin: Japanese gardens.

Description: A dense mound 36 in. wide × 20 in. high (90 × 50 cm). Leaf blade 12 × 6 in. (30 × 15 cm), of good substance, dark green, irregularly margined pure white with some transitional celadon streaking, satiny above and shiny below, some dimpling when mature, veins deeply depressed, edge dramatically rippled, leaf arching, oval with a distinctly twisted cuspidate tip and heart-shaped pinched lobes. Petiole narrow, dark green, finely outlined in white. Flower funnel-shaped, palest lavender, on a drooping, leafy, green, 24- to 36-in. (60- to 90-cm) scape in early summer; seedpods many, fertile.

Cultivation Notes: Site in good light to moderate shade. Slow to establish and difficult to propagate.

The "true" *H.* 'Crispula' is less often seen in cultivation since the 1960s and is used very little as a breeding plant, although its descendent, ★*H.* 'Rocky Mountain High', is one of the few exceptions. Prone to virus infection.

Distinguishing Features: The leaves twist 180 degrees. Decorative, flowerlike bracts extend the length of the scape.

Similar: *H.* 'Enchantment'; ★*H. montana* 'Mountain Snow'; *H.* 'Snow Crust'; *H.* 'Spring Fling' is a larger, superb recent introduction; *H.* 'Zippity Do Dah'.

Sports: *H.* 'Crispula Viridis' has green leaves; *H.* 'Minuet' is smaller.

Hosta 'Crusader' (W. & E. Lachman 1989)

MEDIUM

Origin: *H.* 'Halcyon' hybrid.

Description: A dense mound 36 in. wide × 18 in. high (90 × 45 cm). Leaf blade 6½ × 5 in. (16 × 13 cm), thick, dark green with a blue cast early in the season, narrowly and irregularly margined creamy yellow turning white with some streaking, satiny above and thinly glaucous below, seersuckered when mature, edge undulate, leaf shallowly cupped or convex, widely oval with a mucronate tip and rounded pinched lobes. Petiole slightly oblique, green, outlined in creamy white. Flower funnel-shaped, pale lavender, in a dense raceme, on a slightly oblique, bare, glaucous purple-tinted green, 28-in. (70-cm) scape in late summer; fertility unknown.

Hosta 'Crispula'

Hosta 'Crusader'

Cultivation Notes: If exposed to strong sunlight the upper leaf surface develops a metallic sheen, but if grown in good light to moderate shade, the depth of color is more pronounced. Vigorous, a good increaser. An effective specimen for both leaves and flowers.

Similar: *★H.* 'Tambourine' is larger.

Hosta 'Dark Shadows' (H. Hansen 2004)

LARGE

Origin: Unknown.

Description: An open mound 43 in. wide × 20 in. high (108 × 50 cm). Leaf blade 11 × 7½ in. (28 × 19 cm), thick, emerging blue becoming greener, widely and irregularly margined chartreuse yellow later turning green, matt above and glaucous below, dimpled, edge gently ruffled, leaf broadly ovate with a mucronate tip and heart-shaped open to folded lobes. Petiole dark blue-green. Flower, funnel-shaped, fragrant, pale lavender with a translucent edge, on an upright, leafy, 27-in. (68-cm) scape in midsummer; fertile.

Cultivation Notes: Site in low light to achieve and retain the subtle leaf color contrasts and their changes through the summer. Best in cooler gardens. Moderate to rapid growth rate.

Similar: *H.* 'Blue Shadows' is smaller.

Hosta 'Dark Star' (R. Herold 1999)

SMALL–MEDIUM

Origin: *★H.* 'Swoosh' × *H.* 'Hadspen Heron'.

Description: A rippled mound 24 in. wide × 12 in. high (60 × 30 cm). Leaf blade 7 × 3½ in. (18 × 9 cm), of average substance, smooth, dark green with a blue cast, irregularly margined ivory, with some transitional chartreuse streaks jetting toward the midrib, satiny above and glaucous below, edge widely rippled, leaf arching, narrowly oval with an acute tip and rounded open lobes. Petiole olive green, finely outlined in ivory near the blade. Flower tubular, lavender, on an upright, glaucous red-dotted green, 18- to 24-in. (45- to 60-cm) scape in midsummer; seedpods green, fertile.

Cultivation Notes: Site in light to full shade. Increases rapidly, providing excellent ground cover. Also good in containers.

Distinguishing Features: Leaves widen with maturity so that young plants and mature plants are hardly recognizable as the same hosta.

Similar: *★H. kikutii* 'Kifukurin Hyuga'; *H.* 'Shelley's'.

Hosta 'Decorata' (L. Bailey N/R)

MEDIUM

Origin: Species of convenience originating in Japan.

Description: A rhizomatous mound 36 in. wide × 15 in. high (90 × 38 cm). Leaf blade 6½ × 4 in. (16 × 10 cm), of average substance, smooth, olive to dark green, fairly evenly margined and streaked pure white, matt above and glossy below, veins widely spaced, edge undulate, leaf oblong to oval with a

Hosta 'Dark Shadows'

Hosta 'Dark Star'

sometimes recurved obtuse tip and with rounded open to pinched lobes. Petiole broadly winged, olive green, outlined in white. Flower narrowly bell-shaped, long, white-throated rich purple, on an upright, leafy, green, 24-in. (60-cm) scape in mid-summer; seedpods abundant, fertile.

Cultivation Notes: Site in light to moderate shade. Although it can be difficult in a garden setting, it can be very effective if left alone to increase around trees or in light woodland.

Similar: *★H*. 'Coquette' has smaller, rounder leaves; *★H*. 'Crepe Suzette'.

Hosta 'Decorata'

Hosta 'Déjà Blu'

Hosta 'Déjà Blu' (Walters Gardens 2005)

MEDIUM

Origin: Sport of *★H*. 'Blue Boy'.

Description: A low mound 45 in. wide × 15 in. high (113 × 38 cm). Leaf blade 8 × 5 in. (20 × 13 cm), of average substance, soft glaucous blue-gray turning blue-green, irregularly margined in tricolor shades of chartreuse, narrowly margined cream with gray-green and cream streaking, smooth, attractively veined, edge slightly rippled, leaf broadly ovate with a cuspidate tip and flat to heart-shaped pinched to over-lapping lobes. Petiole thin, pale blue-green, outlined in cream. Flower: see *H*. 'Blue Boy'.

Cultivation Notes: Site in light shade. Vigorous and fast growing. The outstandingly unusual and attractive leaf variegation takes several seasons to become fully apparent.

Distinguishing Features: The "lightning bolt" variegation.

Similar: *H*. 'Bolt Out of The Blue'; *★H*. 'Rosedale Misty Pathways' has larger leaves; *★H*. 'Toy Soldier'.

Hosta 'Delta Dawn' (K. Vaughn N/R)

LARGE

Origin: *H*. 'Aztec Treasure' hybrid.

Description: An open mound 30 in. wide × 20 in. high (75 × 50 cm). Leaf blade 12 × 9 in. (30 × 23 cm), thick, olive green turning chartreuse yellow, widely and irregularly margined cream to ivory white, with some transitional chartreuse streaks

Hosta 'Delta Dawn'

jetting toward the midrib, matt above and glaucous below, some dimpling when young, becoming seersuckered when mature, edge widely undulate, leaf convex, widely oval with a recurved cuspidate tip and heart-shaped pinched lobes. Petiole shallow, chartreuse, finely outlined in cream. Flower widely flared, pale lavender to near white, opening from a purple-gray bud, on an upright, leafy, mauve-green, 24-in. (60 cm) scape in early summer; fertility unknown.

Cultivation Notes: Site in some morning sun to promote the best leaf color contrast. Moderate growth rate. A spectacular hosta.

Distinguishing Features: Extra-wide ivory margins make a superb tonal contrast with the changing base color of the leaves.

Similar: *H.* 'Joshua's Banner' has a brighter leaf base color and is an equally lovely hosta.

Sports: *H.* 'Delta Desire' has yellow leaves; *H.* 'Delta Pride' has streaked leaves.

Hosta 'Diamond Tiara' (T & Z Nursery & M. Zilis 1985)

SMALL

Origin: Tissue-cultured sport of *H.* 'Golden Tiara'.

Description: A spreading mound 25 in. wide × 14 in. high (63 × 35 cm). A spreading mound. Leaf blade 4½ × 3½ in. (11 × 9 cm), thin, mid- to dark green, with irregular pure white margins sometimes jetting toward the midrib, matt above and shiny below, some dimpling when mature, edge slightly rippled, leaf slightly folded, widely oval with a cuspidate tip and rounded open to pinched lobes. Petiole green, outlined in pure white. Flower: see *H.* 'Golden Tiara'.

Cultivation Notes: Site in good light to moderate shade. A moderate to rapid increaser. Ideal for edging. Also good in a container.

Similar: *H.* 'Touchstone' appears identical.

Sports: *H.* 'Pearl Tiara' is smaller and has a wider leaf margin.

Hosta 'Diamond Tiara'

Hosta 'Don Stevens' (M. Seaver 2004)

MEDIUM

Origin: *H.* 'Neat Splash' hybrid.

Description: A neat, tight mound 40 in. wide × 18 in. high (100 × 45 cm). Leaf blade 9 × 6½ in. (23 × 16 cm), of average substance, dark green, widely and irregularly margined and streaked rich yellow turning ivory to white, glossy above and satiny below, dimpled, veins widely spaced, edge widely undulate and sometimes upturned when mature, leaf broadly ovate with an acute to cuspidate tip and heart-shaped pinched lobes. Petiole light olive green, outlined in cream. Flower funnel-shaped, lavender, on an upright, leafy, red-dotted dark green, 31-in. (78-cm) scape in late summer; fertility unknown.

Cultivation Notes: Site in light to full shade. A moderate to rapid increaser.

Distinguishing Features: Juvenile leaves can be streaked before settling down to variegated margins. The margin can be ¾ in. (2 cm) wide in mature leaves.

Similar: ★*H.* 'Queen Josephine' has larger leaves.

Sports: *H.* 'Don Juan' has white-centered, green-margined leaves; ★*H.* 'Don Quixote' has green margins and a streaked center.

Hosta 'Don Stevens'

Hosta 'Dress Blues' (W. Zumbar 1995)

MEDIUM

Origin: ★*H.* "Breeder's Choice F1" × ★*H.* 'Halcyon'.

Description: An upright, open mound 36 in. wide × 24 in. high (90 × 60 cm). Leaf blade 7 × 3½ in.(18 × 9 cm), thick, smooth, gray-tinted blue-green, irregularly margined creamy yellow, with some transitional celadon streaks jetting toward the midrib, matt to glaucous above and glaucous below, closely veined, edge slightly rippled, leaf arching, lanceolate to oval with an acute tip and tapered pinched lobes. Petiole flattish, gray-green, outlined in ivory, dotted in purple at the base. Flower tubular, pale lavender, on an upright, leafy, glaucous green, 34-in. (85-cm) scape in late summer; fertile.

Cultivation Notes: Site in light to full shade. Increases rapidly but can revert to blue-green if not regularly divided.

Similar: ★*H.* 'Chantilly Lace'.

Sport: *H.* 'Moonstruck' has white-centered blue leaves and is vigorous for this type of hosta.

Hosta 'Eagle's Nest' (R. Lydell 2000)

LARGE

Origin: Tissue-cultured sport of ★*H.* 'Sum and Substance'.

Description: An impressive mound 30 in. wide × 18

Hosta 'Dress Blues'

in. high (75 × 45 cm). Leaf blade 12 × 10 in. (30 × 25 cm), very thick, bright chartreuse to mid-green, widely margined and streaked yellow to cream sometimes jetting toward the midrib, glossy above for part of the season and glaucous below, seersuckered and puckered, edge slightly undulate, leaf deeply cupped, nearly round with a strongly cuspidate to mucronate tip and heart-shaped folded lobes. Petiole short, thick, green, outlined in cream. Flower: see *H.* 'Sum and Substance'.

Cultivation Notes: Site in morning sun in cooler climates to achieve the brightest leaf color. Moderate growth rate. Pest resistant. Ideal for an exotic border that also includes *Miscanthus sinensis* 'Zebrinus' and *Hemerocallis* 'Yellow Angel'.

Distinguishing Feature: Unlike most other sports of *H.* 'Sum and Substance', the leaves are smaller with distinct cupping and the plant is somewhat slower growing. Blooms are tightly clustered just above the foliage mound.

Similar: *H.* 'Lodestar' has leaves with conspicuously rippled edges and even more exaggerated tips.

Hosta 'Earth Angel' (H. Hansen 2002)

VERY LARGE

Origin: Sport of *H.* 'Blue Angel'.

Description: A huge, undulating mound 61 in. wide × 36 in. high (152 × 90 cm). Leaf blade 12 × 9 in. (30 × 23 cm), thick, blue-green with wide pale green splashes, widely and irregularly margined and feathered yellow turning ivory white, matt above and glaucous below, slightly dimpled when mature, veins closely ribbed, edge shallowly undulate, leaf broadly ovate to cuneate with a mucronate tip and heart-shaped pinched lobes. Petiole leaning, blue-green, outlined in cream. Flower: see *H.* 'Blue Angel'.

Cultivation Notes: Site in some morning sun in cooler climates, followed by light shade. Best as a specimen with space to increase over the years. Moderate growth rate. Divide regularly. Not suitable for containers. One of the largest and most outstanding cream-margined blue-leaved hostas. Named Hosta of the Year by the American Hosta Growers Association in 2009.

Similar: *H.* 'Duke of Cornwall'.

Hosta 'El Capitan' (W. & E. Lachman 1987)

LARGE

Origin: *H.* 'Beatrice' hybrid.

Description: An open mound 42 in. wide × 24 in. high (105 × 60 cm). Leaf blade 10 × 9 in. (25 × 23 cm), thick, dark sage green, widely and irregularly margined and streaked creamy yellow, matt above and powdery below, seersuckered and puckered, prominently veined, edge slightly undulate, leaf kinked at the lobes, slightly arching or convex, oval to round with a mucronate tip and heart-shaped open to pinched lobes. Petiole dark green, outlined in cream. Flower bell-shaped, rich mauve, opening from a gray-mauve bud, on an upright, bare, 34-in. (85-cm) scape from mid- to late summer; fertile.

Hosta 'Eagle's Nest'

Hosta 'Earth Angel'

Hosta 'El Capitan'

Hosta 'Electrum Stater'

Hosta 'El Niño'

Cultivation Notes: Site in some morning sun except in the hottest climates, where it needs light to full shade. Increases rapidly. Reasonably pest resistant. Useful as a border specimen or for background planting. Lovely with blue-leaved hostas.

Distinguishing Features: Transitional celadon streaking and misting.

Similar: ★*H.* 'Carnival'; *H.* 'Standing Ovation'.

Hosta 'Electrum Stater' (A. Malloy 1997)

MEDIUM

Origin: Sport of ★*H.* 'Abiqua Recluse'.

Description: A dense mound 26 in. wide × 12 in. high (65 × 30 cm). Leaf blade 7½ × 6½ in. (19 × 16 cm), thick, shiny chartreuse to bright golden yellow, irregularly margined cream-yellow turning pure white, with some transitional chartreuse streaks jetting toward the midrib, seersuckered and puckered, edge slightly rippled, leaf cupped or convex, widely oval to nearly round with a mucronate tip and heart-shaped overlapping lobes. Petiole chartreuse yellow, outlined in cream. Flower: see *H.* 'Abiqua Recluse'.

Cultivation Notes: Tolerates sun all day except in the hottest climates, where two hours of morning sun is sufficient. Increases rapidly. Pest resistant.

Distinguishing Features: The tri-toned foliage at different stages of its color changes and the streaks jetting into the leaf center.

Similar: *H.* 'Gaiety' is slightly smaller and needs shade; *H.* 'June Moon' has smaller, more puckered leaves; ★*H.* 'Saint Elmo's Fire'; *H.* 'Sunshine Glory' has wider margins and is more puckered; *H.* 'Zodiac'.

Sport: *H.* 'Rich Uncle' has lutescent yellow leaves.

Hosta 'El Niño' PP14,632 (P. Warmerdam 2003)

MEDIUM

Origin: *H.* 'Halcyon' hybrid.

Description: A graceful mound 30 in. wide × 20 in. high (75 × 50 cm. Leaf blade 6 × 4½ in. (15 × 11 cm), of good substance, smooth, intense blue-gray, irregularly margined white with celadon streaking, matt above and glaucous below, veins closely spaced, edge slightly undulate, leaf ovate with an attractively cuspidate tip and open to pinched lobes. Petiole blue-gray, narrowly outlined in white. Flower bell-shaped, purple-striped lavender, on an upright, leafy, glaucous blue-gray 24-in. (60-cm) scape from mid- to late summer; sterile.

Cultivation Notes: Site in low light to dappled shade to retain the best leaf color. Good in containers or at the edge of light woodland. Ideal where pure white variegation is required.

Distinguishing Features: The attractive variegated margin widens considerably over the years.

Similar: *H.* 'Aristocrat' has wider leaves and is slower growing.

Hosta 'Emily Dickinson' (W. & E. Lachman 1987)

MEDIUM

Origin: ⋆*H.* 'Neat Splash' × ⋆*H. plantaginea*.

Description: A dense mound 41 in. wide × 18 in. high (102 × 45 cm). Leaf blade 6½ × 4 in. (16 × 10 cm), of average substance, medium green, widely and irregularly margined yellow turning creamy white, with streaks jetting toward the midrib, satiny above and shiny below, smooth, edge slightly undulate, leaf oval with an occasionally kinked, acute tip and with rounded pinched lobes. Petiole green, finely outlined in creamy white. Flower funnel-shaped, fragrant, rich lavender, on an upright, leafy, green, 28-in. (70-cm) scape in late summer; fertility unknown.

Cultivation Notes: Site in some morning sun in cooler climates and provide moisture. Increases rapidly.

Similar: *H.* 'Austin Dickinson' has narrower leaves; ⋆*H.* 'Bold Edger' has rounder leaves; *H.* 'Lacy Belle'

needs shade all day since it has bluer leaves; ⋆*H.* 'Tambourine'.

Hosta 'Emma' (D. & J. Ward 1999)

SMALL–MEDIUM

Origin: *H.* 'Sum and Substance' hybrid.

Description: A dense mound 18 in. wide × 9 in. high (45 × 23 cm). Leaf blade 5 × 3½ in. (13 × 9 cm), of good substance, medium green, widely margined creamy yellow to ivory white, with transitional celadon streaks jetting toward the midrib, satiny above and matt below, veins closely ribbed, edge rippled, leaf arching, oval with a cuspidate tip and flat to rounded open to pinched lobes. Petiole green, outlined in cream. Flower tubular, near white, on an upright or leaning, green, 14- to 15-in. (35- to 38-cm) scape in high summer; seedpods green, fertile.

Cultivation Notes: Site in two hours of morning sun except in warmer climates where it needs moderate shade. A good increaser.

Hosta 'Eventide' (W. & E. Lachman 1992)

MEDIUM

Origin: *H.* 'Tokudama Aureonebulosa' hybrid.

Description: A tiered mound 40 in. wide × 17 in. high (100 × 43 cm). Leaf blade 10 × 7 in. (25 × 18 cm), thick, matt, rich olive green, narrowly and irregularly margined white, with some transitional celadon streaks jetting toward the midrib, prominently veined, edge conspicuously and evenly rippled, leaf slightly arching,

Hosta 'Emily Dickinson'

Hosta 'Emma'

widely oval with a cuspidate tip and heart-shaped pinched lobes. Petiole green, outlined in white. Flower flaring, palest lavender to near white, with contrasting mauve anthers, on an upright, stout, leafy, green, 34-in. (85-cm) scape from mid- to late summer; fertile.

Cultivation Notes: Site in light to full shade. Moderate to good growth rate. Pest resistant. An outstanding hosta.

Distinguishing Features: Interesting leaf surface texture, white rippled leaf edge, and white flowers on scapes with white-variegated leafy bracts.

Hosta 'Fantabulous' (E. Elslager 1999)

MEDIUM–LARGE

Origin: *H.* 'Fascinator' hybrid.

Description: A vase-shaped, open, cascading mound 38 in. wide × 26 in. high (95 × 65 cm). Leaf blade 9½ × 6 in. (24 × 15 cm), of good substance, dark spinach green, very widely and irregularly margined ivory white with celadon streaking, satiny above and glossy below, seersuckered, veins widely spaced, edge almost flat, leaf lightly twisted, ovate with an acute tip and heart-shaped pinched to folded lobes. Petiole stout, streaked and margined white. Flower funnel-shaped, purple-striped lavender, on an upright, leafy, dark green, 24-in. (60-cm) scape in midsummer; sterile.

Cultivation Notes: Site in moderate shade as a specimen plant. Average growth rate. Lovely with *Brunnera* 'Langtrees' and silver-variegated asarums early in the season.

Distinguishing Features: The variegated margin gradually turns creamy yellow, especially in hot climates and bright light.

Similar: ★*H. ventricosa* 'Aureomarginata' has larger leaves.

Hosta 'Fool's Gold' (R. Bowden/P. Ruh 2002)

MEDIUM–LARGE

Origin: Sport of *H.* 'Fortunei' originating in Europe. Now thought to be *H.* 'Fortunei Stenantha Variegata', an invalid name.

Description: A dense mound 36 in. wide × 24 in. high (90 × 60 cm). Leaf blade 8½ × 7½ in. (21 × 19

Hosta 'Fantabulous', a juvenile plant

Hosta 'Fool's Gold'

Hosta 'Eventide'

cm), of average substance, mid-green with a grayish cast, irregularly margined muted yellow, matt above and glaucous below, strongly veined, dimpled when mature, edge slightly undulate, leaf arching, oval with a cuspidate tip and heart-shaped open to overlapping lobes. Petiole narrow, gray-green, finely outlined in cream. Flower long, funnel-shaped, lavender, on an upright, leafy, green, 40-in. (100-cm) scape in mid-summer; fertility unknown.

Cultivation Notes: Tolerates some sun but the leaf color will fade. Looks best when grown in light to moderate shade. Vigorous. Its dimensions will increase if given optimum growing conditions. There is another hosta of the same name but this one was registered first so it has priority.

Distinguishing Features: The muted butterscotch-khaki leaf margin holds all season and provides a different emphasis in a border with its unusually contrasting variegation.

Similar: *H.* 'Brass Horn' is identical; *H.* 'Heliarc', although said to be a sport of ★*H.* 'Fortunei Hyacinthina', is remarkably similar; *H.* 'Fortunei Obscura Variegata' has darker, more seersuckered leaves.

Sports: *H.* 'Rhapsody' has large, pendant, dark green leaves with white margins.

Hosta 'Formal Attire' (K. Vaughn 1988)

LARGE

Origin: ★*H.* 'Breeder's Choice' × ★*H. sieboldiana* 'Frances Williams'.

Description: An open mound 60 in. wide × 26 in. high (150 × 65 cm). Leaf blade 10 × 8 in. (25 × 20 cm), of good substance, intense blue-green, widely and irregularly margined creamy yellow turning white, with transitional celadon streaking, matt above and glaucous below, seersuckered, veins widely spaced, edge slightly rippled, leaf convex, widely oval with a mucronate tip and heart-shaped pinched to overlapping lobes. Petiole green, outlined in cream. Flower widely funnel-shaped, pale lavender, on an upright, leafy, green, 38-in. (95-cm) scape in high summer; fertility unknown.

Cultivation Notes: Site in light to moderate shade. Moderate to good growth rate. Useful as a specimen or in a large container. Prized by flower arrangers for its contrasting leaf color and pebbled surface texture.

Similar: *H.* 'Robert Frost' has more streaking in its leaves; ★*H. sieboldiana* 'Northern Exposure' has a smoother, less seersuckered leaf.

Hosta 'Fortunei Albomarginata' (N. Hylander & AHS 1887)

MEDIUM–LARGE

Origin: Sport of *H.* 'Fortunei'.

Description: A dense mound 51 in. wide × 22 in. high (127 × 55 cm). Leaf blade 10 × 6½ in. (25 × 16 cm), of good substance, dark green, irregularly margined white, with streaks jetting toward the midrib,

Hosta 'Formal Attire'

Hosta 'Fortunei Albomarginata'

satiny above and thinly glaucous below, smooth, strongly veined, edge rippled and curved toward the tip, leaf slightly arching, oval with a cuspidate tip and rounded pinched lobes. Petiole dark green, outlined in white. Flower narrowly funnel-shaped, 2 in. (5 cm) long, pale lavender, in a dense raceme, on an upright, leafy, green, 32-in. (80-cm) scape in high summer; slightly fertile.

Cultivation Notes: Site only in shade all day with plenty of moisture at its roots, even in cooler climates. Now surpassed in garden value by some of its selections and sports, which are less fussy about their cultural conditions. Has a tendency to throw sports with variable white margins. Late to emerge in spring.

Similar: *H.* 'Carol' has leaves that are cupped when mature; *H.* 'Zager's White Edge'.

Sports: ★*H.* 'Francee'; *H.* 'North Hills' is smaller.

Hosta 'Fortunei Aureomarginata' (N. Hylander & AHS 1987) ♛

MEDIUM–LARGE

Origin: Natural sport of *H.* 'Fortunei'.

Description: A dense mound 51 in. wide × 22 in. high (127 × 55 cm). Leaf blade 8½ × 6½ in. (21 × 16 cm), of good substance, dark olive green, irregularly margined and streaked rich golden yellow turning cream, satiny above and thinly glaucous below, smooth, edge almost flat, leaf slightly convex, oval with a cuspidate tip and heart-shaped pinched lobes. Petiole olive green, outlined in creamy yellow. Flower narrowly funnel-shaped, 2 in. (5 cm) long, pale lavender, on an upright, leafy, green, 30-in. (75-cm) scape from high to late summer; marginally fertile.

Cultivation Notes: Late to emerge in spring. Tolerates plenty of sun, although the leaf color will fade somewhat. Vigorous, easy to cultivate. Ideal for covering large areas because it is inexpensive. Has been superseded in many gardens by modern introductions. Still considered a classic hosta. A favorite of flower arrangers.

Hosta 'Fortunei Aureomarginata'

Hosta 'Fragrant Dream'

Hosta 'Fragrant Bouquet'

Distinguishing Features: Bracts subtending the flowers are ornamental even after flowering is over.

Similar: *H.* 'Ansley' has leaves with heavier seersuckering; *H.* 'Karin' PP12,663; *H.* 'Royal Flush'; *H.* 'Viette's Yellow Edge' has longer leaves.

Sports: *H.* 'Anne'; *H.* 'Ellerbroek'; ★*H.* 'Twilight'.

Hosta 'Fragrant Bouquet' (P. Aden 1982)

LARGE

Origin: ★*H.* 'Fascination' × *H.* 'Summer Fragrance'.

Description: An open mound 26 in. wide × 18 in. high (65 × 45 cm). Leaf blade 8½ × 6½ in. (21 × 16 cm), of moderate substance, chartreuse to apple green, widely margined yellow to creamy white, satiny above and thinly glaucous below, some dimpling when mature, conspicuously veined, edge widely undulate, leaf convex, widely oval with a cuspidate tip and heart-shaped open to pinched lobes. Petiole pale green, outlined in cream. Flower large, widely funnel-shaped, very fragrant, near white, radially arranged, occasionally with large variegated bracts toward the raceme, on an upright, pale green, 36-in. (90-cm) scape in late summer; usually sterile.

Cultivation Notes: Site in full sun all day, except in the hottest climates, to produce the best leaf color and the most prolific display of flowers. Requires moisture at the roots. Increases rapidly. This cultivar was registered as having streaked leaves but all the plants offered for sale have marginal variegation. Named Hosta of the Year by the American Hosta Growers Association in 1998. An important parent.

Similar: ★*H.* 'Crystal Moon'; *H.* 'Sugar and Cream'.

Sports: ★*H.* 'Color Parade'; *H.* 'Fragrant Dream' has darker green leaves with a brighter yellow margin; ★*H.* 'Guacamole'; *H.* 'Sweet Bouquet' has yellow leaves; ★*H.* 'Sweetie'; ★*H.* 'Sweet Innocence'.

Hosta 'Francee' (M. Klopping & AHS 1986) ♔

MEDIUM

Origin: Sport of ★*H.* 'Fortunei Albomarginata'.

Description: A dense mound 51 in. wide × 21 in. high (127 × 53 cm). Leaf blade 8½ × 5 in. (21 × 13 cm), of average substance, rich dark green, crisply and narrowly margined white with some transitional celadon streaks, matt above and glaucous below, dimpled when mature, edge almost flat, leaf widely oval with a cuspidate tip and heart-shaped open or folded lobes. Petiole dark green, outlined in white. Flower narrowly funnel-shaped, pale lavender, on an upright, leafy, green, 28-in. (70-cm) scape from high to late summer; a few viable seeds.

Cultivation Notes: Tolerates morning sun in all but the hottest climates, but the leaf color will fade to palest olive green. Increases rapidly and thus is excellent for landscaping. Superb in a large container. A classic hosta.

Distinguishing Features: Distinctive, bright purple shoots emerge very late in the season, as they do with all hostas of the Fortunei Group. The narrowly funnel-shaped flowers do not always open at the tips of the scapes.

Similar: *H.* 'Carol' has a slightly wider margin and a more glaucous leaf surface; ★*H.* 'Fortunei Albomarginata'; *H.* 'Fringe Benefit' and *H.* 'Green Gold' have yellow to cream margins; *H.* 'North Hills'; ★*H.* 'Rhino Hide' has a thicker substance and a more defined margin; *H.* 'Zager's White Edge'.

Sports: *H.* 'Academy Fire' emerges with yellow leaves turning light green; *H.* 'Jade Beauty'; *H.* 'Matrix' has a central variegation that emerges golden yellow, becoming white flecked with green; *H.* 'Minuteman'; *H.* 'Pathfinder' occasionally produces a misted effect in the center of the leaf; ★*H.* 'Patriot'; *H.* 'Trailblazer' displays a sharp contrast between the wide, creamy white margin and the dark green center.

Hosta 'Francee'

Hosta 'Francheska' (R. Livingston N/R)

MEDIUM

Origin: *H.* 'Harmony' hybrid. The pod parent was likely to have been ★*H.* 'Marbled Cream'.

Description: A dense mound 36 in. wide × 15 in. high (90 × 38 cm). Leaf blade 7 × 4 in. (18 × 10 cm), of good substance, glaucous blue-influenced bright green, margined yellow turning frosty ivory, with paler green feathering, veins widely spaced, edge widely rippled, leaf arching, broadly elongate with a distinctive acuminate tip and tapered open to pinched lobes. Petiole short, arching, green, finely outlined in cream. Flower funnel-shaped, lavender, on a semi-upright, lavender, 19-in. (48-cm) scape in midsummer; fertility unknown.

Cultivation Notes: Site in moderate shade to retain the blueness in the leaf color. Vigorous. Increases readily. A most attractive new introduction.

Similar: ★*H.* 'Wolverine' does not have the strongly undulate leaf edge.

Hosta 'Frosted Jade' (L. Maroushek 1978)

LARGE–VERY LARGE

Origin: *H. montana* hybrid.

Description: An upright, arching mound 60 in. wide × 28–32 in. high (150 × 70–80 cm). Leaf blade 14 × 10 in.(35 × 25 cm), of good substance, dark sage green, narrowly and irregularly margined pure white, with some transitional celadon streaks jetting toward the midrib, matt above and thinly glaucous below, strongly veined, edge closely rippled, leaf oval with a

mucronate tip and heart-shaped pinched lobes. Petiole deeply channeled, green, outlined in white. Flower funnel-shaped, near white, in a dense raceme, on a leaning, leafy, green, 40-in. (100-cm) scape in mid-summer; seedpods abundant, fertile.

Cultivation Notes: Site in light to moderate shade. Use as a specimen or at the edge of woodland. A classic and still the best of its type.

Distinguishing Features: A slightly upturned leaf edge sets it apart from similar hostas.

Similar: ★*H. montana* 'Mountain Snow'; *H. montana* 'Snow Crust'; *H. montana* 'Summer Snow' has even, white margins and darker green leaves; *H. montana* 'White On'.

Hosta 'Frosted Jade'

Hosta 'Francheska'

Hosta 'Frozen Margarita'

Hosta **'Frozen Margarita'** (R. Solberg 2003)

MEDIUM

Origin: Sport of *H.* 'Fried Bananas'.

Description: An open, arching mound 40 in. wide × 18 in. high (100 × 45 cm). Leaf blade 8 × 6 in. (20 × 15 cm), thick, leathery, glossy, golden yellow, narrowly and irregularly margined white, moderately seersuckered, veins widely spaced, edge slightly undulate, leaf broadly ovate with a recurved cuspidate tip and pinched to folded heart-shaped lobes. Petiole long, chartreuse green, finely outlined in white. Flower: see *H.* 'Fragrant Bouquet'.

Cultivation Notes: Tolerates sun all day, except in the hottest climates, given sufficient moisture to prevent leaf scorch. Ideal in containers in cooler gardens sited to appreciate the fragrance of the superb flowers. Increases rapidly.

Similar: *H.* 'Joshua's Banner'.

Hosta **'Gay Blade'** (W. & E. Lachman 1988)

MEDIUM

Origin: Seedling of ★*H.* 'Resonance' × ★*H.* 'Halcyon'.

Description: A rippled mound 41 in. wide × 18 in. high (102 × 45 cm). Leaf blade 8½ × 2¾ in. (21 × 7 cm), of good substance, gray-green, irregularly margined ivory to pure white, with streaks jetting toward the midrib, satiny above and glaucous below, smooth, edge widely rippled, leaf undulate, elliptic with an acute tip and heart-shaped pinched lobes. Petiole oblique, gray-green, finely outlined in white. Flower 2 in. (5 cm) long, funnel-shaped, lavender, on an upright, leafy, purple-dotted gray-green, 28-in. (70-cm) scape in late summer; fertility unknown.

Cultivation Notes: Site in light to full shade all day as the margins can burn if exposed to strong sunlight, even in cooler climates. Vigorous, easy to grow.

Distinguishing Features: Leaves last well into autumn.

Similar: ★*H.* 'Chantilly Lace' has thinner leaves; *H.* 'Everlasting Love'; *H.* 'Lacy Belle'.

Hosta **'Gemini Moon'** (V. Wade N/R)

MEDIUM–LARGE

Origin: Sport of ★*H.* 'Abiqua Moonbeam'.

Description: A dense, somewhat asymmetrical mound 40 in. wide × 20 in. high (100 × 50 cm). Leaf blade 8 × 7½ in. (20 × 19 cm), thick, matt dark green, very widely and irregularly margined chartreuse becoming soft yellow then glowing golden yellow with chartreuse streaking, seersuckered and puckered, strongly veined, edge slightly undulate, leaf slightly convex when mature, broadly ovate to nearly round with a recurved cuspidate tip and heart-shaped open to pinched lobes. Petiole dark green, outlined in yellow. Flower: see *H.* 'August Moon', the parent of ★*H.* 'Abiqua Moonbeam'.

Cultivation Notes: Site in some morning sun in cooler climates, or in light shade in warmer climates. Vigorous. Moderate growth rate. Sometimes throws all-yellow leaves which should be removed to prevent reversion. Grow with ferns or blue-leaved hostas.

Hosta 'Gay Blade'

Hosta 'Gemini Moon'

Distinguishing Features: Leaf color more pronounced and leaf margin wider than its parent. One of the best of the many descendents of ★*H*. 'August Moon'.

Hosta 'Ginko Craig' (J. Craig & A. Summers & AHS 1986)

SMALL–MEDIUM

Origin: Imported from Japan, now considered to be identical to *H. helonioides* 'Albopicta'.

Description: A dense, spreading mound 44 in. wide × 14 in. high (110 × 35 cm). Leaf blade 5 × 2 in. (13 × 5 cm), thin, dark green, crisply margined pure white with some transitional celadon streaking, matt above and slightly shiny below, some dimpling

Hosta 'Ginko Craig'

Hosta 'Sarah Kennedy'

when mature, edge rippled, leaf arching, slightly convex, elliptic with an acute tip and tapered open lobes. Petiole shallow, green, distinctly outlined in white. Flower open funnel-shaped, dark purple-striped purple, on an upright, bare, green, 22-in. (55-cm) scape from late summer to early autumn; very fertile.

Cultivation Notes: Site in light to moderate shade. The supreme edging hosta since it is vigorous and easy to grow. Displays a very noticeable difference between the narrow, rippled, lanceolate, juvenile leaf blades and the mature elliptic to oval ones.

Similar: *H*. 'Allen P. McConnell'; *H*. 'Blade Runner'; *H*. 'Bunchoko'; *H*. 'Excalibur' is identical; *H*. 'Ground Master'; *H*. 'Jadette' has a creamier margin; *H*. 'Lime Fizz' is smaller; ★*H*. 'Little Wonder'; *H*. 'Peedee Laughing River' has slightly wider and more rippled leaves; *H*. 'Princess of Karafuto' is virtually identical.

Sports: ★*H*. 'Hi Ho Silver'; *H*. 'Sarah Kennedy' has significantly wider margins.

Hosta 'Ginsu Knife' (R. Solberg 2002)

MEDIUM

Origin: *H*. 'Iron Gate Supreme' × ★*H*. 'Green Fountain'.

Description: A cascading mound 28 in. wide × 14 in. high (70 × 35 cm). Leaf blade 10 × 3½ in. (25 × 9 cm), of average substance, shiny, olive green, widely and irregularly yellow-margined fading to near white, with transitional chartreuse streaking, veins ribbed,

Hosta 'Ginsu Knife'

edge serrated, leaf conspicuously undulate, arching, elliptic with an acute twisted tip and tapered open to slightly pinched lobes. Petiole flat, olive green, outlined and streaked cream and chartreuse, rippled. Flower open, flared, with reflexed petals, fragrant, white, on an upright to arching, bare, green, 20-in. (40-cm) scape in late summer; fertility not established.

Cultivation Notes: Site in morning sun in cooler climates, otherwise in light shade. Dimensions are likely to increase in optimum growing conditions. The leaves can be rather flaccid. Unstable variegation can produce streaking into the center of the blade and has now produced a streaked form. *Hosta* 'Ginsu Knife' is a superb, distinct, recent introduction.

Distinguishing Features: A dramatically arching, serrated leaf accentuated by an exaggeratedly twisted tip.

Sports: *H.* 'Ginsu Knife Supreme' has streaked leaves; *H.* 'Machete' has green leaves.

Hosta 'Gloriosa' (G. Krossa & A. Summers & AHS 1986)

MEDIUM

Origin: Thought to belong with the *H.* 'Fortunei' assemblage.

Description: A dense mound 42–46 in. wide × 18 in. high (105–116 × 45 cm). Leaf blade 7 × 4 in. (18 × 10 cm), of average substance, dark green, very narrowly and regularly margined pure white, matt above

and thinly glaucous below, dimpled when mature, veins ribbed, edge almost flat, leaf slightly cupped when mature, elliptic to oval with a cuspidate to mucronate tip and tapered open lobes. Petiole olive green, very finely outlined in white. Flower: funnel-shaped, pale lavender on an oblique, leafy, olive green, 38 in. (95 cm) scape in late summer; sterile.

Cultivation Notes: Site in light to moderate shade. Although the variegation is usually uniform, it occasionally throws white streaks toward the midrib. Vigorous, easy to grow.

Distinguishing Features: Leaves have a distinctly upturned stance when mature. The raceme is bunched toward the top of the scape.

Similar: *H.* 'Change of Tradition'.

Hosta 'Goddess of Athena' (Kuk 1987)

MEDIUM

Origin: *★H.* 'Decorata' selfed.

Description: A spreading mound 30 in. wide × 16 in. high (75 × 40 cm). Leaf blade 7 × 4½ in. (18 × 11 cm), of good substance, dark green, consistently margined creamy yellow to ivory white with occasional streaks, satiny above and glossy below, widely and conspicuously veined, slight dimpling toward the base, edge slightly undulate, leaf oblong to oval with an obtuse tip and rounded open lobes. Petiole narrow, dark green, clearly outlined in cream. Flower attractive, bell-shaped, rich purple, on a leaning, bare, green, 34-in. (85-cm) scape in late summer; fertile.

Hosta 'Gloriosa'

Hosta 'Goddess of Athena'

Cultivation Notes: Site in light to moderate shade. Superb for woodland planting or ground cover as it increases fairly rapidly.

Distinguishing Features: Leaf margin is creamier than its parent. Plant is more rhizomatous than most hostas.

Similar: ★*H.* 'Bold Edger'; ★*H.* 'Queen Josephine'.

Sports: *H.* 'First Impressions' has streaked leaves; *H.* 'Green Smash' has green leaves.

Hosta 'Golden Tiara' (R. Savory 1977) ♔

SMALL–MEDIUM

Origin: Once thought to be a radiation-induced mutation of ★*H. nakaiana* but now considered to be of ★*H. capitata* origin.

Description: A spreading mound 38 in. wide × 16 in. high (95 × 40 cm). Leaf blade 5 × 4½ in. (13 × 11 cm), of moderate substance, mid-green, irregularly margined chartreuse turning yellow then fading to cream, with transitional chartreuse streaking, matt above and shiny below, some dimpling when mature, edge slightly rippled, leaf widely oval with an acute to mucronate tip and heart-shaped open to pinched lobes. Petiole olive green, outlined in cream. Flower widely funnel-shaped, rich lavender to purple, in a dense cluster, on an upright, leafy, olive green, 22- to 25-in. (55- to 63-cm) scape in late summer; seedpods few, fertile.

Cultivation Notes: Site in good light to light shade. Increases rapidly and will exceed these dimensions

given optimum growing conditions. Leaves are variable in shape, the outer ones being oval, the inner ones sometimes almost round. Flowers turn a deeper purple when exposed to sunlight. Some rebloom is possible if spent scapes are removed. Among the most important hostas ever introduced. Lovely in a container. Winner of the 1994 Alex J. Summers Distinguished Merit Hosta Award.

Sports: ★*H.* 'Diamond Tiara'; *H.* 'Emerald Scepter'; *H.* 'Glen Tiara'; ★*H.* 'Golden Scepter'; ★*H.* 'Grand Tiara'; *H.* 'Jade Scepter'; ★*H.* 'Platinum Tiara'; *H.* 'Ribbon Tiara';★*H.* 'Royal Tiara'.

Hosta 'Gold Heart'

Hosta 'Golden Tiara'

Hosta 'Grand Tiara'

Hosta '**Grand Tiara**' (A. Pollock 1991)

SMALL—MEDIUM

Origin: Polyploid tissue-cultured sport of ★*H.* 'Golden Tiara'.

Description: A dense mound 36 in. wide × 14 in. high (90 × 35 cm). Leaf blade 5 × 4½ in. (13 × 11 cm), thick, mid-green, very widely and irregularly margined chartreuse to yellow, later fading to ivory, matt above and shiny below, some dimpling when mature, veins widely spaced, edge almost flat, leaf widely oval with a mucronate tip and heart-shaped pinched lobes. Petiole green, outlined in chartreuse. Flower: see *H.* 'Golden Tiara'.

Cultivation Notes: Site in morning sun to promote good leaf color. Vigorous. Increases rapidly. Prefers a loose, friable soil. Lovely with *Tricyrtis* 'Lightening Strike'. The first of the polyploid hostas of the Tiara Series which is capable of passing on leaves of thicker substance to its progeny.

Sports: *H.* 'Amber Tiara'; *H.* 'Crystal Tiara'; *H.* 'Gilded Tiara' has white-margined golden-yellow leaves; *H.* 'Gold Heart' has reverse variegation with more vivid coloring; *H.* 'Grand Gold' has golden-yellow leaves; *H.* 'Grand Prize'; ★*H.* 'Heavenly Tiara' is smaller than most of the hostas of the Tiara Series and has golden-yellow leaves margined ivory white; *H.* 'Topaz Tiara'.

Hosta '**Great Escape**'

Hosta '**Great Escape**' PP19,003 (J. van den Top 2006)

MEDIUM

Origin: Sport of ★*H.* 'Halcyon'.

Description: A broadly spreading mound 12 in. wide × 6 in. high (30 × 15 cm). Leaf blade 5 × 3 in. (13 × 8 cm), of good substance, gray-influenced blue-green, very widely and irregularly margined ivory, with a few celadon streaks jetting toward the midrib, thinly glaucous above and glaucous below, smooth, veins widely spaced, edge nearly flat with occasional shallow kinks in mature plants, leaf broadly ovate with a mucronate tip and flat to heart-shaped open to pinched lobes. Petiole gray-green, finely outlined in ivory. Flower: see *H.* 'Halcyon'.

Cultivation Notes: Site in moderate shade. Moderate growth rate. Looks superb in a container or as a foreground specimen grown with cerise Japanese azaleas. Registered as a very young plant so is likely to greatly exceed the stated dimensions. A splendid newer introduction deserving of a prominent place in any collection.

Distinguishing Features: Shapely leaves with very wide ivory margins.

Similar: *H.* 'Aristocrat' is less vigorous; *H.* 'Valley's Glacier' has cream margins and is just as spectacular.

Hosta '**Great River Sonata**' (Dubuque Regional Hosta Society/M. Zilis 2004)

LARGE

Origin: Sport of *H.* 'Moonlight Sonata'.

Description: An open mound 50 in. wide × 24 in. high (126 × 60 cm). Leaf blade 11 × 9 in. (28 × 23 cm), thick, leathery, green-gray with a slight blue cast, narrowly and irregularly margined ivory, satiny above and glaucous below, smooth, veins widely spaced, edge shallowly undulate, leaf flat, broadly ovate with a cuspidate tip and open to pinched lobes. Petiole dark green, finely outlined in ivory. Flower funnel-shaped, fragrant, violet-flushed pale lavender, on a leaning, leafy, green, 18-in. (45-cm) scape from late summer to early autumn; fertility unknown.

Cultivation Notes: Best in cooler climates in shade. The blue cast gradually disappears from the leaf leaving a dark green color. The variegated margins are an added enhancement to its plain-leaved parent, and the heavy flower trusses are a bonus if grown with blue-flowered asters and mauve-flowered colchicums, providing a delightful sight in the autumn garden. Alternatively, contrast it with ★*H.* 'Fire Island' whose harsh golden leaves and red petioles will create a lively picture. The gift plant for the Mississippi River Hosta Society convention in 2004.

Hosta 'Hampshire County' (W. & E. Lachman 1993)
MEDIUM–LARGE

Origin: (*H.* 'Banana Sundae' × *H.* 'Sea Drift') × *H.* 'Blue Shadows'.

Description: An overlapping mound 30 in. wide × 24 in. high (75 × 60 cm). Leaf blade 9 × 6 in. (23 × 15 cm), of good substance, dark green, very widely and irregularly margined yellow turning white, with many paler streaks, matt above and glaucous below,

Hosta 'Great River Sonata'

Hosta 'Hampshire County'

seersuckered, prominently veined, edge randomly undulate, leaf convex, broadly ovate with a mucronate tip and heart-shaped open to pinched lobes. Petiole dark green, outlined in cream to white. Flower funnel-shaped, near white, opening from a palest lavender bud, on a stout, upright, leafy, green, 28-in. (70-cm) scape in midsummer; fertile.

Cultivation Notes: Site in good light to moderate shade to retain the blueness in the leaf. Although it is an older introduction, it has been hard to find; now that its availability has improved, it is sure to be greatly in demand.

Distinguishing Features: A very noticeable seasonal change in leaf color, as leaves emerge blue-green with a pale yellow margin and by midsummer turn dark green with a white margin.

Hosta 'Hanky Panky' PP16,217 (Shady Oaks Nursery/H. Hansen 2004)
SMALL–MEDIUM

Origin: Sport of ★*H.* 'Striptease'.

Description: A strikingly variegated mound 33 in. wide × 13 in. high (83 × 33 cm). Leaf blade 7 × 3 in. (18 × 8 cm), of average substance, matt, dark olive green, widely and irregularly margined pale chartreuse green with a randomly marked silver-white halo separating the margin from the center, the base color gradually turning creamy yellow and the margin turning ivory with a pale green overlay, some olive green retained mostly toward the tip, seersuckered, edge almost flat, leaf ovate with a cuspidate

Hosta 'Hanky Panky'

tip and tapered open to pinched lobes. Petiole olive green, outlined in chartreuse. Flower: see *★H.* 'Fortunei Hyacinthina'.

Cultivation Notes: Site in good light to dappled shade for optimum leaf color, which is most outstanding in early summer when the white halo is most clearly visible. Excellent in containers. Vigorous. Fast growing. The complex variegation may disappear unless the plant is frequently divided.

Distinguishing Features: Probably the most interesting of the many similar sports from *★H.* 'Striptease'.

Similar: *H.* 'Cabaret' has green leaves very widely margined cream.

Hosta 'Happy Camper' (G. Johnson N/R)

MEDIUM

Origin: *★H.* 'Neat Splash' × *H. sieboldiana* 'Northern Halo'.

Description: An open mound 26 in. wide × 12 in. high (65 × 30 cm). Leaf blade 8 × 5 in. (20 × 13 cm), of good substance, rich dark green, widely and irregularly margined white, with occasional pale green transitional streaks jetting toward the midrib, satiny above and glaucous below, seersuckered, edge gently ruffled, leaf rounded with a mucronate tip and heart-shaped pinched lobes. Petiole dark green, outlined in white. Flower funnel-shaped, pale lavender, on an upright, leafy, green, 18-in. (45-cm) scape in high summer; fertility unknown.

Cultivation Notes: Site in moderate shade. Slow to moderate growth rate but will probably exceed its

registered dimensions. Pest resistant. An outstanding new border plant.

Distinguishing Features: Rounded leaves with sharp variegational contrast and seersuckering.

Hosta 'Harpoon' (R. Herold 2000)

MEDIUM

Origin: *★H.* 'Swoosh' × *★H. yingeri*.

Description: An open mound 24 in. wide × 14 in. high (60 ×35 cm). Leaf blade 11 × 3½ in. (28 × 9 cm), of average substance, mid- to dark green, irregularly margined and streaked cream, glossy above and satiny below, dimpled, prominently veined, edge unevenly rippled, leaf arching, shallowly undulate, lanceolate to ovate with an acute tip and tapered open to pinched lobes. Petiole narrowly-channeled, green, finely outlined in yellow to cream. Flower spider-shaped, violet with a contrasting white center, widely spaced on an upright, green, leafy, 40-in. (100-cm) scape from mid- to late summer; fertility unknown.

Cultivation Notes: Site in morning sun followed by light shade in cooler gardens. The margin fades from yellow to cream. Vigorous. A multi-award winner.

Similar: *★H.* 'Cordelia'; *★H.* 'Don Stevens'.

Hosta 'Hawkeye' (L. Maroushek 1999)

SMALL

Origin: Sport of *★H.* 'Gold Edger'.

Description: A diffuse mound 25 in. wide × 10 in. high (63 × 25 cm). Leaf blade 3½ × 2½ in. (9 × 6 cm), thick, bright mid-green, widely and irregularly

Hosta 'Happy Camper'

Hosta 'Harpoon'

margined yellow, satiny above and matt below, slightly dimpled, edge flat, leaf folded, upward-facing, nearly round with a mucronate tip and heart-shaped open lobes. Petiole narrow, green, finely outlined in yellow. Flower: see *H.* 'Gold Edger'.

Cultivation Notes: Site in morning sun except in warmer climates. Seen at its best in a container or a rock garden. Moderate growth rate.

Similar: *H.* 'Radiant Edger'; *H.* 'Timothy'.

Hosta 'Heartbeat' (D. Dean 1999)

SMALL–MEDIUM

Origin: *H.* 'Liberty Bell' × ★*H.* 'Dorset Clown'.

Description: A dense mound 31 in. wide × 11 in. high (78 × 28 cm). Leaf blade 6½ × 5 in. (16 × 13 cm),

Hosta 'Hawkeye'

Hosta 'Heartbeat'

thick, mid-green, irregularly margined cream to golden yellow, shiny above and glaucous below, dimpled, veins ribbed, edge slightly undulate, leaf shallowly cupped or convex, widely oval with a cuspidate tip and heart-shaped overlapping lobes. Petiole narrow, light green. Flower bell-shaped, lavender, on an upright, leafy, pale green, 20-in. (50-cm) scape in late summer; sterile.

Cultivation Notes: Site in light to moderate shade. Average growth rate. Grow in containers or at the front of the border for a colorful effect and nicely textured leaves.

Hosta 'Heavenly Tiara' (Walters Gardens 1998)

SMALL

Origin: Tissue-cultured sport of ★*H.* 'Grand Tiara'.

Description: A spreading mound 36 in. wide × 14 in. high (90 × 35 cm). Leaf blade 4 × 3½ in. (10 × 9 cm), thick, chartreuse to golden yellow, widely and irregularly margined cream, with streaks jetting toward the midrib, dimpled when mature, edge flat, leaf folded to cupped, oval with a mucronate tip and tapered open to pinched lobes. Petiole narrow, chartreuse, finely outlined in cream. Flower: see ★*H.* 'Golden Tiara'.

Cultivation Notes: Best grown in good light under a north wall. Much tougher than its delicate coloring suggests. Moderate growth rate.

Distinguishing Features: Leaf color brightens by early summer and the margins turn ivory. Has reverse variegation of *H.* 'Crystal Tiara'.

Similar: *H.* 'Olympic Edger'.

Hosta 'Heavenly Tiara'

236

Hosta 'Hi Ho Silver' (Walters Gardens 1997)

SMALL

Origin: Tissue-cultured sport of ⋆*H.* 'Ginko Craig'.

Description: A dense, spreading mound 16 in. wide × 12 in. high (40 × 30 cm). Leaf blade 6 × 2 in. (15 × 5 cm), of good substance, mid olive green, widely margined pure white, with some transitional chartreuse streaking, matt above and shiny below, edge conspicuously rippled, leaf slightly folded, linear to lanceolate with an acute tip, tapered open lobes. Petiole green with creamy white streaks. Flower: see *H.* 'Ginko Craig'.

Cultivation Notes: Site in light to moderate shade. Moderate growth rate. Useful as a contrast in front of large blue-leaved hostas.

Distinguishing Features: Maintains its smaller leaves, eventually having wider margins than its parent.

Similar: ⋆*H.* 'Ginsu Knife'.

Hosta 'His Honor' (S. Wilkins/J. Wilkins 2000)

LARGE

Origin: Seedling of *H.* 'Herb Benedict'.

Description: A dome-shaped mound 49 in. wide × 24 in. high (122 × 60 cm). Leaf blade 14 × 11½ in. (35 × 29 cm), of average to good substance, mid-green, widely and irregularly margined chartreuse turning creamy white, satiny above and matt below, edge widely rippled when juvenile and almost flat when mature, leaf slightly convex, widely oval with a mucronate tip and heart-shaped overlapping lobes. Petiole green, outlined in chartreuse. Flower tubular, lavender-striped near white, on an upright, leafy,

green, 37- to 42-in. (94- to 105-cm) scape in high summer; seedpods green, fertile.

Cultivation Notes: Site in good light to light shade. Moderate growth rate.

Distinguishing Features: Muted chartreuse leaf margins.

Hosta 'Hot Diggity Dog' (E. Elslager 1998)

SMALL–MEDIUM

Origin: *H.* 'Sea Prize' hybrid.

Description: An upright mound 18 in. wide × 15 in. high (45 × 38 cm). Leaf blade 7 × 6 in. (18 × 15 cm), thick, satiny, rich chartreuse, widely and irregularly margined ivory turning golden yellow, intensely seersuckered, edge flat, leaf cupped, nearly round with

Hosta 'His Honor'

Hosta 'Hi Ho Silver'

Hosta 'Hot Diggity Dog'

237

a mucronate tip and heart-shaped open to pinched lobes. Petiole olive green, outlined in ivory. Flower funnel-shaped, white, on an upright, leafy, ivory-green, 18- to 24-in. (45- to 60-cm) scape from mid- to high summer; seedpods green, fertile.

Cultivation Notes: Site in morning sun in cooler climates to promote the best leaf color, elsewhere in shade all day. Slow to increase. A superb introduction that deserves more recognition.

Similar: *H.* 'Citation' of which *H.* 'Excitation' is a reverse sport; *H.* 'June Moon'.

Hosta 'Hush Puppie' (T. Avent 2005)

SMALL

Origin: ((*H.* 'Beatrice' × open-pollinated seedling) × open pollinated seedling) × *H. venusta*.

Description: A dense mound 16 in. wide × 5½ in. high (40 × 14 cm). Leaf blade 2½ × ¾ in. (6 × 2 cm), of average substance, medium green, irregularly margined yellow turning cream with some feathering, matt above and thinly glaucous below, slight dimpling, veins reasonably prominent, edge slightly rippled, leaf lightly cupped, broadly ovate with a mucronate tip and tapered open lobes. Petiole green, outlined in yellow, dotted in mahogany on the reverse. Flower funnel-shaped, deep purple, on an upright, bare, green, 8-in. (20-cm) scape from mid- to high summer; fertile.

Cultivation Notes: Site in light shade. Very vigorous and fast-growing. An extremely attractive little hosta for edging and ground cover. Also makes an attractive container specimen. A superb recent introduction for the smaller garden.

Distinguishing Features: Leaf shoots with mahogany-purple sheaths.

Sports: *H.* 'Lakeside Scamp' has more prominent leaf tips.

Hosta 'Ice Cream' (R. Rossing 1998)

SMALL

Origin: Tissue-cultured sport of ★*H.* 'Vanilla Cream'.

Description: A low, rhizomatous mound 12 in. wide × 9 in. high (30 × 23 cm). Leaf blade 3 × 3 in. (8 × 8 cm), thick, satiny, mid to dark olive green, widely and irregularly margined muted golden yellow, slightly dimpled, veins widely spaced, edge almost flat, leaf slightly convex, widely oval to round with a mucronate tip and heart-shaped open to pinched lobes. Petiole short, shallowly channeled, green, outlined in creamy yellow. Flower: see *H.* 'Vanilla Cream'.

Cultivation Notes: Site in morning sun to high, filtered shade in cooler climates. Moderate rate of growth. Reasonably pest resistant. Lovely against a background of blue-leaved ornamental grass.

Hosta 'Hush Puppie'

Hosta 'Ice Cream'

Hosta 'Jack of Diamonds' (R. Savory 1985)

MEDIUM

Origin: ★*H. sieboldiana* 'Elegans' × a seedling mutation.

Description: A dense, overlapping mound 20 in. wide × 16 in. high (50 × 40 cm). Leaf blade 7 × 6 in. (18 × 15 cm), very thick, leathery, rich blue-green, irregularly margined yellow turning cream, matt above and glaucous below, seersuckered, edge slightly undulate, leaf shallowly cupped or convex, widely oval with a mucronate tip and heart-shaped folded lobes. Petiole light green, outlined in cream. Flower funnel-shaped, near white, in a dense raceme, on an upright, leafy, glaucous gray, 16- to 17-in. (40- to 43-cm) scape from early to midsummer; fertile.

Cultivation Notes: Site in high, filtered shade for best leaf color, although the golden-yellow margin does not scorch. Slow to increase. Pest resistant.

Distinguishing Features: Smaller, with flatter leaves than ★*H. sieboldiana* 'Frances Williams'.

Similar: *H.* 'Bingo'; ★*H.* 'Brave Amherst'; *H.* 'Cartwheels'; *H.* 'Fleeta Brownell Woodroffe'; *H.* 'Kara'; *H.* 'Lake Hitchcock'; *H.* 'Lakeside Legal Tender' has white-margined green leaves; *H.* 'Merry Sunshine'; *H.* 'Wagon Wheels'.

Hosta 'Jewel of the Nile' (K. Walek 2000)

MEDIUM–LARGE

Origin: Sport of ★*H.* 'Dee's Golden Jewel'.

Description: An upright mound 24 in. wide × 28 in. high (60 × 70 cm). Leaf blade 8 × 6½ in. (20 × 16 cm), thick, blue-green, irregularly margined golden yellow turning cream, with streaks jetting toward the midrib, shiny above and glaucous below, dimpled with slight puckering when mature, edge widely rippled, leaf widely oval with a cuspidate tip and heart-shaped pinched lobes. Petiole light green, tinted pink, outlined in yellow. Flower: see *H.* 'Dee's Golden Jewel'.

Cultivation Notes: Tolerates plenty of sun, even in warmer climates, but the hotter the sun the more the leaf color will fade. A moderate increaser. Pest resistant. A superb hosta for all climates. Easily stabilizes to all-yellow leaves, so regular division of the clump is necessary.

Sport: *H.* 'Bell Bottom Blues' has blue leaves.

Hosta 'Jubilation' (S. Wilkins/J. Wilkins 2000)

VERY LARGE

Origin: *H.* 'Sagae' seedling.

Description: A diffuse, upright mound 70 in. wide × 30 in. high (175 × 75 cm). Leaf blade 15 × 12 in. (38 × 30 cm), thick, blue-influenced green, irregularly margined chartreuse green with some streaks, satiny above and glaucous below, seersuckered, prominently veined, edge gently undulate, leaf mostly convex, broadly ovate with a mucronate tip and heart-shaped pinched lobes. Petiole dark green. Flower tubular, pale lavender, on a semi-upright, leafy, lighter green, 42- to 50-in. (105- to 126-

Hosta 'Jack of Diamonds'

Hosta 'Jewel of the Nile'

cm) scape in high summer; seedpod green; fertility unknown.

Cultivation Notes: Site in dappled to full shade to preserve the blueness in the leaf color. Suitable as a background hosta or grown in semi-woodland but would be spectacular as a single specimen in a shaded courtyard with only paving or stonework as a contrast. Plenty of moisture essential. Slow to increase. Moderately pest resistant.

Distinguishing Features: A noticeable seasonal change in leaf color as the leaves turn dark green and the margins become more yellow.

Hosta 'Kalamazoo' (J. Linneman N/R)

MEDIUM

Origin: Stable sport of *H.* 'Valley's Top', a streaked seedling of *H. kikutii*.

Description: A graceful, arching mound 32 in. wide × 20 in. high (80 × 50 cm). Leaf blade 6 × 4 in. (15 × 10 cm), of average substance, mid- to dark green, irregularly margined yellow turning white, with celadon streaks, satiny above and thickly glaucous below, smooth, prominently veined, edge randomly undulate or rippled, leaf arching, ovate with an acuminate tip and heart-shaped pinched lobes. Petiole dark green, outlined in yellow to ivory. Flower funnel-shaped, lavender, on an oblique, leafy, green, 28-in. (70-cm)

scape from mid- to high summer; seedpods dark purple, fertile.

Cultivation Notes: Site in dappled to moderate shade. Moderate to good growth rate but needs several seasons for the leaves to expand to their full width. A colorful and shapely hosta. A superb new introduction that sometimes produces streaked seedlings.

Distinguishing Features: The heavily ribbed cascading leaves.

Similar: ★*H. kikutii* 'Kifukurin Hyuga' has narrower leaves; *H.* 'Shelley's'.

Hosta 'Key Lime Pie' (H. Hansen 2003)

LARGE

Origin: Sport of ★*H.* 'Squash Casserole'.

Description: A dense mound 60 in. wide × 23 in. high (150 × 58 cm). Leaf blade 11½ × 9 in. (29 × 23 cm), of good substance, muted light green turning to chartreuse yellow, widely and irregularly margined chartreuse turning ivory, with pale chartreuse streaking, matt above and glaucous below, moderately seersuckered, prominently veined, edge attractively rippled, leaf slightly convex, broadly ovate to rounded with a mucronate tip and open heart-shaped lobes. Petiole stout, light green, finely outlined in ivory. Flower: see *H.* 'Squash Casserole'.

Hosta 'Jubilation'

Hosta 'Kalamazoo', a juvenile plant.

Cultivation Notes: Ideal for hotter climates and does well in morning sun in cooler regions if given sufficient moisture. Fast growing. Divide regularly.

Distinguishing Features: Differs from its parent in having yellow-margined leaves.

Similar: ★*H.* 'American Icon' has a longer leaf of brighter colors but is not so suitable for gardens in warmer climates; *H.* 'Jujen'.

Hosta 'Lady Isobel Barnett' (D. Grenfell 1996)

VERY LARGE

Origin: First registered sport of ★*H.* 'Sum and Substance'.

Description: A dense mound 60 in. wide × 30 in. high (150 × 75 cm). Leaf blade 18 × 10 in. (45 × 25 cm), thick, light olive green, irregularly margined golden yellow turning cream, satiny above and glaucous below, edge slightly undulate, leaf widely oval to nearly round with a strongly cuspidate to mucronate tip and heart-shaped overlapping lobes. Petiole leaning, stout, light green, outlined in cream. Flower: see *H.* 'Sum and Substance'.

Cultivation Notes: Grows equally well in sun or shade provided adequate moisture is available; even if grown in a container, adequate moisture will encourage deep seersuckering and puckering of the leaves. Moderate to good growth rate. Pest resistant. Yellow

margins of similar cultivars are said to be visible earlier in the new season's growth, but once they are all in full growth, there is virtually no difference in the width or the color of the margins. Lovely with orange daylilies but impressive as a specimen in a huge container.

Similar: *H.* 'Beauty Substance'; *H.* 'Bottom Line'; *H.* 'David A. Haskell'; *H.* 'Small Sum'; *H.* 'Something Good'; *H.* 'Sum It Up'; *H.* 'Sum of All'; *H.* 'Sum Total'; *H.* 'Titanic'; *H.* 'Vim and Vigor'.

Hosta 'Lakeside Cha Cha' (M. Chastain 1994)

MEDIUM

Origin: ★*H.* 'Fascination' × ★*H. montana*.

Description: A semi-upright, diffuse, tiered mound 27 in. wide × 14 in. high (68 × 35 cm). Leaf blade 8 × 6 in. (20 × 15 cm), thick, soft golden chartreuse, widely and irregularly margined creamy white, satiny above and glaucous below, dimpled, veins widely spaced, edge slightly rippled, leaf moderately undulate, widely oval with a cuspidate tip and heart-shaped pinched lobes. Petiole stout, chartreuse, outlined in cream. Flower funnel-shaped, pale lavender, on an upright, leafy, light green, 28-in. (70-cm) scape from mid- to late summer; sterile.

Cultivation Notes: Lutescent. Site in morning sun in cooler climates.

Hosta 'Key Lime Pie'

Hosta 'Lady Isobel Barnett'

Distinguishing Features: Leaves gradually assume a bright yellow glow, but the variegation can sometimes disappear.

Similar: *H.* 'Gin and Tonic'; ⋆*H.* 'Saint Elmo's Fire' has leaves that turn from a vivid yellow to a soft green; *H.* 'Sunny Smiles' has wider variegation.

Hosta '**Lakeside Dragonfly**' (M. Chastain 1997)

SMALL–MEDIUM

Origin: Unknown.

Description: Matures into a very tight, arching mound 30 in. wide × 18 in. high (75 × 45 cm). Leaf blade 7× 3½ in. (18 × 9 cm), thin, medium blue-green, widely margined chartreuse turning ivory white, with celadon streaking, satiny above and matt below, edge shallowly undulate, leaf broadly lanceolate with an acute tip and tapered pinched lobes. Petiole narrowly channeled, blue-green, outlined in ivory. Flower funnel-shaped, pale lavender, on an upright, bare, blue-influenced green, 30-in. (75-cm) scape from high to late summer; fertile.

Cultivation Notes: Site in light shade to retain the blue leaf color. Good in containers or toward the front of a border with astilbes, dicentras, and liriopes.

Distinguishing Features: A very wide margin for a narrow leaf. The thinness of the leaves can cause some leaf blade edges to roll inwards, giving a canoe-like effect.

Similar: *H.* 'Soft Shoulders' has wider leaves but a narrower variegation.

Hosta '**Lakeside Kaleidoscope**' (M. Chastain 1994)

SMALL

Origin: Unknown.

Description: A compact mound 15 in. wide × 8 in. high (38 × 20 cm). Leaf blade 6 × 4 in. (15 × 10 cm), thick, shiny, blue-green, widely and irregularly margined creamy white, with many transitional celadon streaks jetting toward the midrib, strongly veined, edge variably undulate, leaf widely oval with a cuspidate tip and heart-shaped pinched lobes. Petiole blue-green, outlined in creamy white. Flower tubular,

Hosta 'Lakeside Kaleidoscope'

Hosta 'Lakeside Cha Cha'

Hosta 'Lakeside Dragonfly'

near white, on an upright, leafy, green- and white-streaked, 24-in. (60-cm) scape in late summer; fertile.

Cultivation Notes: Site in shade all day, though tolerates most conditions. Vigorous and quickly forms clumps. An extremely attractive small hosta with striking color combinations.

Distinguishing Features: A very wide-feathered margin; sometimes over 50 percent of the leaf is variegated. Leaves markedly widen as the plant matures.

Hosta 'Lakeside Rocky Top' (M. Chastain 1999)
SMALL

Origin: Unknown.

Description: A low, rippled mound 8 in. wide × 4 in. high (20 × 10 cm). Leaf blade 5 × 3 in. (13 × 8 cm), of average substance, rich, dark green, evenly margined ivory cream, satiny above and matt below, prominently veined, edge widely undulate, leaf lightly folded, wavy, ovate with a cuspidate tip and rounded open to pinched lobes. Petiole short, dark green, outlined in cream. Flower bell-shaped, white, on an oblique, leafy, olive-green, 8- to 12-in. (20- to 30-cm) scape in high summer; seedpods green, fertility unknown.

Cultivation Notes: Site in light to moderate shade in a border accompanied by ★*H*. 'Hadspen Blue' or ★*H*. 'Eye Catcher' for contrast. Moderate to fast growth rate.

Distinguishing Features: The distinctively undulating leaves of this shape are unusual in a small hosta.

Hosta 'Leading Lady' (J. & J. Wilkins 1995)
LARGE

Origin: Sport of a *H*. 'William Lachman' seedling.

Description: An upright, moderately dense mound 40 in. wide × 23 in. high (100 × 58 cm). Leaf blade 14 × 10 in. (35 × 25 cm), thick, dark olive green, narrowly and irregularly margined rich golden yellow turning creamy white, satiny above and glaucous below, dimpled and puckered, prominently veined, edge widely undulate, leaf convex toward the tip, widely oval with a cuspidate tip and heart-shaped pinched to overlapping lobes. Petiole narrow, pale green, finely outlined in cream. Flower tubular, pale lavender, on an upright, leafy, glaucous green, 39-in. (98-cm) scape in late summer; fertility unknown.

Cultivation Notes: Site in light to full shade. Moderate growth rate. A superb specimen hosta.

Similar: ★*H*. 'Sagae' has a wider leaf margin.

Hosta 'Leola Fraim' (W. & E. Lachman 1986)
MEDIUM

Origin: *H*. 'Swoosh' hybrid.

Description: A symmetrical mound 17 in. wide × 10½ in. high (43 × 27 cm). Leaf blade 8 × 6 in. (20 × 15 cm), of good substance, dark gray-green, widely and

Hosta 'Lakeside Rocky Top'

Hosta 'Leading Lady'

243

irregularly margined white with some celadon splashing, matt above and glaucous below, seersuckered, edge slightly undulate, leaf cupped or convex, widely oval with a mucronate tip and heart-shaped open to folded lobes. Petiole flattish, gray-green, outlined in white. Flower funnel-shaped, lavender, on an upright, bare, 28-in. (70-cm) scape in late summer; fertile.

Cultivation Notes: Site in high, filtered shade. Moderate growth rate. Lovely in a container and for flower arrangements.

Distinguishing Features: Leaves more seersuckered than those of H. 'Minuteman', ★H. 'Patriot', or H. 'Trailblazer'. On most leaves the margin is narrower toward the lobes.

Similar: H. 'Circle of Light' is about half the leaf size and can tolerate more sun, a full day's sun in northern Virginia; H. 'Columbus Circle' has a slightly narrower leaf margin; H. 'Heart's Content'; H. 'Mildred Seaver'.

Hosta 'Liberty' PP12,532 (J. Machen Jr. 2000)

LARGE

Origin: Tissue-cultured sport of ★H. 'Sagae'.

Description: An upright mound 39 in. wide × 28 in. high (98 × 70 cm). Leaf blade 12½ × 9 in. (31 × 23 cm), of good substance, dark blue-green turning green, widely margined golden yellow turning ivory cream jetting toward the midrib, matt to glaucous above and glaucous below, edge flat, leaf folded, widely oval with a mucronate tip and heart-shaped open to overlapping lobes. Petiole narrow, green, outlined in cream. Flower: see H. 'Sagae'.

Cultivation Notes: Site in light to moderate shade. Slower to increase than its parent. Use as a specimen in the border, with plenty of moisture available to encourage the leaf to widen. May need extra care to achieve its potential.

Distinguishing Features: The spectacular 2½-in. (6-cm) wide leaf margin. The midseason's golden-

Hosta 'Leola Fraim'

yellow variegated new leaves make an attractive contrast to the first flush with their faded ivory margins.

Similar: *H.* 'Clifford's Forest Fire' PP17,644; *H.* 'Ivory Coast' has a rippled leaf edge; *H.* 'Magic Fire' has larger leaves; *H.* 'Majesty' has more robust leaves.

Hosta 'Li'l Abner' (J. Hadrava/M. Vanous/M. Zilis 2003)

MEDIUM–LARGE

Origin: Stable sport of *H.* 'Rosedale Daisy Mae'.

Description: An open mound 40 in. wide × 18 in. high (100 × 7 cm). Leaf blade 7 × 4 in. (18 × 10 cm), of average substance, matt, medium green, very widely and irregularly margined yellow turning orange-gold with paler streaks sometimes outlined white, dimpled, veins widely spaced, edge flat, leaf broadly ovate with a mucronate tip and heart-shaped pinched to folded lobes. Petiole green, finely outlined yellow. Flower large, funnel-shaped, violet-striped near white, on an upright, leafy, green, 20- to 30-in. (50- to 75-cm) scape in high summer; fertility unknown.

Cultivation Notes: Site in light to moderate shade. Requires hot summers to assume the subtle changes in variegation of which it is capable. Increases rapidly.

Distinguishing Features: The silver-white flashes at the transitional changes of the variegation.

Similar: *H.* 'Rosedale Misty Pathways'; *H.* 'Winter Warrior' has slightly longer leaves.

Hosta 'Mack the Knife' (J. Dishon 1996)

SMALL

Origin: *H.* 'Galaxy' × *H.* 'Hadspen Heron'.

Description: An open mound 15 in. wide × 5 in. high (38 × 13 cm). Leaf blade 5 × 2¾ in. (13 × 7 cm), thick, dark green, widely and irregularly margined deep golden yellow to almost orange, with paler streaks jetting toward the midrib, satiny above and matt below, slightly dimpled when mature, edge rippled, leaf slightly convex, oval with a cuspidate tip and tapered open to pinched lobes. Petiole shallow, dark green, outlined in yellow. Flower funnel-shaped, pale lavender, on an upright, bare, green, 13-in. (33-

Hosta 'Li'l Abner'

Hosta 'Liberty'

Hosta 'Mack the Knife'

245

cm) scape in high summer; fertility unknown.

Cultivation Notes: Site in morning sun in cooler climates, otherwise light to moderate shade. Slow to increase. Best suited to containers or rock gardens.

Distinguishing Features: The orange-yellow margin color fades toward the end of the season.

Hosta 'Mardi Gras' (O. Petryszyn 2001)

LARGE

Origin: ★*H.* 'Christmas Tree Gala' × ★*H.* 'Elatior'.

Description: A wide-spreading mound 60 in. wide × 28 in. high (150 × 70 cm). Leaf blade: 14 × 11 in. (35 × 28 cm), thick, mid- to dark green, irregularly margined ivory, with paler green streaking, glossy above and matt below, prominently veined, edge randomly kinked, leaf broadly ovate to rounded with a cuspidate tip and heart-shaped folded to pinched lobes. Petiole green, outlined in ivory. Flower funnel-shaped, palest lavender to almost white, on an upright, leafy, pale green, 36-in. (90-cm) scape in early summer; fertile.

Cultivation Notes: Site in light to moderate shade. Slow to establish but ultimately very large. Pest resistant. A superb background hosta. Grow with ★*H.* 'Daybreak' to light up a dark corner. The leaves retain a blue overlay in low light.

Distinguishing Features: Subtle tonal variegation which is lacking in the leaf of its sibling *H.* 'All That Jazz'.

Similar: ★*H.* 'Mike Shadrack'; ★*H.* 'Sagae'.

Hosta 'Memories of Dorothy' (H. Hansen/H. Gowen 2002)

MEDIUM–LARGE

Origin: (★*H.* 'Dorothy Benedict' × ★*H. pycnophylla*) × ★*H. montana* 'Aureomarginata'.

Description: A dense mound 42 in. wide × 18 in. high (105 × 45 cm). Leaf blade 10 × 7 in. (25 × 18 cm), of average substance, mid-green with a blue cast, irregularly margined and streaked chartreuse gradually turning ivory, satiny above and glaucous white below, dimpled, veins closely spaced, edge slightly undulate, leaf broadly ovate with a mucronate tip and heart-shaped folded or pinched lobes. Petiole reddish. Flower funnel-shaped, white-striped lavender, on an oblique to upright, sometimes-branched, leafy, dark greenish-brown, 32-in. (80-cm) scape from high to late summer; seedpods green, fertile.

Cultivation Notes: Site in light shade to maintain the blueness of the leaf. Moderate growth rate. The seasonal, subtle tonal contrasts make this hosta a worthy contender for a place in every collection.

Similar: *H.* 'Heavenly Beginnings'.

Hosta 'Mike Shadrack' (Kuk 2001)

MEDIUM

Origin: ★*H. sieboldiana* 'Great Expectations' × *H.* 'Rock and Roll'.

Description: A vase-shaped mound 24 wide × 18 in. high (60 × 45 cm). A vase-shaped mound. Leaf blade 10 × 9 in. (25 × 23 cm), thick, gray-green,

Hosta 'Mardi Gras'

Hosta 'Memories of Dorothy'

irregularly margined creamy yellow, with transitional celadon splashes jetting toward the midrib, matt above and glaucous below, seersuckered, edge almost flat, leaf cupped or convex, widely oval to round with a mucronate tip and heart-shaped pinched lobes. Petiole wide, gray-green, outlined in cream. Flower widely flared, near white, on a stout, upright, leafy, gray-green, 20-in. (50-cm) scape with variegated leaf and flower bracts in midsummer; seedpods mid-green, fertile.

Cultivation Notes: Site in good light or high, filtered shade. Moderate growth rate is increased by copious watering. Pest resistant. A great recent introduction.

Distinguishing Features: Very showy variegated leaf and flower bracts.

Hosta 'Millie's Memoirs' (H. Hansen & Shady Oaks Nursery 1999)

MEDIUM

Origin: Tissue-cultured sport of ★*H.* 'Aspen Gold'.

Description: An open mound 36–41 in. wide × 18–20 in. high (90–102 × 45–50 cm). Leaf blade 9 × 6¾ in. (23 × 17 cm), very thick, mid-green, very widely margined and splashed chartreuse to rich yellow jetting toward the midrib, matt above and glaucous below, intensely seersuckered, edge almost flat, leaf deeply cupped, nearly round with a mucronate tip and heart-shaped overlapping lobes. Petiole shallow, green, outlined in yellow. Flower: see *H.* 'Aspen Gold'.

Cultivation Notes: Site in morning sun to turn the margins yellow; however, the more subtle late spring coloring of bluish green leaves with chartreuse margins can be maintained if grown in shade. Very slow to increase but easy to grow in all climates. Pest resistant.

Similar: *H.* 'Aardvark' has the reverse variegation in a muted color contrast; *H.* 'Tranquility'.

Hosta 'Moonlight' (P. Banyai 1977)

LARGE

Origin: Sport of ★*H.* 'Gold Standard'.

Description: A dense mound 50 in. wide × 20 in. high (126 × 50 cm). Leaf blade 9 × 5 in. (23 × 13 cm), of average substance, olive green turning chartreuse

Hosta 'Millie's Memoirs'

Hosta 'Mike Shadrack'

Hosta 'Moonlight', turning from green to yellow.

247

Hosta 'Moon River'

Hosta 'Mount Tom'

Hosta 'Mourning Dove'

yellow, irregularly margined pure white, strongly veined, dimpled when mature, edge slightly rippled, leaf concave or slightly convex, widely oval with a cuspidate tip and heart-shaped open lobes. Petiole chartreuse green, outlined in white. Flower: see ★*H.* 'Fortunei Hyacinthina'.

Cultivation Notes: Site carefully in good light to light shade since the changes of leaf color over the season are the main attraction. A rapid increaser. A classic hosta, one of the first with a yellow leaf center and a white margin but grown less often now.

Similar: *H.* 'Moon Glow' tolerates some sun; ★*H.* 'Patriot's Fire'.

Hosta 'Moon River' (W. & E. Lachman 1991)
MEDIUM

Origin: ★*H.* 'Crepe Suzette' × ★*H.* 'Blue Moon'.

Description: A dense, rounded mound 30 in. wide × 10 in. high (75 × 25 cm). Leaf blade 4¾ × 4 in. (12 × 10 cm), thick, glaucous dark blue-green, irregularly and widely margined yellow turning ivory white, with some streaks jetting toward the midrib, seersuckered, edge flat, leaf shallowly cupped, almost round with a mucronate tip and heart-shaped pinched or overlapping lobes. Petiole dark green, outlined in cream. Flower flared, lavender, on an upright, leafy, 16-in. (40-cm) scape from mid- to late summer; sterile.

Cultivation Notes: Site in good light to light shade. Slow to increase.

Similar: *H.* 'Cherub' is slightly smaller and has narrower margins; ★*H.* 'Pilgrim'.

Hosta 'Mount Tom' (W. & E. Lachman 1995)
MEDIUM–LARGE

Origin: *H.* 'Flamboyant' × ★*H.* 'Christmas Tree'.

Description: A well-poised, semi-upright mound 36 in. wide × 19 in. high (90 × 48 cm). Leaf blade 11 × 10 in. (28 × 25 cm), thick, blue-influenced dark green, very widely and irregularly margined ivory with chartreuse streaks and splashes, matt above and glaucous below, seersuckered, edge randomly kinked, leaf broadly ovate to rounded with a mucronate tip and pinched to folded lobes. Petiole stout, dark green, outlined in ivory. Flower tubular, palest lavender to near white, in a dense raceme, on an upright, leafy, dark green, 24-in. (60-cm) scape from mid- to high summer; fertile.

Cultivation Notes: Site in light to moderate shade to preserve the blue-toned leaf. Slow to increase. Pest resistant. Divide regularly to retain the balance between the margin and the base color.

Distinguishing Features: Attractive leaf shape and striking variegation make this hosta stand out in any border.

Hosta 'Mourning Dove' PP17,311 (H. Hansen 2005)

MEDIUM

Origin: ★*H. kikutii* 'Ozaki Special' (streaked leaves) × ★*H.* 'Blue Jay'.

Description: A low, spreading mound 31 in. wide × 12 in. high (78 × 30 cm). Leaf blade 8 × 4 in. (20 × 10 cm), of good substance, soft blue-gray, irregularly margined muted chartreuse turning creamy yellow, with paler streaking, glaucous above with a silvery white indumentum below, edge almost flat, leaf arching, lanceolate to ovate with an acute tip and tapered to heart-shaped open to pinched lobes. Flower funnel-shaped, pale lavender with violet markings, on an arching, bare, glaucous blue-gray, 16- to 20-in. (40- to 50-cm) scape in late summer; fertile.

Cultivation Notes: Site in low light to moderate shade. Slow to establish. Lovely in a container or grown with ferns and shade-loving yellow grasses such as *Millium effusum* 'Aureum' and *Carex elata* 'Aurea'. Divide frequently.

Similar: ★*H.* 'Wolverine' has larger leaves and is more vigorous.

Hosta 'Oh Cindy' (H. Benedict N/R)

LARGE

Origin: Stable sport of *H.* 'Outrageous'.

Description: An open mound 36 in. wide × 18 in. high (90 × 45 cm). Leaf blade 10 × 8 in. (25 × 20 cm), thick, shiny, dark green, very widely and irregularly margined golden yellow turning ivory white, with many chartreuse streaks jetting toward the midrib, dimpled, prominently veined, edge flat to slightly kinked, leaf slightly convex, broadly ovate with a mucronate tip and heart-shaped pinched lobes. Petiole dark green, finely outlined in ivory. Flower funnel-shaped, pale lavender, on an upright, pale green,

40-in. (100-cm) scape in late summer; sterile.

Cultivation Notes: Site in light shade. Slow to increase but eventually becomes a large hosta. Although the color of the leaf margin varies widely from brilliant, golden yellow to ivory white depending upon light and heat levels and progression of the summer, this large hosta is always attractive and eye-catching.

Distinguishing Features: The reverse sport of ★*H.* 'My Child Insook'.

Hosta 'Opipara Bill Brincka' (W. Brincka 1988)

LARGE

Origin: A clone of *H.* 'Opipara' from Japan.

Description: A rhizomatous, dense, asymmetrical mound 60 in. wide × 28 in. high (150 × 70 cm). Leaf blade 10 × 8 in. (25 × 20 cm), of good substance, waxy, bright olive green, widely and fairly evenly margined rich yellow turning ivory, slight dimpling when mature, edge undulate to twisted, leaf arching, oval with a cuspidate tip and flat to tapered open lobes. Petiole shallow, short, olive green, outlined in cream. Flower tubular, rich purple-striped deep lavender, on an upright, leafy, green, 30-in. (75-cm) scape, held well above the leaf mound, in late summer; fertile.

Cultivation Notes: Site in light to moderate shade. Increases rapidly. Not suitable for container growing.

Hosta 'Oh Cindy'

Distinguishing Features: A virus-free clone of *H.* 'Opipara', registered to distinguish it from its parent which was originally thought to be virus-prone.

Similar: *H.* 'Opipara Koriyama' is smaller in leaf and stature; *H.* 'Patrician'.

Hosta 'Orange Crush' (E. Elslager 2000)

MEDIUM

Origin: *H.* 'Sea Prize' × *H.* 'Maekawa'.

Description: An upright mound 33 in. wide × 24 in. high (83 × 60 cm). Leaf blade 10½ × 9 in. (27 × 23 cm), thick, rich golden yellow, widely and irregularly margined creamy white with some streaking or

Hosta 'Opipara Koriyama'

feathering, satiny above and glaucous below, heavily seersuckered, edge slightly rippled, leaf cupped, nearly round with a mucronate tip and pinched to folded heart-shaped lobes. Petiole narrow, chartreuse with a well-defined cream margin. Flower tubular, purple-striped pale lavender, on an upright, leafy, glaucous green, 30- to 34-in. (75- to 85-cm) scape in late summer; seedpods green, fertile.

Cultivation Notes: Site in some morning sun in cooler climates, in good light to dappled shade in the hottest climates. Increases rapidly. Reasonably pest resistant. An outstanding recent introduction with an attractive pebbled and crumpled leaf texture.

Distinguishing Features: Orange-yellow leaves with a noticeably lighter toned midrib rimmed by a 1⅛-in. (3-cm) margin that is widest toward the petiole.

Hosta 'Parhelion' (Walters Gardens 1997)

VERY LARGE

Origin: Tissue-cultured sport of ★*H.* 'Sum and Substance'.

Description: A dense mound 60 in. wide × 36 in. high (150 × 90 cm). Leaf blade 15 × 12 in. (38 × 30 cm), very thin, bright chartreuse to light green, narrowly and irregularly margined white, shiny above and thinly glaucous below, dimpled to seersuckered, edge gently rippled, leaf shallowly cupped or convex, widely oval with a cuspidate tip and rounded open to

Hosta 'Opipara Bill Brincka'

Hosta 'Orange Crush', the color deepening as summer progresses.

pinched lobes. Petiole narrow, chartreuse, finely outlined in white. Flower: see *H.* 'Sum and Substance'.

Cultivation Notes: Site in morning sun in cooler climates, otherwise in moderate shade. The margin sometimes disappears altogether in parts of the leaf edge. Increases rapidly but is not as robust as other sports of *H.* 'Sum and Substance'.

Distinguishing Features: Very different from all other sports of ⋆*H.* 'Sum and Substance' because of its thin, pale green leaves and narrow white margin.

Similar: *H.* 'Chariots of Fire' is smaller; *H.* 'Zebson' has more leaf substance and the margin, from which there is streaking, is wider.

Hosta 'Patriot' (J. Machen Jr. 1991)

MEDIUM–LARGE

Origin: Sport of ⋆*H.* 'Francee'.

Description: A dense mound 51 in. wide × 20 in. high (127 × 50 cm). Leaf blade 6½ × 5 in. (16 × 13 cm), of good substance, dark green, widely and irregularly margined ivory turning white, with some celadon streaks jetting toward the midrib, satiny above and glaucous below, dimpled, edge slightly rippled, leaf widely oval with a cuspidate tip and rounded open to pinched lobes. Petiole dark green, edged in white. Flower: see *H.* 'Francee'.

Cultivation Notes: Site in good light to moderate shade. Moderate to fast growth rate. Leaves emerge late from rich violet shoots. Among the most popular variegated hostas ever introduced. Superb in the border and in containers. Named Hosta of the Year by the American Hosta Growers Association in 1997.

Similar: *H.* 'Bold Intrigue' has slightly rounder, more seersuckered leaves; *H.* 'Minuteman' has slightly darker green leaves, purer white margins, exceptionally large flowers for a hosta of *H.* 'Fortunei' ancestry, and is somewhat smaller at maturity.

Sports: ⋆*H.* 'Fire and Ice'; *H.* 'Loyalist'; *H.* 'Midnight Ride' has green leaves; *H.* 'Patriot's Fire'; *H.* 'Patriot's Green Pride'; *H.* 'Paul Revere'.

Hosta 'Patriot's Fire'

Hosta 'Parhelion'

Hosta 'Patriot'

Hosta **'Peace'** (P. Aden 1987)

SMALL–MEDIUM

Origin: *H.* 'Love Pat' hybrid.

Description: A neat, overlapping mound 9 in. wide × 4½ in. high (23 × 11 cm). Leaf blade 5 × 3½ in. (13 × 9 cm), thick, dark blue-green, irregularly margined cream to white, with transitional celadon streaks jetting toward the midrib, matt above and a powdery bloom below, seersuckered, edge almost flat, leaf slightly cupped, widely oval to nearly round with a mucronate tip and heart-shaped open to pinched lobes. Petiole narrow, blue-green, outlined in cream. Flower well-spaced, rich lavender, poised at right angles on an upright, glaucous green, 12-in. (30-cm) scape in late summer; fertile.

Cultivation Notes: When grown in shade, the leaf center is bluer; when grown in some sun, a magnificent display of flowers emerges. Slow to increase but can eventually become larger than its registered dimensions given optimum growing conditions. Pest resistant.

Distinguishing Features: Flower scapes stand well above the leaf mound for a hosta of this type, and the flowers are a deeper color.

Similar: *H.* 'Little Doll'.

Hosta **'Percy'** (H. Benedict N/R)

MEDIUM

Origin: Unknown.

Description: A dense, cascading mound 36 in. wide × 15 in. high (90 × 38 cm). Leaf blade 7½ × 4 in. (19 × 10 cm), of average substance, medium to dark green, very widely and irregularly margined rich yellow turning ivory white with some chartreuse streaking, matt above and satiny below, slight dimpling toward the tip, veins closely ribbed, edge flat to randomly kinked near the base, leaf slightly convex, ovate with an acuminate tip and heart-shaped pinched lobes. Petiole dark green, outlined in yellow to ivory. Flower funnel-shaped, lavender, on an upright, leafy, green, 20-in. (50-cm) scape in midsummer; fertility unknown.

Hosta 'Percy'

Hosta 'Pilgrim'

Hosta 'Peace'

Cultivation Notes: Will tolerate some morning sun but is also well suited to growing in the mid-ground of a shaded border or in light woodland surrounded by plainer-leaved plants to accentuate and frame its strikingly variegated foliage. Increases rapidly.

Similar: ★*H.* 'Yellow Splash Rim' has wider leaves and a less clearly defined, less-elegant shape.

Hosta 'Pilgrim' (G. Rasmussen/A. Malloy 1997)

SMALL

Origin: *H.* 'Flamboyant' seedling.

Description: A dense mound 21 in. wide × 8 in. high (53 × 20 cm). Leaf blade 4 × 3 in. (10 × 8 cm), of average substance, matt, gray-green to dark green, widely and irregularly margined golden yellow turning creamy white, veins ribbed, edge flat to occasionally kinked, leaf widely oval with a cuspidate tip and flat to heart-shaped open to pinched lobes. Petiole green, very finely outlined in cream. Flower tubular, lavender, on an upright, bare, dark green, 20-in. (50-cm) scape in midsummer; seedpods green, fertile.

Cultivation Notes: Site in good light to moderate shade. Vigorous, a rapid increaser. Easily exceeds its registered dimensions. An excellent front-of-the-border specimen and good in containers.

Similar: *H.* 'Cherub'; ★*H.* 'Moon River'.

Sports: *H.* 'Pilgrim's Progress' has an even more dramatic marginal contrast and a leaf margin up to 2 in. (5 cm) wide.

Hosta 'Platinum Tiara' (Walters Gardens 1987)

SMALL

Origin: Tissue-cultured sport of ★*H.* 'Golden Scepter'.

Description: A dense, overlapping mound 36 in. wide × 16 in. high (90 × 40 cm). Leaf blade 4 × 3½ in. (10 × 9 cm), thin, chartreuse to golden yellow, narrowly margined pure white, with occasional streaks jetting toward the midrib, smooth, veins widely spaced, edge slightly rippled, leaf widely oval with a cuspidate tip and rounded pinched lobes. Petiole narrow, chartreuse, finely outlined in white. Flower: see ★*H.* 'Golden Tiara'.

Comments: Site in good light to promote the golden-yellow base color. Slower growing than many other hostas in the Tiara Series, making it an ideal pot plant. Winner of the 1989 Alex J. Summers Distinguished Merit Hosta Award.

Similar: *H.* 'Olympic Edger'.

Hosta 'Praying Hands' (G. Williams 1996)

MEDIUM

Origin: Unknown.

Description: An upright mound 16 in. wide × 14 in. high (40 × 35 cm). Leaf blade 7 × 2 in. (18 × 5 cm), of average substance, olive green with a very narrow

Hosta 'Platinum Tiara'

Hosta 'Praying Hands'

253

yellow-gold margin, satiny above and glossy below, smooth, prominently veined, edge rippled, leaf furled, lanceolate with an acute tip. Petiole narrow, dark green, finely outlined in yellow, mahogany-purple at the base, almost decurrent with the leaf blade. Flower bell-shaped, lavender, on an upright, bare, green, 16-in. (40-cm) scape in late summer; sterile.

Cultivation Notes: Site in light to moderate shade. Grow at eye level to get the best effect from the unusual leaf habit. Plant with a collection of ferns or small hostas with contrasting, heart-shaped leaves. Not just an interesting hosta but an unusual and interesting foliage plant.

Distinguishing Features: Leaves are folded and rolled tightly in an upward, outward stance.

Hosta '**Prima Donna**' (J. & J. Wilkins 1995)

LARGE

Origin: *H. 'William Lachman'* sport.

Description: A compact mound 56 in. wide × 21 in. high (140 × 53 cm). Leaf blade 14 × 10 in. (35 × 25 cm), of good substance, dark green, golden yellow

margined turning cream, with occasional streaks jetting toward the midrib, satiny above and glaucous below, some puckering when mature, conspicuously veined, edge widely undulate, leaf slightly folded, widely oval with a cuspidate tip and heart-shaped pinched lobes. Petiole dark green, outlined in yellow. Flower long, tubular, pale lavender, on an upright, glaucous green, 45-in. (113-cm) scape in late summer; sterile.

Cultivation Notes: Site in moderate to full shade with plenty of space around it so that the undulating leaves can be fully appreciated. Increases rapidly.

Distinguishing Features: Flower bracts are tricolored cream, green, and lavender.

Hosta '**Queen Josephine**' (Kuk 1991)

MEDIUM

Origin: Sport of *H. 'Josephine'*.

Description: A vase-shaped mound 34 in. wide × 16 in. high (85 × 40 cm). Leaf blade 7 × 5½ in. (18 × 14 cm), of average substance, glossy, dark green, widely and evenly margined golden yellow turning

Hosta 'Prima Donna'

creamy white, with streaks jetting toward the midrib, smooth, conspicuously veined, edge almost flat, leaf oval with an obtuse tip and heart-shaped open to pinched lobes. Petiole dark green, outlined in yellow. Flower: see ★*H.* 'Joseph'.

Cultivation Notes: Site in morning sun in cooler climates, otherwise good light or moderate shade.

Distinguishing Features: Rated the best glossy leaved hosta.

Similar: *H.* 'Abiqua Delight'; *H.* 'Anglo Saxon' has rounder leaves; *H.* 'Antoinette'; ★*H.* 'Bold Edger'; ★*H.* 'Cordelia'; ★*H.* 'Don Stevens'; ★*H.* 'Emily Dickinson'; ★*H.* 'Goddess of Athena'.

Hosta 'Regal Supreme' (J. van den Top N/R)

LARGE

Origin: Tissue-cultured sport of ★*H.* 'Krossa Regal'.

Description: A stately, vase-shaped mound 36 in. wide × 34 in. high (90 × 85 cm). Leaf blade 11 × 6¾ in. (28 × 17 cm), thick, glaucous gray-blue, very widely and irregularly margined yellow to creamy

white, with some streaks jetting toward the midrib, veins closely ribbed, edge rippled, leaf arching, folded, oval with a cuspidate tip and tapered to pinched lobes. Petiole light green, outlined in cream. Flower: see *H.* 'Krossa Regal'.

Hosta 'Regal Supreme'

Hosta 'Queen Josephine'

Cultivation Notes: Site in good light to light shade. Moderate to good growth rate. Pest resistant. A striking specimen and superb in antique stone containers giving a quite regal appearance.

Similar: *H.* 'Regal Splendor' has narrower margins and was voted Hosta of the Year by the American Hosta Growers Association in 2003.

Hosta 'Resonance' (P. Aden 1976)

MEDIUM

Origin: Unknown.

Description: A spreading mound 30 in. wide × 9 in. high (75 × 23 cm). Leaf blade 6 × 2½ in. (15 × 6 cm),

Hosta 'Regal Splendor'

thin, dark green, irregularly margined yellow turning creamy white, matt above and shiny below, edge rippled, leaf arching, widely lanceolate with an acute tip and tapered open lobes. Petiole dark green, outlined in yellow. Flower funnel-shaped, lavender, on an upright, light green, 20-in. (50-cm) scape in late summer; fertile.

Cultivation Notes: Site in light to moderate shade. Increases rapidly, making it a useful ground cover. Not suitable as a pot plant. Very susceptible to pest damage. Much used as a breeding plant.

Similar: *H.* 'Bold Ribbons'; ★*H.* 'Candy Cane'; ★*H.* 'Crested Surf'; *H.* 'Ground Master' seems identical; *H.* 'Suzanne'.

Sports: *H.* 'Austin Dickinson'; ★*H.* 'Gay Blade'.

Hosta 'Rocky Mountain High' (Kuk 1991)

MEDIUM

Origin: ★*H.* 'Crispula' × ★*H. sieboldiana* 'Elegans'.

Description: An upright mound 16 in. wide × 16 in. high (40 × 40 cm). Leaf blade 8 × 5½ in. (20 × 14 cm), thick, leathery mid-green, irregularly margined chartreuse, with streaks jetting toward the midrib, satiny above and glaucous below, seersuckered to puckered, edge closely rippled, leaf arching, convex, widely oval to nearly round with a twisted tip and heart-shaped overlapping lobes. Petiole stout, wide,

Hosta 'Resonance'

Hosta 'Rocky Mountain High'

pale green, outlined in chartreuse. Flower funnel-shaped, rich lavender, on an upright, leafy, pale green, 28-in. (70-cm) scape in early summer; fertile.

Cultivation Notes: Site in light to moderate shade. Moderate growth rate. Known to exceed its registered dimensions. A superb plant and one of the few introductions involving ★*H*. 'Crispula'. Deserves to be better known.

Distinguishing Features: Attractively rippled, strongly pebbled leaves.

Hosta 'Rosedale Misty Pathways' (J. Hadrava 2000)

LARGE

Origin: A cross of two numbered seedlings from Jerry Hadrava's breeding program.

Description: An overlapping mound 40 in. wide × 19 in. high (100 × 48 cm). Leaf blade 8 × 6 in. (20 × 15 cm), of good substance, matt, dark green, very widely margined golden yellow, with tri-toned paler green feathering at the junction between the marginal variegation and the base color, seersuckered, veins widely spaced, edge flattish with occasional undulations, leaf shallowly cupped, broadly ovate with a mucronate tip and pinched to overlapping lobes. Petiole pale green, outlined in cream. Flower pale lavender, on an upright, leafy, green, 26- to 28-in. (65- to 70-cm) scape in late summer; fertility unknown.

Cultivation Notes: Site in moderate shade where the leaves, with their most attractive complex tonal variegations, may be seen close up. The best tonal effect is achieved in hotter climates; it takes about four seasons of growth for the full effect to be achieved. The margin lightens to paler yellow during the summer.

Distinguishing Features: The tri-tone effect at the junction of the variegated margin and the base color. The large, variegated inflorescence leaves.

Similar: ★*H*. 'Toy Soldier' is smaller.

Hosta 'Sagae' (K. Watanabe 1996)

LARGE–VERY LARGE

Origin: Unknown. Formerly known incorrectly as *H. fluctuans* 'Variegated'.

Description: An impressive mound 71 in. wide × 30 in. high (178 × 75 cm). Leaf blade 14 × 10 in. (35

× 25 cm), thick, blue-tinted mid-green turning gray-green, widely and irregularly margined bright yellow turning creamy white by midsummer, with celadon streaks jetting toward the midrib, matt above and glaucous below, smooth, veins widely spaced, edge widely undulate, leaf flat to slightly folded, widely oval with a cuspidate tip and heart-shaped open to pinched lobes. Petiole narrow, green, barely outlined in cream. Flower funnel-shaped, lavender, in profusion, on a thick, oblique, leafy, intensely glaucous, 49-in. (122-cm) scape from high to late summer; fertile.

Cultivation Notes: Site in light to moderate shade. It emerges early and is slow to establish and to show

Hosta 'Rosedale Misty Pathways'

Hosta 'Sagae'

its potential, but eventually makes a huge specimen. A superb classic hosta. Named Hosta of the Year by the American Hosta Growers Association in 2000. Winner of the 1995 Alex J. Summers Distinguished Merit Hosta Award.

Similar:★*H.* 'Silk Kimono'; *H.* 'Unchained Melody'; *H.* 'Victory' has paler green leaves with yellow margins.

Sports: *H.* 'Clifford's Forest Fire'; *H.* 'Emerald Emperor' has green leaves; *H.* 'Fat Cat' and *H.* 'Golden Flame' have yellow leaves; *H.* 'Ivory Coast' and *H.* 'Liberty' have wider, thus more dramatic variegation; *H.* 'Magic Fire' PP17,524; *H.* 'Majesty' is virtually identical.

Hosta 'Magic Fire'

Hosta 'Satisfaction' (C. Wasitis/Bridgewood Gardens 2000)

LARGE

Origin: Natural sport of ★*H.* 'Piedmont Gold'.

Description: An arching mound 49 in. wide × 25–30 in. high (122 × 63–75 cm). Leaf blade 9 × 7 in. (23 × 18 cm), of good substance, satiny, very dark green, widely and irregularly margined rich gold, with celadon streaks jetting toward the midrib, closely veined, seersuckered, edge rippled, leaf slightly undulate, arching, widely oval with a cuspidate tip and heart-shaped pinched lobes. Petiole long, dark green, outlined in yellow. Flower: see ★*H.* 'Piedmont Gold'.

Cultivation Notes: The leaf base has a slightly blue tint early in the season if sited in good light to moderate shade. Moderate growth rate. A stunningly beautiful hosta.

Distinguishing Features: A margin that covers nearly one-third of the leaf blade, up to nearly 2 in. (5 cm.

Similar: *H.* 'Tyler's Treasure'.

Hosta 'Savannah' (M. Zilis 2003)

MEDIUM–LARGE

Origin: Unknown.

Description: A dense mound 60 in. wide × 25 in. high (150 × 63 cm). Leaf blade 11 × 7½ in. (28 × 19 cm), of average substance, olive green, irregularly margined creamy yellow turning white, with some streaks jetting toward the midrib, matt above and glossy below, smooth, edge slightly rippled, leaf

Hosta 'Satisfaction'

Hosta 'Savannah'

arching, slightly folded, oval with a cuspidate tip and rounded pinched lobes. Petiole narrow, olive green, finely outlined in cream. Flower funnel-shaped, somewhat fragrant, lavender, on an oblique, leafy, olive-green, 36-in. (90-cm) scape from late summer to early autumn until the first frosts in cooler climates; fertility unknown.

Cultivation Notes: Site in morning sun in cooler climates and provide adequate moisture. Increases rapidly and therefore suitable for landscaping. Also good in containers.

Similar: *H.* 'Edwin Bibby' has slightly streaked leaves and is a useful breeding plant; *H.* 'Sugar and Cream'; *H.* 'Summer Fragrance'.

Sports: *H.* 'Savannah Emerald' has green leaves; *H.* 'Savannah Supreme' has streaked leaves.

Hosta 'Scooter' (H. & D. Benedict 1990)

SMALL

Origin: *H.* 'Yellow Splash' hybrid.

Description: A dense, arching mound 16 in. wide × 8 in. high (40 × 20 cm). Leaf blade 6 × 4 in. (15 × 10 cm), of average substance, dark green, widely and irregularly margined creamy white, with celadon streaks jetting toward the midrib, matt above and shiny below, dimpled when mature, edge slightly rippled, leaf arching, lanceolate to oval with an acute tip and heart-shaped open lobes. Petiole very rippled when young, dark green, outlined in cream. Flower lavender, on a 24-in. (60-cm) scape in late summer.

Cultivation Notes: Site in light to moderate shade. Early to emerge. Makes an excellent ground cover.

Similar: *H.* 'Ground Master' and ★*H.* 'Resonance' both have slightly narrower leaves.

Hosta 'Sea Dream' (M. Seaver 1984)

MEDIUM–LARGE

Origin: Open-pollinated seedling of *H.* 'Neat Splash'.

Description: An overlapping mound 49 in. wide × 24 in. high (122 × 60 cm). Leaf blade 9 × 6½ in. (23 × 16 cm), of average substance, emerging green, soon turning yellow, with a variable narrow ivory white to pure white margin, matt above and shiny below, dimpled, edge shallowly undulate, leaf arching, widely oval with a cuspidate tip and heart-shaped open lobes.

Petiole narrow, pale green, very finely outlined in cream. Flower funnel-shaped, pale lavender, opening from a darker bud, on an upright, chartreuse, 30-in. (75-cm) scape, held well above the leaf mound, in late summer; fertility unknown.

Cultivation Notes: Viridescent. Site in morning sun in cooler climates to achieve the best leaf color, then good light to dappled shade. Protect the thinnish leaves from strong wind. Increases rapidly.

Similar: ★*H.* 'Electrum Stater' has a heavier leaf substance; *H.* 'Golden Torch' has thicker, more seersuckered leaves; ★*H.* 'Saint Elmo's Fire' is more noticeably seersuckered; *H.* 'Zodiac'.

Sport: *H.* 'Winfield Gold' has yellow leaves.

Hosta 'Scooter'

Hosta 'Sea Dream'

259

Hosta 'Sergeant Pepper' (Bridgewood Gardens 2001)

MEDIUM

Origin: Unknown.

Description: An open mound 36 in. wide × 16 in. high (90 × 40 cm). Leaf blade 6 × 5 in. (15 × 13 cm), thick, matt, bright, pale green very widely and irregularly margined chartreuse turning golden yellow, seersuckered, strongly veined, edge rippled, leaf widely oval with a cuspidate tip and heart-shaped pinched to overlapping lobes. Petiole olive green, widely outlined in creamy yellow. Flower tubular, lavender-tinted near white, on an upright, leafy, green, 22-in. (55-cm) scape in midsummer; fertility unknown.

Cultivation Notes: Tolerates sun in most regions, except in the hottest climates.

Distinguishing Features: There is more gold margin than green center to the leaf.

Hosta 'Shade Parade' (G. Goodwin 2005)

SMALL

Origin: Sport of a seedling of *H.* 'Sea Prize'.

Description: A dense, low mound 12 in. wide × 8 in. high (30 × 20 cm). Leaf blade 3 × 3 in. (8 × 8 cm), of good substance, satiny, chartreuse yellow, widely margined palest green to ivory with chartreuse streaks, dimpled, edge flat with occasional undulations, leaf moderately cupped, round with a vestigial tip and heart-shaped open to pinched lobes. Petiole chartreuse, outlined in cream. Flower funnel-shaped, near-white to pale lavender, opening from a balloon-shaped violet bud, on an upright, leafy, green, 15-in. (38-cm) scape in midsummer; fertile.

Cultivation Notes: Site in two hours of morning sun in cooler climates to retain the chartreuse base color of the leaves, otherwise moderate shade. Plant in a rock garden or raised bed with any of the more vigorous very-small leaved or miniature hostas, such as ★*H.* 'Popo', as a color contrast. Moderate growth rate. An outstanding recent introduction for the smaller garden.

Distinguishing Features: The virtually round leaves with their attractive contrasting leaf margins.

Hosta 'Shazaam' (G. Jones N/R)

MEDIUM

Origin: *H.* 'William Lachman' hybrid.

Description: A dense, asymmetrical mound 24 in. wide × 12 in. high (60 × 30 cm). Leaf blade 7½ × 5 in. (19 × 13 cm), of good substance, dark olive green, very widely and irregularly margined ivory-chartreuse

Hosta 'Sergeant Pepper'

Hosta 'Shade Parade'

turning white, with chartreuse streaks, matt above and thinly glaucous below, seersuckered, edge with occasional kinks toward the base, leaf folded, cuneate with a recurved cuspidate tip and flat to heart-shaped pinched to folded lobes. Petiole dark olive green, finely outlined in ivory. Flower funnel-shaped, lavender, on an oblique to upright, bare, green, 24-in. (60 cm) scape in midsummer; fertility unknown.

Cultivation Notes: Site in morning sun followed by light shade. Vigorous and easy to grow. Best planted amid plainer-leaved plants to accentuate the contrast between the dark green center and the eye-catching variegated margin.

Distinguishing Features: The ¾-in. (2-cm) margin is unusually wide on a smallish hosta.

Similar: *H.* 'Honeysong'; *H.* 'Mama Mia'; ★*H.* 'Wide Brim'.

Hosta sieboldiana 'American Halo' (V. Wade 1999)

VERY LARGE

Origin: Sport of *H. sieboldiana* 'Northern Halo'. Initially known as *H. sieboldiana* 'Northern Halo' (Wade's Form).

Description: A dense mound 70 in. wide × 22 in. high (175 × 55 cm). Leaf blade 14 × 10 in. (35 × 25 cm), thick, glaucous dark blue-green, irregularly margined yellow turning ivory white, strongly veined, seersuckered, edge randomly undulate, leaf broadly ovate with a mucronate tip and heart-shaped overlapping lobes. Petiole stout, light green. Flower: see: ★*H. sieboldiana* 'Elegans'.

Cultivation Notes: Tolerates some morning sun in cooler climates but may lose the blue-green leaf color sooner. Slow to establish but eventually becomes a huge mound. Pest resistant. Winner of the 2002 Alex J. Summers Distinguished Merit Hosta Award.

Distinguishing Features: Larger than its parent with a wider leaf margin.

Similar: ★*H. sieboldiana* 'Barbara Ann'.

Hosta sieboldiana 'Barbara Ann' (Park Green Nursery N/R)

LARGE–VERY LARGE

Origin: Sport of ★*H. sieboldiana* 'Elegans'

Description: An overlapping mound 50 in. wide × 30 in. high (126 × 75 cm). Leaf blade 12 × 11 in. (30 × 28 cm), thick, glaucous gray-influenced blue-green, widely and irregularly margined cream turning white with some celadon streaks, seersuckered, edge almost flat, leaf flat to slightly folded or convex, broadly ovate with a mucronate tip and heart-shaped

Hosta 'Shazaam'

Hosta sieboldiana 'American Halo'

overlapping lobes. Petiole pale green, outlined in ivory. Flower: see *H. sieboldiana* 'Elegans'.

Cultivation Notes: Site in good light to light shade in cooler climates; otherwise shade all day. Slow to establish but leave plenty of space around it. Pest resistant.

Distinguishing Features: Leaves more rounded than those of *H. sieboldiana* 'Northern Halo'.

Similar: *H. sieboldiana* 'Silver Spray'.

Hosta sieboldiana 'Frances Williams' (F. & C. Williams 1986) ♀

LARGE–VERY LARGE

Origin: Sport of ★*H. sieboldiana* 'Elegans'.

Description: A dense mound 51 in. wide × 32 in. high (127 × 80 cm). Leaf blade 12 × 11½ in. (30 × 29 cm), thick, glaucous blue-green, widely and irregularly margined yellow turning creamy beige, seersuckered, strongly veined, edge almost flat, leaf slightly cupped, widely oval to nearly round with a mucronate tip and heart-shaped folded lobes. Petiole stout, light green, outlined in creamy yellow. Flower: see *H. sieboldiana* 'Elegans'.

Cultivation Notes: Site in light to moderate shade to prevent the leaf edges from scorching, but they will scorch in the warmest climates even in full shade. Impressive in a large container but needs dividing every three years. Margins are chartreuse, the base color a darker blue if grown in low-light conditions. Slow to establish but nonetheless among the most popular hostas ever introduced. Breeding with this cultivar often produces streaked offspring. Winner of the 1986 Alex J. Summers Distinguished Merit Hosta Award.

Similar: ★*H.* 'Alvatine Taylor' has longer leaves and they do not scorch; *H.* 'Olive Bailey Langdon' has leaf edges that do not scorch; *H. sieboldiana* 'Eldorado'; *H. sieboldiana* 'Gilt Edge'; *H. sieboldiana* 'Samurai' appears to be slightly more vigorous, but otherwise identical; *H.* 'Wagon Wheels' is smaller and also can scorch at the edges.

Sports: *H. sieboldiana* 'Aurora Borealis'; *H. sieboldiana* 'DuPage Delight'; *H. sieboldiana* 'Golden Circles'; *H. sieboldiana* 'Linda Sue'; *H. sieboldiana* 'Time Tunnel' PP16,435.

Hosta sieboldiana 'Northern Exposure' (Walters Gardens 1997)

LARGE–VERY LARGE

Origin: Tissue-cultured sport of ★*H. sieboldiana* 'Elegans'.

Description: A dense mound 70 in. wide × 36 in. high (175 × 90 cm). Leaf blade 13 × 11 in. (33 × 28 cm), thick, glaucous blue-green, widely and irregularly margined cream turning ivory white, seersuckered, edge almost flat, leaf flat to slightly folded or

Hosta sieboldiana 'Barbara Ann'

Hosta sieboldiana 'Frances Williams'

slightly convex, widely oval with a mucronate tip and heart-shaped overlapping lobes. Petiole light green, outlined in cream. Flower: see *H. sieboldiana* 'Elegans'.

Cultivation Notes: Site in good light to high, filtered shade in cooler climates, otherwise shade all day. Slow to establish but well worth the wait. Pest resistant.

Similar: *★H. sieboldiana* 'Frances Williams'; *H. sieboldiana* 'Northern Halo'.

Sports: *H. sieboldiana* 'Eskimo Pie' has centrally variegated leaves of ivory, bordered by chartreuse and margined in rich blue-green.

Hosta 'Silk Kimono' (H. Hansen & H. Gowen 1999)

LARGE

Origin: *★H.* 'Dorothy Benedict' × *★H. montana*.

Description: An upright, tiered mound 60 in. wide × 18 in. high (150 × 45 cm). Leaf blade 13 × 9 in.

(33 × 23 cm), of good substance, matt, gray-green, widely and irregularly margined creamy white, with many celadon streaks jetting toward the midrib, smooth, veins widely spaced, edge rippled, leaf

Hosta sieboldiana 'Eskimo Pie'

Hosta sieboldiana 'Northern Exposure'

Hosta 'Silk Kimono'

Hosta 'Silverado'

Hosta 'So Sweet'

undulate, widely oval with a cuspidate tip and heart-shaped pinched lobes. Petiole sage green, outlined in cream. Flower tubular, purple-striped pale lavender, on an upright, leafy, green, 36-in. (90-cm) scape from mid- to high summer; seedpods green, fertility unknown.

Cultivation Notes: Site in light to moderate shade.

Distinguishing Features: Leaf tips arch down conspicuously.

Similar: *H.* 'Sagae'.

Hosta 'Silverado' (Kuk 1987)

MEDIUM

Origin: Possible sport of *H.* 'Lancifolia'.

Description: An arching mound 33 in. wide × 12 in. high (83 × 30 cm). Leaf blade 6½ × 2 in. (16 × 5 cm), thin, mid-green, narrowly margined chartreuse turning white, glossy above and shiny below, closely veined, edge rippled, leaf arching, lanceolate with an acute tip and tapered open lobes. Petiole narrow, green, finely outlined in cream. Flower funnel-shaped, purple, on an upright, leafy, green, 24-in. (60-cm) scape from late summer to early autumn; fertility unknown.

Cultivation Notes: Site in light to full shade. Lovely in a container.

Distinguishing Features: Flowering earlier than *H.* 'Lancifolia' and the color is a deeper purple.

Similar: *H.* 'Gaijin'; *H.* 'Silver Lance'; *H.* 'Silver Lining'.

Hosta 'So Sweet' (P. Aden 1986)

MEDIUM

Origin: *H.* 'Fragrant Bouquet' hybrid.

Description: An open mound 22 in. wide × 14 in. high (55 × 35 cm). Leaf blade 7 × 4½ in. (18 × 11 cm), of average substance, mid- to dark green, irregularly margined yellow turning creamy white, with light chartreuse streaks jetting toward the tip, satiny above and glossy below, edge slightly undulate to kinked, leaf slightly arching, oval with an acute tip and tapered pinched lobes. Petiole dark green, outlined in cream. Flower: open funnel-shaped, very fragrant, pale lavender, on an upright, leafy, green, 22-in. (55-cm) scape from late summer to early autumn; barely fertile.

Cultivation Notes: Site in morning sun, followed by good light to light shade. Leaves are much narrower in juvenile plants. Increases rapidly and soon reaches maturity. Superb in containers, especially when sited near the house so that its fragrant flowers, which can last until the frosts in cooler climates, can be appreciated. Named Hosta of the Year by the American Hosta Growers Association in 1996.

Similar: *H. 'Bold Edger'.

Hosta 'Spartan Glory' (J. & S. Wilkins 2000)

LARGE

Origin: *H.* 'Elatior' hybrid.

Description: An open mound 62 in. wide × 27 in. high (157 × 68 cm). Leaf blade 14 × 11 in. (35 × 28 cm), of good substance, light green, irregularly margined yellow turning pure white, satiny above and

glaucous below, dimpled to seersuckered, veins distinctively marked, edge lightly rippled, leaf slightly folded, broadly ovate with a mucronate tip and heart-shaped pinched to overlapping lobes. Petiole light green, outlined in cream. Flower bell-shaped, lavender-striped near white, on an upright, bare, green, 35- to 45-in. (88- to 113-cm) scape in high summer; seedpods green, fertile.

Cultivation Notes: Site in moderate to full shade. Grow in light woodland or as a specimen plant at the back of the border. Plenty of moisture needed to reveal the interesting surface texture of the leaves. Moderate growth rate.

Distinguishing Features: The deeply furrowed veins which appear when the plant has matured.

Hosta 'Spinach Souffle' (R. Solberg 2006)

MEDIUM

Origin: Sport of *H.* 'Garden Treasure'.

Description: An upright mound 30 in. wide × 14 in. high (75 × 35 cm). Leaf blade 8 × 8 in. (20 × 20 cm), of heavy substance, glaucous blue-green turning intense, rich green, very widely and irregularly margined golden yellow, with streaks jetting toward the midrib, seersuckered, prominently veined, edge widely undulate, leaf lightly undulate, convex when

Hosta 'Spartan Glory'

Hosta 'Spinach Souffle'

mature, rounded with a mucronate tip and flat to heart-shaped open to pinched lobes. Petiole green, outlined in yellow. Flower funnel-shaped, near white, on a stout, upright, leafy, green, 16- to 18-in. (40- to 45-cm) scape in midsummer; fertility unknown.

Cultivation Notes: Site in light to moderate shade to preserve the best leaf color. Slow to increase, but will probably exceed its registered dimensions over time. Pest resistant.

Distinguishing Features: Smaller than its parent. Leaves very colorful and shapely, evincing ★*H. sieboldiana* 'Elegans' heritage.

Hosta 'Stepping Out' (K. Vaughn N/R)

⅞EDIUM

Origin: ★*H.* 'Breeder's Choice' × *H.* 'Blue Shadows'.

Description: A dense mound 36 in. wide × 16 in. high (90 × 40 cm). Leaf blade 7 × 5 in. (18 × 13 cm), thick, rich blue-green, irregularly margined golden yellow with paler streaking, glaucous above and satiny below, dimpled, veins furrowed, edge almost flat, leaf shallowly cupped, nearly round with a vestigial tip and heart-shaped overlapping lobes. Petiole stout, blue-green, outlined in cream. Flower funnel-shaped, pale lavender, on an upright, leafy, glaucous green

20-in. (50-cm) scape from mid- to high summer; fertility unknown.

Cultivation Notes: Site in moderate shade to help retain the softer leaf coloring. Slow to increase. Pest resistant.

Distinguishing Features: The leaf color changes dramatically by midsummer to shiny dark green with an ivory margin.

Similar: *H.* 'Snow Cap' has ovate leaves that retain their color for longer.

Sport: *H.* 'Mardi Gras Parade' has heavily streaked leaves.

Hosta 'Stetson' (Walters Gardens 1997)

MEDIUM

Origin: Tissue-cultured sport of ★*H.* 'Wide Brim'.

Description: An open mound 25 in. wide × 16 in. high (63 × 40 cm). Leaf blade 7½ × 6½ in. (19 × 16 cm), of good substance, glaucous dark green with a slight blue cast, widely and irregularly margined yellow turning creamy white, with celadon streaks jetting toward the midrib, edge slightly undulate and conspicuously furled, leaf widely oval with a cuspidate tip and heart-shaped overlapping lobes. Petiole dark green, outlined in creamy white. Flower: see *H.* 'Wide Brim'.

Hosta 'Stepping Out'

Hosta 'Stetson'

Cultivation Notes: Site in light to moderate shade but not under a tree canopy. Increases fairly rapidly. Best used as a feature plant in a large container.

Distinguishing Features: The edge is so markedly furled that the glaucous underside of the leaf offers another point of interest.

Similar: *H.* 'Red Hot Poker' has a shiny green leaf margined creamy white.

Sports: *H.* 'Cowrie' is said to have even more markedly upturned leaves.

Hosta **'Stiletto'** (P. Aden 1987)

SMALL

Origin: *H.* 'Amy Aden' × *★H. pulchella* 'Kifukurin Ubatake'.

Description: A low, cascading, dense mound 32 in. wide × 12 in. high (80 × 30 cm). Leaf blade 5½ × 1½ in. (14 × 4 cm), thin, satiny, mid to dark olive green, narrowly margined yellow to creamy white, a hint of dimpling on mature leaves, prominently veined, edge distinctly rippled, leaf slightly arching, lanceolate with an acute tip, no junction between the blade and the petiole. Petiole ripple-edged, flattish, green, outlined in cream. Flower slightly bell-shaped, purple-striped, on an upright, thin, leafy, green, 25-in. (63-cm) scape from mid- to late summer; fertile.

Cultivation Notes: Site in good light to moderate shade all day. Increases rapidly. An excellent edging or ground cover hosta. Needs dividing every four to five years to retain the rippled edge.

Similar: *★H.* 'Crested Surf' has wider leaves; *H.* 'Roller Coaster Ride' has slightly streaked leaves; *H.* 'Sumi' is smaller; *H.* 'Wiggle Worms' has narrower leaves.

Sport: *H.* 'Boogie Woogie' is a streaked form.

Hosta **'Sultana'** (W. Zumbar 1988)

SMALL

Origin: Sport of *★H.* 'Little Aurora'.

Description: A compact mound 30 in. wide × 16 in. high (75 × 40 cm). Leaf blade 5½ × 4½ in. (14 × 11 cm), thick, dark green, widely margined rich yellow turning creamy white, satiny above and thinly glaucous below, seersuckered when mature, edge almost flat to slightly kinked, leaf shallowly cupped or convex, widely oval with a cuspidate tip and heart-shaped pinched lobes. Petiole narrow, outlined in yellow. Flower: see *H.* 'Little Aurora'.

Cultivation Notes: Site in morning sun in cooler climates, otherwise light to moderate shade. Slow to moderate growth rate. Pest resistant. A most strikingly variegated small hosta suitable as a specimen plant for the border or a container.

Distinguishing Features: Scapes bear attractively variegated leafy bracts.

Sports: *H.* 'Border Favourite' has darker leaves with narrower yellow margins.

Hosta **'Stiletto'**

Hosta **'Sultana'**

Hosta 'Summer Breeze'

Hosta 'Sundance'

Hosta 'Sweetie'

Hosta **'Summer Breeze'** (J. Diesen/M. Zilis/1999)

MEDIUM–LARGE

Origin: Sport of ★*H.* 'Summer Music'.

Description: An open mound 50 in. wide × 22 in. high (126 × 55 cm). Leaf blade 8½ × 7 in. (21 × 18 cm), thin, dark green, widely and irregularly margined and splashed chartreuse yellow, matt above and satiny below, dimpled to moderately seersuckered, edge occasionally undulate, leaf lightly wavy, widely oval with a mucronate tip and heart-shaped pinched lobes. Petiole short, wide, green, outlined in chartreuse. Flower: see *H.* 'Summer Music'.

Cultivation Notes: Site in light to moderate shade all day to produce the best leaf color. Moderately rapid growth rate. Susceptible to pest damage.

Distinguishing Features: The leaves emerge green, the variegation appears slowly.

Hosta **'Sundance'** (Walters Gardens 1984)

MEDIUM

Origin: Tissue-cultured sport of *H.* 'Fortunei Aoki'.

Description: A dense mound 36 in. wide × 22 in. high (90 × 55 cm). Leaf blade 9 × 5 in. (23 × 13 cm), of good substance, gray-green with blue overtones in early summer, irregularly margined creamy yellow turning ivory white, with some celadon streaks jetting toward the midrib, matt above and glaucous below, dimpled to seersuckered, edge slightly rippled, leaf convex to arching, widely oval with a cuspidate tip and heart-shaped pinched to folded lobes. Petiole dark green, outlined in cream. Flower funnel-shaped, lavender-gray, on an upright, leafy, green, 36-in. (90-cm) scape in high summer; fertility unknown.

Cultivation Notes: Site in two hours of morning sun in cooler climates. Variegation colors change with different light levels, remaining more yellow in deeper shade.

Distinguishing Features: The variegated leafy bracts are conspicuously large.

Hosta **'Sweetie'** (P. Aden 1988)

MEDIUM

Origin: ★*H.* 'Fragrant Bouquet' × *H.* 'Fragrant Candelabra'.

Description: An unruly mound 30 in. wide × 20 in. high (75 × 50 cm). Leaf blade 8 × 5 in. (210×

13 cm), of average substance, yellow turning bright chartreuse, widely and irregularly margined ivory to white, satiny above and thinly glaucous below, veins ribbed, some dimpling when mature, edge conspicuously undulate, leaf arching, oval with a cuspidate tip and heart-shaped overlapping lobes. Petiole pale green, outlined in ivory. Flower funnel-shaped, white, on an upright, leafy, green, 32-in. (80-cm) scape in late summer; fertile.

Cultivation Notes: Viridescent. Leaves stay yellow longer if grown in sun for most of the day. Vigorous. Moisture at the roots is essential especially in hotter climates. A superb hosta which should be better known.

Distinguishing Features: Leaves are longer and narrower than those of ★*H*. 'Fragrant Bouquet'.

Similar: *H*. 'Sugar and Cream' has greener, less-undulate leaves.

Sports: *H*. 'Fragrant Surprise', a most attractive new introduction, has green leaves margined white with celadon transitional splashes; *H*. 'Sweet Blonde Babe' has twisted pale green leaves with a very wide white margin; *H*. 'Sweetness' has green leaves.

Hosta **'Sweet Innocence'** (H. Benedict N/R)
MEDIUM–LARGE

Origin: Tetraploid sport of ★*H*. 'Fragrant Bouquet'.

Description: A colorful, undulating mound 24 in. wide × 12 in. high (60 × 30 cm). Leaf blade 8 × 6 in. (20 × 15 cm), of heavy substance, light green, very widely and irregularly margined ivory to white with celadon streaking and splashing, satiny above and slightly glaucous below, slightly dimpled, veins conspicuous, edge shallowly undulate, leaf convex, broadly ovate with a recurved mucronate tip and heart-shaped pinched lobes. Petiole deeply channeled, dark green, outlined in ivory. Flower large, very fragrant, pale lavender, on a thick, upright, pale green, 24-in. (60-cm) scape, with occasional large, variegated bracts, in late summer; usually sterile.

Cultivation Notes: Except in the hottest climates, site in full sun all day to produce the best leaf color and most prolific display of flowers. Requires moisture at the roots. Moderate growth rate. Superb in containers placed where the fragrance can be enjoyed, although this is less apparent in cooler climates.

Distinguishing Features: Leaf substance is greater, margins are wider and better defined, and pest resistance is greater than its parents.

Similar: ★*H*. 'Crystal Moon'.

Hosta **'Tambourine'** (W. & E. Lachman 1987)
MEDIUM

Origin: (*H*. 'Resonance' × seedling) × *H*. 'Halcyon'.

Description: A dense mound 24 in. wide × 13 in. high (60 × 33 cm). Leaf blade 6 × 5 in. (16 × 13 cm), of good substance, mid-green, widely and irregularly margined yellow turning ivory to pure white, with chartreuse streaks jetting toward the midrib, satiny above and thinly glaucous below, dimpled, veins

Hosta **'Sweet Innocence'**

Hosta **'Tambourine'**

widely spaced, edge almost flat, leaf widely oval with an acute tip and flat to heart-shaped pinched lobes. Petiole narrow, dark green, outlined in ivory, rosy mauve on back . Flower funnel-shaped, lavender, in a dense raceme, on an upright, leafy, green, 20-in. (50-cm) scape in late summer; fertile.

Cultivation Notes: Leaves assume a blue-green overtone if grown in good light but not direct sun. Increases rapidly. Makes a good ground cover.

Distinguishing Features: The tightly packed leaf mound causes the edges to turn up.

Similar: *H. 'Emily Dickinson'; *H. 'Torchlight'.

Hosta 'Tea and Crumpets'

Hosta 'Thumbs Up'

Hosta 'Tea and Crumpets' (W. & E. Lachman N/R)

SMALL

Origin: *H.* 'Carnival' seedling × *H.* 'Crepe Suzette' seedling.

Description: An open mound 16 in. wide × 10 in. high (40 × 25 cm). Leaf blade 5 × 4½ in. (13 × 11 cm), thick, dark sage green, irregularly margined creamy white, matt above and glaucous below, seer-suckered, edge almost flat, leaf shallowly cupped, nearly round with flat open to pinched lobes. Petiole shallow, dark green, outlined in cream. Flower tubular, dark lavender, on a thick, upright, leafy, glaucous purple, 12- to 16-in. (30- to 40-cm) scape, with variegated leafy bracts, from mid- to late summer; fertile.

Cultivation Notes: Site in good light to moderate shade. Suitable for the front of a border or in a container.

Distinguishing Features: Leaves are unusually spoon-shaped.

Similar: *H. 'Coquette'; H. 'Cream Cheese'; *H. 'Crepe Suzette'.

Sports: *H.* 'Champagne and Caviar'.

Hosta 'Thumbs Up' (J. Schwarz 1999)

SMALL

Origin: Sport of *H.* 'Achy Breaky Heart'.

Description: An upright mound 14 in. wide × 12 in. high (35 × 30 cm). Leaf blade 4 × 3 in. (10 × 8 cm), of average substance, satiny, mid-green, irregularly margined cream turning pure white, with some streaks jetting toward the midrib, slight dimpling, edge flat, leaf oval with a cuspidate tip and rounded pinched lobes. Petiole short, green, outlined in white. Flower tubular, lavender, on an upright, bare, green, 16- to 20-in. (40- to 50-cm) scape in high summer; seedpods green, fertile.

Cultivation Notes: Site in good light to moderate shade in a container, gravel, or rock garden leaving plenty of space to emphasize the upright habit of the leaves. Slow to moderate growth rate.

Hosta 'Tokudama Flavocircinalis' (F. Maekawa & AHS 1987)

MEDIUM

Origin: Natural sport of *H.* 'Tokudama'.

Description: An open mound 48 in. wide × 17 in.

high (122 × 43 cm). Leaf blade 7½ × 5½ in. (19 × 14 cm), thick, glaucous blue, widely and irregularly margined yellow to beige, with streaks jetting toward the midrib, seersuckered, edge flat to slightly undulate, leaf shallowly cupped, widely oval with a cuspidate tip and round pinched lobes. Petiole blue-green, outlined in yellow. Flower: see *H.* 'Tokudama'.

Cultivation Notes: Site in light to moderate shade. Slow to increase. Pest resistant. A classic hosta which does not scorch at the leaf margins.

Similar: *H.* 'Fleeta Brownell Woodroffe'; ★*H.* 'Jack of Diamonds'; *H.* 'Lake Hitchcock; *H.* 'Sunnybrook'.

Sports: *H.* 'Cool Hand Luke' has gray-green leaves and does not scorch at the margins; *H.* 'Tootie Mae' has a strikingly wide cream margin.

Hosta 'Tokudama Flavocircinalis'

Hosta 'Tom Schmid' (T. Schmid 1995)

MEDIUM–LARGE

Origin: Sport of ★*H.* 'Krossa Regal'.

Description: An upright mound 36 in. wide × 25 in. high (90 × 63 cm). Leaf blade 11½ × 7½ in. (29 × 19 cm), thick, emerging gray-blue turning dark green by midsummer, widely and irregularly margined white, matt above and glaucous below, dimpled, veins closely ribbed, edge rippled, leaf slightly folded, oval with a cuspidate tip and rounded pinched lobes. Petiole stout, glaucous pale green. Flower: see *H.* 'Krossa Regal'.

Cultivation Notes: Site in good light to full shade all day. Moderate to rapid growth rate. Use as a border specimen. Superb in a large container.

Similar: *H.* 'Regal Splendor' has a wider leaf margin.

Hosta 'Tom Schmid'

Hosta 'Torchlight' (W. & E. Lachman 1990)

MEDIUM

Origin: *H.* 'Halcyon' hybrid.

Description: An upright or vase-shaped mound 34 in. wide × 14 in. high (85 × 35 cm). Leaf blade 5½ × 4½ in. (14 × 11 cm), of good substance, dark olive green, irregularly margined ivory turning white, with chartreuse streaks jetting toward the midrib, satiny above and shiny below, scarcely dimpled, veins widely spaced, edge widely rippled, leaf slightly cupped, almost round with a cuspidate tip and heart-shaped open lobes. Petiole narrow, olive green, outlined in ivory, red-streaked along the back

Hosta 'Torchlight'

Hosta 'Toy Soldier'

Hosta 'Triumph'

Hosta 'Twilight'

and toward the base in the channeling. Flower flared, funnel-shaped, rich lavender, on an upright, leafy, dark green, 22-in. (55-cm) scape in late summer; seedpods green, fertile.

Cultivation Notes: Site in light to full shade. Good growth rate. Use as a specimen with contrasting foliage, such as ferns or grasses. Equally good in a container. A superb hosta.

Distinguishing Feature: Burgundy-red petioles from the crown into the base of the leaf. Densely red-dotted scapes from the crown into the base of flower bud. White-margined green leafy bracts each containing a flower bud evenly spaced along the scape.

Similar: *H. 'Chantilly Lace'; *H. 'Tambourine' is larger.

Hosta 'Toy Soldier' (R. Solberg 2001)

SMALL

Origin: Tissue-cultured sport of *H. 'Blue Cadet'.

Description: A compact mound 24 in. wide × 10 in. high (60 × 25 cm). Leaf blade 4 × 3 in. (10 × 8 cm), thick, glaucous blue-green, irregularly margined chartreuse and creamy white, strongly veined, slight dimpling, edge randomly undulate, leaf flat, widely oval with a mucronate tip and heart-shaped open lobes. Petiole narrow, blue-green, outlined in creamy chartreuse. Flower: see H. 'Blue Cadet'.

Cultivation Notes: Site in light to moderate shade all day to preserve the subtle leaf coloring. Increases rapidly. Lovely with lacy ferns.

Distinguishing Features: A fascinating and quite distinct bicolored leaf margin, the outer margin chartreuse with white transitional feathering, the colors strengthening as the summer progresses. This effect is not always apparent in cooler climates.

Similar: *H. 'Déjà Blu'.

Hosta 'Triumph' (A. Tower 2002)

LARGE–VERY LARGE

Origin: H. 'Color Fantasy' hybrid.

Description: A dense, overlapping mound 51 in. wide × 30 in. high (127 × 75 cm). Leaf blade 15 × 12 in. (38 × 30 cm), of good substance, dark green, widely and very irregularly margined yellow turning ivory, with transitional chartreuse streaks jetting toward the midrib, satiny above and glaucous below, some dimpling when mature, edge slightly undulate, leaf ovate with a recurved cuspidate tip and heart-shaped pinched lobes. Petiole dark green, outlined in ivory. Flower funnel-shaped, pale lavender, on an upright, leafy, green, 36-in. (90-cm) scape in high summer; fertility unknown.

Cultivation Notes: Site in good light to high, filtered shade. Requires plenty of moisture to boost the already wide margins. A superb recent introduction which should be better known.

Similar: *H.* 'Majesty'.

Hosta 'Twilight' PP14,040 (G. Van Eijk-Bos & D. Van Erven 1997)

MEDIUM

Origin: Tissue-cultured sport of ★*H.* 'Fortunei Aureomarginata'.

Description: An open, elegantly poised mound 32 in. wide × 20 in. high (80 × 50 cm). Leaf blade 10 × 7½ in. (25 × 19 cm), very thick, leathery, very dark green, widely and irregularly margined creamy yellow, with light olive green streaks jetting toward the midrib, satiny above and matt below, slightly dimpled, strongly veined, edge slightly undulate, leaf oval to round with a cuspidate tip and rounded open to pinched lobes. Petiole narrow, dark olive green, finely outlined cream. Flower: see *H.* 'Fortunei Aureomarginata'.

Cultivation Notes: Site in light to moderate shade. Moderate to good growth rate. Pest resistant. Plant with *Millium effusum* 'Aureum', whose seeming fragility is a perfect foil for this bold hosta.

Distinguishing Features: Among the most striking green-leaved hostas with creamy yellow margins to be introduced. Exceptionally thick leaf substance. A tetraploid having higher fertility than the parent plant.

Similar: *H.* 'Anne' PP10,661 is possibly larger; ★*H.* 'Fortunei Aureomarginata'.

Sports: ★*H.* 'Morning Light'.

Hosta 'Undulata Albomarginata' (AHS 1987)

MEDIUM–LARGE

Origin: Natural sport of ★*H.* 'Undulata'.

Description: A dense mound 36 in. wide × 18 in. high (90 × a45 cm). Leaf blade 7 × 4½ in. (18 × 11 cm), thin, mid-green, irregularly margined ivory white, with transitional celadon splashing, matt above and glossy below, slightly dimpled when mature, edge slightly rippled, leaf elliptic with a curved cuspidate tip and rounded pinched lobes. Petiole green, outlined in ivory. Flower: see *H.* 'Undulata'.

Cultivation Notes: Site in light to moderate shade. Vigorous. Susceptible to pest damage. Adaptable to many situations. Especially useful for covering large areas.

Distinguishing Features: Leaves less twisted and less undulate than those of ★*H.* 'Crispula', with which it is often confused.

Sport: *H.* 'Undulata Erromena' has slightly wider, green leaves.

Hosta 'Unforgettable' (Kuk 1999)

MEDIUM–LARGE

Origin: Sport of ★*H.* 'Gold Regal' × ★*H.* 'Golden Medallion'.

Description: An upright mound 24 in. wide × 22 in. high (60 × 55 cm). Leaf blade 8½ × 7 in. (21 × 18 cm), thick, dark green, widely margined and splashed chartreuse turning golden yellow, with streaks jetting toward the midrib, satiny above and glaucous below, dimpled, edge slightly rippled, leaf folded or convex, oval with a mucronate tip and rounded pinched lobes. Petiole green, outlined in yellow. Flower tubular, lavender, on a stout, upright, green, 32-in. (79-cm) scape in high summer; seedpods green, fertile.

Hosta 'Undulata Albomarginata'

Cultivation Notes: Site in good light to light shade. Moderate growth rate. Pest resistant. The contrast between the marginal variegation and the darker leaf blade is exceptionally striking. A superb introduction.

Distinguishing Features: The tall flower scapes,

inherited from the ★*H.* 'Gold Regal' parent, make this hosta more attractive than many others with ★*H.* 'Tokudama' parentage.

Sports: *H.* 'Skyrocket' has soft yellow leaves with a contrasting dark green midrib.

Hosta 'Vera Verde' (P. Aden & Klehm Nursery 1990)

SMALL

Origin: Sport of ★*H. gracillima.*

Description: A rhizomatous, diffuse mound 26 in. wide × 12 in. high (65 × 30 cm). Leaf blade 4 × 1¼ in. (10 × 3 cm), leathery, olive green, narrowly margined creamy yellow turning ivory white, satiny above and glossy below, smooth, edge randomly undulate, leaf arching, elliptic to lanceolate with a recurved obtuse tip, blade decurrent with the petiole in juvenile plants, developing tapered open lobes when mature. Petiole flattish, narrow, olive green, with occasional white flashes along the margin.

Hosta 'Unforgettable'

Hosta 'Vera Verde'

Flower: funnel-shaped, lavender, on a semi-upright, bare, pale green, 28-in. (70-cm) scape from high to late summer; fertility unknown.

Cultivation Notes: Site in good light to light shade. Vigorous. Covers a large area quickly.

Distinguishing Features: Leaves flatten at the edge and widen as the plant matures.

Similar: *★H. gracillima* 'Kifukurin Ko Mame' is smaller and has more pointed leaves.

Sport: *H.* 'Cheesecake' has unstable, central variegation.

Hosta 'Verna Jean' (W. & E. Lachman 1990)

SMALL

Origin: *H.* 'Flamboyant' selfed.

Description: A dome-shaped, compact mound 16 in. wide × 8 in. high (40 × 20 cm). Leaf blade 4 × 2½ in. (10 × 6 cm), of good substance, chartreuse, irregularly margined yellow turning ivory, with some pale chartreuse streaks, matt above and thinly glaucous below, dimpled, edge slightly undulate, leaf ovate with a cuspidate tip and open heart-shaped lobes. Petiole chartreuse. Flower slightly flared, on an upright, bare, chartreuse, 14-in. (35-cm) or more scape in high summer; seedpods many but sterile.

Cultivation Notes: Site in good light but not deep shade to retain the attractive leaf color. Moderate growth rate. Easily exceeds its registered dimensions if given optimum growing conditions. Use as an edging, ground cover, or rock garden plant.

Distinguishing Features: Like a mini *H.* 'Shade Fanfare' which is the stable sport of *H.* 'Flamboyant'.

Similar: *H.* 'Sunny Smiles' is larger.

Hosta 'Veronica Lake' (F. Riehl 1993)

SMALL–MEDIUM

Origin: Sport of *★H.* 'Pearl Lake'.

Description: A dense mound 42 in. wide × 18 in. high (105 × 45 cm). Leaf blade 5 × 4 in. (13 × 10 cm), of average substance, gray-green, irregularly margined yellow turning cream, matt above and glaucous below, some dimpling when mature, edge occasionally kinked, leaf slightly folded, widely oval with a mucronate tip and heart-shaped pinched lobes. Petiole narrow, gray-green, outlined in cream. Flower: see *H.* 'Pearl Lake'.

Cultivation Notes: Site in fairly low light or dappled shade to achieve a more subtle and attractive coloring, as the leaves fade to cream with an ivory margin if exposed to bright light or sunlight. Increases rapidly. A foreground specimen and lovely in a pot.

Distinguishing Features: The overlapping dome-shaped mound with many scapes towering above.

Similar: *H.* 'Tango', a sport of *H.* 'Pasture's New', has leaves with a downward stance.

Hosta 'Verna Jean'

Hosta 'Veronica Lake'

275

Sports: *H.* 'Snowy Lake', a probable tetraploid, has much wider leaf margins and is of thicker substance.

Hosta 'Warwick Choice' (L. Jones 1993)

LARGE

Origin: ⋆*H.* 'William Lachman' selfed.

Description: A symmetrical, dome-shaped mound 48 in. wide × 22 in. high (120 × 55 cm). Leaf blade 10 × 8 in. (25 × 20 cm), thick, mid-green, widely and irregularly margined bright golden yellow turning pure white, satiny above and matt below, veins ribbed, edge flat near the base and slightly rippled toward the tip, leaf widely oval with a cuspidate tip and heart-shaped pinched to overlapping lobes. Petiole dark green, outlined in cream. Flower tubular, near white, on an upright, leafy, green, 38-in. (95-cm) scape in midsummer; fertile.

Cultivation Notes: Site in light to moderate shade. Moderate growth rate. Use as a background specimen or in a shrub border.

Hosta 'Warwick Curtsey' (L. Jones N/R)

SMALL

Origin: ⋆*H.* 'Dorothy Benedict' × ⋆*H. nakaiana*.

Description: A neat, well-proportioned mound 37 in. wide × 15 in. high (94 × 38 cm). Leaf blade 5 × 4½ in. (13 × 11 cm), of good substance, dark

Hosta 'Warwick Curtsey'

Hosta 'Warwick Choice'

blue-green turning green, irregularly margined and splashed yellow turning cream, matt above and thinly glaucous below, dimpled when mature, edge nearly flat, leaf flat to slightly convex, widely oval with a mucronate tip and heart-shaped open to pinched lobes. Petiole thin, dark green, outlined in cream. Flower long, funnel-shaped, lavender, on an upright, thin, leafy, dark green, 26-in. (65-cm) scape in mid-summer; fertility unknown.

Cultivation Notes: Site in good light to moderate shade. Increases rapidly. Use as a foreground specimen. Also very effective in a large container.

Similar: *H. 'Veronica Lake'.

Hosta 'Warwick Edge' (L. Jones 1993)

SMALL–MEDIUM

Origin: *H. 'William Lachman' × *H. nakaiana.

Description: A dense, neat mound 30 in. wide × 16 in. high (75 × 40 cm). Leaf blade 6½ × 5 in. (16 × 13 cm), thick, matt blue-green, irregularly margined pure white, with some celadon streaks jetting toward the midrib, dimpled, moderately prominently veined, edge smooth, leaf slightly folded, near round with a mucronate tip and flat open lobes. Petiole narrow, green, finely outlined in white. Flower tubular, purple, on an upright, green, 14-in. (35-cm) scape in midsummer; fertile.

Cultivation Notes: Site in light to moderate shade all day. Vigorous. A superb foreground or container plant.

Hosta 'Waukon Thin Ice' (R. Axmear N/R)

MEDIUM

Origin: Sport of *H. 'Topaz'.

Description: A diffuse mound 33 in. wide × 16 in. high (83 × 40 cm). Leaf blade 6 × 5 in. (16 × 13 cm), of good substance, glaucous intense blue, irregularly margined chartreuse, with some streaking, smooth, veins widely spaced, edge slightly undulate, leaf slightly folded, broadly ovate with a cuspidate tip and heart-shaped pinched lobes. Petiole long, pale green, outlined in chartreuse. Flower funnel-shaped, lavender on an upright, leafy, glaucous blue-green, 16- to 18-in. (40- to 45-cm) scape in high summer; fertility not established.

Cultivation Notes: Site in light to moderate shade

to preserve the waxy coating and the subtle contrast between the leaf center and margin. Moderate to rapid growth rate. A superb new introduction.

Distinguishing Features: The leaf margin becomes yellow making a greater contrast between it and the leaf center.

Hosta 'Wide Brim' (P. Aden 1979) ♀

MEDIUM

Origin: *H*. 'Bold One' × *H*. 'Bold Ribbons'.

Description: A dome-shaped mound 45 in. wide × 18 in. high (113 × 45 cm). Leaf blade 8½ × 6½ in.

Hosta 'Warwick Edge'

Hosta 'Waukon Thin Ice'

(21 × 16 cm), of good substance, dark green with a blue cast, widely and irregularly margined pale yellow to cream, with streaks jetting toward the midrib, matt to glaucous above and thinly glaucous below, dimpled, edge flat with occasional kinks, leaf flat to slightly folded, widely oval with a cuspidate tip and heart-shaped pinched lobes. Petiole dark green, outlined in cream. Flower funnel-shaped, violet-striped pale lavender, in a dense raceme, opening from an attractive pale lavender-gray bud, on an upright, bare, glaucous, green, 24-in. (60-cm) scape in late summer; fertile.

Cultivation Notes: Site in good light to high, filtered shade to retain the attractive leaf colors. Increases rapidly. Very popular with flower arrangers because of the pleasing outline, the rugosity, the distinctive wide margin, and the contrasting dark base color. The leaf margin reaches up to 1⅜ in. (3.5 cm) in optimum growing conditions. A classic hosta.

Similar: H. 'Hilda Wassman' has a narrower leaf margin; H. 'Honeysong'; H. 'Jambeliah' in its margined form is larger and has more distinctly cupped leaves; H. 'Mama Mia' is slightly larger.

Sports: H. 'Cowrie' has narrowly variegated leaves with a very exaggerated brim; H. 'Ivy Parody' has leaves with a fancied resemblance to an ivy leaf; H. 'Java' is a shapely all-green form; H. 'Kissing Cousin' has leaves that narrow toward the tip; ★H. 'Stetson'.

Hosta 'Wide Brim'

Hosta 'Winter Snow'

Hosta 'Winter Snow' (Winterberry Farms/J. Anderson 2003)

VERY LARGE

Origin: Sport of ★H. 'Sum and Substance'.

Description: An open mound 60 in. wide × 36 in. high (150 × 90 cm). Leaf blade 16 × 14 in. (40 × 35 cm), thick, leathery, strong chartreuse green, narrowly and irregularly margined cream turning pure white, glossy above and glaucous below, prominent veins widely spaced, edge evenly undulate, leaf slightly folded to cupped, widely oval with a strongly cuspidate tip and heart-shaped pinched to overlapping lobes. Petiole stout, chartreuse to green, outlined in creamy white. Flower: see H. 'Sum and Substance'.

Cultivation Notes: Site in morning sun with plenty of moisture at the roots. Vigorous, but takes several seasons to establish before assuming a good growth rate. Becomes slightly smaller than the parent. A worthy addition to the many marginal sports of ★H. 'Sum and Substance'.

Distinguishing Features: The leaf surface is lustrous and has the appearance of being oiled. The margin is very attractively fluted. A quite distinct sport differing in the surface texture and pure white marginal variegation of the leaf.

Sports: ★H. 'Blizzard'.

Hosta **'Wolverine'** (J. & J. Wilkins 1995)

MEDIUM

Origin: Hybrid of a *H.* 'Dorset Blue' sport.

Description: A dense, cascading mound 38 in. wide × 15 in. high (95 × 38 cm). Leaf blade 10 × 5½ in. (25 × 14 cm), of good substance, blue-tinted green, widely and irregularly margined and splashed cream to white, with celadon streaks jetting toward the midrib, satiny above and glaucous below, smooth, edge slightly rippled, leaf arching, widely lanceolate with an acute tip and tapered open lobes. Petiole flattish, green, faintly outlined in cream. Flower tubular, pale lavender, on an upright, bare, green, 20-in. (50-cm) scape in late summer; fertility unknown.

Cultivation Notes: Site in good light to moderate shade. Vigorous, a rapid increaser. Grow as a foreground specimen or in a tall terracotta chimney pot to accentuate the arching leaves.

Distinguishing Features: Unusual blue-green color in a leaf of this shape.

Similar: *★H.* 'Francheska'.

Sports: *H.* 'Curtain Call' has superb, rich, dark blue-green leaves; *H.* 'Striped Weasel' has leaves splashed and streaked white.

Hosta **'Woolly Mammoth'** (K. Queller-Zilis/M. Zilis 2003)

LARGE–VERY LARGE

Origin: Sport of *H.* 'Blue Mammoth'.

Description: A dense spreading mound 60 in. wide × 28 in. high (150 × 70 cm). Leaf blade 12 × 9 in. (30 × 23 cm), thick, glaucous light blue, widely and irregularly margined chartreuse turning cream, moderately seersuckered, edge slightly undulate, leaf slightly convex, broadly ovate with a distinct mucronate tip and heart-shaped pinched lobes. Petiole stout, light blue-green, outlined in creamy yellow. Flower funnel-shaped, near white, opening from a lavender bud, on an upright, bare, 32-in. (80-cm) scape in midsummer; fertile.

Cultivation Notes: Site in light shade in rich, well-drained soil to achieve best leaf coloring. Slow to increase but eventually becomes huge if given enough moisture. The slightly arching leaves accentuate the lighter midribs. The leaves fold and pleat toward the tip in well-grown plants.

Distinguishing Features: As with some hostas of similar coloring, the marginal variegation does not burn.

Similar: *H. sieboldiana* 'Great Arrival'.

Sport: *H.* 'Golden Tusk'.

Hosta **'Yellow Splash Rim'** (AHS 1986)

MEDIUM

Origin: Stable sport of *H.* 'Yellow Splash'.

Description: A spreading mound 43 in. wide × 18 in. high (108 × 45 cm). Leaf blade 7½ × 3½ in. (19 ×

Hosta 'Wolverine'

Hosta 'Woolly Mammoth'

Hosta 'Yellow Splash Rim'

Hosta 'Yin'

9 cm), thin, mid-green, widely and irregularly margined yellow turning ivory white, with streaks jetting toward the midrib, matt above and glossy below, smooth, conspicuously veined, edge occasionally kinked, leaf slightly arching, elliptic with an acute tip and tapered pinched lobes. Petiole green, dotted in red, outlined in ivory. Flower funnel-shaped, rich lavender, on an upright, bare, green, 28-in. (70-cm) scape in late summer; fertile.

Cultivation Notes: Site in light to moderate shade. Increases rapidly, covering large areas of ground. Not suitable as a pot plant.

Similar: *H.* 'Minnie Bell' and *H.* 'Neat Splash Rim' both are slightly smaller.

Hosta 'Yin' (J. & S. Wilkins 2002)

MEDIUM

Origin: Sport of *H.* 'Maize and Blue'.

Description: A dome-shaped mound 28 in. wide × 10 in. high (70 × 25 cm). Leaf blade 7 × 5 in. (23 × 13 cm), of very good substance, blue-green, widely and irregularly margined ivory, with celadon streaks jetting toward the midrib, glossy above and glaucous below, dimpled, prominently veined, edge very slightly rippled, leaf slightly folded, broadly ovate with a cuspidate tip and flat open to pinched lobes. Petiole blue-green, outlined in ivory. Flower funnel-shaped, mid-lavender, on an upright, bare, green, 15- to 18- in. (38- to 45-cm) scape in high summer; seedpods green, fertility unknown.

Cultivation Notes: Site in dappled to moderate shade to retain the blue-green base color. A most attractive border hosta. Lovely planted with amber-gold-leaved *Hosta* 'Cerveza' and *Heuchera* 'Caramel'.

Distinguishing Features: Has the reverse variegation of *H.* 'Yang' and is better suited to containers than in borders.

Hosta 'Ooh La La'

Hosta 'Rhino Hide'

10

Hostas with Medio-Variegated Leaves

M edio-variegated hostas are those whose variegation is in the center rather than on the margin of the leaf. Since the 1990s they have become by far the most popular; however, they are usually not as vigorous as hostas with variegated margins because so much of the central portion of the leaf blade lacks sufficient chlorophyll to enable the plants to thrive. A proportion of hostas with this type of variegation are listed with the connoisseur plants in chapter 12 since they are more suited to regular tender loving care than to taking their chances with other garden plants, which is how most hostas can be grown.

*An asterisk before a name indicates that the plant is fully described elsewhere in this book.

The leaves of many blue-margined, medio-variegated hostas unfurl with only mid-green color and do not assume their expected variegation for several weeks. *Hosta* 'Paul's Glory' is an example. By contrast, *H. sieboldiana* 'Great Expectations' unfurls with its leaf colors sharply delineated.

In this chapter I describe the flowers of sports only if they differ from the parent plant or if the parent plant is not included. For example, *Hosta* 'High Noon', the parent of *H.* 'Five O'Clock Shadow', includes a description of the flowers because they are different from the parent flowers.

Hosta 'Americana' (Walters Gardens 2006)

SMALL

Origin: Sport of *H.* 'Loyalist'.

Description: A dense, unruly mound 24 in. wide × 14 in. high (60 × 35 cm). Leaf blade 6½ × 4½ in. (16 × 11 cm), thick, ivory to pure white, very widely and very irregularly margined dark green, with celadon streaks jetting toward the midrib, matt above and glaucous below, slightly dimpled when mature, veins widely spaced, edge almost flat, leaf twisted and randomly folded, broadly ovate with a mucronate tip and rounded pinched to folded lobes. Petiole ivory, widely outlined in dark green. Flower funnel-shaped, pale lavender, on an upright, leafy, pale green, 20- to 22-in. (50- to 55-cm) scape in high summer; fertility unknown.

Cultivation Notes: Site in two hours of morning sun in cooler climates, otherwise shade all day. Grow at eye level so that the unusual central variegation and the glaucous undersides of the leaves can be fully appreciated. Moderate growth rate. The central variegation does not "melt out." Divide regularly to retain the unusual variegation.

Distinguishing Features: The eye-catching flaring variegation at the center of the leaf.

Similar: *H.* 'Lakeside Paisley Print'.

Hosta 'American Sweetheart' (H. Hansen 2002)

MEDIUM

Origin: Tetraploid sport of *H.* 'Sea Thunder'.

Description: A tight, upright mound 24 in. wide × 20 in. high (60 × 50 cm). Leaf blade 9 × 7 in. (23 ×

Hosta 'Americana'

18 cm), thick, chartreuse to buttermilk cream turning parchment white, irregularly and widely margined dark green, with streaks jetting toward the midrib, satiny above and shiny below, slight dimpling when mature, prominently veined, edge flat, leaf arching to upright, broadly ovate with a cuspidate tip and rounded open to pinched lobes. Petiole ivory cream, dotted in red, outlined in green. Flower widely funnel-shaped, purple, on an upright, leafy, ivory, 36-in. (90-cm) scape in late summer; fertility not known.

Cultivation Notes: Site in light shade in hot climates, elsewhere tolerates some morning sun. Slow to increase, but eventually becomes a superb border specimen. Flourishes in containers if given adequate moisture. Divide frequently to maintain the attractive balance between the leaf colors.

Distinguishing Features: Differs from the parent in having thicker leaves with a much wider margin and a central variegation that does not scorch or melt out. The flowers are also larger.

Similar: *H. 'Ann Kulpa'; H. 'Indian Feather'; *H. 'Lakeside Love Affaire'; H. 'Lakeside Meter Maid'; *H. 'Night before Christmas'.

Hosta 'Andrew' (H. Hansen 2006)

MEDIUM–LARGE

Origin: Sport of *H.* 'Blue Mammoth'.

Description: A colorful, layered mound 32 in. wide × 20 in. high (80 × 50 cm). Leaf blade 9 × 7 in. (23 × 18 cm), thick, pure white, widely and irregularly margined deep turquoise blue-green, with paler turquoise streaks jetting toward the midrib, glaucous above and below, seersuckered, edge almost flat but kinked toward the base, leaf broadly ovate with a mucronate tip and heart-shaped noticeably pinched and folded lobes. Petiole stout, ivory, finely outlined in blue-green. Flower narrowly funnel-shaped, lavender-striped white, opening from a lavender bud, subtended by pinkish ivory bracts outlined in blue-green, on an upright, leafy 25-in. (63-cm) scape in midsummer; sterile.

Cultivation Notes: Tolerates morning sun in cooler climates but the bluish margins turn green sooner than when sited in dappled to light shade. Slow to increase, but eventually well exceeds its registered dimensions. Very slow to increase until the wide margin fully develops. Pest resistant. Divide frequently.

Distinguishing Features: The eye-catching leaf displays an embroidered effect at the junction of the variegation and the margin.

Similar: *H. sieboldiana* 'American Masterpiece'.

Hosta 'Ani Machi' (P. & J. Ruh 2002)

MEDIUM

Origin: Thought to be *H. sieboldii* × *H. rectifolia*. From Japan and well known there, but usually known in the United States as *H.* 'Geisha', although it is not the hosta registered in 1983 as *H.* 'Geisha'.

Hosta 'American Sweetheart'

Hosta 'Andrew'

Description: An upright, unruly mound 36 in. wide × 18 in. high (90 × 45 cm). Leaf blade 7½ × 3½ in. (19 × 9 cm), of average substance, glossy, golden yellow, widely and evenly margined dark olive green, with occasional streaks jetting toward the midrib, smooth, edge slightly rippled, leaf twisted toward the tip, elliptic to narrowly oval with a recurved acute tip and tapered open lobes. Petiole shallow, yellow, outlined in dark green. Flower bell-shaped, light violet, on an upright, leafy, purple-dotted green, 26-in. (65-cm) scape in late summer; fertile.

Cultivation Notes: Viridescent. Site in light to moderate shade. Slow to increase and needs good cultivation and hot summers to maintain a steady growth rate. Leaf center turns pale green at or before flowering time.

Hosta 'Ani Machi'

Hosta 'Ann Kulpa'

Distinguishing Features: The graceful poise of the leaves emphasizes their dramatic coloring.

Similar: ★*H.* 'Mary Marie Ann' is slightly smaller and has cream-centered leaves.

Sports: *H.* 'Apple Court' is a weak grower with smaller leaves that have a white center but are even more contorted; *H.* 'Geisha Satin Ripples' is the flat-leaved green form.

Hosta 'Ann Kulpa' (J. Kulpa 1999)

MEDIUM–LARGE

Origin: *H.* 'Pin Stripe Sister' hybrid.

Description: A layered mound 24 in. wide × 20 in. high (60 × 50 cm). Leaf blade 8 × 6 in. (20 × 15 cm), of good substance, satiny, yellow turning ivory white, very widely and irregularly margined light green turning dark green, with a blue cast in early summer, and with celadon streaks jetting toward the midrib, dimpled, strongly veined, edge flat to slightly undulate, leaf folded, widely oval with a cuspidate tip and heart-shaped pinched lobes. Petiole ivory white, striped dark green. Flower bell-shaped, lavender with translucent edges, on an upright, leafy, ivory white, 28-in. (70-cm) scape from mid- to high summer; sterile.

Cultivation Notes: Site in morning sun in cooler climates. Vigorous, a moderate increaser. Needs frequent division to retain the centrally striped effect.

Similar: *H.* 'Sharply Dressed Man'.

Hosta 'Banana Boat' (W. & E. Lachman 1991)

SMALL–MEDIUM

Origin: *H.* 'Reversed' hybrid.

Description: An upright mound 20 in. wide × 9 in. high (50 × 23 cm). Leaf blade 6 × 4½ in. (15 × 11 cm), thick, leathery, ivory white, irregularly and widely margined dark green, with conspicuous chartreuse streaks jetting toward the midrib, matt above and glaucous below, dimpled, edge flat, leaf folded to slightly cupped, elliptic to narrowly oval with a cuspidate tip and kinked open to pinched lobes. Petiole narrow, flattish, ivory, outlined in dark green. Flower bell-shaped, violet, sparsely arranged, on a slightly oblique, leafy, ivory, 13-in. (33-cm) scape in midsummer; sterile.

Cultivation Notes: Site in morning sun in cooler climates. Slow to increase. Needs careful placing so that it will get sufficient sun to provide vigor but not so much that it burns the leaf center. Slow to increase but it has a better constitution than many hostas of this type.

Distinguishing Features: Slightly inward-folding leaves create a "boat-shaped" outline. Slight sheen to upper leaf surface. Attractively margined and slightly streaked leaves and variegated leafy bracts add to the charms of this colorful hosta.

Hosta 'Brenda's Beauty' (R. Keller 1992)

MEDIUM

Origin: Sport of *H*. 'Gold Standard'.

Description: An open mound 41 in. wide × 18 in. high (102 × 45 cm). Leaf blade 8 × 5 in. (20 × 13 cm), of moderate substance, emerging pale chartreuse turning yellow and finally ivory, irregularly margined mid- to dark green, with streaks jetting toward the midrib, matt above and glaucous below, slightly dimpled, strongly veined, edge undulate, leaf slightly cupped, widely oval with a cuspidate tip and heart-shaped pinched lobes. Petiole chartreuse to ivory, outlined in dark green. Flower: see *H*. 'Fortunei Hyacinthina'.

Cultivation Notes: Site in good light to moderate shade in cooler climates to achieve the best leaf color, elsewhere shade all day. Vigorous. Among the best of the many medio-variegated sports from *H*. 'Gold Standard'.

Distinguishing Features: Conspicuous netted veining is visible in the variegated portion of the leaf.

Similar: *H*. 'Okay Dokey' has more-rugose leaves; *H*. 'Something Different' has more contrast of its leaf colors and has a rippled leaf edge.

Hosta 'Bright Lights' (P. Aden & Klehm Nursery N/R)

MEDIUM

Origin: Clone of *H*. 'Tokudama Aureonebulosa'.

Description: An overlapping mound 51 in. wide × 18 in. high (127 × 45 cm). Leaf blade 9 × 7 in. (23 × 18 cm), thick, glaucous, cloudy chartreuse to yellow, widely margined blue-green, with streaks jetting toward the midrib, seersuckered, edge flat to occasionally kinked, leaf folded, oval with a cuspidate tip and heart-shaped open to pinched lobes. Petiole chartreuse. Flower: see *H*. 'Tokudama'.

Cultivation Notes: Site in light to moderate shade

Hosta 'Brenda's Beauty'

Hosta 'Banana Boat' before the leaves have reached their mature shape.

Hosta 'Bright Lights'

to achieve the most subtle color contrast. Leaves emerge blue slowly assuming the subtle variegation. Very slow to increase. Pest resistant.

Similar: *H.* 'Abiqua Hallucination' has longer, larger leaves; *H.* 'Blue Shadows' is a selected form of *H.* 'Tokudama Aureonebulosa' in which the blue margin and streaking are much darker, almost navy blue, giving a greater contrast; ★*H.* 'Dark Shadows'; *H.* 'Saybrook Surprise' has somewhat rounder leaves.

Sports: ★*H.* 'Heatwave'.

Hosta 'Brother Stephan' (O. Petryszyn 1998)

LARGE

Origin: ★*H.* 'King Tut' × *H.* 'Mildred Seaver' seedling.

Description: An open mound 35 in. wide × 22 in. high (88 × 55 cm). Leaf blade 11 × 10 in. (28 × 25 cm), thick, golden yellow, very widely and irregularly margined medium green, with chartreuse streaks jetting toward the midrib, matt above and glaucous below, seersuckered, edge flat, leaf lightly cupped, nearly round with a vestigial tip and heart-shaped pinched to folded lobes. Petiole stout, green, outlined in yellow. Flower bell-shaped, pure white, in a dense raceme, on an upright, leafy, gray-green, 26-in. (65-cm) scape in early summer; fertile.

Cultivation Notes: Site in light shade. Moderate growth rate. Pest resistant. Grow in a foliage border where it will stand out among plain green leaves. Not suitable for containers. Divide frequently.

Distinguishing Features: The attractive variegation resembles the "hand print" or "maple leaf" pattern.

Similar: *H.* 'Inniswood'; ★*H.* 'Paradigm'; ★*H.* 'September Sun'.

Hosta 'Cadillac' (E. Skrocki/T. Avent 1998)

SMALL

Origin: Unknown.

Description: A dense mound 20 in. wide × 10 in. high (50 × 25 cm). Leaf blade 6 × 4½ in. (15 × 11 cm), thick, golden yellow, widely margined green, with streaks jetting toward the midrib, intensely seersuckered, edge flat, leaf slightly cupped, widely oval to nearly round with a mucronate tip and heart-shaped pinched lobes. Petiole long, chartreuse. Flower tubular, near white, on an upright, bare, green, 16- to 20-in. (40- to 50-cm) scape from early to midsummer; fertile.

Cultivation Notes: Lutescent. In warmer climates, site in light to moderate shade to achieve the best color, elsewhere it tolerates morning sun. Slow to increase. Pest resistant.

Hosta 'Captain Kirk' (K. Brill 1999)

MEDIUM

Origin: Sport of ★*H.* 'Gold Standard'.

Description: An overlapping mound 36 in. wide × 20 in. high (90 × 50 cm). Leaf blade 9 × 7 in. (23 × 18 cm), of good substance, emerging chartreuse turning first yellow then ivory, widely margined bright

Hosta 'Brother Stephan'

Hosta 'Cadillac'

mid-green, matt above and glaucous below, dimpled, strongly veined, edge almost flat, leaf slightly arching, slightly convex, widely oval with a cuspidate tip and heart-shaped pinched lobes. Petiole flattish, cream, finely outlined in dark green. Flower: see ★*H.* 'Fortunei Hyacinthina'.

Cultivation Notes: Some morning sun is beneficial but it needs careful placing in the garden. Vigorous, a fairly rapid increaser. The margin can be up to 2¾ in. (7 cm) wide. Requires regular division of the clump to keep the most pleasing proportion between the leaf blade and margin.

Distinguishing Features: Differs from its parent in having thicker leaves and a narrower central variegation, and in holding its color better.

Similar: ★*H.* 'Ann Kulpa'; *H.* 'Center of Attention'; ★*H.* 'Prime Meridian'.

Sports: *H.* 'Enterprise' has green-margined ivory leaves with attractive transitional chartreuse streaks; *H.* 'Starship' has cream-margined green leaves; *H.* 'Vulcan' has green-margined pure white leaves and is very vigorous.

Hosta 'Cathedral Windows' PP17,295 (H. Hansen 2005)

MEDIUM–LARGE

Origin: Tetraploid sport of *H.* 'Stained Glass'.

Description: An open, dome-shaped mound 34 in. wide × 19 in. high (85 × 48 cm). Leaf blade 10 × 9 in. (25 × 23 cm), of good substance, chartreuse turning golden yellow, very widely and irregularly margined spinach green, with chartreuse feathering and streaking, shiny above and glaucous below, dimpled, veins widely spaced, edge almost flat, leaf usually convex, broadly ovate to rounded with a recurved vestigial tip and flat to heart-shaped open to pinched lobes. Petiole chartreuse, outlined in dark green. Flower: see ★*H.* 'Fragrant Bouquet'.

Cultivation Notes: Lutescent. Tolerates full sun all day except in the hottest climates. Requires abundant moisture to produce a prolific display of the superb flowers. Increases rapidly. Must be divided frequently to retain the balance between the variegation and the wide leaf margins.

Distinguishing Features: Differs from its parent in

Hosta 'Captain Kirk'

Hosta 'Vulcan'

Hosta 'Cathedral Windows'

having thicker leaves with much wider leaf margins which entirely changes the balance of the leaf colors.

Similar: *H.* 'Avocado' and *H.* 'Holy Molé' have slightly wider leaf margins.

Sports: *H.* 'The Shining' has yellow leaves.

Hosta 'Chinese Sunrise' (R. Schaeffer/A. Summers/P. Ruh 1992)

SMALL–MEDIUM

Origin: Thought to be a sport of *H. cathayana*.

Description: A dense, arching mound 28 in. wide × 14 in. high (70 × 35 cm). Leaf blade 6½ × 3 in. (16 × 8 cm), thin, chartreuse yellow fading to light olive green, narrowly and irregularly margined dark olive green, glossy above and satiny below, smooth, prominently veined, edge slightly undulate, leaf lanceolate with an acute tip and tapered open lobes. Petiole narrow, olive green. Flower bell-shaped, light purple, in clusters, on a thin, semi-oblique, very leafy, 28-in. (70-cm) scape in late summer; fertile.

Cultivation Notes: Site in morning sun to good light to retain the variegation for as long as possible. Best planted in clumps 12 in. (30 cm) apart as an edging plant, where the leaves gradually change color through the season making attractive tonal contrasts. Also effective in pots.

Distinguishing Features: One of the first hostas to emerge in spring.

Hosta 'Chinese Sunrise'

Hosta 'Christmas Candy' (G. Van Eijk-Bos & D. Van Erven/D. Van Eechaute 2002)

MEDIUM

Origin: Sport of ★*H.* 'Night before Christmas'.

Description: An upright mound 24 in. wide × 18 in. high (60 × 45 cm). Leaf blade 7½ × 3 in. (19 × 8 cm), thick, emerging chartreuse turning ivory, widely and irregularly margined dark green, with random chartreuse streaks jetting toward the midrib, satiny above and shiny below, visible veins widely spaced, edge slightly rippled and undulate to twisting on young plants but flatter in maturity, leaf ovate with a cuspidate tip and flat open to pinched lobes. Petiole flattish, ivory, finely outlined in dark green. Flower: see ★*H.* 'White Christmas'.

Cultivation Notes: Site in morning sun followed by light shade. Tolerates more sun in cooler climates provided adequate moisture is available. The base leaf color remains pristine ivory throughout the season. The flower heads die less than gracefully so remove them as they start to wither. Lovely with asarums and tradescantia. Divide frequently.

Distinguishing Features: Smaller than its parent. A weak chartreuse overlay is apparent in the whitish variegation toward the petiole.

Similar: *H.* 'Christmas Cookies' has a slightly paler green margin; ★*H.* 'Undulata'; ★*H.* 'White Christmas' has thinner leaves.

Hosta 'Cornbelt' (J. Anderson N/R)

LARGE

Origin: Sport of ★*H.* 'Jimmy Crack Corn'.

Description: A diffuse, upright mound 48 in. wide × 20 in. high (120 × 50 cm). Leaf blade 8 × 5 in. (20 × 13 cm), of good substance, chartreuse to bright golden yellow, very widely and irregularly margined mid- to dark green, with chartreuse and dark green streaks jetting toward the midrib, satiny above and thinly glaucous below, dimpled to seersuckered when mature, edge heavily rippled, leaf slightly folded and arching, ovate with a cuspidate tip and heart-shaped pinched lobes. Petiole chartreuse, outlined in dark green. Flower funnel-shaped, near white, in a dense cluster, on an upright, leafy, chartreuse, 24- to 30-in. (60- to 75-cm) scape in early summer; fertile.

Cultivation Notes: Site in good light or dappled

shade followed by full shade in the hottest regions. Moderate growth rate. Pest resistant. A dramatic specimen better suited to a sophisticated shade border than a wilder woodland setting. The prominently piecrusted edges and extravagantly wider margins make it one of the best large-leafed introductions.

Distinguishing Features: On mature leaves the deeply seersuckered areas resemble blistering.

Similar: *H.* 'Journey's End' PP16,895 has narrower margins.

Hosta 'Dancing in the Rain' PP15,977 (Walters Gardens 2004)

LARGE

Origin: Sport of ★*H.* 'Blue Umbrellas'.

Description: An upright mound 49 in. wide × 28 in. high (122 × 70 cm). Leaf blade 11 × 9 in. (28 ×

23 cm), very thick, ivory white, narrowly and very irregularly margined blue-green turning dark green, with lighter green streaks randomly jetting toward the midrib, matt above and glaucous below, seersuckered and puckered, veins widely spaced, edge nearly flat, leaf convex or cupped, almost round with a mucronate tip and heart-shaped folded to overlapping lobes. Petiole stout, white, outlined in blue-green. Flower: see *H.* 'Blue Umbrellas'.

Cultivation Notes: Site in morning sun in cooler climates to increase vigor, but light to moderate shade produces a better contrast between the margin and the central variegation. Slow to start but needs regular division once established. Pest resistant.

Distinguishing Features: The leaf center develops pale green frosting in extreme summer heat.

Similar: ★*H. sieboldiana* 'American Masterpiece'.

Hosta 'Delia' (R. & M. Ford 1995)

SMALL

Origin: Sport of ★*H.* 'Golden Prayers'.

Description: A compact mound 18 in. wide × 6 in. high (45 × 15 cm). Leaf blade 3 × 2 in. (8 × 5 cm), thick, light yellow, irregularly margined mid-green, with some streaks jetting toward the midrib, matt above and glaucous below, seersuckered, veins moderately prominent, edge flat to slightly rippled, leaf folded, widely oval with a cuspidate tip and heart-shaped pinched lobes. Petiole chartreuse to yellow. Flower: see *H.* 'Golden Prayers'.

Cultivation Notes: Site in morning sun in cooler

Hosta 'Christmas Candy'

Hosta 'Cornbelt'

Hosta 'Dancing in the Rain'

climates, otherwise light to moderate shade. Very slow to increase. Pest resistant.

Similar: *H.* 'Goldbrook Grace'.

Hosta 'Dick Ward' (H. Hatfield 1991)

MEDIUM–LARGE

Origin: Sport of ★*H.* 'Zounds'.

Description: A dense mound 40 in. wide × 18 in. high (100 × 45 cm). Leaf blade 9 × 9 in. (23 × 23 cm), thick, glaucous chartreuse yellow turning golden yellow, irregularly margined dark green, seersuckered, edge wavy, leaf cupped, widely oval to nearly round with a mucronate tip and heart-shaped overlapping

Hosta 'Delia'

Hosta 'Dick Ward'

open to pinched lobes. Petiole chartreuse with a dark green margin. Flower: see *H.* 'Zounds'.

Cultivation Notes: Site in morning sun in cooler climates, then good light to moderate shade. Slow to establish but well worth the wait. Pest resistant.

Distinguishing Features: Becomes a brassy yellow if exposed to full sunlight.

Similar: *H.* 'Midwest Magic' has a narrower, less intense dark green margin; ★*H.* 'Paradigm'; ★*H.* 'September Sun' has slightly smaller leaves.

Hosta 'Dinky Donna' (G. Heemskerk N/R)

SMALL

Origin: Sport of *H.* 'Radiant Edger'.

Description: A dome-shaped mound 25 in. wide × 12 in. high (63 × 30 cm). Leaf blade 3½ × 2½ in. (9 × 6 cm), of moderate substance, chartreuse to muted golden yellow, very widely and irregularly margined dark olive green, with many streaks jetting toward the midrib, matt above and thinly glaucous below, smooth becoming slightly dimpled when mature, edge almost flat, leaf slightly folded, broadly ovate with an acuminate tip and heart-shaped pinched to folded lobes. Petiole muted yellow, outlined in green. Flower: see ★*H.* 'Gold Edger'.

Cultivation Notes: Site in dappled to full shade. Moderate growth rate. Useful as a front-of-the-border or edging hosta but equally suitable for a container.

Distinguishing Features: The attractive and unusual variegation. The leaves have longer tips than those of the parent.

Hosta 'Dylan's Dilly' (Walden-West N/R)

SMALL

Origin: Sport of *H.* 'Fortunei'.

Description: A wide-spreading mound 20 in. wide × 15 in. high (50 × 38 cm). Leaf blade 8½ × 5 in. (21 × 13 cm), of good substance, pale chartreuse to cream, irregularly margined dark green, with some streaks jetting toward the midrib, matt above and glaucous below, edge flat to slightly rippled, leaf shallowly cupped, oval with a cuspidate tip and rounded open to pinched lobes. Petiole chartreuse, finely outlined in dark green. Flower funnel-shaped, lavender, on an upright, leafy, light green, 20-in. (50-cm) scape from mid- to high summer; sterile.

Cultivation Notes: Some morning sun in cooler climates followed by good light results in the best leaf color, so it needs careful placing in the garden. Variegation is constant and stable. Vigorous, a moderately rapid increaser.

Distinguishing Features: Leaves are paler in color than those of ★*H.* 'Gold Standard' and the clump is tighter.

Similar: *H.* 'Geneva Stark', which came from the same cross, has very white central variegation.

Hosta 'Emerald Ruff Cut' (J. Anderson 2003)
MEDIUM
Origin: Sport of *H.* 'Sea Angel Wings'.
Description: A colorful, cascading mound 24 in. wide × 20 in. high (61 × 50 cm). Leaf blade 9 × 7 in.

(23 × 18 cm), of good substance, bright golden yellow, irregularly margined rich emerald green, with some chartreuse streaking, satiny above and matt below, very seersuckered, prominently veined, edge distinctively ruffled, leaf arched, cuneate to ovate with an acute tip and heart-shaped pinched lobes. Petiole yellow, outlined in emerald green. Flower funnel-shaped, pale lavender, on an upright, leafy,

Hosta 'Dinky Donna'

Hosta 'Dylan's Dilly'

Hosta 'Emerald Ruff Cut'

Hosta 'Emerald Tiara'

Hosta 'Eye Declare'

Hosta 'Fire and Ice'

olive-green, 24- to 28-in. (60- to 70- cm) scape in high summer; fertility unknown.

Cultivation Notes: Best in cooler gardens in morning sun following by light shade. Leaves reflush in midsummer but the color is best earlier in the season. Divide regularly.

Distinguishing Features: The deep seersuckering resembles blistering on the leaf surface.

Hosta 'Emerald Tiara' (Walters Gardens 1988)

SMALL

Origin: Tissue-cultured sport of ★H. 'Golden Scepter'.

Description: A dense, spreading mound 34 in. wide × 14 in. high (85 × 35 cm). Leaf blade 4½ × 3½ in. (11 × 9 cm), of average substance, muted gold, irregularly margined rich dark green, with some streaks jetting toward the midrib, smooth, veins widely spaced, edge flat to occasionally kinked, leaf widely oval with a cuspidate tip and heart-shaped open to pinched lobes. Petiole chartreuse, outlined in dark green. Flower: see ★H. 'Golden Tiara'.

Cultivation Notes: Site in some morning sun followed by good light to light shade. Leaf colors become more muted as the season progresses. More vigorous than its parent and easy to grow. A good foreground plant and also suitable for containers.

Similar: H. 'Emerald Scepter' emerges with a gold center and gradually lightens to near white, is less vigorous, and can scorch in sun more easily than other hostas of the Tiara Series; H. 'Stolen Kiss', once thought to be a sport of ★H. 'Cheatin Heart', is now considered a tissue-cultured sport of H. 'Emerald Scepter', following a mix-up in a tissue-culture laboratory; H. 'Topaz Tiara' has a darker central variegation, less of a color contrast, and a thicker substance.

Sports: H. 'Flemish Tiara' has leaves with much wider margins.

Hosta 'Eye Declare' PP18,466 (A. Bergeron/ Walters Gardens 2005)

MEDIUM

Origin: Sport of ★H. 'Sea Fire'.

Description: An arching, overlapping mound 16 in. wide × 12 in. high (40 × 30 cm). Leaf blade 7 × 4 in. (18 × 10 cm), of good substance, satiny, pale yellow, narrowly and irregularly margined and streaked medium green, moderately seersuckered, edge flat, leaf broadly ovate with a mucronate tip and rounded pinched lobes. Petiole chartreuse, dotted in red, finely outlined in medium green. Flower: see *H.* 'Sea Fire'.

Cultivation Notes: Viridescent base color, the variegation becoming greenish yellow. Site in light to full shade. At its best from spring to early summer. Grow with dark green foliage to emphasize the vivid leaf color contrasts accentuated by the red flower buds, shoots, and petioles.

Distinguishing Features: Smaller than its parent.

Hosta 'Fire and Ice' (H. Hansen & Shady Oaks Nursery 1999)

MEDIUM

Origin: Reversed sport of ★*H.* 'Patriot'.

Description: An upright mound 12 in. wide × 8 in. high (30 × 20 cm). Leaf blade 6 × 4 in. (15 × 10 cm), of good substance, creamy ivory to white, widely and irregularly margined dark green, splashed several shades of green jetting toward the midrib, satiny above and shiny below, smooth, edge kinked, leaf moderately folded to lightly twisted and curved at the acute tip, widely oval with rounded open lobes. Petiole ivory white, finely outlined in olive green. Flower: see ★*H.* 'Francee'.

Cultivation Notes: Site in strong light in the morning. Avoid hot afternoon sun. Seemingly vigorous for a medio-variegated hosta.

Distinguishing Features: Scapes are white and purple-dotted toward the raceme. The seedpods, when they are produced, are greenish white with occasional purple lines. The clump is taller than most hostas of this type.

Similar: *H.* 'Abba Irresistible'; *H.* 'Flash of Light' has a more open habit and shows good vigor; *H.* 'Loyalist' has thicker leaves; *H.* 'Paul Revere'.

Sports: *H.* 'Alternative' is ivory white with very wide green margins.

Hosta 'Five O'Clock Shadow' (R. Solberg 2000)

LARGE

Origin: Sport of ★*H.* 'High Noon'.

Description: An upright, spreading mound 36 in. wide × 22 in. high (90 × 55 cm). Leaf blade 10 × 8

in. (25 × 20 cm), moderately thick, bright pale yellow, irregularly margined muted light green, satiny above and glaucous below, seersuckered to pebbled, strongly veined, edge shallowly undulate, leaf slightly folded or slightly convex, widely oval with a cuspidate tip and heart-shaped pinched lobes. Petiole narrow, chartreuse. Flower funnel-shaped, near white, on an upright or oblique, bare, glaucous yellow, 36- to 40-in. (90- to 100-cm) scape in early summer; seedpods green, fertile.

Cultivation Notes: Site in morning sun to achieve the best leaf color. Moderate growth rate. Pest resistant.

Distinguishing Features: Very muted margin can attain a width of 1 in. (2.5 cm).

Similar: *H.* 'Rascal' has larger leaves in a tighter clump.

Sports: *H.* 'Five O'Clock Somewhere' is a tetraploid and therefore has thicker leaves, which have very wide green margins.

Hosta 'Fortunei Albopicta' (N. Hylander & AHS 1987) ♛

MEDIUM–LARGE

Origin: Natural sport of *H.* 'Fortunei'.

Description: An overlapping mound 45 in. wide

Hosta 'Five O'Clock Shadow'

× 22 in. high (113 × 55 cm). Leaf blade 10 × 6 in. (25 × 15 cm), of average substance, chartreuse to pale yellow, irregularly margined dark green with slight blue undertones, and with some pale chartreuse streaks jetting toward the midrib, matt above and glaucous below, moderately seersuckered when mature, edge slightly undulate, leaf slightly folded or convex, widely oval with a cuspidate tip and heart-shaped pinched lobes. Petiole chartreuse, outlined in dark green. Flower funnel-shaped, purple-streaked

Hosta 'Fortunei Albopicta'

Hosta 'Royal Golden Jubilee'

Hosta 'Gold Standard', the leaves have more muted coloring when grown in shade.

lavender, on an upright, leafy, glaucous green, 40-in. (100-cm) scape from mid- to high summer; barely fertile.

Cultivation Notes: Viridescent. Variegation is maintained for longer if grown in light shade in a cooler climate. Exposure to full sun early in the season will bleach the central variegation to ivory white. At its best soon after the leaves unfurl. Late to emerge. Vigorous, easy to grow.

Distinguishing Features: Veins appear like netting across the lighter portion of the leaf. By the end of the season the leaf blade is a dull two-tone green.

Similar: *H.* 'Whirligig' is smaller and has more twisted leaves.

Sports: *H.* 'Chelsea Babe' is smaller in all its parts; ★*H.* 'Fortunei Albopicta Aurea' ♀ has viridescent yellow leaves.

Hosta 'Gold Standard' (P. Banyai 1976)

MEDIUM–LARGE

Origin: Sport of *H.* 'Fortunei Hyacinthina Variegata'.

Description: A dense, overlapping mound 41 in. wide × 22 in. high (102 × 55 cm). Leaf blade 8 × 5 in. (20 × 13 cm), of good substance, chartreuse turning yellow then ivory, irregularly margined dark green, with some streaks jetting toward the midrib, matt above and glaucous below, seersuckered, edge slightly rippled, leaf slightly cupped, widely oval with a cuspidate tip and heart-shaped pinched to overlapping lobes. Petiole chartreuse, outlined in dark green. Flower: see ★*H.* 'Fortunei Hyacinthina'.

Cultivation Notes: Albescent. Is very sensitive to light levels so site in bright light to moderate shade, depending on summer heat and the leaf color required. Emerges late from purple shoots. Vigorous, easy to grow. A colorful specimen in the border and excellent in containers. Winner of the 1993 Alex J. Summers Distinguished Merit Hosta Award. Has probably produced more worthwhile sports than any other hosta. A classic.

Similar: *H.* 'Fan Dance'; *H.* 'Janet' is less vigorous and not easy to grow; *H.* 'Okay Dokey'.

Sports: ★*H.* 'Brenda's Beauty'; ★*H.* 'Captain Kirk'; *H.* 'Collector's Banner'; *H.* 'Darwin's Standard'; *H.* 'Fire Opal' and *H.* 'Flip Flop' both have leaves that

change color; *H.* 'G String' has streaked leaves; ★*H.* 'Moonlight'; *H.* 'Paradise Standard'; ★*H.* 'Richland Gold' has yellow leaves; *H.* 'Royal Golden Jubilee' has leaves that emerge bright gold with a green margin and retain this color throughout the season; *H.* 'Silver and Gold'; *H.* 'Something Different'; *H.* 'String Bikini' and *H.* 'Work of Art' both are white-margined green; ★*H.* 'Striptease'.

Hosta 'Guacamole' (R. Solberg 1994)

LARGE

Origin: Sport of ★*H.* 'Fragrant Bouquet'.

Description: An overlapping mound 51 in. wide × 24 in. high (127 × 60 cm). Leaf blade 11 × 8½ in. (28 × 21 cm), of good substance, chartreuse turning old gold, irregularly margined dark green, with chartreuse streaks jetting toward the midrib, glossy above and thinly glaucous below, prominently veined, edge almost flat, leaf slightly convex, widely oval with a mucronate tip and heart-shaped pinched to overlapping lobes. Petiole chartreuse, faintly outlined in dark green. Flower: see *H.* 'Fragrant Bouquet'.

Cultivation Notes: Site in full sun all day in cooler climates, elsewhere in morning sun only. Increases rapidly. Named Hosta of the Year by the American Hosta Growers Association in 2002.

Distinguishing Features: The leaf margin is barely visible in cooler climates even if exposed to sunlight.

Sports: ★*H.* 'Fried Green Tomatoes' has dark green

Hosta '**Guacamole**'

leaves; *H.* 'Holy Molé' has wide green margins; *H.* 'Paradise Sunshine' has green leaves margined yellow, the margins appearing late but not fading; *H.* 'Stained Glass' has more vividly colored leaves and was named Hosta of the Year by the American Hosta Growers Association in 2006.

Hosta 'Heatwave' (J. van den Top N/R)
MEDIUM
Origin: Sport of ★*H.* 'Bright Lights'.
Description: An open mound 36 in. wide × 14 in. high (90 × 35 cm). Leaf blade 9 × 7 in. (23 × 18 cm), thick, leathery, glaucous chartreuse yellow, widely and irregularly margined rich blue-green, with lighter green streaks jetting toward the midrib, heavily seersuckered, edge flat to occasionally kinked, leaf

Hosta 'Holy Molé'

Hosta 'Stained Glass'

folded, broadly ovate with a cuspidate tip and open to pinched heart-shaped lobes. Petiole chartreuse, outlined in dark blue-green. Flower: see ★*H.* 'Tokudama'.

Cultivation Notes: Although it tolerates some morning sun in cooler climates, it is best sited in light to moderate shade to achieve the most subtle color contrast. Divide frequently to prevent reversion to all-blue leaves. Robust but slow to increase. Pest resistant.

Distinguishing Features: Differs from the parent in having a definite differentiation between the wide margin and the base color. Has exaggeratedly mucronate leaf tips.

Similar: *H.* 'Summer Joy' has a paler base color.

Hosta 'High Society' PP17,313 (H. Hansen 2004)
SMALL–MEDIUM
Origin: Sport of ★*H.* 'June'.
Description: A dome-shaped mound 24 in. wide × 12 in. high (60 × 30 cm). Leaf blade 5 × 4 in. (13 × 11 cm), thick, glaucous golden yellow fading to ivory, very widely margined intense blue-green, with streaks jetting toward the midrib and some transitional chartreuse streaks, dimpled, veins closely spaced, edge flat with an occasional kink, leaf cupped, broadly oval with a cuspidate tip and heart-shaped pinched to folded lobes. Petiole chartreuse to ivory, outlined in blue-green. Flower bell-shaped, near white, in a dense raceme, on a stout, upright, bare, glaucous light green, 18-in. (45-cm) scape in midsummer; seedpods blue-green, fertility unknown.

Hosta 'Heatwave'

Cultivation Notes: Site in light to moderate shade. Slow growth rate. Pest resistant. Simple, elegant containers accentuate the dramatic variegation. Also makes an eye-catching and colorful specimen. Divide regularly to retain the attractive balance of leaf color.

Distinguishing Features: Differs from its parent in having a more upright habit and thicker leaves.

Similar: *H.* 'Catherine'; *H.* 'Touch of Class' PP17,313 has very thick leaves and at registration had much wider blue-green margins but this can change depending upon how often it is divided.

Hosta 'Julie Morss' (J. Morss 1983)

MEDIUM–LARGE

Origin: Breeder states this is a seedling of *H. sieboldiana* 'Frances Williams', but other authorities have claimed it is a viridescent seedling of an unknown *H.* 'Fortunei'.

Description: A dense mound 44 in. wide × 20 in. high (110 × 50 cm). Leaf blade 9 × 7 in. (23 × 18 cm), thick, chartreuse turning pale yellow, widely and irregularly margined mid-green with a blue cast, with celadon streaks jetting toward the midrib, matt above and glaucous below, dimpled, edge almost flat, leaf slightly cupped, widely oval with a mucronate tip and heart-shaped pinched lobes. Petiole pale yellow, outlined in green. Flower bell-shaped, lavender-white, on an upright, bare, glaucous yellow, 22-in. (55-cm) scape from high to late summer; fertile.

Cultivation Notes: Site in somewhat low light or moderate shade all day for the best color in cooler climates. Foliage is most colorful in early summer before the variegation fades. Slow to moderate growth rate. Lovely planted among cerise and purple rhododendrons and azaleas.

Hosta 'June' (Neo Plants 1991) ⚱

MEDIUM

Origin: First tissue-cultured sport of ★*H.* 'Halcyon'.

Description: A symmetrical, overlapping mound 30 in. wide × 15 in. high (75 × 38 cm). Leaf blade 6 × 4 in. (15 × 10 cm), of good substance, chartreuse turning yellow then ivory, irregularly margined blue, with streaks jetting toward the midrib, matt above and glaucous below, smooth, edge almost flat, leaf slightly cupped, oval with a cuspidate tip and heart-shaped pinched lobes. Petiole chartreuse yellow. Flower: see *H.* 'Halcyon'.

Cultivation Notes: For the most subtle chartreuse and blue color, site in light shade in cool climates. For a stronger, harsher contrast of leaf colors, site in morning sun. Indeed, the difference between plants grown in good light and plants grown in shade is so marked they look like different plants. Moderate to rapid growth rate. Easy to grow. A superb foreground specimen. Lovely in a shiny blue ceramic pot. Named Hosta of the Year by the American Hosta Growers Association in 2001.

Similar: *H.* 'Grand Marquee' PP15,961 has more solid margins and is one of the first hostas to flower;

Hosta 'High Society'

Hosta 'Julie Morss'

H. 'Katherine Lewis'; ★*H.* 'Paradise Joyce'; ★*H.* 'Punky'.

Sports: *H.* 'Early Times' has yellow leaves; *H.* 'English Sunrise' has yellow leaves; *H.* 'Frosted June' PPAF is a sport of *H.* 'June Fever' and has frosted chartreuse-margined blue-green leaves; both ★*H.* 'High Society', which is smaller and slow-growing, and *H.* 'Touch of Class' have very wide blue-green margins with streaks and splashes toward the midrib and an ivory to white leaf center; *H.* 'June Fever' PP15,340

is an extraordinarily brazen yellow with some transitional chartreuse splashes and random thin, dark green streaking around the margin; ★*H.* 'May' has yellow leaves; ★*H.* 'Remember Me' is yellow turning ivory white with transitional chartreuse streaks and an irregular blue margin; *H.* 'Valley Lemon Ice' has yellow leaves;

Hosta 'Kiwi Full Monty' (B. Sligh 2000)

MEDIUM

Origin: Sport of ★*H.* 'Striptease'.

Description: An open mound 36 in. wide × 18 in. high (90 × 45 cm). Leaf blade 6 × 3½ in. (15 × 9 cm), of good substance, glaucous chartreuse turning creamy yellow to ivory, widely margined rich blue-green with occasional silver flecks at the junction between the center and the margin, slightly dimpled, edge almost flat, leaf folded, oval with a cuspidate tip and tapered open to pinched lobes. Petiole narrow, chartreuse, outlined in dark blue-green. Flower: see ★*H.* 'Fortunei Hyacinthina'.

Cultivation Notes: Site in good light to light shade to maintain the rich but subtle variations in leaf color. Vigorous, a rapid increaser. Lovely in a container against gray stonework.

Distinguishing Features: Differs from similar introductions by the dark blue-green margins.

Similar: *H.* 'Blue Without You' does not have such pronounced contrast between the leaf center and margin; *H.* 'Gypsy Rose'; ★*H.* 'Striptease'.

Hosta 'June'

Hosta 'Kiwi Full Monty'

Hosta 'Gypsy Rose', which has virtually no white transitional flashing.

Hosta 'Lady Guinevere' PP15,591 (G. Heemskerk 2005)

MEDIUM

Origin: Sport of *H.* 'Elisabeth'.

Description: A graceful, colorful mound 18 in. wide × 10 in. high (45 × 25 cm). Leaf blade 8 × 4 in. (20 × 10 cm), of average substance, chartreuse becoming golden yellow, narrowly and very irregularly margined mid-green with paler streaks, matt above and glaucous below, dimpled, veins widely spaced, edge evenly piecrusted, leaf flat, elliptic to ovate with a recurved cuspidate tip and heart-shaped pinched lobes. Petiole chartreuse to yellow with a green underside. Flower abundant, funnel-shaped, purple, on an upright, grayish-purple-dotted, 20-in. (50-cm) scape from high summer to autumn; fertility unknown.

Cultivation Notes: Site in light shade. Slow to average growth rate. Care is need to avoid pest damage. Best in a border with yellow-leaved hostas and dark green ferns. Divide regularly.

Distinguishing Features: Noticeably rippled leaf edges are unusual in a medio-variegated hosta and add greatly to its attraction.

Hosta 'Lakeside Love Affaire' (M. Chastain 1997)

LARGE

Origin: Unknown.

Description: An upright, flaring mound 36 in. wide × 18 in. high (90 × 45 cm). Leaf blade 9 × 7 in. (23 × 18 cm), thick, white, widely margined dark green, with lime-green streaks jetting toward the midrib, satiny above and matt below, prominent veins widely spaced, edge slightly rippled, leaf widely oval with a cuspidate tip and heart-shaped open to pinched lobes. Petiole white, sharply outlined in dark green. Flower tubular, near white, on an upright, bare, light green, 22-in. (55-cm) scape from mid- to late summer; seedpods green, fertile.

Cultivation Notes: Site in light to moderate shade all day. Moderate growth rate. Unusually large for a medio-variegated hosta. Lovely with the gray-leaved *Athyrium otophorum* var. *okonum* or *A.* 'Ghost'.

Distinguishing Feature: Great sculptural qualities as well as a striking tricolor effect on the leaves.

Hosta 'Lakeside Shore Master' (M. Chastain 1998)

MEDIUM

Origin: Unknown.

Description: An open mound 30 in. wide × 14 in. high (75 × 35 cm). Leaf blade 10 × 8½ in. (25 × 21 cm), thick, ivory rapidly turning light green to rich yellow, very widely and irregularly margined dark blue-green, with some streaks jetting toward the midrib, matt above and satiny below, intensely seersuckered, edge flat, leaf slightly cupped, oval with a cuspidate tip and pinched to overlapping lobes. Petiole chartreuse yellow, outlined in dark green. Flower funnel-shaped, pale lavender, on an upright, leafy,

Hosta 'Lady Guinevere'

Hosta 'Lakeside Love Affaire'

chartreuse, 18- to 22-in. (45- to 55-cm) scape in high summer; seedpods green, fertile.

Cultivation Notes: Site in good light to moderate shade. Increases rapidly. Pest resistant. A very colorful hosta with a pleasing leaf habit.

Similar: ★*H.* 'Reversed'.

Sports: *H.* 'Lakeside Beach Captain' has thicker leaves and thus is probably tetraploid; *H.* 'Lakeside Tycoon' has blue-green leaves.

Hosta 'Lakeside Symphony' (M. Chastain 1988)

MEDIUM–LARGE

Origin: First known sport of ★*H.* 'Piedmont Gold'.

Description: A billowing mound 60 in. wide × 25 in. high (150 × 63 cm). Leaf blade 11 × 9 in. (28 × 23 cm), of good substance, pale chartreuse turning yellow gold, widely and irregularly margined chartreuse, with some old-gold streaks jetting toward the midrib, slightly dimpled, prominently veined, edge slightly

Hosta 'Lakeside Shore Master'

Hosta 'Summer Serenade'

Hosta 'Lakeside Symphony', noted for its muted leaf margin.

undulate, leaf convex, widely oval with a twisted and sometimes pinched, cuspidate tip and with heart-shaped open to pinched lobes. Petiole chartreuse to yellow. Flower: see *H.* 'Piedmont Gold'.

Cultivation Notes: Site in good light to light shade. Moderate to rapid growth rate. Among the first-known hostas with this particular leaf color combination. Makes an impressive specimen.

Similar: *H.* 'David Stone'; *H.* 'Everglades'; *H.* 'Made You Look' is smaller; *H.* 'Rascal'; *H.* 'Summer Serenade' has more distinct margins.

Hosta 'Little Sunspot' (Briggs Nursery 1996)

SMALL

Origin: Sport of ★*H.* 'Little Aurora'.

Description: A compact mound 30 in. wide × 10 in. high (75 × 25 cm). Leaf blade 5 × 4 in. (13 × 10 cm), thick, rich yellow, widely margined vivid dark green, with subtle transitional dark to light chartreuse streaks, matt above and satiny below, seersuckered, edge slightly rippled, leaf slightly cupped, widely oval to nearly round with a mucronate tip and heart-shaped pinched lobes. Petiole chartreuse. Flower: see *H.* 'Little Aurora'.

Cultivation Notes: Site in morning sun in cooler climates where the leaf center will turn brilliant gold. Site in shade all day in the hottest climates. Outstanding in leaf form and leaf color contrast, but divide frequently to prevent reversion.

Distinguishing Features: The marked contrast between the dark green margins and the bright golden leaves.

Similar: *H.* 'Amy Elizabeth'; *H.* 'Just So' and *H.* 'Not So' both have less-marked leaf color contrast; ★*H.* 'Wylde Green Cream'.

Hosta 'Lonesome Dove' PP17,294 (H. Hansen 2005)

MEDIUM

Origin: Hybrid of *H.* 'Blue Moon'.

Description: An upright mound 32 in. wide × 17 in. high (80 × 43 cm). Leaf blade 6 × 5 in. (15 × 13 cm), of heavy substance, pale chartreuse turning ivory white, very widely and irregularly margined glaucous blue-green, with celadon streaks jetting toward the midrib, seersuckered, edge flat, leaf cupped, rounded with a mucronate tip and heart-shaped pinched

to folded lobes. Petiole leaning, ivory, outlined in blue-green. Flower bell-shaped, pale lavender, on an upright, bare, blue-green, 18-in. (45-cm) scape from mid- to high summer; fertility unknown.

Cultivation Notes: Site in shade or low light in cooler climates as heat and sunlight turn the bluish margins shiny green. Avoid planting under tree canopies as falling debris collects in and damages the deeply cupped leaves. Lovely with ferns and other lacy foliage. Divide frequently.

Distinguishing Features: The flower has a darker lavender pattern on the petal center.

Hosta 'Little Sunspot' sporting back to yellow leaves.

Hosta 'Lonesome Dove'

Similar: *H.* 'Lakeside Beach Captain'; *H.* 'Lakeside Cupcake' is smaller.

Hosta 'Mango Tango' (E. Kinman/Stark Gardens 2007)

MEDIUM

Origin: Sport of *H.* 'Dance With Me'.

Description: A rounded mound 36 in. wide × 20 in. high (90 × 50 cm). Leaf blade 7 × 8 in. (18 × 20 cm), of good substance, bright yellow, very widely and irregularly margined soft mid-green, matt above and satiny below, dimpled to seersuckered, veins widely spaced, edge flat to lightly kinked, leaf nearly round with a mucronate tip and flat pinched lobes. Petiole chartreuse yellow, outlined in green. Flower: see *★H.* 'Summer Music'.

Cultivation Notes: Site in good light to moderate shade to prevent the leaves from bleaching. Vigorous, with a moderate growth rate. Use as a specimen for a close-up view of the unusual leaf features. Divide often to retain these features.

Distinguishing Features: The yellow central variegation appears to have been "sewn" onto the green margin causing some puckering near the junction of the two colors.

Similar: *★H.* 'Stitch in Time' has the reverse variegation.

Hosta 'Morning Light' (G. Van Eijk-Bos & D. Van Erven 2000)

MEDIUM

Origin: Reversed sport of *★H.* 'Twilight'.

Description: An upright mound 28 in. wide × 18 in. high (70 × 45 cm). Leaf blade 5½ × 3½ in. (14 × 9 cm), thick, rich ivory with occasional green flecks, widely and irregularly margined dark green with chartreuse to olive green streaks, satiny above and matt below, strongly veined, some dimpling on

Hosta 'Mango Tango'

mature leaves, edge flat to kinked, leaf cupped, widely oval with a slightly twisted cuspidate tip and rounded pinched lobes. Petiole narrow, ivory, outlined in dark green. Flower: see ★*H*. 'Fortunei Aureomarginata'.

Cultivation Notes: Site in some morning sun in cooler climates, followed by light to moderate shade. Moderate growth rate.

Distinguishing Features: Leaves emerge pale chartreuse with light olive green margins that darken later. Leaf tips are exceptionally long.

Similar: *H*. 'Geneva Stark' has thinner leaves.

Hosta 'Night before Christmas' (J. Machen Jr. 1994)

MEDIUM–LARGE

Origin: Sport of ★*H*. 'White Christmas'.

Description: A moderately dense, semi-upright mound 30 in. wide × 18 in. high (75 × 45 cm). Leaf blade 8 × 3 in. (20 × 8 cm), of average substance, white, widely and irregularly margined dark olive green, with some streaks jetting toward the midrib, satiny above and shiny below, some dimpling when mature, veins widely spaced, edge slightly rippled, leaf undulate to twisting, oval with a cuspidate tip and heart-shaped open to pinched lobes. Petiole narrow, ivory, finely outlined in dark green. Flower: see *H*. 'White Christmas'.

Cultivation Notes: Site in bright light to moderate shade. Early to emerge. Use as a mid-ground specimen in a border with plain blue-leaved hostas. Needs

dividing every few years to keep the central white stripe at the most pleasing proportion to the dark green margin.

Distinguishing Features: Is larger and stronger than its parent. Has less variegation because there is more chlorophyll in the leaves. Thought to be a tetraploid.

Similar: *H*. 'Undulata Univittata'.

Sports: *H*. 'Christmas Charm' has green leaves with a wide ivory-white margin and is also a tetraploid.

Hosta 'Olive Branch' (S. Moldovan N/R)

SMALL

Origin: Sport of ★*H*. 'Candy Hearts'.

Description: An overlapping mound 24 in. wide × 10 in. high (60 × 25 cm). Leaf blade 3 × 3 in. (8 × 8

Hosta 'Night before Christmas'

Hosta 'Morning Light'

Hosta 'Olive Branch'

305

cm), thin, muted butterscotch yellow, widely margined olive green jetting toward the midrib, satiny above and glaucous below, smooth, veins widely spaced, edge rippled, leaf flat, heart-shaped with a cuspidate tip and overlapping lobes. Petiole narrow, chartreuse, finely outlined in olive green. Flower: see *H.* 'Candy Hearts'.

Cultivation Notes: Site in bright light to moderate shade. Increases rapidly. Prone to pest damage. Divide regularly to maintain the width of the variegation.

Distinguishing Features: Probably the first hosta to have a muted butterscotch-yellow central variegation (at its best it is in the "hand print" pattern), but quite random in width.

Hosta 'Ooh La La' (E. Elslager 2000)

MEDIUM–LARGE

Origin: *H.* 'Sea Prize' × ★*H. hypoleuca*.

Description: A diffuse, colorful mound 41 in. wide × 18 in. high (102 × 45 cm). Leaf blade 9 × 7 in. (13 × 18 cm), of average substance, emerging cream turning ivory white, widely and irregularly margined dark olive green, with lighter green streaks jetting toward the midrib, satiny above and glaucous below, smooth becoming seersuckered when mature, edge almost flat, leaf lightly cupped, broadly ovate to rounded with a mucronate tip and heart-shaped pinched to folded lobes. Petiole green, outlined in cream. Flower funnel-shaped, pale lavender, on an upright, bare, chartreuse, 26-in. (65-cm) scape in high summer; fertility unknown.

Cultivation Notes: Site in light to moderate shade. Vigorous with a moderate growth rate. Divide frequently to prevent the attractive streaked and splashed leaf center from stabilizing to green.

Distinguishing Features: The very attractive tonal streaking.

Hosta 'Ooh La La'

Hosta **'Paradigm'** (Walden-West 1999)

LARGE

Origin: Sport of ★*H.* 'Abiqua Recluse'. Initially known as *H.* 'Abiqua Paradigm'.

Description: A dense mound 46 in. wide × 20 in. high (116 × 50 cm). Leaf blade 11 × 9 in. (28 × 23 cm), thick, chartreuse green turning yellow, widely margined dark green jetting toward the midrib, satiny above and glaucous below, intensely seersuckered and puckered, edge almost flat to slightly rippled, leaf folded to cupped, widely oval with a mucronate tip and heart-shaped pinched to overlapping lobes. Petiole light green. Flower: see *H.* 'Abiqua Recluse'.

Cultivation Notes: Lutescent. Tolerates two hours of morning sun in cooler climates, but the color is more likely to fade. Increases rapidly. Pest resistant. Named Hosta of the Year by the American Hosta Growers Association in 2007.

Similar: ★*H.* 'Dick Ward'; *H.* 'Inniswood'; ★*H.* 'September Sun'.

Sport: *H.* 'Epiphany' has yellow leaves margined green.

Hosta **'Paradise Beach'** (M. Fransen N/R)

SMALL–MEDIUM

Origin: Sport of *H.* 'Weihenstephan'.

Description: An upright, spreading mound 30 in. wide × 12 in. high (75 × 30 cm). Leaf blade 6½ × 3 in. (16 × 8 cm), of thin to moderate substance, light yellow fading slightly through the summer, widely and irregularly margined mid-green, with streaks jetting toward the midrib, matt above and satiny below, slightly dimpled when mature, edge flat to slightly rippled, leaf slightly arching or twisted, elliptic to narrowly oval with an acute tip and rounded open to pinched lobes. Petiole chartreuse, outlined in green. Flower: see ★*H. sieboldii* 'Alba'.

Cultivation Notes: Site in light to moderate shade. Moderate to rapid growth rate. May need protection from pest damage. Prized for its pure white flowers in late summer.

Hosta **'Paradise Joyce'** **PP12,119** (M. Fransen N/R)

MEDIUM

Origin: Sport of ★*H.* 'Halcyon'.

Description: An overlapping mound 36 in. wide × 16 in. high (90 × 40 cm). Leaf blade 6½ × 4 in. (16 × 10 cm), of good substance, medium yellow then ivory, irregularly margined blue, with streaks jetting toward the midrib, matt above and glaucous below, smooth, edge almost flat, leaf slightly cupped, oval with a cuspidate tip and heart-shaped pinched lobes. Petiole chartreuse yellow. Flower: see *H.* 'Halcyon'.

Cultivation Notes: When grown in full sun in cooler climates the leaf coloring is much stronger. Site in shade in warmer climates. Moderate to rapid growth rate. Easy to grow. Makes a superb foreground specimen. Lovely in a container and recently awarded

Hosta **'Paradigm'**

Hosta **'Paradise Beach'**

The Newbold Vase by the British Hosta & Hemero-callis Society for the best Fransen introduction.

Distinguishing Features: Differs from ★H. 'June' in that the leaf emerges solid blue gradually turning cloudy chartreuse to brilliant yellow, finally bleaching to ivory white. Also differs from H. 'Katherine Lewis' in remaining ivory white until the leaves die down in autumn.

Hosta 'Paradise Joyce'

Hosta 'Paradise Power' PP12,117 (M. Fransen N/R)

LARGE—VERY LARGE

Origin: Sport of ★H. 'Sun Power'.

Description: A dense, upright mound 71 in. wide × 28 in. high (178 × 70 cm). Leaf blade 11 × 7½ in. (28 × 19 cm), thick, golden yellow, irregularly margined dark green, with narrow streaks jetting toward the midrib, matt above and thinly glaucous below, slightly dimpled, edge widely undulate, leaf oval with a cuspidate tip and heart-shaped pinched lobes. Petiole chartreuse, finely outlined in dark green, appearing to pierce the blade. Flower: see H. 'Sun Power'.

Cultivation Notes: Tolerates morning sun with abundant moisture at its roots, except in the hottest climates where it needs light shade all day. Moderately fast growth rate. Pest resistant.

Similar: ★H. 'Lakeside Symphony' has a less striking contrast of colors; H. 'Summer Serenade' has darker green margins.

Hosta 'Paradise Power'

Hosta 'Paul's Glory' (P. Ruh & P. Hofer 1987)

MEDIUM–LARGE

Origin: Natural sport of *H*. 'Perry's True Blue'.

Description: A dense mound 41 in. wide × 24 in. high (102 × 60 cm). Leaf blade 9 × 7 in. (23 × 18 cm), thick, chartreuse turning golden yellow, irregularly margined dark blue-green with some streaks, matt above and glaucous below, seersuckered, edge flat to slightly kinked, leaf slightly folded or convex, widely oval with a cuspidate tip and heart-shaped pinched lobes. Petiole narrow, chartreuse, outlined in dark green. Flower funnel-shaped, pale lavender, on an upright, bare, glaucous green, 40-in. (100-cm) scape in high summer; fertile.

Cultivation Notes: Performs well in high temperatures, keeping its leaf color better if sited in light shade. In summer the center turns gold and the leaves turn dark green; the center will bleach to ivory white if exposed to hot sun. Medium to fast growth rate but needs dividing every three to four years to retain the attractive variegation. Named Hosta of the Year by the American Hosta Growers Association in 1999. A colorful specimen or background hosta.

Distinguishing Features: Particularly vivid and dramatic leaf coloring.

Similar: *H*. 'Inniswood' has paler blue margins; *H*. 'Paradise Glory'; ★*H*. 'September Sun' has paler blue margins.

Hosta 'Orange Marmalade'

Hosta 'Paul's Glory', showing some reversion.

Sports: *H.* 'American Glory Be' has wider blue-green margins; *H.* 'Chesterland Gold'; *H.* 'Glory Hallelujah' has the reverse variegation of *H.* 'Paul's Glory'; *H.* 'Marmalade on Toast' is the reverse sport of *H.* 'Orange Marmalade'; *H.* 'Orange Marmalade' PP16,742 has orange-gold variegation in early summer that gradually turns white; *H.* 'Paradise Glory' and *H.* 'Pete's Passion' both have wide blue leaves with green changing to yellow central variegation; *H.* 'Peter Ruh' has yellow-margined green leaves; *H.* 'St. Paul' has yellow leaves margined green; *H.* 'Wheaton Blue' has good blue leaves.

Hosta 'Peppermint Ice'

Hosta 'Pineapple Upsidedown Cake'

Hosta 'Peppermint Ice' (Belle Gardens 1994)

SMALL

Origin: ★*H.* 'William Lachman' × ★*H. montana*.

Description: A moderately dense, semi-upright mound 22 in. wide × 8 in. high (55 × 20 cm). Leaf blade 6 × 3 in. (15 × 8 cm), thick, ivory white turning pure white, widely and irregularly margined dark green, with streaks in several shades of green jetting toward the midrib, glossy above and satiny below, veins moderately prominent, edge almost flat, leaf slightly folded or arching, widely oval with a cuspidate tip and heart-shaped open to pinched lobes. Petiole ivory, outlined in green. Flower funnel-shaped, rich lavender, on an upright, leafy, ivory-flushed burgundy, 21-in. (53-cm) scape in late summer; fertile.

Cultivation Notes: Site in good light to moderate shade. Moderate growth rate. Among the most colorful hostas of this type. Needs dividing every three to four years to retain the wide central variegation with the attractive streaking.

Distinguishing Features: The noticeably ivory-white scapes and the strongly white-margined leafy bracts.

Hosta 'Pineapple Upsidedown Cake' (M. Zilis 1999)

MEDIUM

Origin: Sport of ★*H.* 'Pineapple Poll'.

Description: A rippled mound 51 in. wide × 18 in. high (127 × 45 cm). Leaf blade 9 × 3½ in. (23 × 9 cm), of good substance, chartreuse to rich golden yellow, narrowly and irregularly margined dark green, with some streaks jetting toward the midrib, matt above and glaucous below, smooth, closely veined, edge conspicuously rippled, leaf slightly folded, elliptic with an acute tip and tapered open lobes. Petiole narrow, chartreuse, finely outlined in dark green. Flower funnel-shaped, lavender, on an upright, leafy, gold, 24- to 36-in. (60- to 90-cm) scape in late summer; fertile.

Cultivation Notes: Site in morning sun in cooler climates. Exposure to hot sun can bleach out the variegation. Less vigorous than the parent.

Similar: ★*H. sieboldii* 'Kabitan' and *H.* 'Peedee Gold Flash' are slightly smaller and have thinner leaves.

Sports: *H.* 'Pineapple Juice' has yellow leaves that

can bleach to white if exposed to hot sun; *H.* 'Pineapple Punch' PP18,318 has creamy yellow-margined deep green leaves.

Hosta 'Pole Cat' (R. Lydell N/R)

MEDIUM

Origin: Sport of *★H.* 'Striptease'.

Description: A dense mound 36 in. wide × 17 in. high (90 × 43 cm). Leaf blade 7 × 5½ in. (18 × 14 cm), of average substance, pure white, very widely and irregularly margined mid- to dark green with occasional chartreuse streaks, matt above and glaucous below, moderately seersuckered, edge almost flat, leaf broadly ovate with a cuspidate tip and heart-shaped pinched to folded lobes. Petiole ivory, outlined in dark green. Flower: see *★H.* 'Fortunei Hyacinthina'.

Hosta 'Pineapple Punch'

Hosta 'Pole Cat'

Cultivation Notes: Site in good light to partial shade. Leaves emerge early. The early season blue cast to the green margin gradually disappears but can be enjoyed for longer if protected from sunlight. Correctly placed the white variegation holds for the whole season. Divide frequently. Lovely with *Actaea simplex*.

Distinguishing Features: If well grown, tiny dark green flecks appear in the white variegation.

Similar: *H.* 'Risky Business' seems identical.

Hosta 'Popcorn' (E. Lachman/T. Schmid 1999)

MEDIUM–LARGE

Origin: Unknown.

Description: An upright mound 25 in. wide × 12 in. high (63 × 30 cm). Leaf blade 6½ × 5½ in. (16 × 14 cm), thick, emerging yellow turning ivory cream, very widely and irregularly margined rich turquoise blue, with celadon streaks jetting toward the midrib, satiny above and matt below, seersuckered, edge almost flat, leaf deeply cupped, broadly ovate to round with a mucronate tip and flattish to heart-shaped open to pinched lobes. Petiole flattish, cream, outlined in blue-green. Flower bell-shaped, pale lavender, on an upright, bare, creamy chartreuse, 14-in. (35-cm) scape in high summer; seedpods green, fertility unknown.

Cultivation Notes: Site in moderate shade to obtain the best leaf color. The subtle tonal variegation quickly responds to different light and heat levels so

Hosta 'Popcorn'

the plant may need to be tried in several places before the optimum conditions are found. Slow to increase but well worth the wait as it is one of the most attractive of the Lachman introductions.

Distinguishing Features: The exceptionally thick, cardboard-like leaf substance. The very short scapes, rising only just above the leaf mound.

Sport: *H.* 'Philadelphia' has nearly round, bowl-shaped green leaves.

Hosta 'Prime Meridian' (M. Chastain/G. Goodwin 2005)

LARGE

Origin: Unknown.

Description: An upright mound 60 in. wide × 20 in. high (150 × 50 cm). Leaf blade 12 × 10 in. (30 × 25 cm), of good substance, satiny, emerging bright yellow turning white, very widely and irregularly margined dark olive green, with many streaks jetting toward the midrib, deeply seersuckered, prominently veined, edge undulate, leaf slightly cupped, broadly ovate with a mucronate tip and heart-shaped open lobes. Petiole chartreuse with green streaks, outlined in green. Flower near funnel-shaped, pale lavender, on an upright, ivory, 25- to 40-in. (63- to 100-cm) scape from early to midsummer; seedpods green or streaked, fertility unknown.

Cultivation Notes: Site in good light to light shade. Moderate growth rate. Pest resistant. Requires frequent division to maintain the most pleasing ratio between the yellow center and green leaf margin.

Distinguishing Features: The inflorescence leaves are very small.

Similar: ★*H.* 'Ann Kulpa'.

Hosta 'Punky' (Kuk 1999)

SMALL–MEDIUM

Origin: Sport of ★*H.* 'Blue Wedgwood'.

Description: A dense mound 24 in. wide × 12 in. high (60 × 30 cm). Leaf blade 5½ × 3½ in. (14 × 9 cm), thick, glaucous cream to golden yellow, narrowly and irregularly margined dark blue-green, with streaks jetting toward the midrib, dimpled, edge widely undulate to twisted, leaf cupped, oval with a flat base, cuspidate tip, and open lobes. Petiole chartreuse, outlined in dark green, appearing to penetrate the blade for about 1⅜ in. (3.5 cm). Flower: see *H.* 'Blue Wedgwood'.

Cultivation Notes: Grows equally well in sun or shade in cooler climates, elsewhere in morning sun. Excessive sun bleaches out the leaf color leaving a green skeleton of margin, midrib, and veins. Moderbate growth rate.

Distinguishing Features: A dramatic contrast between the dark margin and the bright, light center of the leaf when grown in full sun.

Hosta 'Prime Meridian'

Hosta 'Punky'

Similar: ★*H.* 'June'; *H.* 'Katherine Lewis'; *H.* 'Olympic Sunrise'; ★*H.* 'Paradise Joyce'; ★*H.* 'Remember Me'.

Hosta 'Rainbow's End' PP17,251 (H. Hansen 2005)

SMALL

Origin: Sport of *H.* 'Obsession'.

Description: A dense, unruly mound 21 in. wide × 11 in. high (53 × 28 cm). Leaf blade 6 × 4 in. (15 × 10 cm), thick, rubbery, yellow turning ivory, widely and irregularly margined dark green, with streaks of olive green jetting toward the midrib, matt above and satiny below, smooth, edge flat, leaf arching, lanceolate with an acute tip and tapered open to pinched lobes. Petiole cream, outlined in olive green. Flower large, funnel-shaped, violet-striped pale lavender, on an upright, leafy, red, 16- to 19-in. (40- to 48-cm) scape from high summer into autumn; fertility unknown.

Cultivation Notes: Site in moderate shade . Slow growth rate. Useful at the front of a border, in a rock garden, or as an edging.

Distinguishing Features: The large, curled, colorful variegated scape bracts stained red at the junction with the scape, the large red-stained flower bracts and red scape.

Similar: ★*H.* 'Red Hot Flash' is not as red.

Hosta 'Red Hot Flash' (J. Machen Jr. 2004)

SMALL

Origin: Tetraploid sport of *H.* 'Peedee Gold Flash'.

Description: A dense, upright mound 21 in. wide × 14 in. high (53 × 35 cm). Leaf blade 12 × 2 in. (30 × 5 cm), of thick substance, matt, pale green to chartreuse turning greenish white to parchment white, widely margined mid-green becoming dark green later with paler streaking, mostly in the marginal area, slightly dimpled, edge slightly undulate, leaf elliptic to narrowly oval with a recurved cuspidate tip and tapered open to pinched lobes, blade decurrent with the petiole in juvenile plants. Petiole short, chartreuse, outlined in dark green, flushed crimson toward the crown. Flower funnel-shaped, white-veined violet, on an upright, leafy, red-flecked mid-green, 22-in. (55-cm) scape from high to late summer; fertility unknown.

Cultivation Notes: Suitable for hotter climates when sited in early morning sun followed by light shade. Moderate growth rate, but reportedly not vigorous in all gardens. Grow with *Heucherella* 'Sun Spot' to echo the leaf color.

Distinguishing Features: The margin variegation varies from regular to irregular along its length, and from leaf to leaf. Differs from its parent in the thickness of the leaf, the wider margin, and the base color.

Similar: *H.* 'Lyme Regis' has white flowers; *H. sieboldii* 'First Mate'.

Hosta 'Rainbow's End'

Hosta 'Red Hot Flash'

***Hosta* 'Remember Me'** (G. Van Eijk-Bos & D. Van Erven/Walters Gardens 2002)

MEDIUM

Origin: *H.* 'June' hybrid.

Description: A dense mound when mature, 30 in. wide × 12 in. high (75 × 30 cm). Leaf blade 6½ × 4 in. (16 × 10 cm), thick, glaucous bright ivory white to creamy yellow, irregularly and narrowly margined mid-green, with blue and chartreuse splashes jetting toward the midrib, smooth, edge flat, leaf widely oval with a cuspidate tip and heart-shaped pinched lobes. Petiole narrow, cream outlined in dark blue-green. Flower tubular, lavender, on an upright, bare, glaucous ivory, 15-in. (38-cm) scape in midsummer; fertility unknown.

Cultivation Notes: For the brightest effect, site in morning sun except in the hottest climates. Slower to increase than its parent. Good pest resistance. An outstanding recent introduction best planted in masses or drifts at the front of the border. The contrast between the large light area and the narrow dark border stands out in a garden setting.

Distinguishing Features: The distinctly blue veining.

Similar: *H.* 'Extacy' PPAF has longer, narrower leaves; *H.* 'Lakeside Cupcake' has bluer margins and rounder leaves; ★*H.* 'Punky'.

Hosta 'Remember Me'

Hosta 'Rhino Hide'

Hosta **'Rhino Hide'** (D. Rawson 2007)

MEDIUM—LARGE

Origin: Unknown.

Description: A rigid, upright mound 30 in. wide × 20 in. high (75 × 50 cm). Leaf blade 8 × 8 in. (20 × 20 cm), exceptionally thick, glaucous bright chartreuse gold turning pale yellow, very widely and irregularly margined blue-green, intensely seersuckered, edge flat with occasional kinks, leaf deeply cupped, nearly round with a mucronate tip and heart-shaped pinched to overlapping lobes. Petiole stout, stiff, flattish, pale green, outlined in blue. Flower funnel-shaped, pure white, on an upright, bare, pale green, 22- to 24-in. (55- to 60-cm) scape; seedpods green, fertile.

Cultivation Notes: Site in moderate shade to retain the subtle leaf coloring and to accentuate the tonal changes in the variegation. Best grown away from a tree canopy to avoid falling detritus damaging the leaves. Moderate growth rate. Pest resistant.

Distinguishing Features: Probably has the thickest leaves of any hosta.

Hosta **'Roy Klehm'** (H. Hansen 2007)

LARGE

Origin: Sport of *H.* 'Summer Serenade'.

Description: An upright mound of horizontal leaves 24 in. wide × 21 in. high (60 × 53 cm). Leaf blade 11 × 9 in. (28 × 23 cm), of good substance, chartreuse yellow, widely and irregularly margined mid-green, with chartreuse-green streaks jetting toward the midrib, matt above and glaucous below, veins widely spaced, edge almost flat with an occasional undulation, leaf convex, broadly ovate to nearly round with an extended mucronate tip and heart-shaped pinched lobes. Petiole stout, chartreuse, outlined in green. Flower: see *★H.* 'Piedmont Gold'.

Cultivation Notes: Site in some morning sun except in the hottest climates. The leaf color changes depending upon the intensity of the light, being a deeper golden yellow in strong sunshine. Moderate growth rate. Pest resistant. An exciting new sport which is thought to be tetraploid.

Distinguishing Features: The distinctively tipped rounded leaves and exceptionally pleasing variegation.

Hosta **'September Sun'** (R. Solberg 1985)

MEDIUM—LARGE

Origin: First registered sport of *★H.* 'August Moon'.

Description: A dense mound 50 in. wide × 24 in. high (126 × 60 cm). Leaf blade 9 × 7½ in. (23 × 19 cm), thick, golden yellow, widely margined midgreen, with occasional streaks jetting toward the midrib, matt above and glaucous below, seersuckered, conspicuously veined, edge slightly undulate, leaf slightly cupped or convex, widely oval with a cuspidate tip and heart-shaped pinched lobes. Petiole chartreuse, outlined in mid-green. Flower: see *H.* 'August Moon'.

Hosta 'Roy Klehm'

Hosta 'September Sun'

Hosta 'Shirley'

Cultivation Notes: Tolerates a considerable amount of sun, which makes the leaf coloring even brighter. Vigorous, a rapid increaser. Easy to grow. Pest resistant. A forerunner of many similar hostas.

Similar: *H.* 'Lunar Magic' has wider, very dark green margins; *H.* 'Lunar Orbit'; ★*H.* 'Paradigm'; *H.* 'Polar Moon'; *H.* 'September Surprise' has a green margin that appears gradually.

Sports: *H.* 'Hub City' has blue-green leaves.

Hosta 'Shirley' (V. Wade 1998)

MEDIUM

Origin: Unknown.

Description: An upright mound 18 in. wide × 12 in. high (45 × 30 cm). Leaf blade 7 × 4½ in. (18 × 11 cm), of average substance, greenish white to

Hosta sieboldiana 'George Smith'

golden yellow, widely and irregularly margined bright mid-green, with some streaks jetting toward the midrib, matt above and satiny below, some dimpling when mature, veins widely spaced, edge rippled, leaf slightly folded when young, convex when mature, widely oval with a cuspidate tip and heart-shaped pinched lobes. Petiole chartreuse, finely outlined in mid-green. Flower bell-shaped, pale lavender, on an upright, bare, pale green, 21- to 27-in. (53- to 68-cm) scape in midsummer; seedpods green, fertile.

Cultivation Notes: Very sensitive to light levels. Site in good light to dappled shade all day. Slow to increase. A very colorful hosta variegated in several shades of green, the colors deepening as the season progresses.

Distinguishing Features: Shallow, even ripples along the leaf edge. The green margins are ¾ in. (2 cm) wide.

Similar: *H.* 'Hotspur'; ★*H. ventricosa* 'Aureomaculata'.

Hosta sieboldiana 'George Smith' (G. Smith 1983)

LARGE–VERY LARGE

Origin: Natural sport of ★*H. sieboldiana* 'Elegans'.

Description: An open mound 50 in. wide × 24 in. high (126 × 60 cm). Leaf blade 12 × 11 in. (30 × 28 cm), thick, glaucous chartreuse to pale yellow, widely and irregularly margined dark blue-green, with celadon streaks jetting toward the midrib, seersuckered, edge almost flat to slightly undulate, leaf cupped or convex, widely oval to nearly round with a mucronate tip and heart-shaped pinched to overlapping lobes. Petiole stout, pale yellow, outlined in dark green. Flower: see *H. sieboldiana* 'Elegans'.

Cultivation Notes: Lutescent or albescent central variegation, but the variegation is barely visible when the leaves emerge. Site in good light to moderate shade all day. Slow to increase. Pest resistant.

Similar: *H.* 'Borwick Beauty' has more-vivid variegation earlier in the season.

Hosta sieboldiana 'Thunderbolt' PP14,232

(Hawksridge Farms N/R)

MEDIUM–LARGE

Origin: Tissue-cultured sport of ★*H. sieboldiana* 'Elegans'.

Description: A dense mound 41 in. wide × 22 in. high (102 × 55 cm). Leaf blade 9 × 8½ in. (23 × 21 cm), very thick, glaucous chartreuse-white turning cream to yellow and finally ivory white, very widely and irregularly margined blue-green, with streaks jetting toward the midrib, seersuckered, edge flat, leaf cupped, widely oval to nearly round with a mucronate tip and heart-shaped overlapping lobes. Petiole ivory, outlined in dark blue-green. Flower: see *H. sieboldiana* 'Elegans'.

Cultivation Notes: The blue-green margins remain much bluer and the central flash remains more yellow if the plant is grown in light shade. Slow to increase. Pest resistant.

Similar: *H. sieboldiana* 'Dream Weaver' has slightly greener margins and a very distinct sunburst splash of creamy yellow in its leaf center, and is less seersuckered.

Hosta 'Sitting Pretty' (P. Aden 1987)

SMALL

Origin: *H.* 'Reiko' × *H.* 'Amy Aden'.

Description: A flattish mound 8 in. wide × 4 in. high (20 × 10 cm). Leaf blade 7 × 1½ in. (18 × 4 cm), thick, chartreuse turning ivory white to yellow, irregularly margined dark and light olive green, glossy above and matt below, dimpled when mature, edge

Hosta sieboldiana 'Thunderbolt'

Hosta 'Sitting Pretty'

Hosta 'Spritzer'

almost flat, leaf oval with a cuspidate tip and tapered pinched lobes. Petiole narrow, chartreuse, attractively outlined in dark green. Flower funnel-shaped, bright purple, disposed at 90 degrees to an upright, leafy, ivory to chartreuse, 12-in. (30-cm) scape from mid- to late summer; fertile.

Cultivation Notes: Site in some morning sun in cooler climates to intensify the leaf color.

Sports: *H.* 'Junior Miss' has dark green leaves margined creamy yellow.

Hosta 'Spritzer' (P. Aden 1986)

MEDIUM–LARGE

Origin: *H.* 'Green Fountain' hybrid.

Description: An upright, arching mound 30 in. wide × 20 in. high (75 × 50 cm). Leaf blade 10 × 5 in. (25 × 13 cm), thin, old gold, widely and irregularly margined olive green, with many streaks jetting toward the midrib, shiny above and glossy below, smooth, prominently veined, edge rippled, leaf arching, twisted, pinched toward the tip, narrowly oval with a cuspidate tip and rounded open lobes. Petiole chartreuse, outlined in olive green. Flower: funnel-shaped, pale lavender on a leaning, leafy, 30-in. (75-cm) scape from late summer to early autumn; fertile.

Cultivation Notes: Site in light to moderate shade. Increases rapidly, but suited to container growing. Is, in effect, the centrally variegated form of ★*H.* 'Green Fountain'.

Distinguishing Features: The subtly variegated leaves on a cascading mound.

Sports: *H.* 'Golden Spritzer' has yellow leaves.

Hosta 'Step Sister' (G. Draheim/G. Trucks N/R)

MEDIUM–LARGE

Origin: Sport of *H.* 'Sunlight Sister'.

Description: An open mound 30 in. wide × 19 in. high (75 × 48 cm). Leaf blade 8½ × 7 in. (21 × 18 cm), thick, chartreuse green turning chartreuse-white, narrowly and very irregularly margined dark green, with some streaks jetting toward the midrib, matt above and glaucous below, seersuckered, prominently veined, edge almost flat, leaf broadly ovate to nearly round with heart-shaped pinched to folded lobes. Petiole pale chartreuse, outlined in green. Flower funnel-shaped, near white, on an oblique to upright, leafy, glaucous

Hosta 'Step Sister'

light green, 28- to 32-in. (70- to 80-cm) scape from early to midsummer; fertility unknown.

Cultivation Notes: Site in moderate to full shade. Slow to increase. Pest resistant. Grow with carmine-pink Japanese azaleas for color contrast.

Distinguishing Features: The virtually pure white flowers.

Similar: *H.* 'Princess Anastasia', a sport of *H.* 'Ryan's Big One', has blue-green leaf margins.

Hosta 'Striptease' (C. & R. Thompson 1991)

MEDIUM

Origin: Sport of ★*H.* 'Gold Standard'.

Description: A dense mound 50 in. wide × 20 in. high (126 × 50 cm). Leaf blade 8 × 6 in. (20 × 15 cm), of good substance, chartreuse turning yellow to ivory, widely margined dark green with a blue cast in early summer, with occasional silver-white flecks at the junction of the center and the margin, matt above and glaucous below, conspicuously veined, edge almost flat, leaf slightly arching, oval with a cuspidate tip and heart-shaped to rounded, open to pinched lobes. Petiole chartreuse, outlined in dark green. Flower: see ★*H.* 'Fortunei Hyacinthina'.

Cultivation Notes: Careful placement in the garden is essential to achieve the most pleasing seasonal and light-level variations in leaf color. Moderate to fast growth rate. Plant as a border specimen or in a large container. Named Hosta of the Year by the American Hosta Growers Association in 2005.

Distinguishing Features: As originally registered, it has only a few silver-white flecks, but later versions can have the flecking nearly all round the blade.

Sports: *H.* 'Alan Titchmarsh' and *H.* 'Blue Without You' have green-margined yellow leaves; *H.* 'Gypsy Rose Tease' has smaller, more folded leaves with a brighter color contrast; ★*H.* 'Hanky Panky'; *H.* 'Juha' has narrow green leaves, with wide white margins and piecrust edges; ★*H.* 'Kiwi Full Monty' has leaf margins that are more blue than green; *H.* 'Lady Godiva' has narrow white-margined green leaves and is a rapid increaser; *H.* 'Math Man' has a white line around a chartreuse center; ★*H.* 'Pole Cat', *H.* 'Risky Business' and *H.* 'White Bikini' have green-margined white leaves; *H.* 'Paradise Stripes' has crisp white-margined green leaves which turn yellow.

Hosta 'Summer Music' (R. Klehm 1998)

MEDIUM

Origin: Sport of *H.* 'Shade Master'.

Description: An overlapping mound 21 in. wide × 14 in. high (53 × 35 cm). Leaf blade 7 × 6 in. (18 × 15 cm), thin, matt, chartreuse turning pure white, widely and irregularly margined olive green, with chartreuse streaks jetting toward the midrib, dimpled to seersuckered, veins widely spaced, edge very slightly rippled, leaf twisted, convex with the tip recurved, widely oval with heart-shaped overlapping lobes. Petiole shallow, ivory, finely lined chartreuse and olive green. Flower flared, pale lavender, in a

Hosta 'Striptease'

Hosta 'Summer Music'

Hosta 'Dance With Me'

Hosta 'Lakeside Meter Maid'

Hosta 'Sweet Home Chicago'

dense raceme, on an upright, leafy, chartreuse, 30-in. (75-cm) scape in late summer; fertile.

Cultivation Notes: Site in good light to light shade all day. Ensure adequate moisture to prevent leaf scorching in very hot weather. Moderate to rapid growth rate. Protect from pest damage.

Distinguishing Features: The dramatic contrast between the pure white leaf center and the varying shades of green widely bordering it.

Sports: *H.* 'Dance With Me'; *H.* 'Lakeside Meter Maid' has white leaves with wide, dark green margins; *H.* 'Last Dance' has chartreuse-green leaves with pale yellow margins.

Hosta 'Sweet Home Chicago' (M. Zilis/P. & J. Ruh 2002)

MEDIUM

Origin: Tissue-cultured sport of ★*H.* 'Birchwood Parky's Gold'.

Description: A compact mound 45 in. wide × 18 in. high (113 × 45 cm). Leaf blade 6½ × 5 in. (16 × 13 cm), of average substance, chartreuse to yellow, widely and irregularly margined mid-green, matt above and slightly glaucous below, dimpled, edge flat, leaf widely oval to nearly round with a mucronate tip and flat open lobes. Petiole chartreuse, outlined in dark green. Flower: see *H.* 'Birchwood Parky's Gold'.

Cultivation Notes: Site in high, filtered light. Vigorous, a rapid increaser. Easy to grow.

Distinguishing Features: The ⅜-in. (1-cm) wide green margin makes a dramatic contrast to the bright leaf center, the colors intensifying as the season progresses. Scapes have attractively variegated leafy bracts near the raceme.

Similar: *H.* 'Parky's Prize' is the reverse-variegated form.

Hosta 'Undulata' (L. H. Bailey/AHS 2001)

MEDIUM

Origin: Japanese gardens.

Description: An unruly mound 30 in. wide × 12 in. high (75 × 30 cm). Leaf blade 6 × 3 in. (15 × 8 cm), thin, pure white, irregularly margined dark green, with streaks jetting toward the midrib, matt above and satiny below, smooth, edge rippled and twisted, leaf oval with a cuspidate tip and rounded open lobes. Petiole ivory white, outlined in dark green. Flower narrowly funnel-shaped, pale lavender, on an upright, leafy, ivory, 25-in. (63-cm) scape in high summer; virtually sterile.

Cultivation Notes: Site in good light to moderate shade. Leaves can scorch if exposed to strong sunlight when wet. Plenty of moisture and feeding are required because it lacks vigor and is slow to increase. Flower habit is poor since only a few flowers open consecutively and the scape begins to decline before flowering is over. Needs regular division of the clump to prevent the stronger, green marginal portion of the leaf from taking over.

Distinguishing Features: The second flush of leaves is mottled green in the center. The variegated scape bracts can be almost the same size as the leaves.

Similar: *H.* 'Banana Sundae' (the stable form); *H.* 'Kiwi Spearmint' has longer leaves; ★*H.* 'White Christmas' is more difficult to cultivate.

Sports: ★*H.* 'Undulata Albomarginata' was formerly known as *H.* 'Thomas Hogg'; *H.* 'Undulata Erromena' ♛ has green leaves; *H.* 'Undulata Univittata' ♛ has leaves with a narrower central variegation.

Hosta 'Upper Crust' (M. Zilis 2004)

MEDIUM

Origin: Sport of *H.* 'Snow Crust'.

Description: A dome-shaped mound 33 in. wide × 14 in. high (83 × 35 cm). Leaf blade 8 × 4½ in. (20 × 11 cm), of average substance, chartreuse yellow, widely margined dark olive green, with many chartreuse streaks jetting toward the midrib, matt above and thinly glaucous below, dimpled, veins furrowed, edge gently undulate, leaf ovate with an acuminate tip and rounded pinched lobes. Petiole chartreuse, outlined in dark green. Flower funnel-shaped, pale lavender, on an oblique, leafy, green, 4-ft. (1.2-m) scape in midsummer; fertility unknown.

Cultivation Notes: Site in light to moderate shade. The base color fades to light green as summer progresses. Moderate growth rate.

Distinguishing Features: The vivid contrast between the dark green margins and sharp yellow base color which is at its brightest in early summer.

Hosta 'Undulata'

Hosta 'Undulata Univittata'

Hosta 'Upper Crust'

Hosta 'Whirlwind' (J. Kulpa 1989)

MEDIUM

Origin: Possible sport of ★H. 'Fortunei Hyacinthina'.

Description: An upright mound 41 in. wide × 18 in. high (102 × 45 cm). Leaf blade 7 × 5½ in. (18 × 14 cm), thick, pale chartreuse becoming ivory to bright yellow then fading to drab green, widely and irregularly margined dark olive green, with celadon streaks jetting toward the midrib, matt above and glaucous below, slightly dimpled, strongly veined, twisted, nearly heart-shaped, recurved at the exaggerated tip, kinked at flat open lobes. Petiole flat toward the blade, which it appears to pierce. Flower funnel-shaped, pale lavender, on an upright, leafy, glaucous gray-green, 20-in. (50-cm) scape, occasionally with large variegated leafy bracts, in late summer; fertility unknown.

Cultivation Notes: Leaf color varies with temperature and the age of the plant. Some morning sun is beneficial. Vigorous and easy to grow. Makes a superb ground cover.

Distinguishing Features: Differs from other medio-variegated hostas by its broad, twisted leaves on long petioles and the conspicuous green veins on the leaf's surface.

Sports: H. 'Cyclone' is cream with a dark green margin; H. 'Dust Devil' has dark green leaves with chartreuse margins that turn ivory; H. 'Eternal Flame' is white with occasional green flecks when mature and has a dark green margin; H. 'Foxfire Snake Eyes' has a jagged white central stripe down its green leaves; H. 'Twister' has very wide green margins; H. 'Whirling Dervish' is dark green with a wide yellow margin which turns pure white later; H. 'Whirlwind Tour' is smaller and lacks the markedly twisted leaves.

Hosta 'Whirlwind'

Hosta 'Whirlwind Tour'

Hosta 'Wylde Green Cream' (J. & E. Stratton 1996)

SMALL

Origin: Sport of ★H. 'Vanilla Cream'.

Description: A compact mound 16 in. wide × 8 in. high (40 × 20 cm). Leaf blade 4 × 3½ in. (10 × 9 cm), thick, chartreuse to yellow, irregularly margined bright dark green, with streaks jetting toward the midrib, matt above and thinly glaucous below, dimpled, prominently veined, edge slightly rippled, leaf widely oval to nearly round with a mucronate tip and heart-shaped pinched lobes. Petiole narrow, chartreuse, finely outlined in dark green. Flower: see H. 'Vanilla Cream'.

Cultivation Notes: Site in morning sun followed by light to moderate shade. Slow to increase. Pest resistant.

Distinguishing Features: An attractive contrast between the pale but bright center and the dark green margin, which resembles a hand-painted decoration.

Similar: *H.* 'Heart and Soul'; *H.* 'Peppermint Cream' has a much paler green margin; *H.* 'Rainforest Sunrise' appears virtually identical.

Sports: *H.* 'Pistachio Cream' has green leaves.

Hosta 'Xanadu' (A. Malloy 2000)

SMALL

Origin: Sport of *H.* 'Island Charm'.

Description: A diffuse mound 14 in. wide × 7 in. high (35 × 18 cm). Leaf blade 4 × 3 in. (10 × 8 cm), of good substance, matt ivory, widely and irregularly margined in three shades of green, darkest at the edges with lighter streaks, edge flat to kinked at the base, especially in young plants, leaf lightly concave, broadly ovate with a cuspidate tip and tapered to heart-shaped open lobes. Petiole narrow, ivory, outlined in green. Flower flared, purple-streaked rich lavender, opening from a pink bud, widely spaced on an upright, leafy, pink-tinted ivory, 18-in. (45-cm) scape; seedpods pink, fertile.

Cultivation Notes: Some morning sun is beneficial in all but the hottest regions, then light shade. An attractive hosta for all climates if carefully sited. Divide frequently. Plant in rock gardens, picking up the color of the petioles with *Heuchera* 'Cathedral Windows'.

Distinguishing Features: Differs from its parent in having greater vigor and a significantly wider margin with less streaking and splashing. The bracts are pink-margined green.

Similar: *H.* 'Fantasy Island', another sport of *H.* 'Island Charm', has improved leaf substance, sun tolerance, and better vigor than its parent; *H.* 'Island Charm' is less suitable for hotter climates as its leaves can scorch; *H.* 'Pink Panther' has wider green margins, more central green streaking, pink petioles, and pink- and green-streaked seedpods.

Hosta **'Wylde Green Cream'**

Hosta **'Xanadu'**

Hosta 'Ghost Spirit'

Hosta 'Gunther's Prize'

11

Hostas with Streaked, Stippled, Flecked, Marbled, Misted, and Unusually Marked Leaves

Many hostas with streaked, stippled, flecked, marbled, misted, and unusually marked leaves are valued not only for their unusual leaf patterns but also as breeding plants. Hybridizers especially cherish streaked hostas for the variability of the seedlings they produce, many having marginal variegation. The odds of getting a variegated seedling from any other sort of hosta, by contrast, are infinitely remote. Streaked hostas themselves are not stable, and in some hostas no two leaves look the same. The streaking will often migrate to the margins or result in the leaves becoming a solid color. Quite often these reversions result in new and possibly very desirable plants.

Hostas with streaked leaves have a small but dedicated following. Usually they are sought after only by those wishing to incorporate genes for variegation into their breeding programs, the streaked hostas being used as the pod parent (since variegation is almost always inherited from the female parent). Clumps of streaky leaved hostas need to be divided every three to five years if this characteristic is to be retained. Unfortunately, it is all too easy to allow the clump to mutate to a centrally or marginally variegated hosta—or even to the original parent.

Fairly uniform streaking can, however, produce a most unusual and arresting effect in the garden border, especially when plants with streaky leaves are grown among others with plain green, yellow, or blue leaves. Most streaky leaved hostas arise from parents that need dappled or full shade (for example, *Hosta* 'Neat Splash'), are often not very vigorous, and need constant attention. Streaky leaved hostas that arise from *H. plantaginea* (especially *H. plantaginea* 'Athena') and its hybrids will tolerate a good deal of sun and are very valuable in an exotically themed garden. Flower arrangers prize streaky leaved hostas when a uniformly streaked clump is not essential, such as when the instant visual appeal of bold streaking is of the essence.

Streaking is caused by colored plastids arising in the middle layer of the leaf, L2, and in the epidermal layer, L3, which determines the margin. The main area of the leaf blade is a mixture of L2 and L3. The relationship of these two parts of the leaf explains why streaky variegation often migrates to the margin of the leaf. Breeders find streaky hostas especially valuable because of the 50-percent chance of getting a variegated seedling. Streaky hostas are used as the pod parents, and the less fertile the pollen parent, the narrower is the line of breeding, thus making these seedlings the most valuable.

The "snow flurry" or mottling effect can be achieved by selfing *Hosta sieboldiana* 'Frances Williams'. Other unusual types of marking in the center of a hosta leaf are caused by viral infection or a chromosome deficiency.

*An asterisk before a name indicates that the plant is fully described elsewhere in this book.

Many of the hostas listed in this chapter are only of interest to breeders and as such are rare and difficult to find. They may be obtained from specialist suppliers.

Hosta 'Allegan Fog' (K. Herrema/P. Ruh 2000)
MEDIUM

Origin: Sport of ★*H.* 'Fortunei Albopicta Aurea'.

Description: A compact mound 18½ in. wide × 13 in. high (46 × 33 cm). Leaf blade 4¾ × 3 in. (11 × 8 cm), thin, greenish white becoming finely flecked dark green, irregularly margined dark green, matt above and glaucous below, edge slightly rippled, leaf twisted, arching, widely lanceolate with a long, curved, acute tip and tapered open lobes. Petiole narrow, white, outlined in dark green. Flower: see ★*H.* 'Fortunei Albopicta'.

Cultivation Notes: Viridescent. Site in light to moderate shade. Careful positioning is important to achieve the best color effect. Surprisingly vigorous, a fairly rapid increaser once it is established.

Distinguishing Features: Central variegation is stippled and flecked olive green to dark green.

Similar: *H.* 'Alley Oop' is smaller.

Sports: *H.* 'London Bridge' has cream-edged green leaves; *H.* 'London Fog' lacks the green margin of its parent.

Hosta 'Allen C. Haskell' (M. Seaver N/R)
MEDIUM

Origin: Unknown. Initially named *H.* 'Monet' because of the many colors in the streaking.

Description: A tight mound 36 in. wide × 18 in. high (90 × 45 cm). Leaf blade 7 × 5 in. (18 × 13 cm), thick, satiny, blue-green, streaked white, cream, golden yellow, and celadon, seersuckered, edge almost flat, leaf folded, widely oval with a mucronate tip and heart-shaped pinched lobes. Petiole blue-green, with some streaking. Flower funnel-shaped, pale lavender, on an upright, leafy, glaucous, green, 26- to 28-in. (65- to 70-cm) scape in midsummer; seldom, if ever, sets seed.

Cultivation Notes: Site in light to moderate shade. Slow to increase. Variegation is unstable so division of the clump is necessary as soon as the streaking starts reverting to only marginal variegation.

Hosta 'Artist's Palette' (Kuk 1986)

SMALL

Origin: *H.* 'Neat Splash' hybrid.

Description: An open mound 4 in. wide × 3 in. high (10 × 8 cm). Leaf blade 2 × ¾ in. (5 × 2 cm), thick, glossy, ivory, randomly streaked and misted deep cream, chartreuse, and dark green, cleanly margined white, smooth, edge kinked, leaf folded, lanceolate to triangular with an acute to cuspidate tip and tapered open lobes. Petiole flattish, streaked and mottled, outlined in white. Flower long, tubular, purple-striped lavender, on an upright, leafy, streaky green, 14-in. (35-cm) scape in late summer; seedpods streaked, fertile.

Hosta 'Allegan Fog'

Cultivation Notes: Registered dimensions are easily exceeded under optimum growing conditions. A useful pod parent for variegated seedlings. Will quickly revert to an attractive, white-margined form if not regularly divided. Very rare and expensive.

Distinguishing Features: Unstable variegation; one season it appears with a marginal variegation, the next with streaked leaves.

Sports: *H.* 'Margin of Error' has dark green leaves crisply margined creamy white.

Hosta 'Beatrice' (F. Williams N/R)

SMALL

Origin: *H. sieboldii* seedling.

Description: An open mound 20–24 in. wide × 12–15 in. high (50–60 × 30–38 cm). Leaf blade 5 × 1⅜ in. (13 × 3.5 cm), thin, olive green, irregularly margined pure white, with streaks jetting toward the midrib, matt above and satiny below, smooth, veins closely ribbed, edge slightly rippled, leaf arching, elliptic with an acute tip and tapered open lobes. Petiole green with cream stripes. Flower funnel-shaped, lavender, on an upright, leafy, olive-green, 22-in. (55-cm) scape in midseason; fertile.

Cultivation Notes: Site in some morning sun then light to moderate shade. It is prone to throw streaked sports. This was the first streaked hosta to be introduced and is now among the best-known breeding plants. Sets seed readily.

Hosta 'Allen C. Haskell'

Hosta 'Artist's Palette'

Hosta 'Beatrice', an almost stable form.

Hosta 'Blizzard'

Hosta 'Blue Lightning'

Distinguishing Features: Extremely unstable variegation produces leaves which can be streaked and mottled. The dark purple anthers contrast well with the palest lavender flowers.

Hosta 'Blizzard' (Winterberry Farms/J. Anderson 2003)

VERY LARGE

Origin: Sport of ★*H.* 'Winter Snow'.

Description: A dense mound 71 in. wide × 30 in. high (178 × 75 cm). Leaf blade 20 × 15 in. (50 × 38 cm), thick, mottled, streaked, and striped cream, green, and yellow, satiny above and glaucous below, smooth, edge slightly rippled and cupped, leaf widely oval with a conspicuous cuspidate tip and heart-shaped pinched lobes. Petiole streaked with cream. Flower: see ★*H.* 'Sum and Substance'.

Cultivation Notes: Tolerates sun for most of the day, except in the hottest climates. The streaked variegation is fairly stable. Is fertile and yields streaked seedlings. The substance is extremely good for a streaked-leaved hosta.

Sports: *H.* 'Winterberry Farm' is a stable, white-margined form; ★*H.* 'Winter Snow' has less streaking.

Hosta 'Blue Lightning' (Walters Gardens 2005)

MEDIUM–LARGE

Origin: Sport of ★*H.* 'Blue Umbrellas'.

Description: An open mound 24 in. wide × 15 in. high (60 × 38 cm). Leaf blade 9 × 4½ in. (23 × 11 cm), very thick, glaucous, streaked, splashed, and misted ivory, cream, yellow, and blue-green, seersuckered and puckered, veins widely spaced, edge flat, leaf usually convex but sometimes cupped, almost round with a mucronate tip and heart-shaped folded to overlapping lobes. Petiole streaked with blue-green and ivory. Flower: see *H.* 'Blue Umbrellas'.

Cultivation Notes: Tolerates some morning sun in cooler climates although the leaf coloring will be more attractive if grown in shade. Becomes more cream or blue-green on the margins and center as summer progresses. The scapes are streaked blue-green and cream to ivory. Increases rapidly. Pest resistant. Reasonably stable for a streaked hosta. A wonderful new breeding plant.

Hosta **'Breeder's Choice'** (K. Vaughan 1987)

SMALL—MEDIUM

Origin: ★*H. sieboldiana* 'Frances Williams' × ★*H.* 'Beatrice'.

Description: A compact mound 16 in. wide × 8–12 in. high (40 × 20–30 cm). Leaf blade 5 × 4½ in. (13 × 11 cm), thick, mid-green, mottled, striped, and streaked creamy yellow turning white, matt above and glaucous below, seersuckered, edge widely undulate, leaf slightly folded, elliptic to widely oval with a mucronate tip and tapered open lobes. Petiole narrow, chartreuse. Flower bell-shaped, pale lavender, on an upright, bare, ivory, 25- to 30-in. (63- to 75-cm) scape in high summer; seedpods sometimes mottled (indicating a high probability of streaky seedlings), fertile.

Cultivation Notes: Site in good light to moderate shade. Slow to moderate growth rate. Variegation will stabilize if the plant is not divided every few years. Among the most prolific of all streaked breeding hostas and the parent of many well-known introductions.

Sports: *H.* 'American Choice' has white-margined green leaves.

Hosta **'Christmas Tree Gala'** (L. Powell 2000)

MEDIUM

Origin: Sport of ★*H.* 'Christmas Tree'.

Description: A dense mound 30 in. wide × 20 in. high (75 × 50 cm). Leaf blade 6 × 4 in. (15 × 10 cm), thick, matt, dark green with a blue cast, mottled, streaked, and striped cream turning yellow, seersuckered and puckered, edge slightly rippled, leaf slightly

cupped or convex, widely oval to nearly round with a mucronate tip and heart-shaped overlapping lobes. Petiole cream, outlined in green. Flower: see *H.* 'Christmas Tree'.

Cultivation Notes: Site in some morning sun except in the hottest climates. Slow to moderate growth rate. More suitable as a garden plant than some streaky-leaved hostas. Is a well-regarded breeding plant for variegated seedlings.

Distinguishing Features: Each leaf is different, giving a colorful display.

Similar: ★*H.* 'Galaxy'.

Hosta **'Color Fantasy'** (P. Aden 1980)

MEDIUM

Origin: Putative *H.* 'Gala' hybrid.

Description: An open mound 18 in. wide × 10 in. high (45 × 25 cm). Leaf blade 6 × 4 in. (15 × 10 cm), thick, blue-green, streaked and striped, chartreuse and

Hosta **'Christmas Tree Gala'**

Hosta **'Breeder's Choice'**

Hosta **'Color Fantasy'**

ivory, matt above and glaucous below, dimpled, edge flat, leaf mostly arching, widely oval with a cuspidate tip and heart-shaped pinched lobes. Petiole ivory, outlined in blue-green. Flower funnel-shaped, lavender, on a thin, upright or oblique, leafy, pale green, 16-in. (40-cm) scape in late summer; barely fertile.

Cultivation Notes: Site in some morning sun except in the hottest climates, then light shade. Among the first of the streaky-leaved hostas introduced.

Distinguishing Features: Some leaves are predominantly blue-green, others are more conspicuously streaked.

Hosta 'Color Parade' (M. Zilis 2000)

MEDIUM–LARGE

Origin: Tissue-cultured sport of *H. 'Fragrant Bouquet'.

Description: A symmetrical mound 25 in. wide × 18 in. high (63 × 45 cm). Leaf blade 8½ × 6½ in. (21 × 16 cm), of average substance, pale olive green to chartreuse yellow, streaked and mottled yellow-cream turning ivory, satiny above and shiny below, prominently veined, edge shallowly undulate, leaf convex, widely oval with a cuspidate tip and heart-shaped pinched lobes. Petiole ivory, outlined in chartreuse. Flower: see *H. 'Fragrant Bouquet'.

Cultivation Notes: Tolerates sun in most regions. Protect from late frost damage. A valuable plant for breeding streaked, sun-tolerant hostas with fragrant flowers.

Distinguishing Features: The streaked leaf center is usually bordered by a distinct pale olive-green to chartreuse-yellow margin.

Hosta 'Crown Prince' (H. Ross & P. Ruh 1987)

SMALL

Origin: Unknown.

Description: An open mound 18 in. wide × 10 in. high (45 × 25 cm). Leaf blade 4½ × 2½ in. (11 × 6 cm), thin, emerging satiny, bright golden yellow turning first muted yellow then cream with bright green streaks, dimpled to seersuckered, edge slightly rippled, leaf oval with a cuspidate tip and tapered open lobes. Petiole flattish, pale green. Flower flared, intense violet, on an upright, leafy, green, 10- to 18-in. (30- to 45-cm) scape in late summer; fertility unknown.

Cultivation Notes: Site in morning sun in cooler climates. Grow among small boulders with pulmonarias and ferns. Moderate growth rate. Easy to grow. Very underrated.

Distinguishing Features: Leaf color changes throughout the season giving a tricolor effect and also a vivid contrast with the rich violet flowers.

Hosta 'Cynthia' (C. Tompkins 1984)

LARGE–VERY LARGE

Origin: *H. montana* seedling.

Description: A dense mound 60 in. wide × 36 in. high (150 × 90 cm). Leaf blade 12 × 10 in. (30 × 25 cm), thick, mid- to dark green, streaked, blotched,

Hosta 'Color Parade'

Hosta 'Crown Prince'

and mottled chartreuse to creamy yellow, matt above and glaucous below, seersuckered, prominently veined, edge piecrusted, leaf slightly arching, widely oval with a cuspidate tip and heart-shaped pinched lobes. Petiole light green, appearing to pierce the blade. Flower funnel-shaped, pale lavender, on an upright, leafy, green, 30- to 34-in. (75- to 85-cm) scape in early summer; fertility unknown.

Cultivation Notes: Site in light to moderate shade. Increases rapidly.

Distinguishing Features: The variegation, which is random and unstable, fades during the summer. The streaking in this hosta is a possible virus infection.

Hosta 'Devon Cloud' (A. & R. Bowden N/R)

MEDIUM

Origin: Sport of ★*H*. 'Invincible'.

Description: An arching mound 41 in. wide × 20 in. high (102 × 50 cm). Leaf blade 8½ × 6½ in. (21 × 16 cm), thick, leathery, glossy, olive green, streaked and clouded yellow, veins widely spaced, edge rippled, leaf folded, wedge-shaped with an acute tip and rounded pinched lobes. Petiole olive green. Flower: see *H*. 'Invincible'.

Cultivation Notes: If an abundance of moisture is available, site in sun for most of the day. Moderate to rapid growth rate. Easy to grow. Useful for breeding somewhat sun-tolerant hostas.

Distinguishing Features: The variegation has a shadowy, muted effect.

Hosta 'Don Quixote' (M. Seaver 2004)

SMALL–MEDIUM

Origin: Streaked form of ★*H*. 'Don Stevens'.

Description: A dense mound 40 in. wide × 15–18 in. high (100 × 38–45 cm). Leaf blade 9 × 6 in. (23 × 15 cm), of average substance, dark olive green, streaked and splashed rich yellow turning ivory white, prominently veined, edge slightly rippled, leaf oval with a cuspidate tip and tapered pinched lobes. Petiole olive green, dotted in red, outlined in creamy yellow. Flower: see *H*. 'Don Stevens'.

Cultivation Notes: Site in good light to moderate shade. Moderate growth rate. A good breeding plant.

Distinguishing Features: The streaking is usually in the center of the green-margined leaf.

Hosta 'Devon Cloud'

Hosta 'Cynthia'

Hosta 'Don Quixote'

331

Hosta 'Dorothy Benedict' (H. Benedict 1983)

MEDIUM–LARGE

Origin: *H. sieboldiana* 'Frances Williams' selfed.

Description: An open mound 51 in. wide × 25 in. high (127 × 63 cm). Leaf blade 14 × 9½ in. (35 × 24 cm), thick, glaucous blue with golden-yellow stripes between the veins and some golden-yellow mottling, heavily seersuckered and puckered, edge flat to slightly rippled, leaf slightly cupped or convex, widely oval with a mucronate tip and heart-shaped pinched to overlapping lobes. Petiole light blue-green. Flower bell-shaped, purple-marked white, in a dense raceme, on an upright, leafy, glaucous green, 27- to 28-in. (68- to 70-cm) scape in midsummer; fertile.

Cultivation Notes: Site in good light to moderate shade. Very slow growth rate. Very rare. Prized as a pod parent in producing seedlings of good substance. Among the most attractive of its type. Makes a striking specimen in the garden.

Similar: *H.* 'Doctor Reath', whose variegation fades during the summer; *H.* 'Homestead'.

Hosta 'Dorothy Benedict'

Hosta 'Dorset Clown' (H. Benedict N/R)

SMALL

Origin: *H.* 'Dorset Blue' Group seedling.

Description: An open mound 12 in. wide × 10 in. high (30 × 25 cm). Leaf blade 5 × 2¾ in. (13 × 7 cm),

Hosta 'Dorset Clown'

thick, green with a blue cast, striped and mottled cream, smooth, edge flat with an occasional kink, leaf folded, widely oval with a cuspidate tip and rounded pinched lobes. Petiole green, outlined in cream. Flower funnel-shaped, lavender-gray, on an upright, bare, glaucous green, 12-in. (30-cm) scape from mid- to high summer; fertile.

Cultivation Notes: Site in light to moderate shade. Slow growth rate. Pest resistant. A much sought-after breeding plant.

Sports: *H.* 'Clown's Collar' has cream-margined rich blue leaves.

Hosta 'Extreme' (J. van den Top/D. Van Eechaute 2005)

SMALL–MEDIUM

Origin: Sport of ★*H.* 'Hadspen Blue'.

Description: A diffuse mound 13 in. wide × 8 in. high (33 × 20 cm). Leaf blade 4½ × 2¾ in. (11 × 7 cm), thick, streaked shades of pale blue to turquoise, randomly marked with narrow white flashes, margined medium blue with some turquoise, edged with a hyaline line, glaucous above and below, slightly dimpled when mature, veins widely spaced, edge slightly undulate, leaf broadly ovate with a mucronate tip and open flattish lobes. Petiole flat, wide, frosted blue-green. Flower: see *H.* 'Hadspen Blue'.

Cultivation Notes: Site in dappled to full shade to retain the best leaf color. Pest resistant. Slow to increase so is likely to remain a rarity. Smaller than

the parent plant. The newly emerging foliage is green.

Distinguishing Features: The unusual variegation and the noticeable white line around the leaf edge.

Similar: *H.* 'Abba Windows' has larger, greener leaves.

Hosta 'Fascination' (P. Aden 1978)

MEDIUM

Origin: *H.* 'Flamboyant' × ★*H.* 'High Fat Cream'.

Description: A dense mound 20 in. wide × 16 in. high (50 × 40 cm). Leaf blade 5 × 4 in. (13 × 10 cm), of good substance, dark green, streaked with chartreuse, yellow, and white, matt above and glaucous below, dimpled, edge almost flat, leaf convex, widely oval with a cuspidate tip and heart-shaped pinched lobes. Petiole chartreuse, outlined in green. Flower flared, palest lavender, on an upright, leafy, chartreuse, 20-in. (50-cm) scape in midsummer; fertile.

Cultivation Notes: Direct sun brings out many shades of yellow in the overlapping layers of variegation. Increases rapidly but is difficult to maintain in its truly streaked form, the plant usually reverting to a marginal variegation if it is not frequently divided. A good breeding plant producing many variegated seedlings.

Similar: *H.* 'Whoopie' also has the reputation of being an excellent breeder.

Sport: *H.* 'Golden Fascination' has yellow leaves; *H.* 'Ozark Welcome' has muted yellow leaves margined green.

Hosta 'Extreme'

Hosta 'Fascination'

Hosta 'Foxy Doxy' (Belle Gardens 1994)

MEDIUM

Origin: *H. 'William Lachman' × *H. *sieboldiana* 'Frances Williams'.

Description: A moderately dense, semi-upright mound 28 in. wide × 16 in. high (70 × 40 cm). Leaf blade 6 × 5½ in. (13 × 14 cm), thick, glaucous blue-green, narrowly streaked yellow and creamy white, seersuckered, edge flat, leaf slightly cupped or convex, widely oval to nearly round with a mucronate tip and heart-shaped pinched to overlapping lobes. Petiole cream, outlined in dark blue-green. Flower tubular, lavender, on an upright, bare, glaucous blue, 21-in. (53-cm) scape in high summer; fertile.

Cultivation Notes: Site in light to moderate shade. Slow to increase.

Hosta 'Foxy Doxy'

Hosta 'Galaxy' (W. & E. Lachman 1987)

MEDIUM

Origin: *H.* 'Beatrice' seedling × *H. sieboldiana* 'Frances Williams' seedling.

Description: An open mound 30 in. wide × 15 in. high (75 × 38 cm). Leaf blade 10 × 8½ in. (25 × 21 cm), thick, dark blue-green, intensely mottled and streaked yellow to cream, matt above and glaucous below, seersuckered to puckered, edge slightly rippled, leaf cupped or convex, widely oval with a mucronate tip and heart-shaped pinched lobes. Petiole green, outlined in cream. Flower widely funnel-

Hosta 'Galaxy'

shaped, purple-striped lavender, on a stout, upright or oblique, leafy, glaucous purple-dotted, 27-in. (68-cm) scape from mid- to late summer; fertile.

Cultivation Notes: Site in light to medium shade with plain blue- or green-leaved hostas to illuminate a dark area. With yellow-leaved hostas it will produce a more jazzy effect. Easily reverts, so frequent division is necessary to retain the particularly attractive streaking and mottling. Among the best hostas with streaked leaves. A well-known progeny is ★*H.* 'Cherry Berry'.

Distinguishing Feature: Leaves can have large areas of the base color, but usually have more mottling than most streaked hostas.

Similar: ★*H.* 'Christmas Tree Gala'.
Sports: *H.* 'Galaxy Light' is smaller.

Hosta 'Gertie' (Riehl N/R)

SMALL

Origin: Sport of ★*H.* 'Veronica Lake'.

Description: A dome-shaped mound 36 in. wide × 16 in. high (90 × 40 cm). Leaf blade 4½ × 3½ in. (11 × 9 cm), of average substance, smooth, dark gray-green, mottled and streaked cream, veins widely spaced, edge slightly rippled, leaf slightly folded, widely oval with a cuspidate tip and heart-shaped open to pinched lobes. Petiole pale chartreuse, outlined in green. Flower: see ★*H.* 'Pearl Lake'.

Cultivation Notes: Site in light to moderate shade. Not as vigorous as its parent. Moderate growth rate.

Distinguishing Features: One of a very few streaky breeders of ★*H. nakaiana* ancestry. Has a fine display of flowers.

Hosta 'Ghost Spirit' (C. Isaacs 1999)

MEDIUM—LARGE

Origin: Sport of *H.* 'Valentine Lace'.

Description: An open mound 42 in. wide × 20 in. high (105 × 50 cm). Leaf blade 8½ × 5 in. (21 × 13 cm), thick, pure white, with creamy white streaking and misting soon appearing, widely margined blue-gray, dimpled, edge rippled and twisted, leaf folded, oval with a cuspidate tip and heart-shaped pinched lobes. Petiole narrow, green, streaked and flecked white. Flower funnel-shaped, pale lavender, on an upright, leafy, near black, 26-in. (65-cm) scape in early summer; fertility unknown.

Cultivation Notes: The unusual color holds best in shade, but the young leaves have the strongest variegation. Moderate growth rate. Prone to pest damage but unusual and worthwhile enough to give it the best care and attention.

Distinguishing Features: Many leaves form a 1-in. (2.5-cm) deeply contrasting margin encircling the white center. Variegation fades during the summer into a faint misting. An unusual, near black scape.

Sports: *H.* 'Ghostmaster' has white-centered leaves with a blue-green margin and streaks jetting toward the midrib.

Hosta 'Gertie'

Hosta 'Ghost Spirit' showing the leaves changing from white to misted blue.

Hosta 'Gunther's Prize' (R. Solberg/G. Stark N/R)

VERY LARGE

Origin: 'Sport of *H. 'Sum and Substance'.

Description: A spectacular mound 60 in. wide × 36 in. high (150 × 90 cm). Leaf blade 18 × 15 in. (45 × 38 cm), thick, light green turning chartreuse, variously streaked, speckled, and splashed yellow, cream, and ivory, shiny to waxy above and thinly glaucous below, veins widely spaced, edge slightly rippled, leaf

Hosta 'Gunther's Prize'

broadly ovate with a strongly cuspidate tip and heart-shaped overlapping lobes. Petiole stout, chartreuse green. Flower: see *H.* 'Sum and Substance'.

Cultivation Notes: Lutescent. The variegation is unstable and varies from year to year. Divide regularly to retain the streaking. A much sought-after plant and still a rarity although some gardeners may wonder why. Slow to moderate increase.

Distinguishing Features: Large, randomly streaked leaves will always attract attention.

Similar: *H.* 'Blizzard' has a more muted variegation.

Hosta 'High Fat Cream' (P. Aden 1976)

MEDIUM

Origin: Unknown.

Description: An open mound 25 in. wide × 18 in. high (63 × 45 cm). Leaf blade 7 × 5 in. (18 × 13 cm), thick, light olive green, streaked and mottled chartreuse, yellow, ivory, and white, matt above and thinly glaucous below, dimpled to seersuckered, edge smooth, leaf widely oval to nearly round with a mucronate tip and rounded pinched lobes. Petiole

Hosta 'High Fat Cream'

white, outlined in chartreuse. Flower bell-shaped to flared, lavender, on an upright, leafy, chartreuse, 18-in. (45-cm) scape in late summer; fertile.

Cultivation Notes: Site in some morning sun in cooler climates to maintain the attractive but very unstable variegation. Slow to increase. Was a very popular breeding plant but since the 1980s has been extremely rare.

Similar: *H.* 'Flamboyant'; *H.* 'Whoopie'.

Sports: *★H.* 'American Dream'; *H.* 'Golden Guernsey' has brilliant golden-yellow leaves.

Hosta 'Ice Age Trail' (M. Zilis 2003)

MEDIUM

Origin: Sport of *★H.* 'Big Daddy'.

Description: An open mound 36 in. wide × 16 in. high (90 × 40 cm). Leaf blade 10 × 7 in. (25 × 18 cm), thick, heavily misted and streaked blue, light green, chartreuse, gold, and ivory, early glaucous bloom above and glaucous below, moderately seersuckered, edge flat, leaf broadly ovate with a mucronate tip and heart-shaped overlapping lobes. Petiole stout, blue-green. Flower: see *H.* 'Big Daddy'.

Cultivation Notes: Site in moderate shade as a specimen or accompanied by plainer green foliage to complement the "jazziness" of the leaves. The glaucous bloom gradually disappears from the upper leaf surface. Slow to increase. Pest resistant. Divide frequently to retain the leaf pattern.

Distinguishing Features: Leaves are a very colorful, but an unstable blend of blue, chartreuse, golden yellow, and pale cream.

Hosta 'Independence' PP17,044 (Walters Gardens 2001)

MEDIUM

Origin: Reverse sport of *★H.* 'Revolution'.

Description: A shapely, upright mound 30 in. wide × 20 in. high (75 × 50 cm). Leaf blade 6½ × 4 in. (16 × 10 cm), thick, satiny, dark spinach green, widely and irregularly margined and streaked pale yellow to ivory with dark green flecking, dimpled toward the tip, edge shallowly undulate at its widest part, leaf broadly ovate with an acute tip and rounded lobes. Petiole flattish, dark green, finely outlined in ivory. Flower: see *★H.* 'Francee'.

Cultivation Notes: Site in morning sun followed by light shade in cooler gardens. Moderate growth rate. Pest resistant. Copious watering and feeding help to achieve the widest margin and accentuate the unusual and attractive flecking but watch for stabilization to green leaves as the flecking is a precursor to this. Superb in containers.

Distinguishing Features: Very conspicuous green flecking in the marginal variegation.

Similar: *H.* 'Olympic Glacier' is smaller and has a narrower leaf.

Sports: *H.* 'Lakeside Zig Zag' is a smaller look-alike; *H.* 'Nougat' has random green speckles on an ivory base but is not easy to grow.

Hosta 'Ice Age Trail'

Hosta 'Independence'

Hosta 'Iron Gate Delight' (V. Sellers 1981)

MEDIUM–LARGE

Origin: Sport of *H.* 'Iron Gate Bouquet'.

Description: An open mound 36 in. wide × 16 in. high (90 × 40 cm). Leaf blade 6½ × 4 in. (16 × 10 cm), thin, shiny, light olive green, irregularly margined yellow to ivory white, with many streaks jetting toward the midrib, smooth, deeply impressed veins widely spaced, edge slightly rippled, leaf arching, widely oval with an acute to cuspidate tip and rounded pinched lobes. Petiole shallow, the narrow variegation extending from the leaf into the petiole for approximately 1 in. (2.5 cm). Flower open funnel-shaped, fragrant, palest lavender, on an upright, bare, 24-in. (60-cm) scape from mid- to late summer; fertile.

Hosta 'Iron Gate Delight'

Hosta 'Kiwi Blue Marble', in its juvenile form

Cultivation Notes: Site in morning sun in cooler climates, but only give two hours of sun in the hottest climates, then light shade. Provide plenty of water throughout the growing season. Vigorous and easy to grow. A mid-ground specimen and suitable as a pot plant.

Distinguishing Features: Although the streaking is random and variable, some marginal variegation is usually present.

Similar: *H.* 'Iron Gate Supreme' has better-shaped leaves but less streaking.

Hosta 'Kiwi Blue Marble' (B. Sligh N/R)

MEDIUM

Origin: Sport of ★*H.* 'Hadspen Blue'.

Description: Matures into a dense mound 41 in. wide × 16 in. high (102 × 40 cm). Leaf blade 7 × 6½ in. (18 × 16 cm), thick, glaucous intense blue, marbled and streaked golden yellow fading to near white, seersuckered when mature, edge almost flat, leaf folded to slightly cupped, widely oval with a cuspidate tip and heart-shaped pinched lobes. Petiole glaucous blue. Flower: see *H.* 'Hadspen Blue'.

Cultivation Notes: Site in light to moderate shade all day. Slow to increase. Pest resistant. Leaf color is at its most intense in early summer, gradually darkening to almost pure blue that then assumes a green tinge.

Similar: ★*H.* 'Spilt Milk' has slightly larger, rounder, greener leaves.

Hosta 'Korean Snow' (R. Solberg 1999)

SMALL–MEDIUM

Origin: Seedling selection of *H. yingeri*.

Description: An unruly mound 30 in. wide × 12 in. high (75 × 30 cm). Leaf blade 6½ × 3½ in. (16 × 9 cm), of good substance, glossy, mid-green, randomly streaked and flecked creamy white giving a misted effect early in the season, slightly dimpled when mature, veins widely spaced, edge almost flat, leaf elliptic to oval with a cuspidate tip and rounded open lobes. Petiole chartreuse, finely outlined in green. Flower small, spider-shaped, dark purple, widely spaced around a thin, upright, leafy, green, 20-in. (50-cm) scape in late summer; seedpods streaked green and white (the speckling being a seed-transmitted trait), fertile.

Cultivation Notes: Site in morning sun in cooler climates, followed by good light to maintain the variegation. Moderate growth rate. Among the first hostas to emerge, which is when its coloring is most striking.

Distinguishing Features: Has a unique streaked and speckled variegation which shows no sign of stabilizing, although some leaves are more green than white.

Hosta 'Lakeside Knickknack' (M. Chastain 1994)

SMALL

Origin: *H.* 'Hydon Sunset' hybrid.

Description: A compact mound 15 in. wide × 8 in. high (38 × 20 cm). Leaf blade 3½ × 2½ in. (9 × 6 cm), of average substance, light olive green, streaked

Hosta 'Korean Snow'

yellow, very irregularly margined darker olive green, satiny above and matt below, edge slightly rippled, leaf oval with an obtuse tip and rounded open lobes. Petiole flattish, yellow, outlined in olive green. Flower tubular, near white, on an upright, leafy, streaked, 17-in. (43-cm) scape in high summer; fertile.

Cultivation Notes: Site in light to moderate shade. Increases rapidly. Makes a good pod parent for variegated progeny.

Distinguishing Features: Flowers have a repeat blooming tendency, sometimes up to three periods each summer, setting seed each time.

Hosta 'Lakeside Party Dress' (M. Chastain 1997)

MEDIUM

Origin: *H.* 'Spritzer' hybrid.

Description: A low, spreading mound 30 in. wide × 7½ in. high (75 × 19 cm). Leaf blade 8 × 3½ in. (20 × 9 cm), of average substance, satiny, emerging chartreuse turning golden yellow and finally chartreuse, irregularly margined creamy white, veins closely furrowed and creamy white, edge conspicuously rippled, leaf widely lanceolate with a cuspidate tip and tapered open lobes. Petiole chartreuse, dotted red at the base. Flower funnel-shaped, lavender, on an upright, bare, chartreuse, 25-in. (63-cm) scape in late summer; fertility unknown.

Cultivation Notes: Viridescent. Site in bright light to light shade. Increases rapidly.

Hosta 'Lakeside Knickknack'

Hosta 'Lakeside Party Dress'

Distinguishing Features: Veins that are, seemingly uniquely, the same color as the leaf margin.

Hosta 'Marbled Cream' (C. Owens 1985)

SMALL–MEDIUM

Origin: *H.* 'Yellow Splash' hybrid.

Description: A dense mound 22 in. wide × 7 in. high (55 × 18 cm). Leaf blade 7½ × 4 in. (19 × 10 cm), of average substance, dark green, randomly marbled, striped, and splashed cream and white, matt above and satiny below, dimpled when mature, veins

Hosta 'Marbled Cream'

Hosta 'Midnight at the Oasis'

closely ribbed, edge distinctly rippled, leaf oval with a cuspidate tip and heart-shaped pinched lobes. Petiole olive green. Flower funnel-shaped, lavender, on an upright, leafy, olive-green, 30-in. (75-cm) scape in late summer; fertile.

Cultivation Notes: Site in light to moderate shade. Moderate growth rate. Forms an attractive garden specimen and breeds good variegated offspring.

Distinguishing Features: The streaks and stripes can run the entire length of the leaf blade.

Hosta 'Midnight at the Oasis' (Naylor Creek Nursery N/R)

MEDIUM

Origin: Sport of *H.* 'Pathfinder'.

Description: A dense mound 50 in. wide × 21 in. high (126 × 53 cm). Leaf blade 8 × 5 in. (20 × 13 cm), of good substance, parchment cream, widely and irregularly margined rich black-green with some streaking, matt above and glaucous below, dimpled when mature, edge almost flat, leaf broadly ovate with a cuspidate tip and heart-shaped open or folded lobes. Petiole parchment cream, flecked greenish black. Flower: see ★*H.* 'Francee'.

Cultivation Notes: Site in good light to moderate shade. Vigorous and a moderate increaser. Grow with *Hakonechloa macra* 'Aureola' for contrast of leaf shape, or with yellow- or green-leaved hostas for color contrast.

Distinguishing Features: As the summer progresses the leaf center becomes darker and darker and the green flecks become more obvious. This phenomenon is most apparent in hot summers.

Similar: *H.* 'Obsession'.

Hosta 'Neat Splash' (P. Aden 1978)

MEDIUM

Origin: Registered as *H.* 'Yellow Splash' × *H.* "Robusta" seedling, but now thought to be of ★*H. sieboldii* ancestry.

Description: A spreading mound 36 in. wide × 12 in. high (90 × 30 cm). Leaf blade 7 × 2½ in. (18 × 6 cm), thin, dark olive green, irregularly margined creamy white, randomly streaked chartreuse and creamy white and mottled toward the midrib, satiny above and glossy below, edge slightly rippled, leaf arching, widely oblong to elliptic with an acute tip and rounded to tapered open to pinched lobes. Petiole flattish, green, outlined in creamy white. Flower semi-bell-shaped, rich purple, on an oblique, leafy, green, 25-in. (63-cm) scape in late summer; fertile.

Hosta **'Neat Splash'**

Cultivation Notes: Site in light to moderate shade. Increases rapidly. Among the first streaked hostas used in breeding and an excellent parent for variegated offspring.

Distinguishing Features: Very unstable variegation, the leaves often having large patches of green with no streaking.

Similar: ★*H.* 'Beatrice'; ★*H.* 'Breeder's Choice'; ★*H.* 'Don Quixote'; *H.* 'Green Marmalade'; *H.* 'Splish Splash'.

Sports: *H.* 'Neat Splash Rim' has a creamy yellow margin; ★*H.* 'Swoosh'; *H.* 'Yellow Splash'.

Hosta **'Pin Stripe Sister'** (K. Vaughn N/R)

LARGE

Origin: Unknown.

Description: A dense mound 36 in. wide × 22 in. high (90 × 55 cm). Leaf blade 11 × 10 in. (28 × 25 cm), thick, dark green with a blue cast early in the season, randomly mottled, streaked, and splashed

Hosta **'Pin Stripe Sister'**

341

yellow turning ivory white, matt above and glaucous below, seersuckered, closely veined, edge slightly rippled, leaf convex, widely oval with a mucronate tip and rounded open to pinched lobes. Petiole flattish, striped green and ivory. Flower funnel-shaped, near white, opening from a violet bud, on a stout, upright, bare, glaucous, green, 30-in. (75-cm) scape from mid- to high summer; fertile.

Cultivation Notes: Site in light to moderate shade. Slow to increase. Among the best-known and most highly regarded breeding hostas ever introduced.

Similar: *H.* 'Pin Stripe' is another important breeding plant.

Hosta 'Revolution'

Hosta 'Ruffed Up'

Hosta 'Revolution' (G. Van Eijk-Bos & Walters Gardens 2000)

MEDIUM

Origin: Tissue-cultured sport of *H.* 'Loyalist'.

Description: An upright mound 41 in. wide × 20 in. high (102 × 50 cm). Leaf blade 7½ × 4 in. (19 × 10 cm), of moderate substance, creamy ivory, conspicuously flecked green, widely margined dark green, with light olive green flecks jetting toward the midrib, satiny above and glaucous below, smooth, edge widely undulate, leaf variably oval or heart-shaped with a cuspidate tip and rounded open to pinched lobes. Petiole ivory white, finely outlined in dark green. Flower: see ★*H.* 'Francee'.

Cultivation Notes: Site in some morning sun except in warmer climates. Careful placement is necessary to achieve the right balance of sun and shade. Can often stabilize to all-green leaves so frequent division is advised.

Distinguishing Features: Differs from its parent in having green flecks in the center of the leaf.

Similar: *H.* 'Pathfinder', which has rounder leaves when mature, thicker substance, and less green flecking, may prove the more consistently better grower of the two.

Hosta 'Ruffed Up' (M. Carlson N/R)

MEDIUM–LARGE

Origin: Seedling of *H.* 'Bottom Line'.

Description: A dense mound 35 in. wide × 25 in. high (88 × 63 cm). Leaf blade 11 × 8½ in. (28 × 21 cm), thick, emerging chartreuse green turning mottled chartreuse and golden yellow in sun, shiny to waxy above and thinly glaucous below, slightly dimpled, veins ribbed, edge slightly undulate, leaf outward-facing, broadly oval with a cuspidate tip and heart-shaped overlapping lobes. Petiole stout, chartreuse. Flower funnel-shaped, pale lavender, on a semi-oblique, leafy, chartreuse, 30-in. (75-cm) scape in late summer; fertility unknown.

Cultivation Notes: Tolerates sun in all except the hottest climates. Rugged and easy to grow although slow to increase. Pest resistant. An interesting new introduction.

Distinguishing Features: The gold and green mottling only appears if exposed to sunlight.

Hosta **'Sharmon'** (T. Donahue & AHS 1986)

MEDIUM–LARGE

Origin: Sport of *H.* 'Fortunei'.

Description: A dense mound 41 in. wide × 24 in. high (102 × 60 cm). Leaf blade 8 × 6 in. (20 × 15 cm), of good substance, mid-green with a blue cast early in the season, streaked and striped cream fading by midsummer to two-tone green, matt above and glaucous below, dimpled when mature, edge almost flat with an occasional kink, leaf slightly folded, widely oval with a cuspidate tip and heart-shaped pinched lobes. Petiole ivory, outlined in green. Flower funnel-shaped, lavender-gray, on an oblique, leafy, glaucous green, 34-in. (85-cm) scape in midsummer; fertility uncertain.

Cultivation Notes: Site in good light to moderate shade. Best in cooler climates, where the central variegation is brighter for longer. Moderate to rapid growth rate.

Distinguishing Features: Central variegation is overlaid with fine, netted veins.

Similar: *H.* 'Phyllis Campbell'.

Hosta **'Subtlety'** (A. Tower 2003)

SMALL

Origin: Sport of ★*H.* 'Little Aurora'.

Description: A dense mound 30 in. wide × 9 in. high (75 × 23 cm). Leaf blade 4 × 3½ in. (10 × 9 cm), thick, golden yellow, irregularly flecked and misted green either side of the midrib, matt above and thinly glaucous below, seersuckered, edge flat with an occasional kink, leaf cupped, widely oval with a

mucronate tip and heart-shaped pinched to overlapping lobes. Petiole narrow, chartreuse yellow. Flower: see *H.* 'Little Aurora'.

Cultivation Notes: Site in morning sun except in the hottest climates. Slow to increase and takes time to establish. Pest resistant.

Distinguishing Features: The narrow central marking distinguishes this sport of ★*H.* 'Little Aurora' from all others and is quite unique.

Hosta **'Swoosh'** (P. Aden 1978)

SMALL–MEDIUM

Origin: *H.* 'Yellow Splash' × ★*H.* 'Neat Splash'.

Description: A dense, cascading mound 20 in. wide × 12 in. high (50 × 30 cm). Leaf blade 6 × 4 in. (15 ×

Hosta 'Subtlety'

Hosta 'Sharmon'

Hosta 'Swoosh'

343

10 cm), thin, dark green, striped and splashed chartreuse, yellow, cream, and white, matt above and satiny below, smooth, edge almost flat, leaf slightly folded, widely lanceolate to elliptic with an acute tip and tapered open lobes. Petiole narrow, green, cream, or striped, dotted purple at the base. Flower funnel-shaped, lavender, on an oblique, bare, purple-dotted green, 25-in. (63-cm) scape from mid- to late summer; fertile.

Cultivation Notes: Site in light to moderate shade. Moderate to rapid growth rate. A rare, much-prized breeding plant. Striping quickly reverts to marginal variegation unless the plant is divided often.

Hosta 'Wahoo' (P. Aden 1976)

MEDIUM

Origin: *H.* 'Tokudama Aureonebulosa' × ★*H.* 'Tokudama Flavocircinalis'.

Description: A dense mound 36 in. wide × 16 in. high (90 × 40 cm). Leaf blade 7½ × 5½ in. (19 × 14 cm), thick, glaucous rich blue, splashed, streaked, and mottled chartreuse, yellow, cream, and white, dimpled to seersuckered, edge flat, leaf convex, widely oval with a mucronate tip and heart-shaped pinched lobes. Petiole striped cream or green, depending on whether the midrib is plain or variegated. Flower: see ★*H.* 'Tokudama'.

Cultivation Notes: Site in light to moderate shade. Very slow to increase. Pest resistant. A rare and sought-after breeding plant.

Distinguishing Features: Extremely unstable variegation, the clump or individual leaves being either basically blue with central markings or mainly streaked with some blue.

Hosta 'White Feather' (G. Heemskerk 2005)

MEDIUM

Origin: Sport of ★*H.* 'Undulata'.

Description: An open mound 25 in. wide × 14 in. high (63 × 35 cm). Leaf blade 6½ × 2½ in. (16 × 6 cm), thin, emerging pure white from palest lavender shoots, gradually becoming mottled and streaked light green, matt above and shiny below, prominently veined, edge slightly undulate, leaf slightly folded, elliptic with an acute tip and tapered open to pinched lobes. Petiole white, becoming streaked with green. Flower: see *H.* 'Undulata'.

Cultivation Notes: Viridescent. Tolerates morning sun in cooler climates. Slow to moderate growth rate. Very vulnerable to pest damage. Dramatic and unusual as the white leaves are, the foliage is also very effective as a streaky-leaved hosta.

Distinguishing Features: As the streaking develops, the outline of the veins appears as a ghostly impression.

Hosta 'White Wall Tire' (T. Avent 1995)

MEDIUM

Origin: *H.* 'Outhouse Delight' hybrid.

Description: A moderately dense mound 44 in.

Hosta 'Wahoo'

Hosta 'White Feather'

wide × 16 in. high (110 × 40 cm). Leaf blade 11 × 5 in. (28 × 13 cm), of good substance, matt, creamy white with green mottling gradually turning light green with darker green, smooth, prominently veined, edge slightly rippled, leaf elliptic with a cuspidate tip and tapered open lobes. Petiole creamy white, mottled green. Flower tubular, pale lavender, on an upright, bare, ivory-green, 40-in. (100-cm) scape from mid- to late summer; sterile.

Cultivation Notes: Viridescent. Site in morning sun in cooler climates, then light to moderate shade. Moderate growth rate.

Similar: *H.* 'Mostly Ghostly'; ★*H.* 'White Feather' has shorter leaves that emerge pure white; *H.* 'Zebra Stripes' has leaves with more distinct green veins.

Hosta '**William Lachman**' (K. Vaughn 1981)

MEDIUM

Origin: ★*H.* 'Breeder's Choice' × ★*H. sieboldiana* 'Frances Williams'.

Description: An open mound 24 in. wide × 18 in. high (60 × 45 cm). Leaf blade 6½ × 5 in. (16 × 13 cm), thick, glaucous green with a blue cast in spring, mottled and streaked yellow and white, barely dimpled, edge slightly rippled, leaf slightly cupped when young, convex in maturity, oval with a mucronate tip and heart-shaped overlapping lobes. Petiole streaked green and yellow. Flower funnel-shaped, lavender, on an oblique, leafy, glaucous green, 18-in. (45-cm) scape in midsummer; fertile.

Cultivation Notes: Site in light to moderate shade. Reverts very easily to a marginal variegation or a plain color. Needs dividing once large areas of solid color begin to appear. A wonderful breeding plant but too unstable to be a successful garden plant.

Distinguishing Features: An almost imperceptible narrow, irregular margin usually borders the leaf blade.

Similar: *H.* 'Yankee Doodle Dandy'.

Sports: *H.* 'Mint Julep' is a stable form with mid- to dark green leaves widely margined creamy white.

Hosta '**White Wall Tire**'

Hosta '**William Lachman**'

Hosta '**Mint Julep**'

Hosta 'Stitch in Time'

Hosta 'Lakeside Paisley Print'

T he *Hosta* species have been placed in this chapter, segregated from the more popular, eye-catching green-leaved cultivars of chapter 6 because, although many are only grown by specialist collectors and hybridizers today, their valuable heritage must be preserved. *Hosta gracillima, H. longissima,*

H. minor, H. pulchella, H. sieboldii 'Shiro Kabitan', and *H. venusta* will be fully described in chapter 13, "Miniature and Very Small Hostas."

Some hosta cultivars will always remain collector or connoisseur plants. The reasons for this are several: the hostas may be difficult to cultivate, difficult

347

to propagate, or new to cultivation, either only just introduced from abroad or so new that they are not even on the market yet. In turn, any of these reasons could make these plants expensive, which is another factor that tends to keep them rare. Many medio-variegated and miniature hostas fall into the connoisseur category, and I have included here only those that are the most difficult to cultivate and only if they have good garden value. Many of the hostas included in this chapter are *Hosta sieboldii* derivatives.

Hosta hypoleuca

HOSTA SPECIES

Hosta species have been classified into three subgenera reflecting geographical distribution. The first, subgenus *Hosta*, consists of only one species, *H. plantaginea*, its most conspicuous characteristic being its particularly long-tubed, exquisitely fragrant, night-opening white flowers. The two remaining subgenera are further divided into sections, each containing several species which are closely related; however, the classification of *Hosta* is fluid and changes as new knowledge becomes available.

Subgenus *Bryocles* is divided into four sections and two subsections. Section *Eubryocles* comprises only one species, *Hosta ventricosa*, indigenous to southern China and northern Korea, noted for its distinctly bell-shaped deep purple flowers.

Section *Lamellatae* consists of small hostas with ridged scapes mainly coming from mainland Korea. This section is divided into two subsections. Subsection *Capitatae* comprises *Hosta capitata* and *H. nakaiana*, which are characterized by their solid scapes and ball-shaped buds. Subsection *Spicatae* comprises *H. venusta* and *H. minor*, which have hollow scapes and spikelike buds. *Hosta minor* is believed to have evolved in the southern and eastern coastal areas of Korea, while *H. venusta* is thought to have come from the island of Cheju, off the southern coast of Korea.

Section *Arachnanthae* comprises two recently collected species, *Hosta laevigata* and *H. yingeri*. These species are known for their small flowers, which have narrow, spiderlike petals, and for their thick, succulent leaves. They were collected from islands off the coast of Korea.

Section *Stoloniferae* has only a single species, *Hosta clausa*, which, because it typically does not open its narrowly bell-shaped purple flowers and its stoloniferous roots allowing the spread of single plants, obviates the need for reproductive pollination.

Subgenus *Giboshi* includes all the Japanese species and is subdivided into three groups with their respective sections. Group 1 is characterized by narrow-tubed, funnel-shaped white or almost white flowers. It includes three sections. Section *Helipteroides* comprises five species from central and northern Japan: *Hosta crassifolia*, *H. fluctuans*, *H. montana*, *H. nigrescens*, and *H. sieboldiana*. These are mostly large or very large hostas. Section *Rhynchophorae* consists of two species, *H. kikutii* and *H. shikokiana*, which were found on the southwestern tip of the Japanese archipelago. These two are characterized by their leaning flower scapes and buds which bear a fancied resemblance to Kutari cranes. Section *Intermediae* comprises three seldom-grown species from central Japan: *H. densa*, *H.*

*An asterisk before a name indicates that the plant is fully described elsewhere in this book.

348

kiyosumiensis, and *H. pachyscapa*. They bear similarities
to the hostas in section *Rhynchophorae* but are distinct
in having green rather than whitish leafy bracts.

Group 2 has narrow-tubed near bell-shaped flowers.
Section *Picnolepis* has eight species all of which come
from central Japan: *H. aequinoctiiantha*, *H. hypoleuca*,
H. longipes, *H. okamotoi*, *H. pulchella*, *H. pycnophylla*,
H. rupifraga, and *H. takiensis*. These are distinguished
by their boat-shaped white or purple bracts and the
lateness of their flowering season.

Group 3 has narrowly bell-shaped, striped flowers.
Section *Nipponosta* A consists of six closely related species, *H. atropurpurea*, *H. calliantha*, *H. clavata*, *H. ibuk-
iensis*, *H. rohdeifolia*, and *H. sieboldii*, which have ellip-
tical leaves and large, leaflike bracts which clasp the
flower stem. Section *Nipponosta* B includes two species
from central and northern Japan, *H. alismifolia* and *H.
rectifolia*, which are quite distinct in that their leaves
are held stiffly erect rather like *Aspidistra* or *Alisma*,
the water plantain. Section *Nipponosta* C comprises
a single species from central Japan, *H. longissima*,
which has linear leaves held erect. Section *Tardanthae*
includes seven species from Japan, Tsushima Island,
southern insular Korea, and northeastern China, *H.
cathayana*, *H. gracillima*, *H. jonesii*, *H. takahashii*, *H. tardiva*, *H. tibae*, and *H. tsushimensis*, distinct on account
of being the latest to flower and all of which have
ovate to cordate leaves.

The following descriptions cover species growing
in gardens and National Collections in the West. The
Kanji names are indicated as an aid to the naming of
the forms and varieties now in common usage.

Hosta capitata Nakai

Iya Giboshi

SMALL—MEDIUM

Origin: Southern Korea and Shikoku Island, Japan.

Description: A dense mound 30 in. wide × 10 in.
high (75 × 25 cm). Leaf blade 5 × 3½ in.(13 × 9 cm),
thin, mid-green, matt above and shiny below, veins
closely ribbed, edge distinctly rippled, leaf oval with
a drooping cuspidate tip and round to heart-shaped
open to pinched lobes. Petiole narrow, lighter green.
Flower narrowly funnel-shaped, purple with a white
throat, on a thin, arching, purplish green, 22-in. (55-
cm) scape in midsummer; fertile.

Cultivation Notes: Site in light to moderate shade.
Useful as a breeding plant for producing piecrust leaf
edges and heavy racemes of purple flowers that cluster
around the scape.

Distinguishing features: Scapes are noticeably
ridged. Flowers buds are tightly ball-shaped.

Similar: *★H. minor*; *★H. nakaiana*.

Hosta clausa var. *clausa* Nakai

Tsubomi Giboshi

MEDIUM

Origin: Korea.

Description: A dense, rhizomatous mound 12 in.
wide × 12 in. high (30 × 30 cm). Leaf blade 6 × 2 in.
(15 × 5 cm), of average substance, shiny mid- to dark

Hosta capitata

Hosta clausa

green, veins closely spaced, edge slightly undulate, leaf narrowly oval to elliptic with an acute tip and tapered pinched lobes. Petiole green, intensely dotted red. Flower a widely spaced purple bud that does not open, on an upright, leafy, green, 30-in. (75-cm) scape in late summer; barely fertile.

Cultivation Notes: Dimensions are usually much exceeded when grown in cultivation. A moisture-lover and best grown alongside river banks where it will soon colonize huge areas.

Similar: Var. *clausa* is a triploid form; var. *stolonifera* (Schmid 1991) has evolved as a non-flowering phrase of it; var. *normalis* has showy purple flowers that open normally and increase by means of creeping rhizomes.

Hosta densa Maekawa

Keyari Giboshi

MEDIUM

Origin: Southwest Honshu, Japan.

Description: A spreading mound 22 in. wide × 26 in. high (56 × 65 cm). Leaf blade 9 × 5 in. (23 × 13 cm), of good substance, matt dark green above and matt lighter green below, veins closely ribbed, edge shallowly and evenly rippled, leaf slightly arching, elliptic to oval with a cuspidate tip and rounded pinched lobes. Petiole upright, green, with purple dots toward the crown. Flower funnel-shaped, purple-tinted near white, on a thick, leaning, leafy, purple-dotted green, 24-in. (60-cm) scape in early autumn; fertile.

Cultivation Notes: Site in light to moderate shade. Rarely grown in gardens. A collector's plant.

Distinguishing Features: A tightly packed raceme, as the specific name indicates.

Similar: *★H. montana* is larger.

Hosta hypoleuca Murata

Urajiro Giboshi

MEDIUM–LARGE

Origin: Aichi and Shizuoka Prefectures, Japan.

Description: A lax, open mound 45 in. wide × 15 in. high (113 × 38 cm). Leaf blade 13 × 9 in. (33 × 23 cm), thick, leathery, mid- to dark green, satiny above and thickly glaucous below, dimpled when mature, prominently veined, edge shallowly rippled, leaf slightly arching, oval with a cuspidate tip and deeply heart-shaped open to pinched lobes. Petiole narrow, arched, green with red dots. Flower bell-shaped, purple-suffused white, on an oblique to recumbent, leafy, purple-dotted light green, 26-in. (65-cm) scape in late summer; fertile.

Cultivation Notes: Tolerates sun but grows equally well in shade. Changes its characteristics more than any other species when grown in cultivation. In the wild it is often found clinging to a rock face in full sun, where it has only one or two very large leaves; in the garden it forms a typical hosta clump, albeit retaining the white back that in the wild acts as protection from the heat reflected off rocks. Much used in hybridizing for introducing thick pruinose coating to the backs of leaves.

Hosta densa

Hosta hypoleuca

Distinguishing Features: Extraordinarily thick, white pruinose coating on the underside of the leaf.

Similar: *H. pycnophylla* is more difficult to cultivate.

Sports: *H.* 'Maekawa' has gray-green leaves and has produced a wonderful new sport, *H.* 'Nutty Professor', which has ivory-margined leaves.

Hosta jonesii M. G. Chung

SMALL

Origin: Several islands off the coast of Korea.

Description: A diffuse, rhizomatous mound 18 in. wide × 8 in. high (45 × 20 cm). Leaf blade 8 × 4 in. (20 × 10 cm), matt mid-green above, shiny, paler green below, edge lightly undulate to rippled, leaf arching toward the tip, elliptic to oval with tapered open lobes. Petiole tapered, very pale green, dotted purple toward the crown, appearing to pierce the blade almost to the tip. Flower near bell-shaped, white-striped purple, on an oblique to upright, sometimes branching, leafy, purple-dotted green, 24-in. (60-cm) scape in late summer; fertile.

Cultivation Notes: Site in moderate shade all day. In cultivation usually seen only in specialist collections.

Similar: *H. tsushimensis*, a close relative, lacks purple dots on the scape, has larger flowers, and is more vigorous.

Hosta kikutii var. *kikutii* Maekawa

Hyuga Giboshi

MEDIUM—LARGE

Origin: Honshu, Shikoku, and Kyushu Islands, Japan.

Description: A dense, fountainlike mound 36 in. wide × 16 in. high (90 × 40 cm). Leaf blade 11½ × 4½ in. (29 × 11 cm), of average substance, bright mid-green, shiny above and whitish and shiny below, deeply impressed veins closely spaced, edge flattish, leaf arching, elongated to oval with an acute tip and heart-shaped overlapping lobes. Petiole narrow, lighter green. Flower funnel-shaped, near-white-stained lavender, reflexing at the tip, on a stiff, long pedicel with distinct silvery bracts clustered at the top of a conspicuously leaning, leafy, green, 24-in. (60-cm) scape in late summer; fertile.

Cultivation Notes: Site in morning sun followed by dappled shade.

Distinguishing Feature: Heavy, dense clusters of flowers droop downward from the scape.

Similar: *H.* 'Fatal Attraction', a *H. kikutii* hybrid, has all the characteristics of that species with the addition of eye-catching wide white leaf margins; *H. kikutii* var. *caput avis* has conspicuous veins on matt olive green leaves, purplish brown dotting on leafy bracts, and flower buds that have a fancied resemblance to a bird's beak; *H. kikutii* f. *leuconota* has leaves half the size of the species, the leaves and

Hosta jonesii

Hosta kikutii

351

petiole emerging with a white pruinose coating, the upper surface of the leaf becoming green during the summer; *H. kikutii* var. *polyneuron* has strongly marked closely spaced veins giving a ribbed effect, matt, dark green leaves, paler green with a satin sheen below, and is very slow growing; *H. kikutii* var. *tosana*, said by some authorities to be a separate species, is a good breeding plant for red petioles; *H. kikutii* var. *yakushimensis* has longer, curled tips to the leaves and the petiole extends into the bright, glossy, green leaf making a delightful tonal contrast.

Sports: *H. kikutii* 'Hyuga Urajiro' has frosty blue lanceolate leaves striped yellow; ★*H. kikutii* 'Kifukurin Hyuga'.

Hosta kikutii 'Kifukurin Hyuga' (P. Ruh 2002)

MEDIUM—LARGE

Origin: Natural sport of ★*H. kikutii* from Japan.

Description: A graceful, open mound 36 in. wide × 20 in. high (90 × 50 cm). Leaf blade 9 × 5–6½ in. (23 × 13–16 cm), of average substance, shiny, mid- to

dark green, irregularly margined yellow turning cream, with some streaks jetting toward the midrib, veins prominently ribbed, edge rippled, leaf arching, oval with a cuspidate tip and heart-shaped overlapping lobes. Petiole narrow, green, outlined in cream. Flower: see *H. kikutii* var. *kikutii*.

Cultivation Notes: Tolerates some morning sun in most regions. Moderate to good growth rate.

Distinguishing Features: Heavily ribbed cascading leaves.

Similar: *H.* 'Shelley's', formerly assigned incorrectly to *H. kikutii* and now considered a natural sport of *H. kiyosumiensis* (perhaps identical to ★*H. kiyosumiensis* "Aureomarginata"), flowers several weeks later.

Hosta kikutii f. *leuconota* (W. G. Schmid 1991)

MEDIUM

Origin: Aichi and Shizuoka Prefectures, Japan. Formerly known as *H. kikutii* 'Pruinose'.

Description: An arching mound 34 in. wide × 15 in. high (85 × 38 cm). Leaf blade 11 × 2½ in. (28 × 6

Hosta kikutii 'Kifukurin Hyuga'

cm), of average substance, gray-green, smooth, veins
deeply impressed, edge slightly undulate, leaf arching,
lanceolate with an acute tip and tapered open lobes.
Petiole glaucous light green. Flower funnel-shaped,
glaucous near white, in a dense raceme, on a leaning,
smooth, leafy, glaucous green, 16-in. (40-cm) scape
in early autumn; fertile.

Cultivation Notes: Site in dappled to moderate
shade. Vigorous, a good increaser.

Distinguishing Features: Leaves are coated in a
thick white indumentum. Flower buds resemble a
bird's head.

Similar: *H.* 'Glacier Cascade' has paler green leaves.

Hosta kiyosumiensis "Aureomarginata"

(F. Maekawa)

Synonym: *Hosta* 'Kifukurin Kiyosumi'

LARGE

Origin: Honshu, Japan.

Description: An open mound 64 in. wide × 22 in.
high (160 × 55 cm). Leaf blade 11 × 5 in. (28 × 13
cm), of average substance, mid-green, irregularly
margined yellow turning green, with streaks jetting toward the midrib, matt above and shiny below,
veins closely ribbed, edge rippled, leaf slightly arching toward the tip, narrowly oval with a long acute
tip and tapered pinched lobes. Petiole oblique, flattish,
pale green, with red dots toward the crown. Flower
narrow, funnel-shaped, lavender, on an upright, leafy,
light green, 36-in. (90-cm) scape from high to late
summer; fertile.

Cultivation Notes: Site in light to moderate shade.
Slow to average growth rate. Rarely seen in gardens
but a sought-after collector's plant.

Similar: ★*H. kikutii* 'Kifukurin Hyuga' is earlier to
emerge; *H.* 'Shelley's'.

Hosta laevigata W. G. Schmid

SMALL

Origin: Islands off the coast of Korea.

Description: A dense mound 30 in. wide × 12 in.
high (75 × 30 cm). Leaf blade 8½ × 2½ in. (21 × 6
cm), thick, emerging chartreuse turning light green,
matt above and satiny below, slightly dimpled, edge
tightly ruffled, leaf arching, narrowly lanceolate with
an acute tip and tapered open lobes. Petiole flat, light

Hosta kikutii f. *leuconota*

Hosta kiyosumiensis 'Nafuku', the leaves
having the reverse variegation.

Hosta laevigata

green. Flower broad, spider-shaped, purple, on an upright, green, 36-in. (90-cm) scape from late summer to early autumn; fertile.

Cultivation Notes: Site in light shade. Pest resistant. Closely related to *H. yingeri. Good for hybridizing as it passes on the ruffled edges and spiderlike flowers. Winner of the 1996 Alex J. Summers Distinguished Merit Hosta Award.

Distinguishing Features: The spider-shaped flowers have very thin petals. The flower buds can produce more than 30 blooms on one scape.

Similar: *H.* 'Sea Octopus' has matt leaves.

Sports: *H.* 'Ray of Hope' has streaks and flashes throughout the leaf blade, and its sport, *H.* 'Roller Coaster Ride', has a rippled white line running down the leaf margin; both will tolerate sun.

Hosta longipes var. longipes f. viridipes

(Franchet & Savatier) Matsumura

Iwa Giboshi

SMALL–MEDIUM

Origin: Honshu Island, Japan.

Description: A rhizomatous mound 20 in. wide × 9 in. high (50 × 23 cm). Leaf blade 8 × 5 in. (20 ×

13 cm), thick, leathery dark green, shiny above and glossy, lighter green below, veins deeply ribbed, edge almost flat, leaf widely oval with a cuspidate tip and flat pinched to folded lobes. Petiole almost horizontal, light green, dotted purple. Flower near funnel-shaped, lavender, on an oblique to horizontal, purple-dotted green, 12-in. (30-cm) scape from late summer to early autumn; fertile.

Cultivation Notes: Site in light shade. Average to fast growth rate. Very variable in the wild, where many natural sports and seedlings are still being found. Many botanical forms are much used in breeding.

Distinguishing Features: A nearly flat, overlapping mound of wide leaves.

Sports: *H. longipes* 'Hypoglauca' has longer, narrower leaves with an intensely glaucous underside and distinctly red-streaked petioles and is the parent of many hybrids to whom it has passed on this characteristic, including *H.* 'Brandywine', *H.* 'Granddaddy Redlegs', and *H.* 'Red Sox'; *H. longipes* 'Latifolia' has a distinctly rippled leaf edges and a long, pointed tip and is now considered to be synonymous with *H. rupifraga* by some authorities; *H.* 'Strawberry Delight'.

Hosta longipes 'Hypoglauca'

Hosta longissima Honda

Mizu Giboshi

SMALL

Origin: Central and western Honshu, Shikoku, and Kyushu, Japan.

Description: A low, arching, dense mound 25 in. wide × 9½ in. high (63 × 24 cm). Leaf blade 8 × 1 in. (20 × 2.5 cm), of average substance, elm green, matt above and shiny below, veins closely spaced, edge flat with occasional kinks, leaf linear to lanceolate with an acute tip, decurrent with the purple-dotted petiole. Flower funnel-shaped, purple, on an upright, leafy, light green, 22-in. (55-cm) scape from early to late autumn; fertile.

Cultivation Notes: Site in shade all day. Needs an abundance of moisture at its roots. Can be grown in garden ponds successfully if the crown is kept above the water line. Is often confused with the narrowest-leaf forms of *★H. sieboldii*.

Distinguishing Features: Strap-shaped leaves are among the narrowest in the genus.

Similar: *★H.* 'Bitsy Green' is a hybrid; *H. longissima* var. *brevifolia* has smaller, somewhat spoon-shaped leaves; *H. longissima* var. *longifolia* (Honda) W. G. Schmid 1991; *H.* 'Purple Lady Finger'.

Sports: *H. longissima* 'Asahi Comet', a sport of var. *longifolia*, is a very rare, broadly cream margined green-leaved form known in Japan as the *mizu* (water) hosta, which grows on rocks in and around springs and streams.

Hosta montana var. *montana* Maekawa

Oba Giboshi

LARGE–VERY LARGE

Origin: Populations spread widely throughout Japan.

Description: An upright mound 48 in. wide × 24 in. high (120 × 60 cm). Leaf blade 12 × 9 in. (30 × 23 cm), thick, olive green, satiny above, glossy below and rough to the touch, slightly dimpled when mature, veins deeply furrowed above, strongly ribbed below, edge shallowly undulate, leaf arching, slightly folded, widely oval with a cuspidate tip and heart-shaped overlapping lobes. Petiole stout, light green. Flower funnel-shaped, suffused lavender to almost white, on a leaning, leafy, 49-in. (122-cm) scape in midsummer; fertile.

Cultivation Notes: Site in light to moderate shade. Very variable in the wild. Usually much larger in cultivation. Emerges much later than its best-known sport, *★H. montana* 'Aureomarginata'. The parent of many large-leaved hybrids.

Distinguishing Features: Very long, dense racemes and numerous leafy bracts. Heavy production of pods weighs the scape down.

Similar: *H.* 'Devon Tor'; *★H.* 'Elatior'; *★H.* 'King Michael'; *H. montana* f. *macrophylla* has much wider leaves.

Sports: *★H. montana* 'Aureomarginata'; *H. montana* 'Emma Foster', a gold-leaved form, is rarely grown

Hosta longissima

Hosta montana

355

because it is not vigorous; *H. montana* 'Ginrei' has green leaves with white margins flecked green and is a welcome recent introduction.

Hosta montana 'Aureomarginata' (AHS 1987)

Kifukurin Oba Giboshi

LARGE

Origin: Natural sport of ★*H. montana*, originally found in Tokyo Prefecture, Japan.

Description: A cascading mound 65 in. wide × 27 in. high (163 × 68 cm). Leaf blade 15 × 8 in. (38 × 20 cm), of average substance, rich dark green, widely and irregularly margined golden yellow to creamy white depending upon the light available, with light olive green transitional streaks jetting toward the midrib, matt above, glossy below and rough to the touch, veins closely spaced, edge slightly undulate, leaf arching, oval with a cuspidate tip and heart-shaped pinched to overlapping lobes. Petiole wide, green, outlined in yellow. Flower funnel-shaped, pale lavender, in a dense raceme, on a leaning, leafy, light green, 38-in. (95-cm) scape from mid- to high summer; seedpods many, fertile.

Cultivation Notes: Site in light to moderate shade. Moderate growth rate. Although not one of the easiest hostas to grow, it is still one of the most eye-catching variegated hostas ever introduced. Among the first to emerge in spring; the vulnerable new shoots may need pest protection. Late frosts can also scorch the leaves. Winner of the 1985 Alex J. Summers Distinguished Merit Hosta Award.

Sports: *H. montana* 'Ebb Tide' is smaller; *H. montana* 'First Love' is streaked on unfurling, then has green margined yellow leaves; *H. montana* 'Hida-no-hana' has green margined cream leaves overlaid with green misting.

Hosta montana 'Choko Nishiki' (Maekawa)

LARGE

Origin: Natural sport of ★*H. montana*, which is found in the wild in Japan.

Description: A tiered mound 49 in. wide × 22 in. high (122 × 55 cm). Leaf blade 13 × 8 in. (33 × 20 cm), of average substance, emerging bright yellow from red-tinted shoots, with a green cast in shade, widely and irregularly margined bright dark olive green, with light olive green streaks jetting toward the midrib, matt above and glossy below, furrowed veins that are rough to the touch, edge shallowly undulate, leaf with an acute, often twisted tip and heart-shaped open to pinched lobes. Petiole chartreuse, clearly outlined in dark green. Flower: see ★*H. montana* var. *montana*.

Comment & Special Needs: Except in the hottest climates, site in some morning sun to help boost plant vigor and provide adequate moisture. Best in hot, humid conditions. Emerges much later than ★*H. montana* 'Aureomarginata'.

Hosta montana 'Aureomarginata'

Hosta montana 'Choko Nishiki', also known as *H.* 'On Stage'.

Similar: *H. montana* 'Kinkaku' is a natural sport; *H.* 'On Stage' is considered identical.

Sports: *H. montana* 'Hollywood Lights', a selection from *H.* 'On Stage', has wider margins; *H. montana* 'Mountain Sunrise' has bright golden-yellow leaves turning medium green by midsummer and is slow growing but has more vigor than *H. montana* 'Emma Foster'.

Hosta montana 'Mountain Snow' (T & Z Nursery & M. Zilis 1988)

LARGE

Origin: Tissue-cultured sport of *★H. montana* (Mount Fuji strain).

Description: A dense mound 60 in. wide × 27 in. high (150 × 68 cm). Leaf blade 12 × 8 in. (30 × 20 cm), of average substance, mid- to dark green, narrowly margined pure white, with many celadon streaks jetting toward the midrib, matt above and shiny below, smooth, veins closely ribbed, edge lightly rippled, leaf arching to convex, oval with a cuspidate tip and heart-shaped pinched lobes. Petiole stout, green, finely outlined in white. Flower: see *H. montana*.

Cultivation Notes: Site in light to moderate shade. Moderate to good growth rate. Useful as a specimen or in woodland. Emerges later than most selections of this species so is not troubled by late frosts. Prized for the delicate feathered margin in combination with the narrowly furrowed leaf. Its provenance is uncertain but probably belongs with *H. montana*.

Similar: *★H.* 'Frosted Jade' has less white streaking than *★H. montana* 'Mountain Snow'; *H.* 'White On'.

Sports: *H. montana* 'Back Light' has yellow leaves.

Hosta montana 'Yellow River' (E. Smith/P. Ruh 1993)

VERY LARGE

Origin: Natural sport of *★H. montana*.

Description: An impressive, semi-upright mound 80 in. wide × 36 in. high (200 × 90 cm). Leaf blade 15 × 9 in. (38 × 23 cm), of good substance, matt, mid- to dark green, widely and irregularly margined yellow turning creamy white, with celadon splashes jetting toward the midrib, strongly veined, edge widely undulate or kinked, leaf twisted and curved toward the tip, widely oval with a cuspidate tip and heart-shaped pinched to overlapping lobes. Petiole stout, dark green, outlined in yellow. Flower: see *H. montana* var. *montana*.

Cultivation Notes: Site in light to moderate shade. Moderate to good growth rate. Late to emerge. Ideal for a woodland planting with shrubs or as a specimen. A classic hosta which has never been overshadowed by modern introductions.

Similar: *★H.* 'Sagae' has leaves that are a grayer green.

Hosta montana 'Mountain Snow'

Hosta montana 'Yellow River'

Hosta nakaiana Maekawa

Kanzashi Giboshi

SMALL

Origin: Southern and central Korea; Saga; Nagasaki and Hyuga Prefectures, Japan.

Description: A dense, overlapping, dome-shaped mound 32 in. wide × 12 in. high (80 × 30 cm). Leaf blade 3½ × 2½ in. (9 × 6 cm), thin, mid-green with a slight gray cast, matt above and satiny below, smooth, veins ribbed when mature, edge undulate, leaf slightly folded, widely oval with a mucronate tip and heart-shaped pinched lobes. Petiole narrow, green. Flower funnel-shaped, purple with a white throat, on an upright, ridged, leafy, pale green, 15- to 23-in. (38- to 58-cm) scape from mid- to high summer; fertile.

Cultivation Notes: Site in light to moderate shade. Increases rapidly. Feed in spring and autumn.

Distinguishing Features: Very floriferous, producing abundant seed from which has emanated some very worthy hybrids. Scapes are noticeably ridged.

Similar: ★*H. capitata*; *H.* 'Harry van Trier'; ★*H. minor.*

Hosta nakaiana

Hosta nigrescens Maekawa

Kuro Giboshi

LARGE

Origin: Northern Honshu, Japan.

Description: A semi-upright, vase-shaped mound 62 in. wide × 30 in. high (157 × 75 cm). Leaf blade 12 × 10 in. (30 × 25 cm), thick, emerging blue-green then turning dark green, intensely glaucous below, seersuckered, edge almost flat, leaf deeply cupped, widely oval to nearly round with a mucronate tip and heart-shaped pinched lobes. Petiole stout, ash gray. Flower small, funnel-shaped, purple-streaked pale lavender, on an upright, glaucous gray, leafy, 44-in. (110-cm) scape in late summer; barely fertile.

Cultivation Notes: Site in light to full shade all day. Moderate growth rate. Pest resistant. Small hostas and other ground-covering plants can be grown at its feet.

Distinguishing Features: Shoots emerge darkly colored, almost black. Scapes tower above the foliage mound.

Similar: *H.* 'Kelly'; *H.* 'Naegato'; *H.* 'Tenryu' has near-white flowers.

Hosta okamotoi Araki

Okuyama Giboshi

MEDIUM

Origin: Kyoto Prefecture, Japan.

Description: A flattish mound 16 in. wide × 12 in. high (40 × 30 cm). Leaf blade 5 × 2¾ in. (13 × 7 cm), leathery, mid-green above and paler, satiny green below, smooth with some puckering when mature, edge flat to undulate, leaf nearly round with a cuspidate tip and heart-shaped open to pinched lobes. Petiole green, with purple dots toward the crown. Flower funnel-shaped, white with purple-suffusions inside,

Hosta nigrescens

on an oblique, leafy, purple-dotted, 18-in. (45-cm) scape in autumn; fertile.

Cultivation Notes: Site in light shade. Pest resistant. In cultivation, usually seen only in specialist collections.

Similar: *H. aequinoctiiantha*, Ohigan Giboshi, has shorter scapes, flowers spaced more closely, and impressive white bracts subtending the flowers.

Hosta pachyscapa Maekawa

Benkei Giboshi

MEDIUM

Origin: Honshu Island, Japan.

Description: A spreading mound 36 in. wide × 20 in. high. (90 × 50 cm). Leaf blade 8 × 6 in. (20 × 15 cm), of good substance, mid- to dark green, satiny above and shiny below, slightly dimpled, veins closely ribbed, edge slightly rippled, leaf arching, oval to elliptic with an acute tip and rounded pinched lobes. Petiole green, slightly dotted purple toward the crown. Flower funnel-shaped, purple-striped pale lavender, on an upward to leaning, leafy, green, 28- to 50-in. (70- to 126-cm) scape, with purple dots near

the crown and at the tip, from high to late summer; fertile.

Cultivation Notes: Grow in light shade at the waterside. Increases rapidly. Rarely seen in cultivation.

Distinguishing Features: An extraordinarily thick scape, which tends to droop toward the end of the flowering period.

Similar: *★H. kiyosumiensis* is larger.

Hosta okamotoi

Hosta pachyscapa

Hosta plantaginea var. *plantaginea* Ascherson

Maruba Tama-no-kanzashi Giboshi

LARGE

Origin: Southern China.

Description: Matures into a dome-shaped mound 60 in. wide × 24 in. high (150 × 60 cm). Leaf blade 11 × 7 in. (28 × 18 cm), thin, pale to mid-green, satiny above and glossy below, slightly dimpled when mature, veins closely ribbed veins, edge slightly rippled, leaf arching, oval with cuspidate tip and heart-shaped pinched lobes. Petiole mid-green. Flower very long-tubed, up to 5 in. (13 cm) , widely funnel-shaped, exceedingly fragrant, white, on an upright to oblique, leafy, chartreuse, 32-in. (80-cm) scape in late summer and autumn; fertile.

Cultivation Notes: Leaves turn chartreuse in sun. Tolerates half to three-quarters of a day's sun in the hottest, humid regions and full sun all day in other

Hosta plantaginea

Hosta plantaginea 'Aphrodite', flower

Hosta plantaginea var. *japonica*, showing its long-tubed flowers.

areas provided it is supplied with enough moisture. Leaves take several weeks to completely unfurl after the shoots first sprout. It passes on its sweet fragrance to many hybrids, but adequate moisture and heat are necessary to set seed. Feed and water regularly throughout the growing season. Does not produce many flowers in cooler climates where it does best planted against a sunny wall. Known affectionately in the United States as grandmother's plant.

Distinguishing Features: Intensely fragrant, nocturnal, waxy, long tubed white flowers.

Similar: *★H. 'Royal Standard'.

Sports: *H. plantaginea* 'Aphrodite' has extra petals, thus creating the effect of a double flower, and needs a hot, humid climate for the flowers to open as the buds usually abort before flowering in cooler climates; *H. plantaginea* 'Athena' has streaked leaves; *H. plantaginea* var. *japonica* ♛, formerly *H. plantaginea* 'Grandiflora', has longer, laxer leaves and flowers with an even longer tube, while its sport *H. plantaginea* 'Chelsea Ore' has yellow leaves narrowly margined dark green and a notably weak constitution needing a hot, humid climate in which to thrive; *H. plantaginea* 'Heaven Scent', a possible tetraploid, has yellow-margined dark green leaves; *H. plantaginea* 'Ming Treasure' has leaf margins that change from chartreuse to white; *H. plantaginea* 'Venus', *H. plantaginea* 'White Fairy', and *H. plantaginea* 'White Swan' all have true double flowers;

Hosta pycnophylla Maekawa

Setouchi Giboshi

MEDIUM

Origin: Oshima Island, Japan.

Description: An open mound 60 in. wide × 18 in. high (150 × 45 cm). Leaf blade 9 × 8 in. (23 × 20 cm), of good substance, glaucous gray-green, thickly white-coated below, smooth, veins widely spaced, edge conspicuously rippled, leaf slightly arching, widely oval with a cuspidate tip and heart-shaped open lobes. Petiole green, with red dots. Flower funnel-shaped, purple-striped lavender, on a recumbent, leafy, red-dotted glaucous green, 30-in. (75-cm) scape from late summer to early autumn; seedpods many, fertile.

Cultivation Notes: Site in morning sun in warmer climates. Tolerates afternoon sun in cooler climates,

provided it is adequately supplied with moisture. A superb parent for white-backed, ripple-edged hostas and now the pod parent of a superb, thick, yellow-leaved hybrid, *H. 'Aliyah's Grace'. Wild specimens are much smaller than those in cultivation, although it is not an easy hosta to grow, seeming to dwindle rather than increase.

Distinguishing Features: Heavy white coating on the leaf underside.

Similar: *H. 'Paradise Red Delight' has intensely red-dotted petioles.

Sports: *H. 'High Kicker' has much frillier edges and is very slow to establish; *H. 'Ogon Setouchi', of which there are several clones, is a natural sport from which the yellow-leaved *H. 'Gilt by Association' was selfed.

Hosta pycnophylla

Hosta 'High Kicker'

Hosta rectifolia var. *rectifolia* Nakai

Tachi Giboshi

MEDIUM

Origin: Northern Honshu and Hokkaido, Japan.

Description: An upright mound 32 in. wide × 14 in. high (80 × 35 cm). Leaf blade 6 × 2¾ in. (15 × 7 cm), thin, mid-green, matt above and glossy below, veins ribbed, edge slightly undulate, leaf convex, pinched at the tip, elliptic to oval with a cuspidate tip and tapered pinched lobes. Petiole green. Flower widely funnel-shaped, purple-striped bright mauve, opening from a darker bud, on a green 39½-in. (99-cm) scape in late summer; fertile.

Cultivation Notes: Site in some morning sun except in the hottest regions. A broad-spectrum species with many attractive variegated forms not yet in commerce. The scapes are known to tower over 7 ft. (2.1 m), a characteristic that could more often be exploited in hybridizing programs.

Distinguishing Features: Tall scapes of late-flowering blooms on a low foliage mound.

Similar: *H.* 'Brian Halliwell', a hefty plant with green leaves approximately 17 in. (43 cm) long and with rhubarb-like scapes over 7 ft. (2.1 m) long, may turn out to be a new species; *H.* 'Decorata Normalis'; *H.* 'Tall Boy', a putative hybrid of *H. rectifolia* × ★*H. ventricosa*, has spectacularly tall scapes up to 70 in. (175 cm) in optimum growing conditions, with long racemes of lavender flowers in late summer.

Sports: *H.* 'Fujibotan' has superb double flowers; *H.* 'Kinbuchi Tachi' has yellow to cream margins which appear later in the season; *H.* 'Nakai' has narrow leaves with a cream margin; *H.* 'Ogon Tachi' has pale yellow leaves; *H.* 'Oze' has small to medium-sized slightly cupped green leaves with a cream margin that turns white; *H. rectifolia* 'Chionea' has white margins and is similar to ★*H.* 'Ginko Craig'; *H.* 'White Triumphator' PP12,662 has superb white flowers.

Hosta rohdeifolia f. *albopicta* Maekawa

Omoto Giboshi

SMALL—MEDIUM

Origin: Originally described from a variegated garden plant, the wild plant having green leaves and known now as *H. rohdeifolia* f. *viridis*, fid. Schmid.

Description: An upright, arching, and spreading mound 30 in. wide × 14 in. high (75 × 35 cm). Leaf blade 6½ × 2½ in. (16 × 6 cm), of average substance, mid-green irregularly margined yellow turning white, matt above and shiny below, smooth, edge almost flat, leaf slightly arching, elliptic with an obtuse tip and tapered open to slightly pinched lobes. Petiole flattish, green, outlined in creamy yellow. Flower almost bell-shaped, purple-striped lavender, opening from a ball-like bud, on an upright, leafy, 30-in. (75-cm) scape in late summer; fertile.

Cultivation Notes: Site in good light or light to moderate shade. An excellent ground cover but not a rampant increaser.

Distinguishing Features: Leaves have a fancied resembled to those of *Rohdea japonica*. The green-leaved form was introduced in 1940 by F. Maekawa.

Hosta rectifolia

Hosta rohdeifolia f. *albopicta*, the form first described

Hosta rupifraga Nakai

Hachijo Giboshi

MEDIUM

Origin: Hachijo Island, Japan.

Description: A widely overlapping mound 25 in. wide × 8–9 in. high (63 × 20–23 cm). Leaf blade 8 × 5 in. (20 × 13 cm), thick, mid-green, glossy above and waxy below, smooth, strongly veined, edge evenly rippled, leaf flat, oval to heart-shaped with a cuspidate tip and heart-shaped open to pinched lobes. Petiole green. Flower bell-shaped, purple striped, in a dense raceme, on an oblique to arching, blue-green, 18-in. (45-cm) scape in autumn; fertile.

Cultivation Notes: Site in light to moderate shade.

Distinguishing Features: Glossy, leathery leaves.

Similar: *H.* 'Maruba Iwa' has longer scapes; *H.* 'Rain Forest'; *★H.* 'Rhapsody in Blue' has leaves with a blue cast.

Hosta sieboldiana (Hooker) Engler

To Giboshi

LARGE

Origin: Central and Northern Honshu, Japan.

Description: A dense mound 60 in. wide × 24 in. high (150 × 60 cm). Leaf blade 17 × 11 in. (43 × 28 cm), thick, green with a slight gray-blue cast early in the season, slightly dimpled, strongly veined, edge slightly undulate, leaf widely oval with a cuspidate tip and heart-shaped pinched lobes. Petiole stout, light green. Flower funnel-shaped, lavender-striped near white, on an upright, glaucous green, 24- to 25-in. (60- to 63-cm) scape in midseason; seedpods many, fertile.

Cultivation Notes: Site in some morning sun in cooler climates. Slow to moderate growth rate. Pest resistant.

Distinguishing Features: Is quite different from the *H. sieboldiana* grown in most gardens today, which

Hosta rupifraga

363

are mostly forms of ★*H. sieboldiana* 'Elegans'. Many of its characteristics resemble *H. montana*, to which it is closely related.

Similar: *H. sieboldiana* 'Mira' has larger, flatter leaves.

Hosta sieboldii 'Alba' (Irving) Hara

Koba Giboshi

SMALL–MEDIUM

Origin: Sport of *H. sieboldii* var. *sieboldii*, occasionally found in the wild in Japan.

Description: A dense, spreading mound 25 in. wide × 11 in. high (63 × 28 cm). Leaf blade 5 × 2½ in. (13 × 6 cm), thin, matt mid- to dark green above and satiny, paler green below, smooth, edge slightly undulate, leaf slightly arching, widely elliptic with an acute tip and tapered open lobes. Petiole pale green. Flower widely flared, white, on a thin, upright, leafy, pale green, 24-in. (60-cm) scape in late summer; fertile.

Cultivation Notes: Site in good light to light shade all day. An excellent ground cover that is usually

Hosta sieboldiana 'Mira'

Hosta sieboldii 'Weihenstephan' is almost identical to *H. sieboldii* 'Alba'.

Hosta sieboldii 'Anne Arett'

grown in gardens for its floral display rather than its leaves.

Similar: *H. sieboldii* 'Weihenstephan' has even larger flowers, and its sport, ★*H.* 'Paradise Beach', has leaves with green margins and yellow centers; *H.* 'Snowflakes'; *H.* 'White Trumpets'.

Hosta sieboldii 'Anne Arett' (A. Arett 1975)

SMALL—MEDIUM

Origin: Sport of *H. sieboldii* 'Subcrocea'.

Description: A low, arching mound 20 in. wide × 10 in. high (50 × 25 cm). Leaf blade 5 ×1 in. (13 × 2.5 cm), very thin, smooth, golden yellow fading to chartreuse, narrowly margined white, satiny above and dull below, edge rippled, leaf arching, lanceolate with an acute tip and tapered open lobes. Petiole narrow, flattish, chartreuse yellow. Flower: see ★*H. sieboldii* var. *sieboldii*.

Cultivation Notes: Site in bright light to moderate shade to prevent the leaves from scorching. Not vigorous. Needs an abundance of food and moisture to maintain it in steady growth. Susceptible to pest damage. Use as a foreground plant in light woodland among primulas and *Adiantum pedatum*. One of the earliest introductions with this coloring and now considered a collector's plant.

Distinguishing Features: Leaf edge becomes less rippled with maturity.

Hosta sieboldii 'Hart's Tongue' (Kuk 1987)

SMALL—MEDIUM

Origin: Sport of ★*H. sieboldii* 'Kabitan'.

Description: An upright, arching mound 12 in. wide × 9–9½ in. high (30 × 23–24 cm). Leaf blade 4 × 1 in. (10 × 2.5 cm), of good substance, bright chartreuse turning olive green by midsummer, satiny above and glaucous below, dimpled, edge conspicuously rippled, leaf narrowly lanceolate with an acute tip and tapered open lobes. Petiole flattish, olive green, decurrent with the leaf blade. Flower: see ★*H. sieboldii* var. *sieboldii*.

Cultivation Notes: Viridescent. Site in light to moderate shade. Grow with hart's tongue fern (*Asplenium scolopendrium*), which it closely resembles, to produce a copycat effect.

Similar: *H.* 'Purple Lady Finger' has flatter-edged leaves and more-significant flowers.

Hosta sieboldii 'Kabitan' (Maekawa & AHS 1987)

SMALL—MEDIUM

Origin: Natural sport of ★*H. sieboldii* var. *sieboldii* found in both Japan and Europe.

Description: An arching, rippled, somewhat rhizomatous mound 32 in. wide × 14 in. high (80 × 35 cm). Leaf blade 6 × 1½ in. (15 × 4 cm) thin, chartreuse, turning rich golden yellow, narrowly and irregularly margined dark green, satiny above and

Hosta sieboldii 'Hart's Tongue'

Hosta sieboldii 'Kabitan'

shiny below, slightly dimpled when mature, edge rippled, leaf arching, lanceolate with an acute tip and tapered open lobes, almost decurrent with the petiole. Petiole flat, chartreuse, outlined in dark green. Flower: see *H. sieboldii* var. *sieboldii*.

Cultivation Notes: Site in good light to light shade. A hot, humid climate is needed to maintain its vigor, when it will increase rapidly, making it suitable as an underplanting to larger hostas or as an edging hosta. In cooler climates, where the leaves will be considerably smaller, it is best grown in a pot with plenty of food and water. Very susceptible to pest damage.

Hosta sieboldii 'First Mate'

Hosta sieboldii var. sieboldii

Similar: *H.* 'Fuji Sunrise' is smaller; *H.* 'On the Marc'; *H.* 'Peedee Gold Flash'; *H.* 'Yellow Eyes'.

Sports: ★*H.* 'Green Eyes' is a selfed *H. sieboldii* 'Kabitan' with a slightly paler leaf center; *H.* 'Green Kabitan'; *H. sieboldii* 'First Mate' has thicker leaves and is probably a tetraploid.

Hosta sieboldii var. *sieboldii* Paxton ♔

Synonym: 'Paxton's Original'

SMALL

Origin: Natural sport of the green-leaved population that is found on moors and meadowlands in many regions of Japan.

Description: A dense, spreading mound 30 in. wide × 13 in. high (75 × 33 cm). Leaf blade 6½ × 2½ in. (16 × 6 cm), of average substance, olive green, narrowly margined pure white, with some celadon streaks jetting toward the midrib, smooth, veins widely spaced, edge flat to just rippled, leaf flat to arching, elliptic with an obtuse tip and rounded pinched lobes. Petiole green, finely outlined in white. Flower widely funnel-shaped, purple-striped lilac, on a thin, upright, leafy, 25-in. (63-cm) scape from high to late summer; fertile.

Cultivation Notes: Site in morning sun or good light to light shade. Easy to grow and eventually spreads into huge clumps. A superb parent for variegated seedlings. Less often seen in domestic gardens since the advent of showier variegated introductions. Leaves emerge early.

Similar: *H.* 'Change of Tradition'; *H.* 'Cotillion'; ★*H.* 'Gaijin' is smaller; ★*H.* 'Gloriosa'; *H.* 'Silver Lance' and *H.* 'Striker' have narrower leaves.

Sports: ★*H. sieboldii* 'Kabitan'; ★*H. sieboldii* 'Shiro Kabitan (aka 'Haku Chu Han'); *H. sieboldii* 'Subcrocea'.

Hosta takahashii Araki

Shihizo Giboshi

MEDIUM

Origin: Mount Ibuki, Shiga Prefecture, Japan.

Description: An overlapping mound 20–26 in. wide × 12 in. high (50–65 × 30 cm). Leaf blade 5–8 × 5–7 in. (13–20 × 13–18 cm), of good substance, elm green, shiny above and glossy below, smooth, prominent veins deeply impressed and widely spaced, edge undulate, leaf broadly ovate with an acuminate tip and tapered to heart-shaped open to pinched lobes. Petiole upright, green with purple dots at the base, paler green above. Flower widely bell-shaped, lavender, opening from a purple-suffused bud, on a purple-suffused pedicel, at the top of an upright, leafy, purple-dotted green, 26- to 32-in. (65- to 80-cm) scape in early autumn; seedpods purple-dotted light green, partially fertile.

Cultivation Notes: Site in light to moderate shade. Related to ★*H. sieboldii* although the leaf shape is different.

Distinguishing Features: A long raceme of flowers. The anthers are also purple-dotted. Sterile bracts clasp the scape.

Similar: *H.* 'Slick Willie'; ★*H.* 'Tardiflora'; ★*H. tardiva*.

Hosta tardiva Nakai

Nankai Giboshi

SMALL–MEDIUM

Origin: Shikoku and Kyushu Islands and the Kii Peninsula, Japan.

Description: An irregular, arching mound 32 in. wide × 16 in. high (80 × 40 cm). Leaf blade 6 × 3 in. (15 × 8 cm), very thin, bright olive green, shiny above and glossy below, prominently veined, edge flat but with an occasional kink, leaf arching, narrowly oval with an acute tip and tapered pinched lobes that are mostly hidden in the foliage mound. Petiole purple-dotted green. Flower bell- to funnel-shaped, rich violet, on an upright, bare, burgundy-dotted, 24-in. (60-cm) scape in autumn; fertility uncertain.

Cultivation Notes: Rarely grown in gardens. A plant for serious collectors.

Similar: *H.* 'Leather Sheen'; *H.* 'Southern Comfort', once incorrectly thought to be *H. tardiva*; ★*H. takahashii*.

Hosta tibae Maekawa

Nagasaki Giboshi

SMALL

Origin: Nagasaki, Kyushu Island, Japan.

Description: A dense mound 44 in. wide × 16 in. high (110 × 40 cm). Leaf blade 8 × 5 in. (20 × 13 cm), of average substance, mid-green, shiny above

Hosta takahashii

Hosta tardiva

Hosta tibae

and glossy below, slightly dimpled when mature, prominently veined, edge lightly rippled, leaf flat, sometimes kinked and pinched at the tip, oval with an acute tip and heart-shaped pinched lobes. Petiole burgundy-dotted mid-green. Flower funnel-shaped, white-striped purple, disposed around an upright, leafy, 24-in. (60-cm) scape in early autumn; fertile.

Cultivation Notes: Site in light to full shade. Valuable for its late flowers.

Distinguishing Features: Thin, multibranched scapes are unusual for *Hosta*.

Hosta tsushimensis Fujita

Tsushima Giboshi

SMALL–MEDIUM

Origin: Tsushima Island, Korean Strait.

Description: A mound of noticeably upright leaves 31 in. wide × 12 in. high (78 × 30 cm). Leaf blade 7½ × 3½ in. (19 × 9 cm), thin, mid-green, satiny above and glossy below, shallow, smooth, veins noticeably ribbed, edge widely undulate, leaf elliptic to oval with an acute tip and tapered open lobes. Petiole intensely burgundy-dotted. Flower funnel-shaped, pale lavender to near white with thin purple lines, on an oblique, burgundy-dotted green, 26- to 30-in. (65- to 75-cm) scape in early autumn; fertile.

Cultivation Notes: Site in light shade. Of interest to collectors of species *Hosta* but not often grown in gardens.

Distinguishing Features: Branching scapes with sparsely displayed flowers.

Similar: ★*H. jonesii.*

Sport: ★*H.* 'Ogon Tsushima' (aka *H. tsushimensis* 'Ogon') is slightly smaller than the species.

Hosta ventricosa Stearn ♈

Murasaki Giboshi

LARGE

Origin: China and North Korea.

Description: A symmetrical mound 51 in. wide × 22 in. high (127 × 55 cm). Leaf blade 9 × 8 in. (23 × 20 cm), thin, dark spinach green, shiny above and glossy below, smooth, veins widely spaced, becoming strongly ribbed when mature, edge evenly rippled to piecrusted, leaf slightly convex with a distinct mucronate tip and heart-shaped overlapping lobes. Petiole deeply channeled, purple-dotted, shiny light green. Flower bell-shaped, rich purple to violet, on an upright then oblique, leafy, satiny, burgundy-dotted pale green, 32- to 38-in. (80- to 95-cm) scape from late summer to early autumn; fertile.

Cultivation Notes: A naturally occurring tetraploid. The only hosta known to come true from seed. Seeds are produced without fertilization by a process known as apomixis. Can be used in breeding as a pollen plant, however, and is the parent of many piecrust-leaved introductions. The very thin leaves can scorch at the edges in warmer climates, even if grown in full shade. Flowers do not begin to open until the scape is fully extended.

Hosta tsushimensis

Hosta ventricosa

Similar: *H.* 'Strawberry Delight'; *H.* 'Taffeta' is a seedling of ★*H. ventricosa* 'Aureomarginata' and has near-black leaves.

Sports: ★*H. ventricosa* 'Aureomaculata'; ★*H. ventricosa* 'Aureomarginata'; *H.* 'Sunny Disposition'.

Hosta ventricosa 'Aureomaculata' (K. Hensen & AHS 1987)

MEDIUM–LARGE

Origin: Natural sport of ★*H. ventricosa*.

Description: A diffuse mound 36 in. wide × 16 in. high (90 × 40 cm). Leaf blade 9 × 8 in. (23 × 20 cm), thin, chartreuse to yellow turning old gold, widely and irregularly margined dark spinach green, with many streaks jetting toward the midrib, shiny above and glossy below, slightly dimpled when mature, veins widely spaced, edge slightly rippled, leaf widely oval with a cuspidate tip and heart-shaped pinched lobes. Petiole chartreuse yellow, outlined in dark green. Flower: see *H. ventricosa*.

Cultivation Notes: Site in moderate shade. Slow to increase but well worth the wait. Variegation gradually fades during the summer, more rapidly in hot climates.

Similar: ★*H.* 'Flame Stitch'; ★*H.* 'Shirley'; *H.* 'Stained Satin'.

Hosta ventricosa 'Aureomarginata' (K. Hensen & AHS 1986) ♛

MEDIUM–LARGE

Origin: Natural sport of ★*H. ventricosa*.

Description: An overlapping mound 45 in. wide × 22 in. high (113 × 55 cm). Leaf blade 10 × 9 in. (25 × 23 cm), thin, glossy, dark spinach green, widely and irregularly margined yellow turning creamy white, with streaks jetting toward the midrib, dimpled when mature, edge rippled, leaf oval with a cuspidate tip and heart-shaped pinched to overlapping lobes. Petiole dark green, outlined in yellow. Flower: see *H. ventricosa*.

Hosta ventricosa 'Aureomaculata'

Cultivation Notes: Site in full shade all day. Slow to moderate growth rate. Susceptible to pest damage. A classic hosta which has never been surpassed in beauty of leaf and flower.

Sports: *H.* 'Paradise Gold Line' has a very narrow, even gold margin.

Hosta yingeri Jones

SMALL–MEDIUM

Origin: Islands off the southwest coast of Korea.

Description: A compact mound 30 in. wide × 9 in.

Hosta ventricosa 'Aureomarginata'

high (75 × 23 cm). Leaf blade 6 × 3 in. (15 × 8 cm), very thick, bright mid- to dark green, glossy above, glossy below with a white coating, smooth to slightly dimpled when mature, edge slightly undulate, leaf arching when mature, oval to wedge-shaped with an acute tip and rounded open to pinched lobes. Petiole oblique, purple-dotted green, appearing to pierce the blade to the tip. Flower thin, spider-shaped, purple, on an upright, leafy, green, 25-in. (63-cm) scape from late summer to early autumn; fertile.

Cultivation Notes: Site in good light to high, filtered shade except in cooler climates where it can tolerate morning sun. Moderate growth rate but can achieve dimensions of 36 × 18 in. (90 × 45 cm) in cultivation. Closely related to *★H. laevigata*. A superb hosta for hybridizing as it passes on its very glossy leaves and spiderlike flowers, three of its best offspring being *★H.* 'Harpoon'; *★H.* 'Sun Catcher' with lutescent bright yellow leaves; and *H.* 'Sweet Tater Pie' with thick, oval leaves in varying shades of chartreuse to gold, topped with deep purple, spiderlike flowers. Moisture at the roots is essential. Pest resistant.

Distinguishing Features: Very thick, lustrous leaves and spiderlike flowers.

Similar: *H.* 'Crystal Chimes' has pure white spiderlike flowers; *H.* 'Sun Worshipper' has greenish-gold leaves which bleach to near white; *H. yingeri* 'Lily Pad' is a seed selection from Korea with spider-shaped flowers and shiny, round leaves that have a blunt tip; *H. yingeri* 'Treasure Island' is a selected form.

Hosta yingeri

Hosta yingeri 'Treasure Island'

HOSTA HYBRIDS FOR CONNOISSEURS

Hosta 'Abba Satellite' (P. Aden N/R)

MEDIUM

Origin: Unknown.

Description: An open mound 28 in. wide × 16 in. high (70 × 40 cm). Leaf blade 6½ × 4 in. (16 × 10 cm), of good substance, yellow with the narrowest possible dark green central flash, matt above and glaucous below, seersuckered, edge almost flat, leaf slightly cupped, widely oval with a cuspidate tip and rounded open lobes. Petiole dark green, outlined in yellow. Flower: no details available.

Cultivation Notes: Site in bright morning light to moderate shade. Not available in the trade at the time of writing, but since this variation has occurred once, it can occur again.

Distinguishing Features: A central green marking that runs from the base of the leaf blade, where it feathers outwards to the tip.

Hosta 'Abiqua Ariel' (J. Hyslop/Walden-West 1999)

SMALL–MEDIUM

Origin: ★*H.* 'Aspen Gold' × *H.* 'Golden Chimes' seedling.

Description: An upright, compact mound 22 in. wide × 8 in. high (55 × 20 cm). Leaf blade 7 × 5 in. (18 × 13 cm), thick, pale grayish yellow, matt above and glaucous below, heavily seersuckered, edge almost flat, leaf cupped, widely oval with a mucronate tip and heart-shaped open lobes. Petiole dull chartreuse. Flower bell-shaped, pink to near white, in profusion, on an upright, bare, grayish yellow, 10- to 15-in. (25- to 38-cm) scape in midsummer; sterile.

Cultivation Notes: Lutescent, but never as brilliant yellow as ★*H.* 'Aspen Gold' or ★*H.* 'Midas Touch'. In cooler climates, site in morning sun to bring out the color, then light shade. Pest resistant. Rare, but worth seeking out for its unusual, subtle leaf color.

Hosta 'Abba Satellite'

Hosta 'Abiqua Ariel'

371

Distinguishing Features: Subtle grayish bloom distinguishes it from those with golden-yellow leaves.

Hosta 'Amber Maiden' (Walters Gardens 1988)

SMALL

Origin: Sport of ★*H.* 'Candy Hearts'.

Description: A dense mound 22 in. wide × 14 in. high (55 × 35 cm). Leaf blade 5 × 4 in. (13 × 10 cm), thin, dark green with a gray cast early in the season,

Hosta 'Amber Maiden'

Hosta 'Beckoning'

irregularly margined chartreuse turning yellow, with chartreuse streaks jetting toward the midrib, matt above and thinly glaucous below, edge almost flat, leaf folded to slightly cupped, widely oval with a mucronate tip and heart-shaped pinched lobes. Petiole gray-green, outlined in yellow. Flower: see *H.* 'Candy Hearts'.

Cultivation Notes: Site in light to moderate shade. Slow growing and lacking in vigor. Flowers are sterile although the parent plant is very fertile. Mostly grown as a collector's plant.

Hosta 'Beckoning' PP18,371 (T. Saville 2002)

LARGE

Origin: Sport of ★*H.* 'Blue Angel'.

Description: An overlapping mound 20–24 in. wide × 18–22 in. high (50–60 × 45–55 cm). Leaf blade 13 × 11 in. (33 × 28 cm), thick, emerging blue-gray becoming chartreuse to yellow, widely and irregularly margined blue-gray, with streaks jetting toward the midrib, matt above and glaucous below, dimpled when mature, prominently veined, edge slightly undulate, leaf folded, broadly ovate with a cuspidate tip and heart-shaped overlapping lobes. Petiole blue-gray turning chartreuse yellow. Flower: see *H.* 'Blue Angel'.

Cultivation Notes: Lutescent. Extremely sensitive to light and heat. In cooler climates the variegation does not appear until early summer when the leaf center becomes lime-green to pale yellow, whereas in hotter climates the variegation appears about three weeks after the leaves emerge and is a brighter yellow. The plant may require moving several times to different sites in the garden to achieve the best results. It may in time exceed its registered dimensions.

Distinguishing Features: Has smaller leaves and a yellow central variegation, but is not as robust as its parent.

Hosta 'Bizarre' (Kuk 1986)

SMALL

Origin: *H. sieboldii* 'Kabitan' seedling.

Description: A diffuse, upright mound 10 in. wide × 8 in. high (25 × 20 cm). Leaf blade 5 × 2½ in. (13 × 6 cm), thin, matt, bright chartreuse to muted gold, narrowly and irregularly margined pure white, dimpled to seersuckered, veins widely spaced, edge slightly undulate, leaf arching, lanceolate with an acute tip and tapered pinched lobes. Petiole narrowly channeled, chartreuse, finely outlined in white. Flower large, funnel-shaped, dark purple-striped purple, on an upright, leafy, pale chartreuse, 18-in. (45-cm) scape in late summer; fertile.

Cultivation Notes: Shade is essential as the leaves will scorch without it. Performs better in cooler gardens. Regular watering helps to keep the leaves in good condition. Increases rapidly but is not robust or easy to grow. The very thin leaves have heavy seersuckering. The tall, pale chartreuse scapes contrast effectively with the violet flower buds.

Distinguishing Features: Has much larger flowers than its parent.

Similar: *H.* 'Fresh' has smoother leaves.

Hosta 'Blue Canoe' (G. Black/P. Ruh 1999)

SMALL—MEDIUM

Origin: Seedling from an open-pollinated pod on *H. sieboldiana* 'Frances Williams', probably crossed with *H.* 'Halcyon'.

Description: An upright mound 19 in. wide × 16 in. high (48 × 40 cm). Leaf blade 6 × 3 in. (15 × 8 cm), thick, blue-green, dimpled, strongly veined, edge slightly undulate, leaf lightly twisted, deeply folded and cupped, widely oval with a mucronate tip and rounded to kinked folded lobes. Petiole light blue-green. Flower funnel-shaped, near white, subtended by long green bracts, on an upright, leafy, light green, 22-in. (55-cm) scape in midsummer; seedpods blue, fertility unknown.

Cultivation Notes: Site in shade and provide plenty of moisture. Moderate growth rate. Pest resistant. Even in cooler climates the leaf turns green early in the season, and in moderate to hot climates, it assumes chartreuse tints.

Similar: ★*H.* 'Abiqua Drinking Gourd' has a shorter, wider leaf and holds its color better; *H.* 'Kayak', a sibling, has smaller, narrower leaves.

Hosta 'Butter Rim' (A. Summers & AHS 1986)

SMALL—MEDIUM

Origin: Uncertain, although considered a ★*H. sieboldii* var. *sieboldii* derivative.

Description: A low, arching mound 33 in. wide × 13 in. high (83 × 33 cm). Leaf blade 6¾ × 2½ in. (17 × 6 cm), thin, satiny, olive green, irregularly margined yellow, with streaks jetting toward the midrib, smooth, edge rippled, leaf arching, narrowly oval with an acute to cuspidate tip and tapered open lobes. Petiole narrow, green, outlined in yellow. Flower funnel-shaped, white, on an upright, bare, green, 30-in. (75-cm) scape in high summer; fertile.

Hosta 'Blue Canoe'

Hosta 'Bizarre'

Cultivation Notes: Site in light to moderate shade. Lacks vigor and succeeds best in a warm, humid climate. Once a highly prized margined hosta, but now only of interest to collectors.

Hosta 'Butter Rim'

Sports: *H.* 'Moon Shadow' has leaves with a creamy white center and green margin.

Hosta 'Calypso' (W. & E. Lachman 1987)

SMALL

Origin: *H.* 'White Christmas' hybrid.

Description: An upright mound 18 in. wide × 10 in. high (45 × 25 cm). Leaf blade 6½ × 2½ in. (16 × 6 cm), thin, chartreuse turning yellow then ivory white, widely and irregularly margined dark green, with streaks jetting toward the midrib, matt above and thinly glaucous below, smooth, edge flat with an occasional kink, leaf arching, folded or convex, lanceolate with an acute tip and tapered open to pinched lobes. Petiole ivory white with dark green stripes. Flower funnel-shaped, lavender, on an upright, bare, ivory white, 15-in. (38-cm) scape in midsummer; fertile.

Hosta 'Calypso'

374

Cultivation Notes: Site in light to moderate shade in a hot climate, but even so it will not thrive as a garden plant and the leaves will probably scorch. Prized as a breeding plant, however.

Hosta 'Cascades' (W. & E. Lachman 1993)

MEDIUM

Origin: *H.* 'Banana Sundae' × ⋆*H. sieboldiana* 'Frances Williams'.

Description: An open, arching mound 26 in. wide × 15 in. high (65 × 38 cm). Leaf blade 11 × 4½ in. (28 × 11 cm), of thin substance, matt, ivory white, widely margined dark green, with some chartreuse streaks jetting toward the midrib, smooth, edge undulate, leaf arching toward the sometimes curved tip, oval with an acute tip and rounded open to pinched lobes. Petiole ivory white, outlined in dark green. Flower funnel-shaped, white, on a leaning, leafy, ivory white, 36-in. (90-cm) scape in early summer; fertile.

Cultivation Notes: Site in two hours of morning sun, followed by light shade, for the best results. Not always easy to grow, as it needs the summer heat of a continental climate and regular feeding to attain its optimum size. For maximum effect, use it in the center of a border of plain green- or blue-leaved hostas.

Distinguishing Features: The spectacular cascading habit shows off the color contrasts of the leaves.

Similar: *H.* 'Falling Waters' has darker green margins and streaks and is a larger plant.

Sports: *H.* 'Foxfire Zulu' has dark green leaves.

Hosta 'Chartreuse Wiggles' (P. Aden 1976)

SMALL

Origin: *H.* 'Ogon Koba' hybrid.

Description: A dense, spreading mound 25 in. wide × 10 in. high (63 × 25 cm). Leaf blade 5 × 1 in. (13 × 2.5 cm), thin, satiny, bright chartreuse to golden yellow, smooth, veins closely ribbed, edge distinctly rippled, leaf arching, elliptic with an acute tip and tapered open lobes. Petiole flattish, chartreuse. Flower bell-shaped, purple-striped lavender, on a thin, upright, bare, pale chartreuse, 18-in. (45-cm) scape in late summer; fertile.

Cultivation Notes: Thrives in a hot climate where the humidity is high and where sufficient moisture at the roots can boost its singular lack of vigor. It can be successful in cooler climates, when grown in a container, despite its somewhat rhizomatous habit. Protect from bright sunlight and strong winds. Creates a restless, sinuous effect when planted as a foreground specimen or edger accompanying larger hostas, either echoing almost linear leaves or contrasting round or heart-shaped leaves.

Similar: *H.* 'Chartreuse Waves' is wider; *H.* 'Lauren'; *H.* 'Sea Wiggles'; *H. sieboldii* 'Subcrocea' is a deeper yellow and has less marginal rippling; *H.* 'Stormy Dance' has more golden leaves; *H.* 'Yellow Submarine' is somewhat larger and easier to cultivate.

Hosta 'Cascades'

Hosta 'Chartreuse Wiggles'

Hosta 'Cherry Berry' (W. & E. Lachman 1991)

SMALL–MEDIUM

Origin: *H.* "Lachman 82-18-1" × *H.* "Lachman 81-9-2."

Description: A diffuse, upright mound 14 in. wide × 10 in. high (35 × 25 cm). Leaf blade 6 × 2½ in. (15 × 6 cm), thin, satiny, emerging yellow turning ivory white, irregularly and widely margined dark olive green, with some chartreuse streaks jetting toward the midrib, smooth, edge with occasional shallow undulations, leaf arching toward the tip, elliptic with an acute, sometimes curved or pinched tip and with tapered open lobes. Petiole flattish, pink-tinted ivory, widely outlined in dark olive green. Flower flared, violet, subtended by cream-colored bracts, on an upright, leafy, glossy, intensely burgundy-red, 28-in. (70-cm) scape in high summer; seedpods red, fertility unknown.

Cultivation Notes: Site in morning sun or very good light. Leaves widen considerably in hot climates where it grows more vigorously. Very susceptible to pest damage.

Distinguishing Features: A tricolor effect is often visible on the leaves in early to midsummer making it worthwhile to give this hosta special care. The burgundy-red scapes and red seedpods are other reasons to persevere.

Similar: *H.* 'Celebration', *H.* 'Gay Feather', and *H.* 'Goody Goody' all lack the striking red petioles, scapes, and seedpods; *H.* 'Hot Lips'; *H.* 'Joyce Trott'

has wider leaves with more undulate edges; ★*H.* 'Xanadu' has slightly larger and wider leaves.

Sports: *H.* 'Cherries Jubilee' has streaked leaves; ★*H.* 'Maraschino Cherry'.

Hosta 'Cross Stitch' (W. Zumbar/P. Ruh 1992)

LARGE

Origin: *H.* 'Hirao Supreme' selfed.

Description: A cascading mound 37 in. wide × 20 in. high (94 × 50 cm). Leaf blade 14 × 10 in. (35 × 25 cm), of good substance, glossy, rich olive green, satiny above and glossy below, edge shallowly undulate, leaf pinched along the midrib toward the tip, widely oval with a cuspidate tip and heart-shaped pinched lobes. Petiole paler green. Flower flaring, lavender, on an upright, leafy, green, 34-in. (85-cm) scape in late summer; fertile.

Cultivation Notes: Site in light to moderate shade. Moderate growth rate. Makes an interesting specimen whose leaves should be seen at close range.

Distinguishing Features: Veins have a gathered, stitchlike effect producing heavy seersuckering in the spaces in between.

Hosta 'Crystal Moon' (Tower Perennial Gardens/A. Tower 2002)

LARGE

Origin: Sport of ★*H.* 'August Moon'.

Description: An open mound 30 in. wide × 18 in. high (75 × 45 cm). Leaf blade 8½ × 6 in. (21 × 15

Hosta 'Cherry Berry'

Hosta 'Cross Stitch'

cm), of good substance, chartreuse to apple green, irregularly margined creamy white, with many celadon streaks jetting toward the midrib, smooth, veins widely spaced, edge almost flat to slightly rippled, leaf convex, heart-shaped to rounded with a recurved mucronate tip and heart-shaped pinched lobes. Petiole light green, outlined in ivory. Flower long-tubed, widely funnel-shaped, fragrant, pure white, on an upright, bare, pale green. 28-in. (70-cm) scape from mid- to high summer; fertility unknown.

Cultivation Notes: Morning sun in cooler climates. Vigorous, a moderate to rapid increaser. A superb recent introduction, still rare but deserves a higher profile.

Distinguishing Features: The flower, which has also mutated, is white, and deliciously fragrant, 2¾ in. (7 cm) diameter across the mouth of the perianth.

Similar: ★*H*. 'Fragrant Bouquet' has smaller flowers and thinner leaves.

Hosta 'Cupid's Arrow' (Walters Gardens 1988)
MEDIUM

Origin: Tissue-cultured sport of ★*H*. 'Candy Hearts'.

Description: A dense mound 18 in. wide × 10 in. high (45 × 25 cm). Leaf blade 5 × 4 in. (13 × 10 cm), of average substance, matt, ivory white, widely and irregularly margined dark green, with some chartreuse streaks jetting toward the midrib, smooth, edge kinked, leaf arching and twisted with a curved tip, widely oval with heart-shaped pinched lobes. Petiole white, finely outlined in green. Flower: see *H*. 'Candy Hearts'.

Cultivation Notes: Site in good light to moderate shade. Very slow to increase. Requires careful cultivation.

Distinguishing Features: Leaves become much wider over the years (although the plant was named when it was in its juvenile phase).

Similar: ★*H*. 'Undulata' has longer leaves with narrower margins.

Hosta 'Diana Remembered' (J. Kulpa 1997)
MEDIUM

Origin: Tissue-cultured sport of *H*. 'Seventh Heaven'.

Description: An open mound 24 in. wide × 15 in. high (60 × 38 cm). Leaf blade 7 × 6 in. (18 × 15 cm), of good substance, blue-green, widely and irregularly margined creamy white, with transitional celadon streaks jetting toward the midrib, satiny above and matt below, dimpled, veins widely spaced, edge slightly rippled, leaf folded, widely oval with a mucronate tip and heart-shaped pinched lobes. Petiole green, crisply outlined in white. Flower 3 in. (8 cm) long, tubular, fragrant, near white, waxy, on a stout, upright, leafy, green, 22-in. (55-cm) scape in late summer; fertile.

Hosta 'Crystal Moon'

Hosta 'Cupid's Arrow'

Hosta 'Diana Remembered'

Hosta 'Eleanor Lachman'

Cultivation Notes: In cool climates, site in sun for most of the day. In hotter climates, site in morning sun only and provide plenty of moisture . A vigorous, rapid increaser. This superb hosta has many attributes although it can be difficult to cultivate. A late spring frost can decimate the first flush of leaves and greatly retard and distort the second flush.

Distinguishing Features: Large, striking, variegated bracts subtend the raceme.

Similar: ★*H.* 'Crystal Moon' is more robust; *H. plantaginea* 'Ming Treasure'.

Sports: Sometimes produces sports with streaked leaves.

Hosta 'Eleanor Lachman' (W. & E. Lachman 1995)

SMALL

Origin: (★*H.* 'Neat Splash' × *H.* 'Flamboyant') × *H.* 'Robert Frost'.

Description: An open, semi-upright mound 15 in. wide × 5½ in. high (38 × 14 cm). Leaf blade 4 × 3 in. (10 × 8 cm), of heavy substance, ivory white, widely and irregularly margined blue-toned dark green with some streaking near the margin, matt above and glaucous below, smooth, veins moderately prominent, edge flat, leaf arched and slightly folded, broadly ovate, with a vestigial tip and rounded lobes. Petiole chartreuse. Flower bell-shaped, lavender, on an upright, leafy, greenish ivory 8- to 11-in. (20- to 28-cm) scape in high summer; seedpods ivory; fertile.

Cultivation Notes: Site in good light but not hot afternoon sun which can cause "melting out." Slow to increase. A delightful hosta but not always easy to grow.

Similar: *H.* 'Gene Summers'.

Sports: *H.* 'Eleanor Roosevelt' has shapely green leaves.

Hosta 'Embroidery' (P. Aden N/R)

MEDIUM

Origin: Sport induced by radiation.

Description: An upright, outward-facing mound 30 in. wide × 15 in. high (75 × 38 cm). Leaf blade 10 × 8 in. (25 × 20 cm), of average substance, yellowish white turning chartreuse to light olive green, satiny above and slightly glaucous below, seersuckered and puckered, margined with a slightly darker green stitched effect, prominent veins irregularly spaced, edge randomly rippled, leaf kinked and twisted at the tip, widely oval with a cuspidate tip and heart-shaped pinched lobes. Petiole wide, light green, faintly dotted purple near the crown. Flower funnel-shaped, near white faintly striped purple, opening from a purple-tipped bud, surrounded by prominent purple-tipped flower bracts, on a stout, oblique to drooping, leafy, green, 24-in. (60-cm) scape, purple-dotted near the crown, in high to late summer; sterile.

Cultivation Notes: Site in good light to moderate shade. A collector's plant which might best be grown with ferns or grasses rather than in a hosta border. Very prone to pest damage.

Distinguishing Features: The exaggerated stitched and crimped effect along the junction of the ¾- to 1-in. (2- to 2.5-cm) margin and the center of the leaf.

Similar: *H.* 'Collector's Banner'; ★*H.* 'Emerald Necklace'.

Sports: ★*H.* 'Green Velveteen' has smooth leaves with distinctly rippled edges.

Hosta 'Emerald Crust' (M. Zilis & T & Z Nursery 1988)

SMALL–MEDIUM

Origin: Uncertain.

Description: An overlapping mound 38 in. wide × 16 in. high (95 × 40 cm). Leaf blade 11 × 6½ in. (28 × 16 cm), of average substance, chartreuse turning ivory white, widely and irregularly margined dark

green, with streaks jetting toward the midrib, dimpled when mature, prominently veined, edge slightly rippled, leaf slightly arching, oval with a cuspidate tip and heart-shaped pinched lobes. Petiole ivory white, outlined in dark green. Flower funnel-shaped, pale lavender, on an upright, leafy, ivory, 42-in. (105-cm) scape in high summer; fertility unknown.

Cultivation Notes: Site in good light to moderate shade.

Similar: ★*H.* 'White Christmas' has more-twisted leaves of less substance.

Hosta 'Emerald Necklace' (Kuk 1994)

MEDIUM

Origin: Sport of a *H.* 'Tardiflora' seedling.

Description: A moderately dense, semi-upright mound 32 in. wide × 16 in. high (80 × 40 cm). Leaf blade 5 × 3 in. (13 × 8 cm), thick, chartreuse-white turning mid-green, widely and irregularly margined dark blue-green, satiny above and shinier below, closely veined, edge rippled, oval with an acute tip and conspicuously twisted, rounded pinched lobes. Petiole narrow, chartreuse to green. Flower funnel-shaped, violet-striped lavender, on an upright, bare, olive-green, 30-in. (75-cm) scape in late summer; fertile.

Cultivation Notes: Not a difficult hosta to cultivate in the right situation. Careful placement between too much sun and too much shade is necessary for the interesting color changes. More significant color

Hosta 'Embroidery'

Hosta 'Emerald Crust'

Hosta 'Emerald Necklace'

Hosta 'Fair Maiden'

Hosta 'Flame Stitch'

contrast in hotter climates. Grow as a foreground specimen or on a raised bed for best effect.

Distinguishing Features: The conspicuously puckered margin and the leaf center with crimping at the junction between the two give an embroidered appearance to the leaf. At its best in midsummer while the contrasting colors of the center and margin are at their height.

Similar: *H.* 'Collector's Banner'; ★*H.* 'Embroidery'.

Sport: *H.* 'Ivory Necklace' has ivory-white margins without any crimping or puckering, although the center of the leaf is seersuckered.

Hosta 'Fair Maiden' (Walters Gardens/C. Falstad 1993)

SMALL

Origin: Tissue-cultured sport of ★*H.* 'Amber Maiden'.

Description: A compact mound 18 in. wide × 14 in. high (45 × 35 cm). Leaf blade 6 × 5 in. (15 × 13 cm), of average substance, dark green, irregularly margined yellow turning ivory, with streaks jetting toward the midrib, matt above and thinly glaucous below, smooth, veins widely spaced, edge almost flat, leaf slightly cupped, widely oval with a distinct cuspidate tip and heart-shaped pinched lobes. Petiole ivory outlined in green. Flower: see ★*H.* 'Candy Hearts'.

Cultivation Notes: Site in good light to light shade. Very slow to increase and lacking in vigor, which is disappointing since it is such an attractive small hosta.

Hosta 'Flame Stitch' (Walters Gardens & C. Falstad 1991)

MEDIUM

Origin: Tissue-cultured sport of ★*H. ventricosa* 'Aureomarginata'.

Description: An open mound 24 in. wide × 18 in. high (60 × 45 cm). Leaf blade 8½ × 6½ in. (21 × 16 cm), thin, glossy, emerging chartreuse turning yellow then ivory white, widely and irregularly margined dark spinach green, with conspicuous streaks jetting toward the midrib, veins widely spaced, edge almost flat, leaf widely oval with a twisted cuspidate tip and heart-shaped open to pinched lobes. Petiole ivory, outlined in dark green, with an inner line of chartreuse. Flower: see ★*H. ventricosa*.

Cultivation Notes: Very slow and can even dwindle, although a new flush of leaves appears in mid-summer. The white leaf center can scorch unless the plant is carefully sited between good light and just enough shade. Water and feed copiously.

Distinguishing Features: The leaves are more conspicuously heart-shaped than most hostas with this leaf patterning. The heavily streaked margin is tri-tone green varying from very dark to pale chartreuse.

Similar: *H.* 'Stained Satin'.

Hosta 'Guardian Angel' (C. & R. Thompson 1995)

LARGE–VERY LARGE

Origin: Sport of *★H.* 'Blue Angel'.

Description: A moderately dense mound 36 in. wide × 24 in. high (90 × 60 cm). Leaf blade 16 × 10 in. (40 × 25 cm), thick, emerging greenish white turning light blue-green and finally mid-green, widely and irregularly margined dark blue-green, with streaks jetting toward the midrib, matt above and glaucous below, dimpled when mature, prominently veined, edge conspicuously rippled, tip twisted when young, leaf folded, widely oval with a cuspidate tip and heart-shaped overlapping lobes. Petiole chartreuse-white. Flower: see *H.* 'Blue Angel'.

Cultivation Notes: Viridescent. May need re-siting more than once to obtain the maximum effect from the unusual variegation. Divide frequently.

Distinguishing Features: The twisted appearance of the leaf is more apparent in young plants before the leaf has flattened and expanded with maturity. The variegation is not visible on the second flush of leaves.

Sports: *H.* 'American Angel' emerges in spring with broad white-centered leaves which soon turn blue-green; *H.* 'Angel Eyes'; *H.* 'Fallen Angel' has leaves that are misted gray and white before turning blue-green; *H.* 'Fire and Brimstone' has leaves streaked in three shades of green and cream (see photo on page 20).

Hosta 'Hoosier Harmony' (Indianapolis Hosta Society 1995)

MEDIUM–LARGE

Origin: Sport of *★H.* 'Royal Standard'.

Description: A lax, diffuse mound 36 in. wide × 18 in. high (90 × 45 cm). Leaf blade 8 × 6 in. (20 × 15 cm), of average substance, chartreuse to old gold, irregularly margined dark green, with streaks jetting toward the midrib, satiny above and shiny below, smooth, prominently veined, edge shallowly undulate, leaf slightly arching, folded, oval with an acute tip and tapered open lobes. Petiole chartreuse, finely outlined in dark green. Flower: see *H.* 'Royal Standard'.

Cultivation Notes: Lutescent. Site in morning sun, applying plentiful amounts of food and water. Requires heat and humidity to thrive.

Hosta 'Guardian Angel' early in the growing season

Hosta 'Hoosier Harmony'

Hosta 'Koryu'

Hosta 'Lakeside Looking Glass'

Hosta 'Lakeside Paisley Print'

Distinguishing Features: Large, white, fragrant flowers make this hosta worth the trouble of growing it.

Similar: *H. plantaginea* 'Chelsea Ore'.

Hosta 'Koryu' (S. Hirao N/R)

SMALL

Origin: Japanese gardens. Formerly known as *H.* 'Fused Veins'.

Description: A diffuse mound 15 in. wide × 7 in. high (38 × 18 cm). Leaf blade 5 × 1 in. (13 × 2.5 cm), thick, leathery, shiny light green with thick dark green margins "fused" onto the leaf surface, smooth, edge rippled, leaf twisted, narrowly lanceolate with an acute tip and tapered open lobes. Petiole light green. Flower funnel-shaped, lavender with paler petal margins, disposed around an upright, bare, light green, 12-in. (30-cm) scape from late summer to early autumn.

Cultivation Notes: Site in light to moderate shade in a raised bed or a container so that the unusual leaves can be enjoyed close up. Grown by serious hosta collectors rather than general gardeners.

Distinguishing Features: The swollen areas, which are a stable genetic trait, are more prominent in some leaves than others and give the leaf a somewhat contorted effect (*koryu* means "swollen variegation").

Similar: ★*H.* 'Emerald Necklace'; *H.* 'Hamada Contorted' may be identical.

Hosta 'Lakeside Looking Glass' (M. Chastain 1997)

MEDIUM

Origin: *H. yingeri* hybrid.

Description: A fairly dense mound 12 in. wide × 10 in. high (30 × 25 cm). Leaf blade 8 × 5½ in. (20 × 14 cm), thick, leathery dark green, shiny above and very glossy below, dimpled, light green veins widely spaced, edge rippled, leaf arching, widely elliptic with an obtuse tip and rounded pinched lobes. Petiole flattish, blue-black. Flower spider-shaped, bright purple, on an arching, very leafy, light green, 12-in. (30-cm) scape in midsummer; seedpods green, fertile.

Cultivation Notes: Site in light to full shade to keep the leaves a better color. Can be prone to late spring frost damage in colder climates. Increases rapidly if given moist, heavy loam and fed well but does not thrive everywhere.

Distinguishing Features: Very glossy, lustrous leaves. Green leafy bracts form toward the top of the flower scape, which is slightly purple-dotted at the base. The flower scape, when elongating, presents a star-burst of closely packed bracts, each one shielding an immature flower bud.

Similar: ★*H. laevigata*; *H. yingeri* 'Treasure Island'.

Hosta 'Lakeside Paisley Print' (M. Chastain 2006)

MEDIUM

Origin: Unknown.

Description: An upright mound 30 in. wide × 10 in. high (75 × 25 cm). Leaf blade 6½ × 6 in. (16 × 15 cm), of average substance, rich green with cream streaks shooting up from the base of the petiole, satiny above and matt below, dimpled to seersuckered, prominently veined, edge attractively rippled, leaf cupped, broadly ovate to heart-shaped with a mucronate tip and tapered open to pinched lobes. Petiole cream, widely outlined in green. Flower funnel-shaped, purple-striped pale lavender, on an upright, leafy, cream-colored, 21- to 24-in. (53- to 60-cm) scape in high summer; seedpods pale green, fertility not established.

Cultivation Notes: Site in moderate shade. Increases rapidly. Divide frequently to retain the striking and unusual central variegation. Still very expensive and hard to obtain.

Distinguishing Features: The flaring streaks of cream rising from the base of the leaf surrounded by a darkish green background.

Similar: ★*H.* 'Americana', a sport of *H.* 'Loyalist'; ★*H.* 'Ann Kulpa' has less-white feathering from the midrib.

Hosta 'Lucy Vitols' (M. Seaver 1989)

MEDIUM

Origin: Sport of ★*H.* 'Christmas Gold'.

Description: A congested mound 36 in. wide × 14 in. high (90 × 35 cm). Leaf blade 10 × 9 in. (25 × 23 cm), very thick, chartreuse to golden yellow, widely and irregularly margined rich blue-green, with streaks jetting toward the midrib, matt above and glaucous below, intensely seersuckered, edge slightly rippled, leaf shallowly cupped or convex, widely oval to round with a mucronate tip and heart-shaped pinched lobes. Petiole chartreuse. Flower: see *H.* 'Christmas Gold'.

Cultivation Notes: Site in morning sun except in the hottest regions. Very slow to establish and increase so a plentiful supply of water is important. Pest resistant.

Distinguishing Features: The crumpled and puckered mature leaves almost reach a state of distortion, a feature much prized by flower arrangers.

Similar: *H.* 'Spinning Wheel' has less-twisted leaves.

Hosta 'Mary Marie Ann' (L. Englerth 1982)

SMALL

Origin: Sport of *H.* 'Fortunei Aoki'.

Description: An open, dome-shaped mound 30 in. wide × 14 in. high (75 × 35 cm). Leaf blade 6½ × 3½ in. (16 × 9 cm), of average substance, emerging creamy yellow turning ivory then chartreuse to light green, with some olive green transitional

Hosta 'Lucy Vitols'

Hosta 'Mary Marie Ann'

streaks, widely margined darker green, satiny above and thinly glaucous below, veins green, edge flat to kinked with ripples on the flat of the margin, leaf narrowly oval with a curved, acute tip and rounded pinched lobes. Petiole cream, finely outlined in dark green. Flower: see ★*H.* 'Fortunei Hyacinthina'.

Cultivation Notes: Site in morning sun to maintain the yellow central variegation. The leaf blade will expand and exhibit its curious characteristics better in a hot, humid climate. Very prone to pest damage but well worth the trouble to keep the attractive leaves intact. Lovely in a round or oval, antique stone bowl.

Distinguishing Features: The leaf margin is seersuckered, growing at a different rate from the lighter center, causing the blade to twist and distort and the margin to pucker.

Similar: ★*H.* 'Little Caesar' is smaller and has paler variegation.

Hosta 'My Child Insook' (H. & D. Benedict 1995)

MEDIUM–LARGE

Origin: Sport of *H.* 'Outrageous', which is a seedling of ★*H.* 'Dorothy Benedict' × ★*H. montana* 'Aureomarginata'.

Description: A semi-upright mound 30 in. wide × 28 in. high (75 × 70 cm). Leaf blade 10 × 8 in. (25 × 20 cm), of good substance, shiny ivory white, widely and irregularly margined dark green, with chartreuse streaks jetting toward the midrib, dimpled, prominently veined, edge nearly round, lobes heart-shaped and pinched. Petiole white, finely outlined in dark

green. Flower funnel-shaped, pale lavender, on an upright, pale green, 41-in. (102-cm) scape in late summer; sterile.

Cultivation Notes: Site in light to moderate shade. Among the most beautiful of the centrally variegated hostas and, although a fairly rapid increaser, is still rare and seen only in the gardens of serious collectors.

Hosta 'Ogon Tsushima' (P. Ruh 2002)

MEDIUM

Origin: Natural sport of ★*H. tsushimensis*, found in cultivation in Japan.

Description: A diffuse, pendulous mound 26 in. wide × 10 in. high (65 × 25 cm). Leaf blade 6½ × 3 in. (16 × 8 cm), thin, chartreuse turning light yellow, matt above and shiny below, veins noticeably ribbed, edge slightly rippled, leaf arching to pendulous, widely lanceolate with an acute tip and tapered pinched lobes. Petiole long, narrow, chartreuse to yellow, with burgundy dots toward the crown. Flower large, widely funnel-shaped, with reflexed tips, white-striped purple, on an upright, sometimes branched, burgundy-dotted green, 30-in. (75-cm) scape in late summer; fertile.

Cultivation Notes: Lutescent. Tolerates sun in cooler climates. In warmer climates, site it in high, filtered shade and provide a plentiful supply of moisture. Still rare in cultivation.

Similar: ★*H.* 'Whiskey Sour' has red petioles and leaf tips from its *H.* 'Ogon Tsushima' parent, and thicker, more glossy leaves from its ★*H. yingeri* parent.

Hosta 'My Child Insook'

Hosta 'Ogon Tsushima'

Hosta **'Regalia'** (K. Anderson 1992)

LARGE

Origin: Sport of *H.* 'Krossa Regal'.

Description: An upright mound 47 in. wide × 24 in. high (118 × 60 cm). Leaf blade 10 × 7½ in. (25 × 19 cm), thick, light blue-green, widely margined dark blue-green, matt above and glaucous below, slightly dimpled when mature, prominently veined, edge heavily and widely undulate to twisted, leaf widely oval to nearly round with a mucronate tip and rounded open to pinched lobes. Petiole stout, shallow, glaucous light green. Flower: see *H.* 'Krossa Regal'.

Cultivation Notes: Site in light to moderate shade. The leaf color, especially the deeper-toned margin, will be bluer if grown in full shade. Slower to increase than its parent but this majestic yet understated hosta deserves wider recognition. Impressive in a large container. Will always be a rare hosta as it does not come true from micropropagation and needs to be increased by division.

Distinguishing Features: The 1-in. (2.5-cm) wide heavily undulate margins.

Similar: *H.* 'Emerald Necklace' has similar coloring.

Hosta **'Reversed'** (P. Aden 1978)

MEDIUM

Origin: Sport of *H.* 'Splish Splash'.

Description: A dense mound 36 in. wide × 16 in. high (90 × 40 cm). Leaf blade 8½ × 6½ in. (21 × 16 cm), thick, chartreuse yellow to ivory-green, widely and irregularly margined dark green with a blue cast

in shade, and with celadon (shade) or chartreuse (sun) streaks jetting toward the midrib, matt above and glaucous below, seersuckered, edge randomly undulate or kinked, leaf folded to slightly cupped, widely oval with a cuspidate tip and heart-shaped pinched lobes. Petiole chartreuse to ivory-green. Flower funnel-shaped, palest lavender, on an upright, bare, ivory-green, 24-in. (60-cm) scape in high summer; fertile.

Cultivation Notes: Site in light to moderate shade and provide plenty of water if moisture is not readily available from high rainfall or constant summer humidity. Slow to increase in all climates. Bluer tones in the margin are more apparent in cooler climates. Divide regularly to maintain the best balance between the margin and central variegation. Although a challenge to gardeners, it is a much-used breeding plant.

Distinguishing Features: Several forms have wider margins and more vigor.

Similar: *H.* 'Gene's Joy'; *H.* 'Lakeside Shore Master' is a faster grower and has more-turgid leaves.

Hosta **'Royal Tiara'** (M. Zilis & T & Z Nursery 1988)

SMALL

Origin: Registered as a sport of *H.* 'Golden Tiara', but now considered by the raiser to be a sport of *H.* 'Gold Edger'.

Description: A diffuse mound 16 in. wide × 8 in. high (40 × 20 cm). Leaf blade 4 × 2½ in. (10 × 6 cm), of good substance, pure white, widely and irregularly margined chartreuse to light green, with streaks

Hosta 'Regalia'

Hosta 'Reversed'

jetting toward the midrib, matt above and glaucous below, smooth, edge widely undulate causing the blade to twist, leaf oval with a cuspidate tip and tapered open to pinched lobes. Petiole white, outlined in light green. Flower: see ★*H.* 'Gold Edger'.

Cultivation Notes: Site in good light to moderate shade. More vigorous than would be expected of a hosta with such twisted leaves.

Sports: *H.* 'Royal Wave' has a grayish silver central variegation but it is usually unstable.

Hosta 'Saint Elmo's Fire' (R. Solberg 1995)

MEDIUM

Origin: Sport of ★*H.* 'Sea Fire'.

Description: A moderately dense mound 45 in. wide × 18 in. high (113 × 45 cm). Leaf blade 7 × 4 in. (18 × 10 cm), of good substance, satiny, emerging sharp acid yellow from red shoots that turn green, narrowly and irregularly margined greenish cream initially then turning pure white, with streaks jetting toward the midrib, matt above and glaucous below,

seersuckered, veins moderately prominent, edge flat to slightly undulate, leaf convex when mature, oval with a cuspidate tip and heart-shaped pinched lobes. Petiole light green, edged in creamy white. Flower funnel-shaped, pale lavender, from deeper lavender buds, on a sturdy, upright, bare, green, 30-in. (75-cm) scape from high to late summer; fertile.

Hosta 'Saint Elmo's Fire'

Hosta 'Royal Tiara'

Cultivation Notes: Viridescent. High temperatures can rapidly effect its ability to change color. Well worth the trouble of finding the most appropriate site with some morning sun followed by good light or dappled shade. An attractive hosta but not very vigorous. Prone to the drawstring effect unless given plenty of water.

Distinguishing Features: Exhibits both yellow and green leaves throughout the growing season, making a colorful display.

Similar: ★*H.* 'Electrum Stater'; ★*H.* 'Lakeside Cha Cha'; ★*H.* 'Sea Dream'; *H.* 'Zodiac'.

Hosta 'Shere Khan' (M. Zilis & W. Zumbar 1995)

MINIATURE

Origin: Sport of *H.* 'Just So'.

Description: A dense, semi-upright mound 15 in. wide × 8½ in. high (38 × 21 cm). Leaf blade 4 × 3½ in. (10 × 9 cm), thick, light green-gold, narrowly margined pure white, with some streaks jetting toward the midrib, matt above and satiny below, seersuckered, prominently veined, edge slightly undulate, leaf broadly ovate with a cuspidate tip and heart-shaped open to pinched lobes. Petiole narrow, pale green, finely outlined in white. Flower: see ★*H.* 'Little Aurora'.

Cultivation Notes: Lutescent. If sited in morning sun, the center of the leaves will turn golden yellow. Moderate growth rate. Pest resistant. Very rare, but a gem for collectors of smaller hostas.

Hosta sieboldiana 'American Masterpiece'

(V. Wade 1999)

LARGE

Origin: Natural sport of ★*H. sieboldiana* 'Northern Mist'.

Description: An open mound 36 in. wide × 24 in. high (90 × 60 cm). Leaf blade 8 × 7 in. (210 × 18 cm), thick, glaucous ivory white, very widely and irregularly margined dark blue-green, with chartreuse streaks jetting toward the midrib, intensely seersuckered, edge shallowly undulate and twisted at the curved tip, lobes heart-shaped and overlapping. Petiole ivory, outlined in blue-green. Flower: see ★*H. sieboldiana* 'Elegans'.

Cultivation Notes: Site in light shade. Although very slow to increase, shows potential vigor. Makes a superb border specimen. Needs regular division of the clump to maintain the most pleasing balance between the leaf blade and margin. Still very rare.

Distinguishing Features: Embroidered, crimped puckering, particularly on the leaf margin of mature plants. Some misting or speckling into the center of the leaf blade on young leaves. Margin is at least 2¾ in. (7 cm) wide.

Similar: *H.* 'Jim Wilkins' has less twisted leaves; *H. sieboldiana* 'Northern Mystery'.

Hosta 'Shere Khan'

Hosta sieboldiana 'American Masterpiece'

Hosta sieboldiana 'Great Expectations'

(J. Bond/P. Aden 1988)

MEDIUM–LARGE

Origin: Natural sport of ⋆*H. sieboldiana* 'Elegans'.

Description: A dense mound 45 in. wide × 25 in. high (113 × 63 cm). Leaf blade 11 × 9 in. (28 × 23 cm), thick, chartreuse yellow turning cream-yellow to ivory white, widely and irregularly margined rich blue-green, matt above and glaucous below, seersuckered, edge almost flat, leaf widely oval to nearly round with a mucronate tip and heart-shaped pinched to overlapping lobes. Petiole stout, creamy, outlined in dark blue-green. Flower: see *H. sieboldiana* 'Elegans'.

Cultivation Notes: Site in two hours of sun followed by light to moderate shade depending on the temperature and on what is desired, a harsher green-yellow or a subtler blue-chartreuse. Subtler colors can be maintained only in cooler climates. In many regions growers find it lacks vigor; indeed, it can dwindle rather than increase in size. Only the arresting tonal variegation of the leaves keeps this hosta in favor.

Sports: *H. sieboldiana* 'Dream Queen' has much wider blue-green margins and resembles ⋆*H. sieboldiana* 'Thunderbolt' as does *H. sieboldiana* 'Dream Weaver'; *H. sieboldiana* 'Great American Expectations' has greener margins and is more vigorous; *H. sieboldiana* 'Great Arrival' has golden yellow-margined blue-green leaves; *H. sieboldiana* 'Richmond Blue'.

Hosta sieboldiana 'Jim Matthews' (Mrs. J. W. Matthews/J. Matthews/B. Sligh 1998)

MEDIUM–LARGE

Origin: ⋆*H. sieboldiana* 'Elegans'.

Description: An open mound 38 in. wide × 15½ in. high (95 × 39 cm). Leaf blade 11 × 8 in. (28 × 20 cm), very thick, glaucous creamy yellow to ivory white, very widely and irregularly margined dark blue-green, with conspicuous chartreuse streaks jetting toward the midrib, prominent veins closely spaced, edge lightly undulate, leaf cupped toward the base, widely oval to round with a mucronate tip and heart-shaped overlapping lobes. Petiole cream, outlined in blue-green. Flower: see *H. sieboldiana* 'Elegans'.

Hosta sieboldiana 'Great Arrival'

Hosta sieboldiana 'Jim Matthews'

Hosta sieboldiana 'Great Expectations'

Cultivation Notes: Leaf color is more attractive if not exposed to direct sunlight since it varies considerably with differing light intensities. Slow to increase.

Similar: *H. sieboldiana* 'Dream Weaver'; ★*H. sieboldiana* 'Great Expectations' has bolder coloring and is more vigorous; ★*H. sieboldiana* 'Thunderbolt'.

Hosta sieboldiana 'Northern Mist' (C. Falstad 1988)

MEDIUM—LARGE

Origin: Tissue-cultured sport of ★*H. sieboldiana* 'Elegans'.

Description: An open mound 41 in. wide × 19 in. high (102 × 48 cm). Leaf blade 10 × 9 in. (25 × 23 cm), thick, creamy yellow turning near white speckled and misted with blue-green, widely and irregularly margined dark blue-green, with streaks in two shades of blue-green jetting toward the midrib, matt above and glaucous below, intensely seersuckered, edge undulate and twisted, leaf widely oval to nearly round, lifted at the heart-shaped pinched lobes. Petiole stout, cream, finely outlined in dark blue-green. Flower: see *H. sieboldiana* 'Elegans'.

Cultivation Notes: Site in light to moderate shade. Very slow to establish and increase. Although the colors will be richer in cooler climates, the plant will be larger and more vigorous with moderate summer heat and humidity rather than intense heat. Makes an excellent breeding plant.

Distinguishing Features: Leaves have a pebbled surface texture and the central variegation has conspicuous netted veining.

Similar: *H. sieboldiana* 'Northern Lights' is even less vigorous but equally attractive.

Sports: ★*H. sieboldiana* 'American Masterpiece'; *H. sieboldiana* 'Northern Mystery', when young, is even more streaked and mottled than its parent;

Hosta 'Spilt Milk' (M. Seaver 1999)

MEDIUM

Origin: *H.* 'Tokudama' hybrid.

Description: A mound 36 in. wide × 20 in. high (90 × 50 cm). Leaf blade 9 × 7 in. (23 × 18 cm), thick, glaucous blue-green, speckled and narrowly streaked milky white through the blade, the base color becoming slightly more chartreuse toward the

midrib, dimpled to crumpled, edge slightly rippled, leaf slightly cupped or convex, widely oval to almost round with a mucronate tip and heart-shaped overlapping lobes. Petiole shallow, blue-green. Flower tubular, near white, on an upright, bare, glaucous green, 24- to 30-in. (60- to 75-cm) scape in midsummer; seedpods green, fertile.

Cultivation Notes: Site in light to moderate shade. Very slow to increase. Although this once-rare hosta is now readily available through micropropagation, plants produced by this method vary considerably. It is therefore worth seeking out originator stock

Hosta sieboldiana 'Northern Mist'

Hosta 'Spilt Milk'

to acquire a specimen which is identical to the first introduction.

Distinguishing Features: The flecking, misting, and streaking are stable, making this hosta instantly recognizable.

Similar: *H. 'Kiwi Blue Marble' has bluer leaves.

Sports: H. 'Pistache' has cream-margined minted-green leaves.

Hosta 'Stitch in Time' PP18,061 (R. Mortko 2004)

MEDIUM

Origin: Sport of *H. 'Summer Breeze'.

Description: A dense, outward-facing mound 24 in. wide × 12 in. high (60 × 30 cm). Leaf blade 4½ × 4 in. (11 × 10 cm), of average substance, dark green, very widely margined and streaked bright yellow, matt above and satiny below, dimpled to moderately seersuckered, edge occasionally undulate, leaf nearly round with a mucronate tip and flat overlapping lobes. Petiole short, wide, dark green, outlined in yellow. Flower: see H. 'Summer Breeze'.

Cultivation Notes: Site in good light to moderate shade. The new leaves emerge solid green, the center gradually turning yellow. This hosta will always be a talking point so should be placed where its interesting leaf can be seen close up.

Distinguishing Features: The green leaf center appears to be "stitched" onto the yellow margin, the irregular vein pattern causing distortion and puckering in this area of the leaf.

Hosta 'Tattoo' PP11,603 (T. Avent 1998)

SMALL

Origin: Sport of *H. 'Little Aurora'.

Description: A compact mound 12 in. wide × 6½ in. high (30 × 16 cm). Leaf blade 2½ × 2½ in. (6 × 6 cm), of good substance, bright golden yellow, irregularly margined light green, matt above and glaucous below, edge almost flat to slightly rippled, leaf almost round with a mucronate tip and heart-shaped pinched lobes. Petiole narrow, chartreuse to yellow. Flower: see H. 'Little Aurora'.

Cultivation Notes: Site in dappled morning sun but move to a different location if it does not thrive. Keep moist and well fed. Plant as a foreground specimen or in a container so that the unusual variegation can be seen close up. A quite distinct modern hosta and much prized by collectors, but it can dwindle rather than increase. Tony Avent advises that it be grown in a container until it has bulked up into a clump, ensuring that new roots are developing.

Distinguishing Feature: Each leaf is tattooed with the outline of a dark green maple leaf in the center.

Hosta 'Tortifrons' (F. Maekawa/AHS 2002)

SMALL

Origin: Japanese gardens. A possible sport of *H. longipes.

Description: An upright mound 17 in. wide × 8½ in. high (43 × 21 cm). Leaf blade 5 × 1 in. (13 × 2.5 cm), thick, uneven, leathery, dark olive green, matt above and glossy below, edge rippled, leaf narrowly elliptic with an acute tip. Petiole narrow, dark green, decurrent with the leaf blade. Flower large, funnel-shaped, lavender, with reflexed tips, on an upright, bare, green, 15-in. (38-cm) scape in autumn; fertile.

Cultivation Notes: Site in light to moderate shade in a container or on a raised bed. Slow to increase. Cannot be successfully reproduced by micropropagation, so it remains a rarity.

Distinguishing Features: The narrow, distorted leaves are held erect and have a distinct twist caused by an aberration in the make-up of the skin cells.

Similar: *H. 'Embroidery'; *H. 'Emerald Necklace'; *H. 'Koryu'; *H. 'Praying Hands'.

Hosta 'White Christmas' (G. Krossa & Palmer/P. Ruh 1999)

MEDIUM

Origin: Stable form of H. 'Fortunei Krossa's Variegated'. Once though to be a sport of *H. 'Undulata'.

Description: An open mound 25 in. wide × 15 in. high (63 × 38 cm). Leaf blade 8½ × 4 in. (21 × 10 cm), thin, ivory to pure white, narrowly and irregularly margined dark green, with some streaks jetting toward the midrib, satiny above and shinier below, edge conspicuously twisted, leaf oval with a sometimes curved, cuspidate tip and with rounded open to pinched lobes. Petiole narrow, ivory, finely lined and margined in dark green. Flower funnel-shaped, drooping, pale lavender, on an upright, leafy, ivory, 25-in. (63-cm) scape in midsummer; sterile.

Cultivation Notes: Early to emerge. Careful siting is essential. Tolerates long periods of good light but not exposure to full sun. Succeeds best in cooler regions and requires expert cultivation.

Distinguishing Features: The raceme is often surrounded by attractive ivory bracts, finely margined dark green.

Similar: ★*H.* 'Eleanor Lachman' is smaller; ★*H.* 'Emerald Crust'; ★*H.* 'Undulata' is often confused with *H.* 'White Christmas'.

Sports: *H.* 'Christmas Charm'; ★*H.* 'Night before Christmas'; *H.* 'Robert's Rapier'; *H.* 'White Elephant'.

Hosta 'Stitch in Time'

Hosta 'Tattoo'

Hosta 'Tortifrons'

Hosta 'White Christmas'

A planting of mixed small hostas.

13
Miniature and Very Small Hostas

Since 2004, there has been an exponential rise in popularity of miniature (mini) hostas. To meet this need breeders are introducing new varieties at a rate never before seen, and many old or long-forgotten cultivars are being brought back into circulation.

The American Hosta Society in fall 2008 adjusted the dimensions of a miniature hosta as follows:

1. Leaf blade area no greater than about 4 sq. in. (26 sq. cm).
2. Leaf blade length no greater than about 4½ in. (11 cm).

Both requirements must be met. There is no restriction on clump spread.

This new Mini Group definition now embraces many of those hostas which were marginally just too large to be included formerly but have the appearance and characteristics of minis. It still leaves a number of other, also very small hostas which look like minis, but which are too large to be included in the mini definition; most of these hostas still require the same growing conditions and specially treated growing areas as minis, such as rock gardens, peat beds, and containers, together with those hostas formerly categorized as minis which have now outgrown the latest mini definition.

As an aid to gardeners who want to get the best from these sometimes-hard-to-cultivate hostas, this revision is creating a new category, Very Small, to fill the gap between those hostas which cannot easily fend for themselves in a garden border, need specialized treatment, or would look out of place, and hostas such as *Hosta* 'Golden Tiara' (small), only slightly larger, which would soon overwhelm their less vigorous brethren, and, anyway, would thrive when grown in any garden setting and with other larger hostas.

This new chapter is divided into two sections, the first being for mini hostas using the American Hosta Society's new definition, and the second being for very small hostas. The mini section includes the tiniest hostas such as *Hosta* 'Awesome', *H.* 'Daisy Doolittle', *H.* 'Lakeside Cricket', and *H.* 'Tot Tot', which always naturally fell into the older definition of a mini, and, secondly, hostas which can now be officially classed as minis, such as the larger forms and sports of *H. venusta*, *H. longissima* 'Manzo', *H.* 'Bitsy Gold', and *H.* 'Bitsy Green', and all the variegated sports from *H.* 'Baby Bunting'.

The remaining small hostas, which are too small and, on the whole, too delicate, to appear in other chapters of the book, are categorized in the second section, the Very Small Group. These include *Hosta* 'Gosan Gold Midget', *H.* 'Masquerade', *H.* 'X-Ray', the more vigorous but still diminutive *H.* 'Blue Mouse Ears' and most of its sports, *H. minor*, and *H.* 'Silver Threads and Golden Needles', all popular and desirable plants which for garden purposes thrive and look their best when grown in the same conditions as mini hostas.

CULTIVATING MINIATURE AND VERY SMALL HOSTAS

What mini and very small hostas require above all else is good drainage. This is most necessary in winter, especially if the hostas are outside in containers, but even a persistently wet summer can cause the roots to rot if moisture does not move through the soil quickly.

The ideal growing medium seems to be very fine bark chippings such as might be used for growing epiphytic orchids; however, this provides perfect drainage so that it is necessary to water the plants, if in pots, daily and often more frequently in the growing season, enriched with a feed. More practical is to amend the soil with grit, bark chippings, or other aggregate materials, and then top off the mix with gravel or bark. Perlite is also helpful in containers where the soil needs to be even more free-draining.

Some of the more robust very small hostas can also be grown in spaces in dry stone walls provided there is enough moisture. These include *Hosta* 'Crystal Dixie', *H.* 'Dew Drop', *H.* 'Gold Drop', and *H.* 'Popo'.

Hostas with rhizomatous root systems such as *Hosta venusta* adapt well to peat beds and look delightful when accompanied by *Acorus gramineus* 'Masamune'; *Asplenium ceterach*, *A. dareoides*, *A. fontanum*, and *A. trichomanes*; *Saxifraga cuneifolia* 'Variegata'; the slow-growing gray willow, *Salix* 'Boydii'; *Ulmus parviflora* 'Hokkaido'; and the white-berried *Sorbus poteriifolia* as focal points. *Hosta gracillima*, whose Japanese name Iwa Giboshi translates as "small rock hosta," and *H. pulchella*, which was found growing along rock ledges, will naturally be at home in rock garden settings, as are their sports and seedlings.

A rock garden in a dedicated area of a large border can be built up in raised beds into which parallel lines of thin walling stone have been placed vertically, 6–10 in. (15–25 cm) apart with 4–5 in. (10–13 cm) of stone above ground level. The gaps between the stones are filled in with a mix of soil-less growing media, grit and builder's sand (in the United States) or silver sand (in the United Kingdom). The area can be covered with grape waste (residue from grape pressings), bark, or gravel to deter slugs and snails. Tufa and other small rocks, local to the area, will also create a pleasing natural rock garden effect. In less formal gardens, pockets in drift-wood, decaying tree trunks, or railroad sleepers can equally well serve as attractive planting sites.

Along a shaded wall, containerized miniature gardens can be built up on different layers or levels (on bases of differing heights) or placed on an étagère or staging, with pots all the same color and shape either contrasting or echoing the background. This will create a most harmonious effect. Watering such plants at least once a day during the growing season is essential.

Before planting and feeding, ensure that all persistent perennial weeds are removed. From then on all annual weeds and newly seeded perennial weeds can be removed using tweezers, which will not disrupt the growth of these tiny plants. Use a seaweed (kelp) fertilizer every two weeks during the growing season to ensure a healthy root system is built up as soon as possible. Do not divide until the plant has at least six crowns, as small divisions frequently fail.

Because the leaves of some tiny hostas are very thin, for example, *Hosta* 'Bitsy Green', ensure that they are not exposed to too much strong sunlight. Conversely some leaves, particularly those with medio-variegation, such as *H.* 'Masquerade', need about two hours of morning sun in cooler climates, to boost their vigor.

Rigorous pest control is vital since some of these hostas are smaller than the slugs and snails themselves and can be decimated very quickly.

GROWING MINIATURE AND VERY SMALL HOSTAS IN CONTAINERS

The choice of containers in which to grow miniature and very small hostas is very wide. The suitability of the container itself depends largely on its compatibility with the surrounding hard landscaping which might be terracotta, brick, stone, concrete, or wood.

For display purposes such as horticultural shows or competitions, wide shallowish ceramic bowls, the sloping sides packed with styrofoam chips, perfectly

The miniature *Hosta* 'Popo' is ideal for rock gardens, sinks, and containers.

set off tiny hostas, especially when combined with a contrasting taller plant such as a dwarf conifer. The bowl must be at least 5½ in. (14 cm) deep to accommodate the plant's root growth.

In the garden a deeper container such as a terracotta

long tom pot (a pot which is twice as long in relation to the width at the top of the pot as compared with a normal pot) is a better solution. Sinks, troughs, boxes constructed with treated wood, and even varying lengths of vertically placed terracotta pipes can support a pot of hostas. A mulch keeps soil from splashing up and spoiling the tiny hosta leaves.

To prevent pest damage, pots should be raised about 1 in. (2.5 cm) above ground level, preferably standing on mats infused with copper wire which protrude about 1 in. (2.5 cm) outside the base of the container (mostly obtainable in the United Kingdom). Before crocks and planting mix are added to the containers, place a fine wire mesh over the drainage hole to prevent mollusk attack from below. From early spring until late autumn keep the surrounding area of hard landscaping as free as possible from pests by regularly applying a 10-percent solution of household ammonia which kills on contact and also destroys eggs hidden in holes and crevices.

A shallow ceramic bowl makes an excellent home for miniature hostas like *Hosta* 'Cat's Eye'

Hosta gracillima

MINIATURE HOSTAS

Hosta 'Abiqua Miniature' (Walden-West 1988)

Origin: Unknown.

Description: A dense mound 7 wide × 3 in. high (18 × 8 cm). Leaf blade 1½ × ⅜ in. (4 × 1 cm), of average substance, bright green, matt above, glossy and whitish green below, slightly dimpled, edge slightly undulate, leaf folded, oval to heart-shaped with an acute tip and tapered open to pinched lobes.

*An asterisk before a name indicates that the plant is fully described elsewhere in this book.

Petiole narrow, light green. Flower funnel-shaped, pale lavender, on an upright, leafy, light green, 7½-in. (19-cm) scape from mid- to late season; fertile.

Cultivation Notes: Site in two hours of morning sun in cooler climates, otherwise shade all day. Moderate growth rate. Ideal for sinks or small containers. The flowers sometimes rebloom.

Similar: ★*H. venusta*.

Hosta 'Awesome' (H. Benedict N/R)

Origin: *H. venusta* seedling.

Description: A tiny, ground-hugging mound 3 in.

wide × 1 in. high (8 × 2.5 cm). Leaf blade 1¼ × 1 in. (3 × 2.5 cm), of average substance, medium olive green, matt above and shiny below, smooth, edge slightly undulate, leaf noticeably folded, narrowly ovate with an acute tip and flat to rounded open to pinched lobes. Petiole narrow, lighter green, appearing to pierce the blade. Flower attractive, widely funnel-shaped, rich purple with a near-white throat, on an oblique, bare, ridged, 12-in. (30-cm) scape in late summer; fertile.

Cultivation Notes: Site in light to moderate shade. Slow to moderate growth rate. Watch carefully for possible slug and snail damage. Grow in a raised border dedicated to the tiniest hostas, a rock garden, or a container, not allowing it to be swamped by other plants. Do not divide until the clump is about five years old and has at least six crowns.

Distinguishing Features: A typical form of ★*H. venusta* but scaled down in size; it is about the same size, or slightly larger, than *H.* 'Uzo No Mai', which

has no petioles and is virtually impossible to keep alive for more than a year or two.

Similar: *H.* 'Paradise Puppet' is larger and the clump has a laxer habit; *H.* 'Tom Thumb' also is larger.

Hosta 'Awesome'

Hosta 'Abiqua Miniature'

Hosta 'Bitsy Green' (R. Savory 1985)

Origin: *H. longissima* hybrid.

Description: A diffuse, spreading mound 12–18 in. wide × 6 in. high (30–45 × 15 cm). Leaf blade 5 × ¾ in. (13 × 2 cm), thin, chartreuse turning yellow, matt above and shiny below, edge slightly rippled becoming more rippled at the petiole, leaf linear to lanceolate with an acute tip. Petiole decurrent with the leaf blade. Flower small, funnel-shaped, lavender, on an upright, leafy, chartreuse, 14-in. (35-cm) scape from mid- to late summer; fertile.

Cultivation Notes: Early to emerge. Tolerates some morning sun in all but the hottest climates. Moisture is its main requirement. Can be grown in a pot plunged in a pond as long as the crown is above water level. The thin leaves are vulnerable to pest damage.

Similar: *H.* 'Bitsy Gold' has yellow leaves; ★*H. longissima*.

Sports: *H.* 'Bitsy Blue' has wider, bluish leaves.

Hosta 'Cat and Mouse' (H. Hansen 2007)

Origin: Sport of ★*H.* 'Blue Mouse Ears'.

Description: A tight mound 6 in. wide × 3 in. high (15 × 8 cm). Leaf blade 2 × 2 in. (5 × 5 cm), very thick, glaucous chartreuse, irregularly margined blue-green, with many lighter streaks jetting toward the midrib, smooth, edge flat, leaf folded, round when mature with a mucronate tip and rounded open lobes. Petiole short, narrowly channeled, chartreuse, narrowly outlined in blue-green. Flower: see *H.* 'Blue Mouse Ears'.

Cultivation Notes: Lutescent variegation. Tolerates two hours of morning sun in cooler climates followed by dappled to full shade. The leaves retain the attractive variegation into early autumn. Slow to moderate growth rate. Pest resistant. This delightful recent introduction is already captivating the collectors of mini hostas. Grow in sinks, troughs, or other small containers.

Hosta 'Bitsy Green'

Hosta 'Bitsy Gold'

Hosta 'Cat and Mouse'

Hosta **Cat's Eye'** (D. Heims N/R)

Origin: Japan. Unknown, but has many characteristics of ★*H. venusta*.

Description: A low, dense mound 6 in. wide × 2 in. high (15 × 5 cm). Leaf blade 1½ × ⅜ in. (4 × 1 cm), thin, matt yellow turning ivory white, irregularly margined dark olive green, with streaks jetting toward the midrib, smooth, edge flat with an occasional kink, leaf folded, lanceolate with an acute tip and tapered open lobes. Petiole narrow, ivory white, edged in dark green. Flower tiny, widely funnel-shaped, rich purple-striped lavender, on an oblique, bare, ridged, 14-in. (35-cm) scape in late summer; fertility unknown.

Cultivation Notes: Albescent. Site in good light to light shade with some morning sun in cooler climates. Until a root system is well established, keep in a pot and do not divide. A free-draining soil will boost turgidity and vigor, but the growth rate will always be much slower than that of a green-leaved ★*H. venusta*. Best suited to a trough, sink, or rock garden in company with other miniature hostas and tiny ferns or echo the variegation with *Sagina subulata* 'Aurea'.

Distinguishing Features: A two-tone effect in the central variegation at midsummer between the first flush of leaves that then assumes a yellow variegation; the new leaves emerge with ivory-white centers.

Sports: *H.* 'Kitty Cat' has green leaves; *H.* 'Schrödinger's Cat' has streaked leaves.

Hosta **'Collector's Choice'** (W. Janssen N/R)

Origin: ★*H. venusta* ancestry.

Description: A tight mound 20 in. wide × 5 in. high (50 × 13 cm). Leaf blade 1½ × ⅜ –1 in. (4 × 1–2.5 cm), of average substance, mid-green with a blue cast, matt above and shiny below, smooth, edge slightly undulate, leaf folded, oval to nearly heart-shaped with rounded open to pinched lobes. Petiole narrow, pale green. Flower: see *H. venusta*.

Cultivation Notes: Site in light to moderate shade to retain the slight blueness in the leaves for longer. Grow with other tiny hostas in a stone sink or ceramic container.

Similar: *H.* 'Tot Tot' has green leaves with a slightly blue cast; ★*H. venusta*.

Hosta **'Country Mouse'** (H. Hansen 2007)

Origin: Sport of *H.* 'Bill Dress's Blue'.

Description: A dense, irregular mound 9 in. wide × 2½ in. high (23 × 6 cm). Leaf blade 2 × 1½ in. (5 × 4 cm), of average substance, glaucous blue-green, narrowly and irregularly margined white, dimpled, veins widely spaced, edge randomly kinked, leaf folded, broadly ovate with a cuspidate tip and flat open to pinched lobes. Petiole shallowly channeled, blue-green to gray-green, outlined in white. Flower bell-shaped, lavender-striped blushed lavender, on an oblique to upright, leafy, dark blue-green, 18-in. (45-cm) scape, towering above the leaf mound, in high summer; fertility unknown.

Hosta 'Cat's Eye'

Hosta 'Collector's Choice'

Cultivation Notes: Site in light shade. Best suited to cooler gardens since the leaves assume a gray-green cast in hotter climates. Suitable for sinks, troughs, and gravel gardens. Grow with yellow-leaved, rippled-edged miniature hostas *H.* 'Osiris Petit Prince' or *H.* 'Bitsy Gold' for contrast.

Distinguishing Features: Not as vigorous or as easy to grow as its parent, from which it differs in having creamy white margined leaves.

Similar: *★H.* 'Daisy Doolittle' is smaller; *H.* 'Woodland Elf'.

Hosta 'Country Mouse'

Hosta 'Daisy Doolittle' (G. Goodwin 2003)

Origin: Stabilized sport of a small streaked hosta of unknown parentage.

Description: Matures into a rosette-shaped mound 3–7 in. wide × 2 in. high (8–18 × 5 cm). Leaf blade 1½ × 1 in. (4 × 2.5 cm), of good substance, medium green, widely and irregularly margined cream, with celadon streaks jetting toward the midrib, matt above and satiny below, smooth, edge slightly undulate, leaf lightly folded, broadly ovate with an acute tip and rounded open lobes. Petiole flat, green, outlined in cream. Flower funnel-shaped, medium lavender to light violet, with petals fading to a lighter throat, on an upright, bare, green, 8- to 10-in. (20- to 25-cm) scape from mid- to high summer; seedpods green, fertile.

Cultivation Notes: Site in good light to moderate shade. Best suited to containers and rock gardens but is vigorous enough to hold its own at the front of a raised border.

Distinguishing Features: Some leaves are wholly celadon streaked over the base color, showing the instability of the variegation inherited from its streaked parent. The flowers are slightly fragrant.

Similar: *H.* 'Carolingian' is much slower growing; *★H.* 'Country Mouse' has rounder leaves and is not as vigorous; *H.* 'Jennifer Bailey' has longer leaves.

Hosta 'Dragon Tails' (W. Zumbar N/R)

Origin: An unknown hybrid.

Description: A low, arching mound 15 in. wide × 7

Hosta 'Bill Dress's Blue'

Hosta 'Daisy Doolittle'

in. high (38 cm × 18 cm). Leaf blade 4–5 × ¾ in. (10–13 × 2 cm), thin, yellow, matt above and shiny below, veins closely ribbed, edge distinctly rippled, leaf arching, lanceolate with an exaggeratedly extended tip. Petiole arching, narrowly channeled, pale chartreuse, decurrent with the leaf blade. Flower funnel-shaped, lavender, on an upright, bare, chartreuse, 10-in. (25-cm) scape in late summer; fertility unknown.

Cultivation Notes: Lutescent. In hotter climates, site in full shade. In cooler climates, site in dappled shade all day to prevent the color from bleaching out. Vigorous when grown in preferred shade. Increases rapidly. Suitable for sinks, troughs, and rock gardens. Lovely with *Carex firma* 'Variegata'.

Distinguishing Features: One of the best of the myriad of tiny yellow hostas both for leaf color and rippled edges.

Similar: ★*H.* 'Chartreuse Wiggles'; *H.* 'Yellow Eyes' has wider leaves, *H.* 'Yellow Ribbons'; *H.* 'Yellow Submarine'; *H.* 'Yellow Waves'.

Hosta 'Ga Ga' (R. O'Harra N/R)

Origin: Unknown.

Description: A diffuse mound 12 in. wide × 6 in. high (30 × 15 cm). Leaf blade 3 × 1 in. (8 × 2.5 cm), thin, glossy, chartreuse turning bright golden yellow, smooth, prominent veins widely spaced, edge rippled, leaf slightly arching, lanceolate with an acute tip and tapered open lobes. Petiole flattish, chartreuse to yellow. Flower tubular, opening from a purple bud, on

an upright, leafy, yellow, 10-in. (25-cm) scape in late summer; fertility unknown.

Cultivation Notes: Lutescent. Site in good light but not direct sunlight. Vivid leaf color and glossy surface will lighten up a shaded border. Still rare but deserves to be better known.

Distinguishing Features: Flowers remain closed.

Similar: *H.* 'Ground Sulphur' has slightly larger leaves; *H.* 'Kiwi Golden Thimble' has long petioles; *H.* 'Little Stiffy' has smaller, narrower leaves and is more rigid; *H.* 'O'Harra' has smaller, greener leaves.

Hosta 'Gaijin' (M. Zilis & W. Zumbar 1992)

Origin: Unknown. Wild-collected in Japan.

Description: A dense, semi-upright mound 12 in. wide × 8½ in. high (30 × 21 cm). Leaf blade 2 × ¾ in. (5 × 2 cm), of average to good substance, olive green, very narrowly margined golden yellow fading slightly as summer progresses, matt above and satiny below, smooth, edge slightly undulate, leaf arching, lanceolate to ovate when fully mature, with a cuspidate tip and tapered open to pinched lobes. Petiole narrow, green, finely outlined in yellow. Flower funnel-shaped, pale lavender, opening from a violet bud, on a semi-upright to upright, bare, green, 10- to 14-in. (25- to 35-cm) scape randomly through the summer; seedpods green, fertile.

Cultivation Notes: Site in dappled to moderate shade in a rock garden or as an edging plant. Also suitable for a dedicated border for the smallest hostas

Hosta 'Dragon Tails'

Hosta 'Ga Ga'

although it will soon outstrip most others and will need regular division to keep in check. Robust and a moderate increaser. Also holds its own at the front of a raised bed. Currently having a resurgence in popularity.

Distinguishing Features: The flowers are widely spaced down the scape. There can be repeat bloom in late autumn.

Similar: ★*H.* 'Vera Verde' is slightly larger and has a more stoloniferous habit.

Hosta gracillima Maekawa

Hime Iwa Giboshi

Origin: Shikoku Island, Japan.

Description: A sinuous, dense, rhizomatous, overlapping mound 10 in. wide × 3 in. high (25 × 8 cm). Leaf blade up to 2 in. × ¾ in. (5 cm × 2 cm), thin, mid-green, shiny above and very shiny below, smooth, edge rippled, leaf elliptic to lanceolate with a gracefully curved acuminate tip and slightly decurrent lobes. Petiole up to 2½ in. (6 cm) long, slender, deeply grooved, light green, profusely dotted burgundy. Flower widely funnel-shaped, dark lavender with a star-shaped white center and reflexed tips, sparsely arranged, disposed to one side of an erect or slightly oblique, burgundy-dotted green, 10- to 12-in. (25- to 30-cm) scape in early autumn; seedpods green, small, cylindrical, fertile.

Cultivation Notes: Site in light to moderate shade at the front of a raised border with accompanying small plants or, better still, in a dedicated border with other mini hostas, such as blue-leaved *H.* 'Bill Dress's Blue' or the green-margined, yellow-centered ★*H.* 'Cracker Crumbs'. Just as delightful grown as a single specimen in a container. The parent of a number of other miniature hostas.

Similar: *H.* 'Rock Princess' has larger leaves.

Sports: *H. gracillima* 'Alba' has white flowers, is rare

Hosta 'Gaijin'

in cultivation, and is similar to, but smaller than, ★*H. gracillima* 'Sugar Plum Fairy'; *H. gracillima* 'Kifuku-rin Ko Mame' (syn. 'Variegata') has white-margined green leaves; *H. gracillima* 'Saizaki Hime Iwa' has golden-yellow leaves and is very rare in cultivation.

Hosta 'Green Eyes' (H. & D. Benedict 1990)

Origin: ★*H. sieboldii* 'Kabitan' selfed.

Description: A dense mound 15 in. wide × 4 in. high (38 × 10 cm). Leaf blade 2½ × 1 in. (6 × 2.5 cm), of average substance, chartreuse to golden yellow, very narrowly and randomly margined dark emerald green, occasionally streaked, matt above and glossy below, deeply impressed veins widely spaced, moderately dimpled when mature, edge undulate, leaf lightly folded, twisted toward the tip, lobes tapered and open to pinched. Petiole narrowly channeled, chartreuse, outlined in green. Flower funnel-shaped, deep purple-striped violet, opening from a deep purple bud, on an upright, leafy, pale green, 15-in. (38-cm) scape in late summer; seedpods brownish purple, fertile.

Cultivation Notes: Lutescent, but the leaf color dulls as summer progresses. Site in light to moderate shade in a rock garden, raised bed, or border dedicated to very small and mini hostas or use as an edging plant. Moderate to rapid growth rate.

Distinguishing Features: Much more robust and a better garden plant than its parent; the leaves are slightly wider and shorter.

Similar: *H.* 'Green with Envy' has thinner, but slightly larger leaves, is very vigorous, and increases rapidly; *H.* 'Twist of Lime' has a narrower leaf blade and is a more subdued color.

Sports: *H.* 'Yellow Eyes'.

Hosta 'Imp' (H. Hansen 2006)

Origin: ((*H.* 'Yellow Splash' × ★*H. tibae*) × ★*H. venusta*) × (★*H. venusta* × ★*H.* 'Shining Tot').

Description: A dense mound 7 in. wide × 3 in. high (18 × 8 cm). Leaf blade 2 × 1 in. (5 × 2.5 cm), thick, dark olive green, narrowly margined cream turning white, with slight feathering at the junction between the margin and base color, matt above and glossy below, smooth, edge lightly rippled, leaf folded, ovate with an acute tip and tapered open to pinched lobes.

Hosta gracillima

Hosta 'Green Eyes'

Hosta 'Imp'

Petiole olive green, finely outlined in creamy ivory. Flower funnel-shaped, pale lavender, on an upright, bare, green, 15- to 16-in. (38- to 40-cm) scape in high summer; seedpods green, fertile.

Cultivation Notes: Site in good light to full shade. Does not thrive in all gardens but seems to enjoy a cooler climate. Moderate growth rate. A superb recent introduction for the fairy garden, rock garden, or container.

Distinguishing Features: The turgidity, thickness, and smoothness of the leaves.

Similar: *H. venusta* 'Kifukurin' has longer leaves in a laxer clump.

Hosta 'Kinbotan' (P. Ruh 2002)

Origin: *H. venusta* seedling from Japan.

Description: A compact mound 8½ in. wide × 4 in. high (21 × 10 cm). Leaf blade 2 × 1 in. (5 × 2.5 cm), of average substance, mid-green, narrowly margined golden yellow turning almost light green, with many streaks jetting toward the midrib, smooth, edge slightly undulate to kinked, leaf folded, oval with a cuspidate tip and tapered open lobes. Petiole narrow, green, outlined in yellow. Flower funnel-shaped, rich lavender, on an upright, bare, leafy, green, 15-in. (38-cm) scape from mid- to high summer; fertile.

Cultivation Notes: Site in good light to light shade. Keep in a pot until the root system is well established. Best grown in a container, sink, or trough with other tiny hostas. Slow to increase and not easy to maintain in vigorous growth.

Distinguishing Features: The scapes tower above the low-growing leaf mound.

Similar: ★*H.* 'Gaijin' is slightly larger; ★*H.* 'Orphan Annie' is more vigorous; *H.* 'Rock Island Line' has longer leaves.

Hosta 'Lakeside Cricket' (M. Chastain 2003)

Origin: *H.* 'Lakeside Knickknack' hybrid.

Description: A dense, upright mound 3 in. wide × 2½ in. high (8 × 6 cm). Leaf blade 1¾ × ¾ in. (4.5 × 2 cm), of average substance, chartreuse yellow turning ivory, crisply margined olive green, with occasional chartreuse streaks jetting toward the midrib, matt above and satiny below, edge almost flat, leaf flat to lightly cupped, ovate with an obtuse tip and tapered open lobes. Petiole very narrowly channeled, ivory, outlined in green. Flower funnel-shaped, pale lavender, on an upright, leafy, chartreuse-ivory, 6- to 7-in. (15- to 18-cm) scape in midsummer; fertility unknown.

Cultivation Notes: In cooler climates, site in two hours of dappled shade to boost vigor, then full shade.

Hosta 'Kinbotan'

Hosta 'Lakeside Cricket'

Grow with other mini hostas in a dedicated border or in a container. Divide as soon as reversion in the leaves appears, which is likely as the parent is streaked and very unstable. Moderate growth rate. Seems more robust than many other centrally variegated mini hostas.

Distinguishing Features: Differs from the parent in having clearly defined variegation and no streaking.

Similar: ★*H*. 'Cat's Eye' is smaller and far more difficult to cultivate.

Hosta '**Lakeside Elfin Fire**' (M. Chastain 2000)

Origin: *H*. 'Little White Lines' seedling.

Description: An open, upright mound 10 in. wide × 5 in. high (25 × 13 cm). An open, upright mound. Leaf blade 2½ × ¾ in. (6 × 2 cm), of average substance, matt, ivory randomly flecked olive green, irregularly margined olive green, with parallel streaks along the base color, dimpled, edge rippled, leaf lanceolate with an acute tip, the blade decurrent with the petiole in juvenile plants, tapered when mature. Petiole ivory, dotted in red, outlined and streaked in green. Flower funnel-shaped, lavender, on an upright, bare, ivory, 16- to 18-in. (40- to 45-cm) scape from high to late summer; fertility unknown.

Cultivation Notes: Site in two hours of morning sun in cooler climates to boost vigor. Moderate

growth rate. Grow with *Saxifraga stolonifera* or *Heuchera* 'Petite Marbled Burgundy'.

Distinguishing Features: Has less green streaking than the parent.

Similar: ★*H*. 'Masquerade' has less flecking.

Hosta '**Little Bo Peep**' (Kuk 1991)

Origin: *H*. 'Neat Splash' hybrid.

Description: A dense mound 8½ in. wide × 3½ in. high (21 × 9 cm). Leaf blade 3½ × 1¼ in. (9 × 3 cm), thin, glossy, bright green, widely and irregularly margined creamy white, prominently veined, edge with occasional undulations, leaf arching, lanceolate with an acute tip and tapered pinched lobes. Petiole green, outlined in creamy white. Flower tubular, rich violet-purple, on an upright, leafy, green, 8½-in. (21-cm) scape in late summer; seedpods striped maroon and green, fertile.

Cultivation Notes: Site in light to moderate shade all day. Increases reasonably rapidly. Good in a pot or a sink garden, especially if contrasted with a hosta with heart-shaped leaves of a single color. Can easily exceed its registered dimensions.

Similar: ★*H*. 'Neat Splash' is more rhizomatous in habit; *H*. 'Striker'.

Hosta '**Little Caesar**' (D. Ward/I. Chrystal/S. Bond 2000)

Origin: *H*. 'Breeder's Choice' seedling.

Description: An upright mound 12 in. wide × 5 in. high (30 × 13 cm). Leaf blade 3 × 1½ in. (8 × 4 cm), of good substance, ivory white, irregularly margined

Hosta 'Lakeside Elfin Fire'

Hosta 'Little Bo Peep'

mid-green, satiny above and glossy below, smooth, edge slightly rippled, leaf undulate to twisted, folded, lanceolate with a cuspidate tip and wedge-shaped to tapered open lobes. Petiole ivory, outlined in green. Flower tubular, violet-striped lavender, on an upright, leafy, light green, 8- to 10-in. (20- to 25-cm) scape from mid- to high summer; fertility unknown.

Cultivation Notes: Among the best of the smaller white-centered, green-margined hostas. Increases rapidly. Has unusually good substance.

Distinguishing Features: Leaves have a more pronounced twist when young.

Hosta 'Little Caesar'

Hosta 'Little Jim'

Similar: ★*H.* 'Medusa' has narrower leaves in a denser mound; *H.* 'Mountain Fog'; ★*H.* 'Surprised by Joy' has less twisted leaves and a creamier colored central variegation, and is a mini version of ★*H.* 'Whirlwind'.

Hosta 'Little Jim' (H. Benedict 1986)

Origin: Sport of ★*H.* 'Saishu Jima'.

Description: A low mound 6 in. wide × 5 in. high (15 × 13 cm). Leaf blade 3 × ¾ in. (8 × 2 cm), of average substance, dark olive green, randomly streaked and splashed yellow, cream, and white, satiny above and shiny below, veins closely ribbed, edge rippled, leaf slightly arching, lanceolate with an acute tip and tapered open lobes. Petiole dark green, finely outlined in cream. Flower funnel-shaped, white-striped lavender, on an upright, bare, olive-green, 12-in. (30-cm) scape in late summer; fertile.

Cultivation Notes: Site in light to moderate shade. Keep potted until the root system is fully established, then plant in a larger container, rock garden, or gravel garden. An excellent breeding plant.

Hosta 'Masquerade' (D. Grenfell N/R)

Origin: Possibly a seedling of ★*H. sieboldii* × ★*H. venusta*. First known as *H. venusta* 'Variegated'.

Description: A dense mound 15 in. wide × 5 in. high (38 × 13 cm). Leaf blade 3½ × 1¼ in. (9 × 3 cm), thin, pure white, irregularly margined dark green, with streaks jetting toward the midrib, matt above and satiny below, smooth, edge widely rippled or kinked, leaf folded, elliptic with an acute tip and tapered pinched lobes. Petiole ivory white, outlined in dark green. Flower funnel-shaped, lavender, striped purple inside, on a thin, upright, leafy, chartreuse, 12-in. (30-cm) scape in midsummer; fertile.

Cultivation Notes: Site in light to moderate shade. Variegation is likely to fade to green in hot climates and the plant will start to produce leaves with flecking in the central variegation. Its main disadvantage is the strong tendency to stabilize, thus producing larger green leaves or streaked and flecked green leaves marring the attractive clump. Grow in rock gardens, sinks, or troughs. Do not divide until a root system is fully established.

Similar: *H.* 'Island Charm' has slightly larger leaves; ★*H.* 'Pinwheel' has flatter, more-twisted leaves; *H. venusta* 'Crater's Heart' is smaller.

Sports: *H.* 'Munchkin' and *H.* 'Vanessa' both have green leaves.

Hosta 'Orphan Annie' (H. Hansen 2002)

Origin: Possibly a natural sport of *H. venusta* from Japan where it is known as Otome Giboshi Fukurin.

Description: An upright mound 6½ in. wide × 3 in. high (16 × 8 cm). Leaf blade 2 × 1 in. (5 × 2.5 cm), of average substance, dark olive green, regularly margined and streaked parchment white, with streaks jetting toward the midrib, matt above and satiny below, smooth, edge flat, leaf folded, widely elliptic with an acute tip and tapered open lobes. Petiole narrow, olive green, finely outlined in parchment white. Flower: see *H. venusta*.

Cultivation Notes: Site in good light to moderate shade. More vigorous than *H.* 'Cat's Eye', but still needs special care and attention. Grow in a container for several seasons to allow a good root system to develop. It should then thrive in a border dedicated to miniature and very small hostas sheltered from hot sun and cold winds. A superb, tiny, rapidly growing hosta but still very rare. It has been known in Japan

Hosta 'Orphan Annie'

Hosta 'Masquerade'

since the early 1990s but only reached the United States about 10 years later.

Distinguishing Features: The rigid leaves have a very perky appearance.

Similar: *H.* 'Cookie Crumbs'; ★*H.* 'Daisy Doolittle'.

Hosta 'Pandora's Box' (H. Hansen & Shady Oaks Nursery 1996)

Origin: Tissue-cultured sport of ★*H.* 'Baby Bunting'.

Description: A loose, diffuse mound 10 in. wide × 4 in. high (25 × 10 cm). Leaf blade 2½ × 1½ in. (6 × 4 cm), thick, glaucous palest chartreuse to creamy white, irregularly margined dark gray-green, with transitional chartreuse streaks jetting toward the midrib, dimpled, edge almost flat, leaf cupped or convex, widely oval to nearly round with a mucronate tip and heart-shaped pinched to folded lobes. Petiole creamy chartreuse, distinctly outlined in green. Flower: see *H.* 'Baby Bunting'.

Cultivation Notes: Emerges early. Site in good light but in high shade to retain the attractive blue cast to the leaf margins. Establish in a container before planting out. Slow to increase; do not divide until the root system is fully developed. Easily reverts to a plain green leaf, so regular division of the clump

is essential. Not an easy hosta to cultivate but well worth any extra trouble taken to ensure that it thrives. Plant to cascade over a small rock for a pleasing effect.

Distinguishing Features: Flower scape is pale pink, and the white-margined buds and the bracts are outlined in green.

Similar: *H.* 'Cameo' has leaves that are streaked blue-green, white, cream, chartreuse, and gold.

Hosta 'Popo' (R. O'Harra/R. Riehl 1993)

Origin: Unknown.

Description: A dense mound 15 in. wide × 7 in. high (38 × 18 cm). Leaf blade 2 × 1½ in. (5 × 4 cm), of good substance, light blue-gray, smooth, edge flat, leaf slightly folded, widely oval with a cuspidate tip. Petiole gray-green. Flower funnel-shaped, pale lavender to near white, on an upright, bare, light green, 12-in. (30-cm) scape in late summer; fertile.

Cultivation Notes: Site in morning sun in cooler climates to boost the vigor, then dappled to light shade. Ideal for rock gardens, sinks, and containers.

Similar: *H.* 'Peedee Graymulkin'; *H.* 'Vercades Two'.

Hosta pulchella Fujita

Ubatake Giboshi

Origin: Mount Ubatake, Kyushu Island, Japan.

Description: An open mound 8 in. wide × 4 in. high (20 × 10 cm). Leaf blade 1½ × ¾ in. (4 × 2 cm), leathery, shiny, mid- to dark green above, pale green below, smooth, edge widely undulate,

Hosta 'Pandora's Box'

Hosta 'Popo'

leaf slightly arching, oval with a cuspidate tip and heart-shaped pinched lobes. Petiole green, dotted in purple on the back, appearing to pierce the blade. Flower funnel-shaped, purple, on an oblique, leafy, burgundy-stained green, 4¾- to 12-in. (12- to 30-cm) scape in early and midsummer; fertile.

Cultivation Notes: Site in light shade all day. Ideal in sinks or small containers with other tiny hostas. The parent of many popular small-leaved hostas.

Distinguishing Features: Blooms very early.

Similar: *H.* 'Academy Verdant Verge' has larger, more undulate leaves; *H.* 'Baby Kim'; ★*H. gracillima*; *H. gracillima* 'Sugar Plum Fairy'; *H. pulchella* 'Bedspread'.

Sports: *H. pulchella* 'Kifukurin Ubatake', of which *H.* 'Sparky' is similar, has creamy yellow-margined leaves; *H.* 'Spartan Arrow'.

Hosta 'Teeny-weeny Bikini' (E. Elslager 2000)

Origin: *H.* 'Aoba Tsugaru Komachi' selfed.

Description: An unruly mound 8 in. wide × 4 in. high (20 × 10 cm). Leaf blade 2¼ × 1¾ in (5.5 × 4.5 cm), thin, chartreuse yellow turning ivory white, irregularly and narrowly margined olive green, with some chartreuse streaks jetting toward the midrib, matt above and satiny below, smooth, veins widely spaced, edge slightly undulate, leaf ovate with an acute tip and tapered open lobes. Petiole ivory, finely outlined and striped in chartreuse and olive green. Flower funnel-shaped, mauve, opening from a purple bud, on an upright, streaky cream, 9-in. (23-cm) scape from

mid- to late summer; seedpods reddish, fertile.

Cultivation Notes: Site in dappled to full shade even in cool climates, otherwise it can "melt out" if the sunshine is strong. The leaves on mature plants are considerably wider than in juvenile plants. Divide frequently to prevent reversion. Vigorous.

Distinguishing Features: Very brightly colored foliage for a miniature hosta, with different color tones in the variegation on the first and second flush of leaves.

Similar: ★*H.* 'Peanut' has a darker green leaf margin.

Sports: *H.* 'Greenie Weenie Bikini'.

Hosta pulchella 'Kifukurin Ubatake'

Hosta 'Teeny-weeny Bikini'

Hosta pulchella

Hosta 'Tet-A-Poo' (P. Aden 1976)

Origin: *H. venusta* × *H.* 'Blue Cadet'.

Description: A low, dense mound 12 in. wide × 3 in. high (30 × 8 cm). Leaf blade 1½ × ¾ in. (4 × 1 cm), of good substance, blue-green, smooth, edge almost flat with an occasional kink, leaf folded, oval with a cuspidate tip and tapered open to pinched lobes. Petiole shallow, green-blue. Flower funnel-shaped, near white, on an upright, bare, light green, 3½-in. (9-cm) scape in midseason; fertility unknown.

Cultivation Notes: Site in some morning sun in cooler climates. Ideal for sink and container growing. Best in a pot until the root system is well established. Among the smallest hostas and now very rare.

Distinguishing Features: The blue-toned leaves are most unusual for a hosta of this size.

Similar: *H.* 'Lakeside Neat Petite' has larger leaves; *H.* 'Tot Tot'.

Hosta 'Tet-A-Poo'

Hosta 'Tiny Tears' (R. Savory 1977)

Origin: *H. venusta* hybrid.

Description: A dense mound 6 in. wide × 2 in. high (15 × 5 cm). Leaf blade 1½ × 1 in. (4 × 2.5 cm), of average substance, olive green, glossy above and matt below, smooth, veins widely spaced, edge widely kinked, leaf folded in young plants, ovate with a cuspidate tip and tapered pinched lobes. Petiole narrow, green. Flower funnel-shaped, purple, on an oblique to upright, leafy, light green, 10-in. (25-cm) scape in early summer; seedpods green, fertile.

Hosta 'Tiny Tears'

Cultivation Notes: Site in dappled to moderate shade. Grow in sinks, troughs, or rock gardens. Increases well and has produced some exceptionally good sports.

Distinguishing Features: The teardrop-shaped leaves.

Similar: Some forms of ★*H. venusta*, including *H.* 'Elsley Runner' which has slightly larger leaves.

Sports: *H.* 'Bread Crumbs' has green-margined ivory leaves and is one of the smallest cultivars; *H.* 'Cookie Crumbs' has white-margined green leaves; *H.* 'Croutons' has streaked leaves; *H.* 'Tears of Joy' has noticeably folded green leaves.

Hosta venusta Maekawa ♛

Otome Giboshi

Origin: Cheju Island, Korea.

Description: A dense, spreading mound 10 in. wide × 2¾ in. high (25 × 7 cm). Leaf blade 1¼ × ⅜–¾ in. (3 × 1–2 cm), of average substance, mid- to dark green, matt above and shiny below, smooth, edge slightly undulate, leaf folded, widely oval with an acute tip and rounded to flat open to pinched lobes. Petiole narrow, lighter green, appearing to pierce the blade. Flower attractive, widely funnel-shaped, rich purple with a near-white throat, on an oblique, bare, ridged, 14-in. (35-cm) scape in late summer; fertile.

Cultivation Notes: Site in light to moderate shade. Increases rapidly. A very variable species in leaf size and shape. More suitable for small containers and rock

Hosta venusta 'Ogon Otome'

Hosta venusta

gardens than a border, where it is likely to become swamped by larger plants.

Similar: *H.* 'Paradise Puppet' is a seedling with ridged scapes; *H.* 'Springarn's Japan' has tiny green leaves; ★*H.* 'Tiny Tears' has teardrop-shaped leaves.

Sports: *H.* 'Elsley Runner' is a selection with larger

Hosta 'Yakushima Mizu'

leaves; *H.* 'Thumb Nail' and *H.* 'Suzuki Thumb-nail' are identical to *H. venusta*, differing only in the shade of lavender of the flowers; *H. venusta* 'Crater's Heart' (white center, green-flecked variegation) and *H. venusta* 'Crater's Rim' (white margins) both have teardrop-shaped leaves; *H. venusta* 'Ogon Otome'; *H. venusta* 'Red Tubes' has a pinkish-red pedicel and flower tube.

Hosta 'Yakushima Mizu' (Benedict N/R)

Origin: Yakushima Island, Japan.

Description: A flattish, diffuse mound 14 in. wide × 6½ in. high (35 × 16 cm). Leaf blade 2¾ × ¾ in. (7 × 2 cm), thin, mid- to shiny dark green, edge rippled, leaf lanceolate with an acute tip and tapered open lobes. Petiole pale green, appearing to pierce the blade. Flower funnel-shaped, lavender, sparsely disposed on an upright, bare, green, 10-in. (25-cm) scape in late summer; fertile.

Cultivation Notes: Site in dappled to full shade. Suitable as an edging along a raised border. Probably a form of ★*H. gracillima* (fide Schmid).

Similar: ★*H.* 'Saishu Jima'.

Hosta 'Dixie Chick'

VERY SMALL HOSTAS

Hosta 'Abiqua Ground Cover' (Walden-West 1988)

Origin: Unknown.

Description: A rhizomatous mound 12 in. wide × 9 in. high (30 × 23 cm). Leaf blade 2½ × 2 in. (6 × 5 cm), of average substance, gray-green, smooth, veins widely spaced, edge slightly undulate, leaf slightly folded, widely oval with a mucronate tip and heart-shaped pinched lobes. Petiole light gray-green. Flower

bell-shaped, lavender, on an upright or oblique, leafy, glaucous gray-green, 15-in. (38-cm) scape in high summer; fertile.

Cultivation Notes: Site in two hours of morning sun in cooler climates, otherwise good light or moderate shade all day. Vigorous, a rapid increaser. A superb hosta for ground cover although not forming dense mounds.

Hosta 'Baby Bunting' (R. Savory 1982)

Origin: *H.* 'Rough Waters' hybrid.

Description: A dense, rounded mound 12 in. wide × 8 in. high (30 × 20 cm). Leaf blade 3½ × 3½ in. (9 × 9 cm), thick, gray-blue, seersuckered, nearly round with a mucronate tip and deeply heart-shaped pinched lobes. Petiole narrow, gray-green. Flower bell-shaped, pale lavender, on an oblique, bare, green, 18-in. (45-cm) scape in midsummer; fertile.

Cultivation Notes: Leaves turn green in very bright light and always become dark green by the end of the season. Grow in a container or as an edging plant in bright light to light shade. Water sparingly until the root system is established. Slow to increase. Pest resistant. Performs better in cooler climates. The parent of several superb, even smaller-leaved sports.

Distinguishing Feature: Among the smallest glaucous-leaved hostas to have distinctly corrugated leaves.

Similar: *H.* 'Blue Beard' has smaller, richer blue leaves; *H.* 'First Class' has greener leaves; ★*H.* 'Tet-A-Poo'.

Sports: *H.* 'Cameo' has a wide yellow margin; *H.* 'Cherish' has dark green-margined streaked yellow leaves which fade to near white by midsummer; *H.* 'Hope' has a yellow-green margin and is not vigorous; ★*H.* 'Pandora's Box'. All of these sports are Minis.

Hosta 'Blue Mouse Ears' (E. & J. Deckert 2000)

Origin: Sport of ★*H.* 'Blue Cadet'.

Description: An open mound of horizontal leaves 11 in. wide × 6½ in. high (28 × 16 cm). Leaf blade 2–3

Hosta 'Abiqua Ground Cover'

Hosta 'Cherish'

Hosta 'Baby Bunting'

Hosta 'Hope'

413

× 2–3 in. (5–8 × 5–8 cm), very thick, almost rubbery, rich blue-green, some dimpling, edge almost flat, leaf shallowly cupped, oval when young, nearly round with a mucronate tip when mature, lobes heart-shaped and open. Petiole stout, shallow, dark green. Flower: bell-shaped, rich violet-striped lavender, in superb clusters, on a thick, upright, leafy, pale green, 8½-in. (21-cm) scape from mid- to high summer; sterile.

Cultivation Notes: Site in some morning sun in cooler climates or in good light to light shade. Moderate growth rate. Reasonably pest tolerant. An excellent specimen for a rock garden, gravel bed, or a container. Already an iconic hosta with many excellent qualities. Named Hosta of the Year by the American Hosta Growers Association in 2008. Has recently spawned a number of exciting sports.

Hosta 'Blue Mouse Ears'

Hosta 'Mighty Mouse'

Distinguishing Features: Racemes are striking especially when in bud. Buds are held horizontally and swell up like mini-balloons before partially opening.

Similar: ★*H.* 'Baby Bunting'; ★*H.* 'Popo'.

Sports: *H.* 'Blue Mouse Ears Supreme' and ★*H.* 'Royal Mouse Ears' have streaked leaves; ★*H.* 'Cat and Mouse'; *H.* 'Green Mouse Ears'; *H.* 'Mighty Mouse' and *H.* 'Snow Mouse' have cream margins.

Hosta 'Cheatin Heart' (W. Zumbar 1995)

Origin: Seedling of *H.* "Subcrocea F2" × *H.* 'Birchwood Gem'.

Description: A compact mound 18 in. wide × 8½ in. high (45 × 21 cm). Leaf blade 3 × 2 in. (8 × 5 cm), thin, matt, chartreuse turning rich golden yellow, slightly dimpled, veins green, edge rippled, leaf folded, oval with a cuspidate tip and heart-shaped to flat pinched lobes. Petiole narrow, pale green. Flower tubular, lavender- on an upright, bare, yellow, 7- to 10-in. (18- to 25-cm) scape from mid- to high summer; fertile.

Cultivation Notes: Site in two hours of morning sun, followed by light shade. Vigorous and exceeds its registered dimensions if conditions are favorable. Color can intensify to orange-gold in sunlight. Thought to have a diploid leaf edge and a tetraploid leaf center. Ideal for a rock garden with dwarf variegated *Saxifraga* ×*urbium* at its feet.

Distinguishing Features: Light sprinkling of red speckles on petiole and scape.

Hosta 'Cheatin Heart'

Similar: *H.* 'Boyz Toys' has leaves with less-rippled margins and small, deep purple flowers.

Sports: *H.* 'Faithful Heart' has green-margined yellow leaves with rippled margins that emphasize the green color, and its sport, *H.* 'Heartbroken', has viridescent, golden-yellow leaves; *H.* 'Illicit Affair' has yellow-margined leaves with centers that gradually becoming dark green; ★*H.* 'Silver Threads and Golden Needles'.

Hosta 'Cracker Crumbs' (R. Solberg 2002)

Origin: Sport of *H.* 'Shiny Penny'.

Description: A low mound 12 in. wide × 6½ in. high (30 × 16 cm). Leaf blade 3 × 2 in. (8 × 5 cm), of good substance, glossy, copper-tinted golden yellow, irregularly margined dark green, with streaks jetting toward the midrib, smooth, prominently veined, edge widely rippled, leaf oval with a cuspidate tip and heart-shaped pinched lobes. Petiole short, chartreuse. Flower funnel-shaped, lavender, on an upright, leafy, chartreuse, 18-in. (45-cm) scape in late summer; seedpods chartreuse, fertility unknown.

Cultivation Notes: Site in morning sun and apply plenty of water. Increases rapidly. Excellent on a raised bed and at the front of a border or in a gravel garden but also but ideal for sinks and troughs. One of the very best of the smaller hostas.

Distinguishing Features: The contrasting dark green margins appear to have been painted onto the leaf. Some residual chartreuse coloring remains at the base of the leaf blade.

Similar: *H.* 'Baby Sunspot' is very rare; *H.* 'Mini Edged'.

Sports: *H.* 'Plug Nickel' has green leaves.

Hosta 'Crepe Soul' (Naylor Creek Nursery N/R)

Origin: Seedling from an open-pollinated streaked *H.* 'Crepe Suzette'.

Description: An upright mound 15 in. wide × 7 in. high (38 × 8 cm). Leaf blade 4 × 1 in. (10 × 2.5 cm), thick, mid- to dark green, widely margined creamy white, with transitional celadon streaking toward the midrib, matt to satiny above and glossy below, dimpled, edge deeply rippled, leaf widely elliptic to oval with an obtuse tip and tapered open lobes. Petiole short, flat, green, widely outlined in ivory white. Flower funnel-shaped, dark lavender, on an upright, leafy, green, 10-in. (25-cm) scape in midsummer; fertile.

Cultivation Notes: Site in light to full shade. Moderate growth rate. Ideal for a rock garden. Easily exceeds the raiser's published dimensions.

Distinguishing Features: The goffering or crimping on the leaf margin continues down the petiole but is less marked as the leaf widens with maturity. The regular, wide, creamy white margin offers a striking effect.

Similar: ★*H.* 'Crepe Suzette' has shorter, wider leaves.

Hosta 'Dixie Chick' (T. Avent 1999)

Origin: ★*H.* 'Masquerade' × ★*H.* 'Invincible'.

Description: A spreading mound 10 in. wide × 4 in.

Hosta 'Cracker Crumbs'

Hosta 'Crepe Soul'

high (25 × 10 cm). Leaf blade 3½ × 1½ in. (9 × 4 cm), leathery, medium green, narrowly margined cream to ivory white with some random streaking, glossy above and matt below, smooth, edge slightly rippled, leaf widely lanceolate with an acute tip and rounded open lobes. Petiole green, finely outlined in white, appearing to pierce the blade. Flower large, tubular, pale lavender, on an upright, bare, green, 12-in. (30-cm) scape in late summer; sterile.

Hosta 'Dixie Chick'

Cultivation Notes: Site in morning sun in cooler climates. Increases rapidly. Makes a useful edging plant. Contrasts well with larger hostas in a border. Often exceeds its registered dimensions.

Distinguishing Features: Green-flecked leaf margin and a leaf tip that can be conspicuously curved.

Similar: *H.* 'Alakazaam' and *H.* 'Herbie' do not have green-speckled margins.

Sports: *H.* 'Crystal Dixie' (aka 'Per') has green leaves, *H.* 'Dixie Chickadee' has a green flecked near-white central variegation and also exceeds its registered dimensions as it matures.

Hosta 'Emeralds and Rubies' (J. Dishon 1994)

Origin: *H.* 'Emerald Carpet' hybrid.

Description: An arching, upright, rhizomatous mound 12 in. wide × 6 in. high (30 × 15 cm). Leaf blade 3 × 1 in. (8 × 2.5 cm), of average substance, mid-green, matt above and glossy below, veins widely spaced, edge slightly rippled, leaf arching, lanceolate with an acute tip and tapered open lobes. Petiole arching, bright red. Flower tubular, purple-striped lavender, on an upright, bare, dark red, 20-in. (50-cm) scape in midsummer; fertile.

Cultivation Notes: Site in light to moderate shade. Moderate growth rate. Grow at eye level so as to appreciate the startlingly red petiole and scape.

Distinguishing Features: The red coloring in the petiole and scape is solid rather than dotted or streaked.

Hosta 'Dixie Chickadee'

Hosta 'Emeralds and Rubies'

Hosta 'Fireworks' **PP16,062** (Walters Gardens 2001)

Origin: Sport of *H.* 'Loyalist'.

Description: An upright, open mound 8–10 in. wide × 7 in. high (20–25 × 18 cm). Leaf blade 5–6 × 1½ in. (13–15 × 4 cm), of good substance, satiny, ivory white, irregularly margined and streaked dark green with some paler green streaks, smooth, edge flat to kinked, leaf folded, lanceolate with an acute tip and tapered open lobes. Petiole ivory, outlined and streaked in dark green. Flower: see ★*H.* 'Francee'.

Cultivation Notes: In cooler climates, site in two hours of morning sun to dappled shade to encourage vigor, otherwise in dappled to full shade. Moderate growth rate. Can exceed its registered dimensions. Grow in rock gardens, fairy gardens, or containers with other very small or miniature hostas.

Distinguishing Features: Smaller than its parent, with sharp contrast between the base color and the marginal variegation.

Similar: ★*H.* 'Lakeside Elfin Fire' has random green flecks in the ivory leaf base color.

Hosta 'Gold Drop' (K. Anderson 1977)

Origin: ★*H. venusta* × ★*H.* 'August Moon'.

Description: An asymmetrical mound 18 in. wide × 5–6½ in. high (45 × 13–16 cm). Leaf blade 2 × 1¼ in. (5 × 3 cm), of moderate substance, chartreuse to muted golden yellow, matt above and thinly glaucous below, smooth becoming slightly dimpled when mature, edge almost flat, leaf folded, oval to heart-shaped with a cuspidate tip and heart-shaped open to pinched lobes. Petiole narrow, chartreuse. Flower near bell-shaped, pale lavender, produced in abundance, on a narrow, oblique to upright, leafy, chartreuse, 10- to 15-in. (25- to 38-cm) scape from mid- to late summer; fertile.

Cultivation Notes: Lutescent. Tolerates sun. Easy to grow and soon exceed its registered dimensions. A useful edging hosta. Has produced many sports and seedlings.

Similar: *H.* 'Honey Moon'; *H.* 'Midwest Magic'.

Sports: *H.* 'Dew Drop' has green leaves with a narrow ivory-white margin; *H.* 'Drip Drop' has chartreuse-white margins'; *H.* 'Gum Drop' has pale

Hosta 'Gold Drop'

Hosta 'Fireworks'

Hosta 'Dew Drop'

417

green-gray leaves and its sport, *H.* 'Forest Shadow', green leaves edged and streaked dark blue-green; *H.* 'Peedee Absinth' has slightly larger, glossier leaves; *H.* 'Pooh Bear' and ★*H.* 'Tick Tock' have green-margined yellow leaves'; *H.* 'Sun Drop' has superb yellow-margined dark blue-green leaves.

Hosta 'Gosan Gold Midget' (W. G. Schmid 1989)

Origin: ★*H. venusta* × ★*H.* 'Golden Prayers'.

Description: A tight mound 5 in. wide × 3 in. high (13 × 8 cm). Leaf blade 1½ × ⅜–1 in. (4 × 1–2.5 cm), of average substance, glossy, yellow turning chartreuse, slightly dimpled when mature, edge flat, leaf oval with an obtuse tip and tapered open lobes. Petiole flattish, yellow turning chartreuse. Flower flaring, lavender, on an upright, bare, sometimes branching, pale chartreuse, 6- to 10-in. (15- to 25-cm) scape in high summer; fertile.

Cultivation Notes: Viridescent. Site in some morning sun to maintain the leaf color. Grow in a fairy garden or rock garden, or at the front of a border taking care not to swamp it with much larger plants.

Hosta 'Hidden Cove' (G. Foster/A. Malloy 1998)

Origin: Unknown.

Description: An upright, diffuse mound 10 in. wide × 4 in. high (25 × 10 cm). Leaf blade 3 × 1½ in. (8 × 4 cm), of average substance, emerging bright chartreuse green becoming rich golden yellow, widely and irregularly margined dark olive green, with pale chartreuse streaks jetting toward the midrib, matt above and shiny below, veins deeply impressed, edge slightly undulate, leaf slightly twisted toward the tip, widely lanceolate to ovate with a cuspidate tip and rounded open to pinched lobes. Petiole narrowly channeled, pale green, finely outlined in olive green. Flower funnel-shaped, purple-striped pale lavender, opening from a deeper lavender bud, on an upright, leafy, green, 15- to 18-in. (38- to 45-cm) scape in midsummer.

Cultivation Notes: Site in light shade all day. Far exceeds its registered dimensions, especially if given fertile, loamy soil and adequate moisture. Lovely with *H.* 'Bluebeard'.

Distinguishing Features: The colorful but unstable leaf markings.

Similar: *H.* 'Lakeside Little Tuft'.

Sports: *H.* 'Hideout' has sinuous white leaves widely margined olive green; *H.* 'Smuggler's Cove' has green leaves; *H.* 'Valley's Secret Cove' has ivory variegation.

Hosta 'Lakeside Zinger' (M. Chastain 1998)

Origin: Unknown.

Description: A low, dense mound 9 in. wide × 6½ in. high (23 × 16 cm). Leaf blade 3 × 1½ in. (8 × 4 cm), thin, satiny, olive green, irregularly margined

Hosta 'Gosan Gold Midget'

Hosta 'Hidden Cove'

pure white, with streaks jetting toward the midrib, smooth, edge randomly undulate, leaf oval with a cuspidate tip and rounded open lobes. Petiole shallow, green, clearly outlined in white. Flower tubular, pale lavender, on an upright, dark, leafy, green, 11- to 18-in. (29- to 45-cm) scape from mid- to high summer; fertile.

Cultivation Notes: Site in good light to moderate shade. Increases rapidly. Can develop entirely green leaves, so regular division of the clump is essential.

Distinguishing Features: Green dots on the leaf margin. Large conspicuous variegated flower bracts.

Hosta 'Lemon Lime' (R. Savory 1988)

Origin: ★*H. sieboldii* var. *sieboldii* derivative.

Description: A tight, dense mound 36 in. wide × 12 in. high (90 × 30 cm). Leaf blade 3 × 1 in. (8 × 2.5 cm), thin, chartreuse turning yellow toward the edges, matt above, glossy and whitish green below, prominently veined, edge rippled, leaf folded, widely lanceolate with an acute tip and rounded to tapered open lobes. Petiole narrow, green. Flower funnel-shaped, deep purple-striped rich violet, opening from a green bud, on an upright, bare, green, 12- to 18-in. (30- to 45-cm) scape in midsummer; fertile.

Cultivation Notes: Does not tolerate sun. Vigorous, one of the fastest-growing hostas. Can easily exceed its registered dimensions. Three flushes of leaves may be produced each season. Some rebloom is possible in late summer if the first scapes are cut to the ground

after flowering. Leaves remain chartreuse unless the hosta is grown in bright light.

Distinguishing Features: Tall scapes rising above dense carpets of pointed leaves.

Similar: *H.* 'Chartreuse Waves'; ★*H.* 'Feather Boa'; *H.* 'Hydon Sunset' does not have purple-dotted petioles; *H.* 'Ogon Koba'.

Sports: *H.* 'Iced Lemon' has white-margined green leaves; *H.* 'Lemon Frost' is as vigorous as its parent; *H.* 'Lemon Sorbet' has white-margined chartreuse leaves; *H.* 'Twist of Lime'.

Hosta 'Limey Lisa' (W. Zumbar N/R)

Origin: Open-pollinated hybrid derived from *H.* 'Ogon Koba'.

Description: A flattish, open mound 26 in. wide × 12 in. high (65 × 30 cm). Leaf blade 2¾ × 2 in.

Hosta 'Limey Lisa'

Hosta 'Lakeside Zinger'

Hosta 'Lemon Lime'

419

(7 × 5 cm), thick, green-chartreuse, matt to satiny above and glossy below, dimpled when mature, veins widely spaced, edge flat but kinked toward the lobes, leaf slightly cupped, round to spoon-shaped with a mucronate tip and heart-shaped open to pinched

Hosta 'Little Jay', juvenile

Hosta 'Little Jay', mature

lobes. Petiole long, flat, pale green. Flower lavender, in mid- to late summer; fertility unknown.

Cultivation Notes: Viridescent. Site in good light but not direct sun except in cooler climates. Fast growing. Ideal for sinks and containers.

Distinguishing Features: Spoon-cupped tiny leaves that remain lime green.

Hosta 'Little Jay' PP19,539 (J. van den Top/D. Van Eechaute 2004)

Origin: Sport of *H.* 'Beauty Little Blue Streaked'.

Description: A rhizomatous mound 7 in. wide × 4 in. high (18 × 10 cm). Leaf blade 3½ × 1 in. (9 × 2.5 cm), of average substance, matt, ivory, narrowly and irregularly margined and streaked medium blue-influenced green, veins deeply impressed, edge rippled between the blade and petiole in juvenile plants, leaf lightly folded, lanceolate becoming ovate, twisted with an acute tip, the blade decurrent with the petiole in juvenile plants. Petiole ivory, with random green lines and streaks. Flower funnel-shaped, pale lavender, on an upright, leafy, ivory, 8- to 10-in. (20- to 24-cm) scape from mid- to high summer; fertility unknown.

Cultivation Notes: Site in morning sun in cooler climates to boost its vigor, elsewhere in dappled to full shade all day. Moderate to rapid growth rate. Soon exceeds its registered dimensions. One of the best and most attractive hostas of this type. Grow with ★*H.* 'Mighty Mite' for contrast in leaf shape.

Distinguishing Features: The blue-toned green leaf edge looks its best early in the season. The leaf widens and flattens as it matures, the lobes becoming tapered.

Similar: ★*H. longissima* 'Manzo' does not have a blue cast in the green margins.

Sports: *H.* 'Little Treasure' has a much wider leaf margin.

Hosta 'Little Wonder' (W. & E. Lachman 1989)

Origin: *H.* 'Neat Splash' seedling.

Description: A low, dense mound 12 in. wide × 5–6 in. high (30 × 13–15). Leaf blade 3 × 2 in. (8 × 5 cm), of average substance, olive green, irregularly margined cream turning white, with some chartreuse streaks, matt above and satiny below, smooth, edge flat to barely undulate, leaf slightly arching, elongate to ovate with an acute tip and sharply tapered open lobes. Petiole narrowly channeled, olive green, dotted in red, finely outlined in cream. Flower funnel-shaped, bright violet, disposed at right angles to an semi-erect to upright, narrow, leafy, red-dotted olive-brown, 14- to 16-in. (35- to 40-cm) scape from high to late summer; sterile.

Cultivation Notes: Site in high, filtered light to moderate shade. A superb rock garden, edging, or ground cover hosta. Probably too vigorous to grow with other very small and miniature hostas in a container.

Similar: *H.* 'Lakeside Miss Muffet' has slightly cupped leaves with wider margins; *H.* 'Lakeside Toy Treasure'; *H.* 'Little White Lines' has rounder, paler green leaves.

Sport: A streaked form exists.

Hosta longissima **'Manzo'** (N/R)

Origin: Japanese sport of ★*H. longissima.*

Description: An upright, widely diffuse mound 10 in. wide × 5 in. high (25 × 13 cm). Leaf blade 4½ × ¾

in. (11 × 2 cm), of average substance, cream turning ivory flecked green, irregularly margined and streaked dark olive green, matt above and shiny below, smooth, edge randomly rippled to kinked depending upon maturity of the clump, leaf linear to lanceolate, twisted toward the slightly recurved acute tip. Petiole

Hosta longissima 'Manzo', recently reclassified as a mini

Hosta 'Little Wonder'

ivory, outlined in green, decurrent with the leaf blade. Flower: see *H. longissima*.

Cultivation Notes: Site in shade all day. Needs an abundance of water at its roots. Is likely to exceed the given measurements.

Similar: *H.* 'Silver Streak' has wider leaves.

Hosta 'Medusa' (R. Herold 1993)

Origin: *★H.* 'Neat Splash' × *★H. gracillima*.

Description: An unruly mound 12 in. wide × 6 high (30 × 15 cm). Leaf blade 4 × 1 in. (10 × 2.5 cm), thin, ivory to pale chartreuse, widely and irregularly margined and splashed emerald green and olive green, matt above and satiny below, smooth, edge widely rippled, leaf folded, oblique to upward-facing, lanceolate with an acuminate tip and tapered open lobes. Petiole rippled, shallow, ivory, widely outlined in two shades of green. Flower funnel-shaped, deep lavender with purple stripes inside, opening from a green bud, on an upright, leafy, chartreuse, 15-in. (38-cm) scape, purple-dotted at the base, in late summer; fertile.

Cultivation Notes: Site in good light to moderate shade. Grow in a pot until the root system is well established before planting out. Best suited to a rock garden or small container with small, round-leaved hostas for contrast.

Distinguishing Features: The leaves are strongly undulate to twisted which causes the base of the blade to fold in the center; the leaves become flatter and wider as the plant matures. Variegated leafy bracts are clasped to the scapes.

Hosta minor Nakai

Keirin Giboshi

Origin: Korea.

Description: A spreading mound 22 in. wide × 8½ in. high (55 × 21 cm). Leaf blade 3½ × 2½ in. (9 × 6 cm), of average substance, mid- to dark green, matt above, shiny and whitish below, edge undulate, leaf arching, slightly folded, oval with a curved tip and tapered open lobes. Petiole narrow, purple-dotted green. Flower funnel-shaped, light violet, widely disposed on an upright, thin, leafy, ridged, green, 18- to 24-in. (45- to 60-cm) scape in midsummer; fertile.

Cultivation Notes: Site in light to moderate shade. Superb trusses of flowers. Very variable in the wild and often wrongly named in cultivation. Ideal for rock and sink gardens and other containers but will also thrive at the front of the border.

Distinguishing Features: Ridged, hollow scapes. Faint purple dotting at the scape base. Reblooming flowers.

Similar: *★H. capitata* and *★H. nakaiana* are larger; *★H. venusta* is usually smaller.

Hosta 'Ops' (A. Malloy 2001)

Origin: *H.* 'Flamboyant' hybrid.

Description: A dense, spreading mound 12 in. wide × 5 in. high. (30 × 13 cm). Leaf blade 2½ × 2 in. (6 × 5 cm), of average substance, satiny, medium green, irregularly margined deep cream turning white, with some chartreuse streaking, smooth, veins widely spaced, edge shallowly undulate, leaf broadly ovate

Hosta 'Medusa'

Hosta minor

with a cuspidate tip and flat to heart-shaped pinched lobes. Petiole open, shallow, green, outlined in near white. Flower funnel-shaped, pale lavender, on an upright, bare, green, 13- to 15-in. (33- to 38-cm) scape from early to midsummer; fertility unknown.

Cultivation Notes: Site in good light to dappled shade. A vigorous, moderately fast-increasing little hosta with a better constitution than many earlier introductions. Best in a raised bed with other small hostas, ferns, and heucheras, or as a container specimen.

Hosta 'Paradise Sunset' (M. Fransen N/R)

Origin: Sport of *H.* 'Hydon Sunset'.

Description: A low, dense mound 14 in. wide × 8 in. high (35 cm × 20 cm). Leaf blade 2½ × 1½ in. (6 × 4 cm), of average substance, mid- to dark olive green, irregularly margined bright golden yellow, with some streaks jetting toward the midrib, matt above and satiny below, smooth, edge rippled, leaf folded, arching, ovate with an acute tip and tapered open lobes. Petiole narrow, dark green, finely outlined in yellow. Flower funnel-shaped, purple, on a narrow, upright, bare, very dark green, 15- to 18-in. (38- to 45-cm) scape in late summer; fertile.

Cultivation Notes: Site in dappled to full shade in a rock garden or raised border. The viridescent margin becomes dull pale green as summer progresses. Has a tendency to revert so frequent division is essential. Moderate to rapid growth rate.

Similar: The very rare yellow-margined form of ★*H. gracillima*, which has narrower leaves.

Hosta 'Peanut' (J. Schwarz 2002)

Origin: Unknown.

Description: A wide-spreading, unruly mound 9 in. wide × 5 in. high (23 × 13 cm). Leaf blade 3½ in. × 2 in. (9 × 5 cm), of good substance, matt, chartreuse to ivory turning pure white, irregularly margined and randomly streaked and striped dark olive green and chartreuse, seersuckered to pebbled, edge undulate, leaf folded, twisted toward the tip, broadly oval with a cuspidate tip and tapered to pinched lobes which eventually become heart-shaped. Petiole flat, ivory, randomly outlined with light and dark green streaks. Flower bell-shaped, purple-striped rich violet, with white markings

Hosta 'Ops'

Hosta 'Paradise Sunset' reverting to *H.* 'Hydon Sunset'

Hosta 'Peanut'

on the petal reverse, opening from a deep violet bud, on a stout, upright, pale green to ivory, 16-in. (40-cm) scape, with variegated leafy bracts, in high and late summer; seeds rare, fertility unknown.

Cultivation Notes: Site in good light to light shade. Ideal for containers since the leaves eventually become attractively heart-shaped exhibiting dark green flecking toward the margin. Moderate growth rate. Divide frequently. The flowers are among the most spectacular of any miniature and the thin leaf tips are echoed in the leafy scape bracts. A superb tiny hosta which won Best Seedling Award at an American Hosta Society's *First Look* event.

Distinguishing Features: A highly colorful tri-tone effect along the marginal area can be observed showing spinach green, olive green, and chartreuse stripes bleeding into the white base color.

Similar: *H.* 'Lakeside Dot Com'.

Hosta 'Pinwheel' (R. Savory 1983)

Origin: Sport of a *H. venusta* seedling.

Description: A low mound 10 in. wide × 7 in. high (25 × 18 cm). Leaf blade 4 × 1½ in. (10 × 4 cm), of average substance, ivory white, irregularly margined mid-green, matt above and satiny below, smooth, edge almost flat, leaf folded or twisted, widely oval with a cuspidate tip and rounded open lobes. Petiole ivory, finely outlined in green. Flower funnel-shaped, lavender, on an upright, bare, ivory, 10-in. (25-cm) scape in midseason; fertility unknown.

Cultivation Notes: Slow to emerge in spring. Site in light to moderate shade. Slow to moderate growth rate. Protect from pest damage. Best established in a pot before planting into a rock or sink garden or into a larger container. Lovely with *Saxifraga stolonifera*.

Distinguishing Features: The twisted leaves form a pinwheel pattern but they become flatter and wider as the plant matures.

Similar: *H.* 'Apple Court' has slightly larger, more twisted leaves.

Hosta 'Pixie Vamp' (D. & J. Ward 1996)

Origin: *H.* 'Pin Stripe' hybrid.

Description: A low, dense mound 12 in. wide × 6 in. high (30 × 15 cm). Leaf blade 2½ × 2 in. (6 × 5 cm), of average substance, dark green, widely and irregularly margined cream to white, with many celadon streaks jetting toward the midrib, matt above and satiny below, smooth, edge slightly rippled, leaf nearly round with a cuspidate tip and heart-shaped pinched lobes. Petiole narrow, green, outlined in cream. Flower funnel-shaped, deep purple, opening from a purple bud, on a thin, upright, leafy, mahogany, 13-in. (33-cm) scape in high summer; sterile.

Cultivation Notes: Site in good light to moderate shade. Slow to average growth rate. A superb front-of-the-border hosta which deserves to be better known.

Distinguishing Feature: Near black scapes and dark purple buds contrast well with the wide light margins.

Hosta 'Pinwheel'

Hosta 'Pixie Vamp'

Hosta 'Royal Mouse Ears' (E. & J. Deckert 2004)

Origin: Sport of *★H*. 'Blue Mouse Ears'.

Description: A low, open mound 9 in. wide × 5 in. high (23 × 13 cm). Leaf blade 2½ × 2 in (6 × 5 cm), thick, blue-green, streaked chartreuse yellow and cream, matt above and glaucous below, smooth, edge flat, leaf slightly arching in its juvenile state, becoming cupped when mature, broadly ovate to nearly round with a vestigial tip and tapered open lobes. Petiole short, flattish, blue-green. Flower: see *H*. 'Blue Mouse Ears'.

Cultivation Notes: Site in moderate shade in rock gardens, raised borders, or areas dedicated to very small and miniature hostas. Moderate growth rate. One of the most prized sports of *★H*. 'Blue Mouse Ears' since, being streaked, it produces interesting sports thus increasing the range of the amazingly good Mouse Ears group.

Distinguishing Features: Leaves sometimes have blue-green margins enclosing the streaked portion of the leaf, which is more cream than green. Sometimes the background of the whole leaf is blue-green with random, paler streaking.

Sports: *H*. 'Frosted Mouse Ears' has ivory-margined blue-green leaves; *H*. 'Holy Mouse Ears' has cream leaves with a blue-green margin.

Hosta 'Saishu Jima' (R. Davidson & A. Summers/P. Ruh 2002)

Origin: Unknown but probably a form of *★H*. *sieboldii* var. *sieboldii*.

Description: An upright mound 20 in. wide × 8 in. high (50 × 20 cm). An upright mound. Leaf blade 3½ × ¾ in. (9 × 1 cm), of average substance, dark green, glossy above and shiny below, smooth, edge rippled when mature, leaf arching, lanceolate with an acute tip and tapered open lobes. Petiole green. Flower bell-shaped, purple-striped lavender, produced in abundance, on an upright, bare, pale green, 6- to 12-in. (15- to 30-cm) scape from late summer to early autumn; fertile although the flowers do not open properly.

Cultivation Notes: Site in light to moderate shade. Fast growing. Ideal for edging or for tubs and containers but also holds its own in borders if not swamped by larger plants. Sometimes reblooming occurs.

Distinguishing Features: Distinctly rippled edges which take time to develop.

Similar: An unnamed variant of *★H*. 'Saishu Jima', whose flowers remain closed, still very rare; *★H*. 'Yakushima Mizu'.

Sports: *★H*. 'Little Jim'.

Hosta 'Shining Tot' (P. Aden 1982)

Origin: *★H*. *venusta* × *H*. 'Rockmaster'.

Description: A low, tight mound 14 in. wide × 3½ in. high (35 × 9 cm). Leaf blade 3 × 2 in. (8 × 5 cm), of good substance, glossy, dark olive green, smooth, edge almost flat with an occasional small kink, leaf folded, ovate with a cuspidate tip and tapered open to

Hosta 'Royal Mouse Ears'

Hosta 'Saishu Jima'

425

pinched lobes. Petiole light olive green. Flower funnel-shaped, purple-striped lavender, on an oblique, leafy, green, 16-in. (40-cm) scape in high summer; fertile.

Cultivation Notes: Tolerates some sun in cooler climates, otherwise site in dappled to light shade. Moderate to good growth rate. An excellent parent which has produced many good cultivars. One of the most vigorous and reliable of the miniature hostas. Exhibits many characteristics of *H. pulchella*; even though it was registered with ★*H. venusta* as the pod parent, this is unlikely.

Distinguishing Features: The highly glossy leaves, a trait which is usually passed on to its offspring.

Similar: ★*H. pulchella*; *H.* 'Radio Waves' has matt, blue-influenced light to medium green leaves with a widely undulate edge.

Hosta sieboldii 'Shiro Kabitan' (AHS 1986)

Origin: Natural sport of ★*H. sieboldii* from Japan. First known as *H. sieboldii* 'Haku Chu Han'.

Description: A low, dense mound 18 in. wide × 6½ in. high (45 × 16 cm). Leaf blade 4½ × 1 in. (11 × 2.5 cm), thin, pure white turning pale green, irregularly margined dark green, with many paler green streaks jetting toward the midrib, matt above and shiny below, edge randomly rippled, leaf elliptic with a sometimes curved, acute tip and tapered open lobes.

Petiole narrow, ivory-green, outlined in dark green. Flower: see *H. sieboldii* var. *sieboldii*.

Cultivation Notes: Needs a hot, humid climate to maintain its vigor. Under such conditions, it increases rapidly. Very susceptible to pest damage. Makes a colorful underplanting to larger blue-leaved hostas or as an edging hosta. Likely to revert to a green-leaved form.

Distinguishing Features: The variegation tends to lose its crisp whiteness toward the end of summer.

Similar: *H.* 'Fuji Sunrise'; *H.* 'Gay Feather' has slightly larger leaves; *H.* 'Island Charm'; ★*H.* 'Masquerade'; *H.* 'Silver Streak' has leaves that are more twisted.

Hosta 'Silver Threads and Golden Needles'

(J. Anderson N/R)

Origin: Sport of ★*H.* 'Cheatin Heart'.

Description: A dense mound 12 in. wide × 6½ in. high (30 × 16 cm). Leaf blade 2½ × 2 in. (6 × 5 cm), thin, rich chartreuse green overlaid with gray frosting and silver speckles, irregularly margined chartreuse becoming bright yellow which can intensify to orange-gold in strong sunlight, matt above and satiny below, dimpled toward the crown, edge rippled, leaf lightly folded, broadly ovate with an acute to cuspidate tip and open to pinched heart-shaped lobes. Petiole purple-dotted chartreuse green. Flower: see *H.* 'Cheatin Heart'.

Hosta 'Shining Tot'

Hosta sieboldii 'Shiro Kabitan'

Cultivation Notes: Site in good light to moderate shade. Suitable for growing with miniature and very small hostas as it is slow growing and does not perform well in all gardens. Requires plenty of space around it to prevent rot. The central markings are not always stable. Probably best in cooler climates. An interesting and unusual hosta well worth the time and trouble to nurture it.

Distinguishing Features: The central portion of the leaf has an unusual variegation: bright chartreuse green noticeably overlaid frosted gray and silver speckled.

Similar: *H.* 'Royal Wave' has less stable central markings; *H.* 'Seneca' has only slight leaf markings.

Hosta 'Small Parts' (D. Van Eechaute 2006)

Origin: *H.* 'Gummy Bear' seedling.

Description: An open mound 12 in. wide × 4 in. high (30 × 10 cm), the leaves held in an outward and upward stance. Leaf blade 2 × 1 in. (5 × 2.4 cm), thick, leathery, light olive green, matt above and glossy below, smooth, veins deeply impressed, edge flat with an occasional kink toward the petiole, leaf slightly folded, ovate with an acute tip and tapered open to pinched lobes. Petiole palest green, outlined in olive green. Flower tubular, violet-flushed pale lavender, opening from a violet bud, on an upright, leafy, green, 12- to 15-in. (30- to 38-cm) scape from late summer to early autumn; sterile.

Cultivation Notes: Tolerates full sun in cooler climates, elsewhere site in light to dappled shade. An excellent new introduction for the smaller garden, placed in a rock garden or front of the border. Rapid growth rate. Pest resistant.

Distinguishing Features: The exceptionally good raceme of flowers extending well down the scape. The junction of the inflorescence leaves and the scape, and the upper scapes are flushed brown.

Hosta 'Surprised by Joy' (A. Malloy 1998)

Origin: *H.* 'Flamboyant' × ★*H. venusta*.

Description: A dense, upright mound 8 in. wide × 4 in. high (20 × 10 cm). Leaf blade 3½–4 × 1½–2 in. (9–10 × 4–5 cm), of average substance, chartreuse yellow turning ivory white, matt above and satiny below, smooth, veins widely spaced, edge widely undulate, leaf folded, lightly twisted, widely lanceolate to ovate

Hosta 'Silver Threads and Golden Needles'

Hosta 'Small Parts'

Hosta 'Surprised by Joy'

with an acuminate tip and rounded open to pinched lobes. Petiole ivory, outlined in green. Flower funnel-shaped, pale lavender, on a semi-erect, leafy, chartreuse-ivory, 8- to 9-in. (20- to 23-cm) scape in early summer; seedpods ivory.

Cultivation Notes: Site in two hours of morning sun in cooler climates, followed by light to moderate shade. The leaf blade widens considerably as the plant matures and the attractive twist is lost. Grow with small forms of *Adiantum pedatum*.

Distinguishing Features: The leaves are distinctively arrow-shaped.

Similar: *H.* 'Lakeside Little Tuft' has a more yellow leaf center.

Sports: *H.* 'Captain Atom' has streaked leaves; *H.* 'Little Bit' has green leaves.

Hosta 'Thumbelina' (D. & J. Ward 1996)

Origin: *H.* 'Pin Stripe Sister' seedling.

Description: A small, tight mound 14 in. wide × 8 in. high (35 × 20 cm). Leaf blade 3 × 2 in. (8 × 5 cm), of average substance, mid-green, irregularly margined creamy white, with some streaks jetting toward the midrib, matt above and slightly shiny below, smooth, edge almost flat, leaf oval with a cuspidate tip and rounded open lobes. Petiole shallow, green, outlined in cream. Flower tubular, pale lavender, on an upright, green, 3-in. (8-cm) scape in midsummer; fertility unknown.

Cultivation Notes: Site in good light shade. Moderate growth rate. Best suited to rock gardens, gravel gardens, or containers.

Hosta 'Tick Tock' (E. Kipplen N/R)

Origin: Sport of ★*H.* 'Gold Drop'.

Description: An asymmetrical mound 18 in. wide × 5–7 in. high (45 × 13–18 cm). Leaf blade 2 × 1¼ in. (5 × 3 cm), of good substance, chartreuse to yellow, irregularly margined dark green, with streaks jetting toward the midrib, matt above and thinly glaucous below, slightly dimpled when mature, edge almost flat, leaf folded, ovate with a mucronate tip and heart-shaped open to pinched lobes. Petiole narrow, chartreuse. Flower: see *H.* 'Gold Drop'; fertility unknown.

Cultivation Notes: Lutescent leaf center. Tolerates sun in cooler climates. Easy to grow and soon exceeds its registered dimensions. Makes an excellent edging plant but also thrives in rock gardens and containers.

Distinguishing Features: The densely packed flower spike with large flowers on a small hosta.

Hosta 'Winsome' (D. & J. Ward 1996)

Origin: *H.* 'Pin Stripe Sister' seedling.

Description: A very compact mound 14 in. wide × 8 in. high (35 × 20 cm). Leaf blade 3 × 2 in. (8 × 5

Hosta 'Thumbelina'

Hosta 'Tick Tock'

cm), of average substance, matt, dark green, widely and irregularly margined creamy white, with celadon streaks jetting toward the midrib, prominently veined, edge slightly rippled, leaf widely oval with a cuspidate tip and rounded open lobes. Petiole shallow, dark green, outlined in white. Flower long, tubular, pale lavender, on an upright, dark green, 16½-in. (42-cm) scape, with variegated leafy bracts, in midsummer; seedpods green, long, in clusters, fertility unknown.

Cultivation Notes: Site in light to moderate shade in a sink, trough, or gravel garden. Suitable for small flower arrangements. A strong and vigorous grower with very large flowers for such a small hosta.

Similar: *H.* 'Lakeside Miss Muffet'; *★H.* 'Little Wonder' does not make such a neat clump.

Hosta 'X-Ray' (R. Simmering 2000)

Origin: Sport of *★H.* 'Gold Edger'.

Description: An upright mound 10 in. wide × 8 in. high (25 × 20 cm). Leaf blade 4 × 1 in. (10 × 2.5 cm), of average substance, ivory streaks, stripes, and misting, widely and irregularly margined mid green, matt above and shiny below, veins deeply impressed, edge heavily rippled on juvenile plants but undulate in maturity, leaf lanceolate with an acute tip. Petiole flat, green, barely variegated, decumbent with leaf blade. Flower: see *H.* 'Gold Edger', although it appears to be a deeper purple, the scapes ivory with purple-dotted variegated leafy bracts.

Cultivation Notes: Site in dappled to full shade. Increases rapidly but not easy to grow in some gardens. Produces exceptionally good flowers. Lovely with *Heuchera* 'Petite Pearl Fairy'.

Distinguishing Features: Although the petiole is decumbent with the leaf blade, the variegation is barely visible. The attractive variegation is at its best early in the season, fading later to several shades of muted green.

Sports: *H.* 'X-Rated' is a mini, has noticeably seersuckered, medio-variegated leaves, and is similar to *H.* 'Xerxes'.

Hosta 'X-Ray'

Hosta 'Winsome'

Hosta 'X-Rated'

429

The garden of Clarence and Betty Owens, Jackson, Michigan.

The garden of Hans Hansen, Waseca, Minnesota.

The Best Hostas for Different Purposes

Hostas for Flower Arrangements

H. 'Chodai Ginba'
H. 'Dragon Wings'
H. 'Fortunei Aureomarginata'
H. 'Francheska'
H. 'Great Escape'

H. 'Jimmy Crack Corn'
H. 'June'
H. 'Krossa Regal'
H. 'Lakeside Black Satin'
H. longissima
H. 'Morning Light'

H. 'Niagara Falls'
H. 'Praying Hands'
H. sieboldiana 'Elegans'
H. sieboldiana 'Frances Williams'
H. 'Wide Brim'

Hostas with Thick Substance

H. 'Alligator Shoes'
H. 'Big Daddy'
H. 'Bubba'
H. 'Cat and Mouse'
H. 'Christmas Tree'
H. 'Dee's Golden Jewel'
H. 'Extreme'
H. 'Grand Slam'
H. 'Green Sheen'
H. 'H. D. Thoreau'
H. laevigata
H. 'Lakeside Looking Glass'
H. 'Potomac Pride'
H. 'Rhapsody In Blue'
H. 'Rhino Hide'
H. rupifraga
H. 'Sea Monster'
H. yingeri

Hostas with Piecrust-edged Leaves

H. 'Candy Dish'
H. 'Clovelly'
H. 'Corkscrew'
H. 'Cornbelt'
H. 'Crispula'
H. 'Cutting Edge'
H. 'Dancing Queen'
H. 'Devon Discovery'
H. 'Ginsu Knife'
H. 'Grand Slam'
H. 'Hacksaw'
H. 'Jimmy Crack Corn'
H. 'Lady Guinevere'
H. 'Manhattan'
H. 'Moon Waves'
H. 'Niagara Falls'
H. 'Queen of the Seas'
H. 'Quill'
H. 'Tutu'

Hostas with Very Wide Margins

H. 'Atlantis'
H. 'Captain Kirk'
H. 'Cathedral Windows'
H. 'Grand Tiara'
H. 'Liberty'
H. 'Millie's Memoirs'
H. montana 'Aureomarginata'
H. 'Patriot'
H. 'Percy'
H. 'Sergeant Pepper'
H. sieboldiana 'American Halo'
H. 'Sultana'
H. 'Twilight'
H. 'Wide Brim'

Hostas Tolerant of Sun

H. 'Abba Dabba Do'
H. 'August Moon'
H. 'Carolina Sunshine'
H. 'Crystal Moon'
H. 'Dalton's Pick'
H. 'Dee's Golden Jewel'
H. 'Diana Remembered'
H. 'Dixie Chick'
H. 'Fragrant Bouquet'
H. 'Gold Regal'
H. 'Guacamole'
H. 'Korean Snow'
H. 'Maya Swingtime'
H. plantaginea
H. 'Sum and Substance'

Hostas for Warmer Climates (Shade Is Essential)

H. 'Alex Summers'
H. 'Alvatine Taylor'
H. 'Antioch'
H. 'Color Parade'
H. 'Daybreak'
H. 'Frosted Jade'
H. 'Hadspen Samphire'
H. 'Harpoon'
H. 'Heavenly Tiara'
H. 'June'
H. 'Key Lime Pie'
H. 'Korean Snow'

H. 'Krossa Regal'
H. 'Lakeside Shore Master'
H. 'Little Sunspot'
H. 'Patriot'
H. 'Piedmont Gold'
H. 'Saint Elmo's Fire'
H. 'Satisfaction'
H. sieboldii 'First Mate'
H. 'So Sweet'
H. 'Sum and Substance'
H. 'Sweetie'
H. 'Tambourine'

Hostas for Breeding

H. 'Beatrice'
H. 'Blue Lightning'
H. 'Breeder's Choice'
H. 'Christmas Tree Gala'
H. 'Color Parade'
H. 'Donahue Piecrust'
H. 'Dorothy Benedict'
H. 'Dorset Blue'
H. 'Dorset Clown'
H. 'Fascination'
H. 'Galaxy'
H. 'Gold Regal'
H. 'Gunther's Prize'
H. 'Halcyon'
H. 'High Fat Cream'

H. hypoleuca
H. 'Katsuragawa Beni'
H. montana
H. 'Neat Splash'
H. pycnophylla
H. sieboldiana
H. sieboldiana 'Frances Williams'
H. 'Sum and Substance'
H. venusta
H. 'William Lachman'
H. yingeri

Hostas with Outstanding Flowers

H. 'Blue Mouse Ears'
H. 'Brother Ronald'
H. 'Carrie Ann'
H. 'Crystal Moon'
H. 'Deep Blue Sea'
H. 'Diana Remembered'
H. 'Fall Bouquet'
H. montana
H. plantaginea and forms
H. rectifolia 'Fujibotan'
H. 'Red October'
H. 'Rosedale Barnie'
H. 'Royal Standard'
H. 'Sweet Sunshine'
H. ventricosa

WHERE TO SEE HOSTAS

Belgium

Arboretum Kalmthout
Heuvel 2
B-2920 Kalmthout
  www.arboretumkalmthout.be

Rob Sneyers
The Hosta Mill
Molenstraat 73
B-2460 Lichtaart
  www.hostamill.be

Canada

Kevin Plumley
2301 First Street Louth
St. Catharines
Ontario L2R 6P7
Tel: 905-684-5931
  (by appointment only)

France

J. F. Thoby
Pépinière Botanique
Chateau de Gaujacq
40330 Gaujacq
  (by appointment only)

Didier Willery
1 Petites Rues
62270 Boubers-sur-Canche
  (by appointment only)

Netherlands

Jeroen Linneman
Hosta Valley
Karperkolk 35
8017 NM Zwolle
  www.hostavalley.com

John Ramsbotham
Op de Haar Gardens
3871 KE Hoevelaken
  www.opdehaar-tuin.nl

Trompenburg Tuinen (Gardens) and Arboretum
Honingerdijk 86
3062 NX Rotterdam
www.trompenburg.nl
  The Netherlands National Collection of Hosta

United Kingdom

HRH The Prince of Wales
Highgrove House
Contact: c/o NCCPG
12 Home Farm
Loseley Park
Guildford
Surrey GU3 1HS
  info@nccpg.org.uk
  National Collection of Very Large Leaved Hosta

John Baker and June Colley
Narra
Frensham Lane
Lindford
Surrey GU35 0QJ
  (by appointment only)

Stephen Baker and Ian Leask
East Kinknockie
Ardallie, Mintlaw
Peterhead AB42 5AX
   hostaman@tiscali.co.uk
   (by appointment only)

Ann and Roger Bowden
Cleave House
Sticklepath
Okehampton
Devon EX20 2NL
   Bowdens2@eclipse.co.uk
   National Collection of Modern Hybrid Hosta

Carol and James Coutts
Newtonairds Lodge
Newtonairds
Dumfries DG2 0JL
   cbearne@toucansurf.com
   jcoutts@toucansurf.com
   National Collection of *Hosta plantaginea* cultivars
   and hybrids

Una Dunnett
Hosta House
44 Windermere Drive
Warndon
Worcester WR4 9JA
   u.dunnett@hotmail.co.uk
   (by appointment only)
   National Collection of Hosta (excl. sect.
   Helipteroides)

Diana Grenfell and Roger Grounds
Upper Merton House
Newnham-on-Severn
Gloucestershire GL14 1AD
Diana@uppermerton.co.uk
   (by appointment only)
   National Collection of Miniature Hosta

Dean Lockwood
Leeds City Council
7th Floor West, Merrion House
Merrion Centre
Leeds LS2 8DT
   dean@deanlockwood.wanadoo.co.uk
   National Collection of Large Leaved Hosta (held at
   Golden Acre Park)

Barbara and Ian Pollard
Abbey House Gardens
The Market Cross
Malmesbury
Wiltshire SN16 9AS
   www.abbeyhousegardens.co.uk

Tim Saville
1 Poplar Road
Penycae
Wrexham, Clwyd LL14 2PY
   TimSaville@breathe.com
   National Collection of Tetraploid Hostas

Denise and Derrick Targett
The Old Rectory
Somerby
Lincolnshire DN38 6EX
   www.hosta.co.uk
   (by appointment only)
   National Collection of Lachman and Mildred
   Seaver Hosta hybrids

United States
Connecticut
Kathy Sisson
20 Buckboard Lane
Avon, Connecticut 06001
   (by appointment only)

Georgia
Toni Wright and Judy Burns
3070 Hudson Way
Decatur, Georgia 30033
   (by appointment only)

Illinois
Illinois Central College Arboretum
1 College Drive
East Peoria, Illinois 61635
    www.icc.edu/ait/horticulture/arboretum.asp

Iowa
Bickelhaupt Arboretum Hosta Glade
340 S 14th Street
Clinton, Iowa 52732
    www.bickarb.org/

Dubuque Arboretum
3800 Arboretum Drive
Dubuque, Iowa 52001
    www.dubuquearboretum.com

Vander Veer Botanical Park, Hosta Glade
215 W Central Park
Davenport, Iowa 52803
    www.cityofdavenportiowa.com/department/
division.asp?fDD=21-223

Maine
Pine Tree State Arboretum
153 Hospital Street
August, Maine 04330
    www.pinetreestatearboretum.org

Michigan
Hidden Lake Gardens
6214 Monroe Road (M-50)
Tipton, Michigan 49287
    www.hiddenlakegardens.msu.edu/

Sandy and Larry Mackle
460 Goodhue
Bloomfield Hills, Michigan 48304
    (by appointment only)

Dr. James and Sandy Wilkins
7469 Hunters Ridge
Jackson, Michigan 49201
    (by appointment only)

Minnesota
University of Minnesota Landscape Arboretum,
Hosta Glade
3675 Arboretum Drive
Chanhassen, Minnesota 55318
    www.arboretum.umn.edu

Nebraska
Lauritzen Gardens at Omaha's Botanical Center
100 Bancroft Street
Omaha, Nebraska 68108
    www.omahabotanicalgardens.org

New Jersey
David and Roberta Chopko
93 Intervale Road
Boonton, New Jersey 07005
    (by appointment only)

New York
Mike and Kathy Shadrack
8399 Zimmerman Road
Hamburg, New York 14075
    H8staman@aol.com
    Irisborer@aol.com

Ohio
Hosta Garden at The 577 Foundation
577 E Front Street
Perrysburg, Ohio 43551
    www.577foundation.org

Toledo Botanical Garden
5403 Elmer Drive
Toledo, Ohio 43615
    www.toledogarden.org

South Carolina
South Carolina Botanical Garden
Clemson University
150 Discovery Lane
Clemson, South Carolina 29634
    www.clemson.edu/scbg/

Tennessee

Memphis Botanic Garden "Hosta Trail"

750 Cherry Road

Memphis, Tennessee 38117

  www.memphisbotanicgarden.com

Wisconsin

Boerner Botanical Gardens

9400 Boerner Drive

Hales Corner, Wisconsin 53130

  www.boernerbotanicalgardens.org

Foxfire Botanical Gardens

M220 Sugarbush Lane

Marshfield, Wisconsin 54449

  www.foxfiregardens.com

Olbrich Botanical Gardens

3330 Atwood Avenue

Madison, Wisconsin 53704

  www.olbrich.org/

Rotary Botanical Gardens, Hosta Hollow

1455 Palmer Drive

Janesville, Wisconsin 53545

  www.rotarygardens.org

Pennsylvania

Longwood Gardens, Idea Garden

1001 Longwood Road (Rt. 1)

Kennett Square, Pennsylvania 19348

  www.longwoodgardens.org

Barbara and Robert Tiffany

Mille Fleurs

27 Cafferty Road

Point Pleasant, Pennsylvania 18950

  (by appointment only)

SOURCES FOR HOSTAS

Belgium

Danny Van Eechaute
Joos Vijdtdreef 16
9800 Deinze
www.hostacollectie.be
(small nursery for unusual hostas; by appointment only)

Canada

Judy and Bruce Cumpson
Olde Towne Gardens
716 Lakeshore Road
Niagara-on-the-Lake
Ontario L0S 1J0
www.oldetownegardens.ca

Dykhof Nurseries and Florist
460 Mountain Highway
North Vancouver
British Columbia V7J 2L2
www.dykhofnurseries.com

Goldenbrook Hostas
14950 Regional Road 57
Blackstock
Ontario L0B 1B0
www.goldenbrookhostas.com

Rideau Woodland Ramble
P.O. Box 348
Merrickville
Ontario K0G 1N0
www.rideauwoodlandramble.com

Shades of Green
48855 John Wise Linda
Aylmer
Ontario N5H 2R4
www.shades-of-green.ca

France

Jane Phillips
Le Jardin Anglais
Cantiran
47230 Montgaillard
lejardinanglais@freesbee.fr

Germany

Friesland-Staudengarten
Husumer Weg 16
26441 Jever/Rahdum
www.friesland-staudengartren.de

Netherlands

Marco Fransen Hostas
Hostakwekerij
Paradijsweg 5
2461 TK Ter Aar
www.hostaparadise.com

Hostaworld
Jan Van den Top
Wesselseweg 46
3771 PC Barneveld
www.hostaworld.nl

New Zealand

Barry Sligh
Taunton Gardens
Allandale, RD1
Lyttleton
   www.tauntongardens.co.nz

United Kingdom

Apple Court
Hordle Lane
Hordle, Lymington
Hampshire SO41 0HU
   www.applecourt.com

Bali-Hai Mail Nursery
42, Largy Road
Camlough, Ballymena
County Antrim
Northern Ireland BT44 0EZ
   www.mailorderplants4me.com

Bowden Hostas
Sticklepath
Okehampton
Devon EX20 2NL
   www.bowdenhostas.com

Brookfield Plants
Bigelle
Sandyhurst Lane
Ashford
Kent TN25 4NX
   www.brookfieldplants.com

Goldbrook Plants
Hoxne
Eye, Suffolk IP21 5AN
Tel: 01379 668770

Mary Green
The Walled Garden
Hornby
Lancaster LA2 8LD
   marygreenplants@aol.com

Hutton Hostas
Rustic House
Howl Lane
Hutton, Driffield
E Yorkshire YO25 9QD
   www.huttonhostas.com

Ava Macgregor
Loch-Hills Plant Centre
Ellon
Aberdeenshire AB41 8DR
   info@loch-hillsplants.co.uk

Mickfield Hostas
The Poplars
Mickfield
Stowmarket
Suffolk IP14 5LH
   www.mickfieldhostas.co.uk

Park Green Nurseries
Wetheringsett
Stowmarket
Suffolk IP14 5QH
   www.parkgreen.co.uk

United States

Connecticut
O'Brien Nurserymen
40 Wells Road
Granby, CT 06035
   www.obrienhosta.com

Georgia
Bentley Gardens
1900 Peeksville Road
Locust Grove, GA 30248
   www.bentleygardens.com

Bloomin Designs Nursery
558 Auburn Road
Auburn, GA 30011
   www.bloomindesigns.com

Pine Forest Gardens
556 Ellison Road
Tyrone, GA 30290
   www.pineforestgardens.com

Silvers-Elbert Nursery
2024 McDaniel Mill Road
Conyers, GA 30094
    www.hostaplants.com

Illinois
Conner Nursery and Gardens
6605 North Smith Road
Edwards, IL 61528

Hornbaker Gardens
1140 N Avenue
Princeton, IL 61356
    www.hornbakergardens.com

The Hosta Patch
23720 Hearthside Drive
Deer Park, IL 60010
    www.hostapatch.com

White Oak Nursery
1 Oak Park Lake
Metamora, IL 61548
    www.WhiteOakNursery.com

Indiana
Dogwood Farm
RR 13, Box 288
Brazil, IN 47834
    www.hostagarden.com

Soules Garden
5809 Rahke Road
Indianapolis, IN 46217
    www.soulesgarden.com

Walnut Grove Nursery
8348 E State Riad 45
Unionville, IN 47468
    www.walnutgrovenursery.net

Iowa
Honey Hill Hostas
3633 Honey Hill Drive, SE
Cedar Rapids, IA 52403
    www.hosta-holic.com

Oakcrest Perennial Gardens & Nursery
22871 Kane Avenue
Glenwood, IA 51534
    www.OakcrestGardens.com

Kansas
Made in the Shade Gardens
16370 W 138th Terrace
Olathe, KS 66062
    www.HostaGuy.com

Maryland
The Azalea Patch
2010 Mountain Road
Joppa, MD 21085
    www.azaleapatch.com

Nature's Reign Nursery
Hampstead
    www.naturesreign.com

Michigan
Garden Crossings
4902 96th Avenue
Zeeland, MI 49464
    www.gardencrossings.com

Schmid Nursery and Gardens
847 Westwood Boulevard
Jackson, MI 49203
    www.schmidgardens.com

Minnesota
Hostas Direct
19 Mid Oaks Road
Roseville, MN 55113
    www.hostasdirect.com

Savory's Gardens
5300 Whiting Avenue
Edina, MN 55439
    www.savorysgardens.com

Missouri
Hilltop Farm
3307 N State Highway F
Ash Grove, MO 65604
    www.hilltop-gardens.com

New Hampshire
New Hampshire Hostas
73 Exeter Road
South Hampton, NH 03827
    www.nhhostas.com

New York

Carlson's Gardens
26 Salem Hill Road
South Salem, NY 10590
  www.carlsonsgardens.com

Cooks Nursery & Eagle Bay Hosta Gardens
10749 Bennett Road
Dunkirk, NY 14048

Glenbrook Farms
142 Brooks Road
Fultonville, NY 12072
  www.glenbrookplants.com

North Carolina

Green Hill Farm
P.O. Box 16306
Chapel Hill, NC 27516
  www.hostahosta.com

Plant Delights Nursery
9241 Sauls Road
Raleigh, NC 27603
  www.plantdelights.com

Ohio

Hosta Homestead
9448 Mayfield Road
Chesterfield, OH 44026
  www.hostahomestead.com

Kuk's Forest Nursery
10174 Barr Road
Brecksville, OH 44141

Meadow View Growers
755 N Dayton Lakeview Road (Rt. 235)
New Carlisle, OH 45344
  www.meadowview.com

Wade and Gatton Nurseries
1288 Gatton Rocks Road
Bellville, OH 44813

South Carolina

Daylily and Hosta Gardens
2396 Roper Mountain Road
Simpsonville, SC 29681
  www.daylilyandhostagardens.com

Vermont

Vermont Flower Farm
256 Peacham Pond Road
Marshfield, VT 05658
  www.vermontflowerfarm.com

Virginia

Bent Tree Hostas
8630 Tuttle Road
Springfield, VA 22152
  www.benttreehostas.com

Bridgewood Gardens
P.O. Box 391
Strasburg, Virginia 22657

Rick's Custom Nursery
Lexington, VA
  www.rickscustomnursery.com

Wisconsin

Klehm's Song Sparrow Perennial Farm
13101 E Rye Road
Avalon. WI 53505
  www.songsparrow.com

Northern Grown Perennials
54779 Helland Road
Ferryville, WI 54628
  www.hostalink.com

Shades of Green
P.O. Box 3134
LaCrosse, WI 54602
  www.shadesofgreenusa.com

Washington

Naylor Creek Nurseries
P.O. Box 309
Chimacum, WA 98325
  www.naylorcreek.com

Hosta 'Orange Marmalade'

HOSTA SOCIETIES AND OTHER RESOURCES

American Hosta Society
P.O. Box 7539
Kill Devil Hills, North Carolina 27948, USA
   www.hosta.org

British Hosta and Hemerocallis Society
c/o Membership Secretary
Chapelmere
Rodley
Westbury-on-Severn
Gloucestershire GL14 1QZ, UK
   www.hostahem.org.uk

Dutch Hosta Society
Secretariaat, Nederlandse Hosta Vereniging
Van Egmondplein 14
3231 CV Brielle, Netherlands
   http://www.hostavereniging.nl

National Council for the Conservation of Plants and Gardens
12 Home Farm
Loseley Park
Guildford
Surrey GU3 1HS, UK
   www.nccpg.com

Useful Websites
www.hostalibrary.org
www.hostalibrary.org/firstlook
www.myhostas.net

GLOSSARY

Acuminate Gradually coming to a point as in *H.* 'Francheska'.

Acute Sharp pointed, as in *H. longissima*, *H.* 'Tardiflora'.

Albescent Becoming white.

Apomictic Of female flowers which form seed without having been pollinated or fertilized.

Bract A modified leaf usually at the base of a flower stem or sometimes forming part of the flower head itself.

Cordate Heart-shaped: strictly applied only to a pair of lobes at the base of the leaf but loosely used of hosta leaves (such as those of *H. sieboldiana*), which have the outline of a romanticized heart.

Cross A hybrid, or as a verb to create a hybrid.

Crown The upper part of the rootstock from which shoots grow and to which they die back in the fall.

Cultivar Short for cultivated variety.

Cuneate Wedge-shaped.

Cuspidate Of a leaf tip, sometimes long and thin arising gradually from an oval leaf, as in *H. montana*.

Decurrent Running together, as when a leaf stalk and leaf blade merge into one another without obvious differentiation.

Dicotyledon A plant whose seedlings have two cotyledons or seed leaves, noticeably different from the normal leaves. One of the two great classes of flowering plants.

Diffuse Of a leaf mound that is wide-spreading but not dense.

Dimpled Of a leaf blade whose surface is pocked by small, round indentations.

Diploid A plant having the normal number of chromosomes for its species or variety.

Drawstring effect The puckering of the edge of a leaf caused by the center of the leaf growing faster than the margin, which causes the margin to look as though it has been pulled tight by a drawstring.

Fasciated A freak condition in which the stem of a plant becomes flattened, giving the impression that several stems have fused together. The flowers at the tip of such a shoot may also be abnormal.

Floriferous Free-flowering.

Forma (abbrev. f.) The lowest taxonomic rank, subordinate to species and variety.

Furrow The bilateral groove on the upper leaf surface.

Glaucous Bluish green or bluish gray or covered with a bluish waxy coating.

Hyaline Glassy, translucent, transparent.

Hybrid The offspring resulting from the mating of two genetically different parents.

Interface The junction between the inner and outer margin of a leaf.

Jetting Refers to a variegation that sends streaks of color, beginning at the leaf margin, toward the center of the leaf.

Lanceolate Lance-shaped.

Lutescent Becoming yellow.

Melting out Although not a disease, this does affect the appearance of hosta leaves. It is the necrosis of portions of the white or light centers of the leaves due to the remainder of the plants' inability to make enough chlorophyll to support the non-producing centers. Portions of the centers will actually disintegrate. Symptoms usually start when the warm nights and days of summer arrive. This is a common problem, particularly in the U.S. Midwest.

Monocotyledon A plant whose seedlings have a single cotyledon or seed leaf, usually similar to the adult leaf.

Mucronate Of a round leaf that is abruptly terminated by a short tip, as in *H*. 'Tokudama'.

Mutation A spontaneous, vegetative variation from the original type caused by accidental changes in the genetic make-up of the plant. Such mutations are usually deleterious to the plant, but when they are decorative, they may be maintained in cultivation by vegetative propagation.

Navel The apparent hole that appears when the lobes at the base of a hosta leaf overlap.

Oblique Of flower stems that lean away from the vertical.

Obtuse Of a leaf tip that is blunt-ended, as in *H*. 'Decorata'.

Ovate Egg-shaped. Of a leaf where the broadest part is nearest the base.

Pedicel The short stalk that connects a flower to a flower stem.

Petiole The stalk joining the leaf blade to the crown or root system.

Polyploid Having more than the normal number of chromosomes for the species.

Pruinose The powdery, velvetlike, white substance that coats the underside of some leaves, such as those of *H. hypoleuca* and *H. pycnophylla*.

Puckering An exaggerated form of seersuckering, making folds in the leaf.

Raceme An elongated, unbranched flower head in which each flower is borne on an individual stalk or pedicel, with the youngest flowers at the apex.

Rhizomatous Having underground stems that last more than one season and that often grow horizontally, producing new plants at the ends furthest from the parent.

Rib The protruding keel-like vein on the underside of the leaf.

Rugose Wrinkled, a term usually applied to the surface of leaves.

Scape A flower stem that arises directly from ground level and bears no leaves. Used to refer to the flower stems of hostas which, though they may bear bracts, are without leaves.

Seersuckered Resembling seersuckered cloth, a lightweight cotton or linen fabric, and characterized by intense, even dimpling.

Sport A gardener's term for a mutation.

Stolon, stoloniferous A stolon is a horizontal stem produced either above or below ground, producing roots and new shoots at its tip.

Subtended Carried below: used of bracts on flower stems that are carried below the flower.

Tetraploid Having double the number of chromosomes of the typical plant.

Undulate Wavy, referring either to the whole leaf blade or to the margin. A margin can also be described as rippled or more closely piecrusted.

Viridescent Becoming green.

Vestigial, rudimentary, barely present

Hosta 'Ooh La La'

BIBLIOGRAPHY

Aden, P., ed. 1992. *The Hosta Book.* 2nd ed. Portland, Oregon: Timber Press.

Barrett, R. 2004. *Hostas: The Complete Guide.* Newton, Devon, United Kingdom: David and Charles; Auckland, New Zealand; David Bateman.

Bond, S. 1992. *Hostas.* London: Ward Lock.

Brickell, C. D. 1968. "Notes from Wisley." *Journal of the Royal Horticultural Society* 93: 365–372.

Brickell, C. D., et al. 2004. *International Code of Nomenclature for Cultivated Plants.* 7th ed. Leuven, Belgium: International Society for Horticulture.

Callaway, D. J., and M. Brett, eds. 2000. *Breeding Ornamental Plants.* Portland, Oregon: Timber Press.

Dirr, M. 1998. *Manual of Woody Plants.* Campaign, Illinois: Stipes.

Fox, R. 1997. *The Gardener's Book of Pests and Diseases.* London: Batsford.

Greenwood, P., A. Halstead, A. R. Chase, and D. Gilrein. 2000. *American Horticultural Society Pests and Diseases.* New York: Dorling Kindersley.

Grenfell, D. 1990. *Hosta: The Flowering Foliage Plant.* Portland, Oregon: Timber Press; London: Batsford.

Grenfell, D. 2005. *Hostas.* Pershore, Worcestershire, United Kingdom: The Hardy Plant Society.

Grenfell, D. 1996. *The Gardener's Guide to Growing Hostas.* Portland, Oregon: Timber Press; Newton Abbot, Devon, United Kingdom: David and Charles.

Grenfell, D. 2002. *Hostas.* RHS Wisley Handbook. London: Cassell Illustrated.

Hensen, K. J. W. 1963a. "De in Nederlandgetweeke Hostas" (Hostas cultivated in The Netherlands). *Mededelingen van de Directeur van de Tuinbow* 26: 725–735.

Hensen, K. J. W. 1963b. "Identification of the Hostas (Funkias) Introduced and Cultivated by von Siebold." *Mededelingen Landbouwhogeschool, Wageningen* 63 (6): 1–22.

Hensen K. J. W. 1985. "A Study of the Taxonomy of Cultivated Hostas." *The Plantsman* 7 (1): 19–21.

Hillier Nurseries. 2007. *The Hillier Manual of Trees and Shrubs.* 3rd ed. Newton Abbot, Devon: David and Charles.

Huxley, A. 1981. *The Penguin Encyclopedia of Gardening.* London: Allen Lane.

Hylander, N. 1954. "The Genus *Hosta* in Swedish Gardens." *Acta Horti Bergiani* 16 (11): 350–366.

Kohlein, F. 1993. *Hosta (Funkien).* Stuttgart: Ulmer. (In German)

Maekawa, F. 1940. "The Genus *Hosta.*" *Journal of the Faculty of Science, Imperial University of Tokyo*, Section 3 Botany, 5: 37–425. (Re-printed in *AHS Bulletin* 4: 12–64 [1972] and 5: 12–59 [1973]).

Mikolajski, A. 1997. *Hostas.* The New Plant Library. London: Lorenz Books.

Schmid, W. G. 1991. *The Genus Hosta: Giboshi Zoku.* Portland, Oregon: Timber Press; London: Batsford.

Stearn, W. T. 1992. *Botanical Latin.* 4th ed. Portland, Oregon: Timber Press.

Taylor, J. 1991. *Gardening in the Shade.* London: Dent.

Wade, V. 2002. *The American Hosta Guide.* Bellville, Ohio: Wade and Gatton Nurseries.

Watanabe, K. 1985. *The Observation and Cultivation of Hosta.* Tokyo: New Science Company. (In Japanese)

Westcott, C. 1973. *The Gardener's Bug Book.* 4th ed. New York: Doubleday.

Zilis, M. R. 2001. *The Hosta Handbook.* Rochelle, Illinois: Q & Z Nursery.

Other Helpful Information

British Hosta and Hemerocallis Society Bulletin. Published by the British Hosta and Hemerocallis Society.

The Green Hill Gossip. Newsletter published by Robert Solberg of Green Hill Farm, Chapel Hill, North Carolina.

The Hosta Finder. Published annually by Steve Greene of Sudbury, Massachusetts.

The Hosta Journal. Published by the American Hosta Society.

Mature hostas

SUBJECT INDEX

447

Hosta 'Daybreak'

INDEX OF HOSTAS

Boldface indicates a main entry. *Italic numbers* indicate photo pages not part of a plant's main description.